国际旅游岛

前厅服务与管理(双语版)

International Tourism Island Front Office Service and Management

主　编◎张璇

副主编◎苏颖　林琦　陈卫琼

图书在版编目（CIP）数据

国际旅游岛前厅服务与管理（双语版）/ 张璇主编. —北京：经济管理出版社，2015.3
ISBN 978-7-5096-3547-6

Ⅰ. ①国… Ⅱ. ①张… Ⅲ. ①饭店—商业服务—双语教学—中等专业学校—教材—英、汉 ②饭店—商业管理—双语教学—中等专业学校—教材—英、汉 Ⅳ. ①F719.2

中国版本图书馆 CIP 数据核字（2014）第 281935 号

组稿编辑：魏晨红
责任编辑：瑞　鸿
责任印制：司东翔
责任校对：王　淼

出版发行：经济管理出版社
（北京市海淀区北蜂窝 8 号中雅大厦 A 座 11 层　100038）
网　　址：www. E-mp. com. cn
电　　话：（010）51915602
印　　刷：三河市延风印装厂
经　　销：新华书店
开　　本：889mm×1194mm/16
印　　张：22.5
字　　数：633 千字
版　　次：2015 年 3 月第 1 版　　　2015 年 3 月第 1 次印刷
书　　号：ISBN 978-7-5096-3547-6
定　　价：45.00 元

前　言

前厅部是星级酒店的重要组成部分，《国际旅游岛前厅服务与管理（双语版）》是中等职业学校酒店专业的核心课程之一。本书编者本着“以就业为导向，以能力为本位，以学生为主体”的教学指导思想，以海南省建设国际旅游岛为背景，依托地方行业，以前厅部主要岗位为主线，结合海南高星级酒店前厅服务和管理的实际情况和在校学生的思维特点，采用中英文对照编写而成。

与传统教材相比，本书具有如下几个特点：

（1）实用性和针对性。本书结合海南省酒店行业现状和学生情况编写而成，较注重岗位实践，尤其是前厅各岗位的实操练习。本书增加了海南当地的风土人情、人文地理相关知识以帮助学生增长见识。

（2）突出职业教育特色，符合目前职业教育的教学规律和学生特点。立体化资源配套，配有多媒体课件、网络课程，更好地为教学提供服务。本书形式活泼、图文并茂、案例众多、内容深浅适中、通俗易懂、参与性强。

（3）以“模块教学”形式呈现。本书以各大任务分解模块，再以小任务分解大任务，层层递进，环环相扣。每一模块均以案例开篇，结合本模块的相关知识点，采用场景模拟和任务驱动的方法，鼓励学生自主学习和探究，每模块均有“学习目标”以便教师灵活运用以及学生分清主次。

由于编者水平有限，加之时间仓促，教材中难免存在不足之处，敬请读者批评指正。

编　者
2014.12

酒店人的行业自豪感
Occupational Pride of Hotel Personnel

欢迎加入酒店人行列！首先，让我们来了解酒店是做什么的？

Welcome to the hotel industry！First，let us know what the functions of hotel are about.

一、酒店是做什么的？——以盈利为目的（What Are the Functions of Hotel?—For the Purpose of Profits）

酒店（又称宾馆、旅馆、旅店、旅社、客店、客栈、饭店），其基本定义是能够为旅居宾客和其他宾客提供住宿、饮食、购物、娱乐等服务综合性服务的企业。酒店的本质特征是能够为宾客提供旅居住宿服务。酒店主要为游客提供住宿服务、其他生活服务及设施（寝前服务）、餐饮、游戏、娱乐、购物、商务中心、宴会及会议等设施。

Hotel（also called as guest house，lodge，inn，hostel，roadhouse and victualing house），the basic definition is the comprehensive service enterprise providing accommodation，food，shopping，entertainment and other services for living guests and other guests. The essential characteristic of hotel is to provide accommodation services for guests. The hotel mainly provides accommodation service，other life services and facilities（before sleeping），food and beverage，games，entertainment，shopping，business center，banquet and conference facilities for tourists.

经营酒店的目的永远只有一个——盈利！酒店不是行政单位，不会管理和维护社会秩序，不可以根据权力发号施令。酒店更不是福利组织，无偿地为人们提供生活所需。酒店的所有活动都是围绕“盈利”这一目的的。

The purpose of the hotel operation is only one—profits! Hotel is not an administrative unit for managing and maintaining social order and can give the command based on its power. Hotel is also not a welfare organization providing people with the necessities of life for free. All the activities of hotel are for the purpose of “profit”.

进入酒店行业就成了酒店人，酒店人的工作特点是什么？

You will become the hotel personnel after entering hotel industry，and what are the characteristics of hotel work?

二、酒店人工作特点——服务（Characteristics of Hotel Work—SERVICE）

我们的收入来自客人的消费，客人是我们的衣食父母。酒店的业务活动并不生产和销售有形的物质产品，而是凭借物质设施向客人提供一种无形的服务。客人最终得到的只是服务的效用和服务过程的一种体验。所以酒店人无论在哪个岗位都只有一个最重要的特点——为客人提供满意的服务！

Our source of income is the guests’ consumption，and guests are the people we rely on for a living.

Hotel business activities do not generate and sale tangible material products in nature, but provides intangible service to the guests through material facilities. The guests will finally get the effective service and experience the service process. So no matter what positions the hotel people are only, they have one most important feature—providing satisfactory service to guests!

S—Smile（微笑） 对每一个人微笑，尤其是陌生人。我们没有可能去选择周围的人，但我们可以选择对每个人微笑，让他们觉得受到我们最真挚的欢迎！

Smile at everyone, especially strangers. We do not have the choice to choose the people around you, but we can choose to smile at everyone, and let them feel our sincerely welcome!

E—Excellence（出色） 把每一件事都做好，并努力做到出色。我们的能力永远是有限的，但我们可以选择对每件事都尽力去做，无论什么样的结果，我们都不后悔，因为我们尽力了！

Do everything well, and strive to do even better. Our capacity is always limited, but we can choose to do our best, no matter what kind of result is it, we will not regret, because we have tried our best!

R—Ready（准备好） 随时准备好为每个人服务；每个人都期待被别人照顾，我们就是那个照顾别人的人，我们随时都准备好为每个人提供最体贴最专业的照顾。

Ready to service for everyone; Everyone is looking forward to being taken care of by others, we are the one who is taking care of others, and we are always ready to provide the most considerate and professional care for everyone.

V—Viewing（看待） 将每个都当成最特别的人去关注；我们细心地关注周围人的需要，用最专业的服务让他们的需要得到满足。

Viewing every one as special; We pay careful attention to the people needing help around you, and satisfy their needs with the most professional service.

I—Inviting（邀请） 我们永远是殷勤好客的，随时邀请每个人来到我们身边，让我们好好照顾他们。

We are always hospitable, welcome everyone coming to our side and take good care of them.

C—Creating（创造） 为周围的人创造温暖舒适的氛围。我们在工作中充分发挥智慧，不断进行创新，力求让每位顾客的不同需要都得到满足。

Create warm and comfortable atmosphere for the people around you. We give full play to our wisdom and continuous innovation in our work, and strive to meet different needs of customers.

E—Eye（眼光） 以热情友好的目光关注周围人的需要；每个人在我们眼里都是贵宾，是否能够满足贵宾的所有需要可以体现我们的专业水准。

Focus on the needs of the people around you with warm and friendly eyes; Everyone is a VIP in our eyes, our professional level can be reflected by we can satisfy all the needs of customers.

酒店业是全球十大热门行业之一。国外有关研究表明，近年来新增的劳动就业人口中，每 25 人中就有 1 人就职于酒店。2013 年，全球酒店业就业人数超过 1200 万人，中国酒店从业人数达 150.24 万人。酒店业有什么样的吸引力？酒店人拥有什么样的行业自豪感？

Hotel industry is one of the Top ten hottest industries in the world. Foreign studies show that in the newly employed population of recent years, one out of every 25 people works in the hotel. In 2013, the employed population of global hotel industry reaches more than 12 million, and Chinese hotel employs 1.5024 million people. What kind of attraction does the hostel industry have? What is the occupational pride of hotel personnel?

三、酒店人的行业自豪感（Occupational Pride of Hotel Personnel）

（一）酒店业的不断持续发展（Sustainable Development of Hotel Industry）

目前，全国已经有超过 11000 家星级酒店，世界著名酒店集团都在中国发展，而海南已经超过北京、上海，成为中国高星酒店和品牌酒店最多的地方。海南全省的酒店则超过 530 家，仅三亚现有各类酒店 800 家，客房总共超过 35000 间。根据规划，新酒店仍在持续、大规模扩张。在海南国际旅游岛建设过程中，海南将成为全国最受境外游客欢迎的地方，大量世界知名酒店的入驻，为国际旅游岛建设奠定了基础，同时，大量国内外游客的到来将为酒店业带来新契机。国际旅游岛将为海南酒店带来大量的和源源不断的客源，使得长期存在的低开房率有所上升。至 2016 年，海南将新增 68 家 5 星级酒店，今后 10 年海南酒店供给仍拥有渐进增长的空间。

At present, there are more than 11000 star-rated hotels across the country, the famous Hotel Groups in the world choose to develop in China. Hainan province has the most high star-rated hotels and famous hotel in China, exceeding Beijing and Shanghai. There are more than 530 hotels in Hainan province, even Sanya has 800 various types of hotels, and the total of rooms are more than 35000. According to the plan, new hotels continue to expand in large scale. In the construction of Hainan international tourism island, Hainan will become the most popular destination for foreign tourists in China, and the lots of world famous hotels lay the foundation for the construction of international tourism island. At the same time, a large number of domestic and foreign tourists bring new opportunities for the hotel industry. The international tourism island will bring a steady and continuous stream of customers for Hainan hotels, increasing the long-standing low occupancy rate. Up to 2016, Hainan will newly increase 68 5-star hotels, and there still are gradual growth spaces for Hainan hotels in the next 10 years.

（二）酒店业提供大量就业岗位，人才供不应求（Hotel Industry Provides a Large Number of Jobs, Talents Are in Short Supply）

据相关统计数据表明，2009~2012 年，酒店对人才需求量在不断上升。2011 年酒店人才需求量同比增长 74.37%，2012 年同比增长 64.32%。求职人才数量增长缓慢，2011 年同比上年增幅仅为 12.23%，2012 年增长幅度也仅为 27.92%。显然，酒店需求量要大于人才求职数。从人才供求比（人才供求比为求职人数与需求人数之比）来看，自 2009 年开始，该数值四年来一路下滑。伴随着酒店业的发展，以洲际酒店集团为例：洲际酒店集团最近两年新增 3 万就业岗位，人才供求矛盾更加突出。2013 年，整个酒店行业人才供求比始终未突破 1:0.75（即酒店需求人数为 1，求职人数为 0.75）。

Relevant statistics show that from 2009 to 2012, talent demand of hotel industry is rising. The talent demand of hotel industry increases 74.37% in 2011 and 64.32% in 2012. But the number of talents increases slowly with year-on-year growth of 12.23% in 2011 and 27.92% in 2012. Obviously, the hotel demand is greater than talent number. Viewing at the talent supply and demand ratio (talent supply and demand ratio is the ratio of the number of applicants to the number of demands), the ratio went down for four years since 2009. With the development of hotel industry, take Intercontinental Hotel Group as an example: the Intercontinental Hotel Group added 30000 jobs in the last two years, which even reflected the contradiction between talent supply and demand. In 2013, the talent supply and demand ratio of the entire hotel industry does not exceed 1 : 0.75 (i.e. hotel demand is 1, and employee number is 0.75).

（三）酒店业的薪酬待遇情况（Compensation and Benefit of Hotel Jobs）

酒店行业越来越重视员工薪酬状况。2013 年 9 月 17 日，海南省酒店与餐饮行业协会、海南省酒店行业工会联合会正式在海南省酒店与餐饮行业工资专项集体合同书上签字，合同覆盖近2万家酒店餐饮企业的29万多名职工。海南省酒店餐饮员工2013年最低工资由27%上升至31%，一类地区增长27%，二类地区增长31%，三类地区增长27%。

The hotel industry pays more and more attention to employee's compensation. On September 17, 2013, Hotel Food and Beverage Industry Association of Hainan province and Federation of Trade Union in Hainan Hotel Industry officially signed on the Hainan Food and Beverage Industry Salary Special Collective Contract. The contract covers nearly 20 thousand hotel food and beverage enterprises and more than 290 thousand employees. Minimum salary of Hainan hotel food and beverage staff rises 27% to 31% in 2013, A-class region growth is 27%, B-class region growth is 31%, and the C-class region is increased by 27%.

另外，酒店行业的待遇还包括企业解决员工食宿。在三亚地区，员工的住宿已经实现“小区化”，住宿条件不断改善。

In addition, some enterprises of hotel industry also provide accommodation for staff. In Sanya, employee's accommodation is developed in the direction of residence community, the accommodation conditions continue to be improved.

（四）酒店人的职业气质（Occupational Temperament of Hotel Personnel）

酒店服务员就是为绅士和淑女服务的绅士和淑女，即酒店服务员就是绅士和淑女。他们通过酒店服务与管理专业的学习和一段时间的酒店行业相关岗位的服务工作，将变成绅士和淑女。

Hotel waiters are the ladies and gentlemen serving for ladies and gentlemen. And the hotel waiters can become the ladies and gentlemen through professional learning of hotel service and management and a period of work experience in hotel industry.

（五）酒店人拥有更高的素质（Higher Quality of Hotel Personnel）

1. 乐观自信（Optimism and Self-confidence）

酒店人在服务工作中总会要求自己做一个生活中的强者，培养乐观、自信的素质，因为乐观和自信是做好服务工作的重要保障。

In the service work, hotel personnel require themselves to be a stronger in life, and cultivate the quality of optimism and confidence, because it is the important guarantee to do service well.

2. 礼貌热情（Politeness and Enthusiasm）

酒店人的服务宗旨就是让顾客满意，获得了顾客的好感，这才是成功的服务工作。酒店人在服务过程中将培养礼貌热情的素质。

The service tenet of hotel personnel is to make customers satisfied, and give customers a favorable impression. This is the successful service. Hotel personnel will cultivate the quality of politeness and enthusiasm in the service process.

3. 真诚友善（Sincerity and Friendship）

真诚友善就是以诚相待，表里如一。酒店人在服务工作中以善良的愿望同对方友好相处，会赢得顾客的信任，很快被顾客所接纳，消除人际之间的陌生感、隔膜感，在短时间内融洽主客关系，促使顾客接受服务。

Sincerity and friendship is to treat other people with all sincerity, inside equals outside. Hotels in service work with sincere good wishes through each other to get along, win the trust of customers, soon to be accepted by the customer, eliminating the strangeness, a sense of interpersonal diaphragm between the host and guest harmonious relationship in a short time, prompting customers to accept service.

4. 豁达宽容（Generosity and Toleration）

酒店业有句警句“顾客总是对的”，这就是培养酒店人待人的宽容态度和处事的豁达胸怀。

Hotel industry saying aphorism “the customer is always right”, which is to foster tolerance hotel who treat people, doing things open-minded mind.

5. 坚强的意志（Strong Will）

服务工作是极其复杂的工作，需要酒店人不断克服主客观方面的各种困难和障碍，所以只有不断地增强意志力，才能做好服务工作，优秀的意志品质有四种：自觉性、果断性、坚韧性、自制力。

Service work is an extremely complex task, requiring the hotel people continue to overcome all difficulties and obstacles subjective and objective aspects, so only continue to enhance the willpower to do service work, excellent quality will have four: consciousness, decisiveness, tenacity, self-control.

6. 出色的能力（Excellent Capability）

酒店人的能力直接影响到服务的效率和服务效果，一个出色的酒店人应该具备以下的一些能力：敏锐的观察力、良好的记忆力、较强的交际能力。

The hotel directly affect people's ability to effect service efficiency and service, an excellent hotel should have some of the following capabilities: observant, a good memory, strong communication skills.

我希望自己能成为一个优秀的酒店人，如何成为一个优秀的酒店人？

I hope I can become a good hotel people, how to be an excellent hotel people?

四、建立酒店人的职业自豪感（The Hotel People Build Professional Pride）

（一）立德（Moral Composition）

1. 诚信（Honesty）

诚实无欺，讲求信用；行事公平合理，遵守合同协议，在不损坏酒店利益的前提下，自觉维护酒店消费者的合法权益。只有真诚公道地对待每一位消费者，向他们提供优质的服务，才能树立起良好的信誉和形象。

Honesty and honest and good faith; to act in a fair and reasonable, to comply with contractual agreements, without damage to the property interests of the premise, and consciously safeguard the legitimate rights and interests of consumers of the hotel. Only sincere fair to treat every consumer, to provide them with quality services, in order to establish a good reputation and image.

岔路口的选择
Choose Fork

一个士兵，非常 not 长跑，所以在一次部队的越野赛中很快就远落人后，一个人孤零零地跑着。转过了几道弯，遇到了一个岔路口：一条路，标明是军官跑的；另一条路，标明是士兵跑的。他停顿了一下，虽然对做军官连越野赛都有便宜可占感到不满，但是仍然朝着士兵的小径跑去。没想到过了半个小时后到达终点，却是名列第一。他感到不可思议，按说自己与其他士兵的能力相比不可能取得名次。但是，主持赛跑的军官笑着恭喜他取得了比赛的胜利。过了几个小时后，大批人马到了，他们跑得筋疲力尽，看见赢得了胜利的士兵，觉得非常奇怪。但是突然大家醒悟过来，在岔路口诚实守信，是多么重要。

A soldier who is not very good at running, so in a cross-country forces quickly fall away after a man ran alone. Turned a few bends, encountered a fork in the road, a road, indicating that officers running; the other way, indicate that soldiers running trails. He paused, though officers do not even have a cheap motocross can stick dissatisfied, but still trails ran towards the soldiers. After half an hour he did not expect to reach the end, it was ranked first. He was not proposed, according to their ability in comparison with the other soldiers could not get ranking. However, presided race officer smiled congratulate him get the victory. After a few hours later, a large number of troops arrived, they ran exhausted and saw soldiers won a victory, and they feel very strange. But suddenly they wake up in the fork honest, how important it is.

2. 感恩（Thanksgiving）

感谢生活给予我们的一切；恩待哺育、培养、教导、支持、帮助过我们的每个人，同时对每一位客人内心怀有一种感激之情，并由衷地欢迎客人的到来。

Thanks for all things that life gives us; thanks for everyone that feeds, trains, guides, supports and helps us, keep a grateful heart to every guest, and sincerely welcome the guests.

3. 操守（Conduct）

遵纪守法、树正气、走正道；在酒店服务工作岗位上，要经得起时间的考验和艰苦的磨炼，自觉培养高尚的节操；靠自己的劳动创造所得，不要把金钱看成自己幸福的唯一源泉，不择手段地赚取钱财。

Personal integrity: abide laws, encourage health trends, and take the right path; in the hotel service, people should stand the test of time and hardship, consciously cultivate noble moral integrity; create wealth on their own labor, do not put money as the only source of happiness and earn money by foul means.

4. 团结（Unity）

团结协作、顾全大局；在一个团队里，如果成员没有团队意识，各行其是，团队的目标将永远无法实现。创建和谐的团队意识，大家只要密切配合，团结协作，就能使团队焕发出生机和活力；酒店工作需要各岗位工作人员高度配合，团结周围的每一个人，学习先进，互相、关心、尊重、支持，密切配合。

Solidarity and cooperation: pay attention to the overall situation. In the teamwork, if the members do not have the sense of team awareness do things in their own ways, the team objective will never be achieved. Members should closely cooperate with each other in order to create the harmonious team awareness and make the team glowing with vigor and vitality; hotel work require highly cooperation of all positions, unity of everyone, learning of advanced spirits, mutual care, respect, support, and close coordination.

地狱与天堂

Hell and Heaven

牧师请教上帝：地狱和天堂有什么不同？上帝带着牧师来到一间房子里。一群人围着一锅肉汤，他们手里都拿着一把长长的汤勺，因为手柄太长，谁也无法把肉汤送到自己嘴里。每个人的脸上都充满绝望和悲苦。上帝说，这里就是地狱。

Pastor asked God: What is the difference between hell and heaven? God brought the pastor to a room. A group of people were around a pot of broth, their hands were holding a long spoon, and they could not put the broth to their mouth because the handle was too long. Everyone's face was full of despair and misery. God said, "Here is the hell".

上帝又带着牧师来到另一间房子里。这里的摆设与刚才那间没有什么两样，唯一不同的是，这里的人们都把汤舀给坐在对面的人喝。他们都吃得很香、很满足。上帝说，这里就是天堂。

God brought the pastor to another room which had no difference with the above room, and the only difference was that the people here put the broth to the others sitting opposite. They eat very happy and satisfied. God said, "Here is the paradise".

同样的待遇和条件，为什么地狱里的人痛苦，而天堂里的人快乐？原因很简单：地狱里的人只想着喂自己，而天堂里的人却想着喂别人。

In the same terms and conditions, Why the people are suffering in hell, and happy in heaven? The reason is simple: the people in hell just want to feed themselves, but people in heaven are thinking of feeding others.

（二）立志（Making Determination）

（1）爱业："热爱是最好的老师"；热爱本职工作，"干一行，爱一行"，认真仔细地履行自己的职业岗位职责；维护酒店的对外形象和声誉，不做任何有损于酒店利益的事。

Love the work: "Love is the best teacher"; love your own job, "love whatever job you takes up" and fulfill your job responsibilities carefully; maintain the hotel image and reputation, don not do any derimental things to the interests of hotel.

（2）敬业：尊重自己，尊重自己的职业；职业没有高低贵贱，劳动最光荣。酒店就是服务客人的，不管别人怎么看待我们，我们都会真诚地给客人提供最好的服务。

Devote to work: Respect yourself, respect your profession; there in neither lowliness nor nobleness in job, work is the most glorious thing, and hotel is to service the guests. No matter how others treat us, we will sincerely provide the best service to the guest.

（3）乐业：在工作中寻找乐趣；我们不可能选择客人，但我们可以选择快乐地面对各种各样的客人，并将这份快乐带给周围的每个人。

Work in contentment: looking for fun at work; we cannot choose the guests, but we can choose to be happy to face a variety of guests, and bring the happiness to everyone around us.

同学们，新的学习生活即将开始，酒店专业就是你的方向，路就是脚下，明天你将亲自体验这份属于酒店人的自豪感……

Students, new learning life will begin soon. Hotel major is your professional direction. The road is on the foot, tomorrow you will personally experience the sense of pride belonging to hoteliers...

目　录

模块一 前厅部概述
Module I Front Office Department Outline

【情境导入】【Scenario Introduction】

不要让疲倦的客人就这么走了
Do not Let Tired Guests Go with a Disappointment

地点：三亚海悦台热带风情主题酒店前台

Place：Reception of Sanya Haiyuetai Redai Fengqing Theme Hotel

一天深夜，两位面带倦容的客人来到前厅接待处，要求登记一间普通标准间。接待员表示标准间刚刚卖完，只有一间刚刚退房，楼层服务员准备清扫，请两位客人稍等片刻。

One late night, two guests who looked very tired came to the Reception and asked for a standard room. One receptionist told them that the standard room has just been sold out, and asked the two guests to wait a moment because there was a vacant dirty room which was ready to be cleaned by the floor attendant.

客人不禁皱起了眉头："不行，刚才机场代表告诉我们是有房间的！"

The guests grimaced and said, "No, the airport representative just told us that you have room!"

接待员："是有的，但请稍等一会儿，我们马上清理出来，请您在大堂吧略坐片刻，我们会通知您的。"

The receptionist said, "Yes, we have. But you need wait a moment and we will make it ready as soon as possible. Please have a break at the lobby bar and we will inform you when it is ready".

客人看了看接待员，一句话都不说地走向大堂吧。接待员赶紧催促客房中心立即清扫普通标准间。15 分钟后，其中的一位客人来到接待处。

The two guests looked at the receptionist and went to the lobby bar without saying a word. The receptionist urged the guestroom center to clean the standard room at once. 15 minutes later, one of the two guests came to the Reception.

顾客："小姐，到底有没有房间，我们坐了 3 个多小时的飞机，真的很累，想休息……"

Guest: "Hello, is the room ready? We are really tired and want to have a rest because we had a three-hour flight..."

接待员连忙安慰客人，立刻又打电话到客房中心询问普通标准间是否清扫好，客房服务员却说："刚清扫好了一间豪华标准间，其他房间还没有。"

The receptionist had to comfort the guest and called the guestroom center to see whether the room was ready. However, the floor attendant said, "we just finished a Deluxe Room and haven't finished others."

接待员："你们在干什么呢，清扫房间那么慢！你们知道客人等得多焦急。"

The receptionist said, " What are you doing on earth? You are so slow that our guests become anxious."

服务员："房间总得一间间打扫吧，哪有那么快。"说完电话挂断了。

The floor attendant said, "We have to finish them one by one. Not so fast.", then hung up the phone.

接待员无奈地放下话筒。又过了15分钟，两位客人再次走向接待处，开口便高声责问接待员："你们到底有没有房间？把我们骗到这儿，根本没房，我们不在你们这儿住了。"说完，便向门外走去。这时，大堂经理走了过来想留住客人，可没等她说话，客人便愤然离去。

The receptionist had to put down the phone. Another 15 minutes later, the two guests came to the reception again and began to shout at the receptionist: "Do you have a room? You cheated us to come here and you do not have room at all. We will not stay here." Then, they walked away. The assistant manager came up and hoped to persuade them to stay at the hotel. However, the guests left in anger before she spoke.

【情境分析】【Scenario Analysis】

案例中，客人这一次不愉快的经历，将影响他们再次进入该酒店。案例中出现的问题，说明该酒店在管理与服务上存在漏洞。首先机场代表在不了解酒店现实房态的情况下向客人许诺。我们常讲一句话：做不到的事情不要说，说了就一定要做到。无论从事管理或是服务，都必须做到这一点。机场代表在接待前，就应了解房态，答应了客人之后，更应该及时联系酒店做出安排，使客人抵达后能够顺利入住。其次接待员处事不够灵活。从客人的话语中，接待员就应该听得出客人的急切心理，在服务过程中，我们应急客人所急，想客人所想。当酒店一时满足不了客人的时候，要及时采取变通措施。楼层服务员的不配合是最根本的原因。从服务员回答的口气里我们可以看出其服务的意识与合作的态度是欠佳的。

In this case, the guests had an unpleasant experience which will prevent them from staying at the hotel again. The problem in this case indicates that the hotel has some loopholes in management and service. Firstly, the airport representative made a promise to the guests without knowing the room status. We always say that when you can't do something, don't say it, and once you said something, put in your best effort to do it. We must always keep it in mind no matter whether you are engaged in management or service. The airport representative should first know the room status before he/she received the guests, and should have contact the hotel to make necessary arrangement after he/she promised to the guests so that the guests could check in with the hotel smoothly. Secondly, the receptionist was not flexible. From the guests' words, she should have known the anxiety of guests. We should worry about what the guests worry and think what the guests think. When the hotel can't meet the guest's need at once, we should be flexible. The root cause was the noncooperation of the floor attendant. We can see from the floor attendant's answer that he/she lack in service awareness and the attitude towards cooperation.

最后，大堂经理也有责任。大堂经理的职责是在营业部门经理下班或不在场的情况下，监管各营业部门的运作，处理非正常运作所引致的住客投诉，处理酒店发生的意外事件或紧急事件，最终达到客人满意。案例中的客人已等候多时以致发脾气要离开了，大堂经理才姗姗出现，其行为是失职的。

Finally, the assistant manager should also have some responsibility. The duty of an assistant manager is to supervise the operation of the business departments and deal with complaints made by guests due to abnormal operations and handle accidents or emergent events so as to meet the guests' satisfaction when the manager is off duty or absent. In this case, the assistant manager came up when the guests wanted to leave in anger, so she behaved in a negligent manner.

本案例中共涉及前厅部门的前台接待员、房务部服务人员以及大堂经理，由于这三个职位的工作人员没有协调沟通好，导致客人愤然离去，可以看出，酒店在日常运营过程中，不同部门工作人员良好的沟通，将会起到事半功倍的效果。

This case involves the receptionist of the Front Office Department, the floor attendant of the Housekeeping Department and the assistant manager. The guests left in anger due to the poor coordination and communication between them. Therefore, good communication between different departments in the daily operation of the hotel will help achieve better results with half the effort.

【学习目标】【Learning Goals】

［知识目标］［Knowledge Objectives］

1. 掌握前厅部岗位工作任务及业务特点。

To master the work tasks and business features of the Front Office Department.

2. 掌握服务礼仪，熟悉语言技巧。

To master the service etiquette and be familiar with language skills.

［能力目标］［Capacity Objectives］

1. 能区分前厅各个岗位的职责和任务，能够按照酒店的标准来纠正自己的仪容仪表。

To be able to distinguish the duties and tasks of all positions of the front office and to correct own grooming and appearance in accordance with the hotel's standards.

2. 能够进行一般性的岗位英语会话。

To be able to have a dialogue in English.

【重点和难点】【Key Points and Difficulties】

熟练掌握前厅部的组织结构和各部门的业务职责。

To be familiar with the organization structure of the Front Office Department and the duties of various departments.

任务一　认识前厅部
Task I　Introduction to Front Office Department

一、前厅部概况（Overview of Front Office Department）

前厅指的是酒店的正门、大厅（大堂）等，属于前厅部管辖范围。前厅是酒店的中心，是酒店中集交通、服务、休息等多种功能于一体的共享空间，是客人与酒店接触的主要场所，是每一位客人抵达、离开酒店的必经之地，也是客人形成对酒店的第一印象和最后印象之处。按功能可将前厅划分为正门及人流线路、服务区、休息区和公共卫生间等主要区域。

Front office refers to the areas which are under the jurisdiction of the Front Office Department including the entrance gate and the hall (lobby), which is the center of a hotel, a shared space integrating multiple functions such as traffic，service and rest，a major place where guests meet the hotel and an essential place where every guest arrive at and leave the hotel and where gives guests the first and final impressions. Classified by function，the front office can be divided into several functional areas including the main entrance and traffic flow lines，service area，rest area and public washrooms.

前厅部又称为总服务台，它是酒店业务活动的中心，是酒店组织客源、销售客房商品、组织接待和协调对客服务，并对客人提供各种综合性服务的部门。前厅部是整个酒店服务工作的核心，是酒店经营管理中的一个重要部门，是协调酒店所有对客服务的部门，涉及酒店提供的对客服务的诸多内容，为客人提供客房预订、入住登记、行李、电话、留言、问询、票务、邮件、商务、外币兑换、委托代办、结账离店等服务项目，使客人在入住、离店、住店过程中均能享受到高效优质、方便舒适、个性化、全过程的服务。

Front Office，also called as reception desk，is the center of hotel activities and a comprehensive service department which is responsible for the organization of guests，sales of guestrooms，organization of reception and coordination of services to guests，and provision of services to guests. Front Office is the core of a hotel's entire service work and also an important department for the operation and management of the hotel，coordinating all departments providing services to guests and involving many service items provided by the hotel to guests，including room reservation，check-in，luggage，telephone，message，information，tickets，e-mails，business affairs，foreign exchange，commission agency，checkouts，etc. to allow guests to enjoy high-efficiency，quality，convenient，comfortable，individualized and total-process services during check-in，checkout and stay at the hotel.

前厅部为客人提供的服务包括从客人抵店前的预订入住，直至客人离店结账以及建立客史档案等，贯穿于客人与酒店交易往来的全过程，是建立良好住客关系的重要环节，住客对酒店的意见和建议往往会通过前厅来反映。前厅部也是酒店管理的关键部门，为总经理和各职能部门的经理提供各种信息、数据等决策依据，其运行的好坏直接影响到酒店的整体服务质量、管理水平、经济效益和市场形象。

The services provided by the front office run through the whole process of transaction between guests and the hotel ranging from room reservation prior to their arrival，check-out and payment to the establishment of stay records，so the front office is an important point in establishing a good relationship with guests. Guests' opinions and suggestions are often made to the hotel through the front office. The front office is also a key department in managing a hotel，which is responsible to provide all kinds of information and data to the general manager and other functional departments as basis for decision making，so the functioning of the front office will directly affect the overall service quality，management level，economic benefit and market image of a hotel.

二、前厅部的重要性（Importance of Front Office）

（一）前厅部的地位（Position of Front Office）

前厅部是现代酒店的重要组成部分，存在着业务复杂、接待服务广泛、专业技术性强的特点。前厅部要求 24 小时运转，全面对客服务，服务方式灵活多样，要求高效运转，担负着销售客房及酒店其他产品的重任，能够妥善处理各种关系，对酒店市场形象、服务质量乃至管理水平和经济效益有至关重要的影响。

Front Office is an important part of a modern hotel and has features like complexity，wide coverage of services and high professionalism. The front office should run 24 hours per day so as to provide total services to guests and should be flexible in ways of rendering services and efficient in operation. It is responsible for the sales of guestrooms and other hotel products and able to deal with all relations. The front office plays an essential role in shaping hotel's image, and in enhancing service quality, even management level and economic benefits.

因此，前厅部在酒店的经营管理中占有举足轻重的地位和作用，主要表现在以下几个方面：

Therefore, the front office is of special importance and role in the operation and management of a hotel. Its position and role can be represented by the following aspects:

1. 前厅部是酒店的形象代表

Front Office Represents is the image of a hotel

任何客人一进店，就会对前厅的环境艺术、装饰布置、设备设施和前厅部员工仪容仪表、服务质量、工作效率等，产生深刻的"第一印象"，而这种第一印象在客人对酒店的认知中会产生非常重要的作用，它产生于瞬间，但却会长时间保留在人们的记忆表象中。客人离店时，经由大堂，前厅服务人员为客人办理结算手续、送别客人时的工作表现等都会给客人留下"最后印象"，优质的服务将使客人对酒店产生依恋之情。酒店的服务质量和档次的高低，从前厅部的服务就可以直接反映出来。前厅是酒店的门面，对于客人及社会公众形成深刻的第一印象及整体印象起着重要作用，酒店形象是公众对于酒店的总体评价，是酒店的表现与特征在公众心目中的反映，酒店形象对酒店的生存和发展有着直接的影响，一个好的形象是酒店巨大的精神财富，前厅部是酒店的形象代表。

When any guest enters a hotel, the guest will have the "first impression" on the environmental art, decoration and arrangement, equipment and facilities, appearance of front office staff, service hotel, work efficiency of the hotel, which may play an important role in the cognition of the hotel. Although it appears momentarily, it will remain in guests' memory. When guests leave the hotel, they must go to the lobby and check out with the reception, so the work performance of the receptionist will give the "final impression" to them. Quality services can result in guests' high attachment to the hotel. The service quality and level of a hotel can be directly reflected from the services rendered by its front office. The front office is the face of a hotel and plays an important role in giving guests and the public a deep first impression and an overall impression on the hotel. The image of a hotel represents the overall comment of the public on the hotel and the reflection of the hotel's performance and characteristics, so it will have a direct effect on the survival and development of a hotel. A good image is huge spiritual wealth to a hotel while its front office represents the image of a hotel.

【案例】【Case】

背后鞠躬

Take a Bow Behind the Back of A Guest

一位学习酒店专业的同学为了完成老师布置的前厅作业，在三亚亚龙湾红树林度假酒店的前厅对服务进行调查。调查中，他看到了这样的一幕：在宾客进进出出的大堂里，一位手提皮箱的客人走进了大厅，行李员立即微笑地迎上去，鞠躬问候，并跟在客人后面问客人是否需要帮助提皮箱，这位客人也许有急事，嘴里说了声："不用，谢谢！"头也没回，径直朝电梯走去，那位行李员朝着那匆匆离去的背影深深地鞠了一躬，嘴里还不停地说："欢迎！欢迎！"这位同学便找到大堂经理问："为什么要这样做？”大堂经理告诉他：“当面给客人鞠躬是为了礼貌服务。”同学又问：“可那位行李员朝客人的背影鞠躬又是为了什么呢？”“既为这位客人，也为其他客人。”经理说：“如果此时那位客人突然回头，他会对我们的热情服务留下印象，同时也是给大堂里的其他客人看的，他们会想，当我转过身去，酒店员工肯定对我一样礼貌。”

A student majoring in hotel management had a service survey at the front office of Yalong Bay Mangrove Tree Resort, Sanya City in order to complete the assignment made by his teacher. During the survey, he saw a scene: In the lobby with guests coming and going, a porter bowed his greeting with a smile to a guest with a leather suitcase in his hand when walking in the lobby and asked the guest whether he needed help. The guest might have something urgent and said to the porter, “No, thanks!”, and then went towards the elevator without a glance behind. The porter took a deep bow to the guest who rushed away and kept saying “welcome, welcome”. The student found the assistant manager and asked “why did he do that?” The assistant manager told him It is polite to take a bow to a guest face to face.” The student further asked. “Why did the porter take a bow behind the guest?” “Not only to this guest but also to others,” the manager said, “If the guest turns around, he must be impressed by our warm services, and when other guests see this scene, they will think: the hotel staff will be also polite to me when I turn around”.

【案例分析】【Case Analysis】

前厅部员工是酒店的形象代表，他们的一言一行关系着酒店的声誉。无论是大型的接待活动，还是细小的肢体动作，无不是完美服务的体现。当面的热情服务，体现了酒店的礼貌服务，而背后的虔诚备至，才是酒店的与众不同之处，为酒店树立了良好的形象。每个前厅部员工发自内心的对客服务，是酒店闪亮的金牌。

The front office employees represent the image of the hotel, so their words and behaviors relates to the reputation of the hotel. Either a large reception activity or a tiny body movement represents the quality of service. The face-to-face service shows the politeness of a hotel to guests, but the sincerity behind the guests shows the difference of the hotel from others, shaping a good image for the hotel. The heartfelt services rendered by the front office shape a shining golden brand for the hotel.

2. 前厅部是客人与酒店联系的纽带（Front Office, A Tie Between Guests and Hotel）

前厅部工作贯穿于客人与酒店交易往来的全过程。客人在酒店整个居留期间，前厅要提供各种有关的服务，通过开展预订客房业务，首先与潜在的客人接触，接着是接待抵店客人，办理登记手续，使客人顺利入住，为住客提供各项前厅服务，管理客账直至送别客人离店。前厅部还为住客建立客史档案，为住客可能的再次光临做好准备。客人遇到困难要找前厅寻求帮助，客人感到不满时也要找前厅投诉。在客人的心目中，前厅便是酒店的全部。而且，在大堂汇集的大量人流中，除住店客人外，还有许多前来就餐、开会、购物、参观游览、会客交谈、检查指导等各种各样的客人，他们往往停留在大堂，对酒店的环境、设施、服务品头论足。前厅部管理成了住客和酒店联络的“桥梁和纽带”，是建立良好住客关系的重要环节。

The front office's work runs through the whole process of the transactions between a guest and the hotel. During their stay at the hotel, the front office will provide various services to them. Through the room reservation, the front office will keep contact with the potential guests, and then receive the guests and go through check-in procedures for them so that they can stay at the hotel smoothly. After doing so, the front office will also provide their services, manage the guest account and see guests off. After a guest leaves the hotel, the front office should establish a record so as to make preparations for future possible stays with the hotel. When a guest encounters some difficulty, he/she may seek help to the front office, and when he/she is not satisfied with the hotel, he/she will also complain to the front office. Guests regard the front office as the representative of the hotel. In addition, as the lobby can gather many people including those who will come to the hotel for catering, meeting, shopping, sightseeing, business discussions with guests and inspection, who will comment on the environment, facilities and services of the hotel during their stay in the lobby. Therefore, the front office will become a "bridge and tie" between the guests and the hotel, and is an important link in establishing a good customer relationship.

绿茶换红茶
Green Tea Changed to Black Tea

酒店的客房内，按常规要为客人准备一种茶叶。海口明光国际大酒店依据大多数客人的习惯，在客房内统一放上绿茶。一次，一位香港客人住进了该酒店，几天后离店时，无意中说道他不喜欢绿茶。不久，该客人第二次入住该酒店，前厅部马上通知客房部，将该客人房间的绿茶换成红茶。该客人走进房间，意外地发现为他准备的红茶，十分高兴。一连几天，服务员都给他放上红茶。他住了三天，临行前的晚上，他对该楼层的服务员说："你们怎么在我房内始终放红茶，而你们服务车上均是绿茶?"服务员微笑道："您上次住这里时说过不喜欢绿茶，喜欢红茶。我们就在您的客史档案上加了一笔"。这位香港客人惊喜地说："你们的工作真细致！这样高水平的服务，酒店肯定发财！"

Hotels always like to prepare some tea in the guestrooms for guests. Haikou Mingguang International Hotel prepared some green tea in the guestrooms based on the habit of most guests. However, a guest from Hong Kong stayed at the hotel. When he left, he told unconsciously that he did not like green tea. That guest stayed at the hotel again and the front office informed the housekeeping department to prepare some black tea instead of green tea. When the guest entered the room and found the black tea, he felt very happy. The servant served black tea for him during his stay. The guest stayed for three nights. The night before he left, he asked the floor attendant "why did you prepare black tea for my room, while I find green tea in your cart?" The attendant smiled and said "you said you didn't like green tea but like black tea last time when you stayed with us, so we added the information to your record." The Hong Kong guest said happily, "How careful you are! I believe you must make a fortune by such high-quality services."

【案例分析】【Case Analysis】

正是前厅部把客人的喜好记录下来，在客人再次来店时及时通知客房部，取得了客人的好评，给客人留下了深刻的印象，提升了酒店的声誉。所以前厅部是酒店的神经中枢，在信息的采集和传递中处于"首脑"地位。

It is because the front office recorded the preference of the guest and informed the housekeeping department in a timely manner when the guest stayed at the hotel again that the hotel was highly commented and gave a deep impression to the guest, thus enhancing the reputation of the hotel. Therefore, the front office is the nerve center of a hotel and plays an important role in collecting and transferring information.

3. 前厅部是酒店创造经济收入的关键部门（The Front Office is the Key Department for Creating Economic Income to A Hotel）

为住客提供食宿是酒店的基本功能，客房是酒店出售的最大、最主要的商品。前厅部销售的主要产品——客房对酒店的创利至关重要，其销售业绩直接关系到酒店的经济效益。通常在酒店的营业收入中，客房销售额要高于其他各项。据统计，目前国际上客房收入一般占酒店总营业收入的50%左右，而在中国还高于这个比例。前厅部的有效运转是提高客房出租率、增加客房销售收入、提高酒店经济效益的关键之一。

It is the fundamental function of a hotel to provide accommodation for their guests, and guestroom is the largest and most important commodity sold by a hotel. Guestroom, the primary commodity sold by the Front Office, is crucial for the creation of profits to the hotel, and the sales performance is directly related to the economic benefits of the hotel. Usually in the operational income of a hotel the sales of guestroom is higher than all the other items. According to statistics, the income from guestroom usually accounts for about 50% of the total business revenue of a hotel in the world, and in China, it is even higher than this proportion. The effective operation of the Front Office is one of the key factors to enhance the occupancy rate of guestroom, increase the sales revenue of guest office and improve the economic benefits of a hotel.

推销商务房
Promotion of Business Room

这周是三亚第18个服装节。周三下午，客人范先生来到海口喜来登温泉度假酒店前台，要求入住一间标准房。接待员小吴看了一下范先生的穿着，礼貌地询问："范先生是来参加服装节活动的吧？"范先生说是的，因为工作忙，所以没有提前订房。

This week was the 18th Clothes Festival of Sanya. In the afternoon on Wednesday, Mr. Fan, a guest, came to the front desk of Sheraton Hot Spring Resort Hotel in Haikou and asked to live in a standard room. Xiao Wu, the receptionist, looked at the clothes of Mr. Fan and asked politely, "Are you here to take part in the activities of the Clothes Festival?" Mr. Fan answered yes and he also stated that he did not book a room in advance due to busy work.

小吴不失时机地说："范先生，您是来参加服装节活动的，我们酒店的商务房特别适合您这样的商务客人，商务房里有免费的网络，方便您联系，客房比较安静，入住商务房的客人到商务酒廊消费是免费的，到健身中心锻炼也是免费的。房间的价格只比标准房贵了260元，您看我就帮您入住商务房，怎么样？"范先生略作思考，便答应了。小吴把酒店里最后的一间商务房给推销出去了。

Xiao Wu cleverly took the opportunity and said, "Since Mr. Fan you are here to take part in the activities of the Clothes Festival, the business room in our hotel is especially suitable for you, in which there is free internet so it is very convenient for you to contact other people. It is quiet in the guestroom and the guests living in the commercial house could consume freely in the commercial wine lounge and for exercise in the fitness center. The price of this room is only RMB260 Yuan higher than standard room. So may I now help you to live in a business room? What do you think about it?" Mr. Fan contemplated for a short while and then agreed. Thus Xiao Wu sold the last business room out.

【案例分析】【Case Analysis】

小吴积极主动地销售客房产品，提高了酒店的客房出租率和平均房价，使酒店收到了良好的经济效益。

Xiao Wu actively took the initiative to sell the product of guestroom, thus had enhanced the occupancy rate and average room price of the hotel and acquired good economic benefit for the hotel.

4. 前厅部是酒店管理的参谋和助手（The Front Office is the Adviser and Assistant for the Management of A Hotel）

作为酒店业务活动的中心，前厅部直接面对市场、面对客人，是酒店中最敏感的部门，收集有关市场变化、客人需求和整个酒店对客服务、经营管理的各种信息，并对这些信息进行认真的整理和分析，每日或定期向酒店管理机构提供真实反映酒店经营管理情况的数据报表和工作报告。前厅部还定期向酒店管理机构提供咨询意见，作为制订和调整酒店计划和经营策略的参考依据。

As the center for business activities of a hotel, the Front Office directly faces the market and the guest as well as the most sensitive department in the hotel. It collects various kinds of information related to market changes, demands from clients, services of the whole hotel to guests, and operational management, then conduct careful sorting and analysis on this information, and provides daily or monthly data report and working report that could truly manifest the operational management status of the hotel to the management department of the hotel. The Front Office also provides regular consulting opinions to the management department of the hotel as the reference for formulating and regulating the plan and operational strategies of the hotel.

前厅部是酒店信息中心和对客服务协调中心，在很大程度上控制和协调整个酒店的经营活动，在这里发出的每一项指令、每一条信息，都将直接影响酒店其他部门对客人的服务质量。因此，前厅部在酒店的经营活动中是承上启下、联系内外、疏通左右的枢纽，可以说是整个酒店业务的活动中心。

The Front Office is the information center and the guest service coordination center of the hotel, controlling and coordinating the operational activities of the whole hotel to a very large extent. Every instruction and every piece of information will directly influence the quality of the service of other departments of the hotel to the guests. Therefore, the Front Office is the pivot for connecting the preceding and the following, linking the interior and exterior, and dredging the left and the right during the operational activities of the hotel. It could be regarded as the center for the activities of the entire hotel.

综上所述，前厅部是酒店的重要组成部分，是加强酒店经营的第一个重要环节。在当今竞争日益激烈的市场经济情况下，前厅的地位和作用日益得到提高和加强。

To sum up, the Front Office is an important constituting part of a hotel and the first important element for strengthening the operation of a hotel. The position and function of the Front Office are increasingly raised and intensified in the increasingly competitive market.

（二）前厅部的主要任务（Major Tasks of the Front Office）

前厅部的地位和作用决定了它在酒店经营中所承担的任务，虽然不同规模的酒店组织机构不同，但其基本任务是一致的，就是推销客房及酒店其他产品，协调酒店各部门向客人提供满意的优质服务，使酒店获得理想的经济效益和社会效益，主要表现在以下几个方面：

The position and functions of the Front Office have determined the tasks it bears in the operation of a hotel. Although hotels of different sizes have different organizational structures, they have almost the same fundamental task that is to promote guestroom and other products of the hotel and coordinate the various departments of the hotel to provide satisfactory and quality services to the guests so as to render the hotel to achieve ideal economic and social benefits, which is mainly manifested in the several following aspects:

1. 市场销售 (Sales)

通过和各客源单位联系建立客源渠道，以及通过预订和在与顾客接触过程中，在客人入住后进行推销，最大限度地销售客房商品。在国际酒店业中，客房收入、餐饮收入和其他收入的比例为5:4:1，客房销售直接影响酒店的经济效益。同时，客房商品具有价值不可储存性的特征，是一种“极易腐烂”的商品。

The Front Office will establish channels for guest resources with various units providing guest resources, make reservations, and contact with the guests so as to conduct promotion after the guests check in for selling the product of guestroom to the maximum degree. In the international industry of hotel, the proportion of income from guestroom, food, and other sources is 5 : 4 : 1, and the sales of guestroom will directly influence the economic benefit of the hotel. In the meanwhile, guestrooms are characterized as having values unable to be stored, so it is a kind of commodity “that is extremely liable to decay”.

因此，前厅部应运用科学的管理手段，高效率地完成客房销售工作，搞好客房销售预测以提高客房部门的销售能力，同时积极参与酒店的市场调研，参与房价及促销计划的制定，配合销售部门进行宣传和促销，开展客房预订业务。前厅销售客房的数量和达成的平均房价水平，是衡量其工作绩效的一项重要的客观标准。

Therefore, the Front Office should apply scientific management measures to finish the work of selling guestroom high efficiently, and in the meantime to actively take part in the investigation and research on the market the hotel as well as the formulation of price and the plans for promotion, coordinate the sales department to conduct propaganda and promotion, and develop business of guestroom reservation. The number of the guestroom sold by the Front Office and the realized average price of guestroom are the important objective standards for measuring their performance of work.

2. 前厅迎接 (Reception)

住客刚抵达酒店时，在酒店大堂的迎接，其中涉及行李员与散客迎接、门卫和电梯迎接员的迎接、团体行李的处理以及其他情况的迎接等，在迎接住客的过程中，给予客人最良好的体验，让客人尽可能最快地熟悉本酒店的环境。

When the guest just arrives at the Hotel, welcoming in the hall of the hotel involves with receiving by the porter, individual guest, doorman, and elevator receiver, treatment of luggage, and reception under other circumstances. During the process of receiving the guest, it is sure to provide the guests with best experience and enable them to get familiarized with the environment of the hotel as fast as possible.

3. 传递信息及了解住客需求 (Transmission of Information and Understanding of Guests' Need)

当一位客人办理入住手续后，前厅收银员必须为其开设一个账户，以记录客人在酒店住宿期间的消费。一般客人账户包括每日的房费、餐厅的消费（采用签单形式）、客房用餐服务费、饮料费（房间迷你酒吧）、洗衣服务费、外卖服务费、电话费等一切在酒店消费的费用。收银员每天负责核算和整理各营业部门收银员送来的客人消费账单，确保酒店的经济利益；同时编制各种会计报表，以便及时反映酒店的营业活动状况。

After a guest finishes the check-in procedures, the Front Office cashier must open an account for him so as to record the consumption of the guest in the hotel during his stay. Usually the account of the guest includes the room fees for all days, consumption in the dining room (in the form of signed receipts), servicing fees for having food in guestrooms, beverage fees (mini bar within the room), laundry service charges, delivery services charges, telephone fees, and all the other fees consumed in the hotel. The cashier is responsible for calculating and summing up the bills of the guests' consumption sent by the cashiers from various business departments so as to ensure the economic interest of the hotel, and in the meanwhile make various kinds of accounting reports so as to timely reflect the status of the operational activities of the hotel.

4. 提供有关酒店经营管理信息，建立客人信息和其他资料档案（Provision of Related Information on Managing Hotels and Establishment of Guest Information and Other Materials and Documents）

由于前厅部处于酒店业务活动的中心地位，每天能接触大量的信息，如有关客源市场、产品销量、营业收入、客人的需求及反馈意见等，前厅部要将这些信息加以处理，向酒店的各级管理部门报告。前厅部通过建立住店客人的资料档案，记录客人在店逗留期间的主要情况和数据，掌握客人动态。

As the Front Office is the center of the business activities of the hotel, it will receive a great deal of information, such as guest sources, sales volume, business revenues, and needs and feedback from the guests, etc., and the Front Office should deal with these information and report to various management departments of the hotel. The Front Office will record the major status and data of guests during his stay in the hotel and master his dynamic statuses by establishing the materials and files of guests living in the hotel.

将客户资料以及市场调研与预测、客人预订、接待情况等信息收存归类，并定期进行统计分析，便形成了以前厅为中心的收集、处理、传递及储存信息的系统，通过已掌握的大量信息来不断地改进酒店的服务工作，提高酒店的科学管理水平。

Information like the materials of the guest's history, market investigation, research and prediction, guest reservation, and reception is collected for classification, and periodical statistics and analysis are conducted on them so as to form a system of collecting, treating, transmitting and storing information with the Front Office as the center so as to constantly improve the servicing work of the hotel and improve the scientific management level of the hotel through the great deal of information that have been mastered.

5. 提供各项前厅日常服务（Provision of Regular Front Office Services）

前厅部作为对客服务的中心，担负着直接对客人服务的繁重工作，如在酒店大门、机场或车站迎送客人的服务，行李搬运服务，接受问询及投诉，商务中心服务，发放客房钥匙，委托代办，贵重物品保管及通过电话总机所提供的各项服务。由于前厅部的特殊地位，使得这些日常服务工作的质量、效率显得非常重要。

As the center for guest services, the Front Office bears the heavy work of directly providing various kinds of services to guests including welcoming the guests and seeing them off at the gate of the hotel, airport or bus stations, delivery of luggage, accepting inquiries and claims, services in the business center, distributing the keys of guestrooms, authorized representation, keeping precious articles, and those provide through switchboards. Due to the special status of the Front Office, the quality and efficiency of these daily services become very important.

完美服务赢得回头客
Perfect Services Winning Returned Guests

王小姐到三亚必然住金茂三亚亚龙湾希尔顿大酒店，她的朋友十分不解。王小姐说这是因为这家酒店的服务给她留下了十分深刻的印象。原来，王小姐第一次出差到三亚，通过朋友介绍选择入住这家酒店，总台不但迅速办理了入住手续，而且当询问三亚有什么好玩的时，总台小姐很热情地一一介绍，还给了她一本三亚旅游指南。

Every time when Miss Wang came to Sanya, she would surely live in Jinmao Sanya Yalong Bay Hilton Hotel. All her friends felt very confused about this. Miss Wang said that this was due to the services of the Hotel that had left her a very deep impression. It turned out to be that Miss Wang chose to live in this hotel through the introduction of her friends when she first went to Sanya on business, during which working staff at the reception desk not only finished the procedures for checking-in quickly but also provided very enthusiastic introductions and gave her a book on the guidance of tourism in Sanya when she asked about recreational things in Sanya.

入住第二天，由于车票的原因，王小姐想延迟退房，致电总台，总台服务员听完之后很友好地告诉她可以延迟到下午2点退房。她印象最深刻，也是她愿意下榻该酒店的最大的原因是：退完房三亚下起了大雨，行李员撑着伞在雨中帮王小姐招呼出租车，叫到车后，行李员虽然半身都被雨淋湿了，但他仍旧热情地帮王小姐提行李，并为王小姐准备了雨伞，当出租车开出好长一段路，王小姐还隐约看到行李员站在雨中向她挥手。这个景象里的行李员就像王小姐的家人一样。这件事让王小姐十分感动，所以每次到三亚，王小姐总选择该酒店。

On the next day, Miss Wang wished to extend the check-out time due to ticket schedule, so she called the reception desk. After hearing her words, the staff at the reception desk told her in a very polite way that she could extend the check-out time till 2pm. The deepest impression as well as the most important reason for Miss Wang would like to live in that hotel lies in that it rained heavily in Sanya after she checked out but the porter held an umbrella in the rain to help Miss Wang call a taxi, after which the porter still kindly helped her to carry her luggage although he had been almost all wet. He also prepared an umbrella for Miss Wang who could still see him standing in the rain and waving to her after the taxi run for quite a long distance. This scene made Miss Wang feel like a family member of Miss Wang. She was greatly touched by this so every time when she came to Sanya, she would always choose to live in that hotel.

【案例分析】【Case Analysis】

行李员处处为客人着想，像家人一样周到细致的服务，让客人有了家的温暖感受，给宾客留下了依依不舍的感觉。优质服务不但表现在技能技巧上，更表现在真诚热情上，所以该行李员的完美服务赢得了回头客。

The porter considers everything for the guests and provides very meticulous service like a family member so as to render the guest feel the warm feeling of being home and thus unwilling to part. Quality service is manifested not only through skills or techniques but also on sincere enthusiasm. Therefore, the perfect service of the port won returned guests.

6. 协调各部门对客服务过程（Coordinating Guest Services Rendered by Other Departments）

协调酒店各部门是现代酒店前厅部的一个重要功能。现代酒店既有分工，又有协作，是相互联系、互为条件的有机整体，酒店服务质量的好坏直接影响住客的满意程度，而住客的满意程度是对酒店每一次具体服务所形成的一系列感受和印象的总和，在对客服务的全过程中，任何一个环节出现差错，都会影响到服务质量，影响到酒店的整体声誉。

Coordination of various departments of the hotel is an important function of the Front Office in modern hotel that is an integrated whole having both divisions of work and coordination as well as interconnections. The quality of the services provided by the hotel will directly influence the degree of satisfaction of the guests, which actually is the total of the series of feelings and impressions resulted from every specific service. During the whole process of servicing the guests, the fault in every link will influence the quality of the service and the reputation of the hotel as a whole.

所以，现代酒店要强调统一协调的对客服务，要使分工的各个方面都能有效地运转，都能充分地发挥作用。前厅部作为酒店的“神经中枢”，承担着对酒店业务安排的调度工作和对客服务的协调工作。主要表现在：

Therefore, modern hotel should emphasize universal and coordinated service to guests so as to make all functions to operate effectively and bring to full play. As the “neural center” of a hotel, the Front Office bears the work of dispatch arranged according to the business of the hotel and coordination on servicing the guests. These are mainly manifested in:

（1）将通过销售客房商品活动所掌握的客源市场、客房预订及到客情况及时通报其他有关部门，使各有关部门有计划地安排好各自的工作，互相配合，保证各部门的业务均衡衔接。

Timely report to other related departments the status of guest source market, guestroom reservation, and arrival of the guests mastered through activities selling the commodity of guestroom so as to render various related department to plan their own works, cooperate with each other, and guarantee the business in every department to link in a balanced way.

（2）将客人的需求及接待要求等信息传递给各有关部门，检查、监督落实情况。

Transmission of the information on the needs and reception requirements of the guests to various related departments so as to examine and monitor the status of implementation.

（3）将客人的投诉及处理意见及时反馈给相关部门，以保证酒店的服务质量。

Timely feedback of the claims and opinions on solution to related departments so as to guarantee the servicing quality of the hotel.

为适应市场需求，增强酒店的竞争能力，酒店的业务内容越来越多，分工越来越细，前厅部的这种协调酒店各部门的功能也就愈发显得重要。

In order to meet the market needs and increase the competitiveness, hotels have more and more businesses and functions, so this kind of function of the Front Office for coordinating the various departments of the hotel seems to be more and more important.

三、前厅部组织结构（The Organizational Structure of the Front Office）

总体来说，前厅部组织机构的设置应既能保证前厅运作的质量和效率，又能方便客人、满足客人的需求。

The arrangement of the organizational structure of the Front Office should not only ensure the quality and efficiency of the operation of the Front Office but also make the guests feel convenient and meet their requirements.

（一）设置原则（Setup Principles）

1. 组织合理（Rational Organization）

前厅部的机构设置、职责划分、人员配备应根据酒店的性质、规模、地理位置、经营特点与管理方式来确定。如规模小的酒店或以内部接待为主的酒店就可将前厅部归入房务部，而不必独立设置前厅部。

The setup of front office, division of responsibility, and staffing of the Front Office should be determined according to the nature, sizes, geographic locations, business features and management styles of the hotel. For those hotels of smaller size or mainly engaging in in-house business, the Front Office could be integrated into the housekeeping department without the need to set an independent front office department.

2. 机构精简（Precise Organization）

前厅部的机构设置应防止出现机构臃肿、人浮于事的现象，应“因事设岗”，而不能“因人设岗”，应避免出现运作过程中的“交叉地带”。但机构精简并不意味着机构的过分简化，不能出现职能空缺现象和“无人问津的地带”。

The arrangement of the organization of the Front Office should eradicate the phenomena of overstaffing. It should “set up positions for business” instead of “setting up positions due to personnel” so as to prevent the occurrence of “crossed regions” during the process of operation. But the precise organization does not mean the over simplification of the organization, and it should not lead to phenomenon of function vacancy and “unwanted area”.

3. 分工明确（Clear Division of Labor）

前厅部各机构及各岗位人员的职责和任务应明确，指挥体系应高效、健全，信息传达的渠道应畅通，应避免出现管理职能的空缺、重叠或相互扯皮现象。

The responsibilities and tasks of various sections and positions of the Front Office should be clarified and the commanding system should be of high efficiency and soundness, the channels for transmission of information should be unblocked, and phenomena like vacancy, overlap or over trifling of management functions should be eradicated.

4. 便于协作（Convenience for Collaboration）

前厅部机构设置不仅要便于前厅部内部各岗位、各环节间的协作，而且要有利于前厅部与其他部门间的协调与合作。

The front office setup should be convenient for not only the collaboration of the various positions and links within the interior of the Front Office but also the coordination and cooperation between the Front Office and other departments.

（二）组织机构（Organization Structure）

前厅部组织机构设置受到酒店类型、规模、等级、劳动力成本、管理模式等因素的影响。因而，各酒店前厅部组织机构设置的形态也有所不同，酒店管理人员应通盘考虑。一般来说，酒店按客房数量和接待规模可分成大型（500间客房以上）酒店、中型（200~500间）酒店、小型（200间以下）酒店。

The organization of the Front Office is affected by factors like the types, sizes, grades, labor cost, and management modes of the hotel. Therefore, the forms of the arrangement of the organizational institutions of the Front Office of various hotels are also not the same, and the managers of the hotel should take all things into consideration. Generally speaking, hotels can be divided into large-sized (more than 500 guestrooms), middle-sized (200~500 guestrooms), and small-sized (less than 200 rooms) ones according to the number of the guestrooms and reception sizes.

酒店前厅部的组织机构是由若干职能不同的部门和管理权力不同的管理层结合而成的，在它们之间存在着纵横交错的关系，正确处理它们之间的关系是保证酒店正常运转的重要条件。根据酒店的规模大小的不同，常见的前厅部的组织机构模式如图 1-1 所示。前厅部的工作任务，是通过其内部各机构分工协作共同完成的。

The organization of the Front Office of the hotel is the combination of the various departments of different functions and management levels of different authority, and there are crisscrossed relationships among them. To correctly deal with the relationship among them is the important conditions for the normal operation of the hotel. See Figure 1-1 for the mode of the commonly seen organizational institution of the Front Office according to the different sizes of the hotels. The working tasks of the Front Office are achieved through the division of work and cooperation of the various interior institutions.

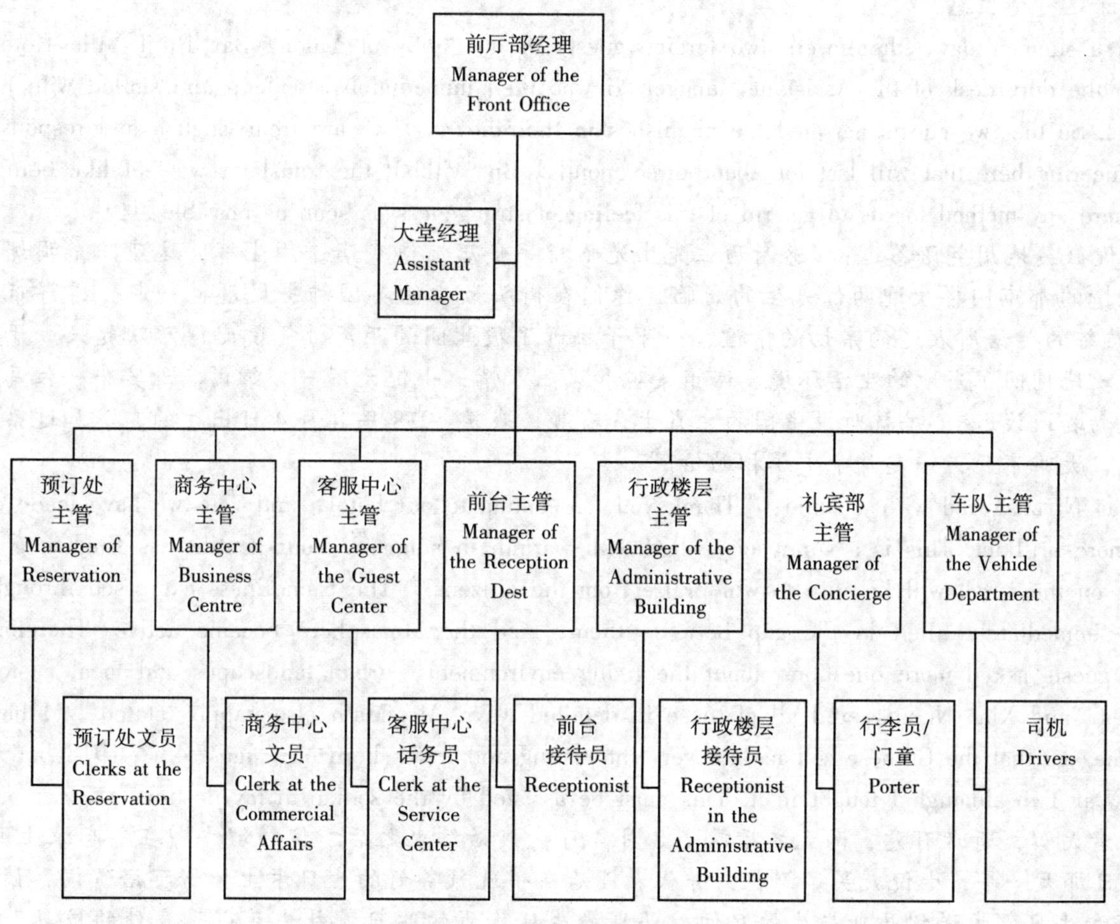

图 1-1 前厅部组织结构

Figure 1-1 The Organizational Structure of the Front Office

任务二　认识前厅服务

Task II Introduction to Front Office Services

【案例】【Case】

客人的生日

Birthday of Guests

夏日，三亚亚龙湾瑞吉度假酒店大堂，两位外国客人向大堂经理值班台走来。大堂倪经理立即起身，面带微笑地以敬语问候，让座后两位客人忧虑地讲述起他们心中的苦闷："我们从英国来，在这儿负责一项工程，大约要三个月，可是离开了翻译我们就成了'睁眼瞎'，不知有什么方法能让我们尽快解除这种陌生感？"

On a summer day，there were two foreign guests in the lobby of Yalong Bay Ruiji Villa Hotel. They came to the duty desk of the Assistant Manager Ni who then immediately stood up and smiled with honorific greetings. So the two guests narrated the anguishes in their heart，"we are from English and responsible for an engineering here that will last for about three months. But without the translator we feel like being blind. So is there any method for us to get rid of this feeling of strangeness as soon as possible?"

小倪微笑地用英语答道："感谢两位先生光临指导我店，使我店蓬荜生辉，这座阳光明媚、充满夏日温情的都市同样欢迎两位先生的光临，你们在街头散步的英国绅士风度也一定会博得市民的赞赏。"熟练的英语所表达的亲切的情谊，一下子拉近了彼此间的距离，气氛变得活跃起来。于是外宾更加广泛地询问了当地的生活环境、城市景观和风土人情，小倪无不一一细说。外宾中一位马斯先生还兴致勃勃地谈道："早就听说中国的生肖十分有趣，我是1918年8月4日出生的，参加过第二次世界大战，大难不死，一定是命中属相助佑。"

Xiao Ni answered with a smile："Thank you for coming to our hotel，and you two have made our hall to be more brilliant. This is a sunny city filled with warmth in summer. Your gentility as English gentlemen walking on the street will be sure to win praise from the citizens." The friendliness expressed through fluent English immediately filled in the gap between them，and the atmosphere became active. Therefore，the foreign guests asked more questions about the living environment，urban landscapes and local customs and practices，and Xiao Ni answered all of these in detailed ways. Mr. Math also happily stated，"I had heard long time ago that the Chinese zodiacs are very interesting and I was born on August 4th，1918 but survived World War Two although I fought in it. This must be assisted by the zodiac in my destiny."

说者无心，听者有意，两天之后就是8月4日，谈话结束之后，倪经理立即在备忘录上做记录。8月4日那天一早，小倪就买了鲜花，并代表酒店在早就预备好的生日卡上填好英语贺词，请服务员将鲜花和生日贺卡送到马斯先生的房间。马斯先生从珍贵的生日贺礼中获得了意外的惊喜，激动不已，连声说道："谢谢，谢谢贵店对我的关心，我深深体会到这贺卡和鲜花之中隐含着许多难以用语言表达的情意。我们在三亚逗留期间再也不会感到寂寞了。"

The speaker had no particular intention in saying something；but the listener reads his own meaning into it. After the completion of the conversation，Assistant Manager Ni made a note. Two days later，that is, on August 4th, Xiao Ni bought fresh flowers and wrote English greeting words on the birthday card he had prepared. Then he asked a service staff to send the flowers and the birthday card to the room of Mr. Math. Mr. Math obtained accidental surprises from the precious birthday gifts and he was so excited that he kept saying: "Thank you very much, thank you for your care to me. I really know the great affections within the cards and flowers that are hard to be expressed in language. We will not feel lonely any more during our stay in Sanya."

【请你分析】【Please Analyze】

1. 是什么原因拉近了客人与大堂经理之间的距离？

What are the reasons making the guests feel more intimate to the assistant manager?

2. 马斯先生为什么在收到生日礼物的时候会如此激动？

Why was Mr. Math so excited when he received the birthday gift?

3. 从这个案例中，你认为大堂服务人员应该具备哪些服务的技能技巧？这些技能技巧对酒店有什么影响？

What skills or techniques do you think a servicing person in the hall should have? What are their effects to the hotel?

【案例分析】【Case Analysis】

本案例中大堂经副理对待两位客人的做法，是站在客人的立场上，把客人当作上帝的出色范例。

What the Assistant Manager Ni had done to the two guests is just to take the position of the guests and treating the guests as the God. This is a perfect example of it.

第一，设身处地，仔细揣摩客人的心理状态。两位英国客人由于在异国他乡逗留时间较长，语言不通，深感寂寞。小倪深入体察、准确抓住了外国客人对乡音的心理需求，充分发挥他的英语专长，热情欢迎外国客人的光临，还特别称赞了他们的英国绅士风度，进而自然而然地向客人介绍了当地的风土人情等，使身居异乡的外国客人获得了一份浓浓的乡情。

Firstly, he had carefully contemplated the psychological status of the guests by taking their positions. The two English guests felt very lonely due to language barriers because they had stayed in a foreign country for a long time. Xiao Ni had made deep observation and correctly understood the psychological needs of the foreign guests for their own languages, so he brought his specialty in English into full play. He warmly welcomed the coming of the foreign guests and specially praised their demeanors as English gentlemen, then introduced the local landscapes and customs to the guests in a very natural way. Therefore, the foreign guests living abroad obtained a strong nostalgia.

第二，富有职业敏感，善于抓住客人的有关信息。客人在交谈中无意中流露生日时辰，小倪的可贵之处在于，能及时敏锐地抓住这条重要信息，从而成功地策划了一次为外国客人赠送生日贺卡和鲜花的优质服务和公关活动，把与外国客人的感情交流推向了更深的层次。因此，善于捕捉客人有关信息的职业敏感，也是酒店管理者和服务人员应该具备的可贵素质。

Secondly, he was sensitive in his work and good at catching related information of the guests. When the guests unintentionally discovered his birthday in conversation, it was very valuable that Xiao Ni timely caught this important piece of information so as to successfully plan a quality service and public-relationship activity of giving birthday card and flowers to foreign guests, thus promoting the communication of affections with foreign guests to a deeper level. Therefore, the professional sensibility of being skilled to catch related information of guests is also a precious quality that should be possessed by hotel managers and servants.

一、前厅部主要岗位工作内容（The Work of the Primary Positions in the Front Office）

如任务一中所述，酒店规模不同，前厅部业务分工也不同，但一般设有以下主要机构：

As stated in Task Ⅰ, hotels in different sizes will have different work for the front office department. Generally, the front office will have the following functions:

（1）预订处。即接受、确认和调整来自各个渠道的房间预订，主要是负责办理订房手续；熟练掌握酒店的房价政策和预订业务；制定预订报表，对预订进行计划、安排和管理；掌握并控制客房出租状况；负责联络客源单位；定期进行房间销售预测并向上级提供预订分析报告；负责与有关公司、旅行社等客源单位建立良好的业务关系；加强与总台接待处的联系，及时向前厅部经理及总台相关岗位和部门提供有关客房预订资料和数据；制定各种订报表（每月、半月、每周和翌日客人抵达预报）；参与制订全年客房预订计划等。

Reservation department. It accepts, confirms, and adjusts the reservations of rooms from various channels, mainly including conducting reservation procedures, getting familiar with the policies of room prices and reservation business, preparing reservation reports and making plans, arrangements, and management for reservations, mastering and controlling the status of occupied rooms, contacting the units having sources of guests, conducting periodical prediction of room sales and providing reports of analyses on reservations to their superior leaders, being responsible for establishing good business relationships with guest source units such as companies and travel agencies, strengthening the relationships with the general reception desk and timely providing materials and data related to the reservation of guestrooms to the managers of Front Office as well as related positions and departments of the general reception desk, preparing various kinds of reports (predictions on the arrival of guests once a month, once half month, once a week and on the next day), and taking part in the formulation of the plans for the reservation of the guestrooms of the whole year, etc.

（2）商务中心。为客人提供打字、翻译、复印、传真、长途电话以及互联网服务（商务服务），根据客人需求提供信息及秘书性服务，提供文件加工、整理和装订服务，提供计算机、幻灯机等的租赁服务等。

Business center. It provides services like typing, translation, copying, faxing, long-distance telephone calls, and internet services (commercial services), information and secretary services according to the requirements of the guests, making, trimming and binding services of files, and renting services of computers, and slide projector, etc.

（3）客服中心。负责接转酒店内外的电话，承办长途电话；回答客人的电话询问；提供电话找人服务、留言服务、叫醒服务、"请勿打扰"（DND）电话服务；受理电话投诉；播放背景音乐；充当酒店出现紧急情况时的指挥中心。

Customer service center. It is responsible for receiving telephone calls from inside and outside of the hotel, making long-distance calls, answering the inquiries from guests through telephone, providing services like looking for persons through telephone, leaving messages, waking up, "Don't Disturb" (DND) calling services, treating claims through telephone, playing background music, and acting as the command center when emergencies occur in the hotel.

（4）前台，包括接待处和问询处。接待处，负责接待抵店的客人，包括团体、散客、长住客、非预期到店以及无预订的客人；办理客人入住手续，分配房间；与预订处、客房部保持联系，及时掌握客房出租变化，准确显示房态；制定开放销售情况报表，掌握住店客人动态及信息资料。问询处，负责回答住客的询问，提供各种有关酒店内部和酒店外部的信息；提供收发、传达、会客等服务；负责保管所有客房钥匙。

Front desk including the reception desk and the inquiry office. The reception desk is responsible for receiving the guests arriving at the hotel, including the guests in groups, individual guests, long-term guests, unexpected guests, and guests not making reservations, conducting checking in procedures for the guests and allocating rooms, keeping in touch with the Reservation Department and guestroom Department so as to timely master the changes in the occupation of guestrooms and correctly displaying the status of rooms, making reports for the status of open sales, and master the dynamic status of the guests living in the hotel and the information materials. The inquiry office is responsible for answering the inquiries of the guests living in the hotel, providing various kinds of information within and from outside of the hotel, providing services like receiving, sending and delivering messages and meeting guests, and keeping keys of all the guestrooms.

（5）行政楼层。行政楼层，又叫贵宾楼层、豪华阁之类，即服务、内部装修与价格均高于普通楼层。与大堂前台接待处相通，但服务对象基本上是行政楼层的客人，可以提供专属的行政楼层待遇，比如说有行政酒廊、免费甜点和下午茶、免费洗衣、延迟离店等，行政楼层可以直接为客人快捷地办理入住及离店手续。

Executive Room Floors. It is also named as VIP floors or luxurious floors, in which the services, interior decorations or prices are all higher than those in common floors. It may share one reception desk with the lobby the targets of their services are almost all the guests in the executive roon floor. It can provide services exclusive to the executive floor, such as the executive lounge, free desserts and afternoon tea, free laundry, and extended check-out, etc., in addition to quick and direct check-in and check-out.

（6）礼宾部。负责在酒店门口或机场、车站、码头迎送住客；调度门前车辆，维持门前秩序；代客人卸送行李，陪客人进房，介绍客房设备与服务，并为客人提供行李寄存和托运服务；分送客人邮件、报纸、转送留言、物品；雨伞的寄存和出租；回答客人问询，为客人指引方向；代办客人委托的各项事宜。

Concierge. It is responsible for receiving and seeing off the guests at the gate of the hotel, or airport, bus stations, and wharf, dispatching vehicles at the gate, maintaining the order at the gate, unloading luggage for the guests, accompanying the guests to enter their rooms, introducing the equipment and services in the guestroom, providing luggage storage and transportation services distributing letters and newspapers to the guests, transferring messages and articles to the guests, depositing and renting umbrellas, answering the guests' questions, showing directions to the guests, and finishing various tasks entrusted by the guests.

（7）车队。负责在机场、车站、码头迎送住客，以及酒店内部部门用车。

Fleet. It is responsible for receiving and seeing off the guests at the gate of the hotel, or airport, bus stations, and wharf as well as cars using of departments within the hotel.

（8）大堂经理。负责前厅服务协调、贵宾接待、投诉处理等服务性工作；负责大堂环境、大堂秩序的维护；发生紧急事件时，必须（在没有请示上级的情况下）做出主动决断的指示；遇危险事故（如火警、匪警等）而没有高层管理人员可请示时，应做出适当决定，需要视情况疏散客人等事项。

Asistant manager. It is responsible for servicing works like coordination of the services in the Front Office, reception of distinguished guests, and treatment of claims, etc., maintenance of the environment and order of the hall, having to taking the initiative to make affirmative instructions (without asking directions from superior leaders) when emergent things happen, and making appropriate decisions to evacuate guests according to the needs of actual conditions when there is no superior higher level of manager for giving instructions when having dangerous risks (like fire or bandits).

二、岗前准备（Preparation Before Work）

（一）前厅部工作人员必备的素质和要求（The Qualities and Requirements Necessary for the Staff Working in the Front Office）

1. 前厅部员工仪容仪表的要求（Requirements on the Appearances of the Staff in the Front Office）

前厅部员工在进入岗位开展对客服务之前，必须先检查自身的仪表仪容，确保符合标准要求，具体内容如下：

Before taking the positions to service the guests, the staff in the Front Office should first check their own appearances so as to ensure the conformity with standards and requirements. Below are the concrete requirements:

（1）发型美观大方，梳理整齐。男员工发际线侧不过耳，后不过领（不超过酒店规定的长度）；女员工长发需用深色发卡束起，不得披肩，不得戴太夸张的发饰，只宜戴轻巧大方的发饰，头发不得掩盖眼部或脸部；头发常洗，不得有头屑。

The hair style should be beautiful and in good taste, and the hair should be combed tidy. For male workers, the hairline should not exceed the ears on the side and collars on the back (not exceeding the length regulated by the hotel); for female workers, the long hair should be swept up with dark-colored hairpins without letting the hair reaching the shoulders or having very exaggerated decorations. Only light and generous hair decorations should be had on, and the hair should not cover the eyes or face; and the hair should be cleaned frequently so there will be no scurf.

（2）面容清洁。男员工经常修面，清爽宜人，不留胡须；女员工化淡妆，不可浓妆艳抹，只宜稍作修饰，淡扫蛾眉，轻涂口红，轻抹胭脂即可。

Clean faces. For male staff, they should usually shave their faces so it looks clear without having any mustaches; for female staff, they should slightly make up and must not put on heavy cosmetics. It is only appropriate for them to make slight decorations, such as slightly draw their eyebrows, lipsticks, and cheeks, etc.

（3）服装须熨烫平整，纽扣齐全，干净整洁，服务工号牌端正地佩戴在左胸处。

The clothes should be ironed to be flat with complete buttons, clean, and tidy. The number plate of the service should be correctly put on the left chest.

（4）应经常洗澡，身上无异味，保持皮肤健康。女员工不要用气味强烈的香料（香水）。

The staff should take showers frequently so as to make their bodies having no unpleasant odors and keep their skin healthy. Female employees must not use perfume with strong odors.

（5）手部保持清洁。男员工不得留长指甲，指甲要干净，指甲内不得藏污垢；女员工不得留太长指甲，不宜涂鲜红指甲油，只允许涂淡色的。

The hands should be kept clean. For male staff, they should not have long fingernails that should be clean and without any dirt inside; while for female staff, they should not have long fingernails or paint their fingers with fresh red enamels (only gray is allowed).

（6）穿鞋统一。男员工要穿清洁的鞋袜，穿黑色袜子，每天上班前要擦亮鞋子；女员工要穿清洁的鞋袜，要穿酒店规定的袜色（大多数为肉色丝袜），每天上班前要擦亮鞋子。

Shoes should be in uniform. For male employees, they should put on clean shoes and socks in black and polish their shoes every day before going to work; while for females, they should put on clean shoes and socks in the color specified by the hotel (most of them are in skin color), and they should shine their shoes every day before going to work.

2. 前厅部员工素质的要求（Requirements for Qualities of Front Office Staff）

前厅部员工在进入岗位开展对客服务之前，必须养成良好的自身素质，确保能够为客人提供优良的服务，具体内容如下：

Before front office staff take their positions to serve their guests, they must have good personal qualities so as to ensure that they are able to provide good services. Below are the concrete requirements:

（1）具有优良端正的品行，作风正派。前厅部的工作政策性很强，经常涉及资金、价格优惠及酒店经营策略方面的机密等，因此，前厅部员工必须有较高的品行修养，坦诚、遵纪守法、原则性强，要为客人保守秘密，也应当为酒店严守商业秘密，同时不能够利用工作之便牟取私利，损害酒店利益。

They should act well and righteously. The work in the Front Office has very strong character in working policies, which usually involves with capital, price discount, and confidentialities in the aspect of operational strategies, etc., therefore, the staff in the Front Office must be of higher morality, honest, obey disciplines and laws, have strong principles, keep secrets for both the guests and the commercial secrets of the hotel, and in the meanwhile should not obtain interest for themselves by taking the advantages of the convenience of work to harm the interest of the hotel.

（2）具有良好的气质，身体健康，五官端正，面带微笑，主动热情，性格外向，反应敏捷，记忆准确，表情自然，具有较强的审美能力。

They should have good temperament, be healthy, with well-featured faces, smile, be initiative, enthusiastic, outgoing, quickly respond, memorize correctly, have natural expressions, and be of rather strong aesthetic abilities.

（3）要有一定学历和文化修养，而且应当有较广的知识面和丰富的专业知识，具有机智灵活的处事能力，具备与各类客人交谈的能力，了解一般的经济、旅游、民族风情、风俗习惯等知识。

They should have some educational background and cultural quality as well as rather wide scope of knowledge and rich professional knowledge, the ability to treat things in wise and flexible ways and communicating with and treating various kinds of guests, and understand common knowledge of economy, tourism, ethnical customs, customs and habit.

（4）应当有较强的语言表达能力，口齿伶俐，语调优美，语速适中，语言技巧熟练，而且至少掌握一门外语，能够用客人使用的语言与客人交流。

They should have rather strong ability of language expression, good tongue, beautiful intonations, and proficient language skills, and even master at least one foreign language so as to be able to communicate with the guests in their own languages.

（5）前厅部工作效率的高低、服务速度的快慢、工作差错的多少，直接关系到酒店的服务质量、管理水平及酒店形象，因此，前厅部员工必须要求业务熟练、工作细心，对待每一项工作都要做到快捷、准确、优质，缺一不可，故要求员工必须掌握业务操作和标准。

The efficiency of the work, the speeds of the services, and the amount of the faults occurring in the works of the Front Office are directly related to the quality of the services, the managing level, and the images of the hotels. Therefore, the staff in the Front Office must conform to the requirements of being skillful and careful in work and quick, correct, and of good quality in every task, and none of them should be lacked of. Therefore, the staff must master the operation and standards of the business.

（6）前厅部员工应该有较好的工作习惯和生活习惯，由于直接面对客人和接触客人的机会较多，因此应当随时保持较好的站姿，做到行为规范，举止大方，谈话音量适中。平时不喝酒，不吃大蒜、韭菜等有刺鼻气味的食物，养成良好的生活习惯。在客人面前始终保持良好的精神面貌和个人形象。

The staff in the Front Office should have rather good working and living habits, and they should always maintain good standing posture because they have more opportunities to directly face and have contact with the guests. They should behave normally and generously and talk in medium voice. They should not drink in common days, do not eat foods with penetrating smells like garlic or leeks, form good living habits, and always show good spirit and personal images in front of the guests.

（7）要有敬业乐业的精神，对客人的要求要敏感、反应快，及时向上级或同事准确地传递信息，应该具有较强的灵活应变能力和吃苦耐劳的能力，具有较强的同情心和爱心，做好每一天的工作。

They should have the spirit of respecting and loving their works, be sensitive and respond quickly to the needs of the guests, correctly deliver information to their superior leaders or colleagues, have rather strong ability of flexible response to changes and hard-working as well as rich sympathy and love so as to do the work of every day well.

（8）前厅部员工必须具有较高的团队合作意识和精神。

The staff in the Front Office should be of rather high awareness and spirit of team cooperation.

【案例】【Case】

这样做，对吗？
Is It Right to Do It in This Way?

某日18时许，三亚鸿洲埃德瑞度假酒店，接待员小吴正忙着为客人办理入住手续。两位客人来到总台对小吴说："我们要一间双人房。"

At about 18 on one day in Eadry Resort Hotel in Hongzhou, Sanya. Xiao Wu, the receptionist was busying conducting the procedures for the guest to check in. Two guests came to the general desk and told Xiao Wu, "We want a double room".

小吴亲切地说道："好的，请稍等，我为这位客人办理完手续后，马上为您安排。"其中的一位客人有些急躁地说："今晚我们要外出签协议，赶时间，你能不能先替我们办理？"

Xiao Wu replied very amiably, "Ok, just a minute, I will arrange one for you immediately after I finish the procedures for this guest." One of the two guests said rather impatiently, "We are now catching time to go out for signing an agreement, so could you do the procedures for us first?"

小吴连忙应答，一边继续办理前一位客人的相关手续，一边用电脑为这两位客人查看空房。不到半分钟，小吴抬头询问道："现在空房还有几间，是海景房的，每晚580元，您看如何?""怎么，上午我电话问过房价，是488元，为什么到了晚上就变成580元？真是漫天要价！"小吴刚要解释，这位客人突然挥拳打向小吴，小吴毫无防备，挨了这一拳，他脸色煞白，正想回敬对方，猛然想到自己在岗，应扮演好岗位角色，心里想到要忍耐！忍耐！绝不可意气用事。

Xiao Wu made a very quick response and he began to check whether there were rooms available for the guest in the computer while continuing to finishing related procedures for the previous guest. In less than half a minute, Xiao Wu raised his head and asked, "There are still several rooms available, and all of them are facing the sea. The price is RMB 588 Yuan per day. What do you think about this?" "What? The price was RMB 488 Yuan when I consulted in the morning through telephone. Why does it turn to be RMB 588 Yuan? This is really a wild speculation!" Xiao Wu was just about to make an explanation, the guest suddenly punched Xiao Wu. Never having expected to defend for this, Xiao Wu was hit. His face turned to be very white. When he was about to do the same thing to the guest, he suddenly remembered that he was still in his position so he should play a good role in the position. So he demanded himself to sustain! Sustain! In no way should he act on impulse without due consideration.

于是，小吴仍然克制自己并用正常语气若无其事地解释道："488元的客房已全部住满了，580元还有几间，是朝向风光大海的，楼层也不一样。我建议你们尽快办理入住手续，还可以准时外出谈生意。请允许我提醒先生，有问题尽可以用语言表达。"

Therefore, he still sustained himself and replied in normal tone as nothing had happened, "The guestrooms at the price of RMB488 Yuan have all been occupied, but there are several rooms at the price of RMB 588 left available and all of them are facing the scenery sea and at different layers of the building. I suggest that you conduct the procedures for checking in as soon as possible so that you still could go out to negotiate for your business in time. Please allow me to remind you, sir, if you have any questions, please try to express in words."

这时在旁边的另一位先生感到他同伴理亏，劝道："这位接待员态度不错，我们赶快住下吧！"那客人见势也软了下来，小吴便为其排房，并让行李员将行李送往房间。

At this time another mister beside him felt that his companion was in wrong, so he persuaded, "This receptionist is really in good attitude, so let's stay at once!" That guest also turned to be soft while seeing this, so Xiao Wu arranged a room for them and let a porter to send their luggage to the room.

事隔两天，那位先生也感到自己的行为不当，在离店结账时向小吴表示歉意。

Two days later, that man also felt himself to be wrong, so he apologized to Xiao Wu when he checked out for leaving.

【请你分析】【Please Analyze】

1. 你为这位接待员感到自豪吗？为什么？请谈谈你的感受。

Do you feel proud of this receptionist? Why? Please tell your own feelings.

2. 前厅部管理人员对此事应持什么态度？

What should be the attitude of the managers of the Front Office to this case?

【案例分析】【Case Analysis】

前厅部员工要有成熟而健康的心理。要善于聆听、观察，善于应变，要有娴熟的服务技能，应掌握一定的推销技巧。希望受人重视是一种人的天性。有的顾客通过抱怨而引起服务生（前台）对他的注意和重视，或者由此引出酒店相关负责人或经理与其见面，使他感觉到自己很重要。

The staff in the Front Office should have mature and healthy psychology, and they should be good at listening, observing, easy to change, have skillful servicing techniques and master some promotional skills. It is natural for human beings hoping to be paid more attentions. Some guests would attract the attentions of the servicers (at the front desk) through complaints or thus having the responsible persons or managers to meet him face to face so that he is made to feel himself is very important.

麻省理工学院的全面质量管理（Total Quality Management，TQM）专家 Dan Maher 和哈佛商学院的教授 Jame L. Heskett 两人在一篇题为《安抚怒气冲冲的顾客》（*Soothing the Savage Customer*）的专题研究中指出：酒店应尽量防止过失发生，防抱怨于未然。一旦出现抱怨，应及时、适当处理，消除顾客怨气，是最后的补救方法。

Dan Maher is an expert on total quality management（TQM）in MIT，and Jame L. Heskett is an expert in Harvard Business School. They pointed out in a monographic study titled "*Soothing the Savage Customer*" that the hotel should try her best to prevent the occurrence of faults，that is，to prevent the complaints from happening. Once it does happen，timely treatment should be conducted in appropriate ways so as to eradicate the grievances of the guests，and this is the last means of redress.

抱怨是一种痛苦的表达方式，人们不愿意抱怨，也避免去抱怨。只有五分之一的客人把抱怨说出来。抱怨是顾客发出的一种信号：我希望下次再来，但请你改进，下次不要再发生问题，给我一个再次回来的理由。

Complaining is a painful expression，people don't like to complain and also avoid to complain. Only 1/5 of the guests will speak their complaints out. Complaining is a signal sent out by a customer：I hope to come back next time，but would you please improve so that next time don't let any problem occur and give me a reason to come back again.

抱怨直接反映了酒店存在的问题，提供了改进及提高的建议。五分之四心存怨气的顾客会不作抱怨，不把问题提出来，这类客人的"回头率"很低，甚至再也不会来了。

Complain directly reflects the problems existing in a hotel，provides the proposal for improvement. 4/5 of the resenting guests will not complain or put forward their issues，but the "return" rate of this kind of guest is very low，and they even never come back again.

（二）岗位职责制定的基本要求（The Basic Requirements on the Establishment of Job Responsibilities）

岗位职责是指对某一特定工作岗位的工作内容和应负的责任，包括这一岗位的工作性质、工作职责、工作内容及工作手段、方法等。酒店前厅部制定岗位职责的目的在于确保各岗位工作内容清晰、目标明确、要求统一、责任到人，从而形成有机统一的运作机制，进一步提高工作效率和服务质量。

Job responsibilities refers to the work content and responsibility of a specific job，including the job nature，responsibilities，working content as well as working measures and methods，and so on. The objective of the Front Office in a hotel is to ensure that the content of the post is clear with confirmed objectives and requirements and specific responsibility to people，thus forming an organic and unified operational mechanism to further improve the work efficiency and service quality.

制定完善且可操作性强的岗位职责是酒店前厅部运行与管理的一项重要的基础性工作。制定岗位职责时应尽量做到：文字通俗易懂，描述客观准确；职责条理分明，要求具体明确；定性与定量相结合；保证各级别、各岗位间的有机联系。

To formulate perfect post responsibility with strong operability is an important basic work in the operation and management of the hotel Front Office. Job responsibilities should be formulated to the following degree as far as possible：The text is easy to be understood，the descriptions are objective and accurate；The responsibilities and requirements are concrete and clear；Qualitativeness and quantitativeness are combined together，and the organic connection between each level and each post is guaranteed.

【实训与评价】【Training and Assessment】

[实训目的][Training Goals]

1. 掌握服务礼仪、语言技巧。

Master the service etiquette and language skills.

2. 能够进行一般性的岗位英语会话，会按照酒店的标准来纠正自己的仪容仪表。

Be able to make general conversation in job in English and, will correct their appearance in accordance with the standards of the hotel.

[实训内容][Training Contents]

前厅服务模拟实训操作：

The training operation simulation of services provided by the Front Office:

1. 以学生为主，让学生分成三组，一组讨论前厅工作人员的仪容仪表的标准；一组讨论前厅工作人员的语言礼仪的标准；一组讨论前厅工作人员的服务礼仪的标准。

This is based on students, and the students are divided into three groups with one group discussing the standards of appearance for the staff working in the Front Office; the second group discussing the standards of the language and etiquette for the Front Office staff; and the last group discussing the standards of the service etiquettes for the Front Office staff.

2. 教师提出要求和注意事项，引导学生观察和思考。

The teachers put forward requirements and matters needing attention and guide students to observe and think.

3. 教师针对学生实训时存在的问题及时加以纠正和进行评述。

In view of the existing problems during the actual practices of the students, the teachers should correct them in a timely manner and conduct review.

4. 各小组派一个代表宣读自己设计的前厅工作人员礼仪标准。

Every team should send a representative to read the standards designed by themselves for the etiquettes of the Front Office staff.

5. 同学们进行补充说明，进行辩论。

The students make complementary explanations and debate.

6. 教师最后纠正并做出评价。

The teachers should do final corrections and give comments.

[实训操作][Training Operation]

全体同学按照标准进行礼仪的实操。

All the students should do actual practices in accordance with the standards of etiquette.

1. 进行仪容仪表的训练，学生两人一组，互相检查仪容仪表，不合要求的地方互相纠正(当然在上节课就要求学生做好准备，男学生过长的头发一定要修剪，女学生有染指甲油的一律洗去)。

The first should be the training of appearance. The students should be put in groups of two to check each other's appearance and correct undesirable points of the other one (of course, in the last class students had been asked to prepare, the long hair of male students must be trimmed, while the female students having nail enamels should get them washed away).

2. 要进行服务礼仪的实操。

Secondly, real practice of servicing etiquettes should be conducted.

①“立如松”是指人的站立姿势要像青松一般端正挺拔。按照酒店的标准，学生安静站立10分钟。

“Standing like a pine tree” refers to the standing posture should be as tall and straight as a pine tree. According to the hotel standards, students should stand quietly for 10 minutes.

②优美的走姿应该是表情自然放松，昂首收颌挺胸，直腰提髋，两臂自然下垂前后摆动，下肢举步、脚尖脚跟相接相送。

Graceful walking posture should include natural and relaxed facial expressions, head held up, jaw retreated, straight chest and waist, raising hips, his arms dropping naturally and swinging back and forth, and when the lower limbs walk, the toe and heel should be connected.

③引领客人的礼仪。

Etiquettes of guiding the guests.

④电梯服务。

Services in elevators.

⑤介绍礼仪。

Etiquettes of introduction.

⑥交换名片礼仪。

Etiquettes of exchanging name cards.

⑦交谈礼仪。

Etiquettes of communication.

⑧握手的礼仪。

Etiquettes of shaking hands.

3. 语言礼仪实操。学生站成两排，由老师带领训练礼貌语言。

The actual practice of language etiquettes. The students stood into two rows to be guided by the teachers for training on polite languages.

①您好，先生/小姐。

Nice to meet you, Mister/Miss.

②先生/小姐，欢迎光临。

Welcome, Mister/Miss.

③这边请。

This way, please.

④先生/小姐，小心台阶。

Mind the stairs, please, Mister/Miss.

⑤对不起，先生/小姐。

Sorry, Mister/Miss.

⑥谢谢您，先生/小姐。

Thank you very much, Mister/Miss.

⑦打搅您了。

Sorry to disturb you.

⑧请问。

Excuse me.

⑨再见，先生/小姐，请走好。

Good bye, Mister/Miss. Have a good trip.

⑩先生/小姐，让您久等了。

Sorry for keeping you waiting，Mister/Miss.

［实训评价］［Comments on Real Practices］

酒店礼仪服务评分标准
Standards for Scoring Etiquette Services in the Hotel

班级：　　　　姓名：　　　　总分：

Class：　　　　Name：　　　　Total Scores：

序号 No.	项目 Items	要求 Requirements	应得分 Full Score	扣分 Scores Deducted	实得分 Final Score
1	仪容仪表 Appearances	(1) 按酒店要求，保持个人良好的仪表、仪容、仪态，着装校服，佩戴校卡。 Maintain good personal appearance and manners dress uniforms, wear the school cards according to the requirements of the hotel.	5		
		(2) 以规范的仪容仪表迎接客人。 Greet the guests with normative appearances.	5		
		(3) 行走、站姿正确，行为规范有礼。 Have correct walking and standing postures as well as normative and polite behaviors.	5		
		(4) 对客人微笑，行注目礼。 Smile to the guests and pay eye solute to the guests.	5		
2	操作技巧 Operational Skills	(1) 礼貌用语的使用。 Usage of polite languages.	10		
		(2) 服务态度热情，友好。 The servicing attitude should be enthusiastic and friendly.	10		
		(3) 操作程序熟练。 Be proficient in operating programs.	10		
3	操作程序 Operational Procedures	(1) 按照酒店的标准，学生安静站立 10 分钟。 The students stand quietly for ten minutes according to the standards of the hotel.	5		
		(2) 优美的走姿。 Beautiful walking postures.	5		
		(3) 引领客人的礼仪。 The etiquettes of guiding guests.	5		
		(4) 电梯服务。 Services in the elevators.	5		
		(5) 介绍礼仪。 Etiquettes of introduction.	5		
		(6) 交换名片礼仪。 Etiquettes of exchanging name cards.	5		
		(7) 交谈礼仪。 Etiquettes of communication.	5		
		(8) 握手的礼仪 Etiquettes of shaking hands. 能根据不同客人的要求安排房间。 Be able to arrange different rooms according to the requirements of the guests.	5		

续表

序号 No.	项目 Items	要求 Requirements	应得分 Full Score	扣分 Scores Deducted	实得分 Final Score
		(9) 语言礼仪实操。 Real practice of language etiquettes.	10		
备注 Remarks		(1) 每一组操作时间不能超过 3 分钟。 The practice of every group should not exceed three minutes. (2) 每一组之间句型内容不能重复。 The contents of the sentence patterns in every group should not be repeated.			

模块小结
Module Summary

1. 简要叙述前厅部的地位和主要工作任务。

Please make simple introduction of the position and major working tasks of the Front Office.

2. 前厅部岗位的业务特点是什么?

What are the characters of the businesses in the post of the Front Office?

3. 你能区分前厅部各个岗位的职责和任务吗?

Can you distinguish the responsibilities and tasks of the various posts in the Front Office?

4. 前厅服务用语有哪几种常用语气? 你能够举例说明前厅服务过程中的常用语言技巧吗?

What are the several kinds of commonly used moods for the servicing languages in the Front Office? Can you give examples to show the common language skills applied into the process of servicing in the Front Office?

5. 你能够按照酒店的标准来纠正自己的仪容仪表吗?

Can you correct your own appearance according to the standards of the hotel?

附录1 知识储备
Appendix 1 Knowledge Reserve

(一) 职场仪态礼仪 (Working Manners and Etiquette)

很多职业人士为了美化外在形象，不惜花重金去美容，购买高档的服饰。爱美之心，人皆有之，这无可厚非。但是，精心打造出来的光鲜夺目的形象，往往会被行为举止上的一些差错而彻底粉碎。修饰你的仪态，从细微处流露你的风度、幽雅，远比一个“衣服架子”更加令人赏心悦目。

A lot of professional people do not hesitate to spend huge sums of money for beauty or buying high-grade dresses in order to make their appearances more graceful. All people have the heart of loving beauty has, for which there is no ground for blame. However, the bright eye-catching images created meticulously, will often be completely crushed to pieces due to some errors in their behaviors. To perfect the beauty of your appearance and reveal your demeanor and elegance in details is far more pleasing to the eye than a frame of clothes.

1. 站姿（Standing Posture）

男士主要体现出阳刚之美，抬头挺胸，双脚大约与肩膀同宽站立，重心自然落于脚中间，肩膀放松。女士则体现出柔和轻盈，丁字步站立。谈话时，要面对对方，保持一定的距离。尽量保持身体的挺直，不可歪斜。依靠着墙壁、桌椅而站；双腿分开的距离过大、交叉，都是不雅观和失礼的行为。手中也不要玩弄物品，那样显得心不在焉，是不礼貌的行为。

To the males, they should show their masculine beauty by raising their heads and straightening their chests with their feet standing in the same width as the shoulder. The center of gravity should naturally fall into the middle of the feet with the shoulder relaxed. As to the females, they should manifest their softness and lightness and stand with their feet looking like the Chinese character of "丁 (Ding)". When speaking, they should face the other party and keep a certain distance. Try your best to maintain the straight body and must not tilt. Stand by leaning on the walls, desks, or chairs. If the distance between the two separated legs is too large or the two legs crossed each other, it will be regarded as ungraceful and impolite. Do not play articles in your hands, which will make you seem abstract-minded and is a behavior not polite.

2. 行走（Walk）

靠道路的右侧行走，遇到同事、主管要主动问好。在行走的过程中，应避免吸烟、吃东西、吹口哨、整理衣服等行为。上下楼梯时，应让尊者、女士先行。多人行走时，注意不要因并排行走而占据路面。

Walk to the right side of the road, and take the initiative to extend greetings to your colleagues and superior leaders. During the walking, do not smoke, eat, whistle, or sort clothes, and similar deeds should be avoided. When getting up and down the stairs, the distinguished persons and ladies should go first. When walking with many other persons, pay attention not to occupy the road due to walking shoulder to shoulder.

（二）体态语（Physique Languages）

1. 目光（Sight）

与人交往时，少不了目光接触。正确运用目光传达信息，塑造专业形象，要遵守以下规律。

When associating with people, no eye contact should be avoided. The correct use of eyes, conveying information, and shaping professional images should abide by the following rules.

PAC 规律：P—Parent，指用家长式的、教训人的目光与人交流，视线是从上到下，打量对方，试图找出差错。A—Adult，指用成人的眼光与人交流，互相之间的关系是平等的，视线从上到下。C—Childen，一般是小孩的眼光，目光向上，表示请求或撒娇。作为职场人士，当然都是运用成人的视线与人交流，所以要准确定位，不要在错误的地点、对象面前选择错误的目光，那会让人心感诧异的。

The PAC rule: P is the "parent", means using parent-like visions to communicate with people in a teaching way. The vision is from up to the bottom so as to try to find some defaults from the other party. A is the "adult", means the communication with people through the vision of an adult. The relationship between them is equal, and the vision is from up to the bottom. C is the "children", which is usually the vision of a child with eyes looking up so as to demand or for coquetry. As a professional person in the vocational field, of course the visions of an adult should be applied to communicate with people, so the positioning should correct. Never choose wrong visions at wrong site and in front of the targets, which will make other people feel surprising.

三角定律：根据交流对象与你关系的亲疏、距离的远近来选择目光停留或注视的区域。关系一般或第一次见面、距离较远的，则看对方的额头到肩膀的这个大三角区域；关系比较熟、距离较近的，看对方的额头到下巴这个三角区域；关系亲昵的，距离很近的，则注视对方的额头到鼻子这个三角区域。

The triangle law: To select the area for lingering of visions or staring according to the intimate degree of the relationships with the targets for communication. For those of common relationship, meeting for the first time, or of longer distance, then look at the big triangle area formed by the forehead and shoulders of the other party; for those of intimate rand closer relationships, look at the triangle areas formed by the part from the foreheads to the cheeks of the other party; for those with intimate relationships, please watch the triangle areas formed by the part from the forehead to the nose of the other party.

时间规律：每次目光接触的时间不要超过三秒钟。交流过程中用60%~70%的时间与对方进行目光交流是最适宜的。少于60%，则说明你对对方的话题、谈话内容不感兴趣；多于70%，则表示你对对方本人的兴趣要多于他所说的话。

Time rules: The time for eye contact for every time should not exceed three seconds. During the process of communication, 60%-70% of the time should be used for eye contact with the other party, which is regarded as the most appropriate. If it is less than 60%, it shows that you are not interested with the topics or the contents of dialogues; while if it is more than 70%, it shows that you are more interested with the person him or herself than what he or she says.

2. 手势运用（Application of gestures）

通过手势，可以表达介绍、引领、请、再见等多种含义。手势一定要柔和，但也不能拖泥带水。

Gestures could express many kinds of meanings like introduction, guidance, pleasing, and farewell, etc. The gestures must be soft, but do not be messy.

（三）定位你的职业形象（Positioning of Your Vocational Image）

得体的穿着，不仅可以显得更加美丽，还可以体现出一个现代文明人良好的修养和独到的品位。

Elegant clothing could not only make a person look more beautiful but also manifest the good accomplishment and unique tastes.

1. 职业着装的基本原则（Basic Principles for Professional Attires）

着装TOP原则：TOP是三个英语单词的缩写，它们分别代表时间（Time）、场合（Occasion）和地点（Place）。

The TOP principles of dressing: TOP is the abbreviation of three English words, which represent time, occasion, and places respectively.

场合原则：衣着要与场合协调。与顾客会谈、参加正式会议等，衣着应庄重考究；听音乐会或看芭蕾舞，则应按惯例着正装；出席正式宴会时，则应穿中国的传统旗袍或西方的长裙晚礼服；而在朋友聚会、郊游等场合，着装应轻便舒适。

The principle of occasion: The dressing should be harmonious with the occasions. During meeting customer and having talks or participation in formal meetings, dressings should be solemn and elegant; when joining concert or ballet, you should be in formal dresses according to the usual practice; for presence at formal dinners, China traditional cheongsam or western dress evening dress should be put on; while in the gathering with friends, hiking and other occasions, the dress should be light and comfortable.

时间原则：不同时段的着装规则对女士尤其重要。男士有一套质地上乘的深色西装或中山装足以包打天下，而女士的着装则要随时间而变换。白天工作时，女士应穿着正式套装，以体现专业性；晚上出席鸡尾酒会就须多加一些修饰，如换一双高跟鞋，戴上有光泽的佩饰，围一条漂亮的丝巾；服装的选择还要适合季节气候特点，保持与潮流大势同步。

The principle of time: The dressing in different periods of time is especially important for women. For man, he only needs to have a fine texture dark suit or Chinese tunic suit to try to do everything all by himself, but women's dress has to change with time. During working in the day, the lady should wear formal suits so as to reflect professionalism; for attending cocktail party at night, then some necessary modification would be added, such as changing into a pair of high heels, wearing shiny accessories, surrounding the neck with a beautiful scarf; the choice of clothing should be also suitable for matching the seasonal climatic characteristics and keeping in pace with the general trend.

地点原则：在自己家里接待客人，可以穿着舒适且整洁的休闲服；如果是去公司或单位拜访，穿职业套装会显得专业；外出时要顾及当地的传统和风俗习惯，如去教堂或寺庙等场所，不能穿过露或过短的服装。

The principle of place: For meeting guests in your own house, you can put on comfortable and neat sportswear; if for visiting the company or organization, wearing a business suit will be professional; while when going out, you should take into account the local traditions and customs, such as that you should not put on the gel or short dress. Guests in their own homes, can be comfortably worn but neat sportswear; if the company or organization is to visit, wear a business suit will be professional; when going out to take into account the local traditions and customs, such as going to sites like church or temple, you should not put on clothes very scanty or too short.

2. 职业女性着装四讲究（The Four Particularities of the Dressing of the Professional Females）

整洁平整：服装并非一定要高档华贵，但须保持清洁，并熨烫平整，穿起来就能大方得体，显得精神焕发。整洁并不完全为了自己，更是尊重他人，这是良好仪态的第一要务。

Clean and smooth: It is not necessary for the clothes to be of high end or luxurious, but they must be maintained clean and ironed to be flat and tidy so as to be dressed in a generous and appropriate way for showing a refreshed spirit. Being tidy is not only for a person himself but also for the needs of respecting others. This is the top priority of good appearance and attitude.

色彩技巧：不同色彩会给人不同的感受，如深色或冷色调的服装让人产生视觉上的收缩感，显得庄重严肃；而浅色或暖色调的服装会有扩张感，使人显得轻松活泼。因此，可以根据不同需要进行选择和搭配。

Skills on colors: Different color can give a person different feelings. For example, dark or cold tonal clothing make the person produce the contractive feeling on the vision, which appears to be solemn and serious; while the clothing of light and warm tones will have the feeling of expansion and make the person seem to be relaxed and lively. As a result, choices could be chosen according to different needs and matching.

配套齐全：除了主体衣服之外，鞋袜手套等的搭配也要多加考究。如袜子以透明近似肤色或与服装颜色协调为好，带有大花纹的袜子不能登大雅之堂。正式、庄重的场合不宜穿凉鞋或靴子，黑色皮鞋是适用最广的，可以和任何服装搭配。

Fully furnishing: Except for the clothes of main body, more considerations should be taken into the matching of shoes, socks and gloves, etc. For example, it would be best if the socks are transparent and almost like the color of the skin or harmonious with the color of the clothes, but those socks with large patterns is not appropriate for attending graceful occasions. In formal and solemn occasions, sandals or boots should not be worn, but black leather shoes are the most widely used ones and they could match all clothes.

饰物点缀：巧妙地佩戴饰品能够起到画龙点睛的作用，给女士们增添色彩。但是佩戴的饰品不宜过多，否则会分散对方的注意力。佩戴饰品时，应尽量选择同一色系。佩戴首饰最关键的就是要与整体服饰搭配统一起来。

Embellishments: Cleverly wearing jewelry can have the effect of making the finishing point and adding colors to ladies. But do not wear too much jewelry, otherwise it will distract others. When wearing jewelries, you should try to choose those of the same color. It is the most critical for wearing jewelry to match and unify with the whole of clothes.

3. 严格禁止的着装（Clothes that Are Strictly Prohibited）

牛仔服（衣、裤）、超短裙、拖鞋（包括时装凉拖）等。

Cowboy suits (clothes and trousers), miniskirts, slippers (including fashionable cool slippers), etc.

（四）日常接待工作（Work of Daily Reception）

1. 迎接礼仪（Etiquettes for Reception）

应立即招呼来访客人：应该意识到大部分来访客人对公司来说都是重要的，要表示出热情友好和愿意提供服务的态度。如果你正在打字应立即停止，即使是在打电话也要对来客点头示意，但不一定要起立迎接，也不必与来客握手。

Guests should be immediately greeted visitors: It should be realized that most visitors are important for the companies, so you should have express a warm and friendly attitude of willing to provide service. If you are typing, you should immediately stop, even when you are on the phone you should also nod to the visitors, but it is not necessary to stand up for greeting and you do not have to shake hands with the visitors.

主动热情问候客人：打招呼时，应轻轻点头并面带微笑。如果是已经认识的客人，称呼要显得比较亲切。

Active and enthusiastic greeting to the guests: You should nod gently and smile when greeting others. If you already know the guest, the salutation should appear to be more cordial.

陌生客人的接待：陌生客人光临时，务必问清其姓名及公司或单位名称。

Reception of strange guests: When the strange guest comes, the names of himself as well as his company or unit must be asked.

2. 接待礼仪（Etiquette of Reception）

接待客人要注意以下几点：

The following several points should be stressed when receiving the guests:

客人要找的负责人不在时，要明确告诉对方负责人到何处去了，以及何时回本酒店。请客人留下电话、地址，明确是由客人再次来酒店，还是我方负责人到对方公司去。

When a guest is looking for the responsible person but actually who is not present, you should clearly tell him where the responsible person in charge has gone and when he/she will return to the hotel. Ask the guest to leave his/her telephone number and address and clarify whether the guest should come to the hotel again or our responsible person to visit his company.

客人到来时，我方负责人由于种种原因不能马上接见时，要向客人说明理由与等待时间，若客人愿意等待，应该向客人提供饮料、杂志。

When the guests arrive but our person in charge cannot immediately meet them for various reasons, you should explain the reasons to the guests for their waiting as well as the time they should wait. If the guest would like to wait, then you should provide beverages and magazine to the guests.

接待人员带领客人到达目的地，应该有正确的引导方法和引导姿势。

When the receptionist guides the guests to their destination, they should have correct guiding methods and gestures.

在走廊的引导方法。接待人员在客人两三步之前，配合步调，让客人走在内侧。

Methods for guiding in the corridors. The receptionist should be about two or three steps ahead of the guests so as to coordinate with the steps of the guests. Let the guest walk in the inner side.

在楼梯的引导方法。当引导客人上楼时，应该让客人走在前面，接待人员走在后面，若是下楼时，应该由接待人员走在前面，客人在后面，上下楼梯时，接待人员应该注意客人的安全。

Guiding methods in the stairs. When the guests are guided to the upstairs, the receptionist should let the guests go ahead but he himself should go at the back; for going downstairs, the receptionist should walk ahead of the guests who should be at the back. When going up and down the stairs, the receptionist should pay attention to the safety of the guests.

在电梯时的引导方法。引导客人乘坐电梯时，接待人员先进入电梯，等客人进入后关闭电梯门，到达时，接待人员按“开”的钮，让客人先走出电梯。

Guiding methods in the elevators. When guiding the guest to take the elevator, the receptionist should enter the elevator first, and after the guests enter, close the door. When the elevator arrives, the receptionist should press the “Open” button and let the guests to get out of the elevator first.

客厅里的引导方法。当客人走入客厅，接待人员用手指示，请客人坐下，看到客人坐下后，才能行点头礼后离开。如客人误坐下座，应请客人改坐上座（一般靠近门的一方为下座）。

Guiding methods in the living rooms. When the guests go into the living room, the receptionist should show hand instructions so as to have the guests sit down, and after seeing the guests sit down, nod for solute and then leave. If the guest takes a wrong inferior seat, he should be directed to a superior one (usually the one closer to the door is regarded as the inferior).

诚心诚意地奉茶。我国人民习惯以茶水招待客人，在招待尊贵客人时，茶具要特别讲究，倒茶有许多规矩，递茶也有许多讲究。

Sincere serving of tea. The people in our nation have been used to entertaining their guests with tea, and when the guests are very distinguished, the tea sets will have special requirements. There are many rules for pouring and delivering teas.

（五）电话礼仪（Telephone Etiquettes）

（1）目的：通过电话，给来电者留下这样的印象：当我们接听电话时应该热情，因为我们代表着公司的形象。

Purpose: It is to leave such an impression to the calling persons through the telephone that we should be hospitable when receiving telephone calls because we are representing the image of the company.

（2）左手持听筒、右手拿笔：大多数人习惯用右手拿起电话听筒，但是，在与客户进行电话沟通过程中往往需要做必要的文字记录。在写字的时候一般会将话筒夹在肩膀上面，这样，电话很容易夹不住而掉下来发出刺耳的声音，从而给客户带来不适。

Holding the listener with the left hand and pen in the right hand. Most people are used to picking up the listener of the telephone with their right hands, but it usually needs to take necessary written notes during the process of communicating with the clients through telephone. When writing, they usually put the listener on their shoulders so that the listener will be clamped and not fall down to produce cacophony, thus making the clients feel uncomfortable.

为了消除这种不良现象，提倡用左手拿听筒，右手写字或操纵电脑，这样就可以轻松自如地达到与客户沟通的目的。

In order to eradicate this bad phenomenon, it is advocated to pick up the listener with the left hand so that the right hand could write or operate the computer so as to realize the goals of communicating with the clients in a very light and freely way.

（3）电话铃声响过三声之内接起电话。

Pick up the phone within three times of the ringing.

（4）注意声音和表情。

Pay attention to the voices and expressions.

说话必须清晰，正对着话筒，发音准确。通电话时，不能大吼也不能喃喃细语，而应该用正常的声音——并尽量用热情和友好的语气。

When speaking, the voice must be clear, face the listener, and pronounce correctly. When speaking in the telephone, do not shout or murmur, and normal voices should be used—and try to use hospitable and friendly tones as much as possible.

还应该调整好表情。微笑可以通过电话传递。使用礼貌用语如"谢谢您"，"请问有什么可以帮忙的吗?""不用谢。"

Expressions should also be adjusted. Smiles could be transferred through telephone. Polite wordings like "Thank you", "What can I do for you?" or "You are welcome" should be used.

（5）保持正确的姿势。接听电话过程中应该始终保持正确的姿势。一般情况下，当人的身体稍微下沉，丹田受到压迫时容易导致声音无法发出；大部分人讲话所使用的是胸腔，这样容易口干舌燥，如果运用丹田的声音，不但可以使声音具有磁性，而且不会伤害喉咙。因此，保持端坐的姿势，尤其不要趴在桌面边缘，这样可以使声音自然、流畅和动听。此外，保持微笑也能够使来电者感受到你的愉悦。

Keep right postures. Right postures should be always maintained during the process of receiving telephone calls. Under general conditions, when the body of a person is slightly sinking, the lower part of the belly will be pressed, thus no voice could come out from this part; and most people speak by using their chest, but in this way it is easy to feel the mouth become dry. If voices from the lower part of the belly could be utilized, it will not only make the voices to be more attractive but also not harm the throat. Therefore, keeping the posture of sit straightly, especially not groveling at the edge of the desk, the voices will seem to be very natural, smooth and pleasant for listening. In addition, keeping smiling will also enable the calling party feel your happiness.

（六）酒店内部的礼仪和秩序（The Etiquettes and Orders Within the Hotel）

（1）离座和外出。前台接待人员工作的特殊性决定了其离座不应该太久，一般不能超过 10 分钟。如果是因为特殊原因需要外出时，应该先找到代办人，并交代清楚接听电话的方法等。

Leave the seats and go out. The specialty of the work of staff in the front desk has determined that they should not leave their seats absent for a very long time. Usually it should not exceed ten minutes. If it needs going out due to particular reasons, an agent should be found first and the methods for receiving telephone calls should be made clear.

（2）严守工作时间。前台接待人员应该严格遵守作息时间，一般情况下，应该提前 5~10 分钟到岗，下午下班应该推迟 20~30 分钟。

Strictly abide by the working time. The receptionists at the front desk should abide by their time for working and rest strictly. Generally speaking, they should arrive 5 to 10 minutes earlier at their positions but leave 20 to 30 minutes after the time point for end of the whole day's work.

（3）应该区分闲谈与交谈。前台人员应该尽量避免长时间的私人电话占线，更不应该出现在前台与其他同事闲谈的场面。

Distinguish chat and communication. The staff at the front table should try best not to let personal calls occupy the telephone lines for a long time, and what is more forbidden is the scene of chatting with other colleagues at the front desk.

附录 2 前厅部主要岗位工作内容
Appendix 2 Job Contents of Key Posts for Front Office

（一） 前厅部经理工作职责（Job Responsibilities of Front Office Manager）

直接上级：总经理

Immediate Superior：General Manager

直接下级：前厅部各岗位主管、大堂经理

Immediate Subordinate：Supervisor and Assistant Manager in Each Position in Front Office

岗位职责：对总经理负责，主持整个前厅部的全面工作，保证本部门员工的对客服务质量，最大限度提高入住率及客房收入。

Job Description：Be responsible for general manager, host the comprehensive work of the front office, and ensure the quality of customer service of staff in department and maximizes to improve the occupancy rate and guest room income.

工作内容（Job Content）：

（1）制定本部门各项规章制度和工作计划，并组织落实。

Make the rules and regulations and work plan of department and put them into effect.

（2）对各分部主管下达工作任务并指导、落实、检查、协调，深入了解员工的服务态度及工作质量，解决各种问题。

Assign work tasks to the supervisor of each branch, and direct, implement, check, coordinate and know the service attitude and job content of staff at deep level.

（3）制订前厅部的培训计划并组织落实，对员工素质、工作效率、服务水准等负有管理和培训的责任。

Make the training program of front office and put it into effect, and take the responsibility of management and training for the quality of staff, work efficiency, service level, etc.

（4）参加酒店各种例会，完成上传下达。

Attend every regular meetings of hotel, report and transmit tasks.

（5）制订部门的物资设备供应计划，对部门的工作计划、督导等负有管理责任。

Make materials and equipments supply plan of department, take management responsibility of the work plan, supervision and other things in department.

（6）组织主持前厅部的每周部门例会，听取跟踪汇报，布置工作，解决问题，同时，主持部门日常会议，及时传达重要信息。

Organize and host the regular meetings of department in each week for front office, hear the follow-up report, assign works and solve the problems, meanwhile, host the daily meetings of department and convey the important information in time.

（7）负责与其他部门的协调，确保部门间的信息沟通和团队协作，协助公安部门协查通缉犯的工作。

Be responsible to coordinate with other departments, ensure the information communication and team cooperation among departments, and assist the public security department to do assistant investigation to the wanted persons.

（8）与财务部协调共同完成账务及信贷方面的工作。

Coordinate with the financial department so as to collectively complete the works in respect of accounting and credit.

（9）与销售部协调安排团队及重要客人的接待，预测市场分配情况。

Coordinate with the sales department so as to arrange the reception of team and VIP guests and predict the allocation condition of market.

（10）与客房部协调合理分配房间，以最大限度提高住房率及客房收入。

Coordinate with housekeeping department so as to reasonably distribute rooms and maximize the rate of room occupancy and income of guest room.

（11）每天检查对 VIP 客人接待工作的准备及落实情况，并跟踪落实。

Check the preparation and implementation of reception for VIP guests in each day, as well as conduct the follow-up work and put them into effect.

（12）了解和掌握当日的房间状况及预订情况，了解欲抵客人资料，抽查分房、排房情况，分析房间状态，力争当天的开房率达到最高水平，并定期做出客房出租率预测报表。

Know and clear the room status and reservation condition in each day, understand the data of guests who are going to arrive, and the condition of random checking, rooms assigning and rooms arranging, analyze the room status, maximize the rate of occupancy in that day and make the projected statement of occupancy rate of rooms at regular intervals.

（13）审阅当日各种报表、各岗位工作日志和各种记录，随时了解客房出租情况，从中发现和了解情况并即使处理或向上级报告。

Review the various statements, work logs and recordings of the day in each post, know the renting condition of rooms at any time, and deal with or report the problems found in the process in time.

（14）检查部署员工的仪容、仪表和仪态以及各分部的工作质量和工作进度，对员工进行现场指导，监督员工的工作表现及实施各种奖惩，负责员工的绩效评估。

Check the staff's appearance and manners, as well as the quality of work and job schedule of each branch, conduct site instruction to staff, supervise the performance of staff, implement all kinds of rewards and punishments, and is responsible for the performance appraisal of staff.

（15）巡视酒店大堂区域，确保大厅的卫生、背景音乐等状态良好。

Inspect the area of hotel lobby so as to ensure that it is clean in lobby, the background music and other items in which are in good condition.

（16）与客人保持良好关系，了解客人反馈意见，处理客人投诉。

Keep good relationships with guests, get feedback opinions from them and deal with their complaints.

（17）检查、负责本部门的安全、防火工作，并负管理责任。

Check and in charge of the security and fire prevention work of department, and have management responsibility.

（18）及时完成总经理或管理部门交办的其他工作任务。

Accomplish other work tasks assigned by general manager or administrative department.

工作流程（Working Process）：

（1）询问住房情况，查看营业日报表。

Inquire the information of occupancy and check the daily statement of business.

（2）参加总经理主持的每日例会。

Attend the regular meeting presided by general manager in each day.

（3）传达酒店最新信息、通知等内容，及时更新销售信息。

Convey the latest information，notice，etc. of hotel，and update the sales information in time.

（4）检查大堂吧卫生工作和报刊架，参加有关计划外会议。

Check the sanitary work and newspaper stand in hobby bar，and attend the related unscheduled conferences.

（5）检查各岗位当班员工在岗时的仪表仪容和服务姿态，检查当日的营业日报和前一日的客房出租率报告。

Check the appearance and service manners of staff at every post on duty，and check the daily business statement of the day and the report of rooms' occupancy rate of the day before.

（6）查阅部门工作日志，及时了解情况。

Consult the work log of department so as to know information in time.

（7）查阅并了解当日进店、住店、离店客人报表。

Consult and understand the statements about the guests who come，check in and check out.

（8）了解每日宴会、会议预订和落实情况。

Understand the condition of daily banquet，conference reservation and implementation.

（9）了解岗位交接班情况。

Understand the condition of duty shifting at each post.

（10）检查当日进店团队、会议、VIP 客人的安排情况。

Check the arrangement about the team who come on the day，and that of conference and VIP guests.

（11）深入现场督导，并检查人手安排情况，随时听取客人意见，处理客人投诉，并随时协调与各部门之间的工作。

Conduct field supervision，check the arrangement of manpower，hear the opinions from guests，handle the complaints from guests at any time and coordinate the work relevant to other departments at any time.

（12）抽查前厅部发出的信息是否准确，保证正常运转。

Random check the information from front office to see whether it is accurate，ensuring the normal running.

（13）整理部门内部资料，按岗位责任开展工作。

Clear up the internal data of department and carry out works according to job responsibilities.

（14）主持前厅部每周工作例会。

Direct the regular meeting in each week for front office.

（二）大堂经理工作职责（Job Responsibilities of Assistant Manager）

直接上级：前厅部经理

Immediate Superior：Manager of Front Office

直接下级：前厅部各岗位主管、领班、员工

Immediate Subordinate: Each Supervisor, Team Leader and Staff in Front Office

岗位职责：协助前厅部经理检查、督导前厅部各下属部门服务工作，代表总经理对酒店各部门服务质量、客房设施等方面进行监督检查，维持酒店形象，听取住客意见，处理住客投诉，并准确制作夜班报表。

Job Description: Assist the manager of front office to check, supervise the service work of every subordinate sectors in front office, supervise and inspect the service quality, facilities in rooms and other matters of each department in hotel on behalf of general manager, keep the image of hotel, hear the opinions from occupants, handle the complaints from occupants and make the statement of night shift accurately.

工作内容（Job Contents）：

（1）巡视大堂及附近公共区域，确保环境整洁有序，员工仪表及行为规范符合酒店要求。

Inspect the lobby and the public area nearby so as to ensure they are clean and orderly, and the appearance of staff and behavioral norms are up to the standards of hotel.

（2）帮助前厅部员工处理棘手的工作，保证前厅工作顺利进行，协助前厅部经理督导下属各岗位员工的服务态度及工作质量。

Help the staff in front office to handle troublesome matters, ensure the work of front office is smooth, assist the manager of front office to supervise the service attitude and work quality of their subordinate staff at each post.

（3）保持与前厅各部分良好的团队精神及协调部门间的关系以最大限度提高工作效率。

Ensure each part of front office has good team spirit, and coordinate the relationships among departments so as to maximize to improve the work efficiency.

（4）对外代表总经理接受客人对酒店所有部门和区域的投诉，并及时圆满解决客人投诉，兼顾酒店及客人利益，确保问题得到妥善及时的解决。

On behalf of general manager, receive the complaints about each department and area of hotel from guests, and satisfactorily solve the complaints in time, which gives consideration to the benefits of hotel and guests so that the problem is solved properly and in time.

（5）代表总经理迎送住客，落实检查 VIP 抵店前的准备工作，落实接待的每一细节，并迎接客人的到来，认真做好离店送别。

On behalf of general manager, implement and inspect the preparatory work for VIP guests coming into hotel, implement every detail of reception, greet the coming guests and see off the guests.

（6）负责迎接及带领 VIP 客人到指定的房间，并介绍房间设施，落实贵宾接待的每一细节。

Be responsible to greet and lead VIP guests to the specified rooms, introduce the facilities condition in room to them and implement every detail of reception for VIP guests.

（7）了解酒店各部门的最新信息准确解答客人问询，帮助客人解决困难，对于酒店范围外的要求，给予最大限度的帮助，发生紧急事件时，必须（在没有请示上级的情况下）做出主动决断的指示，为生病或发生意外事故的客人安排送护等事宜。

Understand the latest information of each department in hotel so as to answer the inquiry of guests, and help guests to solve problems. For the demand beyond the responsibilities of the hotel, offer the maximum help. In case of an emergency, shall initiatively make the decision, and take the guest who falls ill or has an accident to go to hospital, etc.

(8) 完整地记录工作范围内和当值时间内的重要事件及投诉记录，将特殊或重要的内容以书面形式上报于部门，以便管理层进行跟进处理。

Perfectly record the important events and complaints happened within scope of work and happened in periods on duty, report the special or important contents to department in written form so as to do follow-up by the managers.

(9) 应尽量参与接待工作，了解当天及以后房间的销售状况，巡查酒店内外部以保证各项功能正常运行，及时排除隐患。

Try to participate in the reception work, understand the occupancy status of rooms in the day, inspect the inside and outside of hotel so as to ensure every function to be in normal operation and eliminate the hidden danger in time.

(10) 维护大堂秩序，确保酒店和客人的人身及财产安全，熟知酒店的消防程序及安全知识，发生火警或火灾时立即赶赴现场并向有关领导汇报请示，协助指挥处理。

Maintain the order of lobby, make sure the safety of guests and their properties, know well the fire protection procedure and safety knowledge of hotel, in case of a fire alarm or fire, should rush to the site and report to the related leader for instructions, and assist to conduct command and treatment.

(11) 协助保安部及公安人员进行与客人相关的安全调查。

Assist the security department and public security officers to conduct the security investigation relevant to guests.

(12) 做好交接班工作，仔细阅读交班记录本内容，确保须跟进事宜的妥善解决。

Do well the duty shifting, carefully read the record of duty shifting so as to handle the follow-up matters properly.

(13) 负责万能钥匙的保管，熟悉酒店紧急事件处理制度和程序。

Be responsible to keep the master key and familiar with the treatment system and procedure of emergencies in hotel.

(14) 了解员工的思想动态，协助部门经理做好员工技术培训和业务考核的工作。

Understand the ideological trends of staff, and assist the department manager to conduct the technical training to staff and do business assessment work.

(15) 与财务人员配合，追收仍在酒店住宿客人拖欠的账款，必要时可以指挥其他部门人员协助工作。

Coordinating with financial staff, recover the defaulting money from the guests who are still living in hotel, if necessary, can direct the staff in other departments to assist works.

(16) 完成上级交办的其他任务。

Complete other tasks assigned by superiors.

工作流程 (Working Process)：

(1) 认真阅读交班内容，检查各岗位员工的仪表仪容、交接班情况，做好交接工作。

Carefully read the duty shifting record, check the appearance of staff, duty shifting condition and properly complete the duty shifting work.

(2) 了解昨日客房经营情况及当日会议预订、VIP到店情况，并及时做好记录，供当班和下一班使用。

Understand the business condition of guest room on the day before, and the condition of conference reservation and VIP coming into hotel, and make the record in time so as to be used by the staff on duty and the following shift.

（3）检查大厅灯光、背景音乐、室温等是否符合酒店要求，并按酒店规定进行开关。

Check the lights, background music, indoor temperature, etc. in lobby to see whether they are up to the standard of hotel, and switch them as per the requirements of hotel.

（4）完成上一班转交的未完成事宜，并做好记录。

Complete the unfinished matters delivered by the previous shift colleagues and make record properly.

（5）听取住客意见，接受住客投诉，及时处理并做好记录。

Hear the opinions from occupants, receive the complaints from occupants and handle them in time and make record properly.

（6）协助各岗位各部门开展日常工作，并做好记录。

Assist each post and each department to carry out the daily work, and make record properly.

（7）定期巡视大厅清洁卫生、设施设备完好情况，发现问题督促有关人员迅速解决。

Inspect the condition of lobby at regular intervals so as to ensure it is clean and the facilities and equipments are in good condition, if there are any problems, urge the personnel concerned to handle them quickly.

（8）留意大厅内客人动向，维护大厅秩序，控制大厅气氛。

Notice the guests in lobby so as to maintain the order and control the atmosphere in lobby.

（9）中班人员负责将当日发生的最具代表性的事件以及客人的意见、建议归纳整理，上报部门办公室。

Middle shift staff is responsible to sum up and sort out the most representative events and opinions from guests on the day, and report to office of department.

（三）预订处主管工作职责（Job Responsibilities of Supervisor of Reservation Desk）

直接上级：前厅部经理

Immediate Superior: Manager of Front Office

直接下级：预订处文员

Immediate Subordinate: Clerks at Reservation Desk

岗位职责：负责酒店客房预订的全面工作，包括制订前厅部客房预订工作计划，培训、检查、督导下属员工工作，考核员工工作表现，确保前厅部客房预订各项工作的正常开展。

Post Responsibilities: Be responsible to the comprehensive work for room reservation, including that work out the work plan of room reservation for front office, train for staff, inspect and supervise the work of subordinate staff, assess the job performance of staff, and ensure the normal work of room reservation for front office.

工作内容（Job Contents）：

（1）协助前厅部经理，制定预订处的规章制度、服务工作程序，健全岗位职责。

Assist the manager of front office to make the rules and regulations, working procedure of service for reservation desk so as to perfect the job responsibilities.

（2）熟悉酒店经营政策、营业指标、市场动态及其他酒店的订房情况。

Familiar with the business policy, business index of hotel, market dynamics and room reservation condition of other hotels.

（3）参加前厅部经理主持召开的前厅部各项定期例会及其他有关会议，向前厅部经理提供准确的预订信息。

Attend the various regular meeting and other related meetings of front office which held by manager of front office, and offer accurate reservation information to the manager of front office.

（4）主持预订处每日晨会，传达部门例会内容，安排客房预订日常工作。

Direct the daily morning conference at reservation desk, convey the content of regular meeting of department and arrange the daily work for room reservation.

（5）检查、督导本部门员工出勤、仪容仪表、礼貌服务情况。

Check and supervise the attendance, appearance and manner of staff in department.

（6）掌握各类预订信息，随时检查可用房间，掌握房间状态，合理控制房间预订，确保预订信息及电脑输入的准确无误。

Master various reservation information, inspect the usable rooms at any time, master the room status, rationally control the room reservation so as to the reservation information and information input the computer is accurate.

（7）确保下属员工以友善、热情的态度接听酒店内部及外部来电，按照规定程序回复、确认、处理各种电话预订。

Make sure the subordinate staff to answer the interior and external calls in hotel with a friendly and enthusiastic attitude, and reply, affirm and handle various reservation by phone according to the established procedure.

（8）合理安排下属员工的班次，制订员工业务培训计划，组织实施下属员工业务技能培训，并定期进行绩效评估。

Arrange the duty shifting for subordinate staff, make the business training plan for staff, organize and implement the professional skill training for subordinate staff, and conduct performance evaluation at regular intervals.

（9）完成部门规定的各种报表及预测。

Complete the various statements and predictions specified by department.

（10）完成上级交办的其他任务。

Complete other tasks assigned by superiors.

（四）预订处文员工作职责（Work Responsibilities of Reservation Office Staffers）

直接上级：预订处主管

Immediate Superior: Reservation Office Supervisor

岗位职责：按照规定程序热情、友善处理预订工作。

Post Responsibilities: To handle with reservation-related work in a passionate and friendly manner following regulated procedures.

工作内容（Work Contents）：

（1）按照酒店规定接听电话预订，确保客人信息的准确完整，并及时输入电脑。

To pick up phone reservation following hotel regulations, ensure accuracy and completeness of guests information and timely input it to the computer.

（2）随时查看电脑显示的房间状态，合理分配预订的房间。

To timely check room status revealed in the computer and rationally allocate reserved rooms.

（3）准确及时处理客人对预订的更改、取消等特殊要求。

To accurately and timely handle with such particular requirements by guests on change, cancellation and so on of reservation.

（4）按照规定程序处理团队预订、旅行社或公司传真预订及酒店网站上预订。

To handle with team reservation, fax reservation by travel agency or company and on-line reservation in accordance with established procedures.

（5）通过升级销售及交叉销售积极向客人推销酒店设施及服务，以增加酒店收入。

To actively promote hotel facilities and services to guests through upgraded sales and overlapping sales for the purpose of increasing hotel revenues.

（6）对重要的或有问题的预订或传真，及时请示上级主管进行处理。

To timely ask for instructions from high authorities on disposal of big or problematic reservation or fax.

（7）酒店客满期间，将客人列入等候名单或向客人推荐其他酒店。

To list guests in the Waiting List or recommend other hotels to guests during full house status.

（8）做好交接班工作，仔细阅读交班记录本内容，确保须跟进事宜的妥善解决。

To accomplish shifting of duty, carefully review contents in record book related with shifting of duty and ensure proper addressing of matters needing follow-up.

（9）完成上级交办的其他任务。

To complete other tasks assigned by superiors.

（五）商务中心主管工作职责（Work Responsibilities of Business Center Supervisor）

直接上级：前厅部经理

Immediate Superior: Front Office Department Manager

直接下级：商务中心文员

Immediate Subordinate: Business Center Staffers

岗位职责：负责商务中心的日常运作，制订工作计划，培训、督导员工，确保商务中心的良好运转，为客人提供高效的商务服务。

Post Responsibilities: Be responsible for daily operation in the Business Center, preparation of work planning, training and supervising of staffers, ensuring fine operation of the Business Center, and providing of high efficient business services to guests.

工作内容（Work Contents）：

（1）协助前厅部经理，制定商务中心的规章制度、服务工作程序，健全岗位职责。

To assist Front Office Department Manager to prepare regulatory framework and service work procedure of the Business Center and to perfect post Responsibilities.

（2）参加前厅部经理主持召开的前厅部各项定期例会及其他有关会议。

To participate in various routines convened at regular intervals and other related conferences in the Front Hall Department presided over by Front Hall Department Manager.

（3）制订商务中心工作计划，定时填报当月工作报表，合理安排下属员工的班次。

To prepare work planning of the Business Center, to fill in work statement for the month at a fixed time and to rationally arrange shifts of subordinate staffers.

（4）制订员工业务培训计划，组织、实施下属员工业务技能培训，并定期进行绩效评估。

To prepare business training schedule of staffers, organize and implement training on business skills of subordinate employees and carry out performance evaluation at fixed term.

（5）检查员工交接班情况，跟踪落实有关事项。

To check condition related with shift change and to follow and put into force relevant matters.

（6）检查、督导本部门员工出勤、仪容仪表、礼貌服务情况，确保员工行为规范符合酒店要求。

To check and supervise attendance, looks and matters, and politeness service of staffers of the department to ensure staffers behaviors conform to hotel requirements.

（7）参与商务中心对客服务，检查、督导员工工作，考核员工工作表现，保证商务中心服务质量。

To take part in customer services in the Business Center, check and monitor work by staffers, evaluate performance of staffers and ensure service quality of the Business Center.

（8）合理安排下属员工的班次，负责对下属的岗位技能培训并定期进行绩效评估。

To rationally arrange shifts of subordinate staffers and be responsible for training for post skills on subordinates and conduction of performance evaluation at regular intervals.

（9）有效解决预订及为客人提供商务服务中的问题和困难，确保商务设施的完好。

To effectively address issues and difficulties related with reservation and business services provided to guests and ensure that business facilities be in good condition.

（10）确保商务中心与前厅部其他部分的密切配合。

To ensure close coordination between Business Center and Front Hall Department and other departments.

（11）完成部门规定的各种报表及预测。

To complete all kinds of statement and forecast of the Department.

（12）完成上级交办的其他任务。

To complete other tasks assigned by superiors.

（六）商务中心文员工作职责（Work Responsibilities of Business Center Staffers）

直接上级：商务中心主管

Immediate Superior: Business Center Manager

岗位职责：按照规定程序热情、友善地为客人提供打字、复印、传真等商务服务。

Post Responsibilities: To provide such business services as typewriting, copying, faxing and so on to guests in a passionate and friendly matter.

工作内容（Work Contents）：

（1）热情、友善、及时、准确地为客人提供打字、复印、接发传真等商务服务。

To provide such business services as typewriting, copying, fax sending and receiving to guests in a passionate, friendly, timely and accurate manner.

（2）接受客人的文字翻译服务，并联系翻译公司以满足客人的要求。

To take in services for translation from guests and contact translation companies to live up to their demands.

（3）接受客人电脑文字处理的要求，并确保准确无误。

To take in requirements on computer word processing and ensure accuracy.

（4）保管电话磁卡，并做好销售工作。

To take care of phone magcard and do well in sales.

（5）处理客人的特快专递要求。

To handle with express mail service requirement from guests.

（6）定时上网查询电子邮件并通知相关人员。

To log on the internet to inquire e-mail and notify relevant staffers at regular intervals.

（7）熟练掌握商务中心所有服务价格。

To master price of all services in the Business Center.

（8）掌握火情等紧急情况下的酒店防范措施。

To master hotel precautionary measures in times of emergency.

(9) 做好交接班工作，仔细阅读交班记录本内容，确保须跟进事宜的妥善解决。

To come off work related with shift change, carefully review contents in record book of shift change and ensure proper addressing of follow-up matters.

(10) 完成上级交办的其他任务。

To accomplish other tasks assigned by the superior.

（七）客服中心主管工作职责（Work Responsibilities of Call Center Supervisor）

直接上级：前厅部经理

Immediate Superior: Front Office Department Manager

直接下级：客服中心话务员

Immediate Subordinate: Call Center Telephone Operators

岗位职责：负责客服中心的正常运转，安排对下属员工的培训计划并组织落实。

Post Responsibilities: To be responsible for normal operation of the Call Center, arrange training plan on subordinate staffers and organize the implementation.

工作内容（Work Contents）：

(1) 协助前厅部经理，制定客服中心的规章制度、服务工作程序，健全岗位职责。

To assist Front Office Department Manager to prepare regulatory framework and service procedure of the Call Center and to perfect post Responsibilities.

(2) 制定客服中心的工作程序、标准和管理规定，在执行过程中加以改进。

To prepare work procedure, standard and management rules of the Call Center and make amendment during implementation process.

(3) 督导和协调客服中心的各项工作，监督所有话务员的仪容仪表和工作表现符合酒店规定。

To supervise and coordinate work in the Call Center, supervise appearance, manners and performance of all telephone operators that should conform to hotel rules.

(4) 确保所有话务员在铃响三声内接起电话，并顺利、正确、迅速地转接电话。

To make certain that all telephone operators pick up the phone call within three rings and transfer calls smoothly, correctly and quickly.

(5) 合理安排下属员工的班次，负责对下属的岗位技能培训、组织落实，并定期进行绩效评估。

To reasonably arrange shifts of subordinate staffers, be responsible for training of post skills on subordinates and its implementation, and carry out performance evaluation at regular intervals.

(6) 参加前厅部早会，及时将酒店重大信息传达给所有话务员。

To participate in morning meetings of the Front Office Department and timely deliver important information of the hotel to all telephone operators.

(7) 与前厅部其他部分及相关部门保持良好的合作关系，确保信息沟通渠道的畅通。

To maintain fine cooperative partnership with other departments in the Front Office Department and relevant departments and ensure an unimpeded information communication channel.

(8) 和电信局建立良好的合作关系，确保客人和外界的通信联系。

To establish good partnership with Telecommunications Bureau and ensure communication and contact of guests with the outside world.

(9) 确保所有话务员精通酒店传呼系统及闭路电视播放系统。

To ensure that all telephone operators excel in hotel paging system and closed circuit television broadcast system.

(10) 确保将客人账单准确无误地输入电脑，为客人提供商务服务的准确性。

To ensure that bills of guests be correctly input to the computer and accurate business services be provided to guests.

(11) 确保叫醒服务的及时和系统的正常运行。

To ensure timeliness of morning call and normal operation of the system.

(12) 制定酒店的分机表，包括客房、办公室等分机号，并定期更新。

To prepare extension set form of the hotel including device number of guest rooms, office and so on with regular updates.

(13) 帮助客人解决疑难和紧急的问题，准确答复有关世界时间、天气状况等的问询。

To help guests solve difficulties and urgent matters and accurately answer questions concerning zebra time and weather condition, etc.

(14) 服从由前厅部经理批准的工作日程安排，并监督检查话务员的出勤情况。

To comply with work schedule approved by Front Hall Department Manager and supervise attendance condition of telephone operators.

(15) 完成上级交办的其他任务。

To complete other tasks assigned by superiors.

(八) 客服中心话务员工作职责 (Work Responsibilities of Call Center Telephone Operators)

直接上级：客服中心主管

Immediate Superior: Call Center Supervisor

岗位职责：熟练掌握电话交换机的使用，准确、及时处理各种电话转接；准确使用酒店内线传呼系统和闭路电视播放系统。

Work Responsibilities: To have a good command of use of phone switchboard, accurately and timely handle with call transfers and correctly use interior wiring call system and closed circuit television broadcasting system.

工作内容 (Work Contents)：

(1) 保持仪容仪表、工作程序符合酒店规章制度和部门要求。

To maintain that appearances, manners and work procedures conform to hotel regulations and department requirements.

(2) 负责接听所有的外线电话及酒店的内线电话，正确操作交换机，准确运用礼貌用语，为客人提供准确、热情、周到的话务服务。

To be responsible for picking up all exterior wiring phone and interior wiring calls, correctly operate switchboard, accurately apply polite words and provide accurate, warm and thoughtful call services to guests.

(3) 遵循电话保密原则，正确、及时、顺利地转接电话，提供热情友善的服务。

To correctly, timely and smoothly switch calls in accordance with phone confidentiality principle and provide warm and friendly services.

(4) 为客人提供留言服务，确保客人留言服务的准确、及时，并在电话上有所显示。

To provide message-leaving services to guests, ensure accuracy and timeliness of message-leaving services and display it on phone.

(5) 受理客人的叫醒服务，并填写清楚叫醒服务表格。

To take in morning services for guests and fill in forms of morning services clearly.

（6）熟知酒店的消防程序和安全知识，以及酒店内部传呼系统的使用。

To excel in fire control procedure and safety knowledge of the hotel and use of interior call system.

（7）准确回答客人关于天气、时间、酒店设施等方面的问询。

To accurately answer inquiries on weather，timing，hotel facilities and so on from guests.

（8）每天按照闭路电视节目单次序播放内线碟片。

To play interior wiring disc following the sequence of closed circuit television program.

（9）遵守酒店工作要求，服从上级合理的班次安排和变动。

To comply with reasonable shift change and arrangement by superior by observing work requirements of the hotel.

（10）当电话机房机器设备出现故障时，立即向客服中心主管或当值领班汇报，保持和维护酒店的形象。

To timely report Call Center Manager or supervisor on duty when malfunction of machinery equipment in telephone exchange occurs for maintaining and keeping the hotel image.

（11）做好交接班工作，仔细阅读交班记录本内容，确保妥善解决需要跟进的事宜。

To accomplish work related with shift change，carefully review contents in record letter of duty change and ensure proper addressing of matters needing follow-up.

（12）完成上级交办的其他任务。

To complete other tasks assigned by the superior.

（九）前台主管工作职责（Work Responsibilities of Reception Supervisor）

直接上级：前厅部经理

Immediate Superior：Front Office Department Manager

直接下级：前台领班

Immediate Subordinate：Reception Desk Foreman

岗位职责：负责办理客人进离店手续、回复问询、接受预订等日常工作，督导前台员工的对客服务态度及工作效率，维护酒店带给客人的良好印象。

Post Responsibilities：Be responsible for daily work including check in and check out procedures of guests，response to inquiry and reception of reservation，supervise reception staffers’ attitudes to guests and their work efficiency and maintain good image brought about by the hotel to guests.

工作内容（Work Contents）：

（1）协助前厅部经理，制定前台的规章制度、服务工作程序，健全岗位职责。

To assist Front Office Department Manager to prepare regulatory framework and service work procedures for reception desk，and perfect post Responsibilities.

（2）主持每天前台交接班会议，检查交班记录，并确保当班员工熟知酒店新的规定、指示。

To preside over meetings for shift change in the reception desk，check duty shift records and ensure that staffers on duty excel in new rules and instructions of the hotel.

（3）监督前台员工的仪容仪表和服务态度符合酒店规章制度和部门工作要求。

To monitor that appearance，manner and service attitudes of reception desk staffers conform to hotel regulatory framework and work requirements of the department.

（4）每天检查所有预抵客人预订，根据房间状态合理分配房间，并根据客人的特殊要求做好必要的准备工作。

To check reservation of expected arrivals on the daily basis, reasonably allocate rooms according to room status, and ensure necessary preparation in accordance with particular requirements acquired by guests.

(5) 帮助和监督员工为客人办理快速登记入住和结账离店手续，检查登记单的填写及电脑的输入是否准确。

To assist and monitor staffers to transact procedures concerning rapid check-in and check-out for guests and to check accuracy of fill-in of registration bills and input to computers.

(6) 按照财务政策和程序检查当班期间前台账务情况，确保当班内的收入准确、完整，员工有无长短款情况。

To check accounting conditions in the reception during the day on duty in accordance with financial policies and procedures and ensure accuracy and completeness of incomes and whether staffers have coverage and shortage or not.

(7) 确保前台电脑设备完好，常用物品的及时补充，负责前台区域的干净、整洁。

To ensure that reception desk computers be in good condition, common articles be timely supplemented and reception desk be clean and tidy.

(8) 合理安排员工班次，制订前台员工的培训计划组织落实，并根据员工的表现，定期进行绩效评估，及时报告前厅部经理。

To reasonably arrange shift of staffers, prepare training plan on reception staffers and organize its implementation, regularly conduct performance evaluation in accordance with performance of employees and timely report it to Front Office Department Manager.

(9) 与前厅部各部门保持良好的团队精神，同时，协调部门间的关系以最大限度提高工作效率。

To maintain a positive teamwork spirit with each department of the Front Office Department and coordinate interdepartmental relations to improve work efficiency to the maximum degree.

(10) 对于房间钥匙发放做好严格记录和控制。

To keep strict record and control on issuing of room keys.

(11) 了解当日宴会、会议及餐饮的推广项目。

To know promotion projects on feast, meeting and catering of the day.

(12) 准确及时完成部门要求的各种报表。

To accurately and timely complete all statements required by the department.

(13) 掌握当天房间状况，最大限度地出租房间。

To master room status of the day to rent out rooms to the maximum degree.

(14) 参加前厅部早会，及时将更新信息传达给所有前台员工。

To take part in morning meeting of the Front Office Department and timely deliver updated information to all staffers at the reception desks.

(15) 完成上级交办的其他任务。

To finish other tasks assigned by superior.

(十) 前台接待员工作职责 (Work Responsibilities of Receptionists)

直接上级：前台主管

Immediate Superior: Reception Supervisor

岗位职责：按酒店政策及部门工作要求为客人办理登记及离店手续，并将所有信息输入电脑，为客人解答疑问、提供正确信息，保证为客人提供优质高效的服务。

Post Responsibilities: To transact registration and check-out procedure following hotel policy and work requirements of department, input all information to the computer, answer guests' questions, provide accurate information and ensure quality and efficient services be provided to guests.

工作内容（Work Contents）：

（1）检查所有预抵客人预订情况，根据房间状态，为预抵客人合理分配房间。

To check reservation of all expected arrivals and reasonably allocate guests for expected guests in accordance with room status.

（2）做好入住接待、为客人办理登记入住手续，并输入电脑，确认登记填写所有信息的准确完整。

To accomplish check-in reception, transact registration and check-in procedures for guests and input them to the computer, and affirm accuracy and completeness of information related with registration.

（3）回顾当天到达客人种类、预订单，熟悉客人姓名、特殊要求及注释，做好相应准备。

To review varieties and advance order of expected guests of the day and get familiar with guests' names, particular requirements and comments with corresponding preparation.

（4）阅读前台接待员交接班记录本，熟知所有新的记录，完成需要做完的工作，同时，下班前将重要的需跟进的事件记在交班记录本上，并积极跟进落实。

To read record book of shift change of receptionists, get familiar with all new records, complete work needing to be done and in the meantime, and write all important matters needing follow-up in the record book of shift change with active implementation and follow-up.

（5）保证为客人提供热情、周到的服务，电话铃响三声内接起客人来电，帮助处理客人的问题，满足客人合理的要求。

To ensure warm and thoughtful services be provided to guests, guests' calls be picked up within three rings, problems related with guests be assisted for disposal and reasonable requirements from guests be satisfied.

（6）了解当日到达贵宾和团队的详细资料，提前做好准备工作，同时，通知前台或值班经理 VIP 入住情况，请他们陪同客人办理入住。

To know detailed information of arriving distinguished guests and teams of the day and get ready in advance; meanwhile, to notify reception desk or duty manager on VIP check-in status and invite them to escorts guests to transact check-in procedures.

（7）确保客人消费账目及时输入房账，为财务部提供所有必需的单据。

To make certain that consumption accounts of guests be timely incorporated to room charge and all necessary receipts be provided to Financial Department.

（8）为客人提供外币兑换、保险箱、留言等服务。

To provide such services as foreign currency exchange, safe box, message-leaving and so on to guests.

（9）处理客人投诉，对于解决不了的问题，要及时汇报，交管理人员处理。

To handle with guests' complaints and timely report issues that cannot be addressed to administrative staff.

（10）快速准确地为客人办理离店手续，确保所有账目及单据的清晰完整。

To speedily and accurately transact check-out procedures for guests and ensure distinct and completed accounts and receipts.

（11）准确填写公安局发放的登记簿并及时送交，及时将客人相关信息输入公安局电脑，配合公安做好协查通缉工作。

To correctly fill in and timely deliver directory issued by the Public Security Bureau, input guests-related information to computers of Public Security Bureau, and assist the Public Security Bureau on work concerning wanted poster.

(12) 积极推销酒店服务设施及正在实施的各项宴会及餐饮促销活动。

To actively promote hotel service facilities and all undergoing feasts and coupon activities on dining.

(13) 保持前台区域卫生。

To maintain sanitation in reception regions.

(14) 完成上级交办的其他任务。

To finish other tasks assigned by the superior.

(十一) 行政楼层主管工作职责 (Work Responsibilities of Administration Floor Supervisor)

直接上级：前厅部经理

Immediate Superior: Front Office Department Manager

直接下级：行政楼层接待员

Immediate Subordinate: Receptionists of the Administration Floor

岗位职责：全面负责行政楼层的运营工作，包括行政楼层客人的抵离店手续的办理，用餐及下午茶的接待等，制定有效的行政楼层培训计划，对行政楼层的日常工作进行积极监督和检查，协调行政楼层与前厅其他部分的工作。

Post Responsibilities: To take full charge of operation work of the administration floor covering transaction of check-in and check-out procedures of guests for the administration floor, reception of dining and afternoon tea and so on, prepare effective training plan for the administration floor, carry out active monitoring and inspection on routine work of the administration floor, and coordinate other work of the administration floor and Front Office.

工作内容 (Work Contents):

(1) 协助前厅部经理，制定行政楼层的规章制度、服务工作程序，健全岗位职责。

To help Front Office Department Manager prepare regulatory framework and service work procedures of the administration floor and perfect post responsibilities.

(2) 帮助和监督员工准确迅速地为客人办理登记入住手续，确保登记单及电脑输入的准确性。

To help and monitor staffers to speedily transact check-in procedures for guests and ensure accuracy of registration letter and computer input.

(3) 确保贵宾到达前的各项准备工作并亲自为其办理入住手续。

To ensure all preparatory work before arrival of distinguished guests and transact their check-in procedures in person.

(4) 检查预抵客人房间，确保欢迎果篮及相关物品在客人入住前摆放到位。

To check rooms for expected guests and make sure welcoming fruit basket and relevant articles be placed in the proper place before their check-in.

(5) 认真、耐心地听取客人的意见，热情友善回答客人问询，帮助客人解决问题，同时，亲自接受客人投诉，及时有效地处理问题。

To carefully and patiently listen to guests' opinions, passionately and friendly answer their inquiries, help guests address issues and take in and effectively dispose with complaints from guests.

(6) 为行政楼层的客人建立客史档案并不断加以更新和补充。

To set up records of guests for the administration floors and continuously update and supplement them.

(7) 对于房间钥匙发放做好严格记录和控制。

To strictly record and control the issuing of room keys.

（8）检查高额欠款客人信贷状况和跟进预离店房间，每月为长住客结清一次账单。

To check credit status of guests with premium debt, follow up rooms to be checked out, settle an account statement for long-time residents on the monthly basis.

（9）确保行政楼层电脑设备完好，常用物品的及时补充，行政酒廊的干净、整洁。

To make sure that computers on the administration floor be in good condition, commonly-used articles be timely supplemented and administration lounges be clean and tidy.

（10）合理安排员工班次，制订行政楼层员工的培训计划并组织落实，根据员工的表现，对下属做出绩效评估并及时报告前厅部经理。

To reasonably arrange shifts of staffers, prepare training plan of staffers on the administration floor and organize its implementation, follow employees' performance to work out performance evaluations on subordinates and timely report them to Front Office Department Manager.

（11）参加前厅部早会，及时将更新信息传达给所有行政楼层接待员。

To participate in morning meeting of the Front Office Department and timely deliver the updated information to all receptionists of the administration floor.

（12）根据每天行政楼层交接班会议，检查交班记录。

To check records on shift change in accordance with daily shift change meeting of the administration floor.

（13）与前厅部各部门保持良好的团队精神，同时，协调部门间的关系以最大限度提高工作效率。

To maintain good teamwork spirits with all departments under the Front Office Department and coordinate relations between departments to improve work efficiency to the maximum degree.

（14）对所管辖的行政楼层的运营负责，监督行政楼层员工的仪容仪表及工作表现。

To be responsible for operation of all presidial administration floors and monitor appearance, manners and work performance of employees on the administration floor.

（15）完成上级交办的其他任务。

To finish other tasks assigned by the superior.

（十二）行政楼层接待员工作职责（Work Responsibilities of Administration Floor Receptionists）

直接上级：行政楼层主管

Immediate Superior: Administration Floor Supervisor

岗位职责：按工作要求迎接客人及为客人办理登记入住及离店结账手续，为入住行政楼层的客人提供优质服务。

Post Responsibilities: To receive guests in accordance with work requirements, transact check-in and check-out procedures for guests, and provide quality services to guests checking in the administration floor.

工作内容（Work Contents）：

（1）查看所有预订情况，掌握房间状态，及时为预抵客人分配房间，确保欢迎果篮及相关物品在客人入住前摆放到位。

To check all reservations, master room status, timely allocate rooms to expected guests and ensure that welcoming baskets and relevant articles be placed in proper places.

（2）要负责准备客人登记入住时所需要的物品（例如：登记单、欢迎卡、钥匙等），为重要客人抵达前事先做登记，确保准确迅速地为客人办理登记入住及结账离店手续。

To be responsible for preparing all articles needed for check-in of guests (such as registration letter, welcoming cards and keys, etc.), make registrations for VIP guests before their arrivals, and make sure to accurately and speedily transact check-in and check-out procedures.

(3) 负责向行政楼层主管汇报所有即将抵达的重要客人的情况，以便进行特殊的安排。

To be responsible for reporting conditions related with expected VIP guests to administration floor supervisor for particular arrangement.

(4) 认真、耐心地听取客人的意见，热情友善回答客人问询，帮助客人解决问题。

To carefully and patiently listen to guests' advice, warmly and friendly answer inquiries from guests and help guests address problems.

(5) 负责为行政楼层的客人建立客史档案并不断加以更新和补充。

To be responsible for setting up records of guests with continuous updates and supplementation for guests on the administration floor.

(6) 负责接受行政楼层会议室的预订，并提供茶水服务。

To be responsible for taking in reservation for conference room on the administration floor and providing tea services.

(7) 确保行政楼层电脑设备完好，行政接待台区域的整洁。

To make sure that computers on the administration floor be in good condition and administration reception areas be clean and tidy.

(8) 热情问候前来行政酒廊的客人并提供茶水服务。

To warmly send regards to guests to the administration lounge and provide tea services.

(9) 认真完成其他班次须跟进的任务并详细记录，同时，将当班期间未完成的任务仔细记在交班日志上，认真做好交接班工作。

To carefully complete tasks needing follow-up by other shifts with detailed records and carefully record unfinished tasks during the day on duty in daily record of shift change.

(10) 了解酒店消防和安全程序，并要负责行政楼的安全。

To learn fire prevention and safety procedures of the hotel and be responsible for safety of the administration floor.

(11) 完成上级交办的其他任务。

To finish other tasks assigned by the superior.

(十三) 礼宾部主管工作职责 (Work Responsibilities of Concierge Supervisor)

直接上级：前厅部经理

Immediate Superior: Front Office Department Manager

直接下级：行李员/门童

Immediate Subordinate: Baggage Clerk/Doorman

岗位职责：负责礼宾部的正常运作，确保为客人提供高效优质的服务，包括寄存行李、接送客人、邮寄包裹、递送客人留言和邮件、确认机票和接机服务、预订酒店车辆服务等。

Post Responsibilities: To be responsible for normal operation of Concierge, ensure efficient and quality services be provided to guests including left luggage, pick-up of guests, delivery of messages and mails from guests, confirmation of air ticket and airport pickup services and reservation of hotel vehicle services, etc.

工作内容 (Work Contents):

(1) 协助前厅部经理，制定礼宾部的规章制度、服务工作程序，健全岗位职责。

To assist Front Office Department Manager to prepare regulatory framework, service work procedure of

Concierge and perfect post Responsibilities.

（2）监督检查所属员工执行酒店工作程序、标准及规章制度情况，包括仪容仪表、行为规范等，合理安排班次，明确分工。

To Supervise and check that affiliated staffers implement hotel work procedures, standards and regulatory framework status including appearance, manners, behavioral rules and so on, reasonably arrange shifts and determine labor division.

（3）检查交接班记录、行李存放记录，确保所有记录的完整和准确，同时，在工作日志上记录下所有特殊事件，并每日递交给前厅部经理，以便采取必要措施。

To check records of shift change and luggage storage, guarantee completeness and accuracy of all records and write all special matters in daily work record to be delivered to Front Office Department Manager on the daily basis for adopting necessary measures.

（4）负责检查分发给客人和办公室的报纸及其他资料，保证及时、准确地传送。

To be responsible for checking newspaper and other materials issued to guests and offices and ensure timely and accurate delivery.

（5）保持礼宾部值班台区域和行李房的干净整齐，以及所有行李车的光亮整洁。

To maintain cleanliness and orderliness of duty desk area and baggage room of the Concierge and keep all luggage barrows bright and tidy.

（6）监督协调礼宾部各环节的正常运转，确保客人传真和信件的及时处理。

To supervise and coordinate normal operation of all links in the Concierge and guarantee timely handling of fax and mails by guests.

（7）礼貌热情回答客人的问询，对所有入店和离店客人给予及时、有效的安排和照顾，及时帮助客人解决困难。

To politely and warmly answer inquiries from guests, give timely and effective arrangement and care to all check-in and check-out guests and timely help guests address troubles.

（8）负责向客人推销酒店豪华轿车服务并接受预订，帮助客人预订机场班车接送服务。

To be responsible for promoting hotel luxury car services to guests, taking in reservation and helping guests reserve airport bus pickup and delivery services.

（9）制定礼宾部培训计划并组织落实，不断提高员工素质和工作技能，并根据员工的表现，定期进行绩效评估，及时报告前厅部经理。

To prepare training plan of Concierge and organize its implementation, gradually improve staff's quality and work skills, and conduct performance evaluation at regular intervals in accordance with staff's performance to be timely reported to Front Office Department Manager.

（10）经常与客房部、前台经理、预订处主管及前台接待员协调联系，以便了解团队、散客和贵宾的入店和离店情况，确保合作渠道的畅通。

To coordinate and contact with Room Department, Reception Manager, Reservation Office Supervisor and receptionists on a often-time basis for knowing check-in and check-out status of teams, individual travelers and VIP guests and ensuring an unimpeded cooperation channel.

（11）保证礼宾部工作台随时有员工在岗，特别是在工作繁忙的时候，安排有足够的员工上班，根据房间状态及预抵客人情况，合理分配人手。

To make sure that Concierge Workbench have staffers on duty around the clock, particularly during busy hours, arrange sufficient staffers to go on duty and reasonably allocate human resources in accordance with room status and conditions of expected guests.

（12）参与前厅部会议，将信息及时传达给员工。

To take part in Front Office Department meetings and timely deliver information to staffers.

（13）完成上级交办的其他任务。

To finish other tasks assigned by superior.

（十四）行李员/门童工作职责（Work Responsibilities of Baggage Clerk / Doorman）

直接上级：礼宾部主管

Immediate Superior: Concierge Supervisor

岗位职责：帮助进店、离店客人搬运行李，送留言、报纸、邮件和包裹给住店客人，存取行李，热情迎接到店、离店客人，推销酒店设施，确保酒店大厅交通通畅。

Post Responsibilities: To help check-in and check-out guests carry luggage, deliver message, newspaper, mail and package to check-in guests, store and pick up luggage, warmly receive check-in and check-out guests, promote hotel facilities and ensure unobstructed traffic of the hotel lobby.

工作内容（Work Contents）：

（1）提前到达所在岗位向礼宾部主管报到，并由其检查仪表仪容等方面的情况。

To arrive at the assigned posts in advance and report for duty to Concierge Manager who would check such conditions as appearance, manners and so on.

（2）阅读工作记录，熟知酒店所有新的规定，提示需要下一班继续完成的工作。

To review work records, know well all new rules of the hotel and hint work needing continuation by follow-up shift.

（3）以友好、热情、整洁的姿态迎接酒店的每一位客人，为客人提供优质、快捷的服务，给客人树立良好的第一印象。

To receive all guests in the hotel in a friendly, warm and clean posture, provide quality and speedy services to guests and establish a good first impression on guests.

（4）负责准确迅速地运送进店、离店的团队及散客的行李，负责帮助换房客人运送行李及完成客人的其他合理要求，同时负责为客人寄存行李，并确保记录细节的准确无误。

To be responsible for correctly and speedily deliver luggage of check-in and check-out teams and individual travelers, helping room-change guests deliver luggage and complete other reasonable requirements by guests, storing luggage for guests and ensuring that all records be free from errors.

（5）确保及时派送客人及酒店其他部门的报纸、留言、传真、快递、包裹等，负责为客人邮寄信件、包裹或其他物品。

To guarantee that newspapers, messages, faxes, mails, packages and so on be timely delivered to guests and other departments of the hotel and be responsible for mailing letters, packages or other articles for guests.

（6）了解酒店宴会、会议及餐饮推广项目，还有酒店服务设施及客房设施，准确回答客人的问询。

To know hotel feast, meeting, dining-related promotion projects, hotel service facilities and guest room facilities, and correctly respond to guests' inquiries.

（7）负责机场接送服务，负责为客人提供订车服务，推销酒店豪华轿车租用服务。

To be responsible for airport pickup and delivery services, providing reception car services to guests and promoting luxury car lease services.

（8）认真做好交接班工作，跟进其他班次未完成事宜。

To carefully accomplish work related with shift change and follow up matters left undone by other shifts.

（9）认真做好雨伞租用服务，完善登记手续。

To carefully accomplish umbrella lease services and perfect registration procedures.

（10）认真做好岗位的清洁及行李车辆的清洁。

To carefully accomplish cleanliness of posts and luggage vehicles.

（11）认真完成上级交办的其他任务。

To carefully finish other tasks assigned by the superior.

（十五）车队主管工作职责（Work Responsibilities of Motorcade Supervisor）

直接上级：前厅部经理

Immediate Superior：Front Office Department Manager

直接下级：司机

Immediate Subordinate：Drivers

岗位职责：全面负责对司机的管理和车辆的调配与保养，并与交通管理部门和汽车维修厂家保持良好的合作，确保酒店的交通安全工作；协助前厅部经理进行人员、车辆的调配，监督司机的仪容仪表和工作表现。

Post Responsibilities：To take full charge of management of drivers and allocation and maintenance of vehicles，maintain good cooperation with traffic management departments and auto repair plant，guarantee traffic safety work of the hotel，assist Front Office Department Manager to conduct allocation of human resources and vehicles，and monitor appearance，manners and work performance of drivers.

工作内容（Work Contents）：

（1）协助前厅部经理，制定预订处的规章制度、服务工作程序，健全岗位职责。

To assist Front Office Department Manager to prepare regulatory framework and service work procedures for the Reservation Office，and perfect post Responsibilities.

（2）根据用车预订情况，负责提供每日班车服务、酒店客人交通服务和酒店内部用车服务，合理分配人员和车辆，确保出车任务的完成。

To be responsible for providing daily shuttle bus services，transport services to hotel guests and use of vehicles inside the hotel，reasonably allocate staffers and vehicles and guarantee completion of car-use tasks.

（3）负责组织司机定期进行车辆保养，确保酒店所有车辆保持良好的车况。

To be responsible for organizing drivers to carry out auto maintenance at regular intervals and guarantee that all vehicles be in good condition.

（4）确保酒店所有车辆的行驶证件和驾驶员执照的有效。

To ensure that driving certificates and drivers' license for all vehicles be valid.

（5）负责监督油料耗费记录、控制成本，提供最新的车辆运行记录、油耗记录等各种业务报表。

To be responsible for monitoring oil consumption records，controlling costs，and providing latest vehicle operating records，oil consumption record and all kinds of business forms.

（6）协助车队主管完成各种业务报表，统计每月车队收入，及时做出报表上报前厅部经理。

To assist Motorcade Supervisor to finish all business forms，calculate revenues of the motorcade on the monthly basis，and timely work out the statement to be submitted to Front Office Department Managers.

（7）根据车辆的预订情况为司机排班，合理调配人手，并认真做好出车记录。

To arrange shifts to drivers according to reservation status of vehicles，reasonably deploy employees and make careful records on auto use.

(8) 负责维修费、油费、养路费等车辆费用的申请。

To be responsible for application of such vehicle charges as maintenance cost, oil cost and road toll, etc.

(9) 制定车队培训计划，为酒店司机提供礼貌和驾驶技术的培训。

To prepare training plan for motorcade and provide training to hotel drivers on courtesy and driving skills.

(10) 确保司机严格遵守酒店规章制度和交通法规，在工作中有良好的仪容仪表和工作表现。

To make sure that drivers strictly observe hotel regulatory framework and traffic rules and maintain good appearance, looks and work performance during work.

(11) 认真完成上级交办的其他任务。

To finish other tasks assigned by the superior.

(十六) 司机工作职责 (Work Responsibilities of Drivers)

直接上级：车队主管

Immediate Superior: Motorcade Supervisor

岗位职责：驾驶酒店车辆，为客人及酒店各部门提供安全运输服务。

Post Responsibilities: To drive hotel vehicles and provide safe traveling services to guests and all hotel departments.

工作内容 (Work Contents):

(1) 负责检查班前车辆状况，做好出车准备。

To be responsible for checking auto status before shifts and get ready for driving.

(2) 严格执行交通法规，严禁酒后驾车，确保安全行车，完成驾驶任务。

To strictly observe traffic rules, prohibit drunk driving, ensure safe driving and complete driving tasks.

(3) 认真做好出车记录。

To carefully complete car-use records.

(4) 保持车辆干净、整洁。

To maintain cleanliness and tidiness of vehicles.

(5) 定期对车辆进行维护和保养，及时发现并解决问题，保持良好的车况。

To carry out repair and maintenance on cars at regular intervals, timely discover and address problems and maintain good vehicle conditions.

(6) 当班期间，在仪容仪表及个人行为上保持酒店标准，维持酒店职业形象。

To conform to hotel standards in terms of appearance, manners and conducts during the period on duty to maintain the professional image of the hotel.

(7) 认真做好交接班工作，跟进其他班次未完成事宜。

To carefully accomplish work related with shift change and follow up matters left undone by other shifts.

(8) 完成上级交办的其他任务。

To complete other tasks assigned by the superior.

模块二 客房预订
Module Ⅱ Room Reservation

【情境导入】【Scenario Introduction】

酒店客满

No Vacancy

地点：三亚南中国大酒店前台

Venue: Reception Desk of Sanya South China Hotel

正值旅游旺季，由于某旅游团临时增加用房数量，三亚南中国大酒店的客房出租率已经达到100%。晚上，两位来自北京的客人到达酒店前台，接待员小张微笑向客人问好。客人说："我们预订了一个标准间。"小张查看了预订登记表，对客人说："您的预订记录确实在这儿，但实在抱歉，酒店今天已经满房，请两位谅解。"客人有些生气，接待员接着解释："我们已经与本市的三亚柏瑞精品海景酒店联系过了，他们还有几间空房，我已经为两位订了房。虽然那里的设施设备比我们酒店好，房价也比我们高，但你们只需按预订的价格付款，超出的房价由我们支付。如果你们不介意的话，我这就派车送两位过去暂住一个晚上。等明天我再派车接你们回来，一定为你们安排满意的房间。"

It's a peak tourist season. A tourist group temporarily decided to occupy more rooms, making the room occupancy rate reaching 100% of Sanya South China Hotel. In the evening, two guests from Beijing arrived at the reception desk of the Hotel. Zhang, the receptionist, greeted the guests with a smile. The guests said: "We've booked a standard room here." Zhang checked the Reservation Form and said to the guests: "We do have your reservation record here. But terribly sorry, the hotel is fully occupied now. We beg your pardon." The guests were a little bit angry. The receptionist continued: "But we have contacted Barry Boutique Hotel Sanya. They still have some vacant rooms. I've booked one for you. Though they have better facilities than us and the room rate is higher, you only need to pay the reserve price and we'll assume the excess price. If you don't mind, I'll arrange a car to take you there right away for one night. And I'll assign a car to take you back tomorrow. I promise to arrange a satisfying room for you."

客人听到付四星级酒店的房费可以住知名的五星级酒店，何乐而不为，于是欣然同意。

On hearing that they can reside a renowned five-star level hotel with a four-star level hotel room rate, the guests agreed with delight.

【情境分析】【Scenario Analysis】

上述案例说明，酒店接受客人的预订，就应该为客人保留房间。如果确实有特殊情况导致预订客人到店后无房，酒店必须找到妥善办法，安排好客人的住宿，令客人满意。

As shown in the abovementioned case, the hotel should reserve the room for the guest as long as it accepts the reservation from the guest. In case that no room is available after the guest arrives under special circumstances, the hotel must find appropriate methods and arrange the accommodation for the guest until the guest is satisfied.

【学习目标】【Learning Goals】

［知识目标］［Knowledge Objectives］

1. 掌握酒店预订意义、预订方式和种类及预订程序。

To master the significance, methods, types, and procedures of hotel reservation.

2. 掌握控制预订各类情况，熟练掌握酒店超额预订相关知识及预订失约行为处理语言技巧。

To master and control various circumstances in room reservation; be acquainted with related knowledge on overbooking and language skills disposing failure to reserve the room for the guest.

［能力目标］［Capacity Objectives］

1. 熟练掌握预订渠道及预订种类，能够按照酒店的标准来处理各类预订。

To fluently master the reservation channels and types and be able to dispose reservations of various types according to the standards of the hotel.

2. 能够控制各类预订情况，熟练处理酒店超额预订情况。

To be able to control various types of reservations; to be fluently dispose overbooking conditions of the hotel.

3. 能够熟练处理酒店预订失约行为。

To be able to fluently dispose the failure of the hotel to reserve the room for the guest.

【重点和难点】【Key Points and Difficulties】

1. 熟练操作不同情况下的酒店预订。

To be acquainted to hotel reservation under different circumstances.

2. 掌握酒店预订失约行为的处理办法和技能。

To master the disposal methods and techniques in failure of the hotel to reserve the room for the guest.

任务一　认识预订的方式和种类

Task Ⅰ　Understanding Methods and Types of Reservation

【情境导入】【Scenario Introduction】

预订缩水

Reservation Deduction

某日，一位英国客人詹姆斯先生委托本地旅行社订房入住三亚国光豪生度假酒店，要一个标准间预订两天。但在总台办理入住手续时，接待员告诉詹姆斯先生，他的预订只有1天。现在又正值旅游旺季，第二天的标准间难以安排。詹姆斯先生听后很生气，强调自己让本地接待单位在为他订房时是明确要住两天的，订房差错的责任肯定在酒店。由此，接待员与客人在总台形成了僵持的局面。

One day, a British guest Mr. James entrusted a local travel agency to reserve one standard room for two days in Howard Johnson Resort Sanya Bay. However, when Mr. James checked in at the reception desk, the receptionist told Mr. James that his reservation was only for one day. It's the peak tourist season, and standard room for the next day was hard to be arranged. Mr. James was quite angry. He stressed that he had clarified with the local reception unit that he would stay for two days, and it was definitely the hotel that made something wrong. Then, the receptionist and the guest were stalemated on the Reception Desk.

接待员该如何妥善处理此事？分析造成詹姆斯先生生气的原因。

So, how should the receptionist properly deal with this? Let's first analyze why Mr. James is angry.

【情境分析】【Scenario Analysis】

首先，稳定客人情绪，听取客人意见，耐心做出解释，提醒客人追究责任并不是主要问题，尽快解决入住问题才是当务之急。标准房紧张，建议次日换住一间套房，并给予适当优惠。若查明责任在酒店一方，更应安排客人升级入住或给予套房优惠折扣。若责任在当地代订公司，且与酒店是关系良好的协议单位，接待员无法调整同类房的情况下，应请示上级，同意给予客房升级，从而保证酒店与协议公司之间长期的友好协作关系可以顺利发展。有时代订公司为了今后的长期合作，也会主动承担责任。

First, calm down the guest and listen to him. Explain patiently to the guest and remind him that to call to account is not the matter, and to solve the problem as soon as possible is beyond everything.As the standard rooms are in short supply, it is recommended to change the room to a suite with appropriate discount granted. If it's proved that the hotel should assume the liability, the guest should be offered upgraded room or given preferential discount. If it is the local agency that should be assume the responsible and the local agency is a contracted unit having favorable relationship with the hotel, where the receptionist is unable to adjust another room of the same type, he/she should report to the higher management to consent room upgrading. This aims to guarantee the favorable development of the long-term friendship and partnership between the hotel and the contracted unit. Sometimes, the agency would initiatively assume the responsibility for long-term cooperation in future.

客房预订是前厅部的一项重要业务内容，它是整个对客服务中的重要一环。客房预订是指客人或代理机构为住店客人在抵店前的一种预期出租或使用客房的协议。客人可通过电话等各种方式与酒店联系预约客房，酒店可根据客房的可供状况，决定是否满足客人的订房要求。预订一经酒店的确认，酒店与客人之间便达成了一种具有法律效力的预期使用客房的协议，酒店有义务以预订确认的价格为客人提供所需客房。

Room reservation is an important business of the Front Office Department as well as an important link among services to the guests. Room reservation refers to an agreement to guarantee anticipated renting or occupation of guest room before the guest arrives at the hotel by the guest in person or through an agency. The guest may contact the hotel to reserve the room by various means for example telephone. The hotel may decide whether or not to satisfy the room reservation request of the guest based on the availability of the guest rooms. Upon the confirmation of the hotel, reservation between the hotel and the guest will become an agreement with legal force for the anticipated room occupation. The hotel is obliged to provide the room (s) required by the guest at the price confirmed in the reservation.

一、客房预订的意义（Significance of Room Reservation）

酒店前厅部开展客房预订业务，对宾客和对酒店都有着重要的意义。对于客人而言，通过客房预订可以有效地计划自己的行程，节约宝贵的时间，免遭酒店客满的风险；可以提出自己想要的房间的具体要求，让酒店做好接待的准备，使自己的旅行更舒适方便，特别是在旅游旺季，可以使客人提前避免客满无房的风险。对于酒店而言，预订可以帮助酒店更好地提供对客服务，良好的客房预订能够为酒店争取客源，有利于提高酒店客房出租率。同时，酒店可以根据预订情况预测今后一段时间内的客源情况，便于酒店对人力、物力、财力等做好计划和安排，特别是在酒店业务量比较大的时间段，避免出现由于人手紧张和物料准备不足而影响服务工作的正常运转，开展酒店预订，也是酒店保持、提升、扩大自己品牌知名度的重要手段。主要体现在以下几方面：

Room reservation service provided by the Front Office Department of the hotel bears important implication for both the guest and the hotel. As for the guests, they can effectively plan the travel by room reservation, save valuable time and avoid the risk of full occupancy of the hotel. They may also propose specific requirements on the rooms they desire and get the hotel prepared for reception so as to make the travel more comfortable and convenient. Especially in peak tourist seasons, room reservation may keep the guests away from the risk that no roomsare available. As for hotels, reservation may better assist the hotels in providing guest services. Satisfying room reservation may attract more guests and increase the occupancy rate of the hotel. Meanwhile, the hotel may predict the guest source conditions in a period forward, which may facilitate proper planning and arrangement on labor, material and property of the hotel. Especially when the business volume is relatively great, this may protect the normal service operation of the hotel from being affected by insufficient labor and material preparation. Room reservation is also an important method for the hotel to maintain, enhance and expand the brand popularity. The functions of room reservation are mainly reflected in the following aspects:

1. 延展客户的广度和深度，提高酒店服务质量（Extend the Width and Depth of the Guests, Improve the Service Quality of the Hotel）

开展对客预订业务，通过预订员对酒店及客房、房价、各项服务设施和服务项目的介绍，拓展了对客服务在时间、内容等方面的范围，形成了更完整的为客人提供全面服务的概念，从而提高了酒店的服务质量。

By the introduction of the hotel, guest rooms, room rates, various types of service facilities and items by the reservationist, room reservation may expand the scope of guest services on aspects of time, content, etc., establish more complete concept on providing more comprehensive guest services and further enhance the service quality of the hotel.

2. 良好的宣传途径，吸引更多的客源（Provide Favorable Publicity Channels, Attract More Guests）

酒店通过将客房预订信息发到网络、中介机构、报纸杂志等，扩大宣传范围，主动与更多的潜在客源进行信息交流，改变了原来被动等客人上门来入住的局面，有利于酒店提前占领客源市场，提高客房出租率。

The hotel publishes the room reservation information to the website, intermediaries, newspapers, magazines, etc. to expand the scope of publicity and positively make information exchange to more potential guests. This can shift the original scenario of waiting for the guests in a passive manner, assist in proactive efforts in guest competition and improve the occupancy rate of the hotel.

3. 更好地预测未来客源市场（Better Predict Future Guest Market）

通过客房预订业务的展开，酒店可以提前了解酒店在未来一段时间内客源的充沛情况，把握市场导向，为销售部门制定、调整营销策略提供依据；同时通过提前与客人的沟通，将获取的客人的需求变化的信息进行整理分析，可以为酒店未来经营决策提供科学依据。

By the deployment of room reservation business, the hotel may understand the client availability in a period in future, grasp the market trends and provide basis for the formulation and adjustment of the marketing strategies of the Sales Department in advance. Meanwhile, by proactive communication with the guests, the hotel may sort up and analyze the information related to variation of guest demands and provide scientific basis for future operation decision-making of the hotel.

4. 提前做好宾客抵店的准备工作（Get Prepared in Advance before the Arrival of the Guest）

通过客房预订业务的开展，各部门可以在宾客抵店前按其预订要求进行各项接待准备，在人力、物力等方面进行合理的安排，有利于提高酒店的管理水平和服务质量。

By deployment of room reservation business, various departments of the hotel may make reception preparation according to the reservation requirements and make reasonable arrangements on aspects such as labor and material, which will be favorable to enhance the managerial level and service quality of the hotel.

二、预订渠道和方式（Reservation Channel and Method）

（一）预订渠道（Reservation Channels）

酒店住客一般可以通过下列渠道预订客房：

Generally, hotel guests may make the reservation by the following channels:

1. 直接渠道——不经任何中间环节，直接向酒店订房

Direct Channel—Reserve a room from the hotel without any intermediate links

A.客人（或委托人）直接向酒店预订客房。

The guest (or the assignee) makes the reservation directly from the hotel.

B.旅游团体或会议组织者等直接向酒店预订客房。

The tour group, conference organizer, etc. makes the reservation directly from the hotel.

C.与酒店签订商务合同的公司向酒店预订客房。

The company signing business contract with the hotel makes the reservation directly from the hotel.

2. 间接渠道——通过中间环节向酒店订房

Indirect Channel—Reserve a room from the hotel with intermediate links

A. 通过旅行社等中间商订房。

Make room reservation by intermediary business such as travel agency.

B. 连锁酒店或合作酒店相互推荐客房。

Mutual room recommendation among chain hotels or cooperative hotels.

C. 国际订房网络组织订房。

Make room reservation under the organization of the international room reservation network.

D. 向航空公司或其他交通运输部门预订。

Make room reservation from airlines and other transportation departments.

E. 向专门的会议组织机构预订。

Make room reservation from professional conference organizations.

F. 由政府机关或企事业单位预订。

Make room reservation by government agencies, enterprises or public institutions.

（二）预订方式（Reservation Method）

客人预订酒店客房有电话预订、传真预订、互联网预订、面谈预订、团队预订等多种方式。每种预订方式都各有特点，客人可以根据自身的设备条件以及对客房需要的时间紧迫与否，选择自己喜欢的预订方式。对于酒店而言，预订渠道通常有散客自订房、旅行社订房、其他组织订房等多种形式；每个酒店应该充分把握自己目标市场客源通常采用的预订方式，积极地采取有效的措施和方法及时准确地受理客人的预订。

The guest may reserve a room by various means such as telephone, fax, Internet, on site and by group. Each reservation method has its own characteristics. The guests may select their preferred reservation methods according to the actual equipment conditions and the time and urgency on rooms. For the hotels, reservation channels often involves multiple methods such as independent reservation by individual guest, room reservation by travel agency and room reservation by other organizations; Each hotel should fully understand the common reservation methods of the guests in the targeted markets and take positive and effective measures and methods to accurately handle guest reservation.

1. 电话预订（Telephone Reservation）

订房人通过电话向酒店订房，这种方式应用最为广泛，特别是提前预订的时间较短时，这种方式最为有效。其优点是直接、迅速、清楚地传递双方信息，可当场回复客人的订房要求，是最常见的订房方式；缺点是容易出错。在电话预订的过程中，预订员应注意如下事项：A.要求口齿清晰，表达准确；B. 准确掌握订房资料；C. 及时给订房人明确答复。

The reserving person makes the reservation by telephone. This is the most widely used method and is most effective especially when time available is relatively short. Telephone reservation has the superiority to directly, quickly and clearly transmit information from both sides and the hotel may immediately reply the reservation request from the guest. It is the most common reservation method. However, it has the shortcoming that a mistake would easily occur. When making telephone reservation, the reserving personnel must pay attention to the following precautions: A. Be articulate with accurate expression; B. Accurately master room reservation information; C. Timely reply the reserving personnel.

2. 信函预订（Letter Reservation）

信函预订是宾客或其委托人在离预期抵店日期尚有较多时间的情况下采取的一种传统、古老而正式的预订方式。此方式较正规，如同一份合约，对宾客和酒店起到一定的约束作用。在受理此方式预订时，预订员应注意做到以下几点：

Letter reservation is a traditional, ancient but formal reservation method adopted by the guest or his/her assignee where the time is still sufficient to the anticipated date of arrival. The method is relatively formal and is regarded as an agreement that is binding upon the guest and the hotel to some extent. The reservationist should note the following instructions when handling reservation in such manner:

（1）及时复信。确保 24 小时内回函，越早让宾客收到回信，越能赢得宾客好感。

Timely reply. A reply should be guaranteed within 24 hours. The earlier the guest receives the reply, the better impression he/she will have towards the hotel.

（2）避免给宾客留下公函式信件的印象。

Try to avoid a official document type reply.

（3）复信的格式必须正确，注意中英文书信格式的差异。

The format of the written reply should be accurate, Pay attention to the difference between Chinese and English letters.

（4）复信的内容明确，简洁且有条理。

The reply should contain clear contents and in a precise and logical manner.

（5）复信的地址、日期要书写完整、准确。

The address and date of the reply should be complete and accurate.

（6）注意信纸、信封的质量，邮票的选择及复信者的亲笔签名。

Attach importance to the quality of the letter paper and envelope as well as the selection of stamp and the personal signature of the replier.

3. 面谈预订（Hotel Reservation）

面谈订房是指客人直接来到酒店，与订房员面对面地洽谈订房事宜。其优点是能使预订员沟通方便，通过观察客人的神态、表情等，洞察其心理因素，有机会详尽地了解客人的需求，并当面解答客人提出的问题。同时，便于预订员推销客房，必要时甚至可以安排客人参观客房以促使客人做出选择。这种订房方式有利于推销酒店产品。

The hotel reservation refers to the circumstance that the guest directly comes to the hotel and negotiates the room reservation affairs face-to-face with the reservationist. The superiority is that it can facilitate convenient communication for the reservationist, enable the reservationist to understand the guest demands at length by observing the bearings, expressions, etc. of the guest and perceiving his/her mental activities and give the opportunity to reply the guest face to face. Meanwhile, it will facilitate the reservationist to promote different guest rooms. Where necessary, the reservationist may even arrange the guest to visit the guest rooms to push them to make a decision. This reservation method is favorable in marketing the hotel products.

与客户面谈订房事宜时，预订员应注意：

When making face-to-face negotiation on room reservation, the reservationist should:

（1）仪表端庄、举止大方，要求讲究礼节礼貌，态度热情，语音、语调适当、婉转，不厌其烦。

Have good appearance and natural behaviors, be polite, enthusiastic with appropriate and tactful voice and tone, be patient.

（2）把握客户心理，运用适当的销售技巧，灵活地推销客房和酒店其他产品，必要时，还可向客人展示房间及酒店其他设施与服务，以供客人选择。

Understand the mentality of the guest, apply appropriate sales tactics, promote the guest rooms and other products of the hotel in a flexible manner, where necessary, show the guest rooms as well as other facilities and services of the hotel for the guest to make selection.

（3）受理此方式时，清楚书写订单，注意避免向宾客做具体房号的承诺。同时，取消预订时限是每天的18:00。

When handling in such a manner, write down the order clearly, and avoid promising the specific room number to the guest. Meanwhile, the deadline to cancel reservation is 18:00 every day.

4. 传真预订（Fax Reservation）

传真是一种现代通信技术，目前已经得到广泛使用，此方式最为常见，也是最理想的订房手段之一，旅行社等团体常用。其特点是：操作方便，传递迅速，即发即收，内容详尽，并可传递发送者的真迹，如签名、印鉴等，还可传递图表，不易出现纠纷，因此传真成为订房联系最常用的通信手段。在使用这种预订方式的时候，预订员要注意收发传真后必须严格按时间要求进行运作接待。

Fax is a modern communication technology that has been widely applied presently. Fax reservation is one of the most common and ideal reservation methods and is often used by groups such as travel agency. Features: Easy operation, quick transmission, real-time reaction, detailed content. It can transmit undistorted information of the sender such as signature and seal; it can also transmit tables and graphics, unlikely resulting in disputes. Therefore, fax has become the most common telecommunication method in room reservation.When handling room reservation by fax, the reservationist should pay attention that the time required in the fax must be strictly followed in operation and reception.

5. 网络预订（Network-based Reservation）

随着我国酒店业连锁化、集团化进程的加快，不少酒店纷纷加入了国际或国内酒店集团的连锁经营。大型的酒店连锁集团公司都拥有中央预订系统，即 CRS（Central Reservation System）。随着互联网的推广使用，越来越多的上网宾客开始采用这种方便、快捷、先进而又廉价的方式进行预订。酒店也越来越注重其网站主页的设计，以增强吸引力。近年来，原先主要采用电话订房方式的系统都实现了在国际互联网上的在线预订。此种预订方式的优势是信息全、选择面宽、成本低、效率高、直面客户、房价一般低于门市价、适合散客等，这些特点使其越来越受到客户及酒店的青睐。同时，可以把客人的预订资料原封不动地保存下来，不容易出现纠纷，这是目前国际上，尤其是高星级酒店常用的订房方式。随着现代电子信息技术的迅猛发展，通过国际互联网向酒店订房的方式正迅速兴起，它已成为酒店业在 21 世纪发展趋势的重要组成部分。

With the acceleration of chain-oriented and group-oriented process in the hospitality industry in China, many hotels have successively participated in the chain operation of internal or domestic hotel groups. Large-sized hotel chain groups have their own central reservation systems（CRS）. With the generalization of Internet, more and more Netizens have started such convenient, quick, advanced and cheap method to make reservation. Hotels are attaching more and more importance on the homepage design to strengthen the appeals. In recent years, all the systems originally applying telephone reservation method have included on-line reservation on the international Internet. With superiorities such as complete information, extensive options, low cost, high efficiency and direct connection with guest, lower prices compared with market prices generally and suitability to individual guests; such reservation method has been preferred by more and more guests and hotels.Meanwhile, it can save the reservation data of the guest in the integrity, which lowers the possibility of disputes. Network-based reservation is a common reservation method globally, especially in high star-level hotels. With the rapid development of modern electronic information technology, hotel room reservation based on international Internet is now quickly emerging and has become an important part in the development trends of the hospitality industry in the 21st century.

三、预订种类（Reservation Types）

酒店预订类型包括临时性预订、确认性预订和保证性预订三种，具体如下：

Hotel room reservation involves three types, which respectively is temporary reservation, confirmed reservation and guaranteed reservation. The specific descriptions of each type are as follows:

（一）临时性预订（Temporary Reservation）

临时性预订是指客人在即将抵达前或在抵达当天的预订，与抵店时间很接近，酒店一般没有足够的时间给予书面确认，无法预付定金，因此比较难以确认，均予以口头确认。但须问清联系方式、抵达具体时间、提醒客房预订保留时间。一般按照国际惯例实行：为客人保留客房的时间期限为当天的 18:00。

Temporary reservation refers to the reservation when the guest is about to arrive or on the very day of arrival. As the interval between the reservation and the arrival is quite short, generally the hotel doesn't have enough time to make written confirmation and is available to collect the deposit. Therefore, it is relatively hard to make confirmation except oral confirmation. However, the contact information and specific arrival time should be asked. And the guest should be reminded the validation time of the reservation. Generally, the international practice is adopted: To keep the reserved room for the guest till 18:00 of the reservation day.

（二）确认性预订（Confirmed Reservation）

确认性预订是指酒店答应为客人保留客房至某一事先声明的规定时间，但如果到了这一规定时间，客人仍未抵店，也无任何声明，则在用房紧张时期，酒店可将所保留的客房出租给未经预订而直接抵店的客人或等候名单的客人。对于确认性预订客人，酒店一般是向其声明为其保留客房的时间期限（一般是当天 18:00），过了规定时间，如客人未抵店，也未与酒店联系，酒店就有权将预订的客房出租给其他客人。书面确认的预订，只要地址被验证，信任度较高。

Confirmed reservation refers to that the hotel agrees to reserve the room for the guest till the prescribed time previously declared. However, if the guest fails to arrive at the hotel upon the prescribed time without any declaration, in the peak period, the hotel may offer such room to the guest coming to the hotel directly without reservation or guest on the waiting list. For guest applying for confirmed reservation, the hotel generally declares the deadline for the room reservation (generally 18:00 of the same day). If the guest fails to arrive at the hotel without contacting the hotel, the hotel reserves the right to offer the reserved room to other guests. The reservation confirmed in writing is provided with relatively high credit as long as the address has been validated.

确认预订的方式有两种：一种为口头确认，另一种为书面确认。通常使用书面确认，如邮寄、传真回复确认书等。口头确认一般只用于客人订房时间与抵店时间很接近时。无论是口头确认还是书面确认，都必须向客人明确申明酒店规定的抵店时限。

The confirmed reservation may be made by two methods: One is oral confirmation and the other is written confirmation. Generally written confirmation is applied, for example, confirmation letter replied by mail or fax, etc. Oral confirmation is generally used when the reservation is quite close to the anticipated arrival of the guest. No matter for oral confirmation or written confirmation, declaration must be made to the guests on the deadline time of arrival prescribed by the hotel.

书面确认与口头确认相比有如下优点：

Compared with oral confirmation, written confirmation is provided with the following superiorities:

（1）能复述客人的订房要求，使客人了解酒店是否已正确理解并接受了其订房要求，让客人放心。

Be able to repeat the reservation requirements of the guest; enable the guest to know whether the hotel has accurately understand and accept his/her reservation requirements and make the guest feel assured.

（2）能申明酒店对宾客承担的义务及有关变更预订、取消预订以及其他有关方面的规定，以书面形式确立了酒店和客人的关系。

Be able to declare the obligations assumed by the hotel towards the guest as well as other provisions on reservation alternation, cancellation and other affairs; be able to establish the relationship between the hotel and the guest by writing.

（3）能验证宾客所提供的个人情况，如姓名、地址等。所以持预订确认书的客人比未经预订、直接抵店的客人在信用上更可靠，大多数酒店允许其在住店期间享受短期或一定数额的赊账服务待遇。

Be able to validate the personal information provided by the guest such as the name and address. Therefore, guests with reservation confirmation letter are more reliable than those come directly without reservation. Most hotels allow them to enjoy the service on credit in a short term or up to a fixed amount during their stay in the hotel.

（三）保证性预订（Guaranteed Reservation）

保证性预订是客人通过支付一定数量的预付款、与酒店签订订房合同或用信用卡授权等形式向酒店保证前来投宿，否则将承担经济责任。酒店则必须在任何情况下都保证优先落实此类预订——保留客房至抵店日期的次日退房结账时间。如果没有接到订房人取消订房的通知，应将此类客人的房间保留到退房时间，否则酒店将承担经济责任。

Guarantee reservation refers to that the guest guarantees his/her stay in the hotel by paying certain amount of deposit, signing the reservation contract, giving authorization of credit card, etc. Failure to stay in the hotel will result in financial responsibilities. The hotel must, in any case, give priority to such type of reservation, which is, to reserve the room till the check-out time on the next day of the anticipated arrival. Without receiving the notice to cancel such reservation from the guest, the hotel must reserve the room till the check-out time. Or, the hotel must bear financial responsibilities thereof.

保证性预订在酒店与未来住客之间建立了更牢靠的关系，可以通过预付款担保、信用卡担保、合同担保等形式运作，既可约束双方，也能保护双方利益，具体担保形式如下：

Guaranteed reservation establishes more stable and reliable relationship between the hotel and potential guests and may be achieved by means of prepayment guarantee, credit card guarantee, contract guarantee, etc. Guaranteed reservation may not only bind both parties but also protect interests of both parties. The specific guarantee forms are as follows:

1. 预付款担保（Prepayment Guarantee）

对于酒店来说，最理想的保证性预订方法是要求客人通过现金、支票、汇款等酒店认可的形式预付订金，要求不少于一天的房费，以此获订房保证。这样即使客人在规定时间内不来，可以从订金中收取房费，避免损失。

For hotels, the most ideal guaranteed reservation is that the guest makes prepayment by means approved by the hotel such as cash, cheque and remittance to guarantee the reservation. The prepayment should be no less than room rate for one day. In this way, even if the guest fails to arrive within the prescribed time, the room rate may be charged from the prepayment to avoid losses.

预付金可以由预订处收取后交财务部，也可由财务部收取后通知预订处。

The prepayment may be collected by the Reservation Desk and then handed over to the Financial Department, or be collected by the Financial Department and notified to the Reservation Desk.

2. 信用卡担保（Credit Card Guarantee）

客人在订房时向酒店声明，将使用信用卡为所预订的房间付款，并把信用卡的发卡公司、号码、有效期及持卡人的姓名告诉酒店并做授权。如客人在预订日期未抵达酒店，酒店可以通过信用卡公司获得房费收入的补偿。

When making room reservation, the guest declares to the hotel to pay the room rate for the reserved room with a credit card. The guest informs the issuing company, number, validation date and card holder name of the credit card and makes authorization thereof. If the guest fails to arrive as scheduled, the hotel may be compensated with the deserved room rate from the credit card company.

3. 合同担保（Contract Guarantee）

订立商业合同是指酒店与有关客户单位签订的订房合同。合同内容主要包括签约单位的地址、账号以及同意对因为失约而未使用的订房承担付款责任的说明，合同还应规定通知取消预订的最后期限，如签约单位未能在规定的期限通知取消预订，酒店可以向对方收取房费等。

The conclusion of a commercial contract refers to the reservation contract signed between the hotel and related guest organization. The contract mainly involves the addresses and account numbers of the signing organizations as well as provisions on payment responsibilities in case of failure to obey the contract and use the room. The contract should also stipulate the deadline of reservation cancellation by notice as well as the provision that the hotel may charge room rate if the singing organization fails to cancel the reservation within the prescribed time limit.

由于各地区、各酒店的实际情况不同，担保的方法也不尽相同。有些酒店将其认可的个人名誉担保视为订房担保；有些酒店目前尚无法接受以信用卡作为订房担保，故采取何种有效的订房担保，应视情况而定。

As the case may be, the guarantee methods are varying according the actual conditions of different regions and hotels. Some hotels accept guaranteed reservation with personal frames in approved forms; while some hotels don't accept the credit card as guarantee. Therefore, the type of effective guaranteed reservation depends on the specific cases.

需要说明的是，在实际工作中，我们会发现一些客人有时会因各种原因无法按期抵达酒店或者取消订房，这其中有相当一部分客人不会将变更信息及时、主动地通知酒店。因此我们在客人抵达酒店之前要通过电话或者书信等方式主动与客人进行多次核对，一旦获悉变更信息，应及时调整并通知相关部门，以便将闲置的客房重新出租给其他客人。

It should be noted that, in practice, we've found that some guests cannot arrive the hotel as schedules for various reasons or would cancel the reservation, of which quite a number of guest wouldn't notify the updated information to the hotel in a timely and positive manner. Therefore, we should make repeated examination with the guest positively by means of telephone or letter before the arrival of the guest. Once modification is noticed, timely make adjustment and inform related department to enable the vacant room to be offered to other guests again.

知识链接

Knowledge Link

（一）预订员必须掌握的其他业务知识（Other Business Knowledge to be Mastered by the Reservationist）

（1）掌握酒店客房的分布情况及各种房间的类型、特征、价格标准。

Master the distribution of the guest rooms as well as the types, features and rate standards of each type of room.

（2）掌握各种房型的价格及优惠政策。

Master the prices and preferential policies of various room types.

（3）熟练掌握前厅、客房常用专业术语。

Be proficient in common terminology used in the lobby and guest rooms.

客房状态除了用文字表示外，为了操作时直观方便，通常在计算机管理系统界面上用不同的颜色来表示不同的房态，如红色表示维修房；绿色表示在住房；白色表示空净房；绿色与灰色相间表示占用脏房；白色与灰色相间表示脏空房。

More than word expressions, for intuitive and convenient operation, generally different colors are used on the interface of the computer management system to indicate different room status, for example, red for OOO, green for OCC, white for V, green embedded with grey for OD and white embedded with grey for VD.

（4）熟记与酒店签有合同的公司、单位的房价标准。

Bear in mind the room rate standards for companies and organizations signing contracts with the hotel.

（5）熟悉预订部常用表格、报表并能准确填写。

Be familiar with the commonly used forms and statements of the Reservation Department and be able to fill the forms and statements accurately.

（二）前台与客房部常用专业术语（Common Terminology for Front Desk and Housekeeping Department）

1. *客房状态术语*（Terminology for Room Status）

住客房：客人正在住用的房间。

Occupied（OCC）：A room that is being occupied by the guest.

走客房：表示客人已结账并已离开客房。

ChCCk out（C/O）：The guest has checked out and left the room.

空房：昨日暂时无人租用房间。

Vacant（V）：A room that is not occupied for the previous day.

未清扫房：表示该客房为没有经过打扫的空房。

Vacant dirty（VD）：The guest room is unoccupied and not cleaned yet.

外宿房：表示该客房已被租用，但住客昨夜未归。

Sleep out（S/O）：The room is occupied but not used by the guest on the previous night.

维修房：亦称病房。表示该客房因设施设备发生故障，暂不能出租。

Out of order（OOO）：Also called "Sick Room"；referring to a room not available for rent due to failure of facility or equipment.

请勿打扰房：表示该客房的旅客因睡眠或其他原因而不愿服务人员打扰。

Do not disturb（DND）：The guest（s）in the room is/are unwilling to be disturbed by the service personnel for reasons such as sleeping.

贵宾房：表示该客房住客是酒店的重要客人。

Very important person（VIP）：The guest（s）of the room is/are of great importance for the hotel.

长住房：长期由客人包租的房间。又称"长包房"。

Long staying guest（LSG）：A room rented by the guest successively for a long term, also called "long chartered room".

请即打扫房：表示该客房住客因会客或其他原因需要服务员立即打扫的房间。

Make up room（MUR）：The room is required to be cleaned immediately by the service personnel as the guest is about to receive a visitor or for other reasons.

轻便行李房：表示住客行李很少的房间。为了防止逃账，客房部都应及时通知总台。

Light baggage（L/B）：Referring to a room with the guest carrying light baggage. To avoid evader, the Housekeeping Department should timely inform the Reception Desk.

无行李房：表示该房间的住客无行李。应及时通知总台。

No baggage（N/B）：The guest has noluggage. The Housekeeping Department should timely inform the Reception Desk.

准备退房：表示该客房住客应在当天中午 12：00 以前退房，但现在还未退房。

Expected departure（E/D）：The guest of the room is supposed to check out before 12：00 that day but has not checked out yet.

2. 预订状态术语（Terminology for Reservation Status）

预抵

Arrivals The guest is about to arrive

已到店

Arrived The guest has arrived

在店

Stay Over The guest stays over in the hotel

预离

Due Out The guest is due to check out

3. 房间类型术语（Terminology for Room Type）

（1）按床具种类分（According to the bed type）。

单人床

Twin-size Bed Single bed

双人床，包括大号双人床（Queen-size Bed）和特大号双人床（King-size Bed）

Double-size Bed Double bed，including Queen-size Bed and King-size Bed

隐蔽床

Murphy Bed Hidden bed

婴儿床

Baby Bed Bed for the baby

加床

Extra Bed Rollaway Bed Additional bed

（2）按客房类型分（According to room type）。

单人间：就是指房内只有一张床的房间，行内简称单间。

Single Room：A room with only a single bed，"Single Room" for short.

标准间：放置两张单人床，我国酒店的大多数客房属于这种类型。

Standard Room：A room with two single beds，which is typical in hotels in China.

大床间：该房间放置一张双人床，一般适合夫妻或商务客人使用。新婚夫妇使用时称"蜜月客房"。

Double Room：A room with a double bed，commonly suitable for couples and business guests. When used by a newly-married couple，it is also called"Honeymoon Room".

三人间：一般是房内放置三张单人床，供三位宾客同时入住，属经济房间。目前在中高档酒店中此类房间极少，多以在双人间加一张床的方式来满足三人同住一间客房的要求。

Triple Room：Generally，the room is provided with three singled beds to allow three guests simultaneously. It is a type of economic room. Presently，such type is quite rare in middle and high ranking hotels. Generally，an extra bed is provided in the Double Room to satisfy the requirements of one room for three guests.

任务二 预订服务的结构与流程
Task Ⅱ Structure and Flow of Reservation Service

【情境导入】【Scenario Introduction】

沟通不足导致的投诉
Complaints Arising from Insufficient Communication

海南皇马假日大酒店大堂经理接到某旅行社电话，要求为客人预订一间套房。大堂经理根据客人抵达日期查询电脑后，确认有房，将房间设施和价格电话告知对方，并请对方发传真到预订部确认。对方发来的传真预订房间的数量由一个套间变为一个套间和一个标准间，并注明两间房为连通房。大堂副理和预订员由于没有理解客人的要求，为客人订了一个套间和与套间相邻的标准间。当旅行社的客人到店入住后，发现房型与预订要求不符，提出投诉。

The Assistant Manager（AM）of Hainan Huangma Holiday Hotel received a call from one travel agency on reservation of a suite for the guest. The Assistant Manager checked on the computer according to the anticipated arrival date of the guest and confirmed that a suite is available. So the AM informed the room facilities and prices to the travel agency through the telephone and required the caller to send a fax to the Reservation Department for confirmation. However，in the fax reservation by the opposite side，the rooms required were shifted from one suite to one suite and one standard room and it was indicated that the two rooms should be connected. The AM and reservationist failed to understand the requirements of the guest and booked one suite and a standard room next to it for the guest. Upon the arrival of the guests of the travel agency，they found the room types were inconsistent with the reservation requirements and raised a complaint.

【情境分析】【Scenario Analysis】

"在一次做一件事的时候，就把事情做好。"这是印在维也纳万豪酒店《品质手册》封面上的一句口号。我们的对客服务只有保证从第一个环节到最后一个环节都不出差错，才能为宾客提供优质服务。万豪酒店《品质手册》的封面口号应该对我们有所启发。上述案例中，由于大堂经理和预订员在第一次做预订的时候，就没有搞清楚客人的预订要求，根据客人的要求，连通房是可以不经走廊在两室之间自由往来的房型。相邻房是两间靠在一起，互不相通的房间。

"Do it，and do it better." This is a slogan printed on the cover of the *Quality Manual* of Vienna Marriott Hotel. Only if we guarantee no mistake from the first link to every link in guest services can we provide high quality services to the guests. We should learn something from the slogan printed on the cover of the *Quality Manual* of Vienna Marriott Hotel.In this case，the AM and the reservationist fail to understand the reservation requirements of the guests when making the first reservation. According to the guests，two connected rooms should be the rooms interlinked freely without the need to passing the corridor. However，the neighboring rooms are next to each other but not connected.

（1）大堂经理和预订员应准确理解客人的预订要求，按照客人的房型需求做好预订工作，如无所需房型应及时与客人联系商洽。

The AM and the reservationist should accurately understand the reservation requirements and handle the reservation properly according to the requirements on room types of the guest. Contact and negotiate with the guest if the required room type is not available.

（2）当客人入住后如发现房型与要求不符，前台接待员应在可能的范围内尽量迅速为客人调换房间，争取满足客人的要求。

If the guest detects that the room type served is not consistent with the room type required, the receptionist of the Reception Desk should change the room for the guest as possible within the applicable scope and try the best to satisfy the guest's demands.

（3）客房部、前厅部有关人员应具有解决相关投诉的能力。

The personnel of the Housekeeping Department and the Front Office Department should be capable to solve related complaints.

一、预订服务结构（Reservation Service Structure）

前厅客房预订是酒店专设的服务项目，是前厅部销售客房的重要手段和途径。它要完成的主要任务有：

Lobby room reservation is a service item specially designed in the hotel as well as an important method and means for the Front Office Department to sell the guest rooms. The main tasks are as follows:

（1）接受。处理并确认的订房要求。

Reception. Dispose and confirm the reservation requirements.

（2）记录、整理、储存预订资料。

Record, sort up and store reservation data.

（3）检查、控制预订过程。

Inspect and control the reservation process.

（4）完成宾客抵店前的准备工作。

Get prepared in advance before the arrival of the guest.

为了促进酒店销售，提高客房的出租率，预订员在接受与确认预订的过程中，需要掌握口头确认、书面确认、保证性预订、婉拒预订等预订确认的技能；在预订控制方面，需要掌握预订的变更、预订的取消、预订过程的检查和控制以及接收、处理和控制超额预订的技能；在预订确认后，需要记录和整理排放预订资料，然后在客人抵达酒店前做好核对次日抵达酒店客人预订内容、预分排房、制作报表的工作，同时还必须具有做好预订失误处理以及预订常见问题的能力。

To boost hotel sales and enhance the occupancy rate of the hotel, in the process of receiving and confirming the reservation, the reservationist should master related skills on reservation confirmation such as oral confirmation, written confirmation, guaranteed reservation and polite declining of reservation. On aspect of reservation control, the reservationist should master related skills such as reservation alternation, reservation cancellation, inspection and control on reservation process as well as the reception, disposal and control of over-booking. Upon the confirmation of the reservation, the reservationist must record and settle the reservation data and make proper examination on the reservation information, allocate the rooms in advance and make related statements for guests to be arrived on the next day. Meanwhile, the reservationist must be provided with abilities on disposal of reservation mistakes and common problems in reservation.

二、预订服务的流程（Reservation Service Flow）

通常，客房预订的程序可概括成下列六个阶段：通信联系→明确客源要求→受理预订或婉拒预订→确认预订→预订资料记录储存→抵店前准备。

Generally, flow of room reservation may be summarized into the following six stages: Communication → Clarifying guest requirements → Accepting or politely declining the reservation → Confirming the reservation → Keeping of reservation records → *Preparation of guest arrival*.

（一）通信联系（Communication）

宾客常以电话、面谈、传真、互联网、信函等方式向酒店前厅部客房预订处提出订房要求。

The guests often propose reservation requests to the Room Reservation Desk of the Front Office Department of the hotel by means of telephone, face-to-face talk, fax, Internet, letter, etc.

（二）明确客源要求（Clarifying Guest Requirements）

预订员须将宾客的订房要求填入统一印制的订房单，以明确酒店在处理预订中所需的各种信息，如宾客姓名、人数、国籍、抵离店日期及时间、车次或航班、所需客房的种类和数量、价格、付款方式、预订代理人姓名、单位或地址、电话号码、特殊要求等信息。使用订房单记录客人的订房要求有以下作用：

The reservationist must fill in the uniform reservation sheet with the reservation requirements to clarify various types of information required in disposal of reservation, for example, the name, number, nationality, check-in/check-out date, vehicle number, type and number of room required, room rate, payment method, reservation agent name, unit or address of the reservation assignee, telephone number, special requirements, etc. Recording the reservation requirements with reservation sheet provides the following superiorities:

（1）提醒作用：提醒预订员及时询问客人有关信息或说明有关事项。

Reminding: Remind the reservationist to timely enquire the guest about related information or explain related matters.

（2）检查作用：确保所需资料记录在案。

Inspection: Ensure that all the data required has been recorded.

（3）统一格式，便于存档：因格式统一，使用方便，从而提高了预订工作效率。

Uniform format for archiving: The uniform format facilitates the use and further enhances the reservation efficiency.

（4）宾客如采用电话预订或柜台口头预订，预订员应主动问好，询问客人的需求，主动介绍客房设施设备，并根据客源种类准确报价。无论宾客以何种方式订房，预订员都应做好详细记录，并在口头或书面的确认中重复客人的订房要求。订单资料也为今后的预订确认、订房核对等工作提供准确的信息。

If the guest makes the reservation by telephone or orally at the Reception Desk, the reservationist should initiatively greet the guest, enquire the guest's requirements, positively introduce room facilities and equipments and give room rates accurately according to the type of the guest. The reservationist should make detailed record whatever method is used by the guest in the reservation and should repeat the reservation requirements of the guest orally or by writing. The reservation sheet also provides accurate information for further reservation confirmation, reservation examination, etc.

（三）受理预订或婉拒预订（Receiving or Politely Declining the Reservation）

在接到客人的订房要求后，预订员通过查看预订总表或计算机终端，以判断宾客的预订要求是否与酒店的实际提供能力相吻合，并决定客人的订房要求是否可以接受。在决定是否接受客人订房要求时，应考虑下列几个因素：

Upon receiving the room reservation request, the reservationist checks the reservation schedule or computer client to judge whether the hotel is actually able to satisfy the reservation requirements of the guest and whether to accept the reservation request from the guest. When deciding whether to accept the reservation request, the following factor should be considered:

（1）宾客预期抵店日期。

Expected arrival date of the guest.

（2）所需客房的种类。

The room type required.

（3）所需客房的数量。

The number of rooms required.

（4）宾客住店的天数。

The number of days for the stay of the guest.

根据上述条件，预订员要决定是否接受客人的订房要求。如果客人的要求不能或者不能完全被满足，应建议其做些更改或者列入等候名单。

According to the above mentioned conditions, the reservationist should decide whether to accept the reservation request of the guest. If the guest's requirements cannot be satisfied, in full or in part, the reservationist should advice him/her to make adjustment or include the guest into the waiting list.

（四）确认预订（Confirming Reservation）

预订员在接到客人的预订要求后，要立即将客人的预订要求与酒店未来时期客房的使用情况进行对照，决定是否能够接受客人的预订，如果可以接受，就要对客人的预订加以确认。

Upon receiving the reservation requirements of the guest, the reservationist should immediately compare the reservation requirements of the guest from the future room availability of the hotel to decide whether such reservation can be accepted. If the reservation is accepted, the reservation of the guest must be confirmed.

确认预订的方式通常有三种，即口头确认（包括电话确认）、书面确认和短信确认。在过去，确认了宾客的订房要求后，如果条件允许，只要有充足的时间酒店都会及时发出书面预订确认书，向客人寄发确认函。确认书中应复述客人的订房要求、房价及付款方式，写明酒店对宾客订房变更、取消预订的规定。对确认性预订的客人要写明抵店时限；对保证性预订的客人要说明酒店收取预订金的有关政策；最后，还应向客人选择本酒店表示感谢。但是，新型的、已经成为趋势的确认方法是通过酒店信息化平台，给预订成功的客人发送确认预订短信，同时提醒客人通过短信确定入住反馈，这也是最便捷的确认方式。另外，在某些时候，酒店会通过口头确认（包括电话确认）方式，来和客人确定预订。

Generally the reservation confirmation may be made by three means, which respectively are oral confirmation (including telephone confirmation), written confirmation and SMS confirmation. In the past, after the reservation request of the guest is confirmed, where the conditions allow and the times is sufficient, the hotel would timely issue a written reservation confirmation letter and send the confirmation letter to the guest. The confirmation letter should repeat the requirements, room rate and payment method for the reservation and indicate the provisions of the hotel on room reservation alternation and cancellation. For guests of confirmed reservation, the time limit of arrival should be indicated; the guests of guaranteed reservation, related policies of the hotel on prepayment collection should be indicated. Finally, appreciation should be made to the guests for selecting the hotel. However, as the trend, new-type confirmation method is sending a reservation confirmation message to guest successfully making the reservation by the information-based platform of the hotel and meanwhile reminding to give feedback for the confirmation via SMS. This is the most convenient confirmation method. In addition, under some circumstances, the hotel may confirm the reservation with the guest by means of oral confirmation (including telephone confirmation).

(五)预订资料记录储存(Keeping of Reservation Data)

当预订确认书发出后,预订资料必须及时、正确地予以记录和储存,以防疏漏。预订资料一般包括客房预订单、确认书、预付定金收据、预订变更单、预订取消单、客史档案卡及宾客原始预订凭证等。将有关同一宾客的预订资料装订在一起,将最新的资料存放在最上面,依次顺推,以利于查阅。预订资料的记录储存可采用下列两种方式:

After the confirmation letter is sent out, the reservation data must be timely and accurately recorded and stored and no careless omission should be made. The reservation data generally includes the reservation sheet, confirmation letter, prepayment receipt, reservation alternation sheet, reservation cancellation sheet, guest history file card, original reservation evidence of the guest, etc. Reservation data of the same guest should be bound together with the latest data on top to facilitate reference. Recording and storing of reservation data may be made in the following two methods:

(1)按宾客所预订抵店日期顺序储存。按照宾客所预订的抵店日期顺序,将预订单归档储存,以便随时掌握未来每天的宾客抵店情况。通常,将预订资料放在一个大的卡片箱或抽屉里。

Store according to the sequence of arrival date of the guests. Archive and store the reservation sheets according to the sequence of date of arrival according to the reservation to master daily arrival conditions of the guest. Generally, the reservation data is put into a big filing cabinet or drawer.

(2)按宾客姓氏字母顺序储存。按照宾客姓氏第一个字母的顺序,将预订单归档储存,以便随时查找出宾客的预订资料。同时,前厅部问询处和电话总机也可通过宾客姓氏字母顺序快捷有效地查找相关资料。

Store according to the alphabetical order of the family names of the guests. The reservation sheets are archived according to the alphabetical order of the first letters of the family names of the guests, which may facilitate the retrieving of the reservation data of the guest at any time. Meanwhile, the Information Desk and the Switchboard of the Head Office Department may also retrieve related data according to the alphabetical order of the guests in a quick and effective manner.

(六)抵店前准备(Preparation for Arrival)

小型酒店的抵店前的准备工作通常以口头形式传递并完成;在大型酒店,则通过开协调会或抄送各种表格、计划来完成,可分为如下三个阶段:

Preparation for guest arrival in small hotels is generally communicated and completed orally; while in large hotels, such preparation is made by means of holding the coordination meetings or copying various types of forms and schedules. The preparation may be divided into the following three stages:

(1)提前一周或数日,将主要客情,如贵宾、大型团体会议、客满等信息通知有关部门,以做好相应的准备工作。传递的表格一般有《一周客情预报表》、《贵宾接待规格审批表》等。

Information related to major guest information such as VIP, large-sized group conference and full occupancy should be notified to related departments one week or several days in advance for corresponding preparation. Communication forms generally involve: *Weekly Guest Prediction Form*; *Examination and Approval Form for VIP Reception Standards*, etc.

（2）宾客抵店前，将具体接待安排以书面形式通知有关部门，使各部门做好接待准备工作。通知单有《VIP 接待通知单》等。

Before the arrival of the guest, the specific reception arrangement should be notified to related departments in written forms to enable each department to make proper preparation. The advice notes involve: *VIP Reception Advice Note*, etc.

（3）宾客抵达酒店当天，接待员根据宾客的订房要求提前分配房间，并将有关细节通知有关部门搞好接待，共同完成抵店前的准备工作。

On the arrival date of the guest, the receptionist should allocate rooms in advance according to the reservation requests of the guest and inform corresponding details to the related departments to make proper reception and work collectively for preparation.

三、电话预订服务流程（Telephone Reservation Service Flow）

1. 接电话，问候客人（Answer the Call and Greet the Guest）

（1）铃响三声之内拿起电话。

Pick up the receiver before the telephone rings for three times.

（2）问候语：用标准语言问候客人，早上好/下午好/晚上好。

Greetings: Greet the guest with standard langue: Good morning/afternoon/evening.

（3）报部门：××酒店预订部。

Reporting the department: This is the Reservation Department of ×× Hotel.

2. 聆听客人预订要求（Listen to the Reservation Requirements of the Guest）

（1）问清客人姓名（中英文拼写）、住店日期、离店日期、联系电话、房型、数量等。

Ask for detailed information such as name (spelling of Chinese and English name), check-in/check-out date, contact number, room type and number.

（2）查看电脑及客房预订控制板，看是否可以满足客人预订需求。

Check the computer and the room reservation control board to ensure whether the reservation requirements of the guest may be satisfied.

3. 推销房间（Room Sales）

（1）介绍房间种类和房价，尽量从高价到低价。

Introduce the room types and rates; make recommendation from top price to bottom price as possible.

（2）询问客人是否有协议客户、有 VIP 卡。

Enquire whether the guest is a contracted guest or with VIP card.

（3）查询电脑，确认客人公司名称，以及公司协议是否属于合同单位，便于确定优惠。

Check the computer to confirm the company name, company agreement as well as whether such company is a contracted unit so as to determine preferential policies.

（4）填写订单，包括客人姓名、协议单位、抵离日期、抵离时间、预订人姓名、电话、预订房型、房间数量、房价、付费方式、特殊要求，核实无误后录入电脑。

Fill in the reservation sheet, including information such as name of the guest, agreement unit, check-in/check-out date, name of the reserving personnel, telephone number, room type, number of rooms, room rate, payment method and special requirements. Input the information into the computer after the information is proved to be accurate.

4. 询问客人付款方式（Enquire the Payment Method of the Guest）

（1）询问客人付款方式，在订单上注明。

Enquire the payment method of the guest and indicate on the reservation sheet.

（2）公司或旅行社承担费用者，要求在客人抵达前电传书面信函，做付款担保。

If the payment is assumed by the company or travel agency, the guest is required to fax a written letter before the arrival of the guest to guarantee the payment.

5. 询问客人抵达情况（Enquire the Arrival Information of the Guest）

（1）询问抵达航班及时间。

Enquire the Arrival Flight and Time.

（2）向客人说明房间保留时间，或建议客人做担保预订。

Explain the room reservation time to the guest or suggest the guest to make guaranteed reservation.

6. 询问客人特殊要求（Enquire the Special Requirements of the Guest）

（1）询问客人特殊要求，如是否需要接机服务等，如客人需接机服务，说明收费标准。

Enquire the special requirements of the guest, for example: Whether flight pick-up service, etc. is required; if pick-up service is required, indicate the charging standard.

（2）对有特殊要求者，详细记录并复述，如需要特别订餐、摆设要求、房间朝向等，并向客人解释酒店相关规定及收费标准，做好相应记录并通知相关部门安排。

Make detailed record and repeat the special requirements of the guest, such as special meal, arrangement and room direction of the guest; explain related provisions and charging standards to the guests; make corresponding records accordingly and inform related departments to make arrangements.

7. 询问预订人或预订代理人（Enquire the Reserving Personnel or Reservation Assignee）

（1）询问预订人或预订代理人的姓名、单位、联系方式、电话号码。

Enquire the name, unit, contact information and telephone number of the personnel making the reservation or reservation assignee.

（2）对上述情况做好记录。

Make proper records on the abovementioned information.

8. 复述核对预订内容（Repeat and Examine the Reservation Information）

再次向客人复述以上预订内容，避免造成预订信息不准确。

Repeat the reservation information to the guest to avoid inaccuracy of the reservation information.

9. 向客人致谢（Acknowledgement to the Guest）

感谢客人的致电预订，期待客人的光临，与客人道别。

Express appreciation to the guest for calling for reservation, express the expectation on the guest's arrival and say goodbye to the guest.

10. 记录预订（Record the Reservation）

（1）填写预订单并输入电脑。

Fill in the reservation sheet and input the information into the computer.

（2）按日期存放订单。

Archive the reservation sheet according to the date.

【实训与评价】【Training and Assessment】

［实训目的］［Training Goals］

通过散客和团队电话预订客房的项目模拟练习，掌握电话预订客房的步骤和标准。

Master the telephone reservation procedures and standards by simulation exercise of telephone reservation for individual and group guests.

［实训准备］［Training Preparation］

预订单、笔、电话。

Reservation sheet, pen, telephone.

［实训方法］［Training Method］

小组合作法、任务驱动法、讲授法、引导法。

Group Collaboration Method, Task-driven Method, Expository Method, Guidance Method.

［实训步骤］［Training Procedure］

由学生两人一组，进行散客电话客房预订项目模拟练习。要求：预订员应注意眼神、微笑、说话的语气、言辞的礼貌性。

The students work in pairs to make simulation practice on telephone reservation for individual guests. Requirements: The reservationist should pay attention to the eye contact, smile, tone and the politeness of the wordage.

1. 学生两人一组，模仿教师范例，教师给出评判。

The students work in pairs and simulate the examples of the teachers. The teachers give judgments.

2. 学生可以即兴发挥，老师和学生共同评价，老师给出分数。

The students are allowed to make extemporaneous play, the students and the teachers give comments together, the teachers give the scores.

3. 学生提出问题，老师回答。

The students raise questions for the teachers to answer.

［实训案例］［Training Case］

百特房地产有限公司的 George Smith 先生致电酒店预订部，要求为其公司两位客人预订两间商务单间，住宿时间为本月 15~19 日，共四天。客人将于 15 日早上 11:00 左右到达酒店，两位客人的住宿费由百特房地产有限公司结算，餐费及其他费用客人自理。请受理 George Smith 先生的电话预订业务。

Mr. George Smith from Baite Real Estate calls the Reservation Department of the hotel, requiring to business single rooms for two of its guests. The anticipated stay is four days from 15th to 19th this month. The guests will arrive at the hotel at about 11:00 on the morning of the 15th. The room rates for both guests will be settled with Baite Real Estate. And the guests will assume the meal fees and other expenses. Please handle the telephone reservation for Mr. George Smith.

要求（Requirements）：

1. 正确填写预订登记表、预订确认函。

Fill in the reservation sheet and reservation confirmation letter accurately.

2. 接听电话符合礼仪规范。

Answer the call according to the etiquette patterns.

3. 受理预订模拟演练，要求语言简练、礼貌、动作娴熟，不遗漏预订细节。

Make simulation practice on reservation, be precise in language, polite and skilled in gestures without omitting any reservation details.

（1）学生两人一组，分别扮演客人与预订员，礼貌而规范地受理 George Smith 先生的电话订房业务，并发出预订确认函。

The students work in pairs to respectively act as the guest and reservationist, handle the telephone reservation for Mr. George Smith in a polite and normalized manner and issue the reservation confirmation letter.

（2）不断更换客人的订房要求，请学生按散客电话订房的规范完成预订业务。

Change the reservation requests of the guest continuously, ask the students to complete the reservation according to the standards of telephone reservation for individual guests.

（3）请假设情景，试着向客人介绍酒店的客房类型、相近房型之间的区别及房价。

Image the actual conditions, try to introduce the room types, difference of similar room types and room rates in the hotel.

（4）学生之间角色互换，试着向各种不同的客人推销客房，体验推销客房技巧。

The students swap the roles and try to promote rooms to various types of the rooms and experience the skills of room promotion.

4. 妥善处理预订过程中出现的特殊问题。

Dispose the special questions in the process of reservation.

任务三 预订变更服务

Task Ⅲ Reservation Alternation Service

【情境导入】【Scenario Introduction】

到底该不该取消

Is It Appropriate to Cancel

陈女士从浙江来到三亚旅游。在来到三亚之前，她已在网上安排好自己所有的行程，并预订了亚龙湾天鸿度假村酒店。8 月 17 日当天，由于台风来袭，交通十分不便，几乎无法出行。于是，她便向该酒店提出退房。后来，酒店方表示，团购价不予以退款，并诚恳地表示愿意派车接送，不过得缴纳 150 元车费。“以团购价 260 元预订的房间，不入住酒店也不退房费。”无奈之下，她表示只要酒店愿意接送，她愿意出车费。可是，酒店后来又以司机下班为由，不愿意接送。最后，她去不了该酒店也拿不了退款。陈女士认为，是因天气原因导致交通不便，取消预订房间理所当然。酒店拒绝退款，有霸王条款之嫌。陈女士是通过网上以团购价预订该酒店房间。当时，订房时双方都已有协议，若客观原因造成顾客无法入住，酒店可以退房并退还全款。若因主观原因任意选择退房，属于违约，酒店不会给予退款。该酒店负责人表示，17 日当天陈女士本人已在大东海附近。当时，陈女士致电该酒店表示，因台风天气，某景区不对外营业，所以想要退房。她向陈女士解释不能退房原因后，陈女士又表示因交通不便，无法前往亚龙湾。虽然台风来袭，但并没有导致交通瘫痪。酒店大巴不能对外运营，为了给陈女士提供便利，酒店愿意临时接送陈女士。由于陈女士要求免费接送，酒店也无可奈何。所以，是陈女士违约在先，酒店不存在霸王条款。

Ms Chen took a trip to Sanya from Zhejiang.Before coming to Sanya, she had arranged the entire trip on line and reserved Tian Hong Resort Hotel in Yalong Bay. On August 17, as attacked by the typhoon, the traffic was quite inconvenient and it was hardly possible to make the trip. So, the guest requested to check out to the hotel. The hotel expressed that no refund will be made as the reservation was made at group purchase price. And the hotel sincerely expressed that it is willing to assign a car to pick her up. But the guest should pay for the fee of 150 yuan. "Room reserved at a group purchase price of 260 yuan will not be refunded if no check-in is made." The lady could do nothing but expressing her willingness to pay for the pick-up as long as the hotel was willing to dispatch a car. However, the hotel became unwilling to do so with the excuse that the driver is off work. Finally, she could neither get the room refunded nor check in. Ms Chen held that it was just nature that she canceled the reservation due to inconvenient traffic caused by the bad weather. She also suspected that it was an imparity clause that the hotel refused to refund. Ms Chen had reserved the room of the hotel on line at the group purchase price. According to the agreement, the hotel might accept cancellation and made entire refund if the guest was not available for objective causes. But if the cancellation was made by arbitrary selection for subjective causes, it should be regarded as the default and the hotel may refund the refunding. The responsible personnel of the hotel expressed that, on the 17th Ms Chen had already been next to Dadonghai. At that time, Ms Chen called the hotel and expressed that she'd like to cancel the reservation as a scenic spot was closed. The responsible personnel explained the reason that such cancellation was not available. Ms Chen further expressed that she cannot go to the Yalong Bay due to the inconvenient traffic. Though the typhoon wasstrong, the traffic was not totally disabled. As the hotel bus was not allowed to do business out of the hotel, to facilitate Ms Chen, the hotel expressed its willingness to arrange a car temporarily to pick up Ms Chen. However, Ms Chen required free pick-up, the hotel had no alternative. Therefore, the hotel deemed that it is Ms Chen that breached the agreement and the hotel had no imparity clause.

针对案例中的情况，陈女士和酒店之间到底该如何协调解决？

So, how can Ms Chen and the hotel negotiate to settle the matter according to the conditions mentioned above?

【情境分析】【Scenario Analysis】

首先，针对情境中的冲突，应查明客观存在的问题，比如天气情况，台风是否导致交通不便。如果交通条件可以克服，陈女士没有入住酒店的原因是主观原因，还是客观原因，要调查清楚。其次，在处理这种酒店和顾客之间冲突的过程中，不能有任何偏私，尤其是不能帮助酒店欺负顾客，这样会在顾客心目中留下极差的印象，更严重的话可能会对整个旅游目的地造成不良的影响。最后，在处理这样的矛盾时，最好能让双方都让一步，比如酒店把陈女士接过来，送份早餐，这样陈女士虽然不能去景区游玩，但是心里也会舒服很多。

Firstly, for the dispute in the scenario, objective difficulties should be investigated first, for example, the weather conditions, whether it is the typhoon that causes inconvenient traffic. If the traffic difficulties can conquered, investigation should be made on whether the reason for Ms Chen's failure to check-in is subjective or objective. Secondly, no favoritism should be given when disposing such conflicts between the hotel and the guest, especially no assistance should be made to the hotel to suppress the guest, which would leave quite poor impression to the guest. What's even worse, adverse influence would be caused to the entire tourism destination. Finally, when disposing such conflicts, better practice is that both parties take a step backwards. For example, the hotel picks up Ms Chen and offers her a breakfast for free, which would make her feel more comfortable even if she is not able to tour the scenic spot.

酒店接受并承诺了预订后，由于客人抵店前常会因为各种原因出现取消或更改订房的情况，因此，预订员需要做好订房核对工作，发现问题及时更正或补救，以保证订房工作准确无误。预订员应重视并处理好预订的变更工作，订房核对工作一般分三次进行，分别为客人到店前一个月、一周和前一天。若重要客人或团体提前预订时间长，还应增加核对次数。

After the hotel accepts and commits the reservation, as it is common that the guest cancels or alters the reservation for various reasons before arrival, the reservationist should make proper examination on the reservation and take timely corrective or remedy actions on problems detected to guarantee accurate room reservation services. The reservationist should attach importance to and make proper disposal of the reservation alternation. Generally, examination on one reservation should be made for three times, which respective in one month, one week and one day before the arrival of the guest. In case of VIP guests or large-sized groups with long reservation interval, the frequency of examination should be intensified.

如果宾客变更或取消已确认的预订要求，预订员必须填写预订变更单或预订取消单。将取消的订房资料归入取消类存档，将变更的订房资料与预订变更单汇总，按接受一个新的预订程序处理。同时，还应注意以下方面的工作：

On condition that the guest alters or cancels the confirmed reservation requirements, the reservationist must fill in the reservation alternation sheet or reservation cancellation sheet. Archive the data for cancelled reservation into the "Cancellation" class. Gather the altered reservation data and reservation alternation sheet and dispose as a new reservation procedure. Meanwhile, the following aspects should be noted:

（1）若变更或取消的内容涉及一些原有的工作安排，如接机、房间特殊布置、订餐等，应尽快将变更或取消的内容通知到有关部门。

If the altered or cancelled reservation involves some original work arrangement, such as pick-up, special room arrangement and meal ordering, the alternated or cancelled information should be notified to related departments as soon as possible.

（2）有关团体订房的变更与取消，应按合同规定办理。通常合同规定旅行社取消订房应在团体原定抵达日期前 10 天通知酒店，否则按合约规定收取一定数额的取消费。

Alternation and cancellation of group room reservation should be disposed according to contract provisions. Generally, it is stipulated in the contract that the travel agency should inform the hotel about the cancellation ten (10) days before the expected arrival of the group. Or, the cancellation fee to some amount will be charged as agreed in the contract.

（3）耐心、高效地受理预订的取消并尽量简化手续。宾客花时间通知酒店取消其原来的预订对酒店是有利的，预订员应同样给予热情和耐心，高效地受理。据统计，90%的取消预订的宾客会在今后的旅行中返回原预订的酒店。

Handle the reservation cancellation in a patient and highly effective manner and try to streamline the formalities as possible. It is favorable to the hotel if a guest is willing to spend some time to cancel his/her reservation. The reservationist should also make enthusiastic, patient and highly effective disposal. According to the statistics, 90% of the guests cancelling the reservation would select the hotel he/she once reserves in future tour.

（4）无论是变更还是取消预订，宾客都有其实际原因，预订员应表现出热情和有效的帮助。

No matter for alternation or cancellation of the reservation, the guest would have his/her own actual causes, the reservationist should express the enthusiasm and offer effective assistance.

一、修改预订（Reservation Alternation）

（一）修改预订的流程（Reservation Alternation Flow）

预订客人在实际抵店前，因种种原因可能对其原有预订进行修改，预订员应耐心、高效地对客服务。当客人更改预订后，预订员要根据客人更改的情况进行登记，并做好交接。具体工作流程如表 2-1 所示：

Before the actual arrival of the guest, the original reservation may be altered for various types of reasons. The reservationist should offer patient and highly effectively service to the guest. In case of reservation alternation by the guest, the reservationist should make record in accordance with the alternation of the guest and make proper work handover. The specific work flow is as follows Table 2-1:

表 2-1　更改预订程序

Table 2-1　Reservation Alternation Procedure

程序 Procedure	标准 Standard
1. 接收信息 Receive information	（1）当客人需要更改预订时，找出原预订单后，应先查核如下内容： In case of reservation alternation by the guest, retrieve the original reservation form and first check the following information: 客人姓名（Name of guest）； 原预订期限（Original reservation period）； 原预订房类、房价及房数（Original room type, room rate and number of rooms）； 原预订人情况（Information about the original reserving personnel）。 （2）询问客人想要更改的日期、房数或其他要求。 Enquire the guest the date, number of rooms and other requirements to be altered.
2. 确认更改 Confirm alternation	（1）在确认客人新的订房要求前，首先要查询客房预订状态。 First enquire the reservation status of the rooms before confirming the new reservation request of the guest. （2）在有房间可销售的情况下，为客人确认更改预订，并重新填写预订单。 Confirm the reservation alternation if rooms are available, refill the reservation sheet. （3）记录预订更改人的姓名、联系电话及以何种方式更改。 Record the name, contact number and alternation method of the personnel making the alternation. （4）将更改信息输入电脑。 Input related information to the computer.
3. 注明存档 Indicate alternation and archive	（1）在原预订单上注明"更改"字样。 Note "Altered" on the original reservations sheet. （2）按日期存档。 Archive on date basis.
4. 更改处理 Handle the alternation	（1）如果客人需要更改的日期，酒店已无客房可销售，应及时向客人做好解释。 In case that no rooms are available on the date to be altered by the guest; appropriate explanation should be made timely to the guest. （2）告知客人预订暂时放在候补名单上。 Inform that the reservation of the guest is temporarily included in to the waiting list. （3）如果酒店有空房时，及时与客人联系。 Contact the guests timely if vacant rooms are available.
5. 善后工作 Follow-up work	（1）感谢客人及时通知。 Express appreciation to the guest for timely notice. （2）感谢客人的理解与支持（未确认时）。 Express appreciation to the guest for his/her understanding and support (if alternation is not confirmed).

（二）预订变更的规定（Reservation Alternation Provisions）

每家酒店都会根据自身情况和市场行情，结合客人的需求，对于需要变更的情况，进行限定。例如，某酒店对预订变更的规定如下：

Each hotel would set restrictions on alternations according to its own conditions and market trends and based on the demands of the guests. For example, a hotel has stipulated the reservation alternation as follows:

（1）旅行社变更预订减少的房数允许不超过该团预订房数的 15%，或当日预订总房数的 10%，特约客户单位变更预订减少的房数允许不超过当日预订房数的 15%，否则，应比照上述取消预订的规定承担超过部分的预订房费用。针对散客预订变更的规定，根据酒店客房入住情况来对散客的需求予以变更或取消预订。

The number of rooms to be reduced in reservation alternation by the travel agency should not exceed 15% of the total number of reserved rooms by that travel agency or 10% of the total number of reserved rooms for that day. For contracted organizations, the number of rooms to be reduced in reservation alternation should not exceed 15% of the total number of reserved rooms for that day. Or, the room rates for the exceeding part should be assumed according to the above mentioned provisions on reservation cancellation. As for provisions on reservation alternation by the individual guests, such reservation may be altered or cancelled according to the occupancy conditions of the hotel rooms.

（2）变更减少预付房款或以信用担保的预订，所有单位或个人均须按预订房总房费全额承担费用。

For prepayment reduced by alternation or credit guaranteed reservation, all units or individuals must assume the costs to the total room rates of the reservation.

二、取消预订（Reservation Cancellation）

（一）取消预订的流程（Reservation Cancellation Flow）

预订客人在实际抵店前，因种种原因可能对其原有预订进行取消，预订员也要耐心、高效地对客服务。取消预订后，酒店预订员的具体工作流程如表 2-2 所示：

Before the actual arrival of the guest, the original reservation may be cancelled for various types of reasons. The reservationist should also offer patient and highly effectively service to the guest.The specific work flow for hotel reservationist after the reservation cancellation is listed as follows Table 2-2:

表 2-2 取消预订程序

Table 2-2 Reservation Cancellation Procedure

程序 Procedure	标准 Standard
1. 接收信息 Receive information	（1）询问要求取消预订人的姓名、预订期限、房类并与档案柜中原预订单进行核对。 Enquire the name, reservation period, room type from the personnel requesting the cancellation and compared with the original reservation sheet in the file cabinet. （2）询问并记录取消预订人的姓名、联系电话、取消日期、取消方式及原因。 Enquire and record the name, contact number, date of cancellation, cancellation method and reason from the personnel requesting the cancellation. （3）告知客人取消预订可能会产生的费用，如果是预付款或者是信用卡预订，还应告知客人酒店将怎样退款或做出预付授权。 Inform the guest the possible expenses arising from the reservation cancellation. In case of prepayment or reservation by credit card, the guest should also be informed how to refund or make pre-authorization.

续表

程序 Procedure	标准 Standard
2. 确认取消 Confirm the cancellation	复述以上三项内容以得到取消人的认可。 Repeat the above mentioned three items and obtain confirmation for the personnel requesting the cancellation.
3. 处理取消 Handle the cancellation	（1）感谢订房人将取消预订要求及时通知酒店。 Express the personnel making the reservation to timely inform the hotel the cancellation of the reservation. （2）询问客人是否需要做下一个阶段的预订。 Enquire the guest whether the next stage reservation is required. （3）在原预订单上写明"取消"字样，并在上面记录取消预订人的姓名、联系电话、取消日期、取消方式及原因。 Mark "Cancellation" on the original reservation sheet and indicate the name, reservation period, room type from the personnel requesting the cancellation. （4）将预订取消的信息输入电脑。 Input the related information on reservation cancellation into the computer.
4. 做好存档 Archive	按入住日期，将取消单进行存档。 Archive the cancellation sheet according to the stay period.

（二）取消预订的规定（Reservation Cancellation Provisions）

一般而言，针对不同类型的客人，如果住客取消预订，则根据不同情况采取不同的标准收取房费，例如某酒店的规定如下：

Generally, room rates would be charged according to different conditions as the case may be for different types of guests in case of reservation cancellation. For example, the provisions of one hotel are as follows:

（1）旅游团队：于确认入住日平季提前 3 天、旺季提前 7 天以上取消预订的，可不承担房费，但已交订定金的，不退返订金；于确认入住日前平季 3 天、旺季 7 天内取消预订的，承担 50%的房费；确认入住当日取消预订的，承担 100%的房费。

Tourist Group: Should reservation cancellation is made three (3) days in advance in shoulder seasons or seven (7) days in advance in peak seasons before the expected date of arrival, the guest may assume no room rates. However, the prepayment that has been paid, if any, will not be returned. Should reservation cancellation is made within three (3) days in shoulder seasons or seven (7) days in peak seasons before the expected date of arrival, the guest should assume 50% of the room rates. Should reservation cancellation is made on the expected date of arrival; the guest may assume 100% of the room rates.

（2）会议团队：于确认入住日提前 3 天以上取消预订的，酒店不退还会议订金；于确认入住日前 3 天内取消预订的，承担 50%的房费；确认入住当日取消预订的，承担 100%的房费。

Conference Group: Should reservation cancellation is made more than three (3) days in advance before the expected date of arrival, the prepayment for the conference that has been paid, if any, will not be returned. Should reservation cancellation is made within three (3) days in advance before the expected date of arrival; the guest should assume 50% of the room rates. Should reservation cancellation is made on the expected date of arrival; the guest may assume 100% of the room rates.

（3）特约客户单位的散团：于确认入住日提前 1 天以上取消预订的，可不承担房费，但已交付订金的，不退返订金；确认入住当日取消预订的，承担 100%的房费。

Retail Group of Contracted Guest Organization: Should reservation cancellation is made more than one (1) days in advance before the expected date of arrival, the guest may assume no room rates. However, the prepayment that has been paid, if any, will not be returned. Should reservation cancellation is made on the expected date of arrival; the guest may assume 100% of the room rates.

（4）黄金周、节假日、旺季、平季周末、大型会议和酒店重大活动期间以及某些特殊时期，在提前 10 天以上书面通知的情况下，酒店可实行预付房款或以信用担保的方式预订客房。取消预付房款或以信用担保的预订，所有单位或个人均须按预订房总房费全额承担费用。

For the Golden Week, festivals and holidays, peak seasons, weekends in shoulder seasons, large-sized conference, major hotel events as well as some special periods, the hotel may accept room reservation by means of prepayment or credit guarantee provided that a written notice should be made at least ten (10) days in advance. For prepayment so cancelled or credit guaranteed reservation, all units or individuals must assume the costs to the total room rates of the reservation.

（5）由于不可抗力原因造成的预订取消，订房单位可免责，但应及时以书面形式通知酒店，并提供不可抗力事件的证明。

The reserving unit may be exempted from related responsibilities for reservation cancelled caused by force majeure. However, such unit should timely inform the hotel in written form and provide proof for such force majeure.

【实训与评价】【Training and Assessment】

［实训目的］［Training Goals］

学生能处理客人变更与取消客房预订的需求，能够准确地回答客人的要求，遵循酒店政策规范，能计算超额预订量。

The students are capable to dispose room reservation alternation and cancellation requests from the guests; accurately respond the demands of the guests; follow the policies and norms of the hotel and calculate the amount of overbooking.

［实训准备］［Training Preparation］

预订单、预订预报表、房况表。

Reservation Sheet, Reservation Forecast Sheet, Room Status Sheet.

［实训方法］［Training Method］

小组合作法、任务驱动法、讲授法、引导法。

Group Collaboration Method, Task-driven Method, Expository Method, Guidance Method.

［实训内容］［Training Content］

1. 由教师扮演预订员，请一位学生扮演订房客人，展示一段客人变更和取消预订的情境过程。

A teacher acts as the reservationist and a student acts as the guest reserving the room to represent the scenario of reservation alternation and cancellation by the guest.

2. 学生分析和制定出一套客人预订客房变更和取消的工作程序。

The students analyze and formulate a working procedure for reservation alternation and cancellation by the guest.

3. 由教师扮演预订员，请一位学生来扮演订房客人，展示一段酒店总台处理由于超额预订造成客到无房的情境过程。

A teacher acts as the reservationist and a student acts as the guest reserving the room to represent the scenario that no room is available for the arrived guest due to overbooking.

4. 学生分析和制定出一套客到无房的服务工作程序。

The students analyze and formulate a working procedure for the scenario that no room is available for the arrived guest.

5. 教师评价。

The teacher makes the comments.

[实训步骤] [Training Procedure]

1. 由学生两人一组，进行客人预订客房变更和取消项目模拟练习。

The students work in pairs to make simulation practice on reservation alternation and cancellation by the guest.

要求：预订员应注意眼神、微笑、说话的语气、言辞的礼貌性。

Requirements: The reservationist should pay attention to the eye contact, smile, tone and the politeness of the wordage.

(1) 学生两人一组，模仿教师范例，教师给出评判。

The students work in pairs and simulate the examples of the teachers. The teachers give judgments.

(2) 学生可以即兴发挥，老师和学生共同评价，老师给出分数。

The students are allowed to make extemporaneous play; the students and the teachers give comments together; the teachers give the scores.

(3) 学生提出问题，老师回答。

The students raise questions for the teachers to answer.

2. 由学生两人一组，进行由于超额预订造成客到无房项目模拟练习。

The students work in pairs to make simulation practice on the scenario that no room is available for the arrived guest due to overbooking.

要求：预订员应注意眼神、微笑、说话的语气、言辞的礼貌性。

Requirements: The reservationist should pay attention to the eye contact, smile, tone and the politeness of the wordage.

(1) 学生两人一组，模仿教师范例，教师给出评判。

The students work in pairs and simulate the examples of the teachers. The teachers give judgments.

(2) 学生可以即兴发挥，老师和学生共同评价，老师给出分数。

The students are allowed to make extemporaneous play; the students and the teachers give comments together; the teachers give the scores.

(3) 学生提出问题，老师回答。

The students raise questions for the teachers to answer.

3. 填写实训报告，实训结束。

Fill in the training report and end the training.

[实训评价] [Training Evaluation]

班级：
Class: 姓名：
Name: 总分：
Total Scores:

序号 No.	项目 Item	要求 Requirements	应得分 Full Marks	扣分 Deducted Marks	实得分 Actual Marks
1	仪容仪表 Appearance	(1) 按酒店要求，保持个人良好的仪表、仪容、仪态，着装校服，佩戴校卡。 Keep satisfying personal appearance, presence and bearing as required by the hotel; ware the school uniform and the school card.	5		

续表

序号 No.	项目 Item	要求 Requirements	应得分 Full Marks	扣分 Deducted Marks	实得分 Actual Marks
2	礼貌礼节 Politeness and Etiquette	(2) 以规范的仪容仪表迎接客人。 Receive the guest with normalized appearance.	5		
		(3) 行走、站姿正确，行为规范有礼。 The walking and standing gestures are correct, the behaviors are standard and polite.	5		
		(4) 对客人微笑、行注目礼。 Smile to the guest and salute with eyes.	5		
		(1) 礼貌用语的使用。 Use polite language.	5		
		(2) 服务态度热情，友好。 Be enthusiastic and friendly in service.	5		
3	操作程序 Operation Procedure	(1) 能明确客人有无预订。 Be able to clarify whether the guest has made reservation.	10		
		(2) 预订变更的程序是否标准。 Whether the alternation procedure is standard or not.	17		
		(3) 预订取消的程序是否标准。 Whether the cancellation procedure is standard or not.	17		
		(4) 酒店超额预订的程序是否合理。 Whether the overbooking procedure is standard or not.	17		
		(5) 小组合作是否融洽。 Whether the group work is coordinative.	9		
备注 Remarks		每一组内容不能重复。 The contents of each group should not be repeated.			

任务四　预订失约行为及处理

Task Ⅳ　No-show and Disposal

【情境导入】【Scenario Introduction】

预订主管的困惑

Puzzle of A Reservation Supervisor

2014年“十一”黄金周又要来了，这些天金茂三亚亚龙湾希尔顿大酒店预订处的电话响个不停。到这天为止，酒店的客房已经全部被预订完，可是还有很多客户来电要求订房。预订处的主管小王很纠结，对于这些预订到底要不要接受呢？他陷入两难。

The National Day Golden Week of 2014 was approaching. These days, the telephone at the Reservation Desk of Hilton Sanya Resort & Spa in Yalong Bay was quite busy. Up to this day, all the guest rooms of the hotel had been reserved. However, there're still many guests calling for reservation. Wang, Supervisor of the Reservation Desk was quite entangled: Should such reservations be accepted. It was a dilemma for him.

【请你分析】【Please Analysis】

你能帮小王解决他的难题吗？

Make an analysis. Can you help Wang out?

【情境分析】【Scenario Analysis】

此情景中出现的情况为超额预订，针对这一问题，小王应根据本酒店过去黄金周预订情况，对2014年黄金周入住情况做出预判，根据实际情况，合理地确定超额订房的数量或幅度，既能最大限度地销售客房，增加经济效益，又能满足宾客的订房需求而不产生订房纠纷。同时，确保与相邻酒店随时沟通，对于超额预订的客人，如果到酒店后没有客房，及时将其送往和本酒店同级别或高于本酒店级别的酒店，确保客人能够顺利入住。

The Scenario in this scenario is overbooking. For this problem, Wang should make a pre-judgment on the occupancy of the upcoming Golden Week according on reservation in previous Golden Weeks and rationally determine the amount or extent of overbooking so as to sell the rooms to the greatest extent to increase economic benefits while avoiding reservation dispute by satisfying the reservation requests of the guests. Meanwhile, make sure to keep close communication with neighboring hotels. If a guest arrives with no room available due to overbooking, the hotel should timely send him to a hotel of same or higher level of this hotel to ensure that the guest may make the stay smoothly.

一、超额预订与缺额预订（Over-booking and Under-booking）

（一）超额预订（Over-booking）

酒店的主要商品便是“客房”，酒店为了提供良好的服务，应制定出有关订房程序。虽然客人已缴付订金，但有时客人到达酒店时，酒店却不能供应住宿，这往往是因为超额订房的原因，通常这种情形会令我们的客人非常恼怒，他也许会毫不留情地谩骂向他解释不能给他房间的酒店的工作人员，有些客人更会把那工作人员的姓名记下，并恫吓要向酒店的管理阶层投诉服务员，而作为前台的接待员，当然知道不能给客人房间是因为已经超额订房，所以，处理超额订房是一项极富技巧的工作，必须有经验和足够的耐心。

Rooms are the main commodities of the hotel. To provide satisfying services, the hotel should formulate related reservation procedures. If a room is not available for the arriving guest who has paid prepayment, the scenario is commonly caused by over-booking. Generally, the guest would be quite annoyed. Probably he would scold the working staff explaining that no room is available without mercy. Some guests may even note down the name of the staff and threaten to complain about the attitude of the staff to the hotel management. As the receptionist of the Front Desk, certainly he/she cannot disclose to the guest that such unavailability is caused by over-booking. Therefore, disposal of over-booking is a quite tactful task with requiring experience and determined patience.

1. 超额预订的概念（Concept of Over-booking）

超额预订是指酒店在预订已满的情况下，再适度增加预订的数量，以弥补少数宾客临时取消预订而出现的客房闲置，其目的是充分利用酒店客房，提高开房率。做好超额预订的关键在于掌握有效的超额预订数量和幅度，避免或最大限度地降低因失误而造成的麻烦。按国际酒店的管理经验，超额预订的百分比可控制在5%~20%，超额预订的决策不仅依据管理者的个人经验，而且应来自对市场的预测以及对顾客情况的正确分析。长期以来，由于酒店的管理者关心较多的是如何扩大销售量，为此，各种各样的营销方法应运而生，这当然无可厚非，但另一个问题就往往被忽略了，酒店业是以向客人提供优质服务为营利前提的，即对服务质量不能置之不理。

Over-booking refers to the conduct of the hotel of appropriately increasing the reservation amount after the rooms are fully reserved so as to compensate vacant rooms caused by temporary reservation cancellation by a few guests. It aims to fully utilize the hotel rooms and increase the occupancy rate. The key of over-booking is to master effective amount and extent of over-booking to eliminate or reduce the troubles caused by faults to the greatest extent. According to the management experience of international hotels, the ratio of over-booking may be controlled within 5%-20%. Decision-making of over-booking depends not only on the personal experience of the managerial personnel but also on the correct prediction on the market and analysis on the guest conditions. For quite some time, the management of the hotel concerns more about how to increase the sales. Therefore, various types of marketing techniques have been established. This is understandable. However, another problem has been omitted, hospitality has the premise of profit making by providing high quality service to the guest, in other words, the service quality cannot be overlooked.

2. 影响超额预订的因素（Influential Factors on Over-booking）

影响超额预订的因素有许多，这些因素在各个酒店的状态不一样，其超订率也应不同。关于超额订房的影响因素主要涉及掌握好团队订房与散客订房的比例、淡旺季的差别、预订类别的比例、本地区有无其他同等级同类型的酒店、酒店在市场上的信誉程度等，具体的影响因素如下：

There're many influential factors on over-booking. As the conditions of such factors in different hotels are varying, the over-booking rates should also be different. Influential factors on over-booking mainly involve the ratio of group guest reservation and individual guest reservation, difference in shoulder and peak season, proportions of reservation types, existence of hotels of the same level in the locality, reputation of the hotel in the market, etc. The specific influential factors are:

（1）时间的影响：出租率在不同的年份和月份是不一样的。

Time: Occupancy rate of a hotel varies in different years and months.

（2）酒店类型的影响：一般来说，连锁店凭借完善的统一预订系统和庞大的分店数量，可以适当提高超订率以提高利润；独立经营的酒店则只能保守一点。

Hotel Type: Generally, with consummated uniform reservation system and huge number of branches, chain hotels may increase the over-booking rate appropriately to enhance the profits; while the independently operated hotel can only be more conservative.

（3）预订形式的影响：酒店通常采用三种预订方式：临时性预订、确认性预订和保证性预订。临时性预订的客人如在当天"取消预订时限"（6:00p.m.）还没到达酒店，该预订即被取消，故超额预订的弹性也大。确认性预订有充分的时间给以书面确认，向他们收取欠款的风险较小，同时酒店在违约时的责任也相对较大，故超额预订的弹性就小。保证性预订确保酒店在出现预订宾客不来入住的情况下仍有客房收益，因此，对待保证性预订的那些房间，酒店不应该再超额预订。相反，酒店应保留比预订数量稍多的空房间以确保这种预订的宾客来到时有房可住，这可称为"减额预订"。

Reservation Form: Generally, three reservation forms are applied by the hotel: Temporary reservation, confirmed reservation and guaranteed reservation. For guests of temporary reservation, of the guest fails to arrive in the hotel after the "Deadline for reservation cancellation" (6:00p.m.), the reservation should be cancelled. Therefore, there's great flexibility for over-booking. For confirmed reservation, there's sufficient time to make written confirmation. Therefore, the risk to collect the arrearage is relatively small. Meanwhile, the responsibility of the hotel in case of fault is relatively great. To this end, there's small flexibility for over-booking. In case of guaranteed reservation, the room earnings are guaranteed even if the guest fails to check in. Therefore, the hotel should not make over-booking on rooms under guaranteed reservation. Instead, the hotel should reserve slightly more vacant rooms than the reserved rooms to guarantee that rooms are available when the guests arrive, which may be called "under-booking".

（4）宾客类型：团体预订房间，如果团体不在抵达前的某一合适时间确认所留的全部房间，多数酒店会将预留房取消，但是散客预订通常可以将预订和确订同步进行。很显然，他们的超订率亦不会相同。

Guest Type: For rooms under group reservation, if the group fails to confirm all the reserved rooms at a proper time before the arrival, most of the hotels would cancel such rooms. However, for reservation by individual guest, the reservation and confirmation may be made simultaneously. Obviously, their over-booking rates are different.

（5）天气情况：恶劣的天气常造成航班被取消、渡轮停驶，如这种天气出现在预订到达当天，那么"已经预订的客人到期不出现率"（以下简称"不出现率"）肯定会大幅提高，对天气情况的预测便成为超订率制定的重要依据。

Weather Conditions: Severe weathers would often cancel the flights and ferries. If such severe weather occurs on the very day of expected arrival, the "no-show rate of reserved guest" (hereinafter referred to as the "no-show rate") would rise remarkably. Therefore, prediction on the weather conditions is an important basis for hotel to determine the over-booking rate.

（6）突发性事件：倘若在客人的预订到达期前两三天，其所在地发生不利的突发性事件，肯定会影响客人的行程。但往往由于事发突然，客人来不及取消。对酒店来说，适当增加到达当天的预订量，无疑是明智的。

Unexpected Event: On condition that an unexpected event breaks out in the locality of the guest two or three days before the expected arrival, the journey of the guest would be definitely affected. As the event is emergent and unpredictable, the guests are often unavailable to cancel the reservation. For the hotel, it is obviously prudent to appropriately increase the reservation amount of the expected arrival date.

3. 超额预订计算（Calculation on Over-booking）

超额预订数一般要受预订取消率、预订未到率、提前退房率以及延期住店率等因素的影响。常见的公式有：

The amount of over-booking is generally affected by factors such as reservation cancellation rate, no-show rate, early check-out rate and late check-out rate. Common formula:

超额预订数 = 临时取消预订房数 + 预订而未到数 + 提前退房数 − 延期住店房数 =（应接受预订数 × 预订取消率）+（应接受预订数 × 预订未到率）+（续住房数 × 提前退房率）−（预期离店数 × 延期住店率）

Over-booking amount = number of temporarily cancelled rooms + number of no-show rooms + number of early check-out rooms − number of later check-out rooms = (designed number of reserved rooms × reservation cancellation rate) + (designed number of reserved rooms × no-show rate) + (number of renewed rooms × early check-out rate) − (expected number of check-out rooms × late check-out rate)

假设：超额预订数为 X，酒店客房总数为 A，续住房数为 C，预期离店房数为 D，预订取消率为 r1，预订未到率为 r2，提前退房率为 f1，延期住店率为 f2，则：

Assume that: The over-booking amount is X; the total number of hotel rooms is A; the number of renewed rooms is C; the expected number of check-out rooms is D; the reservation cancellation rate is r1; the no-show rate is r2; the early check-out rate is f1 and the late check-out rate is f2; then:

$$X = (A - C + X) \times r1 + (A - C + X) \times r2 + C \times f1 - D \times f2$$

$X = (A - C + X) \times r1 + (A - C + X) \times r2 + C \times f1 - D \times f2$

$= [C \times f1 - D \times f2 + (A - C) \times (r1 + r2)] / [1 - (r1 + r2)]$

假设：超额预订率为R，则：

$R = [X/(A - C)] \times 100\%$

Assume that: The over-booking rate is R, then:

$R = [X/(A - C)] \times 100\%$

在公式中可以发现每一个决定超额预订数的因素都有预计的字样，要想计算准确，首先要保证对各项指标的预测准确。要解决这一问题的最好方法是建立一种准确的预测模型，通过该模型可以准确预测出最佳超额预订数。目前国际上流行的酒店收益管理系统，都提供了强大的预测功能和专门的超额预订模型。

According to the formula, each factor deciding the over-booking amount is based on estimation. Therefore, to accurately make the calculation, first guarantee should be made on accurate estimation of each indicator. To solve this problem, the best method is to establish an accurate prediction model to accurate estimate the optimal over-booking amount.Presently, all the prevailing revenue management system for hotels in the world is providing powerful prediction functions and special over-booking models.

例：某酒店有可供出租客房（A）400间。在3月18日这天：有续住房（C）200间，预期离店房（D）有150间，该酒店预订取消率（r1）为8%，预订未到率（r2）为7%，提前退房率（f1）为5%，延期住店率（f2）为4%，求该酒店3月18日的：①超额预订房数；②预订房数；③超额预订率。

e.g.: The number of available rooms (A) for a hotel is 400; on March 18: The number of renewed rooms (C) is 200; the number of late check-out rooms (D) is 150; the reservation cancellation rate (r1) is 8%; the no-show rate (r2) is 7%; the early check-out rate (f1) is 5% and late check-out rate (f2) is 4%. Then please work out the following indicators of the hotel on March 18: ①Number of over-booking rooms; ②number of reserved rooms; ③over-booking rate.

解：根据公式 $X = [C \times f1 - D \times f2 + (A - C) \times (r1 + r2)] / [1 - (r1 + r2)]$，可得：

Solution: According to formula $X = [C \times f1 - D \times f2 + (A - C) \times (r1 + r2)] / [1 - (r1 + r2)]$:

①该酒店超额预订房数 $= [(200 \times 5\%) - (150 \times 4\%) + (400 - 200) \times (8\% + 7\%)] / [1 - (8\% + 7\%)]$

Number of over-booking rooms $= [(200 \times 5\%) - (150 \times 4\%) + (400 - 200) \times (8\% + 7\%)] / [1 - (8\% + 7\%)] = [(10 - 6 + 30)] / 0.85 = 40$

②该酒店预订房数 $= 200 + 40 = 240$

Number of reserved rooms $= 200 + 40 = 240$

③该酒店超额预订率 $R = [40/(400 - 200)] \times 100\% = 20\%$

Over-booking rate $R = [40/(400 - 200)] \times 100\% = 20\%$

答：3月18日这天，该酒店应该接受40间超额预订房，超额预订率最佳为20%，总共应接受的预订房数为240间。

Answer: On March 18, the hotel should accept 40 over-booking rooms; the optimal over-booking rate is 20%; and the total number of reserved rooms to be accepted is 240.

总之，通过以上分析，酒店可根据实际情况，合理地确定超额订房的数量或幅度，既能最大限度地销售客房，增加经济效益，又能满足宾客的订房需求而不产生订房纠纷。若要达到预期效果，酒店必须注重资料的收集、数据的统计工作，并在日常工作中不断地总结和积累经验。

To sum up, based on the above mentioned analysis, the hotel may rationally determine the amount or extent of overbooking so as to sell the rooms to the greatest extent to increase economic benefits while avoiding reservation dispute by satisfying the reservation requests of the guests according to the actual conditions of the hotel.To achieve anticipated results, the hotel must attach importance to the collection of information and statistical work on data, and summarize and accumulate experiences in daily work continuously.

【情境导入】【Scenario Introduction】

预订的客房没有了
Reserved Room Gone

李先生携新婚妻子要到三亚度蜜月，并为此早做了安排，于半年前在三亚亚龙湾海景国际度假酒店订了一套蜜月套房。李先生和他妻子在与酒店约定的日期到酒店办理入住手续，接待员查看后，发现他所预订的套房住着一位一周前抵店而延期离店的王先生。李先生一听在半年前预订的房间居然落空，情绪激动，在前台大闹。接待员请来经理，经理了解情况后，立即将李先生请入办公室，递上饮料和毛巾。对酒店的抵店准备工作的疏忽向李先生表示深深的歉意。补救方法是以原房间对折的价格另准备一间更高档次的豪华套房作为李先生的蜜月套房，并且赠送李先生一餐烛光晚餐以表示歉意。李先生勉强接受了酒店的安排。

Mr. Li planned to go on a honeymoon with his newly married wife in Sanya and had made arrangement in advance. He had reserved a honeymoon suite in Holiday Inn Resort Sanya Yalong Bay half a year ago. Mr. Li and his wife arrived at the hotel for check-in on the date as agreed with the hotel. The receptionist checked and found that the room he reserved is now being occupied by Mr. Wang who checked in one week ago and had extended his check-out time. On hearing that the room reserved half a year ago is not available, Mr. Li got raged and made a scene at the Front Desk. The receptionist called the Manager. Upon knowing the circumstance, the Manager immediately guided Mr. Li into the office and served him with drink and towel. The Manager expressed his deep sorry on the omission in arrival preparation by the hotel. The remedy was that the hotel offered a higher level luxury suite as the honeymoon suite for Mr. Li at the half price of the original room as well as a candlelight dinner for free as compensation. Mr. Li accepted the arrangement of the hotel reluctantly.

【请你分析】【Please Analysis】

出现该情况的原因是什么？如何避免此类情况的发生？

What's the cause of such circumstance? How to avoid such circumstance?

【案例小结】【Case Analysis】

这个事件的原因在于接待员在一周前排房时未注意一周后的房间预订情况，或者注意了，但未考虑到客人的延期住店问题。而且在前一天也未及时发现客人的延期离店所引发的问题，若发现，可以在客人要求延期离店时要求客人换房，或者提前想好应变之策。所以接待员需要对一个月后、一周后及一天后的订房情况做仔细的检查，以防万一。

The root of the accident is that the reception fails to pay attention to the room reservation conditions of the following week when arrange rooms one week before; or he fails to consider the possible late check-out of the guest even if he has noticed that reservation. In addition, the receptionist also fails to detect the problem arising from late check-out one day ago. Or, the receptionist may require the guest to shift to another room or prepare countermeasures in advance. Therefore, the receptionist should make detailed inspection on the room reservation status in one month, one week and one day just in case.

（二）缺额预订（Under-booking）

缺额预订是指客房预订的某一时段，酒店所接受的预订数量少于酒店可供房数。如果酒店经常出现缺额预订，会对酒店的经济效益产生颇大影响，在现实经营过程中，酒店很少采用这种经营方式。因此，为了摆脱缺额预订的情况，酒店应拓展客房预订渠道，健全预订程序及方便客人进行预订。

Under-booking refers to the conduct of the company that the number of rooms accepted for reservation is less than the number of available rooms of the hotel. Frequent under-booking would greatly affect the economic benefits of the hotel. Therefore, hotels seldom apply such operation method in the process of actual operation. Therefore, to get rid of the under-booking conditions, the hotel should expand the room reservation channels, consummate the reservation procedures and facilitate the guests to make reservation.

二、预订失约行为的分析（Analysis on No-show Behavior）

（一）产生预订失约的原因（Causes for No-show of Reservation）

（1）酒店未能正确掌握可出租房的数量。

The hotel fails to accurate master the number of available rooms.

主要表现为：与前台分房组、营销部的沟通不良；与预订中心系统及订房代理处的沟通不良；客房状态的显示不正确等。

Major Expression: Poor communication with the Room Allocation Group of the Front Desk and the Marketing Department; poor communication with the Central Reservation System and the room reservation agencies; incorrect room status indication; etc.

（2）记录、储存的预订资料出现差错。

Errors in records and the reservation data storage.

具体有：日期错误；姓名拼写错误；遗漏；存档的顺序错误；变更及取消的处理不当等。

To be specific: Data error; name spelling error; omission; error in archiving sequence; improper disposal on alternation and cancellation.

（3）预订员对房价的变更及有关销售政策缺乏了解。

The reservationist lacks of understanding on the room rate alternation and related sales policies.

（4）未能真正领会客人的预订要求。

The reservationist fails to truly understand the reservation requirements of the guest.

主要原因有：因疏忽、遗忘而未能最终落实客房；对行业术语的理解不一致及业务素质不高而造成的失误。

Main Causes: The guest room is not put into place due to omission and forgetting; faults are made due to inconsistent in understanding of industry-specific terminologies and low business skills.

（5）未能精确统计信息数据及实施超额预订过度。

Failure to make accurate statistics on information data and implementation of excessive over-booking.

表现为：过高估计了预订未到宾客的房间数；过高估计了临时取消预订的房间数；过高估计了提前离店宾客的房间数；过低估计了延期离店宾客的用房数等。

Expression：Overestimation on no -show rooms；overestimation on temporarily cancelled rooms；overestimation on early check-out rooms；underestimation on late check-out rooms；etc.

（二）预订失约行为的处理（Disposal on No-show Behavior）

1. 做好预防准备（Making Proper Prevention and Preparation）

（1）应知道转移客人（Overboarding）去住宿别的酒店是最后的选择，因为这对客人和酒店本身都是非常不好的。

Bear in mind that overboarding to other hotel is the last choice，which is quite adverse to the guest and the hotel itself.

（2）查看当天来客表，试看客人中是否有拼住（Double Up）的可能，如家庭、同游者和互相认识的客人，本是预订多间客房，但当他们登记时，希望争取他们住同一个房间，以减少占住客房。

Check the guest arrival record of the day to try the possibility of Double Up，for example：Families，travel companions and guests knowing each other who have reserved several rooms but expressed the willingness to double up into one room to reduce the number of room required.

（3）联络订房的单位，询问客人到达时间，并解释订房的规定是：如客人未通知店方其到达时间，订房将在下午6时自动取消，提醒订房单位须预缴订金以便保留房间。

Contact the unit reserving the room and enquire the estimated time of arrival of the guest；explain the room reservation provisions：If the guest fails to notice the hotel the arrival time and reservation will be cancelled automatically at 6 p.m. Remind the reserving unit to make prepayment to secure the room.

（4）了解附近同级酒店是否有空房，如有需要则代为预订所需房数。

Get to know whether there're vacant rooms available in nearby hotels of the same level. If any，reserve the rooms required on behalf of the guest.

（5）查看当天来客表，将一些容易接受转移往别的酒店去的客人标注出来。如：自付房费的客人或并非本酒店的常住客人等。

Check the guest arrival record of the day and mark the guests likely to be persuaded to move to another hotel. For example：Self-pay guests，those who are not permanent guests of the hotel，etc.

2. 预订失约行为的处理办法（Disposal on No-show Behavior）

（1）诚恳地向客人道歉，解释原因，请求客人谅解。

Apologize sincerely to the guest；explain the causes and ask the guest to understand.

（2）在酒店客房允许的情况下，视情况给予客人免费升级待遇；如条件不允许，应立即与另一家同等级酒店联系，请求援助。同时，派车免费将客人送往这家酒店。如果找不到相同等级的酒店，可安排客人住在另一家稍高的酒店，高出房费由酒店支付。

Where conditions allow，upgrade to a higher level room for free；if not，contact another hotel of the same level for assistance. Meanwhile，assign a car to take the guest to such hotel for free. If there's no hotel of the same level available，the hotel may arrange the guest to reside in a slightly higher level hotel. And the excessive room fees should be assumed by the hotel.

（3）免费提供交通工具和第一夜房费。

Provide free transportation and the room fees for the first night.

（4）免费提供一至两次的长途电话费或传真费，以使客人能将临时改变住处的信息告知有关方面。

Provide toll-free charges or free fax charges for one or two times so enable the guest to inform the temporary change of residence to related sides.

（5）临时保留客人有关信息，便于为客人提供邮件及查询服务。

Keep related information for the guests temporarily so as to provide mail and inquiry services for the guests.

（6）征得客人同意，并做好搬回酒店的接待工作，如大堂副理或客务经理出面迎接客人或在客房内放致歉信，赠送鲜花和水果等。

Upon the consent of the guest, make proper reception when the guest moves back to the hotel, for example, welcoming the guest by AM or Guest Services Manager, placing an apologizing letter in the guest room, free flowers and fruits, etc.

（7）向预订委托人致歉。

Apologize to the reservation assignee.

（8）向提供援助的酒店致谢。

Express appreciation to the hotel giving the assistance.

（三）预订失约行为的控制方法（Control Method on Reservation No-show）

（1）完善预订各项政策，健全预订程序及其标准。

Consummate various policies for reservation, consummate the reservation procedures and the standards thereof.

（2）建立与接待处等沟通的制度。

Establish system to communication with the Reception Department.

（3）加强与预订中心、预订代理处的沟通。

Enhance communication with the Reservation Center and Reservation Agency.

（4）注重培训、督导预订员，加强其责任心，提高其预订业务素质。

Attach importance in training, supervision on the reservationist, enhance the sense of responsibility of the reservationist and enhance the reservation service level of the reservationist.

（5）由专人负责将预订信息按要求输入计算机或标注客房预订汇总表。

Assign specific personnel to be responsible to input the reservation information into the computer or mark on the reservation summary table.

（6）注意预订细节。

Pay attention to reservation details.

（7）加强预订工作的检查，避免出现差错、遗漏。

Enhance inspection on reservation; avoid mistakes and omissions.

（8）合理配置部门人力资源，做到人尽其用。

Make rational allocation on the human resources of the department; exert the potentials of the staff.

知识链接：“No Show”简介
Knowledge Link: Introduction to No Show

客房服务是不可存储的，然而我们可以这样设想：把酒店的超额预订比喻为仓库中的存货，那问题就可归结为酒店如何确定存储的数量（相当于超订数量），以把因缺货（相当于出现“No Show”）造成的损失降到最低。这类问题我们可运用存储论方法加以解决。

Room service cannot be stored. However, we may image it like this: If over-booking of the hotel is compared to the stock in the warehouse, the problem may be interpreted into how the hotel can determine the amount in stock (equivalent to over-booking amount) so as to reduce the loss of out of stock (equivalent to No Show) to the greatest extent. Such problems may be solved by the Inventory Theory.

团队“No Show”与旅行社有直接关系，可以做如下预防：①要求旅行社在团队抵达前 15 天给酒店发接待计划，计划逾期未到，视为该团预订自动取消。②团队抵达前 5~7 天应与旅行社再确认核对预订。③团队抵达当日，销售人员应随时掌握团队的 Check In 情况，并及时与旅行社联系，询问未到团队及人数的动向。④在旺季，尤其是中国长假期间，对国内旅行团队的预订，要求旅行社缴纳足额订金，以防虚占客房。⑤对 No Show 情况登记和分析，划出旅行社预订信誉等级，以使今后接受预订时掌握主动。

The No Show of the group bears direct relationship with the travel agency. The following preventive measures may be taken: ① The travel agency is required to send the reception plan to the hotel at least 15 days before the arrival of the group. If the travel agency fails to send the reception plant within the time limit, the group reservation should be deemed to be cancelled automatically. ② The hotel should confirm and check the reservation 5-7 days before the arrival of the group. ③ On the arrival date of the group, the sales person should pay close attention to the check-in conditions of the team and timely contact with the travel agency to enquire the dynamics of the group not arrived and the number of guests. ④ In peak seasons, especially the long holiday stipulated by the state laws, for reservation for domestic tourism group, the travel agencies should be required to pay up the down payment to prevent unnecessary occupation of guest rooms. ⑤ Make registration and analysis on “No Show” and rank the reservation credit of the travel agencies to have the initiative in future reservation.

会议“No Show”与团队不同，主要出现在会议报到期间，一些会议由于会议主办方对会议规模和会议代表报到时间不能确切掌握，因而易出现部分预订不到。我们可以采取如下措施来预防：①会议预订必须签订协议。明确双方的权利、义务及违约责任，同时应按会议预订在酒店的消费额的 30%~50%收取订金。②会议入住前几日应该再确认预订。③会议报到当日 18:00 前再与会务组确认核实当日用房数，对确认后仍出现“No Show”的客房按当日全额房费收取赔偿费。④总结不同类型会议的规模和用房情况的特点，在接受会议预订时尽可能减少“水分”。

Different from group guests, conference “No Show” mainly occurs during the registration of the conference. For some conferences, the sponsor cannot get the exact information on the scale of the conference and the registration time of the delegates of the conference. Therefore, some of the guests would likely have rooms unavailable. The following measures may be taken: ① Conference agreement must be signed for conference reservation. The agreement must clearly stipulate the rights, obligations and liabilities for breach of contract. Meanwhile, a down payment of 30%-50% of the amount of consumption under such conference reservation should be charged. ②Confirm the reservation again several days before the conference. ③Confirm the room occupied before 18:00 on the registration date of the conference; for “No Show” rooms after confirmation, the full room fees should be charged as compensation. ④ Summarize the scales and room occupation features of different types of conferences; try to reduce the “exaggeration” as possible when accepting the conference reservation.

对散客“No Show”的可以采取以下措施：①接受预订时，必须了解相关信息，如预订人的姓名、联系方式、入住客人的姓名、联系方式、预计抵达时间等。②声明并坚持没有确切入住时间的预订只保留至当日 18:00，逾期不到视为自动取消。③视情况收取一定比例的订金。如在抵达当日才通知预订取消的，预付款应视为赔偿金来处理。④建立预订信誉等级，使预订信誉等级与订金款额挂钩。

The following measures may be taken for “No Show” of individual guests: ① When accepting the reservation, information such as name, contract information of the personnel making the reservation as well as the name, contact information and estimated arrival time of the guest must be obtained. ② Declare and persist that the reservation without exact check-in time will only be reserved till 18:00 of the same day, and the reservation will be cancelled automatically in case of "No Show" after 18:00. ③ Charge the down payment to a certain proportion as the case may be. If the cancellation notice is made on the arrival date, the down payment should be withheld as compensation. ④ Establish reservation credit ranking and proportionate the credit ranking with the amount of down payment.

【实训与评价】【Training and Assessment】

[实训目的] [Training Goals]

学生能处理客人变更与取消客房预订的需求，能够准确地回答客人的问询，遵循酒店政策规范，能计算超额预订量。

The students are capable to dispose room reservation alternation and cancellation requests from the guests; accurately respond the demands of the guests; follow the policies and norms of the hotel and calculate the amount of overbooking.

[实训准备] [Training Preparation]

预订单、预订预报表、房况表。

Reservation Sheet, Reservation Forecast Sheet, Room Status Sheet.

[实训方法] [Training Method]

小组合作法、任务驱动法、讲授法、引导法。

Group Collaboration Method, Task-driven Method, Expository Method, Guidance Method.

[实训内容] [Training Content]

1. 由教师扮演预订员，请一位学生来扮演订房客人，展示一段客人变更和取消预订的情境过程。

A teacher acts as the reservationist and a student acts as the guest reserving the room to represent the scenario of reservation alternation and cancellation by the guest.

2. 学生分析和制定出一套客人预订客房变更和取消的工作程序。

The students analyze and formulate a working procedure for reservation alternation and cancellation by the guest.

3. 由教师扮演预订员，请一位学生来扮演订房客人，展示一段酒店总台处理由于超额预订造成客到无房的情境过程。

A teacher acts as the reservationist and a student acts as the guest reserving the room to represent the scenario that no room is available for the arrived guest due to overbooking.

4. 学生分析和制定出一套客到无房的服务工作程序。

The students analyze and formulate a working procedure for the scenario that no room is available for the arrived guest.

5. 教师评价。

The teacher makes the assessment.

[实训步骤] [Training Procedure]

1. 由学生两人一组，进行客人预订客房变更和取消项目模拟练习。

The students work in pairs to make simulation practice on reservation alternation and cancellation by the guest.

要求：预订员应注意眼神、微笑、说话的语气、言辞的礼貌性。

Requirements: The reservationist should pay attention to the eye contact, smile, tone and the politeness of the wordage.

（1）学生两人一组，模仿教师范例，教师给出评判。

The students work in pairs and simulate the examples of the teachers. The teachers give judgments.

（2）学生可以即兴发挥，老师和学生共同评价，老师给出分数。

The students are allowed to make extemporaneous play; the students and the teachers give comments together; the teachers give the scores.

（3）学生提出问题，老师回答。

The students raise questions for the teachers to answer.

2. 由学生两人一组，进行由于超额预订造成客到无房项目模拟练习。

The students work in pairs to make simulation practice on the scenario that no room is available for the arrived guest due to overbooking.

要求：预订员应注意眼神、微笑、说话的语气、言辞的礼貌性。

Requirements: The reservationist should pay attention to the eye contact, smile, tone and the politeness of the wordage.

（1）学生两人一组，模仿教师范例，教师给出评判。

The students work in pairs and simulate the examples of the teachers. The teachers give judgments.

（2）学生可以即兴发挥，老师和学生共同评价，老师给出分数。

The students are allowed to make extemporaneous play; the students and the teachers give comments together; the teachers give the scores.

（3）学生提出问题，老师回答。

The students raise questions for the teachers to answer.

3. 填写实训报告，实训结束。

Fill in the training report and end the training.

［实训评价］［Training Evaluation］

班级：　　　　姓名：　　　　总分：
Class:　　　　Name:　　　　Total Scores:

序号 No.	项目 Item	要求 Requirements	应得分 Full Mark	扣分 Deducted Marks	实得分 Actual Marks
1	仪容仪表 Appearance	(1) 按酒店要求，保持个人良好的仪表、仪容、仪态，着装校服，佩戴校卡。 Keep satisfying personal appearance, presence and bearing as required by the hotel; ware the school uniform and the school card.	5		
		(2) 以规范的仪容仪表迎接客人。 Receive the guest with normalized appearance.	5		
		(3) 行走、站姿正确，行为规范有礼。 The walking and standing gestures are correct; the behaviors are standard and polite.	5		
		(4) 对客人微笑、行注目礼。 Smile to the guest and salute with eyes.	5		
2	礼貌礼节 Politeness and etiquette	(1) 礼貌用语的使用。 Use polite language.	5		
		(2) 服务态度热情，友好。 Be enthusiastic and friendly in service.	5		
3	操作程序 Operation Procedure	(1) 能明确客人有无预订。 Be able to clarify whether the guest has made reservation.	10		

续表

序号 No.	项目 Item	要求 Requirements	应得分 Full Mark	扣分 Deducted Marks	实得分 Actual Marks
		(2) 预订变更的程序是否标准。 Whether the alternation procedure is standard or not.	17		
		(3) 预订取消的程序是否标准。 Whether the cancellation procedure is standard or not.	17		
		(4) 酒店超额预订的程序是否合理。 Whether the overbooking procedure is standard or not.	17		
		(5) 小组合作是否融洽。 Whether the group work is coordinative.	9		
备注 Remarks		每一组内容不能重复。 The contents of each group should not be repeated.			

模块小结

Module Summary

1. 简述客房预订的概念。

Brief the concept of room reservation.

2. 简述预订的渠道及预订的方式。

Brief the channels and methods of reservation.

3. 预订员在处理电话订房时应注意哪些细节？

What details should be noticed when the reservationist handles telephone reservation?

4. 客房预订的类型有哪几种？各自的特点有哪些？

What types are room reservations? What are their features?

5. 何为预订失约？产生预订失约的原因有哪些？一旦出现此现象，该如何处理？

What is reservation "No Show"? What are the causes for no-show of reservation? What are the disposals in case of such circumstance?

附：客房预订合同

Attachment: Room Reservation Contract

甲方：____________

Party A: ____________

乙方：____________

Party B: ____________

为了更好地明确双方在合作当中的权利、义务关系，经双方友好协商，特订立本合同，以便共同遵守，进一步合作。

This contract is made by and between both Parties to better clarify the rights and obligations of both Parties in cooperation for mutual obedient and further cooperation.

一、合作方式（Cooperation Type）

乙方为甲方在网络平台上及机场提供宣传和客房预订服务，对于通过乙方提供的有效订房，甲方须向乙方支付相应的佣金。

Party B shall provide publicity and room reservation services on the network platforms for Party A and the airports; Party A shall pay corresponding commissions to Party B on effective room reservation provided by Party B.

二、合作有效期（Validation Period of Cooperation）

从________年________月________日至________年________月________日止。

From（YY/MM/DD）to（YY/MM/DD）.

三、房间及房价（酒店也可自附房价表及相关说明）[Room and Rate（The hotel may also enclose additional room rate sheet and explanations thereof）]

房间类型

Room Type

甲方门市价

Market Price of Party A

给乙方协议价

Negotiated Price to Party B

建议售价

Recommended Sales Price

四、订房确认（Reservation Confirmation）

乙方得到客人订房信息即通过传真告知甲方，甲方则根据当天入住率确认后传真通知乙方。甲方的确认传真号为：________；确认人为：________。

Upon obtaining the reservation information of the guest, Party B shall inform such information to Party A by fax. Party A shall make confirmation according to the occupancy rate of the same day and fax to Party B. Fax No. of Party A for Confirmation: ________; Confirming Personnel: ________.

如果甲方的客房出现满员或价格变动的情况，必须及时通知乙方。

In case of full occupancy or price variation of rooms of Party A, Party A shall timely inform Party B.

五、入住、离店时间（Check-in and Check-out Time）

入住、离店时间均为中午十二时。

The check-in and check-out time available is both 12:00.

六、付款方式（Payment Method）

(一) 客人在离店时，其所发生的费用必须在前台付清。

The guest shall pay up all the expenses arising during the stay at the Front Desk at the time of check-out.

(二) 以下佣金支付方式任选其一：□甲方向乙方提供协议价________%的佣金。□甲方提供协议价（底价）和建议售价，两者之间的差额即为乙方佣金。

Commission payment may be made by either of the following methods: □Party A pays a proportion of ________% of the negotiated price as commission. Party A provides negotiated price (bottom price) and recommended price to Party B; and the difference thereof shall be the commission for Party B.

(三) 乙方于每月20日前向甲方传真网络预订结算清单，当双方的订房数有出入时，以甲方收银记录为准。甲方应于每月25日前将当月通过乙方网络预订系统所发生的所有营业额，按本条第(二)款的结算金额，向乙方支付佣金。

Party B shall fax the network reservation statement to Party A before the 20th day of each month. In case of deviation between the room numbers of both parties, the cashier records of Party A shall prevail. Party A shall, before the 25th day of each month, pay commissions to Party B based on the settled amount in Paragraph 2 of this article for all business turnovers generated by the network reservation system of Party B of the current month.

(四) 乙方保证不将本合同第三条协议价以任何形式透露给第三方。

Party B shall not disclose the negotiated prices stipulated in Article 3 of this Contract to a third party in any manner.

七、取消（Cancellation）

甲方将保留乙方预订的房间至客人到达当天的18:00（客人如有特殊情况未能按时到达可事先与甲方协商），逾期房间将不予保留。

Party A shall keep the room reserved by Party B till 18:00 on the expected arrival date of the guest (Party B may negotiate with Party A in advance under special circumstances that the guest is unable to arrive on time). The room so reserved may not be reserved after such deadline stipulated herein.

八、违约责任（Liabilities for Breach of Contract）

合同双方有违反本合约之规定，而导致异议或纠纷，双方友好协商解决，任何一方当事人都有权向乙方之住所地人民法院提起诉讼。

In case of any disagreements or disputes caused by breach of provisions in the contract by either Party, both Parties shall settle such disagreements or disputes based on friendly negotiation. Either Party may reserve the right to institute legal proceedings to the people's court in Party B's domicile.

以上条款双方均已同意，签字、盖章后生效。本合同一式两份，双方各执一份。具有同等法律效力。

The aforesaid clauses have been agreed by both parties and this contract shall take effective upon signing and sealing of both Parties. The Contract shall be made in duplicate and either shall hold one (1) copy. Both copies shall be of the same legal effects.

甲方（盖章）：________ 乙方（盖章）：________

Party A (Seal)：________ Party B (Seal)：________

代表（签字）：________ 代表（签字）：________

Representative (Signature)：________ Representative (Signature)：________

日期：

Date：

模块三 礼宾服务
Module III Concierge Service

【情境导入】【Scenario Introduction】

细心的行李员，惊喜的客人
Considerate Bellman, Amazed Guest

某日上午，一位女住客急匆匆地来到三亚亚龙湾人间天堂鸟巢度假村大堂的礼宾部，手里还拿着两张发票，她径直走到身着燕尾服的“金钥匙”服务员小方面前：“您是酒店的‘金钥匙’吗？有这样一件事您帮一帮我，今天早上我是乘坐出租车来到你们酒店的，刚才我收拾物品时才发现我把摄影机的架子忘在出租车的后排座位上了，更可气的是司机撕给我的发票是长途汽车的发票，而不是出租车的发票，这让我回去怎么报销呢？”客人语气急促地说。

On one morning, a woman guest hurried to the Concierge Department of Yalong Bay Earthly Paradise Bird's Nest Resort in Sanya with two invoices in her hand. She came directly to Fang, a “Golden Key” waiter in the swallow-tailed coat: “Hello, are you the ‘Golden Key’ of the hotel? Can you do me a favor? I took a taxi to your hotel this morning. When I arranged my belongings just now, I found I forgot my camera mounting on the back seat of the taxi. What's annoying me more is that the invoices the driver gave me are for long-distance coach instead of taxi. It's impossible for me to apply for reimbursement when I return!” The guest said in anxiously.

小方说：“小姐，您别着急，让我们一起想一想办法。请问您早上大约几点到达我们酒店的？”

Fang replied: “Just take it easy, Miss. Let's find a way together. May I ask when did you arrive at the hotel this morning?”

客人说：“具体时间记不清了。”

The guests said: “I cannot recall the exact time.”

“请出示一下您的住房卡好吗？”小方接过客人递过来的住房卡并告诉客人在大堂吧稍候一下，随即到前台接待处，查询了这位客人办理入住的具体时间。又到大门口询问是谁帮助这位客人打开车门的。行李员小卢说：“是我接待这位女士的，当时我上前为这位女士拉车门、护顶，她示意让我到车后尾箱取行李，打开尾箱后一共拿出了两个皮箱，当时我还仔细看了一下没有其他行李，这时后面又有其他的出租车来了，我就赶紧关了车门，并迅速在提示卡上记下了这辆出租车车号交给了她，帮着提着行李来到了前台。”小方分析，一方面，是客人自己遗失了一件行李，她可能怕把摄影架压坏弄脏，自己坐在前排，摄影架没有放在车后尾箱而单独放在了车的后排，下车时忘了提醒行李员；另一方面，行李员也够粗心的，一时疏忽也没有检查一下。现在唯一的办法是看能不能找到出租车司机，那就要通过行李员留给客人的那张提示卡了。小方快步来到大堂吧，那位女士充满期盼地迎了过来。

"Would you please show me your room card?" Fang received the room card of the guest and tells her to wait for a while in the Lobby Bar. Then he went to the Reception Desk and enquired the specific check-in time of the guest. Later on, he went to the entrance and asked who opened the taxi door for the guest. Bellman Lu said: "It's me that welcomed the lady. I opened the door and protected her head. She indicated me to get the luggage in the trunk. I opened the trunk and took out two cases in total. Then I carefully checked the trunk to see whether there's other luggage. At that time, there's another taxi coming. I hurried to close the door and quickly noted the plate number of the taxi on the Reminder Card. I gave the card to the lady and carried the luggage to the Front Desk." Fang analyzed: On one hand, the guest had lost a luggage due to her own reason. Probably she selected to sit on the front seat so as not to damage or contaminate the camera mounting. For the same reason, she put the mounting on the back seat instead of in the trunk. And she forgot to remind the bellman when she got off the taxi; On the other, the bellman was so careless that he didn't check the back seat. Now, the only way was to try to find the taxi driver. And the reminder card that the bellman gave to the guest might be the clue. Fang quickly went to the Lobby Bar. The lady comes up anxiously.

小方说："让您久等了，早上您下车时，行李员给您的那张提示卡还在吗？"

Fang said: "Sorry to keep you waiting. Can you find the reminder card that our bellman gave to you when you get off the taxi in the morning?"

客人："好像还在，我找一下。"说完便在手提包里翻找起来，终于找到了一张团成一团的小小的提示卡。

The guest replied: "Maybe. I'll check." Then she searched in the handbag and finally finds it wrapped into a ball.

"就是这张小小的提示卡，上面有那辆出租车公司的名字和出租车牌号。给我吧，我马上去和该公司联系一下。"小方微笑着说。

"This small reminder card tells us the company name and plate number of the taxi. Give it to me. I'll contact with the taxi company immediately." Fang smiled.

小方立即通过礼宾部联系到了出租车调配中心，找到了这家出租车公司的电话，在电话里向对方说明了情况，对方表示将以最快的速度找到司机，态度诚恳地做出了口头承诺："我们马上派人在半小时内把发票和摄影架送到酒店前厅部，绝不耽误客人的时间，抱歉了。"

Fang immediately contacted the Taxi Dispatching Center through the Concierge Department and found the telephone number of that taxi company. Fang briefed the matter to the taxi company on the phone. The taxi company expressed that they would find the driver as soon as possible and made oral commitment sincerely: "We'll take the invoice and camera mounting to the Front Hall Department of the hotel within half an hour. We promise not to waste the guest's time. Sorry!"

20分钟后，一辆出租车停在酒店门口，司机把发票和摄影架送到了前厅部。小方迎上前去，对司机表示了感谢，司机也向客人表示了歉意。拿到摄影架和发票的客人高兴地笑着说："太谢谢你们了，谢谢你们的细心和周到，还有这张给我留下美好回忆的提示卡。"她感激不已，脸上露出了灿烂的微笑。

Twenty minutes later, a taxi pulled up before the hotel. The driver took the invoice and camera mounting to the Front Office Department.Fang stepped forwards and expressed the thanks to the diver. The driver apologized to the guest. Upon receiving the camera mounting and the invoice, the guest said delightfully: "Thank you very much. Thank you for your carefulness and consideration, as well as this reminder card that leaves sweet memories to me." she was quite grateful with big smiles on her face.

【情境分析】【Scenario Analysis】

这是一个帮助客人及时解决困难的服务案例。

This is a case of timely solving problem for the guest.

在酒店服务程序中，很多酒店在客人上下出租车时，都要作一个提示卡的记录，上面写有出租车公司的名字和车牌号。虽然只是一个简单的服务项目，关键时刻会起到很大作用。在本案例中，小方接到客人的求助之后，就是从一张提示卡着手打开了缺口，帮助客人拿到了摄影架和发票。这充分地说明，酒店向客人发放的提示卡是完善酒店服务中必不可少的服务项目，小小的提示卡在酒店服务中起着重要作用。即使这比较烦琐，也应该这样做。客人求助酒店完成本职以外的工作时，有关人员一定要尽力满足客人的要求，这是十分重要的。

In the service procedures of the hotels, most hotels will record the company name and plate number of the taxi on the reminder card when the guests get in/out of the taxi. This is a simple service item; but it will help a lot at critical moment. In this case, Fang makes breakthrough from the reminder card when he is asked for help by the guest. And finally he succeeds to retrieve the camera mounting and invoice for the guest. This has adequately proved that the issuance of reminder card to the guest is an essential service item to consummate hotel services. A small reminder card plays an important role in hotel services.Though it is relatively tedious, When being asked for work beyond the scope of service, related personnel must try the best to satisfy the guest's requirements, which is quite important.

方便、及时、急人之所急，是客人普遍的心理需求特征，无论是哪种服务消费目的的顾客，都希望能够为他们提供尽量方便的条件和及时的服务。

Convenience, timeliness and consideration are the common psychological needs of the guests. Whatever the consumption or service nature is, the guests would expect convenient conditions and timely services as possible.

【学习目标】【Learning Goals】

［知识目标］［Knowledge Objective］

1. 掌握礼宾部岗位任务及业务特点。

Master the post tasks and business features of the Concierge Department.

2. 掌握礼宾部岗位服务礼仪，熟悉语言技巧。

Master the service etiquettes of the Concierge Department; be familiar with language skills.

3. 掌握酒店外接送服务、门厅迎送服务、行李服务和委托代办服务标准。

Master the standards for pick-up services out of the hotel, entrance hall reception service, luggage service and agency service of the hotel.

［能力目标］［Capacity objectives］

1. 熟练掌握礼宾部岗位职责和任务，能够按照酒店的标准提供礼宾服务。

Have a good command of the post responsibilities and tasks of the Concierge Department; be able to provide concierge service in accordance with the standards of the hotel.

2. 了解"金钥匙"服务标准，在日常工作中，尽可能按照"金钥匙"服务标准为顾客提供满意的服务。

Understand the service standards of the "Golden Key", try to provide satisfying services to the guests according to the service standards of the "Golden Key" as possible in daily work.

【重点和难点】【Key Points and Difficulties】

熟练掌握礼宾部岗位职责，并严格按照相关标准提供服务。

Be familiar with the post responsibilities of the Concierge Department and provide services strictly according to related standards.

随着酒店的定位不断攀升，酒店礼宾服务不断扩大深入，从标准化服务到个性化服务再到定制的私人服务，高端酒店由于酒店礼宾司的存在，渐渐成为旅行者们在世界各地的家。酒店礼宾服务员、门童、行李生、领班、私人管家……所有这一系列称谓，都指向酒店中直接和住客打交道的礼宾部。从入住的第一刻开始，礼宾服务员就成为客人在酒店下榻期间的联络人，他们代表着酒店品牌的软件高度，为奢华的起居空间注入关怀和温度，像艺术家一样谱写出客人的下榻生活画卷。

With the continuous enhancement of hotel orientation, the concierge services of the hotel have also been increasingly expanded and intensified. From standard services, to individual services and then to customized personal services, the Concierge Department in high-end hotel has gradually become the homes of the travelers all across the world. The concierge service staff, doormen, bellmen, head waiters, housekeepers, etc. are all functions under the Concierge Department directly to the guests. Once the guest checks in the hotel, the concierge service staff become the contact person of the guest during his/her stay. They represent the "software" level of the hotel brand and add concerns and warmness into the luxury living space. They're designers of the hotel stay for the guests.

礼宾服务，是由法语"Concierge"一词翻译而来，也可译为委托代办服务。许多高档次的酒店都设立了礼宾部，体现了酒店的档次和服务水准，这个部门隶属前厅部。在一些中小规模的低星级酒店中，则称为行李部。礼宾部是整个酒店的门面，在礼宾部工作的都属于前线人员，他们通常是客人真正面对面接触的第一位酒店人员，礼宾部是给客人留下第一印象的地方，是酒店政策运行的重要环节，为大堂乃至整个酒店的宾客提供高品质、标准化、个性化的服务。

Concierge service is translated from the French word of "Concierge", which is also translated as "agency services". Many high-end hotels have established the Concierge Department, which is a department under the Front Office Department representing the grade and service level of the hotel. And in some small and medium sized low star-level hotels, the Concierge Department is called Concierge Desk. The Concierge Department represents the image of the hotel. Staff working in the Concierge Department are all front-line staff for the hotel. They are often the first staff for face-to-face contact by the guest and leave the first impression to the guest. Therefore, they form an important link of hotel policy operation and provide high quality, standardized and personalized services for the guests in the lobby and even the entire hotel.

礼宾服务是现代酒店对宾客服务中的一种新概念，它把迎送宾客服务和为进出店客人提供行李服务合为一体，并做出具体分工。按照服务程序标准化要求对上述两项服务作合理分工，突出宾客应享受的礼宾待遇。其主要职责就是围绕客人需求提供"一条龙服务"。礼宾部的服务涉及客人的方方面面，几乎贯穿了整个酒店，礼宾部代表酒店直接负责迎送每一位客人，是前台部的一个分部门，为客人提供行李搬运及寄存服务，此外，还整理客人的邮件及整个酒店的报纸和邮件的派送，并负责客人车辆的安排。礼宾部的工作渗透于其他各项服务之中，缺少这项工作，会直接影响到酒店内部沟通以及酒店对外的声誉和形象。

Concierge service is a new concept of guest services in modern hotels. It integrates the guest reception/seeing-off services as well as luggage services to the guests and makes specific job divisions. Rational job divisions are made on the abovementioned two services according to the standardization requirements of the service procedures and the concierge treatments deserved by the guests are highlighted. The main responsibility of concierge service is to provide "one package service" focused on the clients. The services of the Concierge Department involve various aspects related to the guests and cover almost the entire hotel. The Concierge Department welcomes and sees off each guest on behalf of the hotel. As a division of the Front office Department, it is responsible for luggage handling and deposit services for the guests, dispatching of the mails of the guests and newspapers and mails of the entire hotel as well as the arrangement of the vehicles for the guests. The work of the Concierge Department permeates into various types of other services. Without concierge services, the internal communication and the external reputation and image of the hotel would be affected.

礼宾部的工作特点是：人员分散工作，服务范围大。在大中型酒店中，礼宾部一般下设礼宾员、门童、行李员等岗位。礼宾部的工作人员在客人心目中常被视为"酒店代表"，其服务态度、工作效率和质量都会给酒店的经济效益带来直接的影响，直接影响到酒店的声誉，这就要求礼宾部员工要以周到的服务、热情的微笑、恰当的礼貌，随时为客人提供各方面的优质服务，为酒店形象和声誉添砖加瓦。

Operating features of the Concierge Department: Staff are working in a distributed manner and the scope of services is intensive. In large and medium sized hotels, generally posts such as the concierge, doorman and bellman are designed under the Concierge Department. Working staff under the Concierge Department are often regarded as the "representatives of the hotel". And their service attitude, working efficiency and quality would bear direct influence on the economic benefits as well as the reputations of the hotel. To this end, the staff under the Concierge Department must provided high quality services of various aspects with considerate services, enthusiastic smiles and appropriate politeness at any time so as to add weight to the image and reputation of the hotel.

任务一　店外接送服务

Task I　Off-site Pickup and Delivery Service

一、店外接送服务（Off-site Pickup and Delivery Service）

酒店代表代表酒店在机场、车站、码头等主要出入境口岸迎接客人，提供有效的接送服务，及时向客人推销酒店产品，是酒店整体服务的向外延伸和扩展，也是酒店对外宣传的窗口，越来越多的酒店在国际空港设置驻机场代表，使服务更加专业化。

The hotel representatives receive the guests on main entry and exit ports such as the airport, railway station and dock; provide effective pickup and delivery services and timely promote the hotel products to the guest. This is the external expansion and extension of the overall hotel services as well as a window for external publicity of the hotel. More and more hotels are designating airport representatives at international airports to further professionalize their services.

到酒店外进行接送的酒店代表应该具有较高的外语交流水平，熟悉酒店的客情，掌握主要客源国旅游者的生活习俗、礼仪，有较高的应变能力和人际交往能力等。具体的服务程序包括以下几方面：

Hotel representatives offering off-site pickup and delivery services should have relatively high foreign language communication skills，be familiar with the guest conditions of the hotel，be acquainted with the life styles，customs and etiquettes of the tourists from the main source countries and should have relatively excellent flexibility and interpersonal skills and so on. The specific service procedures should involve the following aspects：

（1）熟知当日、次日客情。

Be acquainted with the guest conditions of the hotel on that day and the following day.

（2）根据机场预测报告，安排好巴士或向车队下命令。

Properly arrange the bus service or make instructions to the fleet according to the prediction report of the airport.

（3）客人抵达当日，提前做好接机准备。

Get prepared for the pickup services in advance on the arrival date of the guests.

（4）密切注意航班变化。

Pay close attention to the possible variation of the flights.

（5）接到客人后，主动表示欢迎并介绍自己身份。

Express the welcome and make self-introduction positively upon meeting the guest.

（6）根据客人房号开立账单。

Make bills according to the room number of the guest.

（7）使用电话通知前厅礼宾值班台有关客人抵店信息。

Call the Concierge Duty Desk of the Front Office about information related to the arrival of the guest.

（8）出现误接或在机场找不到客人，立即与酒店取得联系。

Immediately contact the hotel in case of mistaken pickup or failure to find the guest.

（9）客人离店时，驻机场代表与礼宾部行李组及车队取得联系。

When the guest is about to check out，the air representative should contact the Luggage Group of the Concierge Department and the fleet.

（10）协助客人托运行李和办理报关手续。

Assist the guest to consign the luggage and clear customs.

（11）与客人告别，感谢客人光临酒店，并欢迎客人再次光临。

See off the guest. Express the appreciation for the guest's stay in the hotel and welcome the revisit of the guest.

无预订客人的争取：

For temporary guests，best efforts should be made to：

（1）主动迎接，礼貌询问客人是否需要住宿。

Welcome the guest initiatively；enquire whether the guest requires accommodation politely.

（2）主动向客人介绍酒店情况。

Positively introduce the hotel to the guest.

（3）察言观色，灵活推销客房及其他产品。

Carefully observe the reactions of the guest；promote the guest rooms and other products in a flexible manner.

（4）客人确认入住后，办理相关手续，上车去酒店。

If the guest confirms to check in, work on related formalities for the guest and arrange the vehicle to the hotel.

（5）驱车途中，向客人介绍酒店及城市情况。

Introduce the hotel and the city to the guest during the drive to the hotel.

二、店外接送服务流程（Off-site Pickup and Delivery Service Procedures）

为了提高酒店整体的服务质量，向客人提供高效快捷、准确无误的个性化服务，根据酒店接送机（车、船）服务相关规定，接送机（车、船）服务操作流程如下：

To enhance the overall service quality and provide highly effective, convenient and accurate individualized services to the guest, the off-site pickup and delivery services (flight, train and ship) should follow the following procedures according to related provisions on such services of the hotel:

（一）接机（车、船）服务［Pickup Services (flight, train and ship)］

（1）礼宾员每日上班时应先与前台核对当日的接机信息，根据接机信息制作接机牌，将相关接机信息如航班号、抵达时间、客人联系方式等备注在接机牌上；并在航班抵达时间前2个小时开始确认航班确切抵达时间（之后每隔半小时确认一次）。

Before starting the daily work, the Concierge Attendant should check the pickup information for the day with the Front Desk; prepare the pick-up card according to the pick-up information and mark related information such as the flight number, arrival time and contact information of the guest onto the pick-up card; confirm the arrival time of the flight 2 hours before the arrival time (and then every half an hour).

（2）司机提前30分钟至大堂副理处领取车辆钥匙并登记。

The driver should get the vehicle from the Assistant Manager and make registration 30 minutes in advance.

（3）礼宾员准备好接机牌，根据该航班飞机预计抵达时间提前30分钟联系机场问询处，询问该航班飞机抵达的准确时间，礼宾员根据飞机抵达的准确时间请司机及时发车。

The Concierge Attendant prepares the pick-up card and contact the Information Desk of the airport 30 minutes before the estimated time of arrival of the flight for the exact time of arrival. The Concierge Attendant requires the driver to depart according to the exact time of the flight.

（4）礼宾员到达机场后观察候机大厅里的大屏幕，根据大屏幕上所显示的该航班飞机抵达时间适时站在国内抵达点（或国际抵达点）举接机牌等候宾客。

Upon arriving at the airport, the Concierge Attendant should observe the big screen in the Waiting Hall and wait for the guest timely with the pick-up card at the Domestic Arrivals (International Arrivals) according to the time of arrival indicated on the big screen.

（5）礼宾员接到宾客时，应主动上前向宾客给予问候并帮宾客提取行李，与司机一起引导宾客至停车场，请宾客上车就座并将宾客的行李放置稳当。告知宾客车子即刻启程回酒店，请宾客坐好。

After picking up the guest, the Concierge Attendant should positively greet the guest and help the guest with the luggage, guide the guest with the driver to the car park, have the guest seated and properly load the luggage of the guest. Inform the guest that the car will immediately head back the hotel and ask the guest to pay attention.

（6）车子启程后，礼宾员应立刻打电话回酒店，告知前台接待员已在机场接到该宾客（以便前台员工提前准备好该位宾客的房卡，提高对宾客服务效率）。在车子回酒店途中，礼宾员应主动与宾客进行交流，礼宾员应告知宾客近期的天气情况，提醒宾客在住店期间注意天气变化、饮食、饮水，向宾客介绍酒店的服务设施、服务项目等。

After the car sets out, the Concierge Attendant should immediately call the hotel and inform the Receptionist that the guest has been picked up (so that the staff at the Front Desk can prepare the room card for the guest and enhance the efficiency of guest services). On the way back to the hotel, the Concierge Attendant should positively communicate with the guest. The Concierge Attendant should introduce the weather conditions in recent days and remind the guest to pay attention to weather changes, foods and drinking water during the stay in the hotel and should introduce the service facilities, service items, etc. of the hotel to the guest.

（7）礼宾员如接不到客人，应和机场问询处或客人本人取得联系，重新确认接机事宜；如无法联系上客人，应第一时间将情况上报大堂经理，由大堂经理落实客人信息。

If the Concierge Attendant fails to pick up the guest, the Concierge Attendant should contact the Information Desk of the guest to reconfirm the pick-up affairs. If the guest cannot be contacted, immediately report the case to the Assistant Manager and the Assistant Manager should be responsible to double check the guest information.

（8）前台接待员应在客人抵店前准备好房卡和入住登记表，并知会大堂经理。

The Receptionist of the Front Desk should prepare the room card and the *Check-in Registration Form* before the guest arrives at the hotel and inform the Assistant Manager.

（9）客人抵店后，由大堂经理协同礼宾员一起引导客人到总台办理入住手续。

Upon the arrival of the guest, the Concierge Attendant should assist the Assistant Manager to guide the guest to handle the check-in formalities at the Front Desk.

（10）司机安全地将客人接至酒店后应及时将车辆钥匙交还大堂经理，向人事部经理回复送机完成情况。

After safely take the guest to the hotel, the driver should timely return the key to the car to the Assistant Manager and report the progress to the HR Manger.

（二）送机（车、船）服务［Delivery Services (flight, train and ship)］

（1）送机（车、船）服务均遵循两个时间段：10:00a.m.和 15:00p.m.，该时间段为免费提供服务，前提条件是不与接机服务时间有冲突，若酒店所提供的穿梭巴士的出发时间均不适合宾客乘坐，礼宾员应建议宾客乘出租车（特殊宾客除外），如客人强烈要求，应请客人等候，由部门主管或当班大堂副理灵活处理。

Free delivery services (for flight, train and ship) are available at 10:00a.m. and 15:00p.m., provided that it doesn't conflict with the pickup services. If the departure time of the shuttle bus provided by the hotel is not available for the guest, the Concierge Attendant should suggest the guest to take a taxi (except special guests). If the guest resists, the Concierge Attendant should ask the guest to wait for a moment and ask the Department Head or the Assistant Manager on duty to dispose flexibly.

（2）当宾客前来前台或礼宾部预订酒店至机场的穿梭巴士时，需礼貌向宾客询问：宾客所需要的穿梭巴士出发时间、宾客所入住的房间号、乘车宾客的人数、是否需要礼宾员帮其至房间提行李。

When the guest comes to the Front Desk or the Concierge Department to reserve the shuttle bus from the hotel to the airport, enquire the guest politely with the following questions: The required departure time of the shuttle bus; room number of the guest; number of guests; whether the Concierge Attendant is required to get the luggage from the guest room.

（3）告知宾客酒店的穿梭巴士是定时的，请宾客提前发车时间 10 分钟到酒店大堂礼宾部。

Inform the guest the shuttle bus is scheduled and ask the guest to come to the Concierge Department in the Lobby of the hotel 10 minutes before the departing time of the shuttle bus.

（4）若宾客乘坐国内航班，请宾客提前飞机起飞时间 1 小时从酒店出发，若宾客乘坐国际航班，请宾客提前飞机起飞时间 2 小时从酒店出发。若酒店所提供的穿梭巴士的出发时间均不适合宾客乘坐，礼宾员应建议宾客乘坐出租车（特殊宾客除外）。

If the guest is about to take a domestic flight, advice the guest to depart from the hotel 1 hour before the departure time of the flight; in case of international flight, advice the guest to depart from the hotel 2 hours before the departure time of the flight. If the departure time of the shuttle bus provided by the hotel is not available for the guest, the Concierge Attendant should suggest the guest to take a taxi (except special guests).

（5）礼宾员详细填写派车单，请部门主管或大堂经理在派车单上签名，在“接送机记录簿”上做好记录，将派车单送至人事部在“接送机记录簿”上签名。

The Assistant Manager should fill in the Dispatching Order and have the Department Head or the HR Department sign on the Dispatching Order. The Concierge Attendant should also make proper record on the “Pickup and Delivery Log” and have it signed by the HR Department.

（三）注意事项（Notes）

（1）接待员在确认接送机（车、船）信息时，应注意不要超出酒店接送机（车、船）服务规定的时间，若客人需要在规定接送机（车、船）时间之外的接送机（车、船）服务，则按酒店接送机（车、船）服务收费标准执行。

When confirming the pickup/delivery (for flight, train and ship) information, pay attention that the time cannot exceed the prescribed time for pickup/delivery (for flight, train and ship) services. If the guest requires for pickup/delivery (for flight, train and ship) services beyond the scheduled time, fees will be charged according to the charging standard for pickup/delivery (for flight, train and ship) services.

（2）如接机订单人数较多，超过 6 人以上需上报部门主管或大堂经理处理。

If more than 6 guests require pickup service, report to the Department Head or the Assistant Manager for disposal.

（3）如遇周六、周日及临时增加或国家法定休息日接到接送机（车、船）服务时，礼宾部将附上预订传真复印件的派车单交由大堂经理审核，再由大堂经理第一时间致电人事经理提出派车申请（派车单由大堂经理代签，待人事部上班后补送至人事经理处）。

In case of pickup/delivery (for flight, train and ship) services on weekends, legal holidays or on temporary basis, the Concierge Department should submit the Dispatching Order together with the copy of reservation faxing to the Assistant Manager for review. The Assistant Manager should then call the HR Manager to apply for vehicle dispatching (the Dispatching Order should be signed by the Assistant Manager and then submitted to the HR Manager when the HR Department is available on work days).

三、店外接送客人具体服务程序和标准（Specific Service Procedures and Standards for Off-site Pickup and Delivery of Guests）

（一）店外迎接客人服务程序和标准（Service Procedures and Standards for Off-site Pickup of Guests）

一般情况下，机场接机服务的程序与标准分为如下几个程序，如表 3-1 所示。

Generally, the procedures and standards for airport pickup services consists of the following steps, as shown in Table 3-1.

表 3-1 店外迎接客人服务步骤和标准

Table 3-1 Service Procedures and Standards for Off-site Pickup of Guests

程序 Procedure	标准 Standard
1. 准备工作 Getting Prepared	（1）定时从预订处取得需要接站的客人名单。 Obtain the list for guests to be picked up from the Reservation Desk in a scheduled manner. （2）掌握客人的姓名、所乘的航班（车次）、到达的时间、车辆要求及接待规格等情况。 Get to know the name, flight (train) No., arrival time, vehicle requirement, reception level, etc. of the guest. （3）根据预订航班、车次或船次时间提前做好接站准备，写好接站的告示牌，安排好车辆，整理好仪容仪表，提前半小时至 1 小时到站等候。 Get prepared for pickup according to the reserved flight/train/ship No.; prepare the pick-up card; arrange appropriate vehicle; check personal appearance and arrive at the airport/station 0.5-1 hour in advance. （4）备好接机牌，正面刻有酒店的中、英文名称，反面是客人的姓名，牌子手把的长度在 0.5 米左右。 Prepare the pick-up card with the Chinese and English name of the hotel on the front and the name of the guest on the back; the handle of the card should be about 0.5m long.
2. 到达机场迎接客人 Receive the Guest at the Airport/Station	（1）注意客人所乘航班、车（船）次到达时间的变动，若有延误或取消，应及时准备通知酒店总台。 Note possible variation of the flight/train/ship No. of the guest. Timely inform the Front Desk of the hotel in case of delay or cancellation. （2）站立在显眼位置举牌等候、主动问好、介绍自己、代表酒店欢迎客人。 Hold the pick-up card and wait for the guest at a conspicuous position; greet the guest and make self-introduction initiatively; welcome the guest on behalf of the hotel. （3）根据预抵店客人名单予以确认。 Make confirmation according to the list for anticipated guests. （4）帮助客人搬运行李并确认行李件数，挂好行李牌，引领客人前往接站车前。 Help the guest with the luggage and confirm the number of the luggage; put on the luggage card (s) ; guide the guest to the pick-up vehicle.
3. 送客人上车 Guide the Guest onto the Vehicle	（1）开车前 10 分钟应将客人送到开车地点，引导客人上车，协助客人将行李装上车。 Take the guest to the place where the vehicle is waiting 10 minutes before the vehicle departs; guide the guest onto the vehicle and assist the guest to load the luggage. （2）向客人道别，开车时站在车前右方 2 米左右，微笑着并挥手向客人道别。 Say goodbye to the guest, stand about 2m to the right front of the vehicle when the vehicle departs, wave goodbye with smile. （3）如果需要随车同行，在行车途中，可以根据具体情况，或简要介绍酒店服务项目内容和当地风貌，或陪同客人聊天，或放音乐让客人自便。 If accompanying is required, on the way return, brief the service items of the hotel and local features, chat with the guests or have the guest enjoy music as the case may be. （4）将客人接到酒店后，引领客人到总台办理入住手续，并询问客人是否需要提供离店服务，VIP 客人接站到店后，请大堂副经理为客人办理入住登记手续。 When the guest arrives the hotel, guide the guest to the Front Desk to handle check-in formalities, enquire the guest whether delivery services are required. For VIP guests, ask Assistant Manager to work on check-in formalities.

续表

程序 Procedure	标准 Standard
4. 通知客人抵店信息 Inform the Arrival Information to the Hotel	(1) 电话通知大厅值班台客人到店的有关信息：客人姓名、乘车号、离开车站时间、用房有无变化等。 Call the Duty Desk of the Front Hall about information related to the arrival of the guest: guest name, vehicle plate number, time of departure from the airport/station, variation of room use (if any), etc. (2) 若没有接到 VIP 客人或指定要接的客人，应立即与酒店接待处取得联系，查找客人是否已乘车抵达酒店。返回酒店后，要立即与前台确认客人具体情况并弄清楚事实及原因，向主管汇报清楚，并在接站登记簿上和交班簿上写明。 If the hotel fails to pick up the VIP guest or the anticipated guest, contact the Reception Desk of the hotel immediately to check whether the guest has arrived at the hotel individually. Upon return to the hotel, immediately check with the Reception Desk on the specific conditions of the guest and figure out the facts and causes; report clearly to the Supervisor and record the details in the pick-up log and shift log.

（二）贵宾服务程序和标准（Service Procedures and Standards for VIPs）

一般情况下，贵宾接送工作的程序与标准分为如下几个程序，如表 3-2 所示。

Generally, the procedures and standards for airport pickup services of VIPs consist of the following steps, as shown in Table 3-2.

表 3-2　贵宾的接送工作

Table 3-2　Pickup and Delivery Services for VIPs

程序 Procedure	标准 Standard
1. 准备工作 Getting Prepared	(1) 根据贵宾提供的航班或车次，提前 30 分钟到达车站或机场做好接待准备。 Arrive at the station/airport 30 minutes in advance to get prepared according to the flight/train No. provided by the VIP guest. (2) 随时将贵宾乘坐航班的确切到达时间通知礼宾部或大堂经理。 Inform the Concierge Department or Assistant Manager the exact time of arrival of the flight/train of the VIP guest. (3) 必要时，由资深酒店代表直接进入车站或机场的接客禁区内（即站台或停机坪）接待客人。提前与合作单位沟通及做好安排。 When necessary, the Senior Hotel Representative may enter the forbidden zone of the railway station or the airport (platform or parking apron) to welcome the guest. Communication and arrangement should be made in advance with the cooperating organization.
2. 接待重要贵宾 Receive the VIP Guest	(1) 航班到达后，由资深酒店代表负责接待贵宾，其他酒店代表随时将贵宾到达的有关情况报告礼宾部。 Upon the arrival of the flight, the Senior Hotel Representative should be responsible to receive the VIP guest; and other hotel representatives should inform the related information about the arrival of the VIP guest from time to time. (2) 预先安排车辆在出口处停泊。 Arrange the vehicle to park at the exit in advance. (3) 与礼宾车司机保持联系，接到贵宾后，帮助其提取行李，引领其到停车地点，放好行李，核实行李数量，向贵宾礼貌告别及目送贵宾车辆离开。 Contact with the driver of the concierge vehicle; after the VIP guest is picked up, assist the guest to withdraw the luggage, guide the guest to the parking area; load the luggage and check the amount of the luggage; say goodbye to the VIP guest politely and gaze after the guest till the vehicle leaves. (4) 通过电话或手提对讲机知会礼宾部转告有关部门：贵宾正在前往酒店途中，以便酒店方面及早安排迎接贵宾。 Inform the Concierge Department by telephone or walkie talkie that the VIP guest is on the way to the hotel so that the Concierge Department may relay the information to related departments and the hotel may make arrangements to welcome the VIP guest in advance. (5) 酒店代表需与机场和车站的有关部门保持良好的合作关系，以便能向酒店贵宾提供周到的接待服务。 The Hotel Representative should establish and maintain favorable cooperation relationship with related departments at the airport or the railway station to enable the hotel to provide considerate reception services to the VIP guests.

任务二　门厅迎送宾客服务

Task II　Lobby Reception and Seeing-off Services

【情境导入】【Scenario Introduction】

一位常住三亚亚龙湾铂尔曼别墅度假酒店的外国客人从外面回来，当他走到服务台时，还没有等他开口，问讯员就主动微笑地把钥匙递上，并轻声称呼他的名字，这位客人大为吃惊，由于酒店对他留有印象，使他产生一种强烈的亲切感，旧地重游如回家一样。

A foreign frequent guest came back from outside to Pullman Oceanview Sanya Bay Resort & Spa. As he approached the Reception Desk, before he said word, the Receptionist handed over his key and called his name gently with smile. This made the guest quite surprised. As the hotel had recalled him, he felt a great sense of intimacy just like coming back home.

还有一位客人在服务台高峰时进店，服务员问讯小姐突然准确地叫出："××先生，服务台有您一个电话。"这位客人又惊又喜，感到自己受到了重视，受到了特殊的待遇，不禁添了一份自豪感。

Another guest entered the hotel at the busy hour of the Reception Desk, a lady Receptionist suddenly called accurately: "Mr. ××, you have a call at the Reception Desk." The guest was both surprised and pleased. Feeling that he was valued and honored specially, the guest had got a sense of pride.

另外一位外国客人第一次前往三亚亚龙湾铂尔曼别墅度假酒店入住，前台接待员从登记卡上看到客人的名字，迅速称呼他以表欢迎，客人先是一惊，而后作客他乡的陌生感顿时消失，显出非常高兴的样子。简单的词汇迅速缩短了彼此间的距离。

It's the first time for a foreign guest to reside in the Pullman Oceanview Sanya Bay Resort & Spa. The Receptionist caught the name of the guest from the registration card and called the name of the guest for welcome. The guest felt shocked and then his strangeness in an alien land disappeared immediately. The guest was quite delighted. Simple words quickly abridged the distance between the guest and hotel.

此外，一位 VIP（贵宾）随带陪同人员来到前台登记，服务人员通过接机人员的暗示，得悉其身份，马上称呼客人的名字，并递上打印好的登记卡请他签字，使客人感到自己的地位不同，由于受到超凡的尊重而感到格外开心。

Furthermore, one VIP guest came to the Reception Desk with his accompanying personnel for check-in. As implied by the pick-up staff, the Receptionist knew who the guest was. Then the Receptionist called the name out immediately and handed over the printed registration card to the guest for signature. The guest felt his exclusive status and was quite delighted for receiving extraordinary respect.

【情境分析】【Scenario Analysis】

学者马斯洛的需要层次理论认为，人们最高的需求是得到社会的尊重。当自己的名字为他人所知晓就是对这种需求的一种很好的满足。

According to Maslow's Hierarchy of Needs, the supreme desire of people is to be respected by the society. The desire may be greatly satisfied if the name is known to others.

在酒店及其他服务性行业的工作中，主动热情地称呼客人的名字是一种服务的艺术，也是一种艺术的服务。通过酒店服务台人员尽力记住客人的房号、姓名和特征，借助敏锐的观察力和良好的记忆力，做出细心周到的服务，使客人留下深刻的印象，客人今后在不同的场合会提起该酒店如何如何，等于是酒店的义务宣传员。

In hospitality industry and other service trades, calling the name of the guest positively and enthusiastically is an art of service as well as a service of art. The staff at the Reception Desk of the Hotel should try the best to memorize the room number, name and features of the guest and provide careful and considerate services with sharp observation and good memory. This may leave deep impressions to the guests and make the guests willing to comment the hotel on different occasions as the voluntary advocators of the hotel.

目前国内著名的酒店规定：在为客人办理入住登记时至少要称呼客人名字三次。前台员工要熟记VIP的名字，尽可能多地了解他们的资料，争取在他们来店报家门之前就称呼他们的名字，当再次见到他们时能直称其名，这是作为一个合格服务员最基本的条件。同时，还可以使用计算机系统，为所有下榻的客人做出历史档案记录，对客人提供超水准、高档次的优质服务，把每一位客人都看成是VIP，使客人从心眼里感到酒店永远不会忘记他们。

Presently, it is stipulated by domestically renowned hotels that, when handling check-in formalities for the guest, the name of the guest should be called at least three times. Staff at the Reception Desk should memorize the name of the VIP guests and try to know more information about them as possible. Efforts should be made so that the Receptionist may recall the guest name before the guest makes self-introduction and call the name directly when meeting the guest again. This is the basic requirement for a qualified hotel staff. Meanwhile, the computer system may be used to establish historic file records for the guest residing in the hotel. This provides extra high quality and level services for the guests and regards every guest as a VIP, which can make the guests feel that the hotel will never forget them.

一、门厅迎送宾客服务（Lobby Reception and Seeing-off Services）

门厅迎送宾客服务，是对宾客进入酒店正门时所进行的一项面对面的服务。门厅礼宾员(Doorman)，亦称礼宾员或门童，是代表酒店在大门口迎接宾客的专门人员，是酒店的“门面”，也是酒店形象的具体体现。因此，门童必须服装整洁，仪容仪表端正、大方，体格健壮，精神饱满，与保安员、行李员相互配合，保证迎客、送客服务工作的正常进行。礼宾员要承担迎送、调车、协助保安员、行李员等工作的任务，具体如下：

Lobby reception and seeing-off service is a face-to-face service when the guest enters the entrance of the hotel. Doorman is the specialized personnel receiving the guest at the entrance of the hotel on behalf of the hotel. The doorman is the “face” of the hotel and is the specific representation of the hotel image. Therefore, the doorman must wear clean uniform and take on upright and generous appearance. The doorman should also have a robust physique and high spirit, and work cooperatively with the security guard and the bellman to guarantee regular services on guest reception and seeing-off. The bellman should assume tasks such as reception/seeing-off, vehicle dispatching, assisting the security guard and bellman. To be specific, the tasks of the bellman involve:

(1) 迎宾服务。当客人抵店时，门童要主动相迎，为来店客人拉开车门，热情欢迎客人。协助客人下车并卸下行李，提醒客人清点行李以防物品遗留在车上，并招呼前厅行李员，将客人引领入店。

Reception Service. When the guest arrives at the hotel, the doorman should welcome the guest initiatively, open the car door for the guest and greet the guest warmly. Assist the guest to get off the car and unload the luggage; remind the guest to check the luggage in case of any omissions; call the bellman in the lobby and guide the guest into the hotel.

（2）送行服务。当客人离店时，门童要将客人的用车召唤至大门口，协助行李员将客人的行李装上车，并请客人核对行李，协助客人上车坐好，轻关车门，向客人致意送别，并表示欢迎客人再次光临。

Seeing-off Service. When the guest leaves the hotel, the doorman should have the vehicle for the guest waiting at the entrance; assist the bellman to load the luggage, ask the guest to check the luggage, assist the guest to be seated, close the door gently, give regards and say goodbye to the guest and welcome the revisit of the guest.

（3）贵宾迎送服务。贵宾接待，是酒店给下榻的重要客人的一种礼遇。门童要根据预订处发出的通知，做好充分准备，要讲究服务规格并在向贵宾致意时有礼貌地称呼其姓名或头衔。根据接待规格的需要，礼宾员还要负责升降该国国旗、中国国旗、店旗或彩旗等。

VIP Receiving/Seeing-off Service. VIP reception is the courteous reception for VIPs residing in the hotel. The doorman should make sufficient preparation according to the notice issued by the Reservation Desk; pay attention to the service level and politely call the name and title of the VIP guest when greeting the guest. As required by the reception standards, the Concierge Attendant should also be responsible for the raising/lowering the national flag of the guest's country, the national flag of China, the flag of the hotel, colored flags, etc.

（4）安全保卫。负责注意门厅出入人员动向，做好防爆、防盗工作。协助保安人员做好贵宾抵离时的安全保卫工作。

Security. Be responsible to keep an eye on the tendencies of the personnel coming in and out of the hotel; make appropriate protection against explosion and theft. Assist the security guards in security work on the arrival/departure of the VIP guests.

（5）门前调度。确保酒店门前车道畅通，指挥正门前交通及车辆停放事宜。为住客召唤出租车，负责大门口附近车辆的清理工作。

Entrance Dispatching. Ensure that the driveway before the hotel is unblocked; direct the traffic and parking in front of the entrance. Call the taxi for the guest; be responsible to clear up the vehicles near the entrance.

（6）检查环境。负责检查门厅环境卫生及室温。

Environment Inspection. Be responsible to inspect the environmental sanitation and room temperature of the lobby.

（7）机场代表的迎送服务。酒店根据自身的服务规格及要求，在机场、火车站、码头等派出代表，即“酒店代表”（有些酒店在机场、火车站等设有固定的接待点），代表酒店对客人的抵达表示热烈欢迎，并致以亲切问候，热情协助他们去酒店或送客离去。

Reception/Seeing-off Service by Hotel Representative. Hotels may assign representatives at the airport, railway station, dock, etc. according to its own service standards and requirements (such representatives are called "Hotel Representative"). Some hotels would establish fixed reception desks at the airport, railway station, etc. The hotel representatives express the warm welcome on the arrival of the guest, offer kind regards, assist the guest to the hotel or see the guest off enthusiastically on behalf of the hotel.

（8）回答客人问询。因工作岗位所处位置的特殊性，经常会遇到客人问询，对此，应持热情友好的态度，准确地答复客人的问询，对没有把握的问题，应向客人表示歉意，并礼貌地请客人到问询处询问。绝不可使用“不知道”、“不清楚”等简单生硬的否定性语言答复客人。

Guest Enquiry Response. Due to the particularity of the post, the doorman would often encounter enquiries from the guests. The doorman should accurately respond the guests in an enthusiastic and friendly manner. In case of uncertain problems, first apologize to the guest and then ask the guest to enquire at the Information Desk politely. Simple and stiff negative words such as “I don't know” and “I'm not sure” are strictly prohibited.

二、VIP 客人的服务规格标准（Service Specifications and Standards for VIP Guests）

（1）A 级迎送。总经理和部分服务员在大厅门口列队迎送客人。

Level A Reception/Seeing-off. The General Manager and some attendants line up at the entrance to receive and see off the guests.

（2）B 级迎送。总经理、大堂经理、礼宾员等人员在大门口迎送客人。

Level B Reception/Seeing-off. The General Manager, Assistant Manager, Concierge Attendants and other related staff receive and see off the guests at the entrance.

（3）C 级迎送。总经理或副总经理，或大堂经理在大厅门口等候迎送客人。

Level C Reception/Seeing-off. The General Manager, Deputy General Manager or the Lobby Manager waits to receive and see off the guests at the entrance.

三、服务流程（Service Procedure）

（一）门厅迎送客人服务程序（Lobby Reception and Seeing-off Services Procedure）

迎接客人的主要操作步骤和标准如表 3-3 所示：

The main operation procedures and standards of guest reception are shown in Table 3-3:

表 3-3 迎接客人步骤和标准

Table 3-3 Procedures and Standards of Guest Reception

操作步骤 Operation Procedures	主要操作步骤 Main Operation Procedures	注意要点 Key Points
1. 准备工作 Getting Prepared	（1）了解当天即将抵店的重要客人和团队。 Get to know the VIP guests and teams to be arrived on that day. （2）了解酒店当日举行的大型活动。 Get to know the large-sized events to be held in the hotel on that day.	准备工作要充分。 The preparation should be sufficient.
2. 迎接客人 Receiving the Guest	（1）将客人所乘车辆引领到适当的地方停车，以免门前交通阻塞。 Guide the vehicle of the guest to park at appropriate position to avoid traffic blocks before the hotel. （2）趋前开启车门，用手臂挡车门为客人护顶，并协助客人下车。原则是应优先女宾、老年人。 Step forwards to open the door; protect the head of the guest with the arm; assist the guest to get out of the car. In principle, priority should be given to female guests and elderly guests. （3）面带微笑地使用恰当的敬语欢迎前来的每一位客人。 Welcome every guest with appropriate honorific language with smiles. （4）协助行李员卸下行李，注意检查有无遗漏物品。 Assist the bellman in unloading the baggage; note to check whether there're any omissions.	（1）热情礼貌。 Be passionate and polite. （2）动作规范。 Behave to the standards. （3）配合行李员工作。 Assist the bellman in working. （4）老人儿童行动不便的要搀扶。 Support the elderly guests and children who are unable to move freely.

续表

操作步骤 Operation Procedures	主要操作步骤 Main Operation Procedures	注意要点 Key Points
3. 欢送客人 Seeing off the Guests	(1) 离店时，为客人打开大门，问候并询问客人离店后所去地点，调度、召唤出租车，并注意看管随客人而出的行李。 When the guest is about to leave the hotel, open the entrance door for the guest, greet the guest and enquire the destination, dispatch or call the taxi and pay attention to take care of the luggage with the guest. (2) 协助行李员将客人行李放入车后行李箱，为客人拉开车门，护顶，请客人上车，并祝客人旅途愉快。 Assist the bellman to load the luggage into the trunk; open the door for the guest; guide the guest into the vehicle and protect the head; wish a pleasant journey to the guest. (3) 驱散可疑闲杂人员，维持店前秩序。 Drive away suspicious people without fixed duties; maintain the order in front of the hotel.	(1) 根据客人的需要，及时提供服务。 Provide timely services according to the needs of the guest. (2) 送别时挥手示意，直到看不见车为止。 Wave goodbye to the guest till the car is out of vision.

（二）VIP 客人服务接待步骤（Reception Service Procedures for VIP Guests）

关于 VIP 客人的服务接待标准如表 3-4 所示。

The reception service standards for VIP guest are shown in Table 3-4.

表 3-4　VIP 客人的服务操作步骤和标准

Table 3-4　Service Procedures and Standards for VIP Guests

操作步骤 Operation Procedures	主要操作内容 Main Operation Contents	注意要点 Key Points
1. 准备工作 Getting Prepared	(1) 了解当天即将抵店的重要客人和团队。 Get to know the VIP guests and teams to be arrived on the very day. (2) 了解 VIP 客人接待规格。 Get to know the reception standards for the VIP guests.	准备工作要充分。 The preparation should be sufficient.
2. 迎接客人 Receiving the Guest	(1) 将客人所乘车辆引领到店门前停车。 Guide the vehicle of the guest to park before the hotel. (2) 趋前开启车门，用手臂挡车门为客人护顶，并协助客人下车。 Step forwards to open the door; protect the head of the guest with the arm; assist the guest to get out of the car. (3) 面带微笑并使用恰当的敬语欢迎前来的客人。 Welcome every guest with appropriate honorific language with smiles. (4) 协助行李员卸下行李，注意检查有无遗漏物品。 Assist the bellman in unloading the baggage; note to check whether there're any omissions.	(1) 热情礼貌。 Be passionate and polite. (2) 动作规范。 Behave to the standards. (3) 卸下行李。 Unload the luggage.
3. 欢迎仪式 Welcome Ceremony	(1) 按 VIP 客人接待级别，安排接待礼仪规格。 Determine the reception etiquette standards according to the reception standards for the VIP guests. (2) 视 VIP 客人级别安排欢迎仪式：列队欢迎，致欢迎词。 Arrange the welcome ceremony according to the level of the VIP guests. Line up to welcome the guest; give welcoming speech. (3) 驱散可疑闲杂人员，维持店前安全秩序。 Drive away suspicious people without fixed duties; maintain the security and order in front of the hotel. (4) 大堂经理（部门经理或总经理）陪同客人上电梯，到客房。 The Lobby Manager (Department Manager or General Manager) assists the guest to take the elevator and to the guest room.	(1) 提前下发 VIP 客人接待报告。 Distribute VIP guest reception report in advance. (2) 根据 VIP 客人接待报告安排迎接。 Arrange the welcome activities according to the VIP guest reception report.

【实训与评价】【Training and Assessment】

［实训目的］［Training Objectives］

1. 熟悉前厅行李服务的相关知识。

To be acquainted with related knowledge of luggage service.

2. 能够处理前厅在行李服务过程中出现的问题。

Be capable to dispose problems in luggage services in the lobby.

3. 规范自己的言行，正确使用礼貌用语和敬语；能有礼有节、不卑不亢地处理突发事件。

Standardize the words and deeds; correctly use polite and honorific languages; be able to dispose emergent cases in a civilized and neither lowly nor overbearing manner.

［实训准备］［Training Preparation］

1. 前厅服务模拟场景、电脑、打印机、值班记录簿、客人行李等。

Simulated scenario of lobby service, computer, printer, duty log, guest luggage, etc.

2. 学生 6 人分为一组，教师讲解示范后，学生根据教师布置的任务进行实际操作。

Divide the student in group of six. The teachers make explanation and demonstration; then the students make practices according to the tasks assigned by the teachers.

［实训方法］［Training Method］

先观看教师播放的教学课件，然后由教师引导学生分析案例，学生 6 人一组，按照任务驱动的要求进行实际操作，教师巡回指导，实训结束前抽小组进行前厅服务模拟表演。

First view the teaching courseware played by the teachers; then the teachers guide the students to analyze the cases. The students forms groups of six and make practical operations according to the tasks. The teachers walk around for guidance. Before ending the training, randomly select some groups to make simulated performance of lobby services.

［实训步骤］［Training Procedure］

第一步：教师向学生展示前厅行李服务的视频，让学生有一定的感性认识。

The teachers play the video about lobby luggage services to the students so that the students may have some perceptual knowledge about it.

第二步：学生分成 4 人一组讨论，由学生分析，指出正误。

Then divide the students into group of four; have the students to make analysis; point out correctness and errors.

第三步：由学生继续讨论，设计行李服务的工作程序。

The students continue discussion and design the working procedures for luggage services.

第四步：各组学生代表发言说出程序，其他各组学生评价。

Student representatives in each group represent their procedures and students from other groups make comments.

第五步：学生分成两人一组，进行前厅行李的实训。

The students work in pairs to make practical training on luggage services in the lobby area.

第六步：教师评价与回答问题。

The teachers makes evaluations and answer questions from the students.

［实训内容］［Training Content］

1. 前厅服务案例分析。

Case analysis on lobby services.

2. 前厅服务模拟实训操作。

Simulated practical training on lobby services.

［练一练］［Practice］

1. 练习门厅迎接员正确的站姿。

Train the correct standing posture of the doorman.

2. 3~5 人组成小组，分别扮演客人及迎接员角色，练习迎送客人的程序和具体规范。

Form groups of three to five, act respectively as the guests and doorman, practice the procedures and specific standards of reception/seeing-off services of the guests.

任务三　行李服务
Task III　Luggage Service

酒店的行李服务是由前厅部的行李员提供的，在欧美国家的酒店，行李员又被称为“Bell boy”、“Bell-man”、“Bell hop”和“Porter”，其工作岗位位于酒店大堂一侧的礼宾部。那么，行李服务都包括哪些具体要求和程序呢？

The luggage service of the hotel is provided by the bellman of the Front Office Department. In European and American hotels, the bellman is also called bellboy, bell-man, bell hop or porter. The post of the bellman is located in the Concierge Department on one side of the hotel lobby. So, what are the specific requirements and procedures of luggage service?

一、行李服务（Luggage Service）

行李服务是前厅服务的一项重要内容，由行李员负责提供。内容包括客人行李搬运和行李保管服务。由于散客和团队的客人有许多不同的特点，因此，其行李服务的规程也有所不同。

Luggage service is an important item in lobby service and should be provided by the bellman. The luggage service consists of luggage handling and luggage deposit services. As the individual guests and group guests present different features, the respective luggage service procedures are also varying.

（一）散客行李服务（Luggage Service for Individual Guests）

1. 散客入住行李服务（Luggage services for individual guests）

（1）散客乘车抵店时，行李员应主动上前迎接，向客人表示欢迎，帮助客人卸下行李，并请客人清点过目，准确无误后帮客人提携。但对于易碎物品和贵重物品不必主动提携，如客人需要帮助时，行李员要特别小心，注意要轻拿轻放，以防丢失破损。

When the individual guest arrives at the hotel by car, the bellman should initiatively come up to welcome the guest, help the guest to unload the luggage, ask the guest to check the luggage and carry the luggage for the guest if no mistake is made. However, the bellman need not carry fragile and valuable things for the guest. If required by the guest, the bellman should pay special attention and handle with care to avoid missing or damage.

（2）行李员提着行李走在客人的左前方，引领客人到总台办理入住登记手续，如属大件行李，则需要行李车。

The bellman should walk to the front left of the guest with the luggage and guide the guest to the Reception Guest to check in. In case of large luggage, luggage cart should be used.

（3）引领客人到达总台后，行李员应放下行李，站在总台前客人侧后 1.5 米处，并随时听候接待员及客人的召唤。

After guiding the guest to the Reception Desk, the bellman should lay down the luggage, stand 1.5 m on the rear of flank of the guest and ready to answer the call of the Receptionist and the guest from time to time.

（4）客人办完入住手续后，应主动上前从接待员手中接过房卡，引领客人入客房。

After the guest finishes check -in, the bellman should positively receive the room card from the Receptionist and guide the guest to the room.

（5）引领客人到达电梯门时，应放下行李，按电梯按钮。当电梯门打开时，护住电梯门，请客人先进入电梯，然后进入电梯靠右边侧站立并按楼层键。电梯到达后，请客人先出，行李员随后提行李跟出，继续引领客人到所住房间。

When guiding the guest to the elevator door, the bellman should lay down the luggage and press the elevator button. After the elevator door opens, the bellman should secure the elevator door and invite the guest to enter the elevator first. After entering the elevator, the bellman should stand to the right side the press the floor button. Upon the arrival of the elevator to the designated floor, ask the guest to get out first and then follow the guest with luggage. Guide the guest to his/her room.

（6）到达客房门口时，行李员先放下行李，按酒店既定程序敲门、开门，以免碰到重复卖房给客人造成不便。房内无反应再用钥匙开门。

In the doorway, the bellman should lay down the luggage first and then knock at the door and open the door according to the established procedures of the hotel to avoid any inconvenience to the guest caused by repeated room sales. Open the door only if there's no response within the room.

（7）打开房门后，将房卡插入取电盒内使房间通电，开灯，退出客房手势示意请客人先进。

After the room is opened, insert the room card into the power supply box, open the lights, quit the guest room and ask the guest to come in first with gesture.

（8）将行李放在客房行李柜上，然后简要介绍房间设施、设备及使用方法，介绍时手势不能太多，时间不能太长，应控制在 2 分钟以内，以免给客人造成索取小费的误解。如果客人以前曾住过本店，则不必再介绍。

Place the luggage onto the luggage cabinet of the room; brief the facilities and equipments in the room as well as their usage; do not take too much time or use too many gestures when making introduction; the introduction should be controlled within 2 minutes to avoid misunderstanding of the guest that the doorman is asking for tips. Introduction is not necessary for a revisited guest.

（9）房间介绍完毕，应征求客人是否还有吩咐，在客人无其他要求时，应礼貌地向客人道别，并祝客人在本店住得愉快。离开时，将房门轻轻拉上。

After introduction of the room, enquire whether the guest has other instructions. If no, say goodbye to the guest politely and wish a pleasant stay of the guest in the hotel. When leaving the room, close the room door gently.

（10）离开房间后，迅速从员工通道返回礼宾部，填写“散客行李（入店/出店）登记表”。

After leaving the room, quickly return to the Concierge Department from the staff passageway and fill in the *Independent Guest Luggage*（*Check-in/Check-out*）*Registration Form.*

2. 散客离店行李服务（Check-out luggage service for individual）

（1）当礼宾部接到客人离店搬运行李的通知时，要问清客人的房号、姓名、行李件数及搬运行李的时间，并决定是否要带上行李车，然后指派行李员按房号收取行李。

When receiving the notice of luggage service for check-out guests, the Concierge Department should ask the room number, name, number of luggage and time for luggage service for the guest and decide whether the luggage cart is required, and then assign the bellman to collect the luggage according to the room number.

（2）在征得客人同意后方可进入房间，并与客人核对行李件数，检查行李是否有破损情况，如有易碎物品，则应贴上易碎物品标志。

Enter the room only upon the consent of the guest; check the number of luggage with the guest; inspect whether there's any damages of the luggage; put on marks for fragile articles, if any.

（3）弄清客人是否直接离店，若客人需要行李寄存，则填写行李寄存单，并将其中的一联交给客人作为取物凭证，向客人道别，将行李送回行李房寄存保管。待客人来取行李时，核对并收回寄存单。

Make clear whether the guest will leave the hotel directly; in case that luggage deposit service is required, fill in the *Luggage Deposit Form* and give one copy to the guest as the certificate to withdraw the deposited things. Say goodbye to the guest and take the luggage to the Luggage Room for safekeeping. Check and take back the *Luggage Deposit Form* when the guest comes to retrieve the luggage.

（4）如客人需直接离店，装上行李后，应礼貌地请客人离开房客，主动为客人叫电梯，为客人提供电梯服务，引领客人到前厅收银处办理退房结账手续。

If the guest leaves the hotel directly. After the luggage is loaded, politely ask the guest to leave the room; positively call the elevator for the guest and provide service in the elevator; guide the guest to the Cashier's Desk in the lobby and handle the check-out formalities.

（5）客人离店时协助行李装车，向客人道别，并祝客人旅途愉快。

When the guest is about to leave, assist the guest in loading the luggage, say goodbye to the guest and wish the guest a happy journey.

（6）完成行李运送工作后，将行李车放回原处，填写“散客行李（入店/出店）登记表”。

After finishing the luggage service, put the luggage cart to the original place and fill in the *Independent Guest Luggage*（*Check-in/Check-out*）*Registration Form.*

（二）团队客人行李服务（Group Guest Luggage Service）

团队客人的行李一般由单位从车站、码头、机场等地装车运抵酒店，而酒店行李员的工作只是按团队名称清点行李件数，检查行李有无破损，做好交接手续，负责店内行李的运送与收取。

Generally, luggage of group guests is loaded at the railway station, dock, airport, etc. and delivered to the hotel. And the bellman of the hotel should count the number of the luggage on group basis, inspection whether there're any damages, make proper handover formalities and be responsible for the delivery and collection of the luggage within the hotel.

1. 团队入住行李服务（Luggage services for group guests）

（1）团队行李到达时，行李员推出行李车，与行李押运员交接行李，清点行李件数，检查行李有无破损，然后双方按各项规定程序履行签收手续。如发现行李有破损或短缺，应由行李押运单位负责，请行李押运人员签字证明，并通知陪同及领队。如行李随团到达，则还应请领队签字确认。

Upon the arrival of group luggage, the bellman should take out the luggage cart, take over the luggage from the luggage escort, count the number of the luggage, inspect whether there're any damages and then work on sign-off formalities with the other party according to the prescribed formalities. In case of any damage or shortage, the luggage escorting unit should assume the liabilities. The bellman should ask the luggage escort to sign as proof and notify the accompanying personnel and the group leader. If the luggage arrives together with the group, the group leader should be asked to sign for confirmation.

（2）填写团队行李登记表，见表 3-5。

Fill in the *Group Luggage Registration Form*, as shown in Table3-5.

（3）清点无误后，立即在每件行李上贴上行李标签或系上行李牌。如果该团队行李不能及时分送，应在适当地点摆放整齐，用行李网将该团队所有的行李罩在一起，妥善保管。要注意将入店行李与出店行李，或是几个同时到店的团队行李分开摆放，避免出错。

After no mistakes are detected by checking, put on luggage label or tie on luggage tag immediately on each piece of luggage. If the group luggage cannot be delivered timely, it should be placed in order at proper place. Cover the entire luggage of the group with a luggage net and keep it properly. Please note that luggage coming in and going out or luggage of different groups arriving at the same time should be placed separately to avoid mistakes.

（4）在装运行李之前，应再清点检查一次，无误后才能装车，走行李通道送行李上楼层。装运行李时应遵循"同团同车、同层同车、同侧同车"的原则。

Recheck before loading the luggage; load the luggage into the cart if no errors are detected; deliver the luggage to the corresponding floor through the luggage passageway. When loading the luggage, the principle of "Same Group in Same Cart; Same Level in Same Cart; Same Side in Same Cart" should be followed.

（5）将行李送到楼层后，按房号分送行李。

Distribute the luggage according to the room number when the luggage is delivered to the related floor.

（6）送完行李后，将每间客房的行李件数准确地登记在团队入店行李登记表上，并按团队入住单上的时间存档。

After the luggage is distributed, accurately record the number of luggage for each room onto the *Group Guest Luggage Registration Form*, and archive according to the time indicated on the *Group Check-in Sheet.*

表 3-5 某酒店团队行李（入店/出店）登记表

Table3-5 Group Luggage (Check-in/Check-out) Registration Form of XXX Hotel

团队名称 Group		人数 No. of People		入店日期 Check-in Date		离店日期 Check-out Date	
	时间 Time	总件数 Total Number of Luggage		酒店行李员 Bellman	领队 Group Leader	行李押运员 Luggage Escort	车号 Vehicle No.
入店 Check-in							

续表

出店 Check-out							
房号 Room No.	入店件数 Number of Receiving Luggage			离店件数 Number of Leaving Luggage			备注 Remarks
	行李箱 Luggage Case	行李包 Luggage Bag	其他 Others	行李箱 Luggage Case	行李包 Luggage Bag	其他 Others	
合计 Total							

2. 团队离店行李服务（Check-out luggage service for group guests）

（1）根据团队客人入住登记表上的离店时间，做好收取行李的工作安排，带上该团队订单和已核对的登记行李件数的记录表，领取行李车，上楼层搬运行李。

Make arrangement on collection of luggage according to the check-out time on the *Group Guest Check-in Registration Form*; take along the reservation form of the group and the checked record sheet on number of luggage; apply for the luggage cart and go to the designated floor to collect the luggage.

（2）在规定的时间内依照团号、团名及房间号码到楼层收取客人放在房门口的行李，并做好记录。收取行李时要核实行李上所挂或所贴的标签是否一致。

Collect the luggage placed by the guest in the doorway according to the group number, group name and room numbers on the designated floor within the defined time; make appropriate record. When collecting the luggage, check whether the marks or tags on the luggage are consistent.

（3）行李员收取行李时，应从走廊的尽头开始，以避免漏收和走回头路。如有客人的行李未放在门口，应通知该团陪同，并协助陪同通知客人把行李拿出房间，以免耽误时间。对置于房间内的行李则不予运送。

When collecting the luggage, the bellman should start from one end of the corridor to avoid omission or repeated work. If the luggage of a guest is not placed in the door way, the bellman should inform the accompanying personnel of the group and assist the accompanying personnel to urge the guest to take out the luggage to save time. Luggage left in the room will not be collected and delivered.

（4）将团队行李汇总到前厅，再次核对并严加看管，以防丢失。核对实数与记录相符，领队或陪同一起过目，并签字确认。与团队的行李押运员一起检查、清点行李，将行李罩好，并贴上表格。做好行李移交手续；特别要和领队核实该行李总件数是否包含领队的行李。

Collect the group luggage to the lobby; double check the luggage and make strict control to prevent losing. If the actual number checked is consistent with the record, have the group leader or accompanying personnel to make visual inspection and sign for confirmation. Work with the luggage escort of the group to inspect and count the luggage. Cover the luggage properly and paste related forms. Work on handover formalities of the luggage appropriately. Particularly check with the group leader whether such total number of the luggage includes the luggage of the group leader him/herself.

（5）行李集中运到行李部，检查后，在“行李进出店登记单”上签字。

Gather the luggage and deliver the luggage to the Luggage Department. Sign on the *Luggage Entering/*

Leaving Registration Form after inspection.

(6) 行李完成交接后，由领班填写“团队行李（入店/出店）登记表”并存档。

After the handover and takeover of the luggage is finished, the Supervisor should fill in and archive the *Group Luggage* (*Check-in/Check-out*) *Registration Form*.

二、客人行李服务流程（Guest Luggage Service Procedures）

（一）散客的行李服务与标准（Luggage Services and Standards for Individual Guests）

(1) 散客抵店的行李服务与标准，如表 3-6 所示。

Receiving Luggage Services and Standards, as shown in Table 3-6.

表 3-6 散客抵店的行李服务与标准

Table 3-6 Receiving Luggage Services and Standards for Individual Guests

操作步骤 Operation Procedures	主要操作内容 Main Operation Contents	注意要点 Key Points
1. 出门迎接 Welcome the guest outside	(1) 行李员主动迎接抵达酒店的客人，为客人打开车门，请客人下车，并亲切问候。 The bellman should initiatively welcome the arriving guest, open the car door for the guest, guide the guest to get off and greet the guest warmly. (2) 从出租车内取出客人行李，请客人确认行李件数，以免遗漏。 Take the luggage out from the taxi. Ask the guest to check the number of the luggage to avoid omissions. (3) 迅速引导客人走进店门，到前台办理入店登记手续。 Quickly guide the guest into the hotel and handle the check-in formalities at the Reception Desk.	(1) 要热情礼貌。 Be passionate and polite. (2) 易碎或贵重物品请客人自己拿。 Ask the guest to carry fragile or valuable article (s) by him/herself. (3) 检查行李件数。 Inspect the number of luggage.
2. 引领客人入店，办理入店手续 Guide the guest into the hotel and work on check-in formalities	(1) 行李员引领客人至前台，把行李放置在离前台 4 米以外的地方，系好本店行李牌，手背后直立站在行李后方，直到客人办理完毕全部入店手续。 The bellman should guide the guest to the Reception Desk, put the luggage 4 m away from the Reception Desk, tie the luggage tag of the hotel, then stand straight behind the luggage with both hands at the back till the guest finishes all the check-in formalities. (2) 对于住在豪华楼层的客人，需引导客人至豪华楼层办理入店手续，并需帮助客人搬开并放好登记台前的座椅，请客人入座，退后 3~4 米，站立等候客人办完手续。 For guests residing on the luxury floor, guide the guest to the luxury floor for check-in formalities, help the guest to pull out the chair in front of the Registration Desk and ask the guest to sit. Step backwards for about 3-4 m and stand till the guest finishes the formalities.	(1) 用左手提行李，行走时身体要自然。 Carry the luggage with the left hand; walk naturally. (2) 过重、过大的行李要用行李车。 Use luggage cart to carry excessively heavy or large luggage. (3) 等待客人办理入住登记时不可左顾右盼，随时听从客人吩咐。 When waiting for the guest to finish the check-in, do not look around; wait for the instructions from the guest at any time.
3. 引导客人入住房间 Guide the guest into the room	(1) 客人办理完入店手续后，行李员接过客房钥匙，清晰地将房间号码登记在行李牌上。 After the guest finishes the check-in formalities, the bellman receives the key to the guest room and clearly mark the room number onto the luggage tag. (2) 如果几位客人同时入店，应在办理完手续后，请每位客人逐件确认行李，在行李牌上写清客人的房间号码，并礼貌地告诉客人在房间等候，然后迅速将行李送入房间。 If there're several guests checking in at the same time, after the formalities are done, ask each guest to confirm the luggage item by item, note the room number on the luggage tag, ask the guest to wait in the guest room politely, and then take the luggage into the guest rooms.	(1) 准确地在行李牌上写上房号。 Mark the room number correctly onto the luggage tag. (2) 引领时走在客人左前方两三步远，用右手指示方向。 When guiding the guest into the room, be about two or three steps away in the left front of the guest, indicate the directions with the right hand. (3) 边走边向客人介绍酒店的设施和服务项目。

续表

操作步骤 Operation Procedures	主要操作内容 Main Operation Contents	注意要点 Key Points
	(3) 引导客人至电梯厅，按叫电梯。在途中向客人介绍酒店设施和服务项目，使客人初步了解酒店。 Guide the guest to the elevator hall and call the elevator. On the way to the elevator, introduce the hotel facilities and service items to make the guests preliminarily know the hotel. (4) 电梯叫到，请客人先进电梯间，并为客人按下相应楼层示意键，然后将行李提进电梯间，靠边放置在电梯里，继续向客人介绍酒店有关情况，回答客人问讯。 When the elevator is ready, ask the guest to enter the elevator first, press the button for related floor for the guest, carry the luggage into the elevator room and place the luggage into the elevator. Continue the introduction to the hotel and answer the questions from the guest. (5) 电梯到达目的地楼层后，请客人先走出电梯，行李员随后赶上，走在客人之前，引领客人进入客房。 When the elevator reaches the targeted floor, ask the guest to get out first. The bellman should follow the guest out and then walk in front of the guest to guide the guest into the room.	Introduce the hotel facilities and service items to the guest while walking. (4) 介绍安全通道。 Introduce the exit passageway. (5) 上下电梯，客人先进先出。 Have the guest come in/out of the elevator first.
4. 房间服务 Room service	(1) 引导客人到达房间，把行李放在房门外左侧，并简短地向客人介绍紧急出口及客人房间在酒店的位置。 Guide the guest to the room; put the luggage on the left side of the room door in the hallway; brief the emergency exit and the location of the guest room in the hotel to the guest. (2) 开门之前，向客人介绍如何使用钥匙开门及其他钥匙的用途（如小酒吧钥匙）。 Before opening the door, introduce to the guest how to open the door with the key and the other functions of the key (such as the key to the small bar). (3) 为客人打开房门，介绍电源开关，并把钥匙插入开关内。 Open the door for the guest; introduce the power switch and insert the key to the switch. (4) 请客人首先进入房间，行李员把行李放在行李架上。 Ask the guest to come into the room first; place the luggage onto the luggage rack. (5) 向客人介绍如何使用电视和收看各频道节目，以及酒店内提供的节目。 Introduce to the guest how to use the TV and watch programs of different channels as well as the programs provided within the hotel. (6) 向客人介绍电话使用方法，店内各主要服务部门的电话号码及空调、收音机、床头灯等电器设备的使用方法。 Introduce the use of telephone to the guest; introduce the telephone numbers of the main service departments of the hotel as well as the use of the electric appliances such as AC, radio and bed lamp. (7) 告知客人写字桌上放有酒店介绍，以便客人更多地了解酒店服务信息。 Inform the guest that the introduction of the hotel is on the desk so that the guest may know more about hotel services. (8) 向客人介绍小酒吧，并提醒客人注意放在酒吧上的价格表。 Introduce the small bar in the guest room; and remind the guest to pay attention to the price list of the bar. (9) 向客人介绍卫生间内设施，提醒客人注意电源的使用。 Introduce bathroom facilities to the guest; remind the guest to be careful with power supplies. (10) 向客人介绍店内的洗衣服务及电话号码。 Introduce the laundry and its telephone number of the hotel to the guest. (11) 介绍完毕，询问客人是否还有其他要求，最后祝愿客人居住愉快。 Upon finishing the introduction, ask the guest whether he/she has some other requirements. Then wish the guest to have a pleasant stay.	(1) 先敲门，再开门。 Knock the door before opening the door. (2) 按规定介绍房间里的设施设备使用情况。 Introduce the use of equipments and facilities in the room according to related provisions. (3) 如果客人没事，介绍完迅速退出。 Quickly quit from the room after the introduction if the guest has no more questions.

续表

操作步骤 Operation Procedures	主要操作内容 Main Operation Contents	注意要点 Key Points
5. 登记 Registration	(1) 待送完客人后，回到行李台登记房号、行李件数、客人入店时间。 After showing the guest into the room the bellman return to the Luggage Desk and register the room number, number of the luggage and the check-in time of the guest. (2) 如遇到早到而暂时无法进入房间的客人，应将行李放在行李台旁，代客人保管，并标明"入店"字样，待客人房间安排好后，再送入房间。 In case that the gucst arrivers earlier than schedule and no room is available, place the luggage beside the Luggage Desk and keep it properly for the guest. Mark the luggage with the words "checked in". After the guest room is ready for the guest; take the luggage to the room when the guest room is ready. (3) 如果客人没有进入房间，而由行李员将行李送入客房。 If the guest doesn't enter the room, the bellman should take the luggage to the guest room.	记录及时、准确、完整。 The record should be timely, accurate and complete.

（2）散客离店的行李服务与标准，如表 3-7 所示。

Leaving Luggage Services and Standards, as shown in Table 3-7.

表 3-7 散客离店的行李服务与标准

Table 3-7 Leaving Luggage Services and Standards for Individual Guests

操作步骤 Operation Procedures	主要操作内容 Main Operation Contents	注意要点 Key Points
1. 接到通知，收取客人行李 Receive the notice and collect guest luggage	当客人离店打电话要求收取行李时，行李员必须问清客人房间号码、行李件数和收取行李时间。 When the guest is about to leave and calls to require the collection of baggage, the bellman must make clear the room number, number of the luggage and the collection time of the guest.	问清房号、行李件数。 Make clear the room number and number of the luggage.
2. 登记 Make registration	行李员在离店登记单上填写房间号码、时间、行李件数，并根据房间号码迅速去取客人行李。 The bellman fills the room number, time and number of the luggage in the *Check-out Registration Form* and quickly collect the luggage according to the room number.	做好记录。 Make proper record.
3. 收取客人行李 Collect the guest luggage	(1) 在 3 分钟之内到达客人房间，轻敲三下，并告知客人"行李服务"或待客人开后，向客人问候。 Get to the guest room within three minutes; knock the door for three times gently and tell the guest "bell service"; or greet the guest when the door is opened. (2) 和客人一起确认好行李件数，并帮助客人检查是否有遗漏物品。如发现遗留物品，应直接还给客人或交给行李部经理。 Check with the guest the number of the luggage, assist the guest to check whether there're omitted things. The omitted things detected, if any, should be returned to the guest or handed over to the Manager of the Luggage Department. (3) 行李员把客人行李放置在行李台旁边，告知领班客人房间号码，站在一旁等候客人。 The bellman place the luggage of the guest beside the luggage cabinet; inform the room number to the Supervisor and stand aside to wait for the guest.	(1) 及时收取行李。 Collect the luggage timely. (2) 查清行李件数。 Inspect the number of lug-gage. (3) 放好行李，以免拿错。 Place the luggage properly to avoid mistakes.
4. 帮助客人离店 Help the guest to check out	(1) 确定客人已付清全部房费，办理完毕离店手续后，引导客人出店，帮助客人将行李放入出租车内。 Make sure that the guest has paid up the room rates; after the check-out formalities are done, guide the guest out of the hotel and assist the guest to load the luggage into the taxi. (2) 为客人打开车门，并请客人上车护顶。 Open the door of the taxi for the guest and protect the head of the guest. (3) 向客人礼貌告别："欢迎下次再来。" Say goodbye to the guest politely: "Welcome back!"	及时将行李放到车上，热情挥手送客直到远去。 Load the luggage into the car in time; wave warmly till the guest has gone far away.

（二）团队的行李服务与标准（Luggage Services and Standards for Group Guests）

（1）团队进店时的行李服务与标准，如表 3-8 所示。

Receiving Luggage Services and Standards for Group Guests, as shown in Table 3-8.

表 3-8　团队进店时的行李服务与标准

Table 3-8　Receiving Luggage Services and Standards for Group Guests

操作步骤 Operation Procedures	主要操作内容 Main Operation Contents	注意要点 Key Points
1. 接收行李 Receive the luggage	（1）当团队行李送到酒店时，由领班向团队行李员问清行李件数、团队人数，并请团队行李员在入店登记表上登记姓名和行李车牌号等。 When the group luggage arrives the hotel, the Supervisor should ask the bellman for the group clearly about the number of the luggage, number of group members, and ask the group bellman to register the name, luggage vehicle number, etc. on the *Check-in Registration Form.* （2）由领班指派行李员卸下全部行李，并清点行李件数，检查行李有无破损。如遇破损，须请团队行李员签字证实，并通知团队陪同及领队。 The Supervisor should command the bellman to unload all the luggage, count the number of the luggage and inspect whether there're any damages. In case of damage, ask the group bellman to sign for confirmation and inform the accompanying personnel and the leader of the group. （3）整齐排放行李，全部系上有本酒店标志的行李牌，并用网子罩住，以防止丢失、错拿。 Place the luggage in order and completely tie the luggage with the luggage tags with the logo of the hotel. Cover the luggage with net to avoid missing and mistaken taking.	（1）分清团队、人数。 Make clear the group and number of people. （2）分清行李件数。 Inspect the number of luggage. （3）系好行李牌。 Tie the luggage tag approp-riately.
2. 分拣行李 Sort out the luggage	（1）根据前台分配的房间号码分拣行李，并将分好的房间号码清晰地写在行李牌上。 Sort out the luggage according to the room numbers distributed by the Reception Desk; clearly note the room numbers onto the luggage tags. （2）与前台分房处联系，问明分配的房间是否有变动，如有变动，须及时更改。 Contact with the room allocation post of the Reception Desk to clarify whether there' re any variations in room allocation. If so, make timely changes. （3）及时将已知房间号码的行李送至房间。 Timely deliver the luggage with fixed room number to the related room. （4）如遇行李姓名卡丢失，行李应由领队帮助确认。 In case that the name card on the luggage is missing, ask the group leader to help confirm.	（1）分送行李要准确。 Luggage sorting and delivery should be correct. （2）同房间同车，同侧同楼层同车。 Put luggage of the same room onto the same cart; put luggage of the same floor and same side onto the same cart. （3）不同团队的行李分车送。 Delivery luggage of different groups onto different carts.
3. 送行李到房间 Deliver the luggage into the room	（1）将行李平稳摆放到行李车上，在推车入店时，注意不要损坏客人物品和酒店设施。 Place the luggage levelly and stably onto the luggage cart; when pushing the cart into the hotel, attention should be made so as not to damage the guest belongings and the hotel facilities. （2）在进入楼层后，应将行李放在门左侧，轻轻敲门三下，报出"行李员"。 When enter the corresponding floor, place the luggage to the left side of the door. Knock at the door gently for three times and call "Bell Service". （3）客人开门后，主动向客人问好，固定房门，把行李送入房间内，待客人确认后方可离开。如果客人的行李不见了，应婉转地让客人稍候并及时报告领班。 Greet the guest initiatively when the door is opened. Fasten the door, put the luggage into the room and leave upon the confirmation of the guest. In case of luggage missing, ask the guest to wait for a moment euphemistically and timely report to the Supervisor. （4）对于破损和无人认领的行李，要与领队或陪同及时取得联系，以便尽快解决。 For damaged or unclaimed luggage, timely contact the group leader or the accompanying personnel to solve the matter as soon as possible.	（1）运送行李动作要文明。 Deliver the luggage in a civilized manner. （2）按规定敲门。 Knock at the door according to related provisions.

续表

操作步骤 Operation Procedures	主要操作内容 Main Operation Contents	注意要点 Key Points
4. 行李登记 Luggage Registration	(1) 送完行李后，应将送入每个房间的行李件数准确登记在团队入店登记单上。 After the luggage is delivered，accurately register the number of the luggage of each room onto the *Check-in Registration Form for Group Guests*. (2) 如果是开门直接送入，则应注明“开门”字样，并核实总数是否与刚入店时一致。 If the luggage is delivered directly into the room after the guest opens the door，indicate “Opened Door” and check whether the total number is consistent with the number when the luggage arrives at the hotel.	及时记录。 Make timely record.

(2) 团队离店时的行李服务与标准，如表 3-9 所示。

Leaving Luggage Services and Standards for Group Guests，as shown in Table 3-9.

表 3-9 团队离店时的行李服务与标准

Table 3-9 Leaving Luggage Services and Standards for Group Guests

操作步骤 Operation Procedures	主要操作内容 Main Operation Contents	注意要点 Key Points
1. 准备 Preparation	(1) 仔细审阅前台送来的团队离店名单。 Read carefully the list for group check-out distributed by Reception Desk. (2) 提前 3 天将欲离团队的团号、房间号、人数与电脑内的档案核实。 Examine the group number，room number and number of the people of the group about to check out with the files in the computer 3 days in advance. (3) 与团队入店时填写的行李表核对，并建立新表。 Check with the Luggage Table filled when the group checks in and establish a new table. (4) 夜班领班将核实后的表格转交下一班领班。 The Supervisor of the night shift should hand over the verified table to the Supervisor of the next shift.	(1) 查清要离店团队的编号名单。 Make clear the list of numbers of groups about to leave. (2) 夜班编制离店表，交接班时，如有特殊情况要交代清楚。 The night shift should compile the Check-out Table. Clearly explain any special cases when making shifting of duty.
2. 收取行李 Collection of luggage	(1) 依照团号、团名及房间号码到楼层收取行李。 Collect the luggage according to the group number，group name and room number on the corresponding floor. (2) 与客人确认行李的件数。如客人不在房间，则检查行李牌号及姓名。 Check the number of the luggage with the guest. If the guest is not in the room，inspect the luggage tag number and name. (3) 如客人不在房间，又未将行李放在房间外，则应及时报告领班解决。 In case that the guest is not in the room and does not put the luggage in the hallway，timely report the case to the Supervisor for solution. (4) 根据领班指定位置摆放行李并罩好，以免行李丢失。 Place at the designated position by the Supervisor and cover the luggage properly to avoid missing.	(1) 仔细对照名单收取行李。 Collect the luggage carefully to the list. (2) 不同的团队分别收取、摆放。 Collect and place the luggage of different groups separately.
3. 核对 Check	(1) 统计行李件数的实数是否与登记数吻合。 Inspect whether the actual number of the luggage is consistent with the registered number. (2) 由领班与陪同或领队一起确认件数。若无误，请其在团队离店单上签字。 The Supervisor should confirm the number of luggage together with the accompanying personnel or the group leader. If no mistakes are made，have the *Check-out Form for Group Guests* signed. (3) 从前台得到该团行李放行卡后，方可让该团队离开。 The group may be released only if the luggage release card of the group is obtained from the Reception Desk.	(1) 按规定确认、签字。 Confirm and sign according to the provisions. (2) 有放行卡方可放行。 Release the luggage only with the release card.

续表

操作步骤 Operation Procedures	主要操作内容 Main Operation Contents	注意要点 Key Points
4. 行李放行及资料存档 Releasing of luggage and data archiving	（1）由领班问清行李员所取的团队行李的团号和团名。 The Supervisor asks the number and name of the group requiring luggage collection. （2）待团队行李员确认行李件数后，请其在离店单上签上姓名和车牌号。 After the group bellman confirms the number of the luggage, ask him/her to sign the name and vehicle plate number on the *Check-out Form*. （3）领班把团队离店登记单存档。 The Supervisor archive the *Check-out Form* for Group Guests.	记录存档。 Record archiving.

【实训与评价】【Training and Evaluation】

行李服务

Luggage Service

［实训目的］［Training Objectives］

掌握客人抵店时行李员应该提供的服务与相关知识。

To master the services to be provided by the bellman when the guest arrives at the hotel and related knowledge.

［组织形式及要求］［Organization Form and Requirement］

1. 按要求设计预订场景。

To design the reservation scenario as required.

2. 场地要求：前厅服务模拟实训室。

Place requirement: Simulated practical training on lobby services.

3. 全班以两人为一个小组分成若干组，小组两位同学分别扮演行李员和客人。

Divide the class into several groups of two. And the two students in one group act respectively as the bellman and the guest.

4. 完成后小组成员角色互换进行练习。

Swap the role after the practice is done.

5. 角色扮演时要投入、认真，填写好相应的表格。

Be devoted and careful in role play; fill in corresponding forms appropriately.

［训练道具］［Training Property］

行李车、行李登记表、行李卡等。

Luggage cart, luggage registration form, luggage card, etc.

［操作程序与标准］［Operation Procedures and Standards］

参照表 3-6 和表 3-7：散客的行李服务与标准。

See Table 3-6 and Table 3-7: Luggage Services and Standards for Individual Guests.

任务四 委托代办服务
Task Ⅳ Agency Services

一、行李寄存服务（Luggage Deposit Services）

由于各种原因，有的客人希望将一些行李暂时存放在礼宾部。礼宾部为方便客人存放行李，保证行李安全，应开辟专门的行李房，建立相应的制度，并规定必要的手续。

Some guests would like to deposit some luggage temporarily at the Concierge Department for various types of reasons. To facilitate the luggage deposit and guarantee the security of the luggage, the Concierge Department should establish specific Luggage Room, establish corresponding systems and prescribe necessary formalities.

（一）对寄存行李的要求（Requirements on Luggage Deposit）

（1）行李房不寄存现金、珠宝、玉器、金银首饰等贵重物品，以及护照等身份证件。上述物品应礼貌地请客人自行保管，或放到前厅收银处的保险箱内免费保管。已办理退房手续的客人如想使用保险箱，需经大堂经理批准。

The Luggage Room provides no deposit services for valuable articles such as cash, treasures, jades and jewelries as well as identity documents such as passport. In case of such articles, ask the guests to keep by themselves or deposit them for free in to the safe at the Cashier's Desk in the Lobby. If the guest has checked out and requires using the safe, approval from the Assistant Manager is required.

（2）酒店及行李房不得寄存易燃、易腐烂、易碎及具有腐蚀性的物品，不得寄存违禁物品。

No inflammable, perishable, fragile or corrosive articles should be deposited in the hotel and the Luggage Room. No prohibited articles should be deposited.

（3）不接受宠物寄存。一般来说，酒店不接受带宠物的客人入住。

No pet should be deposited. Generally, hotels are not accepting guests with the pet.

（4）提示客人将行李上锁，对未上锁的小件行李需在客人面前用封条封好。

Remind the guest to lock the luggage. For small luggage not lock, the staff should seal the luggage with strip seals before the guest.

（二）行李寄存的注意事项（Precautions for Luggage Deposit）

（1）确认客人身份。

Confirm the identity of the guest.

（2）检查行李。

Inspect the luggage.

（3）必须出示有效证件才可以寄存行李。

Require effective certificate for luggage deposit.

（4）行李寄存与处理一定要按规定的程序进行。

The deposit and treatment of luggage must be made according to the stipulated formalities.

（三）行李寄存程序（Luggage Deposit Procedures）

（1）客人前来寄存行李时，行李员应热情接待礼貌服务。

Receive the guest warmly and provide services politely when the guest comes to deposit the luggage.

（2）应弄清客人行李是否属于酒店不予寄存的范围。

Clarify whether the luggage of the guest is beyond the scope of deposit of the hotel.

（3）问清行李件数、寄存时间、姓名及房号。

Check the number of the luggage，deposit time，name of guest and room number.

（4）填写"行李寄存单"，并请客人签名，上联附挂在行李上，下联交给客人留存，并告知客人下联是领取行李的凭证。见表 3-10。

Fill in the *Luggage Deposit Form* and have the guest sign on the form；put on the original copy onto the luggage and the duplicated copy to the guest；inform the guest that that copy is the certificate for the guest to retrieve the luggage. As shown in Table 3-10.

表 3-10 某酒店行李寄存单

Table 3-10 Luggage Deposit Form of ×××Hotel

行李寄存单（酒店联） LUGGAGE DEPOSIT FORM（Copy for Hotel）		
姓名 NAME:	日期 DATE:	房号 ROOM NO:
行李件数 LUGGAGE:		时间 TIME:
客人签名 GUESTS SIGNATURE:		
行李员签名 BELLBOY's SIGNATURE:		
行李员签名 BELLBOY's SIGNATURE:		
行李寄存单（顾客联） LUGGAGE DEPOSIT FORM（Copy for Guest）		
姓名 NAME:	日期 DATE:	房号 ROOM NO:
行李件数 LUGGAGE:		时间 TIME:
客人签名 GUESTS SIGNATURE:		
行李员签名 BELLBOY's SIGNATURE:		
行李员签名 BELLBOY's SIGNATURE:		

（5）将短期存放的行李，如半天或一天的行李放置于方便搬运的地方；如一位客人有多种行李，应用绳索系在一起，以免拿错。

Place the temporarily deposited luggage（e.g. for half a day or a day）to a place easy for handling. If one guest deposits several items，tie such items up with a rope to avoid mistakes.

（6）经办人须在"行李寄存记录簿"上进行登记，并注明行李存放的件数、位置及存取日期等情况，见表 3-11。如属非客人寄存，客人领取的寄存行李，应通知客人前来确认领取。

The responsible personnel must register the deposit on the *Luggage Deposit Log*，indicating information such as the number of deposited luggage，location and the deposit period，as shown in Table 3-11. If the luggage is not deposited by the guest but to be retrieved by the guest，inform the guest to confirm the retrieval.

表 3-11 某酒店行李寄存记录簿

Table 3-11 Luggage Deposit Log of ××× Hotel

日期 Date	时间 Time	房号 Room No.	件数 Number of Luggage	存单号码 Deposit Form No.	行李员 Bellman	领回日期 Retrieval Date	时间 Time	行李员 Bellman	备注 Remarks

（四）行李领取服务（Luggage Retrieval Services）

（1）客人前来领取行李时，需收回“行李寄存单”的下联，请客人当场在下联单上签名；将上下进行核对，看二者的签名是否相符，核实无误后将行李交给客人，最后在“行李寄存记录簿”上做好记录。

In case that the guest comes to retrieve the luggage, the copy of *Luggage Deposit Form* for the guest must be collected. Ask the guest to sign on that copy on the spot and check both copies for the consistency of both signatures. After verification is proved, hand the luggage to the guest and record properly on the *Luggage Deposit Log*.

（2）如果是客人寄存，他人来领取，需请客人把代领人的姓名、单位或住址写清楚，并请客人告知代领人凭“行李寄存单”的下联及证件前来领取行李，行李员需在“行李寄存记录簿”的备注栏内做好记录。

In case that the luggage is deposited by the guest and retrieved by another person, ask the guest to write down clearly the name, unit or address of the assignee. Ask the guest to inform the assignee to retrieve the luggage with the guest copy of the *Luggage Deposit Form* and related credentials. The bellman should make proper record on the remark column of the *Luggage Deposit Log*.

（3）如果客人遗失了“行李寄存单”，需请客人出示有效身份证件，核查签名后，请客人报出寄存行李的件数、形状特征、原房号等。确定是该客人的行李后，需请客人写一张领取行李的说明并签名（或复印其证件）。

If the guest has missed the *Luggage Deposit Form*, ask the guest to present effective identity document and verify the signature. Then ask the guest to tell the number of the luggage, shape features, original room number, etc. of the deposited luggage. After the luggage is confirmed to belong to the guest, ask the guest to fill in the Note to Luggage Retrieval and sign on it (or have the credential of the guest copied).

（4）来访客人留存物品，让住店客人前来领取的寄存服务，可采取留言的方式通知客人，并参照寄存、领取服务的有关条款进行。

For articles deposited by a visitor and requiring the guest to collect, a message may be left to inform the guest. Related provisions on deposit and retrieval may be referred to.

（5）帮助客人把行李送到指定地方，并礼貌地向客人道别。

Assist the guest to carry the luggage to the designated place and say goodbye to the guest politely.

二、行李寄存和提取流程（Luggage Deposit and Retrieval Procedures）

行李寄存和提取的操作程序见表 3-12。

The luggage deposit and retrieval procedures are shown in Table 3-12.

表 3-12 行李寄存和提取的操作程序
Table 3-12 The Luggage Deposit and Retrieval Procedures

操作步骤 Operation Procedures	主要操作内容 Main Operation Contents	注意要点 Key Points
1. 填写行李寄存牌 Fill in the luggage deposit tag	（1）有礼貌地递给客人行李寄存牌，并向客人介绍需填写的项目，提醒客人本店对散客过期不取行李的保留时间。 Pass the luggage deposit tag politely to the guest; inform the guest items to be filled in; remind the retention time on expired luggage for individual guests. （2）向客人询问所存行李件数和提取行李时间，并亲自在行李寄存牌的上联和下联为客人填写清楚。 Enquire the guest about the number of the luggage and the time of retrieval; fill the information in person on both copies of the luggage deposit tag. （3）请客人填写行李寄存牌，需写清当天日期、客人姓名、房间号码。 Ask the guest to fill in the luggage deposit tag. Information such as the date of deposit, name of guest and room number must be clearly indicated. （4）行李员同时在单据上写清自己姓名，撕下下联收据递给客人，并提醒客人凭此提取行李。 The bellman should also write down his/her name on the voucher; tear down the copy for the guest and hand it to the guest; and remind the guest to retrieve the luggage by presenting this copy as certificate.	仔细检查行李寄存牌，要填写清楚。 Inspect the luggage deposit tag carefully and fill in the information clearly.
2. 保管客人所存的行李 Keep the deposited luggage of the guest	（1）将存放半天或一天的行李放在屋外侧，以便搬运。将长期存放的物品放在存储室的行李架上，如果一位客人有多件行李，应用绳子连在一起，以免错拿。 Place the luggage deposited for half a day or a day close to the door to facilitate handling. Place the articles deposited for a long time on the luggage racks of the Deposit Room. If one guest deposits several items, tie such items up with a rope to avoid mistakes. （2）在行李寄存登记簿上登记所存行李情况，标明位置、件数、日期、颜色及存放人姓名和寄存牌编号等，如有贵重物品，应做明显标志。 Register the information of the deposited luggage on the *Luggage Deposit Log*, indicating information such as the location, number of luggage, date, color and name of the depositing guest, number of the deposit tag, etc. Make visible marks for valuables. （3）如发现客人逾期不取行李，及时通知行李部经理。 If the guest fails to retrieve the luggage within the due time, inform the Manager of the Luggage Department in time.	（1）分类存放。 Deposit on classification basis. （2）存放时间长的行李放里面。 Place the luggage deposited for a long time far from the door. （3）易爆、易腐蚀、易碎等物品不能寄存。 Do not deposit explosive, corrosive, fragile articles, etc.
3. 为客人查找、提取行李 Find and retrieve the luggage for the guest	（1）礼貌地收回客人寄存行李牌下联收据。 Collect the guest copy of the Luggage Deposit Tag politely. （2）礼貌地向客人询问行李的颜色、大小及存放时间，以便查找。 Enquire the guest about the color, size and deposit time of the luggage politely to facilitate locating. （3）根据收据上的编号，翻查行李存放登记本，找到行李。 Check the *Luggage Deposit Log* according to the number on the receipt and find the luggage. （4）把行李取出后，交与客人核实，确认后撕掉行李上的寄存牌和客人的寄存收据，并划去行李存放记录。 Take out the luggage and hand to the guest for verification. Upon confirmation, tear away the luggage deposit tag on the luggage and the luggage deposit receipt of the guest, scratch out the luggage deposit record. （5）如遇客人遗失收据，应报告当班领班，检验客人身份，核对无误后方可领取。 If the guest has missed the receipt, report to the Supervisor on duty. Check the identity of the guest and the retrieval is allowed only if there're no mistakes.	（1）应按寄存单查找行李。 Locate the luggage according to the deposit form. （2）准确将行李交给客人。 Hand the luggage to the guest correctly. （3）对丢失寄存单的客人应自己核对，防止行李被冒领。 Check the identity of the guest who has lost the deposit form to prevent unauthorized retrieval of the luggage.

三、贵重物品保管（Safekeeping of Valuable Things）

酒店不仅为住客提供舒适的客房、美味的菜肴及热情礼貌的优质服务，而且还应对住客的财产安全负责。为此，酒店为住客设置寄存保管贵重物品的场所和设施。

The hotel should not only provide comfortable guest rooms, delicious foods and warm, polite, high quality services. In addition, hotel should be responsible for the safety fo the properties of the guests. To this end, the hotel should design the place and facility for the guest to deposit and keep valuable articles.

（一）贵重物品保管程序（Safekeeping Procedures of Valuables）

1.保管箱的启用程序（Starting Procedures of the Safe Deposit Box）

当客人抵店后，第一次提出启用保管箱时，程序如下：

If the guest requests the use of the safe deposit box for the first time upon arrival of the hotel, the following procedures should be followed:

（1）接待员打开门，等客人进入后，接待员关上门。

The Receptionist opens the door to allow the guest in; after the guest enters, close the door.

（2）查核客人的住房卡或钥匙牌，以确认是否是住店客人。

Check the room card or key card of the guest to check whether the guest is a residing guest of the hotel.

（3）取出记录卡，在下面逐项填写，请客人签字，同时，向客人介绍规定和注意事项；取出保管箱，让客人存入物品。

Take out the record card and fill in item by item; ask the guest to sign on the card; meanwhile, introduce the provisions and precautions to the guest; take out the safe deposit box and ask the guest to deposit belongings.

（4）当着客人的面用两把钥匙将保管箱锁上，一把客用钥匙交给客人保管，总钥匙由接待员自己保管，并礼貌提醒客人注意钥匙的保管与安全。

Lock the safe deposit box with two keys before the guest. Pass the guest key to the guest and retain the master key by the Receptionist. Remind the guest to pay attention to the safekeeping and security of the key politely.

（5）向客人道别，为客人开门、关门。

Say goodbye to the guest; open and close the door for the guest.

（6）将填写过的正卡放入纸袋里，标上箱号、客人姓名、房号，放入存放架子。

Put the filled master card into the paper bag; mark the box number, guest name and room number and put it onto the deposit shelf.

2.保管箱中途开箱程序（Midway Opening Procedures of the Safe Deposit Box）

当客人在店逗留期间，第一次存入贵重物品，后要再次或多次使用时，程序如下：

During the stay of the guest in the hotel, after the first deposit of valuables, the following procedures should be followed if the guest requires using the box once again or in a repeated manner:

（1）接待员打开门，向客人问候，客人进入后，接待员关上门。

The Receptionist opens the door to allow the guest in; after the guest enters, close the door.

（2）请客人出示保管箱钥匙，然后取出记录卡副卡，请客人逐项填写、签字。

Ask the guest to present the key to the safe deposit box; take out the assistant card of the record card; ask the guest to fill in item by item and sign on it.

（3）礼貌、巧妙地取出填写过的签字后，核对客人的签字。

Take out the original signature in a polite and elaborate manner; verify the signature of the guest.

（4）如签字相符，则当着客人面用两把钥匙将保管箱打开，让客人再次使用。

In case that the signatures are consistent; open the safe deposit box with two keys before the guest to enable further use by the guest.

（5）客人存取完毕，再当着客人面用两把钥匙将保管箱锁上，一把客用钥匙交客人保管，并有礼貌地提醒客人注意钥匙的保管和安全。

After the guest finishes the deposit, lock the safe deposit box with two keys before the guest. Pass the guest key to the guest and retain the master key by the Receptionist. Remind the guest to pay attention to the safekeeping and security of the key politely.

（6）向客人道别，为客人开门、关门。

Say goodbye to the guest; open and close the door for the guest.

（7）将填写过的副卡与其正卡一起归放在存放架。

Put the filled assistant card together with the master card onto the deposit shelf.

（8）如客人再次前来使用保管箱，仍应重复以上接待程序，将每次填写的副卡放在一起存放。

In case of repeated use of the safe deposit box by the guest, the abovementioned procedures should be repeated and assistant card filled each time should be kept together.

3. 保管箱的退箱程序（Returning Procedures of the Safe Deposit Box）

（1）服务员打开门，向客人问候，客人进入后，关上门。

The Receptionist opens the door to allow the guest in; greet the guest; after the guest enters, close the door.

（2）请客人出示保管箱钥匙，然后取出记录卡正卡，请客人在反面签字，并与正面核对。

Ask the guest to present the key to the safe deposit box; take out the master card of the record card; ask the guest to sign on the back and check with the front side.

（3）如签字相符，当着客人面用钥匙将保管箱打开，让客人取物。

In case that the signatures are consistent; open the safe deposit box with two keys before the guest to enable the guest to retrieve the deposited articles.

（4）客人取物完毕后，要检查一遍保管箱，以防遗留。

Double check the safe deposit box after the guest retrieves the articles to avoid omissions.

（5）收回保管箱的客用钥匙，锁上该箱。

Collect the guest key of the safe deposit box and lock the box.

（6）向客人致谢道别，感谢其合作，为客人开门、关门。

Express appreciation to the guest; say goodbye to the guest; thank the guest for his/her cooperation; open and close the door for the guest.

（7）将正卡与所有填写过的副卡一起留存，以备查核。

Maintain the master cards and all filled assistant cards for further examination.

（二）贵重物品保管注意事项（Precautions for Safekeeping of Valuables）

（1）弄清客人寄存的要求。

Make clear the deposit requirements of the guest.

（2）填写表单，并向客人介绍其注意事项。

Fill in the form and introduce precautions to the guest.

（3）使用总钥匙与分钥匙同时打开保险箱门。

Open the safe door simultaneously with the master key and the guest key.

（4）将存放盒、寄存单第一联放入保险箱，锁上箱门，并轻轻拉放，确认是否已锁好。

Put the safe deposit box and the original copy of the deposit form into the safe; lock the safe door; pull the door gently to confirm that the safe has been properly locked.

（5）告知客人，启用时需出示该箱分钥匙和寄存单并请客人妥善保管。

Inform the guest that the guest key and deposit form should be presented to use the safe and remind the guest to make proper safekeeping.

（6）填写客用安全保险箱使用登记簿，以备核查。

Fill in the register book for safe use by the guest for further inspection.

（7）注意每开启一次，应请客人在寄存单相关栏内签名认可。

Please note that the guest should be asked to sign on related column for approval each time the safe is opened.

（8）客人退箱时，总台人员应收回该箱分钥匙和寄存单。

When the guest returns the safe, the staff at the Reception Desk should collect the guest key and the deposit form of the safe.

（9）在客用安全保险箱使用登记簿上，做终止记录（日期、时间、经办人等）。

Termination record should be made on the register book for safe use by the guest (date, time, responsible personnel).

【实训与评价】【Training and Evaluation】

行李寄存服务

Luggage Deposit Service

［实训目的］［Training Objectives］

通过行李寄存服务，掌握行李员接受客人寄存行李时所需要的知识、技能和步骤。

Master the necessary knowledge, skills and procedures required when the bellman disposes the luggage deposit by luggage deposit services.

［组织形式及要求］［Organization Form and Requirement］

1. 按要求设计预订场景。

To design the reservation scenario as required.

2. 场地要求：前厅服务模拟实训室。

Place requirement: Simulated practical training on lobby services.

3. 全班以两人为一个小组分成若干组，小组两位同学分别扮演行李员和客人。

Divide the class into several groups of two. And the two students in one group act respectively as the bellman and the guest.

4. 完成后小组成员角色互换进行练习。

Swap the role after the practice is done.

5. 角色扮演时要认真、投入，运用酒店礼宾服务用语和礼貌礼节，填写好相应的表格。

Be devoted and careful in role play; apply concierge service languages and etiquettes of hotels; fill in corresponding forms appropriately.

［训练道具］［Training Properties］

行李、行李寄存牌、笔、行李存放登记簿。

Luggage, luggage deposit tag, pen, Luggage Deposit Log.

［操作程序与标准］［Operation Procedures and Standards］

参照表 3-12：行李寄存和提取的操作程序。

See Table 3-12：The Luggage Deposit and Retrieval Procedures.

【情景模拟对话】【Scenario Simulation Dialogue】

行李员：早上好，小姐。需要寄存行李吗？

Bellman：Good morning，Miss. Do you need depositing luggage?

客人：是的，我现在已经退房，但我是下午三点的飞机，我想把行李寄存几小时，然后到西湖边逛逛。带着行李不方便。

Guest：Yes. I've checked out. But my flight is at 3 p.m. So I'd like to deposit my luggage for several hours to take a tour around the West Lake. It's not convenient for me to carry the luggage.

行李员：好的，你原来是哪个房间的客人？

Bellman：All right！ What's your original room number?

客人：我是 3518 房间的。

Guest：Room 3518.

行李员：是高小姐吧。

Bellman：Miss Gao，right?

客人：是的。

Guest：Yes.

行李员：好的，您有几件行李，有没有什么贵重的东西？

Bellman：OK. Here's your luggage. Are there anything valuable?

客人：就这一件，没什么贵重的东西。

Guest：Just this one，nothing valuable.

行李员：有无易燃易爆的东西？

Bellman：Anything inflammable or explosive?

客人：没有。

Guest：No.

行李员：好的，麻烦在这行李寄存单上面签名。

Bellman：OK. Please sign your name on the *Luggage Deposit Form*.

行李员：好的，高小姐，您要寄存一件行李，并在下午 1 点多点取走。请保管好您的寄存行李牌下联。

Bellman：OK. Miss Gao. You have one piece of luggage deposited，which is supposed to be retrieved at around 1 p.m. Please keep the guest copy of your luggage deposit tag.

客人：好的，谢谢，再见。

Guest：OK. Thanks. See you.

【拓展知识】【Knowledge Extension】

“金钥匙”服务

“Concierge” Service（“Golden Key” Service）

“金钥匙”的全称为“国际酒店金钥匙组织”（UICH），是一个国际性的酒店服务专业组织。“金钥匙”是酒店综合服务的总代理，被誉为“万能博士”，其佩戴的两把交叉的金钥匙，意味着尽善尽美的服务，也象征着为客人解决一切难题。只要找到“金钥匙”，他会竭尽全力为客人安排好一切。金钥匙的服务理念就是满意加惊喜，随着金钥匙服务理念在我国酒店业的普及，目前“金钥匙”已成为酒店服务档次的体现，高档酒店都以拥有“金钥匙”为荣。一个酒店有无“金钥匙”是评定该酒店服务水准的一个标准，同时也将是酒店评报星级的考核内容。

The full name of “Concierge” is Union Internationale Des Concierges D’Hotels (UICH), which is an international hotel service specialized organization. The “Golden Key” is the general agent of the comprehensive hotel services and is praised as the “Jack of All Trades” . They wear two crossing golden keys, which means consummated services as well as the ability to solve all difficulties for the guest. The “Golden Key” is ready to arrange all things for the guest. The service philosophy of golden service is “Satisfaction & Surprise” . With the generalization of the service philosophy of “Golden Key” in the hospitality industry of China, presently the “Golden Key” has become a symbol of the service level of a hotel. High end hotels are citing their “Golden Key” services as the honor. Whether a hotel has the “golden key” or not has become a standard to judge the service level of the hotel. Meanwhile, it is also an aspect in the star-level assessment of the hotel.

一、“金钥匙”的起源（Origin of“Concierge”）

关于“Concierge”一词的来源，一种说法是来源于拉丁文，语意为“保管”、“管理”或是仆人；另一种说法，即古代法语的衍生意思，这个词为“The Comte DES cierges”（蜡烛伯爵，即保管蜡烛的人），是负责满足一些到豪华场所娱乐的贵族们的奇想和渴望以及其他需求的人。古时，遍布在那些荒无人烟的边境地区照顾过往的旅行商队的人被称为“Concierge”，这种职业最终在中世纪传到欧洲，在一些知名的政府建筑、宫廷和城堡里,“Concierge”变成“钥匙的保管人”。1800 年，随着铁路和游轮的增加并初具规模，旅游业欣欣向荣，现代酒店的“Concierge”便诞生了。费迪南德·吉列特先生是“金钥匙组织”的主要创始人，他为金钥匙事业呕心沥血，被尊称为“金钥匙之父”。

As for the origin of the word “Concierge”, one version is that the word is originated from Latin and means “safekeeping”, “management” or servant. The other version is that the word is derived from the ancient French word “The Comte DES cierges” (Candle Earl, the person keeping the candle), which refers to a person to satisfy the fancy ideas, desires as well as other demands of the nobility in luxury recreation places. In ancient time, people in the deserted remote areas serving the trade caravans were called “Concierge” . The occupation was finally transmitted to Europe in the Middle Ages. In the renowned governmental architectures, palaces and castles, “Concierge” became “the key keeper” . In 1800, as the railway and cruise ship gained size and taken shape, the tourism industry was quite flourishing. And the “Concierge” for modern hotels was generated. Mr. Ferdinand Gillet was the main founder of UICH. He had devoted heart and soul in the undertakings of the “Golden Key” and he was respected as “Father of Golden Key” .

“金钥匙组织”是指全球酒店中专门为客人提供“金钥匙服务“并以个人身份加入”国际金钥匙组织”的职员的国际专业服务民间组织。1929 年 10 月，来自法国巴黎 Grand Hotel 酒店的 11 个委托代办建立了“金钥匙协会”，协会章程允许“金钥匙们”通过提供服务而得到相应的小费，他们发现那样可以提高对客服务效率，随之还建立了城市内的联系网络。欧洲其他国家也相继开始建立类似的协会。1952 年 4 月 25 日，来自 9 个欧洲国家的代表在法国东南部的戛纳举行了首届年会，并创办了“欧洲金钥匙大酒店组织”（L’ Union Europe ene DES Portieres DES Grands Hotels，UEPGH）。1997 年变成了今天的名称“UICH”（Union Internationale DES Concierges D'Hotels）。

The UNCH is an international non-governmental organization to provide professional services for hotel staff providing “Golden Key” services and joining in the organization personally from hotels all over the world. In October 1929, eleven agencies from Grand Hotel in Paris, France established the “Concierge Association”. According to the *Articles of Association*, the “Concierges” were allowed to receive tips for their services. They found that this could enhance the guest service efficiency and later on established a contact network within the city. Similar associations were also established successively in other European countries. On April 25, 1952, representatives from 9 European countries held the first annual meeting in Cannes in the southeast of France and established L' Union Europe ene DES Portieres DES Grands Hotels (UEPGH). In 1997, the name was finally changed as Union Internationale DES Concierges D'Hotels (UICH) as we use today.

今天，“金钥匙”已成为世界各国高星级酒店服务水准的形象代表，一家酒店加入了“金钥匙组织”就等于在国际酒店行业获得了一席之地；一家酒店拥有了“金钥匙”这种首席礼宾司，就可显示不同凡响的身价。换言之，大酒店的礼宾人员若获得“金钥匙”资格，他也会倍感自豪。因为他代表着酒店个性化服务的标志，是酒店内外综合服务的总代理。

Nowadays, the “Golden Key” has become the image representative of high star-level service standards all over the world. Joint into UICH means a space for the hotel in the entire international hospitality industry; Provided with a Chief Concierge of “Golden Key”, the extraordinary values of the guest may be highlighted. In other words, if the concierge attendant in the hotel is qualified into UICH, he/she would be extremely pride of it. He/she is the symbol of the individualized services of the hotel as well as the overall agent of comprehensive services within and out of the hotel.

它的服务理念是在不违反当地法律和道德观的前提下，使客人获得满意加惊喜的服务，让客人自踏入酒店到离开酒店，自始至终都感受到一种无微不至的关怀。“金钥匙”的服务内容涉及面很广泛：向客人提供市内最新的流行信息、时事信息和举办各种活动的信息，并为客人代购歌剧院和足球赛的入场券；为城外举行的团体会议做计划，满足客人的各种个性化需求，包括计划安排在国外举行的正式晚宴、为一些大公司做旅程安排、照顾好那些外出旅行客人和在国外受训的客人的子女，甚至可以为客人把金鱼送到地球另一边的朋友手中。现在国际酒店“金钥匙组织”已拥有超过4500名来自34个国家的“金钥匙成员”。

The service philosophy is to provide services of “Satisfaction & Surprise” without violating the local laws and moralities and to provide the guests considerate care from the moment the guests step into the hotel to they leave the hotel. The “Golden Key” services involve quite wide ranges: providing popular information, latest news and event information within the city; buy tickets of opera house or football match for the guest; plan for group conference out of the city; satisfy various types of individualized demands of the guests, including planning and arrangement of formal dinner held overseas; arranging the trips for some big companies; taking care of the children of the guests going out for travelling or receiving trainings in foreign countries; or even passing the goldfish to the friend on the other side of the earth for the guest. Presently, the UICH has over 4500 members from 34 countries.

对比欧洲和美洲，亚洲男性选择从事这一职业占有一定比例的人数，中国的会员数量将近300名（少数为女性）；而在中国旅行的客人正在继续加深对酒店“金钥匙”的认识，以便知道如何获得酒店“金钥匙”的帮助。

Compared with Europe and America, a relatively higher proportion of male hotel staff select to take on such occupation. Presently, there're about 300 members in China, of which only a few are female. Guests traveling in China are continuously deepening their understandings on "Golden Key" so as to learn how to turn to them for help in the hotels.

在中国一些大城市，金钥匙委托代办服务被设置在酒店大厅，它们除了照常管理和协调好行李员和门童的工作外，还负责许多其他的礼宾职责。

In some major cities in China, the Concierge Service of the "Golden Key" is designated in the lobby. More than managing and coordinating the bellmen and doormen, they should assume many other concierge responsibilities.

二、"金钥匙"在中国的发展（Development of Golden Key in China）

国际酒店"金钥匙组织"拥有 34 个成员国和地区，分别是：澳大利亚、奥地利、比利时、巴西、加拿大、中国、丹麦、英国、捷克、法国、德国、俄国、希腊、荷兰、中国香港、匈牙利、爱尔兰、以色列、意大利、日本、卢森堡、马来西亚、墨西哥、摩洛哥、挪威、新西兰、菲律宾、葡萄牙、罗马尼亚、新加坡、西班牙、瑞典、瑞士、美国。在 1997 年 1 月意大利首都罗马举行的"国际金钥匙年会"上，中国被接纳为国际酒店"金钥匙组织"的第 31 个成员国。

Presently, UICH has 34 member countries and regions, which respectively is: Australia, Austria, Belgium, Brazil, Canada, China, Demark, the UK, Czech, France, German, Russia, Greek, Netherland, HKSAR, Hungary, Ireland, Israel, Italy, Japan, Luxembourg, Malaysia, Mexico, Morocco, Norway, New Zealand, the Philippines, Portugal, Rumania, Singapore, Spain, Sweden, Switzerland, the US. In January 1997 on the annual meeting of UICH held in Roma, capital city of Italy, China was officially adopted as the 31rd membership country of UICH.

中国酒店"金钥匙组织"从 1995 年 11 月开始筹备，经过多年的发展，中国酒店"金钥匙组织"由小到大、由起步到合法注册，取得了可喜的发展。酒店"金钥匙服务"在中国的出现，最早是由著名爱国人士霍英东先生倡导引入白天鹅酒店的。在第一届中国酒店"金钥匙服务"研讨会上，他建议抓住时机，发展中国酒店"金钥匙服务"事业，创立中国酒店"金钥匙服务"品牌。同时国家旅游局和中国旅游酒店业协会领导对发展中国酒店"金钥匙服务"投入了大量的精力，给予了大量的扶持和指导。在新闻媒介广泛宣传下，中国酒店"金钥匙服务"事迹引起了同行业及社会各界的重视，中国酒店"金钥匙服务"的发展状况也开始被国际酒店"金钥匙组织"重视。1998 年 12 月，中国酒店"金钥匙组织"经国家旅游局批准成立，划归中国旅游酒店业协会指导，并作为中国旅游酒店业协会下属的一个专业委员会。

The preparation of "Golden Key" organization in China was begun in November 1995. With development for several years, satisfying development has been witnessed from small to large, from preparation to legal registration. The occurrence of "Golden Key" service was first initiated and introduced by the renowned patriotic personage Mr. Fok Ying-tung. On the first China Hotel "Golden Key" Service Seminar, he proposed to seize the opportunity to development the "Golden Key" service among hotels in China and establish China's own "Golden Key" service brands. Meanwhile, the leaders from National Tourism Administration and China Tourist Hotel Association have invested great vigor in "Golden Key" service in hotels of China and give intensive supports and guidance. Under the wide publicity by the media, the "Golden Key" service activities have caught the eyeballs within the industry and all walks of life. The development of "Golden Key" service in China was also valued by UICH. In December 1998, Les Clefs d'Or China was approved to be established by the National Tourism Administration. It is under the guidance of the China Tourist Hotel Association and is a professional committee under the China Tourist Hotel Association.

2001 年 1 月，在国家旅游局、中国旅游酒店业协会和广州市政府的高度重视和精心组织下，在广州市成功举办了第 47 届国际酒店“金钥匙组织”年会。此次年会，在组织、接待、服务等方面，再一次展现了中国酒店精致的服务魅力，获得了国际酒店“金钥匙组织”各成员国主席最高的赞誉，并对国际酒店“金钥匙服务”理念在中国得到发扬光大寄予了厚望。中国酒店“金钥匙”发展没有理由不成功，因为它拥有一个“满意加惊喜”、“在客人的惊喜中找到富有的人生”的崇高服务理念，它得到了一切关心旅游酒店事业的各级政府和领导的支持，得到了广大酒店总经理的关爱和支持，受到了广大宾客的欢迎。每一个“金钥匙”都为实践金钥匙服务理念和精神而不断地努力工作，创造了一个又一个美好的服务传奇，两把交叉的“金钥匙”正在发出更加灿烂的光芒，广大追求服务创新的酒店员工正在为之而奋斗着。

In January 2011, with the highly importance and consideration organization by the National Tourism Administration, China Tourist Hotel Association and the People's Government of Guangzhou, the 47th UICH Annual Conference was successfully held in Guangzhou. This annual conference once again showed the exquisite charms of services of China's hospitality industry no matter on organization, reception or service. Chairmen from each member country of OICH had give top praise on the conference and placed great hope on the generalization of the international "Golden Key" service ideologies in China. The development of "Golden Key" in China is destined to be a success, as it has the lofty philosophy of "Satisfaction & Surprise" and "Appreciating A Colorful Life from Surprise of the Guest". It has been supported by governments and leaders of all levels concerning the tourist hospitality undertakings. It has also received cares and supports from General Managers of the hotels and welcomed by the guests. Every "Golden Key" is making continuous efforts in practicing the ideology and spirit of the "Golden Key" service and has successively been creating service legend one after another. The crossing golden keys are more shining, guiding the hotel staff determined in service innovation to strive for its goal.

酒店“金钥匙服务”已被国家旅游局正式列入星级评定标准，规定三星级以上的酒店都应有“金钥匙服务”。酒店“金钥匙服务”对高星级酒店而言，是一种管理水平和服务水平成熟的标志，是在酒店具有高水平的设施、设备以及完善的操作流程基础上，更高层次酒店经营管理艺术的体现。酒店“金钥匙服务”对城市或地区旅游业而言，将对其服务体系的形象产生深远的影响。因为，中国酒店“金钥匙”是由一群有着丰富的服务经验、对中国旅游业发展和酒店发展负有历史使命感和责任感的人组成的，他们共同的任务是使中国的旅游酒店业能够与国际接轨，同时能够在国际上树起自己的品牌。这样，中国酒店会吸引更多客人的光顾，酒店就有效益，行业就有发展。“金钥匙”不仅给各城市的旅游酒店业的创新服务注入了新的活力，而且对各城市旅游服务业的健康和良性互动发展来说也是一种动力。酒店“金钥匙”在中国的逐渐兴起，是我国经济形势发展以及旅游总体水平发展的需要，将成为中国各大城市旅游体系中的一个品牌，即代表着热情好客独具酒店特色的一种服务文化，并将成为该城市酒店业的一个传统。

The "Golden Key" service of hotels has been formally listed into the star-level evaluation standards by the National Tourism Administration. All three-star level hotels and above should be provided with "Golden Key" services. For high star-level hotels, the "Golden Key" service is a symbol of developed managerial levels and service levels. It is the embodiment of higher level hotel operation and management arts based on the high quality facilities and equipments as well as consummated operation procedures. The "Golden Key" service of hotel will bear profound influence on the image of the service system for the tourism industry of a city or an area. The "Golden Keys" in China's hospitality industry consist of a group of experienced staff bearing the sense of historical mission and responsibility for the development of the tourism industry and hospitality industry of China. They share the common task to make China's tourist hospitality industry keeping pace with international levels and establish the own brands internationally. With such efforts, more guests would be attracted to China, bring benefits to hotels and development opportunities of the industry. The "Golden Key" has not only added new vigor into the innovative service of the tourism hospitality industry in each city. In addition, it is a motivation for the healthy and benign interaction of the tourist service industry among different cities. The emerging of "Golden Key" in China answers the call of the economic development and the overall growth of tourism in China. It will become a brand in the tourism systems in major cities in China, in other words, it represents a service culture with unique characteristic of enthusiasm and hospitality and will be a tradition of the hospitality industry in the city.

"金钥匙"的含义应包含五点内容：第一，"金钥匙"是一种服务标志，两把金光闪闪的交叉钥匙代表着酒店委托代办的两种主要职能：一把金钥匙用于开启酒店综合服务的大门，另一把金钥匙用于开启该城市综合服务的大门，也就是说，这是一种综合服务总代理的醒目标志。第二，"金钥匙"代表着酒店顶级的专业化服务，这种服务虽不是无所不能，但以"追求卓越、尽善尽美"为宗旨，涵盖了宾客所需要的接、送、买、订、寄、取、租、代等广泛的服务内容，凡是不违背法律和社会道德的服务，都是"金钥匙服务"的业务范畴。第三，"金钥匙"是对酒店中专门为宾客提供"金钥匙服务"的个人或群体的称谓，他们是酒店的形象大使和综合服务代言人，只有他们才有资格在由"金钥匙组织"指定的燕尾服上戴上国际酒店"金钥匙组织"的交叉金钥匙徽章，为宾客提供"金钥匙服务"。第四，"金钥匙"是一个以友谊、协作为原则的合作网络，网络成员通过掌握丰富的信息并使用共同的价值观和信息高速公路形成庞大的服务网络，作为提供超常服务的强大保障。第五，"金钥匙"是一个国际性专业化组织，该组织是全球酒店中专门为客人提供"金钥匙服务"并以个人身份加入组织而形成的国际专业服务民间组织。

The meaning of "Golden Key" should involve the following five aspects: Firstly, "Golden Key" is a service mark. The two shining crossing keys represent the two major functions of the Concierge Services of the hotel: One key is used to open the door of comprehensive service of the hotel; and the other is used to open the door of comprehensive service of the city. That is to say, the "Golden Key" is a striking mark of the general agency of comprehensive services. Secondly, the "Golden Key" represents the top level professional service of the hotel. Though the service is not necessarily "all-mighty", with the tenet of "Seeking for Excellence and Consummation", it covers wide ranges such as pickup, delivery, purchase, subscription, postage, reception, leasing and agency. It is within the reach of "Golden Key" services as long as the legal provisions and social moralities are not violated. Thirdly, the "Golden Key" is the name for the individuals or groups providing "Golden Key" services specifically for the guests in the hotel. They're the "image ambassador" and "spokesman of comprehensive service" of the hotel. Only those qualified to wear the crossing golden keys badge of UICH on its designated swallow-tailed coat can provide "Golden Key" services for the guests. Fourthly, the "Golden Key" is a cooperative network based on the principle of friendship and coordination. The members of the network form a huge service network based on the rich information they master as well as the common values and Information Superhighway as a powerful guarantee to provide extraordinary services. Fifthly, the UNCH is an international non-governmental organization to provide professional services for hotel staff providing "Golden Key" services and joining in the organization personally from hotels all over the world.

最权威的酒店管理专家认为，“金钥匙”是高星级酒店管理的“心脏”与“灵魂”，它对优化酒店管理、形成高素质的服务群体意义深远。概括来讲，“金钥匙”在酒店管理、服务中的作用可用“桥梁”、“中心”、“龙头”来形容，具体如下：

According to the most authoritative hotel management experts, the “Golden Key” is the heart and soul of high star-level hotel management. It is of great significance to optimize the hotel management and establish high quality service teams. Generally speaking, the functions of “Golden Key” in hotel management and service may be interpreted as: “Bridge”, “Center” and “Flagship”. To be specific:

1. “桥梁”——沟通宾客与酒店、酒店管理与服务的桥梁（“Bridge”—A Bridge Communicating between the Guest and the Hotel, the Hotel Management and Service）

宾客的需求是以最小的投入换取最好的享受，而酒店的需求毫无例外都是谋求效益的最大化。因此，二者之间的需求需要沟通与磨合才能达到和谐。“金钥匙”给客人提供超值服务，让宾客感到物有所值或物超所值，无疑是加强宾客与酒店沟通的有效途径。“金钥匙”在对宾客服务的过程中，也很好地协调了宾客关系，一改传统的酒店服务中餐饮、客房、娱乐各自为战的局面，为宾客提供吃、住、行、游、购、娱一条龙服务，从而成为酒店服务的代言人和总代理。“有事请找金钥匙”已成为经常入住高星级酒店的高档客人的口头禅，进而达到宾客与酒店的及时沟通。

The demand of guests is to exchange the best enjoyment with the least investment; while the demand of hotels is unexceptionally to seek the maximization of the benefits. Therefore, to reach the harmony, communication and “breaking-in” is required from both parties. The “Golden Key” provides premium services to the guests, makes the guests feel good value for money or even more than that. Therefore, it is no doubt an effective way to enhance the communication between the guests and the hotel. In the process to provide guest service, the “Golden Key” may better coordinate the relationship with the guests. It puts an end to the conventional pattern that the food & beverage, guest room and reaction functions work independently. Instead, it provides the “one package service” of dining, residing, traveling, touring, purchasing and entertaining and therefore making the “Golden Key” the spokesman and general agency of the hotel service. “Find ‘Golden Key’ in case of anything” has become a pet phrase of frequent high-end guests of high star-level hotels. It represents timely communication between the guests and the hotel.

在传统的酒店管理和服务中，一般都实施四级垂直管理模式，一级对一级负责，好处是责任明确、分工细致，但由于管理链和服务链衔接不够紧密，对客服务的时效性、管理的时效性大打折扣，也影响了酒店最大的财富——员工创造力的发挥。“金钥匙”在酒店的出现，很好地弥补了这一不足，由于“金钥匙”提出的“创造性思维”、“越组代庖”、“只重效果、不重过程”的工作理念，使工作时效性大大增强，并以其自身网络优势和综合服务代言人的特殊角色不再烦琐地逐级上报、批复，从而实现了服务链条的优化组合，使服务群体形成一个亲密合作、利益共享的高效群体，进而能以最快捷、最直接的方式把有关服务信息反馈到管理层，使传统的管理、服务沟通更加直接，联系更加紧密。

In traditional hotel management and service, generally a four-level vertical management mode is adopted. A responsibility system is carried out level by level. It provides superiorities such as clear responsibility and detailed job division. However, as the management chain and the service chain are not tightly connected, the timeliness of guest service and management is greatly reduced. This also influences the exertion of the staff creativity, which is the greatest fortune of the hotel. The appearance of “Golden Key” in hotel has favorably made up such defects. The work philosophies of “Creative Thinking”, “Crossing the Border” and “Result Speaks” greatly enhance the timeliness of work. With the inherent network superiority and the special role of spokesman for comprehensive services, the “Golden Key” needs no tedious reporting and approval procedures, which realizes the optimized combination of the service chains and integrates the service groups into a highly effective team that work closely and share the profits. This can give feedback on related services to the management in a most speedy and direct manner and make traditional management and service communication more direct and the connection closer.

2. “中心”——酒店收集社会信息的“信息中心”和了解宾客的“情报中心”(“Center”—The “Information Center” of the Hotel to Collect Social Information and the “Information Center” to Understand the Guest)

在当前的酒店经营中，明智的酒店经营者已把信息管理放到与人、财、物管理同等重要的位置，“金钥匙”利用网络组织无疑在信息管理中占有很大优势：在收集服务信息方面，一方面，“金钥匙”可以通过组织内部的计算机网络了解有关订房信息及国内各地的旅游酒店信息等；另一方面，“金钥匙”可以与本地“金钥匙会员”联合，广泛收集社会服务信息，如酒店所在城市的政治、经济、文化、历史、工农业、商贸、旅游场所及有关业务等。如美国旧金山的“金钥匙”，除利用计算机查询外，还用不同颜色的文件夹对信息进行分类，一般使用蓝色代表酒店，绿色代表旧金山的市情，红色代表酒乡，黄色代表游览胜地。在每一栏都有细分栏目，市情内有音乐、医疗、教育等，音乐包含音乐厅、歌剧院、爵士乐吧、钢琴吧、迪士高、夜总会等，酒店“金钥匙”每月都及时核对时间表，收集整理的信息与酒店各部门联网，为宾客提供准确周到的服务奠定坚实的信息基础。

In current hotel management, prudent hotel operators would regard information management as important as management on labor, finance and property. Based on networked organization, the “Golden Key” is no doubt provided with great superiorities. As for service information collection, on one hand, the “Golden Key” may get to know reservation information as well as tourist hotel information all across the country by the internal network of the organization. On the other, the “Golden Key” may work with the local “Golden Key” members to widely collect the social service information, such as the political, economic, cultural, historical, industrial and agricultural, commerce and trading, tourist sites and related businesses of the city where the hotel is located. For example, a “Golden Key” in San Francisco, USA, more than enquiring with computer, file folders in different colors are used to classify different information. Generally, blue represents the hotel, green represents the city information of the San Francisco, red represents wine lands and yellow represent tourist attractions. There're subdivided items under each classification. For example, the city information involves items such as music, medical service and education, and the music involves music halls, opera houses, jazz bar, piano bar, disco, night club, etc. The “Golden Key” of the hotel timely checks the timetable every month and share the information so collected to various departments of the hotel via the network, which aims to lay firm information foundation for the accurate and considerate services to the clients.

在收集宾客信息方面，由于“金钥匙”是面对面接触客人的服务群体，“金钥匙”的客户档案往往是最精确、最优秀的客档，客人的喜好、生活习惯、性格、脾气都是客档记录的主要内容。如美国一名“金钥匙”能记住1000多辆车号、3000多名宾客姓名，保证了及时主动为客人服务。详实准确的客人信息往往是酒店改进管理、提供超常服务、铸造忠诚客源群体的有力武器。

As for guest information collection, as the “Golden Key” makes direct face-to-face contact with the guest, the guest history records are generally the most accurate and excellent files for the guests. The preference, living habits, characteristics and tempers are all important contents in guest history records. For example, there's a “Golden Key” who can memorize over 1000 vehicle plate numbers and over 3000 guest names. This guarantees timely and positive services to the guests. Detailed and accurate guest information is generally a powerful weapon for hotels to improve management, provide excellent service and cast royal guest groups.

3. "龙头"——引导酒店优质服务良性发展的龙头（"Flagship"—The Flagship to Guide Benign Development of High Quality Hotel Services）

"金钥匙"在许多酒店是服务的明星，他们看上去似乎无所不能，对客人而言，犹如一把万能钥匙，为他们解决一个又一个难题。高涨的工作热情、强烈的责任心、丰富的知识、体贴入微的关怀以及工作性质的要求、与酒店各部门长期所形成的和睦融洽的关系等，都决定着"金钥匙"有意识地或潜意识地，甚至不自觉地引导培育酒店优质服务群体的形成。

The "Golden Key" is the service start in most hotels. They seems "all-mighty" and like a "master key" for the guests to solve problems successively. Factors such as high working passions, strong sense of responsibility, enriched knowledge, considerate care, work requirements as well as long-term harmonious relationship with different departments of the hotel make the "Golden Key" deliberately or even unconsciously guide the formation of the high quality service groups of the hotel.

（1）培训员工。"金钥匙"有较长的工作年限，接触的部门较多，积累了丰富的工作经验，深谙待客之道，是最佳的培训师。因此，"金钥匙"无论是在工作中的言传身教，还是培训中对礼貌礼节、服务意识、服务技巧的示范，都能收到其他部门或个人所达不到的效果。

Staff training. The "Golden Key" has relatively long service years. Working with relatively various departments, they have obtained rich working experience and are good at receiving guests. Therefore, they're the best trainers. Therefore, the "Golden Key" can achieve effects that are not available for other departments or individuals no matter in teaching by personal example as well as verbal instruction, or politeness and etiquette, sense of service or service skills.

（2）对外联络。酒店往往与外界各单位有密切联系，如车站、机场、航空公司、旅行社、报社等。在这些单位中，大多数与委托代办业务直接相关，在与相关单位建立良好关系的同时，"金钥匙"无疑成为酒店对外联系的排头兵，也为酒店外联队伍建设做好了铺路工作。

External liaison. The hotel often bears close relationship with various types of external organizations, for example, the railway station, airport, airlines, travel agencies, newspaper offices. Most of the units have direct relationship with the concierge services. While establishing favorable relationship with related units, the "Golden Key" is no doubt the pioneer for external liaison and clearing of the barriers for the external connection team construction of the hotel.

（3）为前台各部门提供准确、详实的宾客情报和社会信息。在信息化时代，谁拥有丰富的信息，谁就掌握了胜利的武器，"金钥匙"的丰富信息引导着服务更趋个性化，酒店管理更趋科学化，引导酒店的服务群体越来越注重宾客的切身感受，为提升服务质量、强化管理功能提供了第一手资料。

Provide accurate, detailed guest information and social information to various departments of the Lobby. In the times of informationalization, those who master abundant information would be provided with the weapon for victory. The abundant information of the "Golden Key" guides the hotel to achieve more individualized services and more scientific hotel management and guides the service groups of the hotel to increasingly attach importance to the feelings of the guest. This provides firsthand data to enhance service quality and intensify management functions.

（4）组织员工的业余活动，增强集体凝聚力。在酒店组织的一些文体活动和联谊活动中，"金钥匙"利用其自身系统的社会关系，帮助联系和安排，落实活动的各项细节，使之有声有色，丰富了员工生活，加强了员工交流，使服务群体能够和谐配合，达到最佳的合作效果。

Organize spare time activities of the staff to enhance collective coherence. In the some recreational and sports activities as well as parties organized by the hotel, with the social relationship of the own system, the "Golden Key" may assist in liaison and arrangement, implementation of various details and adding vividness into the events. This enriches the life of the staff, enhances staff communication, enables harmonious collaboration of the service groups and reaches optimal cooperation effects.

对于酒店各班组的工作，"金钥匙"往往会予以配合，并提出必要的帮助，使酒店"一条龙"的服务进行得更为顺畅，提高酒店整体的服务质量，进而带动整个酒店的优质服务群体的顺利形成和良性发展。

Generally, the "Golden Key" would cooperate and give necessary assistance in work of each service group or team of the hotel, which smoothens the "one package service" of the hotel, enhances the overall service quality of the hotel and then further drives the favorable formation and benign development of high quality service groups of the hotel.

总之，21 世纪的"金钥匙"一定会更加辉煌，因为这个遍及全世界 34 个国家的国际组织拥有一大批高素质、有朝气、肯进取的酒店从业者，他们具有强烈的使命感和良好的敬业精神，正如国际"金钥匙组织"创始人 Ferdinand Gillet 所说："无论在世界哪个角落，'金钥匙'们都将倾尽全力，去延续我们肩负的使命，真诚服务于我们的职业，我们的酒店乃至整个旅游业。"

To sum up, the "Golden Key" in the 21 century will be more brilliant, as it is an international organization covering 34 countries and regions all over the world and involving a great number of high quality, energetic and pioneering hotel participants. They are equipped with strong sense of mission and excellent professional ethics. Just like what's Ferdinand Gillet, Founder of UICH said: "no matter in which corner of the world, the 'Golden Keys' would do their best to exert the missions we shoulder, sincerely serve our professions, the hotels as well as even the entire tourism industry."

三、国际"金钥匙组织"中国区申请入会条件和程序（Applicant Conditions and Procedure of Les Clefs d'Or China）

（一）基本条件（Basic Conditions）

申请人必须年满 21 岁，品貌端正，是在酒店大堂工作的礼宾部首席礼宾司。需具备至少五年酒店从业经验（在酒店的任何职位均可，且至少有三年以上从事委托代办服务工作经验和必须达到一定的工作水平），至少掌握一门以上的外语，参加过国际"金钥匙组织"中国区的服务培训。

The applicant must be a Chief Concierge of the concierge department who is aged 21 or above, has regular features and works at the hotel lobby. The applicant must have at least five years of working experience in the hotel industry (the applicant can work in any position at the hotel, and must have at least three years of the working experience in the consignment service and reach certain working level), command at least one foreign language, and participate in the service training of Les Clefs d'Or China.

（二）必备文件（Required Documents）

申请人必须把申请书（申请表格）连同七份证明和文件递呈国际"金钥匙组织"中国区总部。

The applicant must submit the application (application form) together seven copies of the certificates and documents to Les Clefs d'Or China.

（1）申请人标准一寸彩色照片两张。

Two standard one-inch color pictures of the applicant.

（2）申请人工作场所照片。

Pictures of the working site of the applicant.

（3）两位会员（具备资格三年以上的正式会员）的推荐信，在一个月内答复申请，如果该地区没有符合资格的推荐人，则应把申请表格直接寄至总部。

Recommendatory letters from two members (formal members who are registered for more than three years). If there are no eligible members in the region, the application form must be directly posted to the headquarters.

（4）申请人所在酒店总经理的推荐信。

Recommendatory letter from the general manager of the hotel where the application works.

（5）参加金钥匙学习的资格证书复印件。

Duplicates of the certificates after participation in the training programs of Les Clefs d'Or China.

（6）在酒店工作的新旧证明文件。

Old and new certificates proving the work at the hotel.

（7）申请人在前厅部期间服务的案例（三篇）。

Service cases of the applicant during the work at the lobby department (three).

（三）批准程序（Approval Procedure）

如果申请人被审核符合入会资格，总部行政秘书会把金钥匙组织的相关资料交给申请人（包括交会员费通知等）。申请人完成以上程序并被审核符合所有申请资格后将收到由总部行政秘书发出的授徽通知。经总部授权专人授徽后，该会员及其酒店才正式成为国际“金钥匙组织”成员。

If the applicant meets the entrance requirements after review, the administrative secretary of the headquarters will post relevant documents of Les Clefs d'Or (including membership fee notice) to the applicant. After completing the aforesaid procedure and meeting the requirements after review, the applicant will receive the notice of badge granting from the administrative secretary of the headquarters. After the special person authorized by the headquarters grants the badge, the member and his hotel will become formal members of Les Clefs d'Or.

相关文件按照程序分别递呈国际“金钥匙组织”中国区主席、国际“金钥匙组织”中国区首席代表、秘书长和申请人所在城市地方的“金钥匙分会”备案。

Relevant documents will be submitted to the Chairman of Les Clefs d'Or China, Chief Representative of Les Clefs d'Or China, Secretary of Les Clefs d'Or China and the Les Clefs d'Or organization in the city of the applicant for filing through relevant procedure.

四、我国酒店“金钥匙组织”会员的能力及业务要求（Ability & Skill Requirements for Members of Les Clefs d'Or China）

（一）能力要求（Ability Requirements）

交际能力：善于与人沟通，亲和力强

Communicative ability: Good at interpersonal communication and strong in affinity

语言表达能力：表达清晰、准确

Linguistic expression ability: Clear and accurate expression

协调能力：能正确处理好与相关部门的合作关系

Coordinating ability: Correctly handle relations with related departments

应变能力：能坚持原则，并以灵活的方式解决问题

Response ability: Adhere to principles and solve problems flexibly

身体素质：身体健康、精力充沛，能适应户外工作及长时间的站立工作

Physical quality: Healthy, energetic and capable to adapt to outdoor work and stand for a long time

（二）业务知识与技能要求（Business Knowledge & Skill Requirements）

（1）熟练掌握本职工作的操作流程。

Skillfully master the operating flow of his work.

（2）普通话标准流畅，至少掌握一门外语。

Speak fluent and standard Mandarin and command at least one foreign language.

（3）熟练掌握中英文打字及计算机文字处理等技能。

Master typewriting in Chinese and English, word processing on computer and other skills well.

（4）熟练掌握所在酒店的详细信息资料，包括酒店的历史、服务设施、设备、服务时间、产品价格等。

Know details of the hotel, including history, service facilities, equipment, service time and product prices.

（5）熟悉本地区三星级以上酒店的基本情况，包括地理位置、主要服务项目、特色及价格水平等。

Know basic information of local hotels rated at three stars and above, including geographical location, major service items, features and price levels.

（6）熟悉本市区的主要旅游景点，包括地点、特色、开放时间及消费价格等。

Be familiar with major scenic spots in the city, including sites, features, opening hours and prices.

（7）掌握本市高、中、低档的餐厅，娱乐场所，酒吧等各5个（小城市3个）的基本情况，包括地点、特色、营业时间、价格水平及联系人电话。

Know the basic information of five restaurants, entertainment sites and bars (3 in small cities) at different levels respectively, including locations, features, business hours, price levels and contact information.

（8）能帮助客人购买各种交通票据；了解售票处的服务时间、业务范围和联系人电话。

Help guests buy traffic tickets and know service hours, business scopes and contact information of ticket offices.

（9）能为客人代办物品修理，如眼镜、手表、小电器、行李箱、皮鞋等，掌握维修处的地点、服务时间等。

Help guests repair articles such as glasses, watches, small electrical appliances, luggage carriers and shoes, and know the locations and service hours of repair centers.

（10）能为客人代办邮寄信件、包裹、快件，懂得办理邮寄事项的要求及手续。

Help guests post letters, parcels and express deliveries, and know the requirements and procedure of the posting affair.

（11）熟悉本市的交通情况，掌握从本酒店到车站、机场、码头、旅游景点、主要商业街的路线、路程及乘出租车的大概费用。

Know local traffic conditions, and master routes, ranges and approximate taxi fares from the hotel to railway stations, airports, docks, scenic spots and major commercial facilities.

（12）能帮助客人查找航班托运行李的去向，掌握相关部门的联系电话和领取行李的手续。

Help guests find the status of registered luggage on the aircraft, and know the telephone numbers of relevant departments and the luggage retrieval procedure.

（13）能帮助外籍客人解决办理签证延期等问题，掌握有关单位的地点、工作时间、联系电话和相关手续。

Help foreign guests solve the extension of visas, and know the sites, working hours, telephone numbers and relevant procedures of relevant authorities.

模块小结

Module Summary

1. 机场代表服务有哪些注意事项？

What are the precautions in services provided by the Airport Representative?

2. 门厅迎送客人服务流程有哪些？

What are the service procedures for reception/seeing-off services at the lobby?

3. 散客和团队客人迎送服务标准有什么不同？

What are the differences in reception/seeing-off service standards between individual guests and group guests?

4. 行李的寄存与提取的程序有哪些？

What are the procedures of luggage deposit and retrieval?

5. 搜集三个行李服务的案例，并做评析。

Collect three cases about luggage services and make comments and analyses thereof.

模块四　入住接待
Module IV　Check-in Reception

【情境导入】【Scenario Introduction】

客人没带身份证
The Guest Forgot to Bring Identity Card

2008年圣诞节前一天的下午，海口喜来登温泉度假酒店公关销售部吴经理正在大堂忙忙碌碌地张罗圣诞节的环境布置，只见一位身穿西装的先生带着一位身穿夹克衫的男子急匆匆地走到他跟前，轻轻地对他说："吴经理，有件事跟您商量一下。我是北京天道公司的总经理，这几天和另一位同事住在贵店，开了一间房。这位先生是我的海口客户，刚才和我一起吃完饭，多喝了点酒，我想给他另开一间房，让他休息一下，晚上住一宿，顺便谈点生意。可前台服务员说我已经开了一间房，不能再开了。而这位客户正好没带身份证，也不让登记。这就麻烦了。吴经理，您就帮忙再开一间房吧。您看，这是我的身份证。"他边说边递上身份证，下面还衬着一张没有填写的住房登记表。"吴经理，您就行个方便吧。"旁边那位男子也递上名片求情。

On one afternoon before the Christmas 2008, Wu, Manager of the PR and Sales Department of Sheraton Haikou Resort, was busy in preparation for the decoration of the upcoming Christmas. A gentleman in business suite hurriedly came to him with a man in jacket. The man gently talked to him: "Mr. Wu. Can you do me a favor? I'm the General Manager of Beijing Tiandao Company. I live in a guest room in this hotel with one of my colleagues for several days. This is a client of mine in Haikou. We just finished lunch together. We drank a little bit more. So I'd like to rent one more room for him. He'll rest and stay over the night so that we can talk about some business. However, the attendant at the Reception Desk told me that I cannot rent another room since I've already rented one. However, this guest doesn't take along his identity card. So he is not able to register by himself. That's the trouble. Manager Wu, could you please help to arrange another room? This is my identity card." He said while passing the identity card, together with an empty *Check-in Registration Form*. "Mr. Wu, please." The man beside the guest also passed his business card and asked for a favor.

此刻，吴经理感到很为难：这位北京天道公司的总经理是本酒店的常客，他的要求应该尽量满足，如果处理不当，就会失掉一个很有潜力的常客，但如果答应让其客户无身份证入住，又不符合酒店住宿的一般规程。他试图找到一个变通办法，便询问那男子："您有没有证明您身份的其他证件？"男子摇了摇头。"那可不行啊。"吴经理显得无可奈何。那位先生有点急了，赶紧说："这是特殊情况嘛，请允许我用我的身份证来担保他入住吧。""好，就这么办吧。"吴经理略一沉思，下了决心答应下来。两位客人喜出望外，连声道谢，表示今后有机会一定再住海口喜来登温泉度假酒店。

Mr. Wu found him in a dilemma: The General Manager of Beijing Tiandao Company was a frequent guest of the hotel. Therefore, his requests should be satisfied as possible. If the situation was not handled properly, the hotel would probably lose a highly potential frequent guest. However, if his customer is allowed to check in without identity document, it would breach the general hotel check-in procedures. So he decided to try some alternative method. He asked the man: "Do you have other credentials proving your identity?" The man shook his head. "That will not do." Mr. Wu expressed that he couldn't do anything. The guest got a little bit impatient, and said in a hurry: "Since it's a special circumstance, please allow me to guarantee his residing with by identity card." "All right. Let's do it this way." Mr. Wu thought for a while and determined to consent. Both guests were overjoyed and thanked Wu again and again. They expressed that they would for sure reside in the Sheraton Haikou Resort in future.

吴经理领两位客人到前台办完入住登记后，又给楼层服务台挂了个电话，向前台服务员介绍了那位新入住客人的特殊情况，请她特别多加注意。

Manager Wu guided to guests to the Reception Desk for check-in registration. Later on, he called the Reception Desk of the corresponding floor, introduced the special circumstance of the new guest and asked the attendant to pay special attention.

【情境分析】【Scenario Analysis】

以上吴经理对客人特殊要求的特殊处理，既拉住了一个重要客源，又确保了酒店平安无事。

In this case, Manager Wu made special treatment on the special requirements of the guest, which not only maintained an important guest but also defended the integrity of the hotel system.

第一，吴经理照顾的客人是一个熟悉了解并信得过的大公司总经理，此事的基础是稳妥可靠的。

Firstly, the guest Manager Wu did a favor for was a General Manager of a credible large-sized company known by the hotel. Therefore, the basis of the treatment was stable and reliable.

第二，公司总经理以自己的身份证担保客户入住的安全，并办理了有效的登记手续，就正式承担了相应的责任，有据可凭，有案可查。

Secondly, the General Manager of the company guaranteed the security of the residing of the guest and worked on valid registration formalities. Therefore, he had formally assumed corresponding responsibilities, providing evidence and basis for the case.

第三，吴经理最后又请楼层服务员对新入住客人特别多加注意，再增加了一条保险措施，可以说是慎之以慎，万无一失。

Thirdly, Manager Wu asked the Room Attendant of the floor to pay special attention, which was an additional insurance measure. Therefore, the solution was sufficiently cautious and absolutely safe.

本案例实际上提出了酒店管理者和服务员如何在维护酒店利益的前提下灵活处理遵守规章制度的问题，值得引起酒店同行的思考。有关的例子是不少的，比如，酒店除了对少数了解熟悉、有信誉的客人，原则上是不予赊账的，但有时对有特殊情况且印象不错的客人，可暂允其赊账；住店客人进房时钥匙给同房朋友带走且身边未带住房卡，但服务员认得出客人，宜先开房让其进去休息；等等。

In fact, this case proposes the problem that how the hotel managers and attendants deal with the rules and regulations flexibly while maintaining the benefits of the hotel. The case is worthy to be considered by the colleagues in the hospitality industry. There're also many similar cases. For example, in principle no consumption on credit is permitted by the hotel except for some known and credible guests. However, consumption on credit would be allowed temporarily under special cases and for guests leaving a good expression to the hotel. If the room key is taken away by the roommate while the guest has no room card with him/her, the attendant may open the room to allow the guest to rest in the room, and so on.

【学习目标】【Learning Goals】

[知识目标] [Knowledge Objectives]

1. 掌握入住接待登记的基本接待程序和登记的各种表格、内容。

Command the basic reception procedures of check-in registration as well as various types of forms and contents related to registration.

2. 熟悉 VIP 客人入住流程。

Be familiar with the check-in formalities of VIP guests.

3. 熟悉问询和留言服务的内容与要求。

Be familiar with the contents and requirements of information service and message service.

4. 掌握客人离店结账程序、外币兑换服务流程及特殊情况处理标准。

Command the check-out and account settlement procedures, foreign currency exchange service procedures as well as special circumstance disposal standards for the guests.

[能力目标] [Capacity Objectives]

1. 具备规范、熟练受理入住登记手续的能力。

Be capable to handle check-in registration formalities in a normalized and frequent manner.

2. 熟练懂得酒店所在地的各方面知识,以满足客人的问询服务与要求。

Be familiar with knowledge of various aspects of the locality of the hotel to satisfy the information service and demand for the guest.

3. 能够快速有效地为客人办理外币兑换、离店结账手续。

Be capable to handle foreign currency exchange and check-out settlement formalities for the guests quickly and effectively.

4. 能够分析酒店前厅综合案例,找出合适的解决方案。

Be capable to analyze comprehensive cases in the Lobby and figure out appropriate solutions.

【重点和难点】【Key Points and Difficulties】

掌握前台入住接待的流程,能够熟练处理入住接待过程中出现的特殊情况。

Master the procedures for check-in reception of the Reception Desk; be able to fluently deal with special circumstances in the process of check-in reception.

任务一 入住登记
Task I Check-in Registration

一、入住登记概述(General Introduction of Check-in Registration)

办理入住登记手续是客人与酒店间建立正式合法关系的最根本环节。因此,住客在入住酒店前,首先要办理入住登记手续。

Check-in registration is the most fundamental link to establish legal relationship between the guest and the hotel. Therefore, the guest should first work on check-in registration formalities before residing into the hotel.

（一）入住登记的目的（Purpose of Check-in Registration）

（1）按照我国有关法律的规定，只有办理入住登记方可住宿。

As stipulated by related laws and regulations in China, residing is permitted only after check-in registration is made.

（2）通过办理入住登记手续，可以使酒店与客人之间的责、权、利用法律手段明确下来，也就是所谓的和客人签订住宿合同。

By handling check-in registration formalities, the responsibilities, rights and benefits between the hotel and the guest may be defined by legal means. This may also be interpreted that the guest signs the residing contract with the hotel.

（3）客人通过入住登记，确定房号、房价、住宿期、付款方式等基本事项，酒店则告知客人消费客房产品应注意的事项，如退房时间、贵重物品保管等。

By check-in registration, basic matters such as the room number, room rate, stay period and the payment method are determined for the guest. The hotel should inform the guest precautions in consumption of the guest room products, such as the check-out time and safekeeping of valuables.

（4）入住登记是酒店取得客源市场信息的重要渠道，通过办理入住登记手续，酒店可获得住客的个人资料，如姓名、职业、国籍、出生年月、兴趣爱好等基本信息，有利于酒店提供个性化服务、建立客史档案及日后推介酒店产品等工作的开展。

Check-in registration is an important channel for the hotel to obtain the market information about the guests. By handling the check-in registration formalities, the hotel may obtain the personal data of the guest, such as basic information of name, occupation, nationality, date of birth, hobby, etc. This will facilitate the hotel to provide individualized services, establish guest history files, promote hotel products, etc.

（5）可以掌握客人的付费方式，保证客房销售收入。

Check-in registration may also help to master the payment methods of the guest and guarantee the sales revenue of the guest rooms.

（6）可以保障酒店及客人生命、财产的安全。

Check-in registration may guarantee the safety of the lives and properties of the hotel and the guests.

（二）入住登记的证件（Acceptable Credentials of Check-in Registration）

在国内，酒店在入住登记过程中，合法的身份证件包括护照、签证、中华人民共和国居民身份证、中国香港特别行政区护照、中国香港居民来往大陆通行证、中国港澳同胞回乡证、中国台湾居民来往大陆通行证、中华人民共和国旅行证、中华人民共和国外国人居留证、警官证、军官证、士官证等。

Domestically, legal identity credentials acceptable for check-in registration involve: Passport, visa, ID card of the People's Republic of China, passport of HKSAR, Mainland Travel Permit for Hong Kong Residents, Home-visit Permit for Hong Kong and Macao Residents, Mainland Travel Permit for Taiwan Residents, Travel Permit of the People's Republic of China, Residence Permit for Foreigners of the People's Republic of China, Police ID Card, Military Officer Certificate, Non-commissioned Officer Certificate, etc.

（三）入住登记项目（Check-in Registration Items）

公安部门规定入住酒店的客人所需登记项目：

The check-in registration items for residing guests of the hotel stipulated by the public security organs:

（1）客人姓名及性别。姓名与性别是识别客人的首要标志，服务人员要记住客人的姓名，并以姓氏去称呼客人。

Name and sex of the guest. Name and sex is the primary marks to identify the guest. The service attendants should remember the name of the guest and call the guest by the family name.

（2）国籍。尤其是对于外国客人，是必须登记的内容。

Nationality. It is a compulsory registration item especially for foreign guests.

（3）房号。房号是核对房间类型和房价的主要依据，注明房号同时有利于查找、识别住店客人及建立客账。

Room Number. Room number is the main basis to check the room types and room rates. Indicating room numbers would facilitate the searching and identification of a residing guest and establish the guest accounts.

（4）房租。房租是客人与接待员协商确定的，建立客账、预测客房收入的重要依据。

Room Rate. Room rate is negotiated and determined between the guest and the Receptionist. It is an important basis to establish the guest account and predict guest room incomes.

（5）付款方式。确定付款方式有利于保障客房销售收入及决定客人住宿期间的信用标准，并有助于提高退房结账的速度，还有利于酒店为其提供一次性结账服务。

Payment Method. The determination of payment method will be favorable to guarantee the sales income of the guest room and decide the credit standards of the guest during the stay in the hotel. It is also favorable to speed up check-out account settlement and one-package settlement service provided by the hotel.

（6）抵离店日期。掌握客人准确的抵离店日期，有助于计算房租；了解客人的预计离店日期，有助于订房部进行客房预测及接待处排房，有助于客房服务中心安排客房清扫顺序。

Check-in/Check-out Date. To master the accurate check-in/check-out time will be favorable to calculate the room rates. To understand the anticipated check-out date of the guest will be favorable to make room predictions by the Reservation Department and the room arrangement of the Reception Desk. It will also facilitate the Room Service Center to arrange the room cleaning sequences.

（7）住址。保存正确、完整的客人永久住址，有助于酒店与客人日后建立联系，并提供如遗留物品处理、邮件转寄等服务。

Address. Save correct and complete permanent address of the guest, which will facilitate the hotel to establish further connection and provide services such as treatment of forgotten articles and forwarding of letters.

（8）有效证件及相关内容等。

Valid credentials, related contents, etc.

（9）酒店管理声明。登记表上的管理声明，即住客须知。告诉客人住宿消费的注意事项，如：规定的会客时间；退房时间为中午 12 点前；建议客人使用前厅收银处的免费保险箱，否则如有贵重物遗失，酒店概不负责等。

Hotel management declaration. The management declaration on the Registration Form, i.e. the *Instructions to Guest*. Inform the guest precautions in hotel consumptions, for example: Prescribed guest meeting time; the check-out time limit is 12:00 at noon; recommendation of the free safe at the Cashier's

Desk; no responsibility of the hotel in case of missing of valuables if the safe is not used, etc.

（10）接待员签名。有助于加强员工的责任心，便于控制和保证服务质量。

Signature of the Receptionist. This would be favorable to enhance the sense of responsibility of the staff and facilitate the control and guarantee of the service quality.

表 4-1　国内酒店住宿登记表

Table 4-1　Typical Check-in Registration Form of A Domestic Hotel

编号：
No.:　　　房间号：
Room Number:　　　房租：
Room Rate:

<table>
<tr><td colspan="2">姓 名
Name</td><td>性别
Sex</td><td>年龄
Age</td><td>身份证或其他有效证件
Identity Card or Other Valid Credentials</td><td colspan="2">证件号码
Credential No.</td></tr>
<tr><td colspan="2"></td><td></td><td></td><td></td><td colspan="2"></td></tr>
<tr><td colspan="2">户口地址
Registered Permanent Residence</td><td colspan="5"></td></tr>
<tr><td colspan="2">抵店日期
Check-in/Check-out Date</td><td colspan="2"></td><td>离店日期
Check-out Date</td><td colspan="2"></td></tr>
<tr><td rowspan="3">同宿人
Roommate (s)</td><td>姓名
Name</td><td>性别
Sex</td><td>年龄
Age</td><td>关系
Relationship</td><td rowspan="3">备注
Remarks</td><td rowspan="3"></td></tr>
<tr><td></td><td></td><td></td><td></td></tr>
<tr><td></td><td></td><td></td><td></td></tr>
<tr><td colspan="6">请注意：
Note:
1. 退房时间是中午 12:00 之前。
Check-out should be made before 12:00 at noon.
2. 贵重物品请存放在前台保险箱内，阁下一切物品之遗失酒店概不负责。
Please keep your valuables into the safe at the Reception Desk. The hotel should assume no liability in case of any losing of your personal belongings.
3. 来访客人请在 23:00 前离开房间。
Visitors should leave the guest room before 23:00.
4. 退房请交回钥匙。
Please return the key when checking out.
5. 房租不包括房间里的饮料。
The room rate does not include beverage in the room.</td><td>结账方式：
Payment method:
现金
Cash
信用卡
Credit Card
支票
Cheque
客人签名：
Guest Signature:
接待员：
Receptionist:</td></tr>
</table>

二、散客入住登记（Check-in Registration of Individual Guests）

散客入住登记主要涉及两类：一类是有预订的散客人员；另一类是无预订的、直接到酒店入住的散客人员。客人来到酒店前台，首先要问他是否有预订。根据不同类型的散客人员，服务流程也有差异，具体流程如下：

Individual guest check-in registration mainly involves two types, of which one is individual guests making reservation in advance and the other is individual guests making no reservation and coming directly to the hotel. When a guest comes to the Reception Desk of the hotel, first enquire whether he/she has reserved or not. The service procedures vary according to different types of individual guests. The specific procedures are as follows:

（一）有预订的散客接待程序与标准（Reception Procedures and Standards for Reserving Individual Guests）

表 4-2 有预订的散客接待程序与标准表

Table 4-2 Table of Reception Procedures and Standards for Reserving Individual Guests

项目 Item	标准 Standard
1. 问候 Greet the guest	(1) 以礼貌、热情、友善的语气问候客人，如果不知道其姓名，称呼其“先生”、“女士”。 Greet the guest with a polite，enthusiastic and friendly tone；call the guest “Mr.” or “Ms.” if the name of the guest is unknown. (2) 尽量熟记客人姓名，如果是经常来的客人，前台接待员要以姓氏或以体现其身份的称呼问候客人（用其姓氏称呼客人至少在对话中使用一次）。 Try to memorize the name of the guest. In case of a frequent guest，the Receptionist of the Reception Desk should greet the guest with his/her family name or a way that can represent his/her social status (Call the guest with his/her family name at least once in the conversation). (3) 地域不同，与客人的熟悉程度不同，要以个性化称呼来向客人打招呼。称呼客人可体现出尊敬感与亲切感。 As the guests may come from different regions and the degrees of familiarity to the guests are different，individualized ways should be used to call the guest. Give the guest a sense of respect and intimacy when greeting the guest. (4) 与客人讲话时面带微笑，保持目光的接触。 Smile when talking with the guest；keep eye contacts.
2. 赠送欢迎茶水 Offer welcoming drink	(1)（夏天）× × 先生/女士，外面天气热，您喝杯冰的酸梅汤解解暑，稍等一下，马上为您办理入住手续。 (In summers) Mr./Ms. × ×，it's hot outside. Please have a cup of cooled plum juice to relieve the summer heat. Just wait for a moment，we'll handle the check-in formalities right away. (2)（冬天）× × 先生/女士，外面天气冷，您喝杯热的柠檬蜂蜜水暖和一下，稍等马上为您办理入住手续。 (In winters) Mr./Ms. × ×，it's cold outside. Please have a cup of hot plum juice to warm yourself. Just wait for a moment，we' ll handle the check-in formalities right away.
3. 询问 Enquire	(1) 问询客人是否提前预订过房间。 Enquire the guest whether he/she had made the reservation. (2) 与客人确认预订相关信息。 Confirm reservation information with the guest. (3) 与客人确认房价时，请回避其他客人，如其他客人在场，必要时将房价信息写在 RC 单上与客人确认，以避免其他客人在房价上引起疑义。 When confirming the room rate with the guest，please try to avoid other guests. If other guests are present，where necessary，write the room rate information onto the RC Sheet for confirmation of the guest so as to avoid objections on room rate from other guests. (4) 对于回头客，根据情况温馨提示客人第几次入住，以表示对客人的重视。 For a returned guest，warmly remind how many time the guest has checked in the hotel as the case may be，to show that the hotel is valuing the guest. (5) 如系统有客人特殊要求的提示，员工要告知客人酒店将尽力为其安排。 In case of special requests of the guest prompted by the system，the staff should inform the guest that the hotel will try the best to arrange for the guest. (6) 对于有过投诉记录的客人，前台要特别注意客人要求，避免事件重复发生，在接待过程中可适当与客人沟通，让客人感受到酒店为其在以往入住过程中出现的不愉快表示歉意（C/I 后立即通知前台经理）。 For guests with complaint records，the Reception Desk should attach special importance to the requirements of the guest to avoid the reoccurrence of the event. Appropriate communication may be made with the guest in the process of reception to have the guest perceive the apology of the hotel for the displeasure of the previous stay of the guest (Inform the Manager of the Reception Desk immediately after C/I).
4. 安排房间并进行入住登记 Arrange the room and make check-in registration	(1) 依照预订的房间类型和要求选择房间，并进行入住登记。 Select the room according to the room type and requirements in the reservation and make check-in registration. (2) 前台需询问客人是否需要无烟房？尽量为其安排，如果当时没有可用的无烟楼层房间，当酒店获悉客人不吸烟的信息，尽可能给客人安排房态较好的房间（或通知客房服务员对房间进行无烟处理），让客人感受到酒店对他的重视（将此信息备注在客人喜好中）。 Ask the guest whether the guest requires a non-smoking room. Arrange for the guest as possible. In case that no room is available on the non-smoking floor，if the hotel knows that the guest does not smoke，try to arrange a room in relatively good conditions for the guest (or inform the room attendant to make non-smoking treatment to the room) so as to make the guest feel that he/she is being valued (Add such information into the remarks as guest preference).

续表

项目 Item	标准 Standard
	（3）客人入住时如暂时未准备好预订的房间，前台接待员应婉转与客人确认是否介意为其更换房型。 If the reserved room is not ready temporarily when the guest makes check-in; the receptionist of the Reception Desk should confirm whether the guest minds to change the room type in a tactful manner. （4）客人入住时如暂时未准备好预订的房间，客人坚持入住此类型房间，前台接待员应详细查询电脑信息，尽可能为其安排（前台可将其他预订未到的客人房间优先安排给客人）。 If the reserved room is not ready temporarily when the guest makes check-in and the guest insists living in such type of the room, the receptionist of the Reception Desk should carefully check the information on the computer and arrange the room for the guest as possible（The Reception Desk may allocate the room reserved by other guests not checked in yet to the guest）. （5）如客人为常住客人，入住时暂时未准备好预订的房间，前台接待员可根据酒店出租率情况，为其免费升级。 If the reserved room is not ready temporarily when the guest makes check-in and the guest is a frequent guest of the hotel, the receptionist of the Reception Desk may offer free upgrading according to the occupancy rate of the hotel. （6）向客人介绍升级房间的特点。 Introduce the features of the upgraded room to the guest.
5. 验证登记 Make validation and registration	（1）请客人出示有效证件，并验证证件有效性（真伪、有效期、人证相符）。 Ask the guest to present valid credentials; verify the validation of the credentials（authenticity, validation period and consistence of the guest and the holder of the credential）. （2）酒店常客人住时可不用每次出示证件，可将其证件复印件留存到前台，待每次入住时使用。 A frequent guest may not be required to present the credentials each time. The guest may keep his copy of the credentials to the Reception Desk and such copy may be used each time. （3）双手接过客人递过的证件并复印证件。 Receive the credential from the guest with both hands and copy the credential.
6. 确认付款方式 Confirm the payment method	（1）确认付款方式。 Confirm the payment method. （2）填写单据（房卡、登记单、押金收据）等并请客人签字确认。 Fill in the vouchers（room card, registration form, deposit receipt）and ask the guest to sign for confirmation. （3）在登记单上让客人留下本人的联系方式，以便客人在退房时有遗落物品能及时与客人取得联系。 Ask the guest to leave the personal contact information on the registration form so that the guest can be contacted in time in case of forgotten articles after the guest checks out. （4）押金收据要与客人确认是本人退款还是凭收据退款。 Confirm with the guest that the guest can get the refund in person with the deposit receipt. （5）如果为承担付账房间，请承担付账人签字确认。 If the room is supposed to be paid by others; ask the person responsible for the payment to sign for confirmation. （6）询问客人是否有贵重物品需要寄存到贵重物品寄存室，酒店可以为其免费提供。 Enquire the guest whether he/she has valuable to be deposited into the Deposit Room for Valuables and inform that the service is for free.
7. 制作房卡并道别 Make the room card and say goodbye to the guest	（1）制作房间钥匙，双手向客人递交房卡，并为客人指示电梯位置（如果客人需要两张房卡，在备注中注明“两把钥匙”，待退房时及时收回）。 Make the room key; pass the room card to the guest with both hands and indicate the position of the elevator（in case that the guest requires two room cards, mark “TWO KEYS” into the remarks and collect the keys in time at the C/O）. （2）在人员准许的情况下，将第一次入住的客人送入房间，为客人做整个酒店的介绍。 Guide the guest residing in the hotel for the first time if the personnel is available; introduce the entire hotel to the guest. （3）可提示外地客人次日天气情况。 Introduce the weather of the following day for nonlocal guests. （4）祝客人居住愉快，目送客人离开后再继续自己的工作。 Wish the guest a pleasant stay; see the guest off and continue the work.
8. 通知相关部门 Inform related departments	（1）如果遇到带有小孩的客人入住，为每一位携带儿童的客人赠送小礼物，并通知客房部，客房部会给带小孩的房间送儿童洗浴用品、拖鞋或玩具等相关物品。 In case of guest with child, give gift to each guest with child. Inform the Room Department. The Room Department would prepare bathroom articles, slippers, toys, etc. in rooms with children. （2）遇有特殊要求，如保密等要及时在电脑中标注并立即通知客服中心。 In case of special requirements such as confidentiality, timely mark in the computer and immediately inform the Customer Service Center.

续表

项目 Item	标准 Standard
9. 建立、更改客户信息 Establish, modify guest history information	及时将客人的信息准确输入电脑。 Input the guest information accurately into the computer in a timely manner.
10. 检查 Make inspection	当班负责人及时检查相关单据。 The responsible personnel should inspect related vouchers in time.
11. 单据存档 Archive the vouchers	一式两联：接待部、前台收银分别存档。 Prepare the voucher in duplicate: The Reception Department and the cashier of the Reception Desk should archive one copy respectively.

（二）无预订的散客接待程序与标准（Reception Procedures and Standards for Non-reserving Individual Guests）

表 4-3 无预订的散客接待程序与标准表

Table 4-3 Table of Reception Procedures and Standards for Non-reserving Individual Guests

项 目 Item	标 准 Standard
1. 问候 Greet the guest	(1) 以礼貌、热情、友善的语气问候客人，如果不知道其姓名，称呼其"先生"、"女士"。 Greet the guest with a polite, enthusiastic and friendly tone; call the guest "Mr." or "Ms." if the name of the guest is unknown. (2) 尽量熟记客人姓名，如果是经常来的客人，接待员要以姓氏或以体现其身份的称呼问候客人（用其姓氏称呼客人至少在对话中使用一次）。 Try to memorize the name of the guest. In case of a frequent guest, the Receptionist of the Reception Desk should greet the guest with his/her family name or a way that can represent his/her social status (Call the guest with his/her family name at least once in the conversation). (3) 地域不同，与客人的熟悉程度不同，要以个性化称呼来向客人打招呼，即称呼客人既要体现出尊敬感，又要体现出亲切感。 As the guests may come from different regions and the degrees of familiarity to the guests are different, individualized ways should be used to call the guest. Give the guest a sense of respect and intimacy when greeting the guest. (4) 与客人讲话时面带微笑，保持目光的接触。 Smile when talking with the guest; keep eye contacts.
2. 赠送欢迎茶水 Offer welcoming drink	(1)（夏天）××先生/女士，外面天气热，您喝杯冰的酸梅汤解解暑，稍等一下，马上为您办理入住手续。 (In summers) Mr./Ms. ××, it's hot outside. Please have a cup of cooled plum juice to relieve the summer heat. Just wait for a moment, we'll handle the check-in formalities right away. (2)（冬天）××先生/女士，外面天气冷，您喝杯热的柠檬蜂蜜水暖和一下，稍等马上为您办理入住手续。 (In winters) Mr./Ms. ××, it's cold outside. Please have a cup of hot plum juice to warm yourself. Just wait for a moment, we'll handle the check-in formalities right away.
3. 询问 Enquire	(1) 问询客人是否提前预订过房间，如未预订过，询问客人是否有过入住记录。 Enquire the guest whether he/she had made the reservation; if not, check whether there's residing record of the guest in the hotel. (2) 前台需询问客人是否需要无烟房间，尽量为其安排，如果当时没有可用的无烟楼层房间，当酒店获悉客人不吸烟的信息，尽可能给客人安排房态较好的房间（或对房间进行无烟处理），让客人感受到酒店对他的重视（将此信息备注在客人喜好中）。 Ask the guest whether the guest requires a non-smoking room. Arrange for the guest as possible. In case that no room is available on the non-smoking floor, if the hotel knows that the guest does not smoke, try to arrange a room in relatively good conditions for the guest (or inform the room attendant to make non-smoking treatment to the room) so as to make the guest feel that he/she is being valued (Add such information into the remarks as guest preference).

续表

项 目 Item	标 准 Standard
4. 介绍并选定房间 Introduce and select the room	（1）对初次入住本酒店的客人，前台接待员应热情地向客人介绍酒店的房型、房价、设施。 Warmly introduce the room types，room rates and facilities for guest checking in the hotel for the first time. （2）与客人确认所喜欢的房间类型，并为客人选定房间。 Confirm with the guest his/her preferred room type and select the room for the guest. （3）如客人需要参观房间，立即通知当班领班带客人看房间。 Immediately notify the Duty Supervisor to show the guest the rooms if the guest requires visiting the rooms. （4）如客人为常住客人，入住时暂时未准备好预订的房间，前台接待员可根据酒店出租率情况，为其免费升级。 If the reserved room is not ready temporarily when the guest makes check-in and the guest is a frequent guest of the hotel，the receptionist of the Reception Desk may offer free upgrading according to the occupancy rate of the hotel.
5. 验证登记 Make validation and registration	（1）请客人出示有效证件，并验证证件有效性（真伪、有效期、人证相符）。 Ask the guest to present valid credentials；verify the validation of the credentials（authenticity，validation period and consistence of the guest and the holder of the credential）. （2）酒店常客入住时可不用每次出示证件，可将其证件复印件留存到前台，待每次入住时使用。 A frequent guest may not be required to present the credentials each time. The guest may keep his copy of the credentials to the Reception Desk and such copy may be used each time. （3）双手接过客人递过的证件并复印证件。 Receive the credential from the guest with both hands and copy the credential.
6. 付款方式 Payment method	（1）确认付款方式。 Confirm the payment method. （2）填写单据（房卡、登记单、押金收据）等并请客人签字确认。 Fill in the vouchers（room card，registration form，deposit receipt）and ask the guest to sign for confirmation. （3）在登记单上让客人留下本人的联系方式，以便客人在退房时有遗落物品能及时与客人取得联系。 Ask the guest to leave the personal contact information on the registration form so that the guest can be contacted in time in case of forgotten articles after the guest checks out. （4）押金收据要与客人确认是本人退款还是凭收据退款。 Confirm with the guest that the guest can get the refund in person with the deposit receipt. （5）如果为承担付账房间，请承担付账人签字确认。 If the room is supposed to be paid by others；ask the person responsible for the payment to sign for confirmation. （6）询问客人是否有贵重物品需要寄存到贵重物品寄存室，可以为其免费提供。 Enquire the guest whether he/she has valuable to be deposited into the Deposit Room for Valuables and inform that the service is for free.
7. 制作房间钥匙并道别 Make the room key and say goodbye	（1）制作房间钥匙，双手向客人递交房卡，并为客人指示电梯位置（如果客人需要两张房卡，在备注中注明“两把钥匙”，待退房时及时收回）。 Make the room key；pass the room card to the guest with both hands and indicate the position of the elevator（in case that the guest requires two room cards，mark“TWO KEYS”into the remarks and collect the keys in time at the C/O）. （2）在人员准许的情况下，将第一次入住的客人送入房间，为客人做整个酒店的介绍。 Guide the guest residing in the hotel for the first time if the personnel is available；introduce the entire hotel to the guest. （3）可提示外地客人次日天气情况。 Introduce the weather of the following day for nonlocal guests. （4）祝客人居住愉快，目送客人离开后再继续自己的工作。 Wish the guest a pleasant stay；see the guest off and continue the work.
8. 送客人至房间 Guide the guest to the room	（1）途中向客人介绍酒店设置。 Introduce the hotel arrangements to the guest on the way to the room. （2）到楼层时，告知客人安全通道的位置。 Inform the guest the position of the exit passageway when reaching the floor. （3）开启房门，请客人先进入房间，告知客人房卡已经插入取电器中，然后根据时间，开启房间照明（晚 6 点后为客人将窗帘关闭）。 Open the room door and invite the guest into the room first；inform the guest that the room card has been inserted into the main switch then open the room lamps according to the time（close the curtain for the guest after 6 pm.）. （4）征询客人同意后开始为其介绍房间（包括电视遥控器、网线、拖鞋的位置；房间 DND 提示灯、电话的使用）。

续表

项 目 Item	标 准 Standard
	Introduce the room to the guest upon the consent of the guest (including the locations TV remote, network wire, slippers; DND lamp of the room; use of the telephone). (5) 询问客人是否对房间满意，祝客人居住愉快，倒退着离开房间。 Enquire whether the guest is satisfied with the room; wish the guest a pleasant stay; leave the room backwards.
9. 通知相关部门 Inform related departments	(1) 如果遇到带有小孩的客人入住，为每一位携带儿童的客人赠送小礼物，并通知客房部，客房部会给带小孩的房间送儿童洗浴用品、拖鞋或玩具等相关物品。 In case of guest with child, give gift to each guest with child. Inform the Room Department. The Room Department would prepare bathroom articles, slippers, toys, etc. in rooms with children. (2) 遇有特殊要求，如保密等要及时在电脑中标注并立即通知客服中心。 In case of special requirements such as confidentiality, timely mark in the computer and immediately inform the Customer Service Center.
10. 建立、更改客户信息 Establish, modify guest history information	及时将客人的信息准确输入电脑。 Input the guest information accurately into the computer in a timely manner.
11. 检查 Make inspection	当班负责人及时检查相关单据。 The responsible personnel should inspect related vouchers in time.
12. 单据存档 Archive the vouchers	一式两联：接待部、前台收银分别存档。 Prepare the voucher in duplicate: The Reception Department and the cashier of the Reception Desk should archive one copy respectively.

注意事项：确定付款方式时，用信用卡的要预先留下信用卡的授权；付现金的则要视信用情况决定是否交押金；收取押金的话，应先将客人的资料输入电脑，然后带客人至收银处交押金，或直接收取。

Precautions: When determining the payment method, in case of credit card, first retain the authorization of the credit card. In case of cash, determine whether deposit is required according to the credit standing of the guest. If deposit is required, first input the guest date into the computer; then guide the guest to the Cashier's Desk to pay the deposit or directly collect the deposit.

三、团队客人入住流程（Check-in Procedures for Group Guests）

团队客人因人数较多，入住前需要更加仔细地对待每一个流程，确保客人能够顺利入住。其中，团队客人来之前，以及到来后，对可能遇到的一些情况，需要加以注意，比如：

As the number of guests is relatively great, before the check-in of the group guests, each procedure should be treated more seriously to guarantee smooth check-in of the guest. Importance should be attached for possible matters before and after the arrival of the group guests, for example:

（1）在团体客人抵店前，接待处应做好一切准备工作。如果是大型团队，在特定区域或特别场所为客人办理入住手续。团体客人临时提出加房、加床的要求，要严格按照合同和操作程序处理。

The Reception Desk should get everything prepared before the arrival of the group guests. In case of large-sized group, handle check-in formalities for the guests in designated area or special site for the guests. Requirements of extra rooms and extra beds temporarily proposed by the group guests should be handled strictly in accordance with the contract and operation procedures.

（2）若团队客人提前一天到达，查看当天客情，确定是否可以安排，通知酒店该旅行团的负责人做好接待。若本酒店无法安排该团队入住，则应先到就近的其他同等级别或以上级别的酒店订房，安排团队客人入住，费用由旅行社负责；若本酒店可以安排，则按一般散客接待入住，房价由上级领导决定。

In case that the group guests arrive one day in advance, check the guest conditions of the day to confirm whether arrangement is available. Inform the responsible personnel of such tourist group in the hotel to make proper reception. In case that the hotel is unable to make arrangement thereof, first reserve rooms from nearby hotels of the same or higher level; arrange the group guests to check in; the expenses should be assumed by the travel agency. If the hotel is available to make such arrangement, receive the group guests as common individual guests. The room rates may be decided by the superior leaders.

（3）团队到达时，要求减少房间数量，首先通知营销部该团队实际订房数量，以便营销部通知收银员为结账做好准备。同时，在团队单上注明取消的房号，取出钥匙，及时更改房态；通知客房中心、礼宾部、总机取消的房号及餐饮具体的用餐人数。

If the group requires reducing the room numbers upon the arrival, first inform the Sales Department the actual number of the rooms occupied, so that the Sales Department may inform the cashier to make preparation for account settlement. Meanwhile, mark the room numbers of the cancelled room on the group reservation form; take out the keys; modify the room conditions in time; inform the Room Center, Concierge Department and the Telephone Exchange the cancelled room numbers and inform the Food & Beverage Department the specific number of people for dining.

团队客人具体入住接待流程如表 4-4 所示。

The specific check-in reception procedures for group guests as Table 4-4.

表 4-4　团队客人接待程序与标准表

Table 4-4　Table of Reception Procedures and Standards for Group Guests

项 目 Item	标 准 Standard
1. 准备工作 Getting Prepared	（1）仔细阅读预订处发来的团队信息，打开团队信息文件夹，将团队预订单以及其他相关信息放在此文件夹中。 Read carefully the group information sent by the Reservation Desk; open the group information folder; put the group reservation form and other information into this file folder. （2）夜班负责按团队预订单的要求分房，尽量将同一个团队安排在相同或相邻的楼层。 The night shift should allocate the rooms according to the Group Reservation Form; try to arrange the same group on the same floor or neighboring floors as possible. （3）早班领班检查团队房卡、欢迎卡、早餐券、宣传品的准备情况，将确认后做好的团队房卡、早餐券放在团队信息夹内。 The Supervisor of the morning shift should inspect the preparation of the room cards, welcome cards, breakfast coupons and publicity materials; put the readily made group room cards and breakfast coupons that have been confirmed into the group file folder. （4）在计算机中输入相关信息，控制已经预排好的房间，将旅行社等接待单位提供的客人名单按房号予以分配，并将团队客人登记表交给团队陪同。 Input related information into the computer; control the prearranged rooms; allocate the room numbers to the guest list provided by reception units such as the travel agency; submit the Group Guest Registration Form to the accompanying personnel of the group. （5）早班领班在团队/会议抵店前 3 小时必须确认完排房；与营销部再次确认团队/会议的预抵时间。 The Supervisor of the morning shift should confirm that the room allocation is ready 3 hours before the arrival of group/conference; reconfirm the estimated arrival time of the group/conference with the Sales Department. （6）在团队抵达前 1 小时，必须再次核实预抵团队/会议房间的房态是否都已是 VC。 Check again whether the room condition of each room is VC for group/conference 1 hour before the arrival of the group.

续表

项目 Item	标准 Standard
2. 主动迎客 Welcome the guest initiatively	(1) 引领客人们到团队入住登记区域，团队客人抵达时，大堂经理致欢迎词，并简单介绍酒店情况。 Guide the guests to the group check-in registration area; upon the arrival of the group guests, the Lobby Manager gives welcome speech and brief the hotel conditions. (2) 前台接待人员应主动与领队或陪同取得联系，向他们询问该团的人数、预订的房间数、用餐情况及叫醒和出行等事宜，协助领队分房。 The Receptionist of the Reception Desk should positively contact the group leader or accompanying personnel; enquire the number of people, number of reserved rooms, dining information as well as other matters such as morning call and travel arrangement; assist the group leader to allocate the rooms.
3. 办理入住 Handle check-in	(1) 拿出准备好的团队登记单与领队或团队陪同确认该团/会议用房数、房型、陪同房号、付费方式、叫醒及用餐信息，并逐一登记于团队确认书上。 Take out the prepared group registration form and confirm the information such as number of rooms, room types, room number of accompanying personnel, payment method, morning call and dining for the group/conference with the group leader or the accompanying personnel; record such information item by item on the Group Confirmation Form. (2) 所有团队/会议用房的房号确认后，在发钥匙之前，必须抄录在前台的团队确认书上，请陪同/领队签收。 After all room numbers for the group/conference are confirmed, before issuing the key, copy the room numbers on the Group Confirmation Form of the Reception Desk; ask the accompanying personnel/group leader to sign for confirmation. (3) 前台接待必须向陪同收取团队/会议名单，确保客人全名、性别、生日、证件号码、签证及对应的房号齐全。 The Receptionist of the Reception Desk must collect the name list of the group/conference from the accompanying personnel and confirm complete information such as the full name, sex, birthday, credential number, visa and corresponding room number of each guest. (4) 如会议团分批入住，必须协同营销负责人及时与会务组确认会议客人具体抵店的时间以及确认该会议团用房最后保留时间。 If the conference group checks in (C/I) in batches, assist the responsible personnel of the Sales Department to confirm the specific arrival time of the conference guests and the final retention time of the rooms for such conference.
4. 通知相关部门 Inform related departments	前台应及时将由领队、陪同确认过的团队单及时分发到餐饮部、房务中心、总机，便于电话叫醒等工作准备。 The Reception Desk should timely distribute the group form confirmed by the group leader and accompanying personnel to the Food & Beverage Department, Room Service Center and the Telephone Exchange for preparation such as morning call.
5. 建立账单 Establish bills	(1) 领队、陪同或会务组房号信息必须在电脑中注明。 Room number information for the group leader, accompanying personnel or the Conference Affairs Group must be indicated in the computer. (2) 按房号录入团队/会议客人的姓名。 Record the name of the group/conference guests according to the room numbers. (3) 检查团队主账的付款方式及团体付费情况。 Inspect the payment method of the master account of the group as well as the payment conditions of the group.
6. 建立、更改客史信息 Establish, modify guest history information	及时将客人的信息准确输入电脑。 Input the guest information accurately into the computer in a timely manner.
7. 检查 Make inspection	当班负责人及时检查相关单据。 The responsible personnel should inspect related vouchers in time.
8. 单据存档 Archive the vouchers	一式两联：接待部、前台收银分别存档。 Prepare the voucher in duplicate: The Reception Department and the cashier of the Reception Desk should archive one copy respectively.

四、VIP 客人入住流程（Check-in Procedures of VIP Guests）

（一）VIP 客人简介（Brief Introduction of VIP Guests）

“VIP”是英语 Very Important Person 的简称，意为非常重要的客人。酒店虽然提倡服务无差别，但不是向每位客人都提供 VIP 服务。酒店通常对每一位客人都按照 VIP 客人的服务模式提供服务，这是在向客人提供翔实的酒店信息，反映酒店接待的艺术与技巧，而提供 VIP 服务的对象主要包括在政治、经济以及社会各领域有一定成就、影响力和号召力的人士，是酒店完善的、标准的接待规格服务对象。VIP 是酒店优质服务体系的集中体现。

VIP is “Very Important Person” for short. Though undifferentiated services are advocated by the hotels; not each guest is provided with VIP services. Generally, hotel would provide service to each guest according to VIP service mode, which aims to provide detailed hotel information to the guest and reflects the receptions arts and skills of the hotel. However, VIP services are honors for persons with certain achievements, influences and appeals in the political, economic and various social fields. The VIP guests are the service objects receiving consummated and standardized reception levels of the hotel. VIP services are the centralized embodiment of the high quality service system of the hotel.

表 4-5 VIP 客人级别简介
Table 4-5 Brief Table on Guest Grades

等级 Grade	资格 Qualification	申请人 Applicant	批准人 Approving Personnel
VA	国家元首、国家部委领导、某省主要负责人 Heads of state, leaders from state ministries and commissions; leading officials of provincial level	酒店总经理、驻店经理、公关营销部经理 General Manager of Hotel, Resident Manager; Manager of the PR & Sales Department	集团董事长、酒店总经理 Group President; Hotel General Manager
VB	各政府部门领导、市主要领导，投资集团、企业高层管理者，同星级酒店董事长、总经理，省级中国国旅、国际旅、青旅总经理，对酒店有过重大贡献的人士，酒店邀请的客人 Governmental leaders of all levels; major municipal leaders; executives of investing groups and enterprises; presidents and general managers of hotels of same star - level; general managers of provincial CITS, CYTS; persons having made great contributions to the hotel; guests invited by the hotel	驻店经理、公关营销部经理 Resident Manager, Manager of PR & Sales Department	酒店总经理 Hotel General Manager
VC	社会名流（演艺界、体育界、文化界），酒店邀请的客人（业务客户） Social celebrities (from entertainment, sports or cultural circles); guest invited by the hotel (business clients)	部门经理以上 Department Manager or higher level	驻店总经理或执行副总经理 Resident General Manager or Executive Deputy General Manager
VD	个人全价入住酒店豪华客房 3 次以上的客人，个人全价人住酒店客房 10 次以上的客人，酒店邀请的客人 Guests residing the luxury room of the hotel at full rate for over three times; guests residing the hotel room at full rate for over ten times; guests invited by the hotel	前台主管以上、管理人员 Reception Desk Supervisor or higher level; managerial personnel	公关营销部经理或前厅部经理 Manager of PR & Sales Department or Manager of Front Office Department

（二） VIP 客人接待流程（Reception Procedures of VIP Guests）

1. VIP 客人入住前（Before the Check-in of VIP Guests）

（1）前台接待人员打印次日 VIP 报表并看预付单，并为次日预抵的 VIP 客人锁好房间。

The Receptionist of the Reception Desk prints out the VIP statement for the next day and check the advance payment form; lock the room for the VIP guest to be arrived for the next day.

（2）如客人晚到应通知 HK 在下班前 17:30 准备鲜花送至房间，保持其新鲜美观，做好协调工作。

If the guest is about to be arrive late, inform the HK to take the fresh flowers to the room at 17:30 before going off duty; keep the freshness and beauty of the flowers; make proper coordination.

（3）次日当班接待人员在电脑上核准房态后，根据客人的国籍以及 VIP 等级打印中英文问候卡，VB、VC、VD 都打印问候卡，VA 打印问候卡和欢迎卡。在客人到店前试用房间钥匙，将欢迎卡和问候卡摆放在客人房间。

After the on-duty receptionist of the next verifies the room conditions on the computer; print the greeting cards in both Chinese and English according to the nationality and VIP grade of the guest. Print greeting cards for VB, VC and VD. Print greeting card and welcome card for VA. Try the room keys before the guest arrives the hotel; place the welcome letter and greeting card into the guest room.

（4）如果 VIP 客人乘飞机到达，接待人员根据客人所乘的航班，与查询台确认飞机落地的准确时间。

If the guest arrives by air, the receptionist should confirm the exact landing time of the flights with the Information Desk according to the flight of the guest.

（5）前台、行李员要熟记预抵 VIP 客人的姓名和预订单所提供的有关客人信息。

The receptionist and bellman should bear in mind the name of the VIP guest as well as guest information provided on the reservation sheet.

（6）如客人有特殊要求，接待人员要亲自到机场做接待工作。

If the guest has special requirements, the receptionist should receive the guest at the airport in person.

2. VIP 客人到店后（After the Arrival of the VIP Guest）

（1）接待人员应在酒店正门迎接 VIP 客人，面带微笑，用客人姓氏称呼客人并自我介绍，送客人至房间，在房间办理入住手续。

The reception personnel should welcome the VIP guest at the main entrance of the hotel with smile; greet the guest with his/her family name and make self-introduction; escort the guest into the room; work on check-in formalities in the guest room.

（2）走在客人侧前方 0.5 米处，为客人带路。

Guide the guest 0.5 m to the laterally front of the guest.

（3）为客人打开电梯，请客人先进入；到达楼层后，请客人先走出电梯。

Open the elevator for the guest; invite the guest to enter the elevator first; ask the guest to go out first when the elevator reaches the floor of the guest room.

（4）在去房间的路上向客人介绍酒店的设施。

Introduce the hotel facilities to the guest on the way to the guest room.

（5）进入房间，按照要求帮客人填写登记单，向客人介绍房间设施等情况。

Enter the room; fill in the registration form for the guest according to related requirements; introduce conditions such as room facilities to the guest.

（6）询问客人的离店时间，询问客人是否需要叫醒、确认机票服务；与客人交换名片。

Enquire the estimated check-out time of the guest; enquire whether the guest requires services such as morning call and air ticket confirmation; exchange business cards with the guest.

（7）向客人告别，祝客人在店期间愉快，将房门轻轻带上。

Say goodbye to the guest; wish the guest a pleasant stay; close the room door gently.

（8）在电脑中办理入住登记，将客人信息输入完整。

Handle check-in registration on the computer; consummate the guest information input.

3. VIP 客人离店时（Upon the Check-out of the VIP Guest）

（1）接待人员打电话与客人确认离店时间。

The reception personnel calls the guest to confirm the check-out time.

（2）通知前台收银员准备账单，并提前为客人安排收取行李。

Inform the cashier of the Reception Desk to prepare bills; arrange luggage collection for the guest in advance.

（3）如 VIP 客人如需要送机服务，应及时与客人确认离店时间，并将确切时间通知司机班提前安排车辆。

If the VIP guest requires airport drop-off services, the GRO should confirm the check-out time of the guest in time; and inform the Drivers Crew the exact time so that the vehicle may be arranged in advance.

（4）在客人离店前询问客人的住店感受，如果客人提出意见要求及时处理落实，要给予充分重视。

Enquire the feelings of the guest for his/her stay before check-out; timely dispose and put into place the recommendations and requirements of the guest and attach sufficient importance to such recommendations and requirements.

（5）将客人的反馈意见及时记录。将客人的意见输入表格，与其他部门员工分享相关内容。

Timely record the feedbacks of the guest. Update the comments of the guest into the profile; share related contents with staff of other departments.

（6）通知市场营业部、大堂经理及相关人员在 VIP 客人离店前 15 分钟在一层正门等候。

Inform the Market & Sales Department Manager; Lobby Manager and corresponding personnel to wait at the entrance of the ground floor 15 minutes before the check-out of the guest.

（7）陪同客人办理离店手续。

Accompany the guest to work on check-out formalities.

（8）送客人至酒店门口，并向客人表达良好祝愿。

Guide the guest to the hotel entrance; express the best wishes to the guest.

（三）常见问题的处理（Disposal of Common Problems）

（1）准备工作时，大堂经理在客人到达前 1 小时检查房间；客人抵达前半小时，大堂经理应准备好客房卡、欢迎卡及住宿登记单，在门厅迎候客人抵店。

When making preparation, the Lobby Manager should inspect the room 1 hour before the arrival of the guest; the Assistant Manager should prepare the room card, welcome card and check-in registration form half an hour before the arrival of the guest and wait for the guest at the lobby.

（2）办理入住手续，要准确掌握当天预抵 VIP 客人姓名；以客人姓名称呼客人，对不同级别的 VIP 客人，相应地通知酒店总经理、驻店经理、前厅部经理及大堂经理等亲自迎接。同时，不同级别的管理人员分别将不同级别的 VIP 客人亲自送至房间，并向客人介绍酒店设施和服务项目。

Work on check-in formalities; accurately know the name of the VIP guest to be arrived for that day;

call the guest by his/her name; inform the hotel General Manger, Resident Manager, Front Office Department Manager, Lobby Manager, etc. accordingly to receive the guest in person to the grade of the VIP guest. Meanwhile, have managerial personnel of corresponding levels to guide the VIP guest of different level in person to the guest room; introduce the hotel facilities and service items to the guest.

(3) 前台接待人员复核有关 VIP 客人资料，并准确输入电脑；在电脑中注明"VIP"以提示其他各部门或人员注意。

The Receptionist of the Reception Desk should recheck the guest data of the VIP guest; input the information accurately to the computer; mark " VIP" in the computer to remind the alertness of other departments or personnel.

(4) VIP 要求换房，如果客人未到达时要求换房，由预订处更改客人的入住信息后及时将房间变更单分发至各个部门。另外，客人入住后要求换房，除按散客换房处理外，必须通知大堂经理或部门管理人员，以确保服务周到。

In case that the VIP guest requires to change the room, if such request is proposed before the arrival of the guest, the Reservation Desk should alter the check-in information of the guest and distribute the Room Alternation Sheet to each department in time. If the request is proposed after the check-in of the guest, more than disposing according to room changing procedures for individual guests, the Assistant Manager or the department managerial personnel must be notified to guarantee considerate services.

五、换房服务（Room Change Service）

客人在办理完入住后，来到房间，可能会因为各种原因，对酒店安排的房间不满意，便会要求换房。

After the check-in of the guest, the guest would be unsatisfied with the room arranged by the room for various reasons, in such case, the guest would require the room change.

（一）换房原因（Reasons for Room Change）

客人申请换房时的具体原因可能如下：对客房方向不满意；对客房层数高低有疑义；远离朋友的房间，造成相互沟通不方便；对床型及房型有疑义（床的大小、标间、单间、套间）；对房价有疑义；客房噪音太大；房间设备有故障；房间的卫生令客人不满意等。

Possible specific reasons for room change by the guest: Not satisfied with room direction; not satisfied with the floor of the guest room; being far away from the friend's room, resulting in inconvenient communication; not satisfied with the bed type and room type (bed size, standard room, single room, suite room); questioning about the room rate; excessive noise of the room; failure of room equipment; not satisfied with room sanitation, etc.

（二）换房流程（Room Change Procedures）

1. 正常情况下的换房操作流程（Room Change Procedures Under Normal Circumstances）

(1) 前台接到换房通知后应了解客人的需求，然后在房态表上仔细查看后选择合适的房间，询问客人在什么时间能把行李准备好，行李员可以在什么时间协助搬迁，并请客人在客房稍等。

Upon receiving the room change notice, the Reception Desk should understand the requirements of the guest and carefully check the room status table and select appropriate room. The Reception Desk should then enquire the guest when the luggage will be ready and when the bellman may come to collect the luggage. Ask the guest to wait for a moment in the guest room.

（2）前台接待应填妥一份房号、房型、房租变更表，此表一式三联，并在换房单上注明时间及换房原因。

The Receptionist at the Reception Desk should properly fill in the *Alternation Form for Room Number/Room Number/Room rate*. The form should be made in triplicate. Indicate the time and reason for room change on the *Room Change Form*.

（3）前台接待应把房型变更表及时交与行李员，连同将要迁入之房间钥匙一并交与行李员，按时前往客房替客人换房。

The Receptionist of the Reception Desk should timely pass the *Alternation Form of Room Type* to the bell man together with the key to the new room. And the bellman should change the room for the guest on time.

（4）行李员替客人换妥后，应请客人在房价变更表上签字，收回原房间钥匙，并在客人签字前提醒客人房价有变动，行李员应在礼宾部经手人一栏签名，再把第三联交与客房服务员，余下两联返回给前台。

After the bellman properly changed the room for the guest, ask the guest to sign on *Alternation Form of Room Rate* and collect the key to the original room. Remind the guest that the room rate has changed before the guest signs the name. The bell man should sign in the "Responsible Person of Concierge Department" column. Give the third copy to the Room Attendant and the remaining two copies to the Reception Desk.

（5）前台接待收回变更表后，把第一联交与前台收款员，以便更新账目及住宿登记表或团体房号表上的相关资料。前台接待应把第二联备存，然后更新房间资料架及其他有关记录，通知总机更改客名资料架上的房号，如有影响预订部的资料（如团体房安排）也应通知预订部。

Upon receiving the *Alternation Form*, the Receptionist at the Reception Desk should give the first copy to the Cashier at the Reception Desk so that the later may update the accounts as well as related information on the Check-in Registration Form and Group Room Number Table. The Receptionist at the Reception Desk should maintain the second copy and update the Room Information Folder and other related records; inform the Telephone Exchange to modify the room number on the Gust Information Folder. Inform the Reservation Department for information affecting the Reservation Department (for example, group room arrangement), if any.

2. 非正常情况下的换房操作流程（Room Change Procedures Under Abnormal Circumstances）

有些时候客人要求转房，但他要马上外出，或因其他原因不能留在房中等待，为了满足住客的要求及不影响酒店的房间调配，酒店有必要为客人及时更换房间。

Sometime, the guest requiring room change is about to go out soon or cannot wait in the room for other reasons, to satisfy the guest requirements and not to influence the room allocation, the hotel has the necessity to change the room for the guest in time.

（1）前台应了解客人对更换房间的要求并告诉客人房价的变更，让行李员把换房表送到客人房间，先请客人确认房价并签字确认（如房价无变更则无须立即请客人签字，可等客人回到前台领取钥匙时再请客人签字）。

The Reception Desk should understand room change requirements of the guest and inform the guest about the change in room rate and ask bellman to take the *Room Change Form* to the guest room. First ask the guest to confirm the room rate and then sign for confirmation (If there's no change in room rate, immediate signature from the guest is not required. And signature from the guest may be requested when the guest returns to the Reception Desk to get the key).

（2）向客人解释不便马上更换的原因（大多是因为房间没有及时清洁或客人还未迁出）。

Explain the reason that it's not convenient to make immediate change (in most cases, the room is not cleaned or the original guest doesn't move out).

（3）如客人需要外出而希望酒店能自动替他换房时，应通知客人预先把行李收拾好。

If the guest needs to go out and hopes the hotel to change the room for him/her, inform the guest to get his luggage prepared in advance.

（4）应避免告诉客人具体的房号，这样可以挑选最早清洁的房间，为他安排。

Avoid telling the guest the specific room number. Thus the room available to be soonest cleaned will be arranged for the guest.

（5）通知客人返回酒店后，可向前台询问及拿取新的钥匙。

Inform the guest that he/she may enquire and get the new key at the Reception Desk when he/she comes out.

（6）前台接待等房间清洁完成后，填完整经客人签字后的房费变更表，然后按正常的换房程序进行操作，但行李员必须由楼层服务员陪同前去客人房间收取客人行李。在行李员从旧房取出行李后，楼层服务员应检查客人有无遗漏物品，然后陪同行李员把行李放在新的房间内的行李架上，最后关门离去并在相关的工作日志本上填写具体的进出客人房间的时间。

After the room is cleaned, the Receptionist at the Reception Desk completes the *Alternation Form of Room Rate* signed by the guest and then works on normal room change procedures. However, the bellman must collect the guest luggage in the guest's room with the accompanying of the Floor Attendant. After the bellman takes out the luggage from the original room, the Floor Attendant should check whether there're any articles omitted in the room, then accompany the bellman to the new room and place the luggage onto the luggage rack. Close the door and fill in the specific time to coming in/out of the guest room on the corresponding work log.

表 4-6　换房工作程序与标准

Table 4-6　Room Change Procedures and Standards

项　目 Item	标 准 Standard
1. 问候 Greet the guest	（1）遇到客人先微笑，以礼貌、热情、友善的语气问候客人，如果不知道其姓名，称呼其“先生”、“女士”。 Smile to the guest; greet the guest with a polite, enthusiastic and friendly tone; call the guest “Mr.” or “Ms.” if the name of the guest is unknown. （2）尽量熟记客人姓名，如果是经常来的客人，前台接待员要以姓氏或以体现其身份的称呼问候客人（用其姓氏称呼客人至少在对话中使用一次）。 Try to memorize the name of the guest. In case of a frequent guest, the Receptionist of the Reception Desk should greet the guest with his/her family name or a way that can represent his/her social status (Call the guest with his/her family name at least once in the conversation). （3）地域不同，与客人的熟悉程度不同，要以个性化称呼来向客人打招呼。即称呼客人既要体现出尊敬感，又要体现出亲切感。 As the guests may come from different regions and the degrees of familiarity to the guests are different, individualized ways should be used to call the guest. Give the guest a sense of respect and intimacy when greeting the guest. （4）与客人讲话时面带微笑，保持目光的接触。 Smile when talking with the guest; keep eye contacts.

续表

项　目 Item	标 准 Standard
2. 确认 Make confirmation	（1）客人换房原因，如果要求合理，按照客人的要求换房。 If the reason for room change is rational，change the room for the guest as required by the guest. （2）客人到前台要求换房时，与客人确认房间是否有行李，如无行李收回原房卡，直接为其更换新房卡；如房间仍有行李，请客人先返回房间整理行李，告知客人，礼宾员会在5分钟内至其房间协助其换房。 If the guest requests the room change at the Reception Desk，confirm with the guest whether there's luggage in the room. If there's no luggage，collect the original room card and change new room card to the guest directly. If there's luggage in the room，first ask the guest to prepare the luggage and the Concierge Attendant will show up in his/her room within five minutes to assist in room change. （3）客人在房间打电话要求换房，告知客人不用离开房间，礼宾员会在5分钟内至其房间协助其换房。 If the guest calls for room change in his/her guest room，tell the guest that he is not required to leave the room and the Concierge Attendant will show up in his/her room within five minutes to assist in room change. （4）客人在店外打电话要求换房，告知客人房间已为其保留，待其返回酒店后为其换房（客人返回酒店参照前两项为其换房）。 If the guest calls for room change out of his/her guest room，inform the guest that the room has reserved for him and room change will be made when he/she returns（for procedures after the guest returns，please refer to the abovementioned two items）.
3. 办理手续 Work on formalities	（1）将换房单一式三联内容填写齐全（客人姓名、原房号、现房号、房价是否变更，填写换房原因，经手人签字）。 Complete the Room Change Form in triplicate（the name of the guest，original room number，new room number，whether the room rate is changed，room change reason，signature of responsible personnel）. （2）将新的房间钥匙一起交给礼宾员，并提醒礼宾员将原房间钥匙取回返还前台。 Pass the new room key to the Concierge Attendant；remind the Concierge Attendant to get the original room key and return the key to the Reception Desk. （3）通知客房部原房号及换房后的房号。 Inform the Room Department the original and new room numbers.
4. 更改电脑信息及存档 Modify computer information and archive	（1）立即更新电脑，并在REMARK中注明换房房号及原因。 Update computer information immediately and indicate the new room number and room change reason in the column of "REMARK". （2）当礼宾员将原房间钥匙返回时，将换房单的"白联"与客人登记卡一同放到客人新房间的档案中，"粉联及蓝联"存档以备查询。 When the Concierge Attendant returns the key of the original room，put the "white copy" of the Room Change Form and the Guest Registration Card together into the file for the new room，Archive the pink copy and blue copy for further reference.
5. 电话确定 Confirm by telephone	客人换到新房间10分钟后打电话给客人。 Call the guest 10 minutes after the guest moves into the new room.
6. 建立客史记录 Establish guest history record	将客人具体要求和喜好输入电脑，待客人下次入住时可提前做好准备。 Input the specific requirements and preferences of the guest into the column of "REMARKS" in the PROFILE of the computer so as to make preparations in advance for future residing of the guest.

（三）换房前注意事项（Precautions Before Room Change）

（1）如更换的客房价格有差异，一定要在客人提出换房要求时即告诉客人，并要提前让客人在房价变更表上签字确认。

In case of variation in room rates，immediately inform the guest once the guest proposes the room change request. Ask the guest to sign for confirmation on the *Alternation Form of Room Rate* in advance.

（2）在客人提出换房要求时一定要弄清楚客人换房的真正原因并在换房单上注明。

When the guest proposes room change request，do make clear the true reason of room change by the guest and indicate the reason on the Room Change Form.

（3）将要安排给客人的房间是否已完全清洁好，如暂时还未清洁好但又没有别的选择，应请客房部提前整理，并问清所需时间，然后向客人说明。

Check whether the new room for the guest has been fully cleaned. If the room is not cleaned up yet and there're no alternatives, ask the Room Department to give priority to the room, get to know the required time and explain to the guest.

（4）未经清洁之房间坚决不可以更换给客人。

Never offer room that is not cleaned to the guest.

（5）当客人不在房间而要求换房时，一定要记住请客人先把行李整理好，以方便行李员为客人搬运行李。

If the guest requests room change when he is out, do remember to ask the guest to prepare the luggage in advance to facilitate the bellman to transport the luggage for the guest.

（6）在客人不在房间时，行李员一定要在楼层服务员的陪同下才可以进入客人的房间，在离开前切记不能让客人有物品遗留在房间，造成客人的损失和投诉。离开客人房间后楼层服务员应该有出入时间的登记备查。

If the guest is not in the room, the bellman must enter the room with the company of the Floor Attendant. Strongly bear in mind that no articles of the guest should be forgotten in the room. Or, losses would be incurred against the guest or complaints would be caused. After leaving the guest room, the Floor Attendant should record the exact in/out time for further reference.

（7）对客人提出的一些无理的换房要求应该及时请管理人员与客人进行沟通。

In case of unreasonable room change requirements by the guest, immediately ask the managerial to communicate with the guest.

（8）对由于酒店的失误造成客人换房，一定要记得向客人表示歉意并对客人的意见表示感谢。

In case of room change caused by the faults of the hotel, do remember to apologize to the guest and thank the guest for his/her recommendations.

六、前台接待处常见问题处理工作流程（Disposal Procedures on Common Problems at Reception Desk）

表 4-7 特殊情况处理流程

Table 4-7 Disposal Procedures Under Special Circumstances

项目 Item	标准 Standard	流程内容 Procedures
客人不愿进行入住登记 The guest is unwilling to make check-in registration	耐心、细致解释 Make patient and detailed explanation	（1）应了解客人的想法，并耐心解释填写住宿登记表的必要性，让其签字认可。 Understand the true thoughts of the guest; patiently explain the necessity of filling in the Check-in Registration Form; have the guest to sign for confirmation. （2）如果客人是有所顾虑，害怕被人打扰，则可向客人耐心解释，并做出保证让其放心。 If the guest hesitates and is afraid to be disturbed; explain to the guest patiently and make promise to the guest to ease the guest.
来访者要求查询住房客人 The visitor requests to enquire about the residing guest	尊重客人意愿 Obey the will of the guest	先查询客人的房号，而后与客人联系，征得客人的同意，然后才能告诉来访者客人的房间号。 First enquire the room number of the guest; contact the guest; tell the visitor the room number of the guest upon the consent of the guest.

续表

项目 Item	标准 Standard	流程内容 Procedures
在房间紧张的情况下客人要求延住 The guest requests extension under room stress	致歉并说明原因 Apologize and explain the reasons	(1) 照顾已住店的客人利益为第一要义，宁可为即将来店的客人介绍别的宾馆，也不能赶走已住店的客人。 Give priority to the benefits of the residing guest. Would rather to introduce new hotel to the upcoming guest than driving away the residing guest. (2) 可以先向客人征求其意见，是否愿意搬到其他酒店延住，如果客人不愿意，则应尽快通知预订处，为即将来店的客人另寻房间，或是联系其他酒店。 First solicit the opinions from the guest about whether he/she is willing to extend the stay in another hotel. If the guest denies, inform the Reservation Desk as soon as possible to find other room for the upcoming guest or contact another hotel.
客人离店时带走房间物品 The guest takes away items in the room	委婉提示或按价赔偿 Remind tactfully or ask the guest to compensate according to the value of the item	个别客人在临走时出于贪小便宜，或是为了留个纪念等心理，常会顺手拿走宾馆的茶杯、毛巾等用品，碰到这种情况，直接向客人索要是不合适的，会令客人尴尬，破坏彼此间已建立起来的和谐关系，聪明的做法是不露痕迹地告诉客人："您房间里的东西找不着了，是不是您一时不注意放在什么地方，忘记恢复原位了，能不能麻烦您帮助我们找一找？" Some guests would take along items such as cup and towel of the hotel for greediness for small advantages or as souvenir when they check out. In such case, it is inappropriate to claim directly from the guest, which would embarrass the guest and damage the harmonious relationship with the guest. A wise solution is to ask the guest naturally: "There's something missing in your room. May I ask if you forgot to restore it to the normal position? Will you please help us to look for it?"

任务二　问询服务
Task II　Information Service

酒店问询服务最主要的任务就是解答客人有关酒店服务、设施及酒店所在城市的交通、游览等内容的询问，以及客人查询、问询、代客留言、找人、联系旅游等内容的服务。

The main task of information service is to respond inquiries on aspects such as hotel services, facilities, traffics and tourism of the city as well as services such as inquiry, information, message, people finding and tourism contact.

一、住客信息咨询服务（Information Service for Residing Guest）

（一）问询服务的业务范围（Scope of Information Service）

(1) 回答客人的咨询，提供准确的信息。

Response inquiries from the guest and provide accurate information.

(2) 做好留言服务。

Provide proper message service.

(3) 处理客人的邮件。

Handle mails for the guests.

(4) 完成客人委托的事情。

Accomplish matters as assigned by the guests.

（二）问询处员工应掌握的信息范围（Scope of Information to be Mastered by Information Personnel）

（1）酒店自身的有关信息：本酒店的位置（应有向导卡），本店所有服务设施、服务项目，酒店的组织体系，各部门办公地点、职责及主要负责人姓名，每天的宴会、会议、展览会等各种活动情况，酒店的有关政策。

Information related to the hotel: The position of the hotel (guide card required); all service facilities, service items of the hotel; organizational system of the hotel; offices, responsibilities and names of leading officials of each department; information about various types of events of the day such as banquets, conferences and exhibitions; related policies of the hotel.

（2）掌握本市有关信息：交通、主要观光娱乐、购物、科教文化等方面的信息及主要企事业单位、银行、医院及政府有关部门的地址、电话等。

Information related to the city: Information on aspects such as traffic, major sightseeing and recreation places, shopping, science, education and culture; addresses, telephone numbers, etc. of main enterprises and public institutions, banks, hospitals and related governmental departments.

（3）天气、日期、时差方面的信息。

Information related to weather, date and time difference.

（4）其他方面的信息。

Information related to other aspects.

（三）问询处要备齐的信息资料（Information and Data to be Prepared at the Information Desk）

（1）飞机、火车、轮船、汽车等交通工具的时刻表、价目及里程表。

Timetables, prices and mileages of transportation vehicles such as plane, train, ship and bus.

（2）地图的准备：本地的政区图、交通图、旅游图及全省、全国乃至世界地图。

Preparation of maps: Local administrative division maps, traffic maps, tourism maps as well as the provincial, national and even world maps.

（3）电话号码薄：本市、全省乃至全国的电话号码薄及世界各主要城市的电话区号。

Telephone directory: Telephone directories of the city, province and even the country; area codes of major cities in the world.

（4）各主要媒体、企业的网址。

Websites of major media and enterprises.

（5）交通部门对购物、退票、行李重量及尺寸规格的规定。

Provisions on shopping, tick refunding, luggage weight and size by the traffic department.

（6）本酒店及其所属集团的宣传册。

Brochures of the hotel and the group governing the hotel.

（7）邮资价目表。

Postage price list.

（8）酒店当日活动安排，如宴会。

Event arrangement (e.g. banquet) of the hotel.

（9）当地著名高等院校、学术研究机构的名称、地址及电话。

Names, addresses and telephone numbers of local renowned colleges and universities academic research institutes.

（10）本地主要娱乐场所的特色及其地址和电话号码。

Feature of major local entertainment venues and their addresses and telephone numbers.

（四）查询服务注意事项（Precautions of Information Service）

（1）接待员应注意聆听客人的问题，主动热情地回答客人提出的问题，对国内外客人要一视同仁。

The Receptionist should carefully listen to and positively and enthusiastically answer the questions raised by the guests; regard the domestic guests and foreign guests equally.

（2）只回答自己权限内的问题，对自己不了解的事情应当向客人表示歉意，同时尽可能请示有关方面的负责人，查询后再答复客人，对于一时查不到的问题应请客人留下姓名、房号，等得到正确信息后再及时转告客人，对于经多方努力仍无法解答的问题，也要及时给客人回音并表示歉意。

Only answer the questions within the scope of authorization; apologize to the guests for the unknown matters; try to seek for instructions from related responsible personnel as possible; for questions not available to be answer temporarily, ask the guest to leave the name and room number and forward the correct information in time to the guest; for questions unable to be answered even after efforts in many ways, reply to the guest and apologize in time.

（3）给予简明准确的回答，注意语气语调，做到热情、耐心，有问必答，百问不厌。

Give precious and correct reply; pay attention to the mood and tone; be enthusiastic and patient to answer all questions.

（4）每位客人的姓名、房号、国籍、活动、房价等资料均属保密范围，接待员不得随意泄露。要求给予保密的客人，对他们的来访者和来电都应委婉拒绝。

Keep information such as the name, room number, nationality, activity and room rate confidential. Do not disclose information about the guest who requires confidentiality randomly. Decline the visitors and calls for such guests tactfully.

（5）对来电、来访者，接待员要先从电脑中查明被访者是否住在本酒店，如被访者不住酒店应礼貌告诉客人，如被访者有预订，可建议来电、来访者留言。

For callers and visitors, the Receptionist should first check whether the guest is residing in the hotel. If the guest is not a guest of the hotel, inform the caller or visitor politely. If the guest has made room reservation in the hotel, recommend the caller or visitor to leave a message.

（6）接待员在问明来访者姓名和单位后，以电话形式通知客人并征询客人意见，同意后方可将电话转入。

After asking the name and unit of the visitor, the Receptionist should call the guest to enquire the opinion of the guest. Transfer the call upon the consent of the guest.

（7）如果电话振铃声之后客房无人接听，可告诉来访者客人不在房间，建议来访者留言，但不可将房号随便告诉来访者。对于询问“××住客叫什么名字?”之类问题的来访者，接待员要特别提高警惕。

If no one answers the phone after the telephone rings, tell the visitor that the guest is not in and recommend the visitor to leave a message. Do not disclose the room number of the guest to the visitor without authorization. Especially raise the alertness for visitor with questions such as “What's the name of the guest in Room ××”.

（8）问询员在回答客人问讯时，必须准确无误，态度温和，不能使用不确定的语言，如“我想可能”、“大概”、“也许”等。

Be correct and gentle when answering the inquiries of the guest. Do not use uncertain expressions such as “I think probably”, “maybe” and “perhaps”.

二、查访住客服务（Inquiry of Guest Information）

有关住客查询是来访客人问询的主要内容之一，通常应在不触及客人隐私的范围内进行回答。问询员应首先从电脑中查看客人是否入住本酒店，然后确认其房号，接着向客房内打电话联系，将有人来访的信息告诉住客，经客人同意后才可将房号告诉来访者。如果客人不在客房内，可视情况通过呼叫等方法在酒店公共区域帮助来访者寻找被访的客人。但是绝不能未经住客许可，便直接将来访者带入客房或直接将房号告诉来访者。酒店必须注意保护客人的隐私，确保住客不受无关人员或不愿接待的访客的打扰。

Inquiry about the guest is one of the main contents of the visitors. Generally response should be made without disclosing the privacy of the guest. The Receptionist should first check whether the guest is residing in the hotel through the computer and then confirm the room number. Call the guest room and inform the guest that he/she has a visitor. Tell the room number to the visitor upon the consent of the guest. If the guest is not in the room, help the visitor to seek for the guest in public areas of the hotel by means of public addressing as the case may be. Never guide the visitor to the guest room or directly disclose the room number to the visitor without the permit of the guest. The hotel must attach importance to protect the privacy of the guest and guarantee that the guest is not disturbed by irrelative personnel or unwelcomed visitors.

（一）查询住客（Inquiry about the Guest）

（1）接到客人电话查询某客人住几号房间时，应问清要查找的住客姓名，通过电脑查出客人房号。

When receiving a call inquiring which room a guest lives in, ask the name of the guest and check the room number by computer.

（2）对住客的房号要注意保密，如果住客在房间，则问清来访者姓名、身份，接通客房电话，将某人来访的信息告诉该客人，说明有人找，征得客人同意后，将此电话转给客人。

Pay attention to the confidentiality of the room number of the guest. If the guest is in the room, ask clearly about the name, identity of the caller. Forward the information of an incoming call to the guest. Transfer the call to the guest upon the consent of the guest.

（3）如果住客不在房间又未留下去向，则询问来访者是否留言。若想继续查找，可按以下方法：问查询者除了提供的名字外，是否还有其他的名字，如英文名字、中文名字或特殊拼法；问清客人是从哪里来，何日何时抵店，何时离店；问清是否是团体，团号是多少，或是否与其他人一起来住店的，如是，问清同行人的姓名再从同行人的姓名中查找；问清是哪个接待单位，哪个公司的客人；如电脑中有相似的名字，可查出房号，然后核对资料；问对方是否有被查询人的名片；还可向接待组同事询问是否熟悉被查询客人的信息，因有时客人刚办理入住手续，还未办理电脑输入工作。如按以上做法，仍查不到客人，应向询问者表示歉意，并说明已通过多种方法查找，同时留下电话号码，一旦查到后马上通知询问者或请询问者留言，一旦找到客人或客人以后来登记时，即将“客人留言单”交给客人。

If the guest is not in and does not inform the hotel his/her track, enquire whether the caller would like to leave a message. For further searching, the follow methods may be used: Ask the enquirer whether the guest is provided with other names other than the provided name, such as English name, Chinese name or special spellings; ask about where the guest comes from, when the time of arrival/departure; ask whether the group is in a group as well as the group number, whether the guest comes together with other people. If so, ask the name of his/her fellow travelers and check from the names of the fellow travelers; ask the reception unit and company o the guest. If there're similar names in the computer, check out the room number and then verify the data; as the enquirer whether he/she has the business card of the guest; ask the Reception Desk whether they are familiar with information about the guest. Sometimes, though the guest has checked in, related input is not made into the computer. If the hotel fails to retrieve the guest according to the abovementioned methods, apologize to the enquirer and explained that all possible means have been tried. Meanwhile, leave the message of the enquirer. Immediately inform the enquirer if information is available or ask the enquirer to leave a message. Once the guest is found or the checks in later on, hand the *Guest Message Form* to the guest.

（4）如果住客预先交代其在酒店某个公共场所，则请行李员举寻人牌去寻找。找到客人后，将具体情况及时转达给客人。

If the guest has informed that he/she is in a certain public area of the hotel, ask the guest to search the guest with the Search Plate. After the guest is found, timely inform specific conditions to the guest.

（二）访问住客（Visit to the Guest）

（1）来访者知道住店客人姓名及房号，直接指引客人上楼。

Direct guide the visitor upstairs if the visitor knows the name and room number of the guest.

（2）来访者只知住店客人姓名不知房号，通过电脑查询，避开来访者与客人联系，在住店客人允许后，才可告诉来访者客人房号；对于来访者只知房号，不知客人姓名，不可以告诉来访者客人的姓名，可让其用电话与客人联系。

If the visitor knows the guest name and doesn't know the room number, check through the computer; contact with the guest evading the visitor; tell the visitor the room number upon the consent of the guest. If the guest knows only the room number and doesn't know the guest name, ask the visitor to contact the guest by telephone.

（3）因公务与酒店有关部门联系来访者，问清来访者姓名及单位，避开来访者，征得有关部门秘书同意后，方可告诉其部门位置，或找大堂副经理帮助客人；官方人员来访交与大堂副经理处理。

In case of visitor requiring contacting with related department of the hotel for official business, first ask the name and unit of the visitor, then seek for the consent of the secretary of related department evading the visitor. Tell the visitor the location of the department only upon the consent or ask the Assistant Manager to assist the guest. Visit of governmental personnel should be disposed by the Assistant Manager.

（三）住客要求保密的处理（Disposal of Confidentiality Requirements by the Guest）

（1）此项目要求问询处处理。

Such request should be disposed by the Information Desk.

（2）问清客人要求保密的程序。

Clarify the confidentiality procedure required by the guest.

（3）在值班簿上做好记录，记下客人姓名、房号及保密程度和时限。

Record properly on the duty log; note down the name, room number as well as the extent and time limit of such confidentiality of the guest.

（4）通知总机室做好该客人的保密工作。

Inform the Telephone Exchange to keep proper confidentiality for the guest.

（5）如有人来访要求保密的客人，或来电查询该客人时，问询员及总机均应以该客人没有入住或暂时没有入住为由予以拒绝。

In case of visiting or calling to the guest requiring confidentiality, the Information Clerk and the

Telephone Exchange Operator should decline such inquiry with the reason that the guest is now or temporarily not residing in the hotel.

（6）如客人要求更改保密程度或者取消保密时，应即刻通知总机室，并做好记录。

In case that the guest request to change the extent of confidentiality or cancel the confidentiality, the Telephone Exchange should be notified immediately and properly record should be made.

（四）查询访客注意事项（Precautions of Service to Inquiring Visitors）

（1）接待员应主动热情回答客人提出的问题，对国内外客人要一视同仁。

The Receptionist should carefully listen to and positively and enthusiastically answer the questions raised by the guests; regard the domestic guests and foreign guests equally.

（2）只回答自己权限内的问题，对自己不了解的事情应当向客人表示歉意，同时尽可能请示有关方面的负责人。

Only answer the questions within the scope of authorization; apologize to the guests for the unknown matters; try to seek for instructions from related responsible personnel as possible.

（3）每位客人的姓名、房号、国籍、活动、房价等资料均属保密范围，接待员不得随意泄露。要求给予保密的客人，对他们的来访者和来电都应委婉拒绝。

Keep information such as the name, room number, nationality, activity and room rate confidential. Do not disclose information about the guest who requires confidentiality randomly. Decline the visitors and calls for such guests tactfully.

（4）对来电、来访者，接待员要先从电脑中查明被访者是否住在本酒店，如被访者不住在本酒店应礼貌告诉客人。如被访者有预订，可建议来电、来访者留言。

For callers and visitors, the Receptionist should first check whether the guest is residing in the hotel. If the guest is not a guest of the hotel, inform the caller or visitor politely. If the guest has made room reservation in the hotel, recommend the caller or visitor to leave a message.

（5）接待员在问明来访者姓名和单位后，以电话形式通知客人并征询客人意见，同意后方可将电话转入。

After asking the name and unit of the visitor, the Receptionist should call the guest to enquire the opinion of the guest. Transfer the call upon the consent of the guest.

（6）如果电话振铃声之后客房无人接听，可告诉来访者客人不在房间，建议来访者留言，但不可将房号随便告诉来访者，对于询问"××住客叫什么名字?"之类问题的来访者，接待员要特别提高警惕。

If no one answers the phone after the telephone rings, tell the visitor that the guest is not in and recommend the visitor to leave a message. Do not disclose the room number of the guest to the visitor without authorization. Especially raise the alertness for visitor with questions such as "What's the name of the guest in Room ××".

三、留言服务（Message Service）

前厅问询处受理的留言主要有两种：访客留言和住客留言。

Messages disposed by the Information Desk at the Lobby mainly involve two types: visitor message and guest message.

（一）访客留言（Visitor Message）

（1）访客留言是指来访客人对住店客人的留言。具有一定的时效性，为确保留言单传递速度，有些酒店规定问询员每隔 1 小时与客房联系。

Visitor message refers to the message left by a visitor to the guest. Such message is provided with defined timeliness. To guarantee the transfer efficiency of the message, it is stipulated in some hotels that the Information Clerk should contact the guest room every other hour.

（2）问询员在接受该留言时，应请访客填写一式三联的“访客留言单”，将被访者客房的留言灯打开，将填写好的访客留言单第一联放入钥匙邮件架内，第二联送电话总机组，第三联交信使或行李员送往客房（将留言单从房门底下塞入房间）。

When accepting the message, the Information Clerk should ask the visitor to fill in the *Visitor Message Form* in triplicate and turn on the message lamp for the room of the guest. The first copy of the completed *Visitor Message Form* should be placed into the key and mail holder; the second copy should be sent to the Telephone Exchange Group and the third copy should be given to the messenger or the bellman to deliver it to the guest room (tuck the message under the room door).

（3）为此，客人可通过三种途径获知访客留言内容：取钥匙时得到留言单；进入客房时发现留言单；看到房内留言灯亮着，通过询问可获悉留言内容。

Thus, the guest may obtain the message from the visitor in three ways: By receiving the key; by entering the guest room; by inquiring the message on noticing the message lamp.

（4）当了解到客人已得到留言内容后，话务员或问询员应及时关闭留言灯。

After knowing that the guest has got the message, the operator or the information clerk should turn off the message lamp timely.

（5）晚班问询员应检查钥匙邮件架，如发现孔内仍有留言单，则应立即检查该房号的留言灯是否已经关闭。如留言灯已关闭，则可将该架内的留言单作废；如留言灯仍未关闭，则应电话与客人联系，将访客留言内容通知客人；如客人不在酒店，则应继续开启留言灯以及保留留言单，等候客人返回。

The night shift information clerk should check the key and mail holder. If the message is still in the hole, immediately check whether the message lamp of the corresponding room has been turned off. If the message lamp has been turned off, invalidate the message; if the message lamp is still on, call the guest and inform the contents of the message to the guest. If the guest is not in the hotel, keep the message lamp on and maintain the message form till the return of the guest.

（二）住客留言（Guest Message）

（1）住客留言是住店客人给来访客人的留言。

Guest message refers to the message left by a guest to the visitor.

（2）客人离开客房或酒店时，希望给来访者（含电话来访者）留言，问询员应请客人填写“住客留言单”，一式两联，问询处与电话总机各保存一联。

Before leaving the guest room or the hotel, if the guest would like to leave a message to the visitor (including caller), the information clerk should ask the guest to fill in the *Guest Message Form* in duplicate. The Information Desk and the Telephone Exchange should keep one copy respectively.

（3）若客人来访，问询员或话务员可将留言内容转告来访者。

In case of visitors, the Information Clerk or the Exchange Operator may forward the content of the message to the visitor.

(4) 由于住客留言单已注明了留言内容的有效时间，若错过了有效时间，仍未接到留言者新的通知，可将留言单作废。

As the guest has indicated the valid period of such message, if such period expires without new message by the guest, the message may be invalidated.

(5) 此外，为了确保留言内容的准确性，尤其在受理电话留言时，应注意掌握留言要点，做好记录，并向对方复述一遍，以得到对方确认。

In addition, to ensure the correctness of the message, especially for telephone message, attach importance to grasp the key points and make proper records. Repeat to the guest once for the confirmation of the guest.

表 4-8 留言服务流程

Table 4-8 Message Service Procedures

项 目 Item	标 准 Standards
1. 问候 Greet the guest	(1) 遇到客人先微笑，以礼貌、热情、友善的语气问候客人，如果不知道其姓名，称呼其“先生”、“女士”。 Smile to the guest; greet the guest with a polite, enthusiastic and friendly tone; call the guest “Mr.” or “Ms.” if the name of the guest is unknown. (2) 尽量熟记客人姓名，如果是经常来的客人，前台接待员要以姓氏或以体现其身份的称呼问候客人（用其姓氏称呼客人至少在对话中使用一次）。 Try to memorize the name of the guest. In case of a frequent guest, the Receptionist of the Reception Desk should greet the guest with his/her family name or a way that can represent his/her social status (Call the guest with his/her family name at least once in the conversation). (3) 地域不同，与客人的熟悉程度不同，要以个性化称呼来向客人打招呼。即称呼客人既要体现出尊敬感，又要体现出亲切感。 As the guests may come from different regions and the degrees of familiarity to the guests are different, individualized ways should be used to call the guest. Give the guest a sense of respect and intimacy when greeting the guest. (4) 与客人讲话时面带微笑，保持目光的接触。 Smile when talking with the guest; keep eye contacts.
2. 确认 Make confirmation	(1) 当接到要求留言的电话后，迅速在电脑中查询客人的姓名、房号是否与要求留言者所提供的信息相符。 When receiving the call requesting message, quickly check on the computer whether the name and room number of the guest is consistent with the information provided by the person leaving the message. (2) 确认客人是否正在住店，或者是否为预计抵店客人，除非客人已结账离店，否则都应做留言。 Confirm whether the guest is residing in the hotel or about to check in later; offer message service for all guests except that the guest has checked out. (3) 在便笺上记录留言方姓名、电话号码、公司名称及留言内容。 Note down the name, telephone number, company name and message content of the person leaving the message. (4) 将对方姓名、住店客人姓名、电话号码、公司名称及留言内容重复一遍，以获得确认。 Repeat the name of the people leaving the message, name of the residing guest, telephone number, company name and message content for confirmation.
3. 通知跟进 Notify follow-up	(1) 将留言内容输入电脑，然后将留言在打印机中打印出来。 Input the message into the computer and print the message by the printer. (2) 将“电脑留言单”装入信封，在 15 分钟之内送往客人房间。 Load the *Computer Message Form* into the envelope and deliver it to the guest room within 15 minutes. (3) 若留言为复杂的中文留言，或遇到电脑出故障时，应采用“手工留言单”，将留言书写在酒店信纸上，并复印一份留在前台存档，然后装入信封，由礼宾员在 15 分钟之内送往客人房间。 In case of complicated message in Chinese or failure of the computer, use *Manual Message Form.* Write down the message onto the letter paper of the hotel; make one copy at the Reception Desk for archiving; load the message into the envelope; have the Concierge Attendant deliver it to the guest room within 15 minutes. (4) 如果客人为预计抵店，应在电脑中“意见”处注明，将其留言存放在前台。 If the guest is about to check in, mark in the column of “COMMENTS” in the computer and keep the message at the Reception Desk.

任务三　客账服务
Task III　Guest Account Service

【情境导入】【Scenario Introduction】

某日夜晚，在三亚亚龙湾环球城大酒店前台处，一位外籍住店客人正在兑换外币，在填写旅行支票时，不慎将名字签错了地方，面对签错的支票，酒店前台外币兑换员对客人说："这张支票签名的地方不对，请换一张。"客人不同意，双方发生了争执，兑换员坚持不予兑换，客人满腹怒气，来到大堂经理处。

On night, at the Reception Desk of Yalong Bay Universal Resort Sanya, a foreign guest was exchanging foreign currency. When filling in the traveler's cheque, the carelessly signed the name at the wrong position. Facing the wrongly signed cheque, the foreign currency exchange cahier at the Reception Desk told the guest: "The signature is at the wrong position, please change another cheque." The guest disagreed and disputed with the cashier. The cashier insisted that it could not be exchanged. The guest was full of anger and came to the Lobby Manager.

经理小夏正在值班，看到气呼呼走过来的客人，小夏迎上前去，问道："先生，能为您效劳吗?"客人说了事情的经过，显得很着急。小夏听罢，心中暗忖，兑换员说不行，怕难以变通，但又不能随随便便将一位寻求帮忙的客人拒之门外，小夏安慰客人道："先生，别着急，事情总可以解决的，您先喝杯咖啡，我帮您想办法。"说着，把客人请到大堂吧稍做休息。

Manager Xia was on duty. On noticing the guest approaching, Xia stepped forwards and asked: "May I help you, sir?" The guest explained what had happened quite anxiously. Xia thought that probably it was hard to make it as the cashier said it was not allowed. However, it was improper to decline a guest seeking for assistance. So he consoled the guest: "Take is easy, sir. Let's find a way out. Just have a cup of coffee and I'll work it out." Then he guided the guest to the Lobby Bar to have a rest.

小夏本身对兑换外币业务并不熟悉，但他想客人之所想，急客人之所急，不熟悉情况先了解这方面的情况，随即，他拨通储蓄所的电话，诚恳地向他们请教。电话接通了："你好，我是××酒店，我们这儿的一位客人在兑换外币时签错了支票，我想请教一下，有没有什么可以补救的办法?"对方听后请小夏打电话到分行询问，小夏道："谢谢!"随后又拨通分行办公室的电话，回答是要问国际兑换台。小夏又一次拿起电话，接通分行国际兑换台，请求帮助。银行方面说办法简单：只要在正确的地方再补签个名就可以了。找到办法后，小夏很快回到客人身边，告诉他解决的办法，并将客人带到前台外币兑换处，向兑换员讲明情况，帮客人顺利地兑换了外币，这时客人带着满意的神情称赞小夏："谢谢你这么快解决了问题，帮了我的大忙，真不愧为客人的知己。"看着客人翘起大拇指，小夏舒心地笑了："这是我们应尽的义务，请不必客气。"客人满意而去。

Xia was not familiar with the foreign exchange business. However, he could put himself to other's position. He decided to get information first since he's not familiar with it. Then, he dialed the number of the savings agency and consulted sincerely. After the telephone put through, he said: "Hello, this is ×× Hotel. We have a guest here signing the signature at the wrong place when making foreign currency exchange. I'd like to sake whether there's any remedies?" The savings agency asked Xia to call the branch bank for consultation. Xia replied: "Thank you!" Then he dialed the office of the branch bank and received the reply that it was the International Exchange Desk that he should consult to. Xia called a third time to the International Exchange Desk of the branch bank for assistance. The bank offered an easy solution: Just signing another name at the correct place. Finding a solution, Xia quickly returned to the guest and told him the solution. He then showed the guest to the foreign currency exchange service at the Reception Desk and explained the case to the cashier. The guest has the foreign currency exchanged smoothly and praised Xia in satisfaction: "Thank you for solving the problem so quickly. You did a great favor for me and you know the guest best!" Seeing the guest thumbing up, Xia smiled joyfully: "This is our duty. Never mind." The guest left with great satisfaction.

【情境分析】【Scenario Analysis】

原本是一件极可能引起投诉的复杂事情，可处理起来就这么简单，几个电话就把它处理妥帖，而且效果相当好。其实，类似的事情在我们平常服务工作中都会遇到。该如何处理？上面的事例就是答案：不能简单地说"不"，不如换一种方式试试，多动动嘴，多跑跑腿，在自己力所能及的范围内多为客人做些努力。

The case seems to be a complicated matter that would possible causing complaint. However it was simply and properly disposed just by several calls with good effects. As a matter of face, we would frequently meet such kind of affairs in daily services. How should we handle this? The case above is the answer. We cannot simply say: "No." Better shift to another method, ask more and do more and make more efforts within the own ability.

这样，即使有些事一时不能得到解决，客人也会谅解的。

With such efforts, the guest would be understanding even of the matter would not be solved temporarily.

前台账务处理是前台收银处的一项日常业务工作。为避免出现工作差错，发生逃账、漏账情况，前台收银处必须有一套完整的制度。前台账务处理的方法和要求如下：

Reception desk account treatment is a daily routine of the Cashier's Desk of the Reception Desk. To avoid mistakes in work as well as conditions such as skippers and omitted accounts, the Cashier's Desk at the Reception Desk must be provided with a set of complete rules. Methods and requirements for Reception Desk accounting treatment:

(1) 账户清楚。前厅接待处给每位登记入住的客人设立一个账户，供收银处记录该客人在住店期间的房租及其他各项花费。它既是客人离店时结算的依据，又是编制各类营业报表的数据来源之一。通常，酒店为散客设立个人账户，团体客人设立团体账户。若团体客人中有不愿受综合服务费标准的限度而有其他消费时，则应另立个人账户。户头应清楚、准确，特别注意姓名、房号必须与住宿登记表内容一致。账户应分类归档，取用方便。

Clear Accounts. The Reception Desk in the Lobby must establish an account for every guest checked in for the Cashier's Desk to record the room rates and other expenses of the guest during his/her stay in the hotel. It is not only the basis for account settlement in check-out but also one of the data sources for the compilation of various types of business statements. Generally, the hotel would establish individual accounts for individual guests and group accounts for group guests. If the a guest within a group is unwilling to be restricted by the comprehensive service fee standards of that group and makes other consumptions, an additional individual account should be established. The account should be clear and accurate. Special attention should be attached to the consistence between the name and room number and the information indicated on the *Check-in Registration Form*. The accounts should be classified and archived to facilitate the access.

（2）转账迅速。由于客人在酒店逗留期较短，发生的费用项目多，又可能随时离店，故要求转账迅速。各业务部门必须按规定时间将客人签字认可后的账单送到前台收银处，以防跑账、漏账现象发生。若采用计算机收银系统，对于客人在店内的任何消费，只要收银员将账单转入收银机，计算机即可同时记下客人当时的转账款项，极大地提高了工作效率。

Quick Transfer. Generally, the stay of the guest in the hotel is relatively short and the number of items of the expenses is relative great, plus that the guest would leave the hotel at any time, the transfer must be quick. Each business department should send the bills signed and confirmed by the guest to the Cashier at the Reception Desk within the stipulated period to avoid skipped or omitted accounts. If computer-based cashier system is used, for any consumptions of the guest in the hotel, the cashier only needs to transfer the bills into the cash register and the computer will simultaneously record the current transfer sums of the guest, which greatly enhances the work efficiency.

（3）记账准确。为客人建立账户后，即开始记录客人住店期间的一切费用。客人的房租采取按日累计的方法每天结算一次。客人离店加上当日应付房租，即为客人应付的全部房租。其他各项费用，如餐饮、洗衣、长途电话、传真、美容美发、书报等项目，除客人愿在消费时以现金结算外，均可由客人签字后由各有关部门将其转入前厅收银处，记入客人的账户。因此，要求记账准确，客人姓名、房号、费用项目和金额、消费时间等应清楚，并和客人账户记录保持一致。

Accurate Accounting. Begin to record all the expenses of the guest during the stay in the hotel after the account is established for the guest. The room rate of the guest should be settled on daily basis in an accumulative manner. When the guest checks out, the total room rates payable should be the record in the computer plus the room rate for that day. Except items that the guest is willing to make cash settlement, other expenses such as food and beverage, laundry, long-distance call, beauty treatment and hairdressing, magazines and newspapers may be transferred to the cashier's desk at the Lobby by the related departments upon the signature of the guest and credited into the accounts of the guest. Therefore, the accounting should be correct; the name, room number, expense items, amounts, consumption time, etc. should be clear; the record should be kept consistent with the account record of the guest.

一、客人离店退房结账服务（Check-out and Account Settlement of the Guest）

客人的付款方式有现金、支票、信用卡、挂账等形式。若客人用外币旅行支票结账，前台不直接收取旅行支票，客人需到外币兑换处依照当天汇率兑换人民币现钞，然后再付清自己的账目；若客人以信用卡付款，当客人离店时，要有礼貌地请客人出示信用卡，要对照客人的信用卡号码、有效期及签字，以确保信用卡的有效性、通用性和真实性，以保证信用卡的正确使用。另外，如果客人住店消费超过有效限额，将通知信用卡授权中心，申请授权号码，所批准的授权号码应写在信用卡单据的右上角。下列是多数酒店可以接受的信用卡：美国运通卡（American Express Card）、大来卡（Dinners Card）、万事达卡（Master Card）、JCB 卡（JCB Card）、签证卡（Visa Card）、长城卡（Great Wall Card）等。如果客人使用外币现钞结账，需先请其到外币兑换处依照当天汇率换成店内可收取的货币，然后转交前台结账；若为公司挂账，接待人员打出电脑明细账单，经客人认可在账单上签字，并找齐所有公司担保付款凭证一起转交至财务部，由财务部和公司进行结算。

Payment methods available for the guests involve cash, cheque, credit card, consumption on credit, etc. If the guest selects to settle the account of the foreign currency foreign currency exchange, the

Reception Desk will not directly collect the traveler's cheque. The guest should be covert the cheque into cash in RMB at the Foreign Currency Exchange Desk and then clear the accounts. If the guest selects to settle the account of the credit card, when the guest checks out, ask the guest to present the credit card politely. Check the number, valid period and signature of the credit card of the guest to guarantee the validity, universality and authenticity of the card so as to further guarantee the correct use of the credit card. In addition, if the consumption of the guest in the hotel exceeds the valid limit, inform the Credit Card Authorization Center to apply for the authorization number. The approved authorization number should noted on the upper right corner of the credit card voucher. Credit cards acceptable by most hotels are listed as follows: American Express Card, Dinners Card, Master Card, JCB Card, Visa Card, Great Wall Card, etc. If the guest selects to settle the account by foreign currency cash, first ask the guest to covert the foreign currency into acceptable currency by the hotel at the Foreign Currency Exchange Desk according to the exchange rate of that day; and then transfer to the Reception Desk to settle the account. In case of account on credit by the company, the Receptionist should print out the detailed bills with the computer. Sign on the bills upon the confirmation of the guest. Collect all the payment vouchers on credit by the company and submit all such vouchers to the Financial Department. The Financial Department will then make settlement with the company.

（一）快速结账服务（Quick Settlement Service）

办理退房结账手续是客人离店前所接受的最后一项服务，应给客人留下良好的最后印象。结账一般要求在两三分钟内完成，酒店一般规定退房结账的最后时间为中午12:00，在此之前通常结账客人比较集中，为了避免客人排队等候，或缩短客人的结账时间，酒店可以提供快速结账服务。

Handling check-out and account settlement formalities is the last service provided to the guest before check-out, which should leave satisfying final impression to the guest. Generally, account settlement should be finished within 2-3 minutes and the deadline of check-out and settlement is 12: 00 at noon. Generally, the guests checking out are relatively concentrated before 12: 00. To avoid waiting of the guest or shorten the settlement time, the hotel may provide quick account settlement service.

1. 客人房内结账（Account Settlement Within the Guest Room）

客人房内结账的前提是，前厅计算机系统与客人房间的电视系统联网，客人通过电视机显示器查阅账单情况，并通知收款处结账。如果客人使用信用卡，收款员可以直接填写签购单，不需要客人到前台去。如客人使用现金，则在房间内核对金额后，结账时直接多退少补，从而简化了手续。一般情况下，房内结账只对信誉较好、采用信用卡结算的客人提供。

The account settlement within the guest room should have the premise that the computer system at the Lobby is interlinked with the TV system within the guest room, the guest may view the bills on the TV and inform the settlement of the Cashier's Desk. If the guest selects to use the credit card, the cashier may directly fill in the slip. The guest is not required to go to the Reception Desk. If the guest selects to use cash, after the guest checks the amount within the room, the guest may have the payment refunded for any overpayment or make a supplemental payment for any deficiency, which streamlines the formalities. Generally, room account settlement is only provided by guests with relatively good credit standing and settling accounts with credit card.

2. 通过填写“快速结账委托书”结账（Account Settlement by Filling in the *Authorization Letter on Quick Account Settlement*）

对于有良好信誉、使用信用卡结账的客人，酒店为其提供此项快速结账服务：客人离店前一天填写好“快速结账委托书”，允许酒店在其离店后办理结账手续。收款员核对委托书的签名与客人签购单、登记表上的签名是否一致，在客人早晨离店时只向客人告知应付费用的大致金额即可，在客人离店后，在闲暇时间替客人办理结账手续，事后按照客人填写的地址将账单收据等寄给客人。

The hotel may provide such quick settlement service to guests with good credit standing and paying with credit card: The guest should fill in the *Authorization Letter on Quick Account Settlement* one day before the check-out so as to allow the hotel to settle the account after he/she leaves the hotel. The cashier should check whether the signature on the *Authorization Letter* is consistent with the signature on the slip and the registration form. The guest just needs to inform the approximate amount of the accrued expenses when he leaves the hotel. Work on the account settlement formalities for the guest in free time; and then mail the bills, receipts, etc. to the address provided by the guest afterwards.

3. 即时消费结账（Immediate Consumption Account Settlement）

即时消费是指客人临近退房前的消费费用，因转送到收款处太迟而没能赶在客人退房前及时入账。在采用电脑操作管理的酒店，类似问题一般不会出现，而对于采用手工转账的酒店，及时核查即时消费，确保不产生漏账损失是一件重要工作。通常做法是，客人结账时，收款员应礼貌询问客人是否有即时消费，或者直接电话询问易产生即时消费的消费点，如总机、餐厅、房务中心等。这种做法一方面取决于客人的诚实度，另一方面当面与客人核查费用问题，让客人产生不信任感，影响客人对酒店的印象。而且，在客人结账时去核查消费会耽误太长时间，影响工作效率，引起客人的不满。

The immediate consumption refers to the consumption occurred just before the consumption that is not entered into the account before the check-out of the guest because it's too late to be transferred to the cashier's desk. Generally, such problems would not occur in hotels applying computer operation management; while for hotels applying manual transfer, it is important work to timely check the immediate consumptions so as to prevent losses of omitted accounts. The common practice is that, when the guest checks out, the cashier should politely enquire whether the guest has immediate consumption politely or directly enquire the consumption points where immediate consumption would easily occur, for example, Telephone Exchange, restaurant, Room Center, etc. Such practice depends on the honesty of the guest. In addition, checking expenses face to face with the guest would make the guest the sense of sense of not being trust, which would affect the impression of the guest of the hotel. Furthermore, consumption examination at the time of check-out would waste too much time, adversely affect the work efficiency and further cause dissatisfaction of the guest.

（二）前台结账流程（Account Settlement Procedures at the Reception Desk）

1. 散客结账服务程序（Check-out Service Procedures for Individual Guests）

（1）当客人到前台结账时，礼貌地询问客人房号，确认客人姓名是否正确，并随时称呼客人的姓氏。

When the guest comes to the Reception Desk to settle the account, enquire the room number of the guest; confirm whether the name of the guest is correct; readily call the family name of the guest from time to time.

（2）接待员主动收取房间钥匙，并问询客人是否发生其他消费。

The Receptionist positively collects the room keys; and enquires whether there're some other consumptions rated to the guest.

（3）客人结账时，前台接待员要及时与客房服务中心联系，请迅速查清客人房间酒水使用情况。

When the guest checks out, the receptionist of the Reception Desk should timely contact the Room

Service Center to quickly check the drink consumption conditions in the guest room.

(4) 委婉地问明客人是否有刚发生的消费费用（如电话费、房内小酒吧饮料费、早餐费等），以免漏账。

Politely ask the guest whether there're personal expenses just occurred (such as telephone bill, drink bill in the small bar within the room, breakfast fee) to avoid omissions of the bills.

(5) 打印出电脑清单，交付客人检查，经其认可在账单上签字，按已约定的付款方式向客人收取费用或转入财务部应收账款。

Print out the list from the computer; give the guests for inspection; have the guest to sign on the bill if the guest bears no doubts; collect the expenses or change to the account receivables of the Financial Department according to the agreed payment methods.

(6) 收回客房钥匙。

Collect the room key (s).

(7) 在结账的同时，要清理客人档案栏，取出登记卡、信用卡复印件，以便其他客人重新使用。

Sort up the guest file during the check-out. Take out the registration card and the copy of the credit card to facilitate further use of the guest.

(8) 客人提前付清账目，但晚些离店时，接待人员要在电脑中注明延迟离店，以便提醒其他部门及人员。

If the guest pays up the bills in advance and leaves the hotel at a later time, the receptionist should indicate "delayed leaving" in the computer system so as to remind other departments and personnel.

(9) 在客人结账时，要查看电脑中所注明的特殊注意事项。

When the guest checks out, examine the special matters needing attention indicated in the computer system.

(10) 确认一切手续，在最短时间内完成结账手续。

Confirm all formalities and finish the check-out formalities as soon as possible.

(11) 在客人结清账款后，在其账单上打印"付费"的印迹，使账单的挂账数为零，然后将一联交给客人做收据，另一联转送会计组，将金额填入现金收入日报。

After the guest has paid up the bills, stamp "paid" on the bills to clear the accounts on credit. Give one copy to the guest as receipt; forward another copy to the Accountant Group. Fill in the amount into the *Daily Cash Income Report*.

(12) 在入住登记表的背面盖上结账日期，连同客房钥匙移交前台接待员，接待员在计算机上做相应处理，将该住客房转换为走客房。

Stamp the check-out date on the back of the Check-in Registration Form; forward the form to the Receptionist at Front Desk together with the keys. The Receptionist make corresponding treatment on the computer and shift the status of the room to C/O.

(13) 微笑有礼貌地为客人迅速、准确地办理离店手续，并表示欢迎客人再次光临本酒店，祝其旅途愉快。

Work on check-out formalities quickly, accurately and politely with smiles; welcome the guest to revisit and wish him/her a pleasant journey.

2. 团队结账服务程序 (Group Check-out Service Procedures)

(1) 在团队离店前一天根据团队要求准备好团队总账。

Prepare the general account for the group one day before the check-out date as required by the group.

（2）登记进店和离店日期、团队名称、房间数、房间类型、房价、餐饮安排、预付款收取等内容。

Register the check-in date, check-out date, name of the group, number of the rooms, types of the rooms, room rates, food and beverage arrangements, collection of advance payment, etc.

（3）在团队离店前，及时与领队联系，随时沟通团队付账情况；经领队认可在总账单上签字，其余账由客人各自付清，领队要保证全队账目结算清楚后方可离开酒店。

Before the guest checks out, timely contact with the group leader, communicate the payment status of the group from time to time; have the group leader sign on the general bill upon approval and have the remaining bills paid separately by the guest; the group leader should ensure that the group may only leave the hotel after the bills of the entire group have been paid up.

（4）团队总账单由领队签字认可后，转交至财务部。

The general bill of the group should be forwarded to the General Ledger upon the signature and approval of the group leader.

（5）财务部将与旅行社联系解决有关付款问题，如有特殊情况，旅行社将在团队到达时现付或预先付订金作为保证。

The Financial Department will then contact the travel agency on related payment issues. In case of special circumstances, the travel agency should make cash payment or make advance payment as guarantee upon the arrival of the group.

（6）检查团队所有账目已付清；收取团队全部房间钥匙；查清账目后，发放行李放行单，作为团队可离店的凭证。

Inspect that all the bills of the group are paid up; collect the keys to all rooms of the group; after the accounts are settled, issue *Luggage Release Form* as credential for the group to leave the hotel.

表 4-9　前台结账服务流程

Table 4-9　Flow Chart for Check-out Services at the Reception Desk

项　目 Item	标　准 Standards
1. 问候 Greeting	（1）遇到客人先微笑，主动热情问候客人（30 秒内）。 Smile to the guest and greet the guest warmly and initiatively (within 30 s). （2）主动收取客人房卡，与客人确认房间号码。 Positively collect the room cards of the guests and confirm room numbers of the guest.
2. 报查房 Requiring room check	立即通知客房部房间退房，并告知员工姓名。 Immediately inform the check-out to the Room Department and inform the name of the staff.
3. 确认消费 Confirming consumption	（1）确认房间酒水消费（如客人清楚记得房间消费，可直接记账）。 Confirm the drink consumption within the room (keep accounts directly if the guest can clearly recall the room consumption). （2）如果客人不确定消费品或非本人入住时，可告知客人稍等 2~3 分钟，酒店立即查房。 If the guest is uncertain about the consumption items or does not live in person, ask the guest to wait for about 2-3 minutes and the hotel will have a check immediately.
4. 打印账单 Printing bills	告知客人账单正在打印，请稍等。 Inform the guest wait for a moment as the bills are being printed.
5. 确认账单及发票 Confirming bills and invoices	（1）请客人确认账单账目并签字（指示签字位置）。 Ask the guest to confirm the items on the bills and sign on the bills (indicate the area for signature) （2）确认开具发票名头，并告知发票开据相关规定（发票只可当次开具，过后作废，并不予补开）。 Confirm the title of the invoice and inform corresponding provisions on invoicing (The invoice can only be issued for the current stay and should be valid if the invoice is issued afterwards; reissue of the invoice is not accepted).

续表

项　目 Item	标　准 Standards
6. 结算 Settling the accounts	(1) 确认结账方式后，为客人结算。 Settle the accounts for the guest after the settlement method is confirmed. 1) 如客人用信用卡结账，请客人出示信用卡，在 POS 机做好离线或销售交易后，告知客人金额，请客人签字，并与卡背面核对签字后，将信用卡双手递给客人。同时提醒客人将信用卡保管好，经客人同意后可当面撕掉做押金的原授权单。 If the guest applies credit card to settle accounts, ask the guest to present the credit card; after making the off-line or sales transaction at the POS machine, inform the amount of the guests, ask the guest to sign his/her name; check with the signature on the back of the card; pass the credit card to the guest with both hands. Meanwhile, remind the guest to properly keep the credit card; tear up the original authorization sheet as guarantee upon the consent of the guest. 2) 如现金结账尚有余额需退还客人，收回押金收据后与 PAIDOUT 核对客人签字无误后将余额退给客人，请客人清点并保管好。 If there's still some balance refundable to the guest in cash settlement, after recovering the deposit receipt, check the signature of the guest. If no errors are found, return the balance to the guest. Ask the guest to count and make safekeeping on it. 如退款人非交押金人，且不是凭签字退款，应让退款人与交押金人取得联系，得到交押金人授权后，方可将余额退还，否则不予退款，可告知客人稍后随时可退款。 In case that the guest receiving the refund is not the guest making the advance payment. Refunding should not be made on signature basis. Instead, the refunding personnel should contact with the personnel making the advance payment. The balance can only be refunded only upon the authorization of the personnel making the advance payment. Or, no refunding should be made. Ask the guest refunding will be available at any time later on. (2) 结账完毕后将账单、信用卡收据及发票装入信封中，双手递给客人，请客人查收（也可根据客人不同要求为客人调整和打印各种明细账单）。 After check-out, put the bill, credit card receipt and invoice into an envelope and pass the envelope to the guest with both hands (or adjust and print various types of detailed bills as requested by the guests). (3) 询问客人是不是以后入住也开现在的这个发票抬头，可将客人发票抬头输入"注释"中，以便下次客人结账时开发票使用。 Ask the guest whether such invoice title will also be used in future. If so, input the title into the REMARK column to facilitate future invoicing.
7. 道别 Saying goodbye	(1) 主动询问客人住店的意见和建议，如对酒店房间或服务有任何建议应详细记录并反馈至当值经理。 Positively enquires the opinions and recommendations from the guest on his/her stay in the hotel, record any suggestions on guest rooms or services in details and give feedbacks thereof to the Duty Manger. (2) 询问客人是否需要叫车服务并确认目的地，如需要，马上通知礼宾部。 Ask the guest whether taxi service is required and confirm the destination; if taxi service is needed, notify the Concierge Department immediately. (3) 如当日天气有雾或下雪，前台接待员要提示客人天气信息、机场信息及道路信息。 In case of fog or snow, the receptionist of the Reception Desk should remind the guest about the weather information, airport information and traffic information. (4) 如得知客人乘火车或飞机，可为客人带上一份当日的报纸，在路上看。 If it is known that the guest is about to leave by train or by air, offer the guest a newspaper for that day to kill time on the way. (5) 感谢客人此次入住酒店并欢迎客人再次光临。 Thank the guest for residing in the hotel and welcome the revisit of the guest. (6) 目送客人离店后，再继续自己的工作。 See the guest off till he/she leaves the hotel and then continue the work.
8. 关注 Showing concerns	(1) 在为客人结账时，如果有其他客人，前台应主动问候，并请客人稍候。 When several guests require check-out services at the same time. When providing services for the first guest, the Reception Desk should positively welcome the other guests and ask them to wait for a while. (2) 整个接待过程，必须在 3 分钟之内完成（特殊情况除外）。 Otherwise under special circumstances, the entire reception must be finished within three minutes.

二、外币兑换服务（Foreign Currency Exchange）

酒店为方便客人，受中国银行委托，开展外币兑换服务。目前，中国银行除收兑换外汇现钞外，还办理旅行支票、信用卡等收兑业务。因此，前台收银员应掌握外币兑换的业务知识，接受这方面的培训。

To facilitate the guests, the hotels may provide foreign currency exchange services as entrusted by the Bank of China. Presently, more than providing exchange for cash, Bank of China also provide acceptance and exchange services for traveler's cheque, credit card, etc. Therefore, the cashier at the Reception Desk should master business knowledge on foreign currency exchange and receive related trainings thereof.

（一）酒店外币兑换工作流程（Work Flow for Foreign Currency Exchange of Hotels）

1. 兑换周转金出入库程序（Procedures for Withdrawal/Deposit of Revolving Funds for Foreign Currency Exchange）

根据酒店与银行签订代兑换外币业务协议内容规定，银行地区分行向宾馆提供一定数量的兑换周转金，由兑换领班专人管理，单设保险柜，并建立严格的出入库手续，确保外币兑换工作的顺利进行。外币兑换周转金通常每天入库一次，出库两次。每笔金额出入库都要做到签字手续齐全，准确无误。

To be stipulated by the contents in the foreign currency exchange agency agreement signed between the hotel and the bank. The regional branch of the bank provides a certain amount of exchange revolving fund. Such fund should be controlled specifically by the Exchange Supervisor and should be stored in individual safe. Strict withdrawal/deposit formalities should be followed to guarantee smooth foreign currency exchange. Generally, the foreign exchange revolving fund should be deposited once and withdrawn twice every day. Each withdrawal/deposit of the revolving fund should be provided with complete and accurate signing formalities.

2. 兑换前准备工作程序（Working Procedures for Preparation Before Exchange）

（1）收银员每天早上要按时收听并记录中国银行公布的外汇牌价，及时更改当天的外汇牌价表。

The cashier should listen to and record the foreign exchange rate issued by the Bank of China on time each morning and change the foreign exchange rate list for the day in time.

（2）领用当天所使用的兑换水单，检查是否连号，是否有短号现象，并办理领用手续。

Receive the exchange memo for the day; inspect whether they're in consecutive numbers and whether there're numbers missing; work on the reception formalities.

（3）领用并配备大小面值的兑换周转金，办理出库手续。

Receive and arrange exchange revolving fund with different face values; handle withdrawal formalities.

3. 外币兑换及承付现金程序（Procedures for Foreign Currency Exchange and Cash Acceptance）

（1）外币现钞。目前，国内酒店外币兑换处承兑的外币种类有美元、英镑、日元、澳大利亚元、加拿大元、瑞士法郎、新加坡元、欧元等。外币现钞兑换程序是：弄清客人的兑换要求；清点查收客人需兑换的外币金额；识别货币真伪；填制水单，请客人在水单上签名；检查复核，确保其正确，核对无误后，将兑换的款额付给客人。

Foreign cash. Presently, the main types of foreign currencies that can be exchanged by domestic hotels involve USD, GBP, YEN, AUD, CAD, SF, SGD, EUR, etc. Foreign cash exchange procedures: Clarify the exchange requirements of the guest; check the amount of foreign currency required to be exchanged by the guest; verify the authenticity of the cash; fill in the exchange memo; ask the guest to sign on the exchange memo; double check the memo; give the exchanged amount to the guest if no errors are found.

（2）旅行支票。旅行支票是一种定额支票，亦称汇款凭证，通常由银行、旅行社为便利国内外旅游者而发行。旅游者在国外可按规定手续，向发行银行（或旅行社）的国内外分支机构、代理行或规定的兑换点，兑取现金或支付费用。收兑旅行支票的服务程序是：弄清客人的兑换要求；检查、核对其支票是否属可兑换之列，有无限制（区域、时间）；与客人核对，清点数额；请客人出示有效证件，并进行复签（应看着客人进行），并检查复签是否与初签相符；查清当日牌价，填制水单，并扣除贴息，准确换算，请客人在水单上签名；检查复核，核对无误后，将支付款额付给客人。

Traveler's Cheque. The traveler's cheque is a kind of quota cheque and is also called payment document. It is generally issued by the banks and travel agencies to facilitate the domestic and overseas tourists. The tourists may exchange for cash or make payment to the domestic and overseas branches, agencies or prescribed exchange points of the issuing banks (or travel agencies) according to the stipulated formalities. Service procedures for acceptance and exchange of the cheque: Clarify the exchange requirements of the guest; inspect and verify whether the cheque is within the exchangeable scope; whether there're any limitations (regions, times); check with the guest; count the amount; ask the guest to present valid credentials; make counter-signature (under the witness of the cashier); check whether the counter signature is consistent with the initial signature; make sure the daily exchange rate; fill in the exchange memo; deduct the interest subsidy; make accurate conversion; ask the guest to sign on the exchange memo; double check the memo; give the exchanged amount to the guest if no errors are found.

（3）信用卡。信用卡是由银行或信用卡公司提供的一种供客人赊欠消费的信贷凭证，上面印有持卡者的姓名、号码、初签等。中国银行自1981年4月起，先后与一些代理行签订协议，代兑由它们发行的信用卡。目前，可兑换的信用卡有：美国运通公司的运通卡（American Express Card）、中国香港汇丰银行的东美卡（签证卡）（Visa Card）和万事达卡（Master Card）、中国香港麦加利银行的大来卡（Federal Card）、日本东海银行的百万卡（Million Card）以及发行的信用卡，包括长城卡、牡丹卡、金穗卡等。

Credit Card. Credit card is a kind of credit credential for the guest to make consumptions on credit issued by the banks or credit card companies. The credit card carries the name of the holder, card number, initial signature, etc. Since April 1981, the Bank of China has successively signed agreements with some agent banks to provide exchange services for the credit cards issued by such banks. Presently, exchangeable credit cards involve: American Express Card issued by American Express; Visa Card and Master Card issued by HSBC HK, Million Card issued by Tokai Bank. The issued credit cards involve Great Wall Card, Peony Card, Golden Spike Card, etc.

4. 外币兑换营业日报表的编制程序（Compilation Procedures of Daily Foreign Currency Exchange Statement）

当一笔兑换业务完成时，由复核员将水单号码、兑换外币种类及金额分别填写在兑换营业日报上，编表要求如下：

After a foreign exchange transaction is done, the reviewer should fill the exchange memo number, type of foreign currency and amount respectively onto the daily foreign currency exchange statement. The compliance requirements for such statements are:

（1）按照流水单顺序号码一一填写。

Fill the information item by item according to the sequence of the exchange memo number.

（2）外币现金、支票分别填写。

Foreign currency cash and cheque should be filled in respectively.

（3）每笔现金、支票金额分别以现钞价或卖价等于兑换的外汇人民币金额填写。

The amount of each cash or cheque should be equal to the foreign exchange equivalent of RMB in form of cash price or selling price.

5. 兑换员下班前，外币及周转金交接程序（Foreign Currency and Revolving Fund Handover Procedures Before Duty Shift of Cashiers）

（1）外币交接程序：兑换营业日报表编制完毕后，兑换员应将外币日报表包捆好装入现金袋内封好，并在口袋封口处签上自己的名字，放在指定保险箱内，待第二天领班查处、清点、汇总。

Foreign currency handover procedures: After the compilation of daily foreign currency exchange statement, the cashier should bind the daily foreign currency exchange statements, put them into the cash bag and seal the bag properly. Sign the name of the cashier on the seal of the bag. Put the bag into the designated safe for the examination, counting and collection of the Supervisor of the following day.

（2）兑换周转金的交接程序是：当 A 班下班后将兑换周转金余额清点好转交给 B 班兑换员，并办理交接签字手续。当 B 班工作结束时，将兑换周转金余额清点好装入现金袋内，袋内现金应与现金袋上的记录及兑换营业日报表周转金余额一致，与外币现金袋一同放到指定保险箱内。

Procedures for handover of revolving funds for foreign currency exchange: When Shift A is about to be off duty, count the balance of the evolving funds for foreign currency exchange and pass it to the cashier of Shift B. Make proper handover and signature formalities. When Shift B is about to be off duty, count the balance of the evolving funds for foreign currency exchange and put the balance into the cash bag. The cash in the bag should be consistent with the record indicated on the bag as well as the balance in the daily foreign currency exchange statement. Put it together with the foreign currency cash bag into the designated safe.

6. 注意事项（Precautions）

（1）酒店的外币兑换汇率是由对应合作的银行每天发传真至酒店以做更新。

The foreign currency exchange rate of the hotel should be faxed to the hotel on daily basis by corresponding cooperative bank for updating purpose.

（2）根据银行对于外币兑换（包括现金与旅行支票）的规定，凡是货币面有破损、涂写等损毁，银行将一律拒收该笔款项。

According to provisions on foreign currency exchange (including cash and traveler's cheque) by the bank, any currency with damages on the surface such as breakage, alternation would be rejected by the bank.

（3）对于兑换旅行支票的住客，必须复印其有效的证件照片页；必须核对清楚住客所签署的签名是否与旅行支票上原本的签名样式一致。

For residing guest exchanging traveler's cheque, copy his/her photo page of the valid credential; carefully verify whether the signature of the guest is consistent with the signature on the original copy of the traveler's cheque.

（4）未经许可，前厅部员工不得私自帮助客人到银行兑换外币，一经发现将追究其法律责任。

Without permission, the staff in the Front Hall Department may not help the guest to exchange foreign currency to the bank. Or, legal responsibilities would be investigated.

（5）不得为非酒店住客兑换外币。

Do not exchange foreign currency for guests out of the hotel.

（6）所有的外币必须以投款的形式上交财务部。

All the foreign currency must be handed in to the Financial Department in form of cash deposit.

（二）关于前厅部兑换外币的操作流程（Operation Procedures of Foreign Currency Exchange in Front Hall Department）

由于执行外币兑换程序需要到相应兑换银行进行一系列的外币兑换程序培训，因此，外币兑换服务只能由前厅部接待处员工处理，其余未经培训的员工一律不具备该兑换资格。兑换外币的操作流程如下：

As the foreign currency exchange procedures require a series of related trainings by the corresponding exchanging bank, such service cannot be provided by the staff at the Reception Desk of the Front Hall Department. Other staff without training are not qualified to offer such services. Operation procedures of foreign currency exchange:

（1）接待处员工收到客人兑换外币的要求后，必须先核实客人是否为住客，若客人不是住客，则婉拒客人并告知客人酒店的外币兑换业务只提供给本酒店住客；若客人是住客，则询问住客的房间号码，核对客人名字是否与系统中登记的名字相符。

Upon receiving foreign currency exchange requirements, staff at the Reception Desk must first verify whether the guest is a residing guest of the hotel. If not, decline the guest politely and inform the guest that the foreign currency exchange service is only available for the guests of the hotel. If the guest is a residing guest of the hotel, enquire the room number and check whether the name of the guest is consistent with the name registered in the system.

（2）待正确核对住客信息之后，接待员咨询住客所需兑换的外币金额，若外币金额过大（最高限额一般按照每房间每天最多兑换 200 美元为对照计算），可建议住客到附近的银行进行兑换。

After checking the guest information correctly, the Receptionist should ask the guest about the amount required to be exchanged. If the amount exceeds the limit (generally 200 dollars every day for one room), recommend the guest to make exchange in a nearby bank.

（3）接待员使用外币验钞机检验货币的真伪，并检查住客所提供的外币是否有破损或涂写的痕迹，一旦发现以上问题，则应婉转地向住客解释并拒绝收取有问题的外币。

The Receptionist should verify the authenticity of the cash with the foreign currency detector and check whether the foreign currency provided by the guest is broken or altered. Upon detecting such problems, explain to the guest politely and decline all questionable foreign currency.

（4）复印住客所提供的有效证件照片页，并按规定填写银行“外币兑换凭证单”，将所有钞票号码记录在“外币兑换凭证单”上方空白处。

Copy the photo page of the valid credential provided by the guest; fill in the *Foreign Currency Exchange Voucher* of the bank; record the numbers of the bank notes into the blank on the top of the *Foreign Currency Exchange Voucher*.

（5）接待员需准确计算出兑换后相应的人民币金额并与客人核实，待住客确认无误之后，先由接待员在“外币兑换凭证单”相应位置签名作证，再请住客在“外币兑换凭证单”的相应位置签名作实。

The Receptionist should calculate the corresponding RMB amount accurately and verify the amount with the guest. If the guest proposes no doubt, the Receptionist should first sign his/her name in the corresponding position of the *Foreign Currency Exchange Voucher* as witness and then ask the guest to sign as approval.

（6）接待员于前厅备用金中数取相应的人民币金额，面值大于 50 元以上的钞票必须用验钞机在住客面前检验以示钞票真伪；待所有钞票检验完毕后，接待员必须再次与住客面点钞票以示金额的准确性。

The Receptionist then takes out the corresponding RMB amount from the revolving funds of the Front Hall. Notes with the face value greater than 50 yuan must be verified by the currency detector before the guest. After all the money is detected, the Receptionist must manually check the notes before the guest to show the correctness of the amount.

（7）最后将“外币兑换凭证单”客人联撕下交给客人留底，第一联记账联与第二联银行联与外币和住客有效证件复印件捆绑在一起上交财务部。

Finally, tear down the guest copy of the *Foreign Currency Exchange Voucher* and give it to the guest as record. The first copy（accounting copy）and the second copy（bank copy）should be tied together with the foreign currency and the copy of the valid credential of the guest and then submitted to the Financial Department.

（8）对于旅行支票的兑换，与外币现金基本一致，其不同点在于：住客必须在接待员面前签署与旅行支票上样式一致的签名；对于面值总额大于100元（包括100元）的旅行支票，必须致电到美国运通旅行支票授权中心取授权号，并将该授权号用铅笔写在旅行支票的右上角。

Exchange of the traveler's cheque is basically consistent with the foreign currency cash, with difference as follows: The guest must sign his/her name consistent with the signatures on the traveler's cheque before the Receptionist; for traveler's cheque with total face value greater than 100（including 100）, call the Traveler's Cheque Authorization Center of American Express for the authorization number. Write down the authorization number with pencil onto the upper right corner of the traveler's cheque.

三、防止客人逃账的有效措施（Effective Measures of Preventing the Bill Escaping）

防止客人逃账、确保酒店应有收入的准确回收是前厅部销售管理的一项重要任务。前厅服务人员应掌握一些防止客人逃账的措施，以保护酒店应有利益。防止客人逃账流程如表7-4所示。

Preventing the bill escaping and guaranteeing the accurate recovery of income is a significant task of the sales management in Font Office. The receptionist shall grasp some measures for preventing the bill escaping, for protecting the interests of hotel. Procedures of preventing bill escaping are shown in Table 7-4.

（1）收取订金不但可以防止因客人“预订不至”而给酒店造成损失，而且，即使客人如期抵店入住，收取的订金也可作为预付款使用，从而有效防止客人逃账。

The down payment can prevent the loss caused by the “reservation with no shows”. Meanwhile, if guests arrive at the hotel as expected, the down payment can also be used as the pre-payment, which may prevent the guest from escaping the bills effectively.

（2）未经预订而直接抵店、信用情况不了解或信用较差的客人，酒店应收取预付款。

For guests arriving at the hotel without reservation, or guests with poor credibility, the hotel shall charge the advance payment.

（3）酒店配以专职的信用经理从事信用审批、核查工作。

Hotels shall employ full-time credit manager to be engaged in the credit approval and inspection.

（4）通过建立详细的客户档案，掌握客户所在单位的性质和履约守信程度，以此决定酒店给予客人的信用政策。

Through establishing detailed guest file, the hotel shall grasp the nature of guest's work unit and honesty, and decide to give the credit policy to guests.

（5）对持信用卡的客人，酒店可采取提前向银行要授权的方法，提高客人的信用限额。

For guests with credit cards，hotels can ask for the authorization method to improve the credit limit of guests.

（6）酒店可以从客人行李的多少、是否列入“黑名单”等发现疑点。

The hotel may discover the doubtful points according to the number of luggage of guests，or if they are on the“blacklist”.

任务四　特殊情况处理

Task Ⅳ　Disposal of Special Circumstances

【情境导入】【Scenario Introduction】

能不能办理续住

Should Extension Be Provided

某住客夜晚11时回来，却怎么也打不开门，便到前台询问。当班的正好是昨天帮他办理入住手续的服务员小王。小王告诉他，因为他昨天办理入住登记时说是住一晚，因此，过了今天中午12时，匙卡就会失效，所以打不开门。这位客人不满地说昨天自己明明说的是住两晚。小王也不示弱，强调自己昨天清楚地听到客人说住一晚。结果为“一晚”还是“两晚”，这位服务员便和客人争执起来。值班经理迅速到场，了解了事情原委后，一方面制止小王别再多说，另一方面不断向这位客人道歉，承认是酒店不对，并主动提出房费可予以八折优惠。在这位值班经理的安抚下，这位客人趋于平静，准备拿匙卡回房休息。但是，没想到不再说话的服务员小王，明显不高兴地将新做好的匙卡从台面推向客人。这使得本已消气的客人又被激怒了，任凭值班经理好话说尽，也不肯原谅，结完账甩袖而去。

A guest came back at 11 pm. but failed to open the room door. So he went to the Reception Desk.The Receptionist on duty happened to be Wang，the exact attendant working on check-in formalities for him the day before. Wang told him，he asked to stay for one night when making check-in formalities the previous day. Therefore，the key card became invalid after 12：00 at noon today. That's why the door wouldn't open. Discontentedly，the guest claimed that he asked to stay for two nights the day before. Wang stood fast and stressed that it was clearly heard that the guest would stay for one night. So they quarreled about whether it's one night or two nights. The Duty Manager turned up immediately. After knowing what happened，on one hand the Manager stopped Wang from talking，and on the other，the Manager apologized repeatedly to the guest，admitted that it's the hotel's fault and positively offers a 20% discount for the room rate. With the consolation of the Duty Manager，the guest gradually calmed down and was about to take the room card and go back for rest. However，beyond the expectation of everyone，Wang pushed the new card to the guest with obvious unhappiness. This irritated the guest who had already cooled down，he refused to forgive the hotel however hard the Duty Manger tried and left the hotel after check-out.

阅读以上材料回答下列问题：

Read the case and answer the follow questions：

1. 小王的做法对吗？请说明原因。

Was Wang Right? Why?

2. 如果你是小王，你会怎么做？

What would you do if you're Wang?

【情境分析】【Scenario Analysis】

第一，现实中有许多服务人员虽然知道“顾客是上帝，顾客总是对的”，而一旦发生纠纷，自己身临其境，却不能把持自己，也许在他们看来顾客是人我也是人，为什么明明是客人不对，反而让我说对不起，这说明了“顾客总是对的”只是贴在墙上，挂在嘴边，并没有真正融入到心里。

In reality, though many attendants know that they should treat the customers as “God” and they're always right, being personally on the scene, they could not control themselves. Probably according to them, the guest and the receptionist are both equally human beings, it makes no sense that the receptionist should apologize in case that obviously it's the fault of the guest. This is the evidence that the rule of “Customers Are Always Right” is just on the wall, by the mouth but not into the heart.

第二，作为服务人员，不能事事与服务对象——为我们发工资的客人寻找心理平衡，明辨是非曲直，而应使自己拥有一颗宽容之心，把“对”让给客人，不要与客人发生争执，要让顾客开开心心消费，高高兴兴离去。

However, as the service personnel, we cannot seek for the balance and insist rightness from wrongness on everything against the service objects—our guests where our wages are sourced from. Instead, we should try the best to bear a generous heart and put the guests in superior position. We should avoid to dispute with the guests and should have the guests make consumptions and check out delightedly.

第三，在此例中服务人员如能在发生争执之前即刻道歉，说句“对不起，也许是我听错了”之类的话，完全可以大事化小，小事化了。

In this case, if the Receptionist could apologize immediately before the dispute and tell the guest “Sorry, probably I was wrong” or something like that. This would relieve or even eliminate the problem.

第四，要让第一线员工树立“顾客总是对的”观念，一方面，通过不断地培训考核，改变或剔除那些不适合从事服务工作的个性员工；另一方面，管理人员也要相信员工，千万不要再去责怪或惩罚已经受了委屈的服务人员。

Ask the first line staff to establish the concept of “Customers Are Always Right” . On one hand, continuous trainings and evaluation should be made to alter or remove the staff with strong personalities that are not suitable to provide services. On the other, the managerial personnel should entrust the staff and do not scold or punish the service attendants who have already suffered from injustice.

一、办理逾期续住服务（Working on Extension Services）

（一）续住的工作程序及步骤（Working Procedures and Steps for Extension）

1. 问候客人（Greeting the Guest）

（1）问候客人并了解客人的需求。

Greet the guest and ask the needs of the guest.

（2）向客人说明续住必须由登记客人前来办理或确认得到登记客人的授权。

Explain to the guest that extension should only be made by or under the authorization from the guest making the registration.

（3）确认客人需要续住后为客人办理续住手续。

Confirm that the guest requires extension and then work on extension formalities for the guest.

2. 办理续住（Handle Extension）

（1）请客人出示房卡和钥匙或身份证件，核对客人身份。

Ask the guest to present the room card, key or identity document; verify the identity of the guest.

（2）询问客人续住天数，通过电脑查询客人续住期间的预订情况，确认此房今后无预订、续住后未超过预订或无维修保养。

Enquire the days of extension; check the reservation conditions of the room during the extension; confirm that the room is not otherwise reserved or to be maintained during such extension.

（3）计算房间账目，确认是否需要补缴押金。

Calculate the room account and confirm whether additional advance payment is required.

（4）将钥匙收回，重新制作钥匙。

Recover the key and remake the key.

（5）将重新制作的钥匙和相关的收据递交给客人，告知客人已经按其要求办理完毕。

Pass on the remade key and related receipts to the guest; ask the guest that extension has been made according to his/her requirements.

3. 结束续住手续（Extension Termination Formalities）

（1）询问客人有无其他需要，确认客人无其他需要后与客人道别，目送客人离开柜台。

Enquire whether the guest has other needs; say goodbye to the guest upon confirming that the guest has no other needs; see the guest off till the guest leaves the Reception Desk.

（2）客人离开柜台后，在电脑中更改离店日期，在客人登记单上加注新的离店日期、预付情况。

After the guest leaves the Reception Desk, change the check-off date in the computer and add new check-out date and advance payment information on the *Check-in Registration Form* of the guest.

4. 特殊情况（Special Circumstances）

（1）客人所住房间无法办理续住（此房有预订或有维修保养计划），则婉转地向客人说明，请客人谅解。有相同类型的房间时，另选房间为客人办理续住；无相同类型的房间时，尽量推荐比原类型档次高的房间或经上级批准后办理升级住房。

If the extension of the guest room is not available (the room is under reservation or maintain schedule), explain to the guest tactfully and ask understanding of the guest. Extend the stay for the guest with another room if a room of the same type is available. If the room of the same type is not available, try the best to promote a room of a higher level or upgrade the room upon the approval of the higher management.

（2）费用非由住店客人本人支付的，要与付款方确认，其中费用由公司支付的，请公司补发传真或汇款或与营销部担保人确认均可；费用由其他客人支付的，与付款人确认；不再为客人支付费用的，请客人自付。

If the expenses are not paid by the guest in person, confirm with the payer. For expenses to be paid by the company, ask the company to resend the fax, make remittance or confirm with the guarantor of the Sales Department. For expenses to be paid by other guests, confirm with the payer. For expenses not paid for the guest, the guest should assume such amount.

（二）其他情况的续住服务（Extension Services Under Other Circumstances）

1. 旅行社凭单结账或已付房费房间的续住处理（Extension Disposal for Rooms Settled by Voucher by the Travel Agency or Paid-up Room）

（1）向客人重申付款方式、房价，如不能享受原优惠房价，向客人说明，必要时请示上级处理。

Restate the payment method and room rate to the guest; explain to the guest if the original preferential rate is not available; report to the superior management for disposal where necessary.

（2）根据电脑资料填写客人登记表，注明续住时间和付款方式。

Fill in the *Check-in Registration Form* of the guest according to the computer information; indicate the extension time and payment method.

（3）请客人重新交预付金，并通知收银处做账务处理。

Ask the guest to pay additional advance payment; inform the Cashier's Desk to keep accounts.

（4）用电脑续住功能修改客人离店日期并输入新房价，办理续住手续。

Modify the check-out date of the guest with extension function by the computer and input new room rate; handle extension formalities.

（5）办理方式与新开房程序相同。

The disposal procedures are the same as the new room procedures.

2. 已交预付金或已预刷银行卡房间的续住处理（Extension Disposal of the Room with Advance Payment or Paid by Credit Card in Advance）

（1）了解房间是否已结账。

Check whether the account for the room has been settled.

（2）根据电脑资料填写（续住登记表）。

Fill in the *Extension Registration Form* according to the computer information.

（3）对交预付金的客人，请客人到收银处重交预付金；对预刷银行卡已结账的客人，重新预刷卡。

If the guest has made advance payment, ask the guest to make additional advance payment at the Cashier's Desk; for guest having settled the account with credit card in advance, pay with the credit card in advance once again.

（4）用电脑续住功能办理续住手续。

Handle extension formalities with the extension functions of the computer.

（5）电话通知客房服务中心续住情况。

Call the Room Service Center to inform the extension information.

3. 换人续住房间的处理（Disposal Procedure for Extended Rooms With Substituted Guest）

（1）了解房间是否已结账。

Check whether the account for the room has been settled.

（2）征得原住客同意，并做好新入住客人的登记，注明换人续住。

Ask for consent form the original guest; register the new guest properly; indicate the stay of the substituted guest.

（3）确认新客人的付款方式。

Confirm the payment method of the new guest.

（4）按规定办理入住手续。

Work on check-in formalities according to provisions.

（5）在原客人“登记表”上注明已退房及退房日期。

Indicate the check-out status and check-out date of the *Registration Form* for the original guest.

（6）将新客人资料输入电脑。

Input the information of the new guest into the computer.

（三）续住服务流程与标准（Extension Service Procedures and Standards）

表 4-10　客人续住服务流程

Table 4-10　Table for Extension Service Procedures for Guests

1	客人要求 Guest raises requests	前台服务员 Reception Desk Attendant	• 客人到前台要求延迟退房 • The guest requests extension at the Reception Desk	• 接受客人要求 • Receive the requests from the guest	• 工作记录簿 • Work log
2	核查是否符合延迟退房标准 Inspect whether the extension standards are met	前台接待员 Receptionist of the Reception Desk	• 询问客人房号、原因并查询该客房当日预订情况，结合酒店延迟退房标准及员工权限 • Enquire the guest room number, reason for extension; check the reservation conditions of the room for that day; dispose according to the extension standards and the staff authorization	• 确认符合可延迟退房的标准，且记录下房号 • Confirm the conformity of extension standards; record the room number	• 工作记录簿 • Work log
3	申请批准 Apply for approval	前台接待员、有相应权限的管理人员 Receptionist of the Reception Desk; managerial personnel with corresponding authorization	• 需前厅经理、大堂副经理、销售经理等管理人员有权限批准的一定要请示对应管理人员并决定是否收取费用 • If approval is required by managerial personnel such as Lobby Manager, Assistant Manager and Sales Manager; application must be made to corresponding managerial personnel to decide whether expenses should be charged	• 已经请示过前厅经理或大堂副经理或销售经理 • Report to the Lobby Manager, Assistant Manager or Sales Manager	• 工作记录簿 • Work log
4	续房卡 Renew the room card	前台接待员 Receptionist of the Reception Desk	• 回复客人并将客人的房卡收回做续卡，房卡有效时间只做到确认客人延迟退房的时间 • Reply the guest; collect the room card of the guest; extend the card; the valid period of the card should only cover such extension	• 已经为客人续房卡至确认延迟退房时间 • Extend the room card to the extension time for the guest	• 工作记录簿 • Work log
5	注明并做好交班 Note and make appropriate shift handover	前台接待员 Receptionist of the Reception Desk	• 在对应房号的电脑备注上注明。如：××同意延迟到 14：00 • Indicate the corresponding room number in the REMARK column on the computer. E.g.: ××Agree to extend to 14：00 for free	• 已经准确打好电脑备注 • Accurately print out the computer remark	• 工作记录簿 • Work log

二、客人延迟结账服务（Extended Account Settlement Service for Guest）

【技能目标】【Skill Objectives】

1. 能够迅速熟练地按要求做好岗前准备工作。

Be able to make proper preparation before taking on the post in a quick and skilled manner.

2. 能够按要求准确地填写各类表单、报表。

Be able to fill in various types of forms and statements as required.

3. 能针对有预订的散客、团队等不同类型的宾客制定客房预分方案。

Be able to formulate guest room pre-allocation schemes according to different types of guests such as individual guests and group guests.

4. 能按要求给不同类型的客人办理入住手续。

Be able to work on check-in formalities for different types of guests.

表 4-11 客人延迟结账服务流程
Table 4-11 Table for Extended Account Settlement Service for Guest

项 目 Item	标 准 Standard
1. 问候 Greet the guest	(1) 遇到客人先微笑，以礼貌、热情、友善的语气问候客人，如果不知道其姓名，称呼其“先生”、“女士”。 Smile to the guest; greet the guest with a polite, enthusiastic and friendly tone; call the guest “Mr.” or “Ms.” if the name of the guest is unknown. (2) 尽量熟记客人姓名，如果是经常来的客人，前台接待员要以姓氏或以体现其身份的称呼问候客人（用其姓氏称呼客人至少在对话中使用一次）。 Try to memorize the name of the guest. In case of a frequent guest, the Receptionist of the Reception Desk should greet the guest with his/her family name or a way that can represent his/her social status (Call the guest with his/her family name at least once in the conversation). (3) 地域不同，与客人的熟悉程度不同，要以个性化称呼来向客人打招呼。即称呼客人既要体现出尊敬感，又要体现出亲切感。 As the guests may come from different regions and the degrees of familiarity to the guests are different, individualized ways should be used to call the guest. Give the guest a sense of respect and intimacy when greeting the guest. (4) 与客人讲话时面带微笑，保持目光的接触。 Smile when talking with the guest; keep eye contacts.
2. 确认 Make confirmation	(1) 确认相关信息（房号、姓名、晚结账时间）尽量满足客人的需求。 Confirm related information (room number, name and extended settlement time); try to satisfy the guest's needs as possible. (2) 根据出租率情况，尽量满足客人要求，根据酒店相关规定进行如下处理： Try to satisfy the guest's requirements as possible according to the occupancy rate of the hotel; make disposal as follows according to related provisions of the hotel: 1) 晚离店至下午 14:00 免收房费。 Extension till 14: 00 PM will be charged for free. 2) 下午 18:00 之前加收半天房费。 Extension till 18:00 PM will be charged half of the daily room rate. 3) 超过下午 18:00 加收一天房费。 Extension after 18:00 PM will be charged full of the daily room rate. 告知客人请提前 10 分钟办理结账手续。 Inform the guest to work on account settlement formalities 10 minutes in advance. (3) 针对客人的特殊要求，前台应灵活处理，可请示当班前台经理，尽量满足客人的要求，请示后立即给客人回复。 In case of special requirements of the guest, the Reception Desk should disposal in a flexible manner. Report the Manager of the Reception Desk on duty and try to satisfy the guest's requirements as possible; reply the guest immediately if instructions are obtained.
3. 更改电脑信息 Modify computer information	在注释中注明备注人姓名、日期。 Indicate the name of the personnel making the remark and the date in the column of “COMMENTS”.

5. 能妥善地办理转房、加床及客人延期续住等手续。

Be able to make room change, extra bed and extension formalities appropriately for the guest.

6. 能够运用酒店计算机管理系统进行客房状况的控制与调整。

Be able to control and adjust the guest room conditions with the computer management system of the hotel.

7. 能够迅速地为客人进行各类结账，准确地为客人兑换外币。

Be able to settle various types of accounts for the guests quickly; be able to exchange foreign currency accurately for the guests.

8. 能够按照操作规范独立受理住客物品积存服务、留言服务、邮件服务等工作，并且能处理问询服务过程中出现的简单突发事件。

Be able to provide services such as deposit services, message services and mail services for the residing guests independently according to the operation procedures and dispose simple and emergent events in the process of information services.

【实训与评价】【Training and Assessment】

［实训目的］［Training Objectives］

1. 熟悉前厅客人入住接待服务程序和规范并为客人提供相应的服务。

Be familiar with check-in reception procedures and norms at the Lobby and provide corresponding services for the guests.

2. 规范自己的言行，正确使用礼貌用语和敬语；能有礼有节、高效地为客人办理入住手续。

Standardize the words and deeds; correctly use polite and honorific languages; be able to dispose emergent cases in a civilized and highly effective manner.

［实训准备］［Training Preparation］

1. 前厅接待模拟场景、电脑、入住登记表、黑色水性笔等。

Simulated scenario of lobby service, computer, check-in registration form, black marker pen, etc.

2. 学生四人分为一组，教师讲解示范后，学生根据教师布置的任务进行实际操作。

Divide the student in group of four. The teachers make explanation and demonstration; then the students make practices according to the tasks assigned by the teachers.

［实训方法］［Training Methods］

先观看教师播放的教学课件，然后由教师引导学生分析工作规范和任务，学生四人一组，按照要求进行实际操作，教师巡回指导，实训结束前抽小组进行迎宾服务的实训。

First view the teaching courseware played by the teachers; then the teachers guide the students to analyze work procedures and tasks. The students forms groups of four and make practical operations according to the tasks. The teachers walk around for guidance. Before ending the training, randomly select some groups to make simulated performance of guest reception services.

［实训步骤］［Training Procedure］

第一步：教师向学生介绍客人入住接待服务程序，让学生有一定的感性认识。

The teachers play the video about guest check-in reception service procedures to the students so that the students may have some perceptual knowledge about it.

第二步：学生分成四人一组讨论，由学生分析，指出正误。

Then divide the students into group of four; have the students to make analysis; point out correctness and errors.

第三步：由学生继续讨论，设计出客人入住接待的工作程序。

The students continue the discussion and design the work procedures for guest reception.

第四步：各组学生派出代表进行角色演练，其他各组学生评价。

Each group assigns representatives to take role play and other groups make comments.

第五步：学生分成两人一组，进行客人入住接待服务的实训。

The students form groups of two and make practical training on check-in reception services.

第六步：教师评价与回答问题。

The teachers make evaluations and answer questions from the students.

[实训内容] [Training Content]

1. 模拟操作散客入住登记手续的受理。

Simulate acceptance on check-in registration formalities for individual guests.

2. 模拟操作团队客人入住登记手续的受理。

Simulate acceptance on check-in registration formalities for group guests.

3. 模拟操作 VIP 客人入住登记手续的受理。

Simulate acceptance on check-in registration formalities for VIP guests.

4. 模拟操作换房的受理。

Simulate acceptance on room change.

模块小结

Module Summary

1. 在办理入住登记时，散客和团队客人之间有什么区别？

What are the differences between the individual guests and group guests in case of check-in registration?

2. 关于住客信息咨询服务，应注意哪些问题？

What are the precautions on information consultation services for the residing guests?

3. 如果有人查访本酒店的住客，酒店服务人员应注意哪些方面？

What are the precautions for the hotel attendants in case that someone enquires about the residing guest of the hotel?

4. 在受理留言服务过程中应注意哪些方面？

What aspects should be concerned in the process of acceptance of message service?

5. 针对不同类型的住客，在结账时如何操作才会更有效？

What are the more effective operations in account settlement for guests of different types?

6. 关于外币兑换服务，应注意哪些问题？

What are the precautions about foreign currency exchange services?

7. 如果住客要办理续住或延时退房，服务人员应如何操作？

What are the operations of the service attendants in case of extension of stay or extension of check-out requested by the guest?

模块五 总机和商务中心服务
Module V Switchboard and Business Center Services

【情境导入】【Scenario Introduction】

"疏忽"的叫醒服务
"Inattentive" Wake-up Service

小明是刚从旅游院校毕业的大学生，到三亚亚龙湾天鸿度假村工作后，因为要从基层接受锻炼，他被安排在房务中心工作。刚到房务中心上班的第二天就轮到他值大夜班。接班没多久，电话铃响了，小明接起电话："您好，房务中心，请讲。""明天早晨5点30分叫醒。"一位中年男子沙哑的声音。"5点30分叫醒是吗？好的。没有问题。"小明知道，叫醒虽然是总机的事，但一站式服务理念和首问负责制要求自己先接受客人的要求，然后立即转告总机，于是他毫不犹豫地答应了。

Xiao Ming, a fresh graduate from a tourism college, was working in Sanya Yalong Bay Tianhong Vacational Village located in. Because he was new that he was arranged to work in the Housekeeping Center. Today was his second working day and he was on the graveyard shift. Few minutes after he took his turn, the phone rang and Xiao Ming answered: "hello, Housekeeping Center, anything I can help?" "Please wake me up at 5: 30 am. tomorrow", a middle-aged man said hoarsely. "5: 30 am., right? Ok, no problem." Xiao Ming knew that wake-up service should be provided by the Switchboard, but one-stop service concept and first-asking responsibility system of the hotel require him to give the guest a positive answer first and then report to the Switchboard immediately, so he agreed without any hesitation.

当小明接通总机电话后，才突然想起来，刚才竟忘了问客人的房号！再看一下电话机键盘，把他吓出一身冷汗——这部电话机根本就没有号码显示屏！小明慌了，立即将此事向总机说明。总机说无法查到房号。于是小明的领班马上报告值班经理。值班经理考虑到这时已是三更半夜，不好逐个查询。再根据客人要求一大早叫醒情况看，估计十有八九是明早赶飞机或火车的客人。现在只好把希望寄托在客人也许自己会将手机设置叫醒；否则，只有等待投诉了。

Only when he got through the Switchboard, did he realize that he forgot to ask the guest about the Room No.! So he made a quick look at the phone keyboard, but there was no number display at all, which scared him out! Like an ant on a hot pan, he explained the whole story to the Switchboard immediately, but the Switchboard could not help either. So the Foreman reported the issue to the Manager on duty promptly. The Manager analyzed that it was inconvenient to interrupt the guests one by one to identify the Room No. and the guest probably needed to catch a plane or train so he had to get up at 5: 30 am. What we could do now was to pray that the guest can set the alarm clock on his phone, otherwise what we would face was nothing but complaints.

早晨7点30分，一位睡眼惺忪的VIP客人来到总台，投诉酒店未按他的要求叫醒，使他误了飞机，神态沮丧而气愤。早已在大堂等候的大堂副经理见状立即上前将这位VIP客人请到大堂咖啡厅接受投诉。

At 7：00 am. in the following morning，a sleepy VIP guest with a frustrated and angry expression on his face，came to the Reception Desk and complained that the hotel did not wake him up as he required，and he missed the plane. The Assistant Lobby Manager who had been waiting in the lobby for a long time went up to the guest immediately and invited him to the Cafe House to entertain his complaints.

原来，该VIP客人是先到三亚过夜，准备一大早赶往机场，与一家旅行社组织的一个旅游团会合后乘飞机外出旅游。没想到他在要求叫醒时，以为服务员可以从电话号码显示屏上知道自己的房号，就省略未报。

According to what the guest said，he was from a county suburb and stayed the night over to catch the plane in the early morning，so as to join a tour group organized by a travel agency. He thought that the waiter could know his Room No. from the phone number display screen，so he did not mention it.

酒店方面立即与这家旅行社联系商量弥补的办法。该旅行社答应可以让这位VIP客人加入明天的另一个旅行团，不过今天这位VIP客人在旅游目的地的客房预订金270元要由客人负责。接下来酒店的处理结果是：为VIP客人支付这笔订金，同时免费让VIP客人在本酒店再住一夜，而且免去VIP客人昨晚的房费。这样算下来，因为一次叫醒失误，导致酒店经济损失共计790元。

The hotel immediately contacted the travel agency to discuss measures should be taken. The travel agency promised to arrange the VIP guest to another group in the next day，but the room（at the travel destination）reservation deposit of 270 Yuan for that day shall be assumed by the guest. Measures taken by the hotel were：paying for the deposit for the VIP guest，letting the guest to stay for another night for free and charging no fees for the last night. So，the hotel lost 790 Yuan in total due to an "inattentive" wake-up service.

【情境分析】［Scenario Analysis］

因为一次叫醒的失误，酒店为此付出了790元的代价。这790元既是成本，也是"投资"——花钱买教训。由本案例得出的教训和应采取的改进措施有二：

An "inattentive" wake-up service caused a loss of 790 Yuan to the hotel. This loss might be normal costs during operation of the hotel，but it was also an "investment" to learn lessons and gain experience. The following two measures should be taken against the above-mentioned case：

第一，所有的"新手"上岗，都应当由"老员工"或领班带班一段时间，关注他们的工作情况。包括哪怕一次电话的全部过程。比如，与客人的对话是否得体完整、是否重复、是否记录等，必要时要做好"补位"工作。

Firstly，all "green hands" should be guided by "senior staff" or the Foreman for a period of time to inspect their performance including even the whole process of a call. For example，if they communicate with the guests appropriately，completely and concisely with necessary information being recorded. When it is necessary，"senior staff" or the Foreman should do relevant work in person.

第二，所有接受客人服务来电的电话机都必须有来电显示屏，并有记忆功能。这样既有利于提高效率、方便客人，也可防止类似本案事件的发生。

Secondly，telephones with call displays and memory functions must be provided to serve the guests to improve service efficiency and avoid similar cases.

要杜绝类似本案事件的发生，是否应当让当事人“埋单”？让当事人的上司负连带责任？对此暂且不论，但是不论怎样处理这两位员工，若不接受教训并采取有效改进措施的话，将来还有可能产生“小明第二”。因此，总结教训，采取相应的改进措施（比如，换有来电显示的电话机，新手由领班“跟踪”一段时间等），防患于未然才是根本，酒店各级管理人员应当充分利用自身的工作经验和教训，有预见性地去寻找问题，并采取预防性措施，这才是提高管理水平和服务质量的关键。

Whether punishing Xiao Ming and his superior can help to avoid similar cases or not? Regardless of this question, without learning lessons and taking effective measures, punishing means nothing to prevent similar cases from happening. Therefore, learning lessons and taking corresponding measures (for example, providing telephones with call displays and guiding the “green hands” by the Foreman for a period of time, etc.), are fundamental to nip similar cases in the bud. Therefore, management personnel at all levels should make full use of their experience to find potential problems and take preventive measures, which is the key to improve the management and service quality of the hotel.

【学习目标】【Learning Objectives】

［知识目标］［Knowledge Objectives］

1. 能够胜任酒店总机服务的基本服务工作和接待工作，能够提高水准、高效率地为客人服务。

Be competent to provide basic services and reception services related to the Switchboard and to serve the guests with high standard and efficiency.

2. 能够熟练提供复印机、打印机、传真机等办公服务，能够根据标准和程序，向客人提供会议室出租服务、翻译和秘书服务及票务服务。

Proficient in providing office service related to copiers, printers, fax machines etc., and providing meeting room rental, translation and secretarial services as well as ticketing services according to appropriate standards and procedures.

［能力目标］［Capacity Objectives］

1. 熟练掌握总机服务的基本知识及总机各项业务的程序与标准。

Master basic knowledge of the Switchboard services and procedures and standards for all businesses related to the Switchboard.

2. 熟练掌握邮件、传真、打印、复印等服务，会议室出租服务、翻译和秘书服务及票务服务。

Be familiar with email, faxing, printing, copying services and meeting room rental, translation and secretarial services as well as ticketing services.

【重点和难点】［Key Points and Difficulties］

1. 熟练完成总机日常工作中的各种任务。

Complete various tasks in daily work related to the Switchboard smoothly.

2. 熟练提供满意的商务服务。

Skilled in providing satisfactory business services.

任务一　总机服务
Task Ⅰ　Switchboard Services

【情境导入】【Scenario Introduction】

凌晨一点多了，前厅部叶经理的床头响起了急促的电话声。睡意朦胧的叶经理很不情愿地拿起了电话，话筒里传来酒店另一位经理急促的声音："叶经理吗？你的总机有20分钟无人接听，是刚才张局长打电话发现的，他在外地没法通知你，只好打我的手机，你赶快过来处理一下吧!"叶经理被这突如其来的消息惊得倦意全无。

It had passed 1:00 am., and the Front Office Manager was waken up from a sound sleep by a sudden phone ring. He reluctantly picked up the phone, "Manager Ye, your Switchboard has been inaccessible for twenty minutes. Director Zhang just called the Switchboard, but there was no answer. He could not inform you because he is in other place, so he called me. Hurry up to come over to deal with it!" Manager Ye was totally sobered up by the sudden bad news.

当他心急火燎地赶到总机房时，接线生陈小丽仍在值班室呼呼大睡。叶经理见状十分生气，立即打电话安排了另一位员工上班，现场辞退了陈小丽。

He came to the Switchboard Room anxiously, but only found that the operator Chen Xiaoli sleep soundly on duty. The Manager was aggravated by what he saw and he immediately made a phone call to arrange another staff on leave to take the duty from Chen Xiaoli at the scene.

【情境分析】【Scenario Analysis】

电话总机是酒店内外信息沟通联络的通信枢纽，每天需处理成千上万个电话业务，且绝大多数客人对酒店的第一印象，是在与接线生的第一次接触中形成的。这次事件且不说与接听电话规范中"铃响三声必须有人接听"的服务要求相去甚远，也不谈当值睡觉是酒店服务之大忌，仅20分钟无人接听电话，在酒店投诉个案中就属罕见。这给客人留下的第一印象只能是遗憾和惋惜。

Switchboard is the communication hub for internal and external information of a hotel, dealing with thousands of calls a day. Besides, the first impression of the hotel left to most of the guests is influenced by their first interaction with the hotel through the operators. Inaccessible for twenty minutes is already pretty rare in hotel complaint cases, not to mention breaking the service requirement of "answering the phone before the phone rings three times" and sleeping on duty. Thus, the guests will feel nothing but regretful.

高度的责任感是优质服务的有力保障，员工陈小丽玩忽职守，严重违反酒店规章制度，受到惩罚是应该的。"谁砸了酒店的牌子，酒店就会砸掉谁的饭碗"。但彻底清除总机服务质量中不稳定的因素，提高总机服务水准才是目的。

High sense of responsibility is a powerful guarantee for quality service. Chen Xiaoli slept on duty, which severely violated rules and regulations of the hotel, so she deserved the penalty. The hotel will fire anyone who damages its reputation. But all measures taken should take removing unstable factors from Switchboard services and improving service quality as the ultimate goal.

夜班员工服务效率不高，又往往疏于管理，加之正值常规酣梦之时，思想本身压力减轻，自我约束能力减弱。因此，诸多因素造成违纪状态潜伏。诚然，夜值员工十分辛苦，坚持良好的服务需要坚韧的毅力。然而，我们都知道，尽职尽责、坚守岗位，是每一位员工必须遵守的劳动纪律，也是酒店从业人员必须充分具备的职业道德。作为一名普通劳动者，工作期间必须有较强的工作热忱和高度的责任感，以及高度的组织纪律性，才能提供高质、高效的劳动成果。作为服务员，则更需要保证强烈的酒店意识和良好的服务质量。夜班员工除做好当值一些日常工作外，还必须警惕意外事件的发生，确保客人、员工的生命和财产安全。

Service efficiency of night-shift staff is relatively low and their performance is often neglected. Besides, at the conventional sleeping time they fell less stressful, thus their self-discipline ability is also weaken. Therefore, there are many factors initiating disciplinary behaviors. Admittedly, it is toilsome to take night-shift and strong perseverance is a necessary for quality service. However, as we all know, fully performing responsibilities and sticking to positions are labor disciplines must be abide by every employee and professional ethics must be possessed by hotel professionals. To provide quality and efficient service, an ordinary worker must be enthusiasm in work and held high sense of responsibility and organizational discipline. For a waiter, it is more important to keep a strong sense of the hotel reputation and quality service. In addition to doing a good job on duty, the night-shift staff must also be alert to any accidents, so as to ensure the life and property safety of the guests and the staff.

夜值员工是酒店夜晚的“保护神”。夜值员工的自律，维系着客人和其他员工的生命。而总机，又是酒店的“第一公关员”，代表着客人对酒店的第一印象。所有酒店的总机服务，都能在客人心目中塑造完美的形象。

Night-shift employees play a role of “patron saint” of the hotel at night. Lives of the guests and other staff hinge on night-shift employees' self-discipline. While, Switchboard is “the first public official” of the hotel, which represents the first impression of the hotel left to the guests. All Switchboard services are able to leave a perfect impression to the guests.

总机，是酒店前厅部的组成部分之一，是酒店内外信息沟通联络的通信枢纽，是一间配置多部服务话机和适量的话务操作台的办公室。总机工作员工通常被称作话务员或者接线员，在对客服务过程中扮演着十分重要的角色。在日常服务中，话务员不与客人直接见面，大多数客人通过声音的传播留下对酒店的第一印象。总机话务员的礼貌服务有独到之处，热情、快捷、高效的对客服务，集中体现在自己的嗓音上。总机话务员以电话为媒介，直接为住客提供各种话务服务，其服务质量的高低，直接影响着住客对酒店的评价，甚至影响到酒店的经济效益。总机的工作看似比较简单，但事实上想做一名优秀的接线员还需要付出很多努力，在接听电话时有很多标准语言需要记忆，这些东西在多次练习熟练之后，可以在很大程度上提高工作效率。

Switchboard, a part of the Front Office, is the communication hub of internal and external information of the hotel. Switchboard is an office with a number of service telephones and a defined amount of telephone traffic operation desks. Workers in the Switchboard are called operators or telephone operators who play a crucial role in daily guest service. They provide guest-service without direct interaction, and their service on the phone always leaves the guests with first impression of the hotel. There is something special in telephone service. Enthusiasm, rapid and efficient customer service is embodied in the tone of the operator, who directly provides service on the phone. The quality of telephone service directly affects the reputation and even economic benefits of the hotel. It seems easy to provide telephone service, but to be an excellent operator, there is still a long way to go. There are lots of standard phrases to be remembered and practiced, so as to significantly improve the work efficiency.

如今，由于移动通信的发展及短信服务业务的开展，电话总机的服务范围，随着酒店的类型、规模及程控电话交换机的功能等有所不同，常见的服务有电话转接服务、电话自动叫醒服务、电话查询、留言服务、应急电话服务等。

Presently, with the development of mobile communication and short message service, hotel types and sizes as well as functions of SPC telephone exchanges have changed. So has scope of Switchboard service, which commonly includes call transferring service, telephone wake-up service, telephone query service, message service, emergency telephone service, etc.

一、电话转接（Call Transfer）

（一）接听报岗（Answer the Phone，Reveal the Post）

接听电话第一步要做的就是报岗，让致电者清楚是哪里在接听酒店电话，具体操作内外线是不一样的。因为话务员一接起电话就要马上反应出报岗内容，所以这段语言必须记忆非常熟悉，达到惯性本能的反应。具体操作如下：

The first thing to do is reveal the post after answering the phone to let the callers know which department is answering the phone. Different words should be said against internal and external lines. Those words must be remembered by the operators who have to blurt those words out immediately after picking up the phone. Specific steps are as follows:

（1）三声铃响前，话务员拿起话筒，按"应答"键。

The operator picks up the phone and presses the "reply" button before the phone rings three times.

（2）话务员问候来电者，并表明身份。

The operator greets the caller and reveals the post.

（3）外线电话：您好，××酒店，请问有什么可以帮您？内线：早上好/下午好/晚上好，电话服务中心，请问有什么可以帮您？

External lines: hello, this is ×× hotel, what can I do for you? Internal lines: good morning/good afternoon/good evening, this is the Telephone Center, what can I do for you?

注意事项：要求声音清晰、口齿清楚，注意语音语调，使人感到悦耳动听。

Notes: speak clearly and make the pronunciation and intonation pleasing to the ear.

（二）电话转接及留言服务（Call Transferring and Message Service）

1. 注意事项（Cautions）

（1）向来电者热情问好，然后认真聆听客人讲话再转接，并说："好的，马上为您转接。"如果客人需要其他咨询、留言等服务，应对客人说："好的，马上为您查询。"

Say hello to the caller enthusiastically, then transfer the call after listening to the guest seriously, and at the same time say: "ok, transfer for you right now." If the guest needs consultation service, message service and other kinds of services, the operator should say: "ok, I will do it for you right now."

（2）在等候转接时，为客人播出悦耳的音乐。

Play a sweet music for the guest when waiting for the transfer.

（3）接转之后，如果对方无人接听，话务员应在铃响五次之后向客人说明："对不起，电话无人接听，请问您是否需要留言？"若是需要留言，则问清客人是要语音留言还是文本留言。多数情况下为语音留言，则马上将电话转至需要留言的房间的话机。若是给酒店管理人员的留言，则由话务员清楚地记录下来，通过寻呼或其他方式尽快将留言转达给有关人员。

When the call is transferred and if no one answers the phone, the operator should explain to the guest after the phone rings five times: "I'm sorry, nobody is answering the phone, would you like to leave a message?" If the guest needs to leave a message, ask about whether the guest wants to leave a voice message or a text message. If the guest wants to leave a voice message (in most cases), the operator should immediately transfer the call to the corresponding room. If the message is for management personnel of the hotel, the operator should clearly write the message down and pass the message to relevant personnel by paging or other ways as soon as possible.

2. 电话转接服务要求（Requirements of Call Transferring Services）

（1）铃响三声内必须接起电话，主动问候，自报店名和身份。

The phone must be answered before it rings for three times, take the initiative to say hello, reveal the hotel and the post.

（2）根据来电人提供的姓名和房号，迅速准确地转接电话。

Promptly and accurately transfer the call according to the name and room number provided by the caller.

（3）当电话占线时，及时向来电人说明占线情况，请住客稍候再试或留言。

If the line is busy, explain the situation to the caller in a timely manner and ask the guest to try again later or leave a message.

（4）如无人接听，向来电人说明电话没人接听的情况；主动征询住客是否愿意稍候再接或留言。

If no one is answering the call, explain the situation to the caller in a timely manner and take the initiative to consult the guest if he/she is willing to try it again later, or leave a message.

（5）如果来电人只提供受话人的姓名，请其稍等，在电脑上查询到房号后，将电话转接过去，但不能告诉来电人住客房号。

If the caller only provides the name of the callee, ask the caller to wait for a moment and transfer the call after checking the room number on the computer, but never tell the caller the room number.

（6）如果来电人只提供房号，则应核实身份，查询住客是否有特殊要求，如房号保密、电话请勿打扰等。

If the caller provides room number only, verify his/her identity and check if the callee has special requirements, such as room number confidentiality, telephone DND, etc.

（7）挂断电话前，要等来电人先挂断，才能切断电路。

Never hang up the phone before the guest.

3. 电话转接程序（Procedures of Call Transfer）

（1）酒店内线电话处理流程。如图 5-1 所示。

Interphone treatment scheme as shown in the Figure 5-1.

（2）市内进线处理流程，如图 5-2 所示。

Treatment scheme of local call, as shown the Figure 5-2.

（三）回答问询及查询服务（Query-Answering Service）

无论是店内还是店外的客人，常常都会向酒店总机提出各种问询，因而，话务员必须了解酒店内外一般的信息资料，特别是酒店各部门及酒店附近的主要有关单位的电话号码，以方便客人。查询电话服务的工作程序如下：

Guests stays in or out of the hotel often raise various kinds of questions to the Switchboard, therefore, the operator must be familiar with general information inside and outside the hotel, telephone numbers of all the departments of the hotel and concerned units near the hotel, so as to facilitate the guest service.

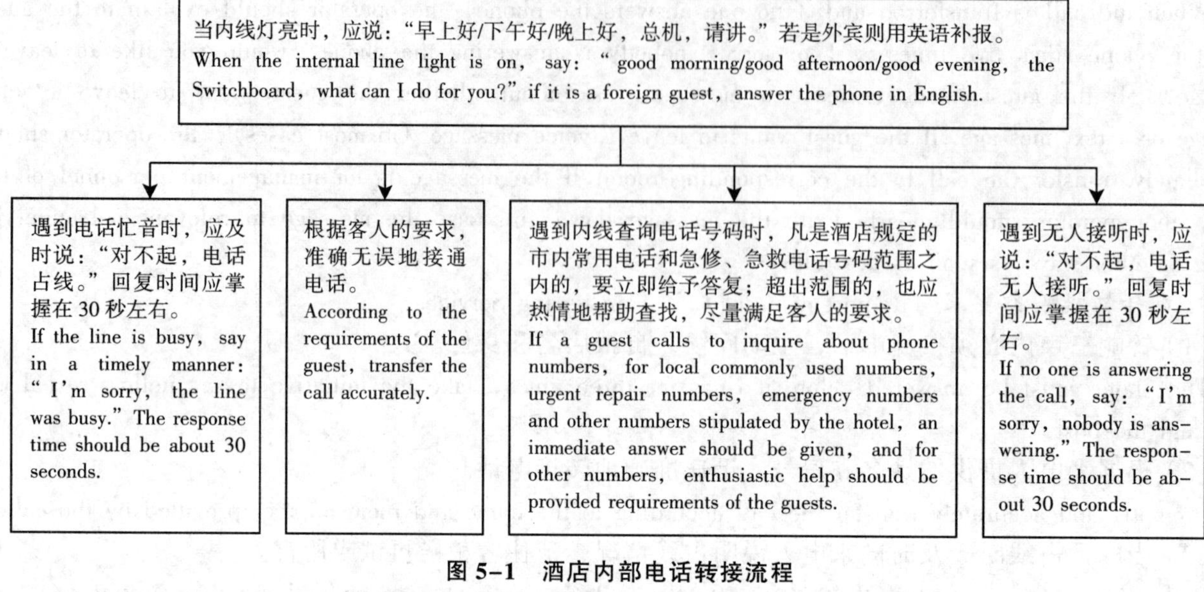

图5-1 酒店内部电话转接流程

Figure 5-1 Flow Chart of Internal Line Transfer

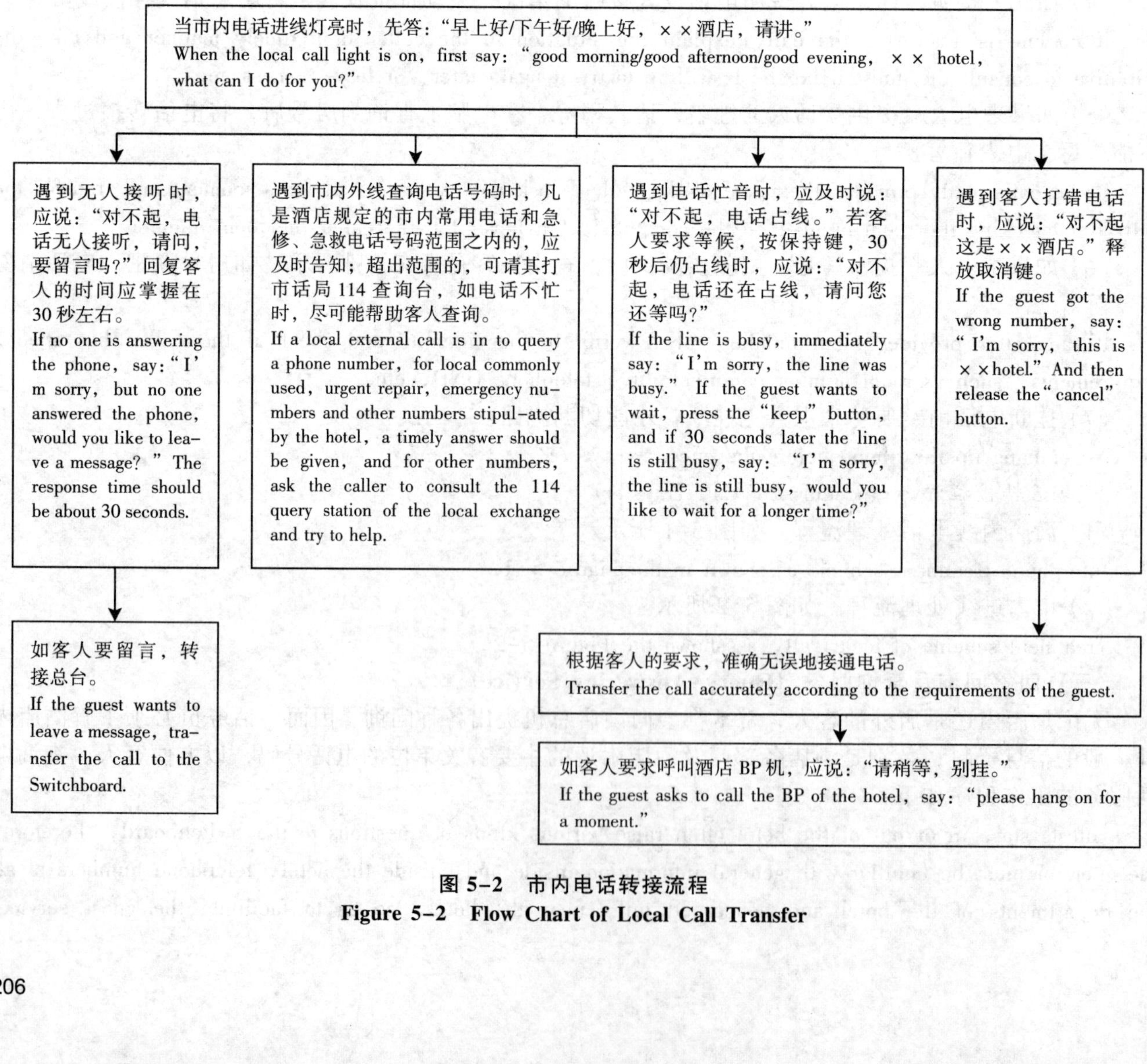

当市内电话进线灯亮时，先答：“早上好/下午好/晚上好，××酒店，请讲。”
When the local call light is on, first say: “good morning/good afternoon/good evening, ×× hotel, what can I do for you?”

遇到无人接听时应说：“对不起，电话无人接听，请问，要留言吗？”回复客人的时间应掌握在30秒左右。
If no one is answering the phone, say: “I'm sorry, but no one answered the phone, would you like to leave a message?” The response time should be about 30 seconds.

如客人要留言，转接总台。
If the guest wants to leave a message, transfer the call to the Switchboard.

遇到市内外线查询电话号码时，凡是酒店规定的市内常用电话和急修、急救电话号码范围之内的，应及时告知；超出范围的，可请其打市话局114查询台，如电话不忙时，尽可能帮助客人查询。
If a local external call is in to query a phone number, for local commonly used, urgent repair, emergency numbers and other numbers stipulated by the hotel, a timely answer should be given, and for other numbers, ask the caller to consult the 114 query station of the local exchange and try to help.

遇到电话忙音时，应及时说：“对不起，电话占线。”若客人要求等候，按保持键，30秒后仍占线时，应说：“对不起，电话还在占线，请问您还等吗？”
If the line is busy, immediately say: “I'm sorry, the line was busy.” If the guest wants to wait, press the “keep” button, and if 30 seconds later the line is still busy, say: “I'm sorry, the line is still busy, would you like to wait for a longer time?”

遇到客人打错电话时，应说：“对不起这是××酒店。”释放取消键。
If the guest got the wrong number, say: “I'm sorry, this is ××hotel.” And then release the “cancel” button.

根据客人的要求，准确无误地接通电话。
Transfer the call accurately according to the requirements of the guest.

如客人要求呼叫酒店BP机，应说：“请稍等，别挂。”
If the guest asks to call the BP of the hotel, say: “please hang on for a moment.”

图5-2 市内电话转接流程

Figure 5-2 Flow Chart of Local Call Transfer

Procedures of providing telephone query service are usually as follows:

（1）如果客人查询的是常用电话号码，话务员需以最快的速度对答，体现工作效率，因此话务员平日应将那些常用的电话号码进行熟记、背诵。

If the guest queries about commonly used phone numbers, the operator should answer as quick as possible to reflect high work efficiency, so the operator must memorize and recite those numbers.

（2）如果客人查询非常用电话号码，话务员必须请客人稍等，保留线路，而后以最有效的方式为客人查询号码，在确认号码正确无误后，再及时通知客人。如果所查询的号码比较难查，一时之间查不出来，则应请客人留下电话号码，等查清后再主动与客人联系，将号码告诉客人。

If the guest queries about uncommon phone numbers, the operator must ask the guest to wait, keep the phone on, and query the number in the most effective way, then inform the guest after confirming the number. If it will take some time to query the number, the operator should ask the guest to leave a contact number so as to take the initiative to contact the guest after finding the number out.

（3）如果来电是查询客人房间的电话，话务员务必要注意为客人保密，不能泄露住客的房号，应先接通，然后让客人直接与来电人通话。来电时如果总台电话占线，话务员可通过电脑为客人查询。

If the guest calls to query a guest room number, the operator must pay attention to the confidentiality of the guest and never disclose the room number. The operator should transfer the phone and then let the guest talk with the caller directly. If the Switchboard is busy, the operator can query the number for the guest through a computer.

（4）若来电找人，则问清要查询的客人是酒店员工还是住店客人，若是酒店员工，则问清要查询人的姓名、部门，确有此人马上将电话转接给相关部门或人员。若查找住店客人，则问清要查找的人的姓名、单位、国籍等相关信息，核对后将电话转入客人房间，如果转接时间在客人休息中，则问清住店客人是否接听，如果接听马上将电话转入，如果不需要接听则告知来电者这个时间段客人不方便接听。

If the caller queries about someone, then make it clear whether the queried person is a hotel staff or a hotel guest. If it is a hotel staff, then ask about the person's name and department, and transfer the call to appropriate department or individual after confirming the person. If it is a hotel guest, ask the caller about the name, unit, nationality and other related information of the queried person and transfer the phone to the relevant room after verifying the information. But if the queried guest is at rest, solicit his/her opinions before transferring the call, and if the guest agrees to answer the call, then transfer it immediately. If not, inform the caller that the guest is not convenient to answer at this time.

（四）注意事项（Cautions）

表 5-1　电话转接服务注意事项

Table 5-1　Cautions for Call Transferring Service

工作任务 Tasks	做法 Method of work	影响业务水平的因素 Factors affecting professional skills
吐字清晰、切勿含糊 Speak clearly	话务员必须发音清晰，表意明确，不说多余的废话。 The operator must speak clearly, definitely and concisely.	客人看不见你，他们说话和理解的70%都是听觉性的。因此，你必须口头表达清楚、简练。 The guests cannot see you, so they understand you mostly based on what you said. So, you must speak clearly.

续表

工作任务 Tasks	做法 Method of work	影响业务水平的因素 Factors affecting professional skills
不要使用俚语和首字母缩写词。 No use of slangs and acronyms	请勿使用下列词语： Never answer the phone using the following phrases： 今天天气不错——什么？ It is a good day today——what? 等一下——为什么？ Wait for a moment——why? 我——再见 I——bye 你是在开玩笑吧——你要留言？ Are you kidding me——you want to leave a message?	只用大家熟知的英语，我们以为所有的人都明白我们说的缩略语的意思，如一名从英国打来电话的人不知道 GST 是什么意思（他们说 VAT）。 Use only English which is familiar to almost every one. Acronyms will be a bad choice, because not everyone uses the same acronym for the same meaning, for example, a British man may not know what GST means because in English the corresponding term is VAT.
接外线 External line	说"早上好/下午好/晚上好。 ××酒店——我是约翰（报你的名字） 我能为您做些什么？" Say "good morning/good afternoon/good evening. ×× hotel，I'm John（reveal your name）What can I do for you?"	在问候时报出酒店和你自己的名字，你实际上是在告诉打电话的人他是否拨对了号码、找对了人。 When revealing hotel name and your name, you are actually tell the caller whether he dialed the right number and find the right person.
如果打电话的人想跟其他人通话 If the caller wants to contact another person	试着得到打电话人的姓名并向酒店住客介绍他们。 Try to ask about the caller's name, and introduce the caller to the guest of the hotel. 打电话的人："请转预订处。" The caller："Please transfer to the Reservation Desk." 话务员："好的，先生/女士，我能告诉他们您是谁吗？" The operator："OK, Mr. / Ms., could I tell the Reservation Desk who you are?" 打电话的人："我是史密斯太太。" The caller："I am Mrs. Smith." 话务员："正在转接，史密斯太太。" The operator："I am transferring the call，Mrs. Smith." 话务员接通预订处，"史密斯太太在一号线。" The operator gets through the Reservation Desk，"Mrs. Smith. is on the first line."	通报打电话的人会使接电话的人更加友好。在刚才的例子中，接待员可以这样回答："下午好，史密斯太太，我能为您做点什么吗？"这当然比仅回答"预订处"要礼貌得多。 If the operator answering the transferred call knows the name of the caller, the operator can answer the call more friendly. In this case, for example, the operator can answer like this："good afternoon，Mrs. Smith，what can I do for you?" This，of course，is much more polite than just answer "This is the Reservation Desk". 这个过程占用话务员较少的时间，可是却能把优质酒店和其他酒店区分开来。 This costs little time, but it can make a distinction between quality hotels and other hotels.
如果你正在接电话又有新电话进来 If another call is in when you are on a phone	不要说"请等一下"，设法从第一个电话抽身几秒，恰当得体地接电话。 Don't say "please wait for a moment", try to answer the phone appropriately by hanging on the first call for several seconds.	这个打电话的人可能来自海外，如果你不给他们时间说清自己的需要，他们可能会非常不满并挂断电话。 The callers may come from overseas，so if you don't give them time to tell their own needs，they may be unhappy and hang up the phone.
如果电话是找酒店的一位客人 If the caller queries about a guest of the hotel	询问打电话人的姓名。 Ask about the name of the caller.	客人享有隐私权，因此一家好的酒店绝对不能不通报就直接把电话接到客人房间。 Guests enjoy privacy，so a qualified hotel never transfers the call to the guest room without notification in advance.
如果客人出去了 If the guest is out	留言，仔细地听，把细节向打电话的人重复一遍，告诉打电话的人你一定会转交留言。 Listen to the message carefully，repeat the details to caller，and tell the caller you will pass the message.	仔细记录留言十分重要，话务员应该拼出不常见的名字和指示，确保信息的准确。 It is important to record the message carefully. The operator should spell out unusual names and instructions to ensure the information is accurate.
如果客人要求不接电话或者已经通知你他们不想被打扰 If the guests require to be free from any calls or they have informed you that he does want to be disturbed	不要告诉打电话的人客人不接电话，说客人现在不在，请留言。保证客人尽快得到留言。 Don't tell the caller that the guest refuses to answer the phone，say that the guest is out right now，please leave a message，I will pass the message to the guest as soon as possible.	在此重申应尊重客人的隐私，保证留言的准确性极其重要。 Again，privacy of the guest should be respected. It is extremely important to ensure the accuracy of the message.

续表

工作任务 Tasks	做法 Method of work	影响业务水平的因素 Factors affecting professional skills
当让打电话的人稍等时 If the caller is asked to wait	至少每30秒回复打电话的人一下，让他们知道原因。如果你正在找人，或许被叫方正在打电话，要主动提出留言。 Reply to the caller every 30 seconds at least to let them know why they are waiting. If you are calling for someone, and the line is busy, take the initiative to ask the caller to leave a message. 一位优秀的话务员会将这些留言记录下来并检查落实，确保将它们交给客人。 An excellent operator will record and verify these messages, and ensure that they have been given to the guests.	挂断电话是最让人不满的经历之一，如果你能避免这个问题，不要这么做。 Someone hangs up your phone is one of the most upsetting experience, so don't do it if it can be avoided. 如果电话是长途或国际长途，不要让对方等待，让对方留言并且答应当他要找的人回来后会给他回电话。 If the call is a long distance or international one, don't let the caller wait, and ask the caller to leave a message and promise to call back when the queried guest is available. 记录并转达留言会使你的酒店显得效率高。 Recording and conveying a message can reflect the high efficiency of a hotel.
如果电话是找员工的 If the caller queries about a hotel staff	留言并转达，同时告诉他这样的事情今后不允许再发生，因为这会占用总机及电话线。 Ask the caller to leave a message and pass the message to the staff and at the same time tell the staff that this are not allowed to happen again, because its take up the switchboard and the telephone line.	留言，不要说“员工工作时不允许接电话”，这只会贬低员工，引起尴尬。如果这样的问题继续存在，应该告知员工的监督人。 Ask the caller to leave a message, don't say "the staff is not allowed to answer the phone at work" which will only diminish the staff, and cause embarrassment. If this problem persists, corresponding supervisor should be informed.
如果客人想了解当地的信息，比如商店什么时候关门 If the guest calls to ask local information, such as the close time of a shop	尽量自己帮助客人，有些酒店直接把电话接到行李台，但是这样会浪费客人的时间。 Try to help the guest directly. Some hotels may transfer the call to the Luggage Service Desk, which will be a waste of time for the guest.	亲自帮助客人显得酒店效率很高。 Help the guest in person can reflect the high efficiency of the hotel.
如果客人找预订部或者想订餐，但是占线 If the guest calls the Reservation Department or wants to order food, but the line is busy	询问客人预订的细节，记下他们的名字和电话（重复一遍，确保准确）。向客人保证预订员或总服务员会尽快回复他们。 Ask the reservation details, write down their names and phone numbers (repeat them to ensure accuracy). Promise the guests that the Reservationist or the waiter will reply them as soon as possible.	如果客人等待的时间太长，他们会挂断电话，一次预订就损失了。记录这类留言时，话务员应亲自落实，和接收人核对信息，确保其得以执行。 The guest may hang up the phone after a long wait, so a reservation will be lost. The operator should record and verify this kind of messages personally; check the information with the receiver to ensure this information is performed.
如果有客人投诉酒店的服务 If the guest calls to make complaints about service of the hotel	如果客人向你投诉，说明他想让你立即采取行动。在有些酒店他们会把电话转到别处，让客人重复，这只会使问题变得更糟糕。 When a guest complains to you, he/she wants you to take relevant actions immediately. In some hotels, complaint calls may be transferred, thus the guest has to repeat the complained issue, which only makes the issue worse. 倾听时给予同情、理解，向客人保证会采取行动。向有关负责人汇报，让他们处理并与客人联系。 Show your sympathy and understanding when listening to complaints and promise to take actions. Report to relevant responsible persons and let them handle the issue and communicate with the guest.	投诉的客人要求立即采取行动，将问题交给他人只会使问题变得更糟。 If the guest requests to take immediate actions, transferring the issue to others will only make the issue worse.

续表

工作任务 Tasks	做法 Method of work	影响业务水平的因素 Factors affecting professional skills
如果客人房间里有维修方面的问题，比方说电视坏了，或者浴室里的毛巾不够 If the guest has maintenance problems, for example, the TV is out of work or towels in the bathroom is not enough	记录细节并亲自与客房部或维修部门联系。一段时间后，比如说 20 分钟后，给投诉的人打电话，询问问题是否已经解决。如果没有，立刻落实。 Record the details and contact the Housekeeping Department or the Maintenance Department. After a period of time, like 20 minutes, call back to the complainer, asking whether the problem has been resolved. If has not, verify the situation immediately.	这样做是为了向客人表示我们关心他们提的问题，再次打电话询问是确保问题已经得到修正，而不是引发一大堆别的工作。客人向我们报告问题说明他们想问题得到立即解决，而不是等到明天。 We do so to show that we care about their problems. We call back the complainer to ensure that their problems have been solved, rather than to cause a lot of other problems. Guests report problems to us with an intention to solve the problems at once rather than until tomorrow.
如果客人有特殊的要求，如想换房间或想坐在餐厅里靠窗的座位 If the guest has special requirements, like changing room or asking for window seats in the restaurant	记录细节，向客人保证会把问题转达给负责人，他会处理。不要向客人承诺任何事情，除非你有 100%的把握能满足他们的要求。 Record the details, and promise the guests that you will convey the problem to relevant responsible person, and the problem will be handled. Don't promise things about which you cannot meet their requirements 100%.	如果你承诺的什么，你其实是拟订了一份口头协议，当然具有法律效力。 Your promise constitutes an oral agreement, which, of course, has the force of law.
感谢打电话的人不怕麻烦给酒店打电话 Show your gratefulness to the guest for calling the hotel	对外界打进的电话，说“谢谢您拨打××酒店的电话，祝您愉快”来结束通话。 For external calls, end them by saying "thank you for calling, wish you a happy day". 在对方挂电话前，不要结束通话。 Never hang up the phone before the caller.	祝愿他们度过美好的一天会使他们对酒店产生好感。 Wishing them a happy day will leave the caller a good impression of the hotel.
如果客人打电话时无礼、粗暴 If the guest speaks rudely on the phone	不要放在心上，保持冷静镇定，不要表现得不耐烦，也不要对对方粗暴，尽可能地使对方满意。如果他们继续无礼，让他们稍等，把情况报告给监督人。 Don't take it seriously, and stay calm, patient and civilized to satisfy the guest as much as possible. If the guest continues to be rude, ask him/her to wait and report the situation to the supervisor.	忽视他们的无礼，像平常一样谈话会显得你是一名真正的专业人士。有一句古谚：“谁先失去耐性谁就会输掉战役。” Ignore their rudeness and talk as normal, which indicates that you are a real professional. An old saying goes like this "he who loses patience first will lose the battle."

二、电话留言（Telephone Message）

电话留言可分为访客留言和住客留言：

Telephone message can be divided into visitor message and guest message:

（1）访客留言。是来访客人给住店客人的留言，可由来访者口述、问询员记录，再请其过目签字，或由来访者自己填写访客留言单，然后问询员签字，再通知被访的住店客人；接受客人留言后，必须在留言单上用打时机打上时间。可以由电话总机话务员开启客人房间的留言灯。

Visitor message is the message left by the visitor to the guest residing in the hotel. The message may be dictated by the visitor, recorded by the inquiry staff, and then be checked and sighed by the visitor or the visitor can fill in a Visitor Message List personally, then the inquiry staff signs on the list, and finally inform the visited guest; after the message is accepted, corresponding time must be stamped on the list and the operator from the Switchboard may open the message light of the guest room.

（2）住客留言。是住店客人给来访客人或其他住客的留言可填写住客留言单，并存放在前台；住客留言单一般一式两联，即问询组、电话总机各保存一联；且要在上面注明留言内容的有效时间。

Guest message is the message left by the guest of the hotel to the visitor or other internal guests. The guest may fill in a Guest Message List and deposit it at the Reception Desk; generally, the Guest Message List is made in two sheets, the Inquiry Group and the Switchboard hold one respectively; and the valid time of the message must be indicated on the list.

表 5-2　访客留言处理服务与规范

Table 5-2　Visitor Message Processing Services and Specifications

流程 Procedures	标准 Standards
1. 留言确认 Confirming the message	(1) 若有来访者或来电找人，接待员应根据其提供的信息在电脑上查找。 If the visitor or the call queries about a person, the receptionist should search on the computer based on the provided information. (2) 若被访者是已住店客人，应先与客人联系，按客人意见处理。 If the person is a hotel guest, the receptionist should contact with the guest first, and conduct related work as the guest required. (3) 若客人一时联系不上或是预订客人，可询问来访者来电者是否留言。 If the guest cannot be contacted temporarily or is a reservation guest, the receptionist should ask if the visitor or the caller wants to leave a message.
2. 记录留言 Recording the message	(1) 到店来访者留言（Visitor message）。 ① 接待员请访客或代为访客填写访客留言单，填好后要仔细检查并请访客签字。 The receptionist should ask the visitor fill in a Visitor Message List or fill in it for the visitor, then check the list carefully and finally ask the visitor to sign on it. ② 及时将访客留言输入电脑。 Input visitor message into a computer in a timely manner. (2) 来电留言（Telephone message）。 ① 接待员要问清留言人的姓名、留言的内容（时间、地点等）、电话号码，必要时留下其公司名称或地址。 The receptionist should be clear about name of the caller, message content (time, place, etc.), telephone number, and ask about his/her company name or address when necessary. ② 记好后应向来电者复述一遍留言的内容。确保准确无误后，将留言按格式输入电脑，检查拼写和语法，确保正确后再打印出来。 After recording all the above-mentioned information, the receptionist should repeat the message content to the caller. After verifying the accuracy of the content, input the message into the computer in the required format, check the spelling and grammar, and then print it out.
3. 传达留言 Passing the message	(1) 若是已住店客人留言，接待员请行李员将留言单的底单装入信封，打上客人姓名、房号和时间戳后送到客房；将面单放入留言柜以备查。 If the message is left by a guest residing in the hotel, the receptionist should ask the bellboy to put the bottom sheet of the message into an envelope and stamp guest name, room number and corresponding time on the envelope, then send it to the guest room; put the top sheet of the message into the message cabinet for reference. (2) 若是当天预计到达的客人留言，把该客人的订单号或团体代号分别抄在文字留言单的底单和面单的左上角，面单放在"将入住"留言柜以备查，底单按散客接待、团体接待或商务楼层入住分类放置。 If the message is of the expected guest on that day, write the order number or group code respectively at top left corners of both the bottom sheet and the top sheet of the message. Put the top sheet into the "expected" message cabinet for reference and the bottom cop should be classified based on the type of the guest, such as FIT, group or business travel. (3) 若是已订房但非当天入住的客人的留言，将订单号或团号分别抄在文字留言单的底单和最上面单的左上角，将底单交给订房部并请其在最上面单上签收；最上面单暂放在"将入住"留言柜里，待客人入住后在最上面单上写上房号再归档备查。 If the message is of the reservation guest who will not stay in the hotel on that day, write the order number or group code respectively at top left corners of both the bottom sheet and the top sheet of the message. Deliver the bottom sheet to the Reservation Department and ask the department sign and accept the sheet; the top sheet should be put into the "expected" message cabinet temporarily, and after the guest checks in, write the corresponding room number on the top sheet and file the sheet for future reference. (4) 要定时检查"将入住"留言柜内的留言，如有已经入住的，则请行李员马上把留言单的底单送到房间并告知客人。 Regularly check messages in the "expected" message cabinet, if relevant guests have checked in, ask the bellboy to deliver the bottom sheets of those messages to corresponding rooms and inform the guests right away. (5) 客人到达或查询留言时，将底单交给客人或将电脑内的留言内容告知客人。 When the guest arrives or queries about the message, hand over the bottom sheet to the guest or show him/her the message content in the computer to the guest.

续表

流程 Procedures	标准 Standards
4. 留言管理 Managing the message	（1）接待员每天将归档柜中的留言条按房号顺序整理并存档，每月清理一次。 The receptionist should sort and archive the message slips in filing cabinet daily on the basis of room number order, and clean them up once a month. （2）长住客人的留言在客人提取留言后一周，由接待主管取消电脑文字记录。 After messages of the long staying guest having been collected for being a week, relevant computer records should be canceled by the Reception Supervisor.

三、电话查询（Telephone Inquiry）

（一）有关酒店内部的问讯（Inquiry about Internal Affairs）

1. 问询服务要求（Inquiry about Service Requirements）

为客人提供及时周到的问询服务，要求提供服务的人员掌握大量的信息，并且有很好的服务意识和对客技巧。在服务过程中需要做到：

Offer timely and thoughtful inquiry services for guests. The staff that provides services should grasp a lot of information, and have good service consciousness and customer service skills. During the service process, the staff should:

（1）对待客人礼貌热情，彬彬有礼并且要一视同仁，避免让客人产生厚此薄彼的感觉。

Treat guests politely, enthusiastically and equally to avoid producing unfair feelings among guests.

（2）对酒店的各项服务项目要非常熟悉，记清酒店各服务部门的电话号码，以便能够及时地与其联系，减少客人等待的时间。

Be familiar with various service items in the hotel, remember phone numbers of various service sectors to keep in contact with them and reduce waiting time for guests.

（3）对于性急的客人或是因着急询问而语无伦次、词不达意的客人，要帮助他们稳定情绪，然后迅速、简明扼要地回答客人的问题。

As with impatient guests or guests who talk in a confused manner due to anxiousness, stabilize their mood and then answer their questions quickly and succinctly.

（4）问询服务员要随时补充、修改、更新自己掌握的信息和资料，以便解答客人的各种问题。

The inquiry staff should add, modify and update the information and data that he/she has in hand to answer various questions raised by guests.

（5）对于熟知的问题，回答时应简明扼要，不要含糊其辞，使客人无法清楚理解。

For familiar questions, the answer should be clear and concise, otherwise it would make guests feel confused.

（6）对于不太了解的问题，应向客人道歉并说明，请客人稍等，然后迅速借助手中资料或互联网等进行查找；如果一时查找不到，请求客人给予谅解，并将客人的姓名、房号及问讯内容记录下来，事后再迅速进行查阅，查到后立即告知客人；如果经过努力仍无查找结果，也应如实向客人说明情况，并请客人谅解。

For unfamiliar questions, make an apology and explain to guests, ask them to wait for a moment, and then quickly search the material in hand or the Internet for answers; if you cannot find the answer for the moment, reach an understanding with guests, and record their names, room numbers and inquiry content, then look up in a quick manner and inform guests once you find the answer; if all your efforts are in vain, get in touch with guests and truthfully explain the situation to them to win their understanding.

（7）问询员在回答客人问询时，必须准确无误，态度温和，不能使用不确定的语言，如“我想可能”、“大概”、“也许”等。

While answering guests' inquiry, the inquiry staff should give an accurate answer with a gentle attitude. Ambiguous language such as “I think it might be”, “probably” and “perhaps” are prohibited.

（8）当几位客人同时进行询问时，应该遵循先问先答、急问急答、有问有答的原则，尽可能使每位客人都能得到热情的接待和满意的解答。

When several guests ask questions at the same time, follow the principle of first question answer first, urgent question answer promptly and answer all questions to give satisfactory answers to every guests in an enthusiastic manner.

（9）要耐心、细致地回答客人的任何询问，做到百问不厌。

Answer all inquiries in a patient and careful manner and do not lose your temper no matter how often guests ask.

2. 在问询服务中，要注意保证客人的隐私权（Safeguard Guests' Privacy During the Inquiry Process）

（1）接待员应主动热情回答客人所提出的问题，对国内外客人要一视同仁。

The receptionist should answer questions raised by guests in an active and enthusiastic manner, and treat domestic and foreign guests equally.

（2）只回答自己权限内的问题，对自己不了解的事情应当向客人表示歉意，同时尽可能请示有关方面的负责人。

Only answer questions within your limits of authority. Make an apology to guests for questions that you do not understand and ask for the instruction of responsible person concerned.

（3）每位客人的姓名、房号、国籍、活动、房价等资料均属保密范围，接待员不得随意泄露要求给予保密的客人的信息，对他们的来访者和来电都应委婉拒绝。

Keep each guest's name, room number, nationality, activities, room price and other information confidential, the receptionist should not disclose guests' confidential information at will and should politely decline all related visitors and calls.

（4）对来电、来访者，接待员要先从电脑中查明被访者是否住在本酒店，如被访者不住酒店应礼貌告诉客人。如被访者有预订，可建议来电、来访者留言。

With respect to calls and visitors, the receptionist should first refer to the computer to ascertain whether the respondent live in the hotel. If the respondent does not live in the hotel, tell the truth to guests politely. If the respondent is occupied, ask the caller or visitor to leave a message.

（5）接待员在问明来访者姓名和单位后，以电话形式通知客人并征询客人意见，同意后方可将电话转入。

The receptionist should query about the visitor's name and unit and then inform guests by telephone to seek for their opinions. Transfer calls to guests only after obtaining their approval.

（6）如电话无人接听，可告诉来访者客人不在房，建议留言，不可将房号随便告诉来访者。对于询问“××住客叫什么名字？”之类问题的来访者，接待员要特别提高警惕。

If the guest does not answer the phone, tell visitors that the guest is not in the room and ask them to leave a message. Do not disclose the room number to visitors. The receptionist should pay special attention to inquiries about “what's the name of ×× guest?”

（二）有关酒店外部的问询（Inquiry about External Affairs）

1. 查询酒店外部的程序和规范（Inquiry about External Procedures and Specifications）

（1）对于常用电话号码，话务员需对答如流，以提供快速查询服务。

The operator should speak out common phone number fluently to provide swift inquiry services.

（2）如遇查询非常用电话号码，话务员需请客人保留线路稍等，以最有效方式为客人查询号码，确认号码正确后，及时通知客人。如需较长时间，则请客人留下电话号码，待查清后，再与客人电话联系，告诉客人。

In case of inquiry about uncommon phone number, the operator should ask guests to hold on for a moment, check the number in the most effective way and inform guests of the number after confirming it. If it takes a long time, ask guests to leave their phone numbers and get in touch with them after ascertain the number.

（3）如遇查询某单位信息的电话，话务员首先需问清客人是否有该单位的电话号码。

In case of inquiry about the information of a certain unit, the operator should first ask guests if they have the phone number of the unit.

（4）如遇客人查询客人房间的电话，在总台电话均占线的情况下，话务员应通过电脑为客人查询。但此时应注意为客人保密，不能泄露住客房号，可接通后让客人直接与其通话。

In case of inquiry about the phone number of the guest room and all lines are busy, the operator should check through the computer for guests. But pay attention not to reveal the room number of guests. Connect the phone and let guests communicate directly by phone.

2. 有关酒店外部查询的主要内容（Main Contents of Inquiry about External Affairs）

（1）酒店所在城市的旅游景点及其交通情况。

Tourist attractions and traffic situation of the city where the hotel is located in.

（2）主要娱乐场所、商业区、政府部门、学校及有关企业的位置和交通情况。

Location and traffic conditions of major places of entertainment, commercial district, government departments, schools and enterprises.

（3）近期内有关大型文艺、体育活动的基本情况。

Basic information about the recent large-scale cultural and sports activities.

（4）市内交通情况，如公共汽车、出租车、地铁、火车等。

Traffic situation in the city, such as buses, taxis, subway, train, etc.

四、叫醒服务（Wake-up Service）

电话叫醒服务是酒店对客服务的一项重要内容，它涉及住客的计划和日程安排，尤其是关系到住客的航班、车次等。因此，不能出任何差错，否则会给住客和酒店带来不可弥补的损失。酒店向住客提供叫醒服务分为人工叫醒和自动叫醒。在采用功能齐全的程控交换机的酒店，多选择电话自动叫醒。

Wake-up service is an important part of the guest service in a hotel, which relates to guests' plan and schedule, particularly flight number, train number and so on. Therefore, you cannot make any mistake; otherwise it would bring irreparable loss for guests and the hotel. Wake-up service is divided into manual wake-up service and automatic wake-up service. Automatic wake-up service is adopted by hotel with full-featured SPC exchange.

(一)接听客人叫醒服务(Receive Wake-up Service)

(1)当客人需要叫醒服务时，将叫醒日期、房号、时间、话务员工号及收到申请的时间都清楚地记录在记录簿上，并把信息输入电脑，检查是否正确。

When guests need wake-up service, record wake-up date, room number, time, operator's employee number and time of receiving the application clearly in the record list, and input the information into the computer for check.

(2)复述客人叫醒要求，以获得客人的确认。

Repeat guests' requirements on wake-up service to obtain guests' confirmation.

(3)检查叫醒房间的种类和客人的种类，如是套房、VIP，必须做出特别提示。

Check the type of room and guests who ask for wake-up service. Pay special attention to a suite or VIP room.

(4)祝客人晚安。

Wish guests good night.

(5)让客房服务员再次对房间叫醒服务做确认，填写叫醒记录簿。

Let room attendant confirm the wake-up service and complete the wake-up record list.

(6)夜班的话务员把叫醒记录按时间顺序整理记录在交接班簿上，注明相关信息并签字。

The night-shift operator should record wake-up record on the shift book according to the time order, specify relevant information and affix his signature.

(二)自动叫醒程序(Automatic Wake-up Procedure)

(1)接到住客要求叫醒服务的电话，话务员要问清住客的房号、姓名及叫醒时间。

After receiving calls for wake-up service, the operator should ask the room number, name and wake-up time.

(2)话务员复述一遍住客的要求，以获得客人的确认，祝住客晚安。

The operator should repeat guests' requirements to obtain their confirmation and wish guests good night.

(3)把叫醒要求输入程控交换机。

Enter wake-up requirements into the SPC exchange.

(4)填写"电话叫醒记录单"，按时间顺序填写住客的房号、叫醒时间及话务员姓名。

Fill the room number, wake-up time and operator name in the "wake-up record list" in the time order.

(5)叫醒时间到，程控交换机会自动接通房间电话，并打印叫醒记录。

SPC exchange will connect the phone automatically at the wake-up time and print wake-up records.

(6)话务员注意查看叫醒记录，对于没有应答的房间应采取人工叫醒，如再无人应答，应通知房务中心派服务员去叫醒。

The operator should pay attention to wake-up records. Manual wake-up call should be adopted for room that gives no answer. If there is still no answer, ask the Housekeeping Service Center to send attendant to wake up guests.

(7)若需要人工叫醒，则接到住客叫醒的电话，信息确认无误后，在叫醒记录上填写清楚，并在电话或钟表上定时以提示叫醒时间到。

If manual wake-up call is needed, specify it in the wake-up record list after confirming the information once receive calls for such service, and set time on the phone or clock to remind you of the wake-up time.

(8)叫醒时使用标准的叫醒语言："早上好，张先生！现在是北京时间7:00。这是您的叫醒服务，今天天气很好，祝您工作愉快！请问您还需要第二次叫醒吗？”

Wake-up service should be provided in accordance with the standard language, “Good morning, Mr. Zhang! This is your wake-up call at 7: 00, Beijing time. Have a nice day. Do you wish to have another wake-up call?”

（9）叫醒后认真在“叫醒记录表”上填写清楚叫醒时间及叫醒人员。若无人应答，则应立即派人去房间查看情况。

When the guest is woke up, record the wake-up time and wake-up staff clearly in the wake-up record list. If no one answers, send staff to check the room immediately.

（三）散客叫醒（FIT Guests Wake-up Call Service）

（1）客人在服务台要求叫醒服务时，应记下客人的姓名、房号和要求叫醒的时间，并在电脑中核对客人的房号与姓名，同时复述一遍要求叫醒的时间，以免发生差错。

When guests request wake-up service at the service desk, write down guest name, room number and wake-up time, check room number and guest name in the computer, and repeat wake-up time to avoid errors.

（2）将记下的内容转交给问询处。

Forward the content recorded to the inquiry desk.

（3）把要求叫醒的房号和时间通知总机。

Inform the Switchboard of room number and wake-up time by phone.

（4）在“叫醒服务记录簿”上做记录，并签上经办人的姓名。

Make a record in the Wake-Up Call Record List, and sign the name of the handler.

（5）在规定时间，把“叫醒服务记录簿”上所有当天要求叫醒服务的记录与总机记录核对一遍，确保其正确性。

Check the records in the Wake-Up Call Record List against the Switchboard records at the specified time to make sure they are correct.

（四）团队叫醒（Group Wake-up Call Service）

（1）接到客人要求将整个旅游团的客人全部叫醒时，应礼貌地请客人到前台登记，如负责人提供团队名单要求叫醒时，要明确是否要求全部客人在同一时间叫醒，并与领队复核一遍。

When the guest request for wake-up service for all members of the tour group, ask the guest to register at the Front Desk. When the group leader provides the name list of group members, ask whether to wake up all guests at the same time and recheck the list with the leader.

（2）受理 23：00 以后的团队叫醒预订，记录团号、叫醒时间、预订人姓名、预订人房号，通知总机做好记录。

As with group wake-up service after 23: 00, record group number, wake-up time, booker name, room number and ask the Switchboard to make a record.

（3）根据前台问询处的叫醒记录，中班话务员负责找出团队用房表，并与“叫醒登记簿”核对，夜班话务员必须再次复核团队。

The middle-shift operator should find out the group rooming list according to the wake-up records of the Inquiry Desk at the Front Desk and check with the Wake-up Register Book. The night-shift operator should recheck such records.

（4）叫醒登记表和团队分房表，然后按要求将团队叫醒时间输入机器。

Check Wake-Up Record List and Group Rooming List, and enter wake-up time into the machine as required.

（5）检查叫醒团队客人的情况，如有问题必须马上纠正。

Check the wake-up situation of the group and make corrections immediately if there is problem.

（五）VIP 叫醒服务（VIP Wake-up Service）

（1）准时叫醒。根据“叫醒服务记录表”上要求的时间和房号，准时拨打房间电话。

Wake up in time: call the room phone timely according to the time and room number in the Wake-up Service Record List.

（2）话务员拿起话筒，问候客人，根据不同的时间、客人、国籍选择不同的问候语，并询问客人是否需要了解当天的天气情况，祝福客人。

The operator should pick up the phone and greet guests with different greetings depending on different time, guests and nationality and ask if guests need to know the weather conditions of the day and express wished to guests.

（3）做好记录。当班话务员将叫醒时间、结果记录在二次叫醒记录簿上签名字。

Make a record: the operator should record the wake-up time and results in the Secondary Wake-up Call List and affix his name on the list.

（4）话务员在没人接听或占线的房号备注写“HSKP”并通知客房服务中心协助，在客人指定的叫醒时间，按下客人的房间号码。

The operator should write down “HSKP” in the remarks column as with unanswered or occupied room, ask Housekeeping Service Center for assistance and call guests in the specified time.

（5）总机领班在协助检查当日所有的叫醒记录后签字。

The Switchboard Foreman should check all wake-up records of the day and affix his name.

（六）注意事项（Cautions）

（1）对每一个来自酒店内部客人的叫醒服务申请，话务员都要进行确认。

The operator should confirm all wake-up service requests from guests living in the hotel.

（2）当班的话务员务必在当日的最早叫醒时间之前先检查叫醒机是否工作正常，一旦发现问题，应及时通知相关的部门进行处理。

The operator on duty must check whether the wake-up machine is working normally before the earliest wake-up time and inform relevant department for treatment once a problem is found.

（3）核对信息。团队、散客全部提供电话叫醒，VIP 客人直接提供人工叫醒服务。

Check information: provide automated wake-up service for group and FIT guests and manual wake-up call service for VIP guests.

（4）团队房提供电脑叫醒时，只需核对叫醒结果记录，没人接听或占线时，先通知客房部后通知领队或陪同，并在团队上注明。

Provide computer wake-up service for group room and check wake-up records. For unanswered and occupied calls, inform HSKP first and then the Foreman or Companion and mark on the records.

（5）听到较“模糊”的声音时，话务员应重新再叫一遍。

If a “blurred” sound is heard, the operator should make another call.

（6）通知客房服务中心帮助叫醒的房间，要求在 5 分钟之内得到反馈，没有收到反馈的，应主动询问，并把结果写在“叫醒服务记录表”上，以备查询。

For guests who are waked up by the Housekeeping Service Center, feedback must be given within 5 minutes. If no feedback is given, take the initiative to ask and write down the results in the Wake-up

Service Record List for query.

（7）如发现漏叫或没有打印出来的客人，话务员必须用电话叫醒客人，并做好记录。

As with guests that is missed from calling or printing out, the operator should wake up them by phone and make a record.

（8）在叫醒时，话务员一旦发现有异常情况，必须立即通知客房中心或大堂经理去客房查看，并准确记录在交接班簿上。

If abnormal situation is found when waking up guests, the operator must immediately notify the Housekeeping Service Center or Assistant Manager to check the situation and make a record in the shift book.

（9）如有客人要求取消叫醒服务，话务员必须在登记簿、电脑上同时做出更正，并上交接簿上说明。

If the guest cancels wake-up service, the operator must make corrections on the registration book and in the computer, and make notes on the shift book.

（10）如有客人要求多次叫醒时，话务员必须在“叫醒登记簿”上做出说明。

If the guest asks for several wake-up calls, the operator must make notes on the Wake-up Call Registration Book.

（11）话务员务必在客人要求的时间准时叫醒客人，如果耽误客人的飞机、会议等重要事件，情况会非常严重。

The operator must wake up guests at the specified time. It will lead to serious circumstances if guests delay in arriving at the airport, for a conference or for other important events.

五、其他服务（Other Services）

（一）设置免打扰服务（DND Service）

1. 注意事项（Cautions）

（1）话务员应将所有提出免打扰要求客人的姓名、房号记录在交接班簿上，同时注明接到客人通知的时间。

When guest asks for DND service, the operator should record the names and room numbers of all the requiring guests on the shift book, and mark the time of receiving the notice.

（2）接到通知的话务员，需将电话号码通过话务台锁上，同时将此信息及时、准确地通知所有的当班人员。

The operator should lock guest's telephone number through Attendant Console, and notify accurate information to all staff on duty in a timely manner.

（3）客人要求取消“免打扰”，或外出的客人回到房间，接到通知的话务员应立即通过话务台释放被锁的电话号码，同时在交接班簿上标明取消符号及时间。

When guests ask to cancel the DND service, or guests come back to the hotel, the operator should immediately release the locked telephone number through Attendant Console, and mark cancel symbol and time on the shift book.

（4）在免打扰期间，如果打电话的人要求与房间客人讲话，话务员应将客人不愿意被打扰的信息礼貌、准确地通知打电话的人，并建议其留言或是等客人取消免打扰服务之后再进行联系。

During DND period, if someone calls to speak to the guest, the operator should politely and accurately notify the caller that the guest does not want to be disturbed at that moment, and recommend that messages can be left for the guest or call again after the DND service is canceled.

2. 免打扰服务工作流程 (Workflow of DND service)

表 5-3 免打扰服务工作流程
Table 5-3 Workflow of DND service

项目 Items	流程内容 Workflow	标准 Standards
1	将所有要求"免电话打扰"服务的客人姓名、房号和具体"免电话打扰"服务时间记录在交接簿上（或注明在记事牌），并写明接到客人通知的时间。 Record the names, room numbers and specific DND period of all guests requiring DND service on the shift book (or the notice board), and mark the time of receiving guest's notice.	准确无误 Accurate
2	将电话号码写在交接簿上，并将此信息准确通知所有其他当班人员。 Write the telephone numbers on the shift book, and notify accurate information to all staff on duty.	记录详细完整 Detailed and complete record
3	在免打扰期间，如果打电话的人要求与住客讲话，话务员应将有关信息礼貌、准确地通知打电话的人，并建议其留言或待取消"免电话打扰"之后再来电话。 During DND period, if someone calls to speak to the guest, the operator should politely and accurately notify the caller that the guest does not want to be disturbed at that moment, and recommend that messages can be left for the guest or call again after the DND service is canceled.	及时、准确传递信息 Timely and accurate information transferring
4	客人要求取消"免电话打扰"后，在交接簿上或记事牌上标明取消记号及时间。 When guests ask to cancel the DND service, mark cancel symbol and time on the shift book or the notice board.	记录详细完整 Detailed and complete record

(二) 挂拨长途电话 (Hang up and Dial Long Distance Calls)

现代酒店一般采用程控直拨电话系统，住客可以在房间内直接拨打国内、国际长途电话。通话后，电脑计费系统自动记录通话时间和费用，并记录到住客账户上。特殊情况下，住客才会要求电话总机代拨长途电话，以国内长途为例：

Modern hotels generally adopt SPC direct dial telephone system. The guest can make DDD&IDD calls in the guest room. Computer cost counting system will produce automatic record for the calling time and cost, and record them in the guest's account. The guest will not ask the Switchboard for help unless there are special circumstances. Take DDD calls for example:

(1) 接到住客要求，话务员问清所要接听电话的人所在省份、城市、电话号码、姓名及住客的房间号码、住客的姓名。

The operator should ask the province, city, phone number and name of the person to whom the guest wants to call and the room number and name of the guest.

(2) 核查住客所提供的有关房间及姓名方面的信息，是否与电脑记录内容相符。

Check whether relevant information about the room number and name of the guest is consistent with computer records.

(3) 填写"挂打国内长途单"。

Fill in the Sheet for Hanging up and Dialing DDD Calls.

(4) 话务员拨打地区代码和电话号码。

Dial the area code and phone number.

(5) 电话接通后，将电话转到住客房间。

Transfer the phone to guest's room after being connected.

(6) 通话完毕，将通话时间和费用通知住客，并将计费单转到收款处。

When the call is over, notify the holding time and expense to the guest, and transfer the Charging Sheet to Cashier's Desk.

（三）应急电话服务（Emergency Telephone Service）

电话总机除了提供对客服务外，在酒店出现紧急情况时，还能作为酒店管理人员的指挥协调中心。话务员在接到火警电话时，千万别急或做出不当的主张，一定要依照下列程序和办法去处理：

In addition to providing customer services, the Switchboard can act as the command and coordination center for hotel management personnel for handling emergencies. The operator should keep calm when receiving a fire call, and react as per the following procedures and measures:

（1）当班的话务员接到火警电话时，要保持极其清醒的头脑，向报警人询问以下内容：A. 报警人姓名；B. 报警人所在部门；C. 出事地点；D. 何物燃烧；E. 火势大小。

The operator should keep calm when receiving a fire call, and ask the informant following information: A. Informant's name; B. Department where the informant is; C. Fire location; D. Things on fire; E. Fire size.

（2）迅速将有关内容准确记录在案；告诉报警人："我们会立即通知有关部门及人员，请您马上寻找紧急出口撤离"。

Record relevant information quickly and accurately; tell the informant: "We will inform relevant departments and personnel immediately. Please evacuate through emergency exit right away."

（3）立即通知消防控制中心以下内容：A. 报警人姓名；B. 报警人所属部门；C. 着火地点；D. 燃烧物；E. 火势大小；F. 话务员姓名；G. 记录受话人姓名。

Immediately notify Fire Control Center the following information: A. Informant's name; B. Department where the informant is; C. Fire location; D. Things on fire; E. Fire size; F. Operator's name; G. recorder's name.

（4）准确地将有关接到处理的报警内容记录在报警簿上并立即向安保部或消防中心报告。

Take an accurate record for received alarms on the alarm book, and report this immediately to the Security Department or the Fire Protection Center.

（5）消防中心立即派人实地查询，若情况属实，会立即从出事地点向总机报警。

Fire Protection Center should immediately send personnel for check. If the case is true, the fireman will call the Switchboard on the fire scene.

（6）通知有关部门：白天需通知客务经理、保卫部值班室、总经理办公室及消防值班领班；夜间需通知呼叫酒店总值班经理、客务经理、保卫部值班室及当日部门值班经理，有关部门及火灾区域部门领导立即赶到火灾发生地点，在通知时要清楚地说明火情及具体地点。

Notify related departments: during the day, Customer Service Manager, Duty Office of Security Department, General Manager Office and Fire Foreman on duty should be notified; during the night, call the General Manager on duty, Customer Service Manager, Duty Office of Security Department and Department Manager on duty. Departments concerned and leaders of departments in the fire area should rush to the spot. Clearly describe the fire and the specific location when notifying.

（7）根据紧急处理预案的要求，做好通信联络工作。

Keep communication and connection work and smooth in accordance with the requirements of Emergency Preparedness and Response Plan.

【实训与评价】【Training and Assessment】

[实训目的] [Training Goals]

通过模拟情境操作明确总机接转电话的服务程序与标准，确保为住客提供全面、高效的电话服务。

Identify service procedures and standards of the Switchboard through simulation scenarios, and provide guests with comprehensive and efficient telephone service.

[实训准备] [Training Preparation]

电话、记录簿、笔、常用电话簿

Telephone, notebook, pen, phone book used frequently

[实训方法] [Training Method]

模拟情景

Simulation scenarios

[实训内容] [Training Contents]

话务员转接电话操作

Operator receives and transfers telephone

[实训步骤] [Training Steps]

准备→转接内线电话（一般直接拨房间号码即可）→转接外线电话

Get ready→transfer internal calls (dial the room number directly in general) → transfer external calls

[实训评价] [Training Evaluation]

模拟电话转接练习：王先生致电××酒店总机，想找303房间的张先生，要求进行电话转接服务。教师请两位学生分别模拟练习。

Simulate telephone transfer: Mr. Wang calls ×× hotel Switchboard to speak to Mr. Zhang in Room303, for which transfer service is required.

Two students are asked to carry out simulation exercises.

任务二 商务中心服务
Task II Business Center Services

【情境导入】【Scenario Introduction】

迟迟到来的机票
A Belated Air Ticket

张先生是大连一家大型企业的业务副总经理。16~18日他计划在三亚参加完交易会后，立即返回大连，因为有一个重要会议在等着他。18日早晨，张先生来到他所入住三亚天域度假酒店的商务中心，首先预订了一张19日上午返回大连的机票，商务中心的刘小姐热情地接待了张先生，立即与航空公司票务中心进行了联系，并承诺最迟在晚上20:00将机票送到客人房间。张先生这才放心外出办事。

Mr. Zhang is the Deputy General Manager of a large enterprise in Dalian. He planned to fly back to Dalian to participate an important meeting after attending the Trade Fair held in Sanya from 16 - 18th day of the month. In the morning of the 18th day, Mr. Zhang came to the Business Center of the hotel he resided in－Sanya Tianyu Resort Hotel. He booked an air ticket to Dalian in the next morning at first, and the attendant Miss Liu warmly received Mr. Zhang, immediately contacting the airline ticket center, and promising to send the ticket to the guest room before 8:00 pm After all those, Mr. Zhang went out trustingly.

白天张先生非常忙，直到晚上9点才返回酒店，他一回到房间就向客房服务员询问机票务之事，客房服务员却回答说："这件事是您自己与商务中心联系的，您还是自己联系。对不起，我帮不了您。"张先生马上将电话打到了商务中心，谁知一位接待小姐说："这里是有一张大连机票，可是我现在还不敢断定是您的，待我再询问一下回答您。"

Mr. Zhang was so busy that he returned to the hotel till 9 pm The first thing he did was asking the room attendant about his air ticket, but the room attendant answered: "you booked the ticket directly through the Business Center, so it might be better for you to contact the Center yourself. I'm sorry, I can't help you." Mr. Zhang immediately called the Business Center, but a receptionist said: "here is a ticket to Dalian, but I'm not sure that it is yours, I will call back after some conformation."

等到了晚上23：30，张先生仍不见机票被送来，于是又致电商务中心，商务中心的接待员又回答说："由于早班人员已下班，我现在联系不上。对不起。再请等一下好吗？"张先生一听很气愤，心想这酒店怎么在服务上这么没有信誉，张先生担心延误明天一大早的返程，又休息不成，便将此事投诉到了大堂副理处。大堂副理经过了解才知道，原来早上接受张先生订票的服务员中午突然因生病去了医院，未及时告知其他人员而登记的内容又有误。大堂副理拿着机票送到客人的房间时已是深夜近凌晨了，尽管他向张先生表示了歉意，但客人仍然是余怒未消。

Until 11: 30 pm Mr. Zhang received nothing, then he contacted the Business Center again, but the receptionist replied: "the morning-shift staff is off duty now, I cannot contact her. I'm sorry, please wait for a moment." Mr. Zhang was annoyed by what the receptionist said and thought that the service of the hotel was poor. Mr. Zhang was so worried about missing the plane that he could not take a rest, therefore he complained about this to the Assistant Manager. After some investigation, the Assistant Manager knew that the attendant booking the ticket for Mr. Zhang was hit by a sudden sick and went to the hospital at noon without informing other staff about the situation and the recorded information was also wrong. It was late at night when the Assistant Manager brought the ticket to the guest. Mr. Zhang felt the lingering anger though the Assistant Manager expressed deep apologies.

【情境分析】【Scenario Analysis】

本案例中发生了特殊情况是可以理解的，但不能对客人没有交代，因疏忽未能及时将机票送达客人而引起客人的不满，是非常严重的失误。票务服务是酒店对客服务的重要组成部分。作为客人，总是希望入住的酒店能提供简捷、优质的代订票服务，以消除"后顾之忧"。代客人订购各种机票、船票、车票、戏票等都要按照客人的要求去办，如果有困难或情况发生变化，一定要及时征求客人的意见，要由客人自己做主。

Special cases in this case are acceptable, but corresponding explanation should never be neglected. It is a serious mistake to make the guest feel discontent because of a ticket failure caused by negligence. Ticketing service is an important part of guest services in a hotel. A guest always hopes that the hotel he stays in can provide a simple and quality ticket booking service to eliminate subsequent worries. The attendant should book tickets like air tickets, steamer tickets, ride tickets, opera tickets, etc in accordance with the requirements of the guest, and if it is difficult for you to do so or the situation has changed, opinions of the guest must be solicited in time and let the guest decide what to do next.

商务中心是酒店前厅部的重要部门，酒店星级的高低，可以通过商务中心的服务来体现，级别越高，为客人提供的服务越具体，带给住客的商务服务越方便。基本而言，酒店的商务中心是能够为客人提供传真、复印、打印、国际国内长途直拨电话、邮件服务、国际互联网接入、特快专递、代购火车票机票等商务服务的岗位。商务中心文员最好要具备办公室秘书的技能，比如打字、帮人复印、代发传真等技能，以便能够方便、高效地为住客提供服务。

Business Center is an important sector of the Front Office, The star level of a hotel can be reflected in the services provided by the Business Center. The higher the star level, the more specific and convenient the services offered by Business Center. Basically, Business Center of a hotel is able to provide business services like faxing, copying, printing, international and domestic direct dial telephone, mail services, international Internet accessing, express mail and ticketing services. It is better for a Business Center clerk to possess office secretarial skills, such as typing, copying and faxing skills to conveniently and efficiently provide service for the guests.

一、复印、传真、打印和邮件服务（Copying，Faxing，Printing and Posting Services）

（一）复印服务（Copying Service）

复印服务是酒店商务中心提供的最基本的服务，同时，也是客人经常会选择的服务。商务中心在提供复印过程中，商务中心文员要严格按照规定为客人提供复印服务。如在服务过程中，要主动热情，在复印前要明确客人的要求，复印后，将客人的复印原件还给客人，同时要严格入账。表面看来，这是一项非常简单的工作，但是不可或缺。具体服务流程如下：

Copying service is the most basic service provided by the Business Center as well as a service frequently chosen by guests. Business Center clerks should provide copy services for guests in strict accordance with relevant provisions. For example, initiative enthusiasm is required in the service process. Before copying, clerks should make clear of the requirements of the guests. After copying, clerks should return guests the original and enter the item in an account strictly. On the surface, copying service is nothing but a very simple task, nevertheless, it is indispensable. Specific service process is as follows:

表 5-4 复印服务程序和标准

Table 5-4 Procedures and Standards for Copying Service

项目 Items	标准 Standards
1. 问候 Greetings	看到客人走入商务中心，马上放下手中的工作，面带微笑，起立问："早上好/中午好/晚上好，先生/女士，请问需要帮忙吗？" When a guest walks into the Business Center，put down the work immediately，stand up and ask with a smile："Good morning/Good noon/Good evening，Sir/Madam，what can I do for you?"
2. 询问 Inquiries	语气柔和，询问客人需要的服务项目，了解客人要求后重复以确认。 Inquiry guest about his or her needed service in a soft tone. Repeat guest's requirements for confirmation.
3. 报价 Quotation	（1）与客人确认复印数量及纸张需要，并报价。 Confirm the number of copies and paper size with guest and quote. （2）如果客人复印数量较多，征询客人意见是在商务中心等候还是复印好后送至房间。如果客人复印多套文件，询问客人是否需要将文件分别装订。 As for large quantity of copies，ask the guest whether he or she wants to wait at the Business Center or needs the copies to be delivered to his or her room after copying. When copying multiple sets of documents，ask guest whether the files need to be stapled separately.

续表

项 目 Items	标 准 Standards
4. 复印 Copy	(1) 开启复印机，选好纸张规格、浓度复印，调整复印机，以确保复印的文件干净、清晰。 Turn on the copier，select paper size and copy concentration，adjust the copier so as to ensure clean and clear copies. (2) 与客人确认复印纸张的尺寸（如 A3 或 A4）及件数。 Confirm paper size（such as A3 or A4）and quantity with the guest. (3) 复印后，检查一下复印的页数、浓淡程度，询问客人是否符合要求。 Check the number of copies and the copy concentration，then ask whether the guest is satisfied. (4) 复印完毕，取出复印原件交给客人，如原件是若干张，不要将顺序搞乱。 After copying，give the original to the guest in order（if the original has many sheets）. (5) 如果客人需要将复印好的文件送到房间，将文件放在大信封里，并打印好客人姓名及房号，由礼宾员送到客人房间。 If the guest requires the copied files be delivered to his or her room，put the files in a large envelope and print the guest's name and room number for the concierge staff to deliver. (6) 检查复印机内是否留有客人的原稿。 Check whether the original files are left in the copier. (7) 如是大量的复印，应先复印一份让客人确认效果。 As for large quantity of copies，copy one first and ask the guest whether it is satisfactory.
5. 检查装订 Check and staple	(1) 检查复印是否达到了客人要求的效果。 Check whether the copy meets the requirements of the guest. (2) 检查复印的数量、放大倍数是否与客人的要求一致。 Check whether the number and magnification are consistent with guest's request. (3) 根据客人的具体要求，分类装订好，并请客人复核认可。 Classify and staple the copies according to guest's specific requirements，and ask for guest's review and confirmation.
6. 结账 Payment	(1) 填写"复印单据"，清楚地写出服务项目以及所需费用。 Fill out service items and relevant charges in the Copy Bill clearly. (2) 如挂账，礼貌地请客人出示房卡，核对姓名、房号及能否挂账，并请其在账单上签字。 If the guest wants to sign the bill，politely ask him or her to show the Room Card，check that whether the name and room number are available for signature，and let the guest sign on the signature form. (3) 账单一式三联，开好后，将第二、第三联撕下，第二联交财务结账处，第三联交给客人，如客人不要，立即碎掉。 The bill is in triple sheets. Give the second sheet to the Financial Department for settlement and hand the third sheet to the guest. Tear up the third sheet immediately if the guest does not want to keep it. (4) 如付现金，客人需要开发票时，为客人开具正式发票。 When the guest asks for invoices for paying cash，issue official invoices.
7. 道别 Farewells	礼貌地与客人道别："欢迎您再次光临商务中心"，并目送客人离开。 Say goodbye to the guest politely："Welcome to the Business Center again，" and watch the guest leave.
8. 入账 Enter in an account	填写日报表，并及时将账单输入电脑。 Fill out the Daily Sheet，and timely enter bills into the computer.

（二）传真服务（Faxing Service）

传真服务也是酒店商务中心最基本的职能之一，在提供收发传真服务过程中，当收发完毕后，要和对方确认，是否收到传真，如果是接收传真，要给对方反馈接收到传真的页数和内容，确保收发传真的准确。当客人来到商务中心要求接收或发送传真时，接待员应根据服务规范向客人说明收费标准，并请客人确定收发传真的内容和要发送的国家、地区及传真号码等。

Faxing service is also one fundamental function of Business Center. After the faxes are sent out，confirm with the counterpart whether it has received the faxes. And after receiving faxes，give feedback to the counterpart about the pages and contents of the received fax to ensure the accuracy. When guests come to the Business Center to receive or send a fax，the receptionist should describe the fax charges according to service standards，and let guests confirm the contents，nation，region and fax number，etc.

1. 接收传真（Fax Receiving）

商务中心文员要根据客人需求，按照商务中心工作标准开展接收传真服务，在接收传真过程中，要认真阅读接收到的传真抬头与前厅确认收件人的姓名及房号，将接收“OK”报告单与来件放在一起，并做好记录，填写“商务中心日传真来报统计报表”，便于统计。如果在接收到传真后，遇到疑难来件应及时请示大堂副理，妥善处理查无此人的来件。具体服务流程如下：

Business Center clerks should provide fax receiving service in accordance with guests' needs as well as Business Center Work Standards. When receiving a fax, clerks should read the header of the received fax carefully, confirm the recipient's name and room number with the lobby, put reception "OK" reports together with incoming fax, make a record, and fill in the Sheet for Daily Incoming Faxes of Business Center for statistics. Once receiving intractable faxes, clerks should ask for instructions from Assistant Manager timely, and properly handle the unidentified incoming faxes. Specific service process is as follows:

表 5-5　接收传真工作标准

Table 5-5　Standards for Fax Receiving

项　目 Items	标　准 Standards
1. 收取 Receive	一般听到机器发出接收完毕信号后，就要注意收取传真，及时地将传真从传真机上取下，保证客人能够及时、准确地接收到传真。 Generally, on hearing the signal that the fax machine receives a fax, prepare to receive the fax and get it out of the machine in a timely manner, ensuring that the guests can receive prompt and accurate faxes.
2. 阅读 Read	(1) 传真接收完毕后，仔细核查传真页码及查看内容是否连贯。准确地记下客人的姓名及房号。 After receiving a fax, check the coherence of the fax pages and contents carefully. Write down the guest's name and Room No. accurately. (2) 同一时间前后接收两次传真，要注意是否连页，是否是给同一客人的。 As for two faxes received around the same time, pay attention to their pages, and make sure whether they are for the same guest.
3. 核实 Verify	(1) 查阅电脑，核实客人的姓名、房号。 Verify the guest's name and room number on computer. (2) 如文稿上没有房号的应在电脑中查找出。 Look for the room number on computer if it doesn't exist on the document.
4. 核实未果 Failed verification	(1) 确认传真的应接收人，如果住店客人中没有，要查询预抵和已离店客人的资料，查询电脑后未能找到客人，有传真号码的，应打电话与对方确认，或注明“查无此人，请重新确认”，并反传回去。 Confirm the recipient of the fax. If there is no such person among those who stay over in the hotel, look up information of guests who are about to arrive or have checked out. Once no such person can be found on the computer, call for confirmation if there is a fax number, or fax back marked with "no such person, please re-confirm". (2) 没有传真号码的，应在交班簿中注明并跟进，3 日后存入柜中，6 个月后销毁。 If there is no fax number, mark out in the shift book and follow up. Three days later, the fax will be stored in the cabinet and be destroyed six months later.
5. 标注 Remarks	(1) 核实无误的传真，将传真内容朝里折叠好，放入传真信封。 As for verified fax, fold the fax content inwards three times, and put it into a fax envelope. (2) 在信封上选择：“INCOMING FAX”。 Write on the envelope: "INCOMING FAX". (3) 用签字笔在信封上注明房间号码及客人姓名，并在信封右下角写明页数。 Room number and guest's name should be marked with sign pen on the envelope, and pages should be indicated in the lower right corner of the envelope.
6. 通知 Notice	(1) 致电客人房间：“您好，××先生/女士。这里是商务中心，收到您的传真，共×页，请问是帮您送到房间还是您方便的时候过来取？” Call the guest's room: "Hello, Mr./Ms××. This is the Business Center. We received your fax, × page (s). Would you like that we deliver it to your room or you come to fetch it when convenient?" (2) 向客人报价。 Offer quotation.

续表

项 目 Items	标 准 Standards
	(3) 客人同意付费后，问清客人的付费方式（挂账或付现金），查看能否挂账。 After the guest agrees to pay, ask about the payment method (signing a bill or in cash), and check whether the signing bill is available. (4) 填写"传真单据"，清楚地写出服务项目以及所需费用。 Fill out service items and relevant charges in the Fax Bill clearly. (5) 联系礼宾部将传真及"传真单据"送至客人房间并请客人在"传真单据"上签字，或存于商务中心等待客人亲自来取。 Contact the Concierge Department to send the fax and Fax Bill to the guest' s room and let the guest sign on the Fax Bill, or wait for guest to collect the fax. (6) 原则上不允许任何人代取传真，如客人坚持要代取，需打电话给收件人确认该客人是否能代取，并请代取人出示有效证件。 In principle, fax collection by anyone other than the recipient is not allowed. If the guest insists for fax collection by other people, call the recipient to confirm whether the guest is authorized, and let the guest present valid document.
7. 通知无人 No such person	房间电话无人接听，填写留言单："商务中心收到您的传真，共×页，请您在方便的时候给商务中心回电。"联系礼宾部将留言单送到客人房间，并在交班簿上做好记录。 If no one answers the phone, fill in a message note: "Business Centre received your fax, × page (s). Please call back when convenient". Contact Concierge Department to send the note to guest's room, and record on the shift book.
8. 入账 Enter in an account	填写接收传真控制表、日报表，并及时将收费传真的账单输入电脑。 Fill out Control Table and Daily Sheet for received faxes, and timely enter bills of charged faxes into computer.

2. 发送传真（Fax Sending）

（1）发送传真注意事项（Cautions）。发送传真前要认真查看客人提供的国家及地区代号，如不清楚，应立即询问客人；同时要向客人说明发传真的价格；如果客人的原稿较小或较薄时建议客人先将原稿复印，再将复印件发出，以免原件太小、太薄在传真的过程中被机器卡住而将原稿损坏；发送传真后，要填写"商务中心日发送传真报表"，以方便统计。

Cautions. Before fax sending, check the country and region code offered by the guest. If there is anything unclear, immediately ask the guest about it; at the same time, tell the guest the fax sending price; if the original is too small or a thin sheet, suggest the guest make copy for the original first, and then send the copy in afraid that the original is jammed and damaged in the machine due to size and thickness; After fax sending, fill in Daily Fax Sending Sheet of Business Center for statistics.

（2）传真计费方法（Fax Charging Method）。

国际收费标准：线路费 =（每分钟价格 + 0.2 元电信费）× 时间

附加费 = 线路费 × 70% + 纸张费　　总计 = 线路费 + 附加费

国内收费标准：线路费 =（每分钟价格 + 0.1 元电信费）× 时间

附加费 = 线路费 × 70% + 纸张费　　总计 = 线路费 + 附加费

International charging standard: circuit fees = (price per minute + RMB 0.2 Yuan of telecommunication fees) × time

Surcharge = circuit fees × 70% + paper costs

Total = circuit fees + surcharge

Domestic charging standard: circuit fees = (price per minute + RMB 0.1 Yuan of telecommunication fees) × time

Surcharge = circuit fees × 70% + paper costs

Total = circuit fees + surcharge

（3）发送传真服务流程（Procedures of Fax Sending Service）。

表 5-6 发送传真服务流程

Table 5-6 Procedures of Fax Sending Service

项 目 Items	标 准 Standards
1. 问候 Greetings	看到客人走入商务中心，应马上放下手中的工作，面带微笑，起立问："早上好/中午好/晚上好，先生/女士，请问需要帮忙吗?" When a guest walks into the Business Center, put down the work immediately, stand up and ask with a smile: "Good morning/Good noon/Good evening, Sir/Madam, what can I do for you?"
2. 询问 Inquiries	语气柔和，询问客人需要的服务项目，了解客人要求后，重复以获确认。 Inquiry guest about his or her needed service in a soft tone. Repeat guest's requirements for confirmation.
3. 报价 Quotation	发送传真是每页××元。 Fax sending is priced at RMB ×× Yuan/page.
4. 发送 Sending	(1) 在发送传真前，将传真的号码朗读出来，如有不清，立即询问，同时，记下客人所发传真的区域及号码。 Before fax sending, read the fax number out. For unclear numbers, ask the guest immediately. At the same time, write down the fax region and fax number that the guest sends for. (2) 将传真内容朝下发送。 Put the fax content downwards when sending. (3) 传真原稿较多时，需守在传真机旁，以免其他原因而导致原稿不能如数发出。 When the originals are numerous, wait beside the fax machine. (4) 保证传真顺利发出并把传真报告给客人看。 Ensure the success of fax sending and present guest with the fax report.
5. 发送失败 Unsuccessful sending	(1) 如果传真发送失败，将在发送报告上显示出来。 Unsuccessful sending will appear on the sending report. (2) 如果客人有疑义，等待发送报告打出，将发送报告出示给客人，征求客人的意见，询问是否需要重新发送，或更换其他号码发送。 If the guest has doubts, show guest the sending report, and ask whether the guest wants to resend, or replace for other number to send the fax. (3) 暂时发不出去时，应礼貌地向客人解释。若客人不急发，告诉客人发出后将把原件送回房间，请客人先签单；若是店外客人，应先付100%押金，将传真发了后通知客人来取。 When fax sending is temporarily unavailable due to crowded guests or line barrier, politely explain to the guests. If the guests are not in a hurry for sending, tell them the original will be delivered back to his or her room after sending, and let guests sign on the bill; 100% deposit is required for external guests, who will be informed to take the originals after the fax sending.
6. 结账 Payment	(1) 将传真发送完毕后，要将传真原件送回双手递送给客人。 After the fax sending, give back the original to the guest by hands. (2) 填写"杂项传票"，清楚地写出服务项目以及所需费用。 Fill out service items and relevant charges clearly on the Miscellaneous Summons. (3) 如挂账，礼貌地请客人出示房卡，核对姓名、房号及能否挂账，并请其在账单上签字。 If the guest wants to sign a bill, politely ask him or her to show the Room Card, check that whether the name and room number are available for signing bills, and let the guest sign on the bill. (4) 如付现金，客人需要开发票时，为客人开具正式发票。 When the guest asks for invoices for paying cash, issue official invoices.
7. 道别 Farewells	礼貌地与客人道别："欢迎您再次光临商务中心"，并目送客人离开。 Say goodbye to the guest politely: "Welcome to the Business Center again," and watch the guest leave.
8. 入账 Enter in an account	填写日报表，并及时将账单输入电脑。 Fill out Daily Sheet, and timely enter bills into the computer.

（4）受理店外客人发送传真流程（Procedures of Fax Sending for External Guests）。

表 5-7 受理店外客人发送传真流程
Table 5-7 Procedures of Fax Sending for External Guests

工作步骤 Work Steps	工作标准及要求 Work Standards and Requirements
1. 店外客人打电话要求收传真 External guests call for fax receiving service	(1)"您好！这里是商务中心的××在讲话，请问我能为您做什么？" "Hello! Here is ×× speaking from Business Center. What can I do for you?" (2) 向客人说明传真号码，并尽量在传真上注明收件人姓名，以便确认，并记下客人联系方式。 Tell guest the fax number, and ask him or her to detail the recipient's name on the fax so that we can confirm it. Write down the guest's contact information.
操作要点（Key operation points）： • 店外客人接受传真收费标准：××元/页。 External guests accept the fax charges: RMB ×× Yuan/page. • 店外客人来电话要求接收传真时：首先告诉客人酒店的传真号码，向客人说明收费标准。 When outside guests call for fax receiving service: firstly, tell hotel's fax number to the guests, and describe the fax charges as well.	
2. 收到传真后通知客人 Notify the guests upon the fax arrival	(1) 您好，先生，我们已经收到您的传真，一共是××页，对吗？ Hello, sir, we have received your fax, ×× pages, all right? (2)我们为您保留传真，请您在方便的时候来取。 We will keep the fax for you. Please fetch it when convenient.
操作要点（Key operation points）： • 如果长时间未收到应及时与客人联系，让客人了解情况，并告诉其他员工，随时关注传真动态。 Contact with the guests if you do not receive the fax after a long moment, and tell other staff to concern about this at any time.	
3. 客人来商务中心取传真 Guest comes to the Business Center for the fax	(1)您好，先生，请问您贵姓？×××先生，这是您的传真，请您查阅。 "Hello, sir, may I have your name?" Mr. ×××, this is your fax. Please have a look. (2)您的费用一共是××元，请问您是付现金还是刷卡？ RMB ×× Yuan in total. Would you like to pay in cash or by card?
操作要点（Key operation points）： • 客人如没有来取传真，将文件妥善收存，等客人来取。 Properly keep the fax until the guest comes for it. • 如果客人来取传真，向取件人询问姓名，确认无误后，开具付款凭证。 When the guest comes to fetch the fax, ask his or her name, and issue a payment voucher after confirmation.	

（三）打印服务（Printing Service）

打印服务包括替客人进行文字录入服务、文件打印服务等，在服务过程中，要和客人确定要打印的文本内容，了解客人要求及特殊格式的安排，看是否有看不清楚的地方或字符，有没有特殊的要求，同时，告知客人大概完成的时间，以确保打印服务顺利完成。同时，打印结束后，要询问客人是否存盘及保留时间，如不要求保留，则删除。具体服务流程如下：

Printing service refers to words inputting, document printing, etc. for the guests. Before printing, confirm with guest the textual content to be printed, ask about the requirements and special formats and look through the text to see whether there are unclear characters and particular requirements of the guest. At the same time, tell the guest about the time needed to print the file. After printing, ask the guest whether to archive the document and its retention time. If the guest doesn't require reservation, delete the file right away. Specific service procedures are as follows:

表 5-8 打印服务流程
Table 5-8 Printing Service Procedures

项 目 Items	标 准 Standards
1. 了解要求 Understand guest's requirements	仔细阅读客人需要打印的文件，不清楚的地方要与客人核实，然后按客人要求确定打印格式。 Read the document carefully, verify with the guest where is not clear, and then define the printing format as per guest's request.
2. 告知价格 Quote	(1) 向客人介绍有关价格。 Make an offer to the guest. (2) 告知客人大概完成时间，然后迅速、准确地按客人要求将文稿打印出来。 Tell the guest about the needed time, and then print the document quickly and accurately as requested.
3. 修改文件 Modify the document	客人需修改文件时，为其修改文件并打印出来，同时，请客人检查确认。 If the guest needs to modify the document, print the document after modification, and let the guest have a check.
4. 文件存盘 File the document	(1) 问清客人是否需保留该文件，如要保留，请其确认保留时间，一般对客人文档在电脑中保留一个月。 Ask the guest whether to keep the document. If he or she would like a reservation, verify the retention time with the guest. Generally speaking, a month of retention time kept in computer is available. (2) 如不要求保留，则删除该文件。 If the guest doesn't require reservation, delete the file.
5. 计费结账 Payment	同收银程序。 Same as checkout procedures.

(四) 邮件服务 (Posting Service)

1. 注意事项 (Cautions)

根据客人的需求，邮件服务也是商务中心提供的服务之一，在邮寄过程中，要注意：

Posting service is one of the services offered by Business Center as well. The matters needing attention are as follows:

(1) 准备不同面值的邮票，根据客人要求，出售所需面值、图案和数量的邮票。

Prepare stamps of different denominations. Sell stamps of required nominal values, designs and numbers to the guests.

(2) 每天早上与前厅交接昨晚或当日所收客人交寄的信件，核对邮票和信件是否相符。

Hand over letters to be posted that day or the day before that day to the Front Office every morning, and check whether the stamps and letters are consistent.

(3) 根据邮件大小、重量，所寄不同国家、省 (市)，贴足邮票。

Properly stamp subject to the post size, weight, countries and provinces.

(4) 对酒店内部所寄邮件，应按部门分类登记，做好原始记录，贴足所需邮票，记好邮资账，以备月底汇总报销。

As for internal posts, classify them on the basis of departments, take original records, have them stamped, and keep postage account to reimburse at the end of the month.

(5) 对于酒店客人所寄的重要邮件，如挂号信、快递、小包裹等，客人需亲自填委托单，并同客人核对所填内容，在确认地址、人名等无误后，请客人交足押金，方可寄出，并将邮局回执、收据复印件留底 (原件交客人)，以备查找。

As for important posts sent by guests, such as registered letters, couriers, small parcels, etc. the guests themselves need to fill in the Commission Sheet. Verify the address, name, etc. with the guests, after which let the guests pay the deposit before sending. Keep the return receipt and voucher copies (the originals being given to the guests) issued by Post Office for references against any subsequent problems.

（6）国外航空信件，应加盖航空字样的章；国内信件需要填好邮政编码。

Foreign airmails should be stamped with the words of aviation; as for domestic letters, help the guests find and fill out the zip code.

（7）当日所收邮件应在当日16：00前寄出，特殊邮件，应收后马上为客人寄出。

Send the incoming letters of that day before 16：00 on the same day. Special posts need to be sent upon receiving.

2. 邮件服务流程（Posting Service Procedures）

表5-9 邮件服务流程
Table 5-9 Post Service Procedures

程序 Procedures	标准 Standards
1. 告知服务 Introduce the service	（1）向客人介绍商务中心提供的邮件服务有平信、包裹、EMS； Introduce the posting service of ordinary mails，parcels and EMS; （2）告知客人，根据邮局规定，商务中心不受理易碎、易燃、易爆、有腐蚀性以及贵重物品的邮寄。 Let the guests informed that posts of fragile，flammable，explosive，corrosive and valuable items are beyond the scope of Business Center according to the provisions of Post Office.
2. 填写邮单 Fill out the mail sheet	（1）请客人在《专递邮件详情单》或《包裹详情单》上用正楷填清地址、国家、城市、代码和目的地，并要填写详尽，同时请客人在标有发件人姓名处签字。 Let guests fill in clear address，country，city，code and destination on the Express Mail Waybill or Parcel Waybill using regular script capitals as explicit as possible，and let guests sign his or her name at the place marked with "sender". （2）帮客人填上原寄局及交寄日期、时间，并签上经办人姓名。 Help guests fill in the original register office and posted date and time，and let the handler affix a signature.
3. 检查邮件 Check the posts	检查邮件是否为违寄物品（易燃、易爆或有毒物品等）。 Check whether the posts belong to contraband（flammable，explosive or toxic substances，etc.）.
4. 称重计价 Wright and price	（1）邮资秤秤好邮件重量以确定邮费。 Weigh the posts to calculate the postage. （2）资费用填在《专递邮件详情单》或《包裹详情单》相应位置。 Fill in postage at appropriate location on Express Mail Waybill or Parcel Waybill. （3）将《专递邮件详情单》第三联（寄件人存根联）交给客人。 Give the third sheet（sender stub sheet）of Express Mail Waybill to the guests.
5. 交接邮件 Hand over posts	（1）将邮件服务内容在"邮件服务交接本"上逐项填写。 Write down the post service contents on the Handover Book Concerning Post Service. （2）当邮局工作人员来酒店收取邮件时，请其确认邮件内容，并在"邮件服务交接本"上签字。 When Post Office staff come to collect posts，ask the postman to confirm the post contents，and sign on Shift Book Concerning Post Service. （3）请邮局工作人员在《包裹详情单》的相应位置签字，并将第一联留下转交给寄件人。 Ask the postman to sign on Parcel Waybill，and give the first sheet to the sender.

二、票务服务（Ticketing Service）

一般来说，酒店商务中心内还设立票务中心，提供机票、火车票等预订受理，极大地方便了客人的出行。通常，在票务服务中，商务中心文员要认真核对客人所要购票的信息，待购票成功后，及时将票送至客人手中，以满足客人的需求。

In Business Center，the guests can always find a Ticketing Center that offers reservation service of air tickets，train tickets，etc. While providing ticketing service，Business Center clerks should verify the ticket information carefully，and deliver tickets to the guest timely.

(一) 代购火车票服务 (Train Tickets)

1. 注意事项 (Cautions)

(1) 在客人委托订购火车票时，商务中心文员应问清客人要订的票务种类和信息，认真填写火车车次、目的地、票价、客人姓名、有效证件号码及联系方式等。

Business Center clerks should ask the guests for ticket type and information and fill in the train number, destination, fare, guest name, valid ID number and contact information carefully.

(2) 商务中心文员要按客人的要求及时到火车站、火车代售点联系或是在互联网上进行订票，确保及时订到票。

Business Center clerks should book ticket at train station, train ticket agency or online according to guest's requests in a timely manner.

(3) 送票员将票送到后，要仔细核对票面信息与订票单是否相符，尤其是发车日期，更要重点关注。

Have a careful check to see whether the coupon information is consistent with the booking form upon receiving the ticket. Special attention should be paid to the departure date.

(4) 商务中心文员通知客人携带证件（护照、身份证、出差证明或工作证）到商务中心取票，客人取票时，要将客人的证件审查清楚，请客人认真核对票上的日期、时间、车次等信息。

Business Center clerks should inform the guests to bring certificate (passport, identity card, proof of business travel or work permit) to get the ticket at Business Center. Review the certificate carefully, and let the guest check the date, time, train number and other information on the ticket.

2. 代购火车票流程 (Procedures of Purchasing Train Tickets)

表 5-10 代购火车票流程

Table 5-10 Procedures of Purchasing Train Tickets

项 目 Items	标 准 Standards
1. 问候 Greetings	看到客人走入商务中心，马上放下手中的工作，面带微笑，起立问：“早上好/中午好/晚上好，先生/女士，请问需要帮忙吗？” When a guest walks into the Business Center, put down the work immediately, stand up and ask with a smile: “Good morning/Good noon/Good evening, Sir/Madam, what can I do for you?”
2. 询问 Inquiries	语气柔和，询问客人需要的服务项目，了解客人要求后，仔细听清楚客人的订票要求，如目的地、张数、车次、日期等，等客人说完后，重复一遍以求得客人的确认。 Inquiry the guest about his or her needed service in a soft tone. Listen carefully to guest's booking requirements, such as destination, number of tickets, train numbers, dates, etc. Repeat guest's requirements for confirmation.
3. 查询报价 Quotation	(1) 为客人查询相关行程的火车票情况，并如实地告知客人订票需另加收手续费。如确认能按客人的要求购到票，则给客人肯定的回答，告知酒店代购火车票手续费的标准。 Look up ticket information, and tell guests about commission charges. If the ticket can be purchased as requested by the guests, give a promise to the guests, and tell him or her the standards of ticket purchasing charges at the same time. (2) 告知客人火车票可以开具铁路专用发票。 Let the guests know that railway special invoice can be issued. (3) 如不能确认，则请客人留下房号/联系电话和姓名，待查明后，再给客人答复。 If the ticket information can't be confirmed, take guests' room number/contact number and name in record. Give the guests a reply upon confirmation. (4) 查明有票后，马上致电话给客人，表示可以按其要求购票，告知酒店代购火车票手续费的标准，如客人确定要订购，请客人到商务中心交订金。 If there are available tickets, call the guests immediately and tell them the standards of ticket purchasing charges as well. If the guests are willing to order, ask the guests to pay the deposit at Business Center. (5) 如查明客人所要求购的车票已售完或其他原因，则也需快速致电客人向其说明原因，并给客人其他建议。 If the tickets have been sold out or if there are other problems, it is also required to call the guests to make explanation, and offer other recommendations.

续表

项　目 Items	标　准 Standards
4. 押金 Deposit	（1）商务中心文员拿出订金单（客票袋），逐项填写清楚，在预收一栏填上预收金额，把白联给客人，叮嘱客人一定要凭订金单白联拿票，交的订金多退少补。 Business Center clerks should fill out the Deposit List（Ticket Pocket） clearly. Write down the amount in the column of advance payments，hand the guests the white sheet，and notify them that they are unable to get the ticket without that white sheet. As for the paid deposit，return the overcharge and demand payment of the shortage. （2）给客人开具的押金收据在上面写清楚订票时间、行程、手续费的费用等，并请客人在押金收据上签字。 Clear booking time，travel route，charges and guests' signature should be included on the deposit receipt.
5. 订票 Ticket booking	（1）征得客人同意后，给火车票代理打电话，并确认送票时间，快捷、细致、准确地为客人订好火车票。 After obtaining the consent of the guests，call the train agency and confirm the ticket delivery time，providing a fast，considerate and accurate ticketing service for the guests. （2）告知客人票到后打电话取票。 Tell guests the Business Center will make a call to him or her to fetch the ticket after ticket arrival. （3）如票务员在外购票，联系票务员告诉其客人已交订金，票务员接到客人订票通知或商务中心文员的通知，并确认客人已在商务中心交了订金后，应马上到相关地方购票，并立刻返回酒店。 Contact to tell the ticket agent that the guest has paid the deposit if the ticket agent is out of the hotel. Ticket agent should purchase the tickets at once upon notice of guest tickets booking or Business Center clerk as well as confirm that the guest has paid the deposit，and return to the hotel immediately. （4）在购票过程如有突发情况，如没有客人所要求的软卧，应马上征得客人意见，并按客人的要求购票。 Immediately contact with the guest for decision when unforeseen circumstances rise in the purchase process，such as there is no soft-seat required by the guest.
6. 通知 Notice	（1）火车票送到后，商务中心文员致电客人，征求客人意见是把票送到客人房间还是客人亲自来取。 Upon the ticket arrival，Business Center clerk should call the guest，and ask whether to deliver the ticket to his or her room or the guest fetches the ticket him or herself. （2）商务中心文员凭订金单给客人拿票，并视票面价给客人多退少补。 Business Center clerk should give guest the ticket based on the Deposit List，and return the overcharge and demand payment of the shortage subject to the par value. （3）开具商务中心收费单据按标准收取手续费，并请票务员签名后入账。 Issue receipt of the Business Center，charge commissions in accordance with relevant standards，and ask ticket agent to sign for account making. （4）如客人要求送票至房间，则由礼宾员代办。 Let concierge delivery the ticket to guest' room if the guest asks so.
7. 道别 Farewells	（1）客人拿到票后，请客人核对火车票。可以询问客人是否需要帮助协调延时退房 1~2 小时（看票面的发车时间而定）。 Let guest have a check of the ticket，and ask whether he or she needs to delay 1-2 hours to check out（dependent on the departure time on the ticket）. （2）礼貌地与客人道别，并目送客人离开。 Say goodbye to the guest politely，and watch the guest leave.

（二）代购机票服务（Air Tickets）

1. 注意事项（Cautions）

（1）在客人委托订购机票时，商务中心文员应问清客人要订的票务信息，认真填写机票航班时刻、目的地、票价、客人姓名、有效身份证件号码及联系方式等。

Business Center clerks should ask the guests for ticket information，such as flight schedule，destination，fare，guest name，valid ID number and contact information，etc.

（2）商务中心文员要按客人的要求及时与航空公司联系，进行订票，确保及时订到票。

Business Center clerks should contact with the airline promptly for booking according to guests' requests.

（3）送票员将票送到后，要仔细核对票面信息与订票单是否相符，尤其是航班起飞时间、航班班次等，更要重点关注。

Have a careful check to see whether the coupon information is consistent with the booking form upon receiving the ticket. Special attention should be paid to departure time, flight number, etc.

（4）商务中心文员通知客人携带证件（护照、身份证、出差证明或工作证）到商务中心取票，客人取票时，要将客人的证件审查清楚，请客人认真核对航班起飞时间、航班班次等信息。

Business Center clerks should inform the guests to bring certificate (passport, identity card, proof of business travel or work permit) to get the ticket at Business Center. Review the certificate carefully, and let the guest check the departure time, flight number and other information on the ticket.

2. 代购机票服务流程（Procedures of Purchasing Air Tickets）

表 5-11　代购机票服务流程

Table 5-11　Procedures of Purchasing Air Tickets

项　目 Items	标　准 Standards
1. 问候 Greetings	看到客人走入商务中心，马上放下手中的工作，面带微笑，起立问："早上好/中午好/晚上好，先生/女士，请问需要帮忙吗?" When a guest walks into the Business Center, put down the work immediately, stand up and ask with a smile: "Good morning/Good noon/Good evening, Sir/Madam, what can I do for you?"
2. 询问 Inquiries	语气柔和，询问客人需要的服务项目，请客人填写委托单，写清客人要订的航班、到达地点、所乘的舱位（头等、公务、普通），重复以获确认。 Inquiry guest about his or her needed service in a soft tone. Ask the guest to write clear flight, destination and seat type (First Class, Business Class, Economy Class) on the commission order. Repeat the above information for confirmation.
3. 查询报价 Quotation	为客人查询相关航段的机票情况，并如实告知客人所需舱位的价格。 Look for ticket information in the required leg for the guest, and tell guest the actual ticket price of the wanted class.
4. 订票 Ticket booking	(1) 快捷、细致、准确地为客人打印出所需的机票。 Provide fast, considerate and accurate ticket printing service for the guests. (2) 请客人认真核查机票的名字、有效证件号码是否正确。 Let guests check the name and valid ID number on the ticket. (3) 为使客人出行方便，把带有天气预报的温情提示卡交给客人。 Offer guests a Tip Card with weather forecast on to ease their travel.
5. 结账 Payment	(1) 如果客人付现金，直接把票款给票务人员，不用填写订票单据。 If guests pay in cash, give the money to the ticket agent directly without filling in the Ticket Order. (2) 如果房间押金充足也可以挂房账，填写"订票单据"，清楚地写出服务项目以及所需费用并请客人签字。 If the room deposit is adequate, the fares can be charged to the room. Write clear service item and charges on the Ticket Order and ask guests to sign on it. (3) 如果客人刷卡，国内和国际卡到前台刷卡，需要商务中心人员事先记录卡号，卡单共三联，客人留存联给客人，商户存根联请客人签字不给客人，此联（相当于现金）晚上投款，结算总计单订账单上。 If guests choose to brush card, domestic and international card can be brushed at the Front Desk. Before that, Business Center staff should record the card number. The sheet is in triple sheets, of which sheet for the guests to keep should be given to the guests, and sheet for the merchants to keep (equal to cash) should be signed by the guests for settlement in the evening.
6. 道别 Farewells	(1) 客人拿到票后，请客人核对飞机票上面的信息。 Let guests check the information on the ticket. (2) 礼貌地与客人道别，并目送客人离开。 Say goodbye to the guest politely, and watch the guest leave.
7. 入账 Enter in an account	(1) 晚间票务人员会把全天的票款金额交给商务中心人员。 Ticket agent will hand over the total fare amount of the day to Business Center staff in the evening. (2) 商务中心人员会把所有票款金额数量输入系统。 Business Center staff will enter all the amount into system. (3) 第二天早班把报表交给财务部。 The statement will be delivered to the Finance Department at morning shift on the next day.

【实训与评价】【Training and Assessment】

［实训目的］［Training Goals］

1. 熟悉前厅票务服务的相关知识。

Be familiar with related knowledge about ticketing services of the Front Office.

2. 能够处理前厅在票务服务过程中出现的问题。

Be competent to deal with the problems happened when the Front Office is providing ticketing services.

3. 规范自己的言行，正确使用礼貌用语和敬语；能有礼有节、不卑不亢地处理突发事件。

Regulate words and deeds, use courtesy and honorific appropriately; be competent to handle sudden events decently.

［实训准备］［Training Preparation］

1. 前厅服务模拟场景、电脑、打印机、值班记录簿、机票等。

Simulation scenarios, computers, printers, notebooks, air tickets, etc. used to provide Front Office services.

2. 学生 6 人分为一组，教师讲解示范后，学生根据教师布置的任务进行实际操作。

Divide the students into group of six persons, and after interpretation and demonstration by the teacher, the students conduct actual operation according to the tasks assigned by the teacher.

［实训方法］［Training Method］

先观看教师播放的教学课件，然后由教师引导学生分析案例，学生 6 人一组，按照任务驱动的要求进行实际操作，教师巡回指导，实训结束前抽小组进行前厅服务模拟表演。

Watch the teaching courseware first and then the students analyze the case led by the teacher. Six students in one group conduct actual operation based on Task -Driven Questions, and the teacher is responsible for guidance. Before the end of the training, select one group to conduct simulation performance of Front Office services.

［实训步骤］［Training Procedure］

第一步：教师向学生展示票务服务的视频，让学生有一定的感性认识。

The teacher plays students the video of ticketing service, giving the students certain perceptual knowledge.

第二步：学生分成四人一组讨论，由学生分析，指出正误。

Divide the students into groups of 4 to discuss and analyze the video, pointing out what is right and wrong.

第三步：由学生继续讨论，设计票务服务的工作程序。

Continue the discussion and design the working procedures of ticketing service.

第四步：各组学生代表发言说出程序，其他各组学生评价。

Representative of each group explains the procedures and other groups present their evaluation.

第五步：学生分成两人一组，进行前厅票务服务的实训。

Divide the students into groups of 2 to conduct Front Office ticketing service training.

第六步：教师评价与回答问题。

The teacher gives evaluation and answers questions.

［实训操作］［Training Operation］

由学生分成两人一组，进行前厅票务服务的模拟练习。

Divide the students into groups of 2 to conduct simulation exercise of Front Office ticketing services.

1. 学生两人一组，模仿标准进行实训，教师给出评判。

Divide the students into groups of 2 to conduct the training by imitating the standards, and the gives corresponding evaluation.

2. 学生可以即兴发挥，老师和学生共同评价，老师给出分数。

The students can extemporaneously play, the teacher and other students give a joint evaluation, and the teacher a score.

3. 学生提出问题，老师回答。

The teacher answers questions of the students.

4. 填写实训报告，实训结束。

Fill in the training report, the training ends.

［实训评价］［Training Evaluation］

1. 能够掌握关于火车票、飞机票以及汽车票等的基本知识。

Master basic knowledge about tickets like train tickets, air tickets and bus tickets.

2. 完整地为客人提供票务服务。

Provide complete ticketing services for the guests.

3. 妥善解决票务服务程序中出现的各种问题。

Properly handle all kinds of problems happened when providing ticketing services.

【案例】【Case】

传真未及时收到
An Overdue Fax

三亚亚龙湾海景国际度假酒店的一位经商的住客弗兰克先生，一天下午 14：45 来到商务中心，告诉早班服务员陈小姐 15：15 将有一份发给他的加急传真，请收到后立即派人送到他房间或通知他来商务中心领取。15：15 这份传真发到了商务中心。15：10 时，中班小张已经上班，15：15 时早班陈小姐正向小张交代刚接收到的一份紧急文件的打印要求，并告诉她有一份传真要立即给客人送去，然后按时下班。恰巧在这时，有一位商务客人手持一份急用的重要资料要求打印，并向张小姐交代打印要求；此时又有一位早上打印过资料的客人因为对打印质量不满而向小张交代修改要求。忙乱之中，小张在 15：40 才通知行李员把传真给弗兰克先生送去。弗兰克先生拒绝收传真。他手指传真说因为酒店商务中心延误了他的传真使他损失了一笔大生意，并立即向大堂副理吴先生投诉。大堂副理吴先生看到发来的传真内容是：如果下午 15：30 没有收到弗兰克先生发回的传真，就视作弗兰克不同意双方上次谈妥的条件而中止这次交易，另找买主。弗兰克自称为此损失了 3 万美元的利润，要求酒店或者赔偿他的损失，或者开除责任人。

Mr. Frank, a business man, once resided in Sanya Yalong Bay Seaview International Resort Hotel. One day, at 14:45 he came to the Business Center and told the morning-shift waitress Miss Chen that there would be an urgent fax to him at 15:15 and he also told the waitress to send the fax to him or inform him to come to collect it immediately after receiving the fax. The middle-shift waitress Xiao Zhang was on duty at 15:10. At 15:15 Miss Chen was telling Xiao Zhang the printing requirements of the urgent fax she received and stressing that the fax should be sent to the guest immediately. Then Miss Chen got off work on time. Happen to be in at that moment, a business guest came with an urgent and important document to be printed, and told Miss Zhang the printing requirements; at that time, another guest who had printed a document but was unsatisfactory about the quality so the guest asked the Xiao Zhang to reprint it according to his requirements. In such a hurry, Xiao Zhang notified the bellboy to send the fax to Mr. Frank at 15:40, which was refused by Mr. Frank. He said that overdue fax from the Business Center caused him a big loss, and he immediately complained to the Assistant Manager. The Assistant manager Mr. Wu saw the content of the fax: if the fax sent back by Mr. Frank is not received before 15: 30, it will be deemed that Mr. Frank disagrees with the negotiated conditions last time and the deal will be suspended. We will find other buyers. Frank claimed that the overdue fax cause him a loss of $30000 in profit and demanded compensation for his loss from the hotel, otherwise the hotel must dismiss the responsible person.

问题：大堂经理吴先生应当怎样处理这件事？

Question: What should the Assistant Manager Mr. Wu do to deal with this event?

[案例提示] [Case Clew]

大堂经理吴先生可以采取的做法有以下几种：

Actions may be taken by the Assistant Manager Mr. Wu are as follows:

1. 按照客人的要求，酒店全额赔偿 3 万美元或至少赔偿 1 万美元。这一做法酒店的损失太大，不能考虑，更何况客人所报的损失也许有虚假成分。

The hotel makes a full compensation of $30000 or at least $10000 as required by the guest. But it is of the question because it a big loss for the hotel. What's more, the loss claimed by the guest might be larger than the actual loss.

2. 经弗兰克同意并指点，由酒店管理人员直接发传真到与弗兰克交易的公司，说明弗兰克未能及时回传真的责任在酒店，请求对方按双方原定的条件进行交易。这种方法可以试一试，但是成功的希望不是很大。

Subject to consent and guidance Frank, the hotel management personnel fax directly to the trading company with Frank to explain that the hotel assumes all the responsibility for the delay and ask the company to make a deal with Frank according to the original conditions. This method can be tried, but there is little hope to success.

3. 按照弗兰克的要求开除商务中心陈小姐、张小姐两位员工。这一做法过于严厉，虽然能够满足客人，但是会沉重地打击员工的工作积极性，非到万不得已，不应采用。

Dismissal Miss Chen and Miss Zhang as the Frank required. Although this approach can satisfy the guest, it is too harsh for the employees which will hurt the work enthusiasm of employees and should only be used when there are no other alternatives.

4. 由酒店总经理或副总经理出面向客人道歉，承认酒店的过错，对客人住店费用酌情予以减免，并送上鲜花、水果及其他一些礼品。告诉客人两位员工责任很大，但是还不至于开除。请求客人同意给予她们留店查看的处分并让她们承担一部分经济损失（例如扣发半年的奖金）以补偿弗兰克先生，并让她们当面向弗兰克先生道歉请求原谅。

The General Manager or the Deputy General Manager apologizes to the guest in person to admit the hotel's fault, reduce the hotel charges appropriately and send him flowers, fruits and other gifts. Explain to the guest that the two guests assume most of the responsibility but they do not deserve to be fired. Request the guest agrees to give them a warning and an economic punishment (such as withholding their bonus of half a year) to compensate for Mr. Frank, and ask them apology to Mr. Frank face to face.

这一方法勉强可行，如果客人不是太不通情达理的人，应该能够接收。当然如果能想到其他可能让客人满意的方法，也不妨一试。通过这件事，应当给酒店带来以下启示：

If the guest is a reasonable people, this approach might be feasible. Of course, other available satisfactory methods might be tried as well. The hotel should learn the following lesson from this case:

1. 酒店平时应当加强对员工的培训，使员工熟练掌握服务技能和技巧，以提高员工的服务效率。在工作忙时，也应当分清轻重缓急，做到忙而不乱，有条不紊。

The hotel should strengthen the training of employees at ordinary times to make employees familiar with service skills and techniques so as to improve the service efficiency. When it is busy, the staff should sets priorities, stays calm and do first thing first.

2. 员工在交接班时很容易出现差错，应当特别小心，要做到工作日志和口头双重交接，以避免出现差错。

Mistakes often happened when shifting duty, to which much attention should be paid. Both work diary and oral handover should be conducted to avoid any mistakes.

3. 如果员工一时忙不过来，可以向上级或同事求援，其他员工应尽量帮忙。

If a certain employee is too busy to deal with all the matters, ask superiors or colleagues for help, and other staff should try to give a hand.

4. 对各种违纪现象的处理应当在员工手册中有明确具体的体现，以使员工少犯错误，也便于在出现问题需要处理员工时有章可循。

Methods to deal with various discipline phenomena should be specified in the Employee Handbook, so as to bind the employees, and it also will make punishment of employees rules-based when it is necessary.

模块小结

Module Summary

1. 熟练掌握总机服务的基本知识及总机各项业务的程序与标准。

Be familiar with basic knowledge related to the Switchboard services and procedures and standards of various businesses about the Switchboard.

2. 能够熟练操作复印机、打印机、传真机、多功能打字机、装订机、碎纸机等办公设备。

Be competent to skillfully operate copiers, printers, fax machines, multi-function typewriter, binding machines, shredders and other office equipment.

3. 能够根据标准和程序，向商务客人提供传真收发服务、电子文件、打印、复印与装订服务。

Be competent to provide business guests with fax sending and receiving services, printing, copying and binding services of electronic files according to relevant standards and procedures.

4. 能够根据标准和程序，为客人提供票务服务。

Be competent to provide guests with ticketing service according to relevant standards and procedures.

模块六 住客关系
Module XI Guest Relations

【情境导入】【Scenario Introduction】

发票事件
Invoice Event

三亚海航铂爵公馆是海南省海航集团下属单位，开据的发票是从省地税局购买的，省地税局2009年的发票没有改版，而其他酒店用的都是三亚市地税局的发票，市地税局的发票在2009年都换成带防伪条码的发票，所以一段时间以来，不断有客人前来投诉或打电话询问发票问题。

As a subordinate unit of HNA Group，SanyaHaihang Earl Mansion purchases invoice from the Provincial Local Taxation Bureau which is the originalvision，while those purchased by other hotels are issued by Sanya Local Taxation Bureau with the anti-counterfeitcodeadded in 2009，which leads to uninterrupted complaints or inquiries from guests.

一日，李经理在酒店中餐收银台值班，在值班过程中，收银员接到外线电话，语气非常难听："你们那是什么破发票，在网上查都查不到，你们知不知道给我造成多大的损失，现在我们公司都以为我拿假发票套钱，你们要给我恢复名誉，否则我就告你们去。"当值收银员听到这里马上感到问题很严重，但由于在日常培训中已做过这方面的培训，所以并没有慌张，而是静下心来耐心听完客人的陈述，对客人进行安抚："先生，您先别生气，您是在三亚地税网站查的吧，我们这里的发票是省地税局的，您在省地税的网站上就可以查到了，如果方便，您记一下网址和电话好吗？网址是×××，进入后点击'发票流向查询'，输入发票代码和号码。查询电话号码是×××××××××，如果您还有疑问，请致电×××××××××，咨询负责发票管理的会计，好吗？"但由于客人非常愤怒，根本不听收银员的解释，而是要求财务负责人给他解释，并且很无礼地说道，这是名誉损失，如果他下班之前没接到答复就要去媒体投诉！收银员很无奈地记下电话再次给客人道歉，并说他们会尽一切办法给予客人答复。

One day，Manager Li was on duty at the Chinese meal cashier. In the course of duty，the cashier received an offensive call："What is wrong with your invoice？I couldn't check it on the Internet.Your fake invoice has caused much damage to me. Now all staff thinks that I angles for money out of fake invoice. You should restore my reputation，or else I'll take actions." The cashier on duty sensed the seriousness of the problem，but since he had received daily training on this aspect，he showed no panic，but listened patiently to the statement of the guests and tried to ease his mood："Sir，please don't get angry. Did you check it on the website of Sanya Local Taxation Bureau？Our invoice is issued by Provincial Local Taxation Bureau. The website is ×××. Click 'invoice query' and enter the invoice code and number after entering the website. The contact number is ×××××××××. If you have any questions，please call the account being responsible for invoice management at ×××××××××, okay?" However, since the guest was so angry that he did not listen to the cashier's explanation but required chief financial officer to explain to him. In addition, he said in a rude tone that such a thing had caused loss of reputation for him. If he didn't receive a reply before getting offwork, he would make a complaint to the media! Xiao Wang had no choice but to write down his phone number and apologize to the guests again, saying that they will give a reply by all means.

收银员把事情反映给李经理后，李经理首先就事情的经过做了一个了解，确认了客人在酒店消费的时间、地点及开票金额，在确认开票属实后，把这个事情向财务负责人做了汇报并请示了领导答复客人的方式。得到领导首肯后，李经理拨打了客人留下的电话，在报明来意后客人还是很愤怒，但鉴于酒店对此事的重视，客人说道，"你们开的发票我们公司在网上查不到，财务的人以为我拿的是假发票，你说这对我的名誉是多大的损失!"李经理首先向客人解释了发票的情况，保证只要是该酒店开出的发票绝对不会假，并再次告知客人查询方式和查询电话！客人听到这里语气已经缓和很多，但要求酒店打电话给他们的财务部门说明情况。为了完善酒店的服务，体现酒店的形象，只要是客人合理合法的要求作为服务业从业者就要给予满意的答复。李经理拨通了客人公司财务部的电话，告知发票的查询方式，表示如果需要其他证明，酒店可以提供。几分钟后，财务确认发票真实有效。

The cashier reported this matter to Manager Li. Manager Li first acquainted himself of the whole thing and then confirmed the time, room and invoiced amount of the guest. After confirming the validity of the invoice, he reported such matter to the chief financial officer and consulted with the leader for the way of reply. After being approved by the leader, Manager Li made a call to the guest. The guest was angry after hearing his reply, but considering that the hotel paid attention to this matter, the guest said, " Our Company couldn't check out your invoice on the internet. The Financial Department thought that it was a fake invoice. This is a great damage to my reputation!" After making a brief introduction to the invoice, Manager Li guaranteed to the guest that the invoice was true and genuine and told him of the query method and the contact phone. The guest eased his mood after hearing this, but asked the hotel to make an explanation to the Financial Department. In order to improve our service and image, we would try out utmost to give a satisfactory reply to the reasonable requirement of the guest. Manger Li called the Financial Departmentand told it of the query method, adding that the hotel would provide other necessary proof. A few minutes later, the Financial Department certified the effectiveness of the invoice.

事后李经理再次拨通了投诉客人的电话来说明情况，客人对酒店的服务表示认可，也对前期的态度表达了歉意，表示以后还会到该酒店消费。

After that, Manager Li made another call to the guest to explain the situation. The guest praised our services, apologized for his attitude and said that he would patronize our hotel.

通过这件事情，客人确实成为了酒店的常客，并在后期与公司签署了挂账协议，给酒店留住了一位长期消费客户。

Since then, the guest becomes our regular guestand signs credit account agreement with the company, helping us to retain a long-term consumer.

【情境分析】【Scenario Analysis】

上述案例说明，客人投诉无小事，虽然有时明知是客人不对，可以不必理会，但作为服务行业这是行不通的，在酒店行业竞争日益激烈的今天，多留住一个客源，或是一个潜在的客户，无疑也会提升酒店的竞争力，您认为呢？

The above case illustrates that guest complaint is no small matter. Though sometimes it is the guest's wrong, which could be ignored, but it is not acceptable for the service industry. In today's increasingly competitive hotel industry, one more guest or potential guest will undoubtedly enhance the competitiveness of the hotel, do you think so?

我们正生活在服务经济时代，服务已渗透到生活中的诸多细节，每个人既是享受服务的“客户”，又是为“客户”提供服务的个体。客户享受服务的经历多了，对酒店的客户服务质量自然会有更高的期待，这就给酒店的客户服务质量管理不断提出更高的要求。客户服务质量是一个管理的过程。客户服务质量的管理要以客户的需求为基础、为中心、为出发点，要以酒店的策略为条件，最终要以客户的感受为结果。

In the era of service economy, service has penetrated into almost all aspects of life. We are both "guests" enjoying services and individuals providing services for "guests". Guest will naturally have higher expectations on the service quality of the hotel with the increase of their experiences, which puts forward higher requirements on the hotel's guest service quality management. Guest service quality is a management process based and centered on guests' needs which is also the starting point of the hotel. The hotel should draw up policies to cater for guests' feelings in the process of management.

【学习目标】【Learning Goals】

［知识目标］［Knowledge Objectives］

1. 掌握构建客史档案的意义、客史档案的基本内容、客史档案的建立流程和管理。

To grasp the significance of establishing guest history file, the basic content of guest history file, the establishing processes and management of guest history file.

2. 掌握酒店客人投诉的基本类型、投诉处理的原则及处理投诉的程序。

To master the basic types of guest complaints, complaints handling principles, and procedures for handling complaints.

［能力目标］［Capacity Objectives］

1. 能熟练地建立客人的客史档案。

To establish guest history file skillfully.

2. 能够熟练地对顾客投诉进行处理，确保客人的投诉能够得到有效回应。

To handle guest complaints skillfully to ensure an effective response to guest's complaints.

【重点和难点】【Key Points and Difficulties】

1. 客史档案的建立和管理流程。

The establishment and management processes of guest history file.

2. 高效处理顾客投诉。

Efficient handling of guest's complaints.

任务一 构建客史档案

Task I Establishment of Guest history file

【情境导入】【Scenario Introduction】

洗发液带来的满足

Satisfaction Brought by Shampoo

一位企业经营者在东京投宿某家酒店，由于他习惯使用某一特定品牌的洗发液，于是就要求前台给他更换浴室里洗发液的品牌。这一要求被迅速地满足了。

A business man checked in a hotel in Tokyo. Since he is used to use a particular brand of shampoo, he asked the front desk to change the shampoo in the bathroom. His request was satisfied without any hesitation.

一个偶然的机会，这位客人到纽约出差。出于上次的体验，他习惯性地来到那家酒店在纽约的连锁店。令他惊奇的是，当他来到房间时发现浴室的洗发液正是上次他要求更换的品牌。这使他由衷地产生一种受尊重的感激之情。从此以后，他每到外地，首选酒店就是该酒店的连锁店。

Occasionally, he went to New York for official business. Due to his past experience, he habitually went to the chain hotel in New York. To his surprise, the shampoo in the bathroom is right what he want. His heart felt gratitude for being respected aroused in him. Since then, he would make the chain hotel as his first choice each time he travels to foreign lands.

【情境分析】【Scenario Analysis】

这家酒店将每位曾经住宿过的客人资料都用计算机存档，把顾客的每一个小小的要求都记录在客史档案中并传输给连锁酒店。通过这种方式，这家酒店集团成功地吸引了一大批稳定的客源。

This hotel records guest data in the computer and even records guests' little requirements in guest history file and transfers them to the chain hotel. In this way, this hotel successfully attracts a batch of long-term guests.

建议酒店对住店客人的基本情况、消费行为、信用状况和特殊要求记录在案，建立客史档案，这是酒店促进销售的重要工具，也是酒店改善经营管理和提高服务质量的必要资料。

The hotel is recommended to record the basic situation, consumer behavior, credit status and special requirements on record and to establish guest history file, which is an important tool to promote the sale of the hotel and also the essential material for the hotel to improve management and service quality.

为了更好地为客人提供服务，酒店对每一位入住客人的信息进行储存，以便为客人下次入住时提供更加个性化、更加完美的服务。这就需要建立客史档案。

In order to better serve the guests, the hotel will record the information for all guests to provide personalized and more perfect service when they check in the next time. This requires the establishment of guest history file.

一、建立客史档案的意义（Significance of the Establishment of Guest History File）

客史档案记录了酒店所需的有关客人的主要资料，包括客人的常规档案、消费特征档案、个性档案及反馈意见档案等信息，可供酒店分析客源市场状况，客人消费项目及能力情况，是酒店研究客人心理、提高酒店的销售能力及服务的针对性的主要依据。建立客史档案对提高酒店服务质量、改善酒店经营管理水平具有重要意义。

Guest history file records the essential information about relevant guests, including guests' routine file, consumption characteristics file, personality file, feedback file and other information for the hotel to analyze guest market conditions, consumption items and abilities. It is the main basis for the hotel to study guest psychology, improve sales capabilities and determine the target of services. The establishment of guest history file plays a significant role in improving the service quality and management level of hotel.

（一）增强酒店的创新能力（Enhancing the Innovative Capacity of Hotel）

酒店产品体系的创新是酒店的生命力所在，而客史档案的科学建立和运用是提升酒店创新能力的基础。通过客史档案的管理和应用，酒店能够及时掌握顾客消费需求的变化，适时地调整服务项目，不断推陈出新，确保持续不断地向市场提供具有针对性、有吸引力的新产品，满足顾客求新、求奇、求特色的消费需要。另外，当每一批顾客到店消费后，不论在哪里，总会有他自己的满意与不满之处，他们的赞扬与不满或者建议，对于改进酒店的不足，发扬他们的优点，有很大的督促作用。

The innovation of product system determines the vitality of hotel. The establishment and scientific use of guest history file is the basis for the enhancement of innovation capacity of hotel. Through the management and application of guest history file, hotel can grasp the changes in guest consumption demand, make timely adjustment on service items and make continuous innovation to provide the market with relevant and attractive new products so as to meet guests' new, odd and distinctive consumption needs. In addition, guests will have their satisfaction and dissatisfaction wherever they go. Their praise and dissatisfaction or suggestion is a great urge for the hotel to overcome their weakness and carry forward their strong points.

（二）提升酒店的服务品质（Improving the Service Quality of Hotel）

客史档案是酒店客户关系管理系统和客户忠诚系统的组合平台，一方面，客户关系管理系统的作用就在于通过对客户信息的深入分析，能够全面了解客户的爱好和个性化需要，开发出“量身定制”的产品，使服务更具人情味，最终达到提高客人满意度和扩大市场占有率的目的；另一方面，客户忠诚系统的作用则体现在通过个性化服务和一系列酒店与客户间“一对一”的情感沟通，客户对酒店会产生信任感，认为在此消费比其他地方更可靠、更安全、更有尊严感，顾客满意将升华为顾客忠诚，酒店服务的品质会得到客户进一步的认同。

Guest history file is a combination platform for guest relationship management system and guest loyalty system. On the one hand, the role of guest relationship management system is to fully understand guest preferences and individual needs through an in-depth analysis of guest information to develop “tailor-made” products, provide personalized services, and ultimately improve guest satisfaction and expand market share; on the other hand, the role of guest loyalty system is that guests will have a sense of trust to hotel and consider it more reliable, safe and respectful than elsewhere through personalized services and a series of “one to one” emotion communication between hotel and guests. Thus, guest satisfaction will be elevated to guest loyalty. The service quality of hotel will gain further recognition of guests.

（三）提高酒店经营效益（Boosting the Operational Effectiveness of Hotel）

客史档案的科学运用将有助于酒店培养一大批忠诚顾客，让更多的忠诚顾客带来更多的顾客，一方面可以降低酒店开拓新市场的压力和投入，另一方面由于忠诚客户对酒店产品、服务环境熟悉，具有信任感，因此他们的综合消费支出也就相应比新客户更高，而且客户忠诚度越高，保持忠诚的时间越长，酒店的效益也就越好。要知道，维护好一个老顾客将会比开发一个新客户提高几倍的利润。

The scientific use of guest history file will be conductive to the cultivation of a batch of loyal guests. Loyal guests will bring more guests for hotel. One the one hand, it reduces the pressure and investment of the hotel to open up new markets; on the other hand, since loyal guests are familiar with products and service environment and have a sense of trust to the hotel, so their comprehensive consumption expenditure is correspondingly higher than new guests. Furthermore, the higher the loyalty degree is, the longer the time to remain loyal will be, so will be the effectiveness of hotel. Old guests will bring several times profits than new guests.

（四）提高酒店工作效率（Raising the Working Efficiency of Hotel）

客史档案为酒店的经营决策和服务提供了扎实的基础材料，使得酒店的经营活动能够有较强的针对性，避免许多不必要的时间、精力、资金的浪费。由于对客户消费情况的熟悉，员工的服务准备更为轻松。良好客户关系的建立，也有助于酒店工作氛围的改善，员工的工作热情、主动精神将有效地发挥，酒店整体的工作效率也将极大地提高。

Guest history file provides a solid basis material for operating decisions and services of hotel, making its business activities targeted, so as to avoid unnecessary waste of time, energy and money. Since hotel is familiar with guest consumption, the preparation work for service will be much easier. The establishment of good guest relationship is also conductive to the improvement of the working atmosphere of hotel. Staff enthusiasm and initiative spirit will be put into effective play and the overall efficiency of hotel will also be greatly improved.

（五）塑造酒店品牌（Building Hotel Brands）

根据客史档案划分、培育忠诚客户，可以为酒店创造更为重要的边际效应及口碑效应。口碑效应是酒店品牌塑造的关键因素，忠诚客户一个显著的特点是会向社会、同事、亲戚朋友推荐酒店。义务宣传酒店的产品和优点，为酒店树立了良好的口碑，带来新的客源。

The division and cultivation of loyal guests according to guest history file will create a more important marginal effect and public praise effect for hotel. Public praise effect is a key factor in brand building. One of the notable features of guest loyalty is to recommend hotel to community, colleagues, relatives and friends. The voluntary advertisement of products and advantages of hotel establishes a good reputation and brings new guests for hotel.

（六）有利于开展促销活动，争取回头客（Conducive to the Implementation of Promotional Activities and the Competition for Repeated Guests）

客史档案上记录了客人的通信地址、出生日期等基本资料，通过了解客史档案，酒店可以向客人邮寄生日贺卡和酒店的宣传资料，及时了解客人的需求，适时提供各种产品与服务，调整经营策略，以扩大潜在的客源市场。

Guest history file records the mailing address, date of birth and other basic information of guests. The hotel may keep track of guests' needs, provide various products and services timely and adjust business strategies to expand the potential market by sending birthday cards and promotional materials to guests according to the guest history file.

总之，酒店如果利用好客史档案，将让酒店的客人关系更加融洽，让越来越多的客户成为“忠诚客户”，为酒店的经营和发展巩固更多的客源。

All in all, if the hotel makes good use of guest history file, it will establish harmonious relationships with guests, retain more “loyal guests” and bring more guests for the operation and development of hotel.

二、客史档案的基本内容（Basic Content of Guest History File）

（一）客户的常规档案（Guest's Routine File）

包括单位客户档案和散客档案。单位客户档案主要有双方协议签订时所提供的单位名称、性质、经营内容、地址、负责人姓名、联系人姓名、联系方式、主要消费需求、认定的房价、消费折扣率、付款方式等信息。散客档案则是指客人在办理预订和入住登记时所留下的第一手资料，主要包括客人姓名、性别、出生日期、所属单位、常住地、有效身份证件类别、号码、联系方式、到达原因、入住房价、入住时间、付款方式等要素。通过收集和保存这些常规档案，有助于酒店了解客源市场的基本情况。

It includes corporate guests file and casual guests file. Corporate guests file mainly includes corporate name, nature, scope of operation, address, name of responsible person, name of contact person, contact information, major consumption demand, agreed price, consumption discount rate, type of payment and other information provided by the two sides when sign the agreement. Casual guests file refers to the first-hand information left by guests in the process of booking and check-in registration, including guest name, gender, date of birth, affiliated unit, permanent residence, type of certificate, certificate number, contact information, reasons of arrival, check-in price, check-in time, type of payment and other information. The collection and keeping of these routine files is conductive to the understanding of the basic situation of guest market.

（二）酒店有意识收集的顾客消费个性化档案（Guest Personalized Consumption File Collected by Hotel in Conscious）

这主要是指在酒店各服务区域，通过不同渠道、方式，酒店有意识、主动去收集的顾客消费需求特点、行为特征、个人嗜好等信息。

It mainly refers to consumption demand characteristics, behavioral characteristics, hobbies and other information collected by hotel in conscious and initiative through different channels and methods in various service regions.

（1）预订档案。包括客人的订房方式、介绍人、订房的季节、月份和日期及订房的类别等，掌握这些资料有助于酒店选择销售渠道，做好促销工作。

Reservation file, including the way of reservation, introducer season, month, and date of reservation and type of room reserved, etc. The information will facilitate hotel to select sales channels and carry out promotional work.

（2）消费档案。包括包价类别、客人租用的房间、支付的房价、餐费以及在商品、娱乐等其他项目上的消费；用房种类、房价、消费情况、信用情况、信用卡及账号等。掌握客人的消费档案，便于酒店了解客人的消费水平、支付能力、消费倾向、信用情况等。

Consumption file, including the type of package price, room rented, price of room, price of meals and price paid on other consumption items such as goods, entertainment and so on; type of room, price of room, consumption conditions, credit conditions, credit card and account number, etc. The consumption file will facilitate hotel to understand the level of consumption, affordability, consumption tendency, credit conditions and some other information of guests.

（3）习俗爱好、特殊要求档案。这是客史档案中最重要的内容，包括客人的旅行目的、爱好、生活习惯、宗教信仰和禁忌、住店期间的额外服务、特殊爱好等。了解这些资料有助于为客人提供有针对性的“个性化”服务。

File for custom, hobbies and special requirements. This is the most important content in guest history file, including the purpose of travel, hobbies, habits, religious beliefs and taboos, additional services during the stay, special interests and so on. These data will help to offer guests "personalized" services.

（4）意见反馈档案。包括客人住店期间的意见、建议、表扬、投诉及处理结果等。掌握客人的投诉内容有助于酒店服务防患于未然。

Feedback file, including comments, suggestions, praise, complaints and handling results during the stay of guests. The understanding of guest complaints will be conductive for hotel to take preventive measures.

（三）客户信息分析档案（Guest Information Analysis File）

客史档案是客户信息的总汇，是客史档案价值的真正体现。客户信息分析主要从以下几方面进行：①客户概况分析，包括客户层次、经济风险、爱好、习惯等；②客户忠诚度分析，主要指客户对酒店各项服务产品的认同度和购买热情；③客户利润分析，主要指客户消费不同产品的附加利润、总利润额、净利润等；④客户未来分析，包括客户数量、类别、潜在消费能力等未来发展趋势，争取客户的手段、方法等；⑤客户促销分析，包括广告、宣传、情感沟通计划等；⑥客户维护服务，客户的店庆、婚庆、厂庆、生日、客户特殊意义纪念节日、儿女升学等。

Guest history file is a summary of guest information, a true reflection of the value of guest history file. Guest information analysis mainly includes: ①Guest profile analysis, including guest consumption level, economic risk, hobbies, habits, etc; ②Guest loyalty analysis, mainly referring to degree of acceptance and consumption enthusiasm of guests for various products and services provided by hotel; ③Guest profitability analysis, mainly referring to additional profit, total profit, net profit for the consumption of different products; ④Guest future analysis, including the number of guests, categories, potential consu-mption capacity and some other future development trends, means and methods of competing for guests, etc; ⑤Guest promotion analysis, including advertisement, promotion, emotional communication plan, etc; ⑥Guest supporting services, store anniversary, wedding celebration, plant celebration, birthday, memorial festivals, children entering into a higher school and so on.

只有上述三项内容有机组成的客史档案才能形成一个完善的体系，构筑起酒店客户关系管理系统和客户忠诚系统的组合平台，为经营决策提供依据。

Only by the organic combination of the above three aspects, can we form a sound guest history file, build a combination platform for guest relationship management system and guest loyalty system and provide basis for business decisions.

三、客史档案的建立与实施（Establishment and Implementation of Guest History File）

在错综复杂、千头万绪的客户信息中提取出有效的信息，形成科学的客史档案是一项十分困难的工作。因此，客史档案的建立必须做到以下几点：

It is difficult to form a scientific guest history file with the valid information collected from complex guest information. Therefore, we must do the following aspects to establish guest history file:

（一）树立酒店的档案意识（Establishing a Sense of Building Files）

客史档案信息来源于日常的对客服务细节中，需要酒店全体员工高度重视，在对客服务的同时有意识地去收集，因此酒店在日常管理、培训中应向员工不断宣传客史档案的重要性，培养员工的档案意识，形成人人关注、人人参与收集客户信息的良好氛围。

The information of guest history file comes from the daily details of guest service. All staff should pay special attention to and collect such information consciously during the process of guest service. Therefore, the hotel should publicize the importance of guest history file in daily management and training to cultivate their sense of building files and form a good atmosphere of collecting guest information.

（二）建立科学的客户信息制度（Establishing a Scientific Guest Information System）

把客户信息的收集、分析作为酒店日常工作的重要内容，在服务程序中将客户信息的收集、分析工作予以制度化、规范化。要求各部门各级管理者及对客服务的员工每天在接触顾客的过程中，必须将客户信息及需求填写到客人意见表中，在日常服务中应给员工提示观察客人消费情况的要点。客房部员工在整理客房时应留意客人枕头使用的个数、茶杯中茶叶的类别、电视停留的频道、空调调节的温度数、客房配备物品的利用情况等。餐饮部员工可注意客人菜品选择的种类、味别，酒水的品牌，遗留菜品的数量，就餐过程中对酱油、醋、咸菜等的要求……从这些细节中能够捕捉到客人的许多消费信息。同时应以班组为单位建立客户信息分析会议制度，每个员工参与，根据自身观察到的情况，对客人的消费习惯、爱好做出评价，形成有用的客史档案，在客人再次来店时可以针对性的实施。

Make the collection and analysis of guest information as an important part of the daily work and standardize the collection and analysis of guest informationin service process. It requires managers at all levels and staff providing services to fill guest information and requirements in guest comments table during their daily contact with guests. Ask staff to observe the key points of guest consumption in daily service. Housekeeping staff should pay attention to the number of pillows, type of tea, television channels, air-conditioning temperature, the utilization of room supplies and so on. Food and beverage staff may pay attention to the type, taste of food, brand of beverage selected by guests, number of left dishes, requirements on soy sauce, vinegar, pickles, etc. Much information may be collected from these details. Meanwhile, establish information analysis meeting system by groups to involve all staff in the process. According to the situation observed, make evaluations on consumption habits and hobbies to form a useful guest history file and implementit when guests arrive the next time.

（三）形成计算机化管理（Forming Computerized Management）

客史档案的管理必须纳入酒店计算机管理系统中。计算机管理系统中的客史档案应具备以下特点：第一，信息共享功能，通过酒店计算机管理系统达到客史档案的资源共享功能是客史管理的基本要求，对客各部门能够相互传递信息，才能发挥相应作用。第二，检索功能，便于随时补充、更改和查询。第三，及时显示功能，在酒店每个服务终端输入客户基础数据，系统能够立即自动显示客人的相关信息资料，并作为对客接待提供依据。

The management of guest history file must be incorporated into the computer management system of hotel. The guest history file incorporated into the computer management system should have the following characteristics: firstly, information sharing function, the realization of resource sharing function through the computer management system is the basic requirement of the management of guest history file. Various guest service departments may play their corresponding role only through the mutual transmission of information. Secondly, search function, easy to add, change and query at any time. Thirdly, timely display function, enter guest data in each service terminal and the system will immediately and automatically show the relevant information of guests, which will serve as a basis for providing guest reception service.

（四）利用客户档案进行常规化的经营服务（Implementing Routine Operational Services with the Use of Guest History File）

酒店营销部门、公关部门应根据客户档案所提供的资料，加强与VIP客户、回头客、长期协作单位之间的沟通和联系，使之成为一项日常性的常规工作；通过经常性的回访、入住后征询意见、客户生日时赠送鲜花、节日期间邮寄贺卡、酒店主题活动、新的菜式产品推出时给予推荐等方式来拉近酒店与客户之间的关系，让客人感到亲切和尊重。

The Marketing Department and Public Relations Department should strengthen communication and contact with VIP guests, repeated guests and long-term cooperative units based on the information provided in guest history file, making it a daily routine; through regular visits, inquiry after arrival, sending flowers at birthday, mailing greeting cards during holidays, themed events, recommendation of new dishes and some other ways to close the relationship between guests and hotel, making guests feel warm and respectful.

总之，酒店客户档案的管理和应用是一项系统性工程，需要酒店高度重视，积极挖掘，形成严密完整的体系，并对客人日积月累的消费记录进行各方面的分析，从而提供有利的决策依据，才能使之成为酒店经营决策的基石。

In short, the management and application of guest history file is a systematic project. The hotel should pay attention to and form an integral system through initiative research. Meanwhile, it shall analyze the cumulative consumption records from various aspects to provide a favorable basis for decision making, so as to make it a cornerstone of business decisions.

四、客史档案的管理（Management of Guest History File）

酒店的客史档案管理工作一般由前厅部承担，而客史信息的收集工作要依赖于全酒店的各个服务部门。客史档案的管理工作主要有以下几个方面：

Generally, the Front Office should be responsible for the management of guest history file. All service departments throughout the hotel should be responsible for the collection of guest history information. The management of guest history file mainly concludes the following aspects:

（一）分类管理（Classified Management）

为了便于客史档案的管理和使用，应对客史档案进行分类整理。经过分类整理的客史档案是客史档案有效运行的基础和保证。

Guest history file should be classified to facilitate its management and use. The classified guest history file serves as a foundation and guarantee for the effective operation of guest history file.

（二）有效运行（Effective Operation）

建立客史档案的目的，就是为了使其在有效运行中发挥作用，不断提高经营管理水平和服务质量。客人离店后，要将客人的客史档案再次输入新的内容，使客史档案的内容不断得到补充。

The purpose of the establishment of guest history file is to make it play a role in the effective operation process, so as to constantly improve the management level and service quality. After the departure of guests, new contents should be entered into guest history file to make constant supplement.

（三）定期整理（Regular Sorting）

为了充分发挥客史档案的作用，酒店应每年系统地对客史档案进行1~2次的检查和整理。检查资料的准确性，整理和删除过期档案。

To give full play to the role of guest history file, the hotel should carry out systematic inspection and sorting 1-2 times every year to check the accuracy of the information and sort out and delete expired files.

五、建立客史档案流程（Establishing Process of Guest History File）

（一）注意事项（Notes）

（1）将住客入住登记表的最后一联作为客史档案卡建档。这种方式比较简单易行，但记载的信息量不大。以手工操作入住登记手续为主的中小型酒店多使用这一方式。

Put the last copy of guest check-in table in guest history file. This method is relatively simple, but the amount of information recorded in the file is small. Generally, small and medium sized hotels implementing check-in registration manually adopt this approach.

（2）填写档案卡片方式（见表 6-1）。

Fill in the fill card (see Table 6-1).

（3）在电脑系统中设定客史档案栏目以电脑方式建档。该方式操作简单，信息储存量大，且易于保存，是建立客史档案的最主要方式。

Set items of guest history file in computer system and establish computerized file. This method is simple and the amount of information recorded in the file is large and easy to store. This is the main way for establishing guest history file.

表 6-1 客史档案卡
Table 6-1 Guest History File Card

客人姓名 Guest name		性别 Gender		国籍 Nationality	
出生日期及地点 Bate of birth and place			证件号码 Certificate number		
职业 Career			职务 Title		
工作单位 Work unit					
单位地址 Unit address			电话 Phone		
家庭地址 Home address			电话 Phone		
其他 Others					

住店序号 Stay No.	住宿期间 Stay period	房号 Room No.	房租 Room price	消费累计 Total consumption	习俗爱好、特殊要求 Custom, hobbies and special requirements	表扬、投诉及处理 Praise, complaints and handling results	预订信息（渠道及介绍人） Reservation information (channels and introducer)	信用卡及账号 Credit card and account number	备注 remarks

（二）建立客户档案流程（Establishing Process of Guest History File）

表 6-2 建立客户档案流程
Table 6-2 Table for Establishing Process of Guest History File

项目 Item	标准 Standards	流程内容 Process content
准备客人登记表 Preparation of guest registration table	详细、准确 Detailed，accurate	汇集前一天办理的客人住宿登记表。 Gathering the guest registration table of the past day.
1. 查询客人的个人资料 Query of guest profile	详细、耐心、细致 Detailed，patient，considerate	(1) 进入电脑程序，选择相应目录可进入客人的历史档案查询网。 Access to the computer program，select appropriate directory and enter into website for guest history file. (2) 选择相应电脑程序，并同时根据客人登记表输入客人姓名的第一个字母或第一个字，即可得到客人个人资料或得知有无电脑记录。 Select an appropriate computer program and enter the first letter or the first character of guest name to obtain guest profile or query whether there are records in the computer.
2. 建立客人历史档案 Establishment of guest history file	详细、完整 Detailed，complete	(1) 选择电脑程序相应一项，输入客人姓名、性别、公司名、家庭地址、邮编、国籍、城市名称、护照号码、签证号码、生日等，以此为据，为客人建立历史档案。 Select an appropriate computer program and enter guest name，gender，company name，home address，zip code，nationality，city name，passport number，visa number，date of birth，etc.，and establish guest history file based on these data. (2) 将客人其他特殊要求输入备注一栏。 Other special requirements of guests should be enter into the remarks.
3. 确认 Confirmation	以免错漏 Avoid mistakes and missing	选择相应键，以检查电脑存储资料是否同客人手写资料相符，确认无误。 Select an appropriate button to check if the information stored in the computer is consistent with the handwriting data and confirm there is no mistake.

【实训与评价】【Training and Assessment】

［实训目的］［Training Goals］

1. 熟悉客史档案相关知识，会做客史档案。

To be familiar with relevant knowledge on guest history file and be able to establish guest history file.

2. 规范自己的言行，正确使用礼貌用语和敬语；能有礼有节、不卑不亢地处理突发事件。

To regulate your behaviors，use proper polite language and honorifics；to be able to handle sudden events politely and restrainedly，neither haughty nor humble.

［实训准备］［Training Preparation］

1. 前厅服务模拟场景、电脑、打印机、值班记录簿、客史资料，黑色水性笔等。

Service simulation scenarios at Front Office，computers，printers，duty log，guest history information，black ink pens，etc..

2. 学生 6 人分为一组，教师讲解示范后，学生根据教师布置的任务进行实际操作。

Students are divided into a group of six. After demonstration，students implement practical operation according to tasks assigned by the teacher.

［实训方法］［Training Method］

先观看教师播放的教学课件，然后由教师引导学生分析案例，学生 6 人一组，按照要求进行实际操作，教师巡回指导，实训结束前抽小组进行客户档案的制作实训。

Watch the teaching courseware played by the teacher, and students analyze the case at the guidance of the teacher. Students are divided into a group of six to implement practical operation. The teacher should give guidance. After the completion of practical training, select a group of students to establish guest history file.

[实训步骤] [Training Procedure]

第一步：教师向学生展示3个客人的客户档案，让学生有一定的感性认识。

The teacher shows the guest history file of three guests to students to make them have some perceptual knowledge.

第二步：学生分成4人一组讨论，由学生分析，指出正误。

Students are divided into groups of four to discuss, point out the right and wrong points and make analysis.

第三步：由学生继续讨论，设计出做客户档案的工作程序。

Students continue to discuss and work out the establishing process of guest history file.

第四步：各组学生代表发言说出程序，其他各组学生评价。

The representative of each group speak out the process and other groups of students make evaluations.

第五步：学生分成两人一组，进行客户档案制作的实训。

Students are divided into groups of two to establish guest history file.

第六步：教师评价与回答问题。

The teacher makes evaluation and answers questions.

[实训操作] [Training Operation]

由学生分成两人一组，进行客户档案制作的模拟练习。

Students are divided into groups of two to establish guest history file.

1. 学生两人一组，模仿标准进行实训，教师给出评判。

Students work in pairs to mimic standard training and the teacher gives judgment.

2. 学生可以即兴发挥，老师和学生共同评价，老师给出分数。

Students improvise, teachers and other students make evaluation and teacher gives scores.

3. 学生提出问题，老师回答。

Students ask questions and teacher gives answers.

4. 填写实训报告，实训结束。

Fill in training reports. The training is completed.

[实训评价] [Training Evaluation]

1. 能够根据要求制作客户档案表格。

Be able to establish guest history file according to requirements.

2. 填写表格内容与搜集客户资料相符。

The contend filled in the table is consistent with the collected guest history information.

3. 可以根据客户资料设计表格。

Be able to design tables according to guest history information.

任务二 投诉及特殊情况处理
Task II Complaints and Handling of Special Circumstances

【情境导入】【Scenario Introduction】

一卷卫生纸引起的投诉
Complaints arising from a roll of toilet paper

某日傍晚，一个香港旅游团结束“三亚一日游”，回到了下榻的三亚国光豪生度假酒店。然而，不到10分钟，旅游团的一位中年女领队就光着脚来到了大堂，怒气冲冲地向前台投诉客房服务员。

One day in the evening, a Hong Kong tour group returned to Howard Johnson Resort Sanya Bay after “one-day tour in Sanya”. However, less than ten minutes later, the tour leader, a middle-aged woman, came barfoot to the lobby, making a complaint to the Front Office about the room attendant.

原来，早晨出发时，这位女领队要求楼层客房服务员为房间加一卷卫生纸，但是这位服务员却只将这位客人的要求写在了交班记录簿上，并没有与交班服务员特别强调指出。结果，下一班的服务员看到客房卫生间内还有剩余的半卷卫生纸，就未再加。结果，这位客人回来后，勃然大怒。无论前台的几位服务员如何规劝、解释，她依然坚持光着脚站在大堂中央并大声说：“你们的服务简直糟透了。”她的话引来许多客人的好奇目光。此时值班经理和客房部经理很快赶到，看到此情此景，他们一边让服务员拿来一双舒适的拖鞋，一边安慰客人说：“我们的服务是有做得不够好的地方，请您消消气，我们到会客室里面坐下来谈，好吗？”这时客人的态度渐渐缓和下来，值班经理耐心地向客人询问了整个事件的经过和解决问题的具体意见，最后值班经理代表酒店向旅游团的每个房间都派了一卷卫生纸，并向这位客人赠送了致歉果盘。事后，经向该团导游了解，这位领队因对旅行社当天的行程等一些事情安排不满，故心情不好，亦是其中原因之一。

It turned out that before leaving the hotel in the morning, the tour leader had asked the room attendant to put a roll of toilet paper in the room, but the attendant only wrote down the requirement on the shift log and didn't emphasize it to the shift-taking attendant. Seeing there was still some toilet paper in the room, the shift-taking attendant didn't bring a new one. As a result, the guest flew into a rage when she came back. Regardless the persuasion and explanation of the attendants, she still stood barefoot in the lobby and said loudly: “Your service is simply awful.” Her words attracted much attention from other guests. At that time, the manager on duty and housekeeping manager arrived. Seeing such a situation, they asked the attendant to bring a pair of comfortable slippers and comforted her by saying: “There is indeed something wrong with our service, please calm down. Let's sit down and have a talk in the reception room, okay?” The guest eased her mood and the managers on duty asked about the whole event and sought for her suggestions on solving the problem. Finally, the manager on duty sent a roll of toilet paper to each room and gifted fruit tray as an apology. Afterwards, from what the tour guide said, we knew that the tour leader was dissatisfied with the other itinerary arranged by the travel agency, which also triggered off the complaint.

【情境分析】【Scenario Analysis】

从心理学的角度来分析，此案例首先是消费者心理个性的特殊反映。因为消费者的心理随时受到社会环境及个人情感、情绪的影响。当他们将个人情感、情绪带到酒店，就势必影响到整个消费过程。由于客房服务员之间的沟通出现问题，导致客人因为半卷卫生纸而大动肝火。事情虽小，但由于客人的心情和心理原因，出现的后果和产生的不良影响却很严重。正所谓心随境转，可能客人在情绪比较正常的状态下，打电话与客服中心联系就可以解决问题。但这时候，客人的心里不舒服、正憋着气，这半卷卫生纸无疑就成了客人不良情绪宣泄的一条导火线。

From psychological perspective, this case is a special reflection of consumers' psychological personality. Consumers' psychology will be influenced by social environment and personal feelings and emotions at any time. When they bring their personal feelings and emotions to the hotel, it is bound to affect the whole process of consumption. Communication problems between room attendants lead to the guest flying into a rage just for a half roll of toilet paper. Though this is a small matter, the adverse effects are serious due to guest's mood and psychological reasons. As the saying goes, our perceptions of the world will change with the changes of heart. Perhaps, the guest will solve the problem by calling the customer service center when she is in a right mood. However, the guest was in mental discomfort and felt oppressed at that time. Therefore, the half roll of toilet paper undoubtedly offers an outlet for her bad mood.

在酒店对客服务中，应时刻关注客人消费时的“求平衡”心理状态：一方面，客人要通过来酒店消费、放松，以舒缓日常生活中的压力。以经营度假村而闻名的“地中海俱乐部”的创始人之一特里加诺说过：“以前，人们注意的是使身体得到调理，增强体力，以便重新投入工作。今天，身体状况已经得到改善，头脑却过于紧张。主要的问题是精神高度疲劳。所以，人们需要用一种生活方式来加以调剂。”现代人为什么要求心理平衡？因为现代人最沉重的负担，不是在体力上，而是在精神上。对于这一点，作为酒店的经营者和服务人员，都应给予足够的重视。千万不要小看客人对半卷卫生纸、一个指甲钳、一个创可贴的需求，酒店向客人提供的，也正如特里加诺所说的，是“另一种生活方式”。另一方面，在酒店消费过程中，客人也需要保持必要的心理平衡，借此获得社会的尊重，并体现自我的尊严或自己的社会地位。所以客人都希望能在整个消费过程中获得轻松、愉快的享受，借此来舒缓日常生活中的压力。

During the process of offering guest service, the hotel should always pay attention to guests' mental state of "seeking balance". On the one hand, guests want to consume and relax in the hotel to relieve their stress. Terry Gano, one of the founders of the famous resort "Club Med", said: "In the past, people focus on the nursing of their body and the enhancement of physical strength to continue with the work. Today, though their physical condition is gradually improved, they are all on wires, resulting in mental fatigue. So, they need a certain kind of lifestyle to make adjustments." Why modern people ask for psychological balance? Because the most heavy burden suffered by them is not the physical one, but the spiritual one. Hotel operators and service personnel should give enough attention to this point. Do not underestimate the simple requirement on a half roll of toilet paper, a nail clipper or a band-aid.What the hotel offers to the guests, as Terry Gano said, is "another way of life". On the other hand, during the consumption process at a hotel, guests seek for necessary mental balance, thereby obtaining the respect of society and reflecting their dignity or social status. So guests aspire for relaxed and joyous enjoyment during the whole process of consumption to relieve their stress.

此外，我们在处理客人的投诉过程时，应有正确的认识，才能做出正确的处理。首先，必须认识到客人肯来投诉，对酒店而言，实在是一次纠正错误的好机会。千万不能把客人的投诉当作有意挑剔或"鸡蛋里挑骨头"。尽可能满足客人的要求，如本案例客人投诉酒店说："你们的服务简直糟透了。"值班经理和客房部经理没有因这样极端的话而生气，反而先为客人拿来拖鞋，并真诚地向客人道歉，以此来缓和客人的情绪。

In addition, while dealing with guest complaints, we should have a proper understanding so as to take the right measure. Firstly, we must realize that it is a good opportunity for hotel to make corrections when guest makes a complaint. Do not think that the guest is too picky or fault-finding. Try to meet the requirements of guests as far as possible. As in this case, when the hearing the guest say: "Your service is simply awful", the manager on duty and housekeeping manager did not get angry for such an extreme sentence, but brought slippers and apologized to the guest to ease her mood.

在处理投诉时，还必须做到诚恳耐心地倾听投诉，在听的同时表示出同情，争取在感情上和心理上与投诉者保持一致，千万不要话没有听完就开始为自己做解释和辩解，这很容易引起投诉者的反感。

In dealing with the complaint, we must listen to the guest sincerely and patiently, and show sympathy to keep in line with him emotionally and psychologically. Do not make explain or defend yourself before guest finishes the complaint, which may easily lead to guest's resentment.

应该说，多数客人都是讲道理的，即使遇到个别因不了解情况产生误会或爱挑剔的客人，也要本着"客人至上"、"客人如归"的宗旨，以平常心去对待客人和理解客人，在不影响其他客人的情况下，有意让客人通过发泄，使其不平静的心情逐渐平静下来。这样有利于弄清楚事情的来龙去脉和问题的顺利解决。

It should be noted that most guests are reasonable. Even if we run into some picky guestsor those who misunderstand us, we should treat them with an ordinary mood and try to understand them under the principle of "guests first" and "guests feel at home". On the premise of not affecting other guests, we should give vent to the bad mood of guests to calm them down. This will help us to clarify the circumstances and to solve the problem properly.

酒店要想赢得客人的满意，就要让他们在这里获得轻松愉快的经历，就必须让客人在与酒店工作人员的交往中，真正获得一种"就像回到自己家里"的感觉，特别是在消费过程中获得轻松愉快的人际交往。

In order to win customers' satisfaction, the hotel should give them relaxed and joyous experience. During the contact with hotel staff, we must make guests "feel at home", especially in the consumption process obtain relaxed and joyful interpersonal communication.

客人投诉是指客人对酒店服务工作感到不满而提出意见，客人投诉管理是酒店客人关系管理的一项非常重要的内容。由于酒店是一个复杂的整体运作系统，而且客人对服务的需求又是多种多样的，因此无论酒店经营得多么出色，都不可能百分之百地让客人满意，客人的投诉也是不可能完全避免的。前厅部在客人心目中是"酒店的代表"，所以前厅部往往是受理客人投诉的所在，可以说，客人是酒店送上门的老师，对于客人的投诉应积极对待，而不是害怕与逃避。酒店投诉管理的目的和宗旨在于如何减少客人的投诉，以及如何使因客人的投诉而造成的危害降到最低程度，最终使客人对投诉的处理感到满意。

Guest complaint refers to the comment proposed by guests due to their dissatisfaction with the service work of the hotel. Guest complaint management is a very important element in guest relationship management. Since the hotel is a complex overall operation system and guests may have various demands for services, it will not make everyone satisfied no matter how outstanding it is, thus guest complaints is unavoidable. As the "representative of the hotel", the Front Office is responsible for the handling of guest complaints. Guest is the home-delivery teacher for hotel. It should take an active attitude towards guest complaints, rather than fear and escape. The aim and purpose of hotel complaint management is to reduce guest complaints and to minimize the harm caused by guest complaints, and finally to make guests satisfied with the handling of complaints.

一、客人投诉分析（Analysis of Guest Complaints）

投诉是指酒店客人将其主观上认为由于服务工作存在瑕疵或者酒店产品不合格等情况而提出的书面或口头上的异议、抗议、索赔和要求解决问题等行为。

Complaints refer to written or oral objections, protests, claims and demands of problem solving proposed by guests due to subjectively suspected defective services or substandard products.

（一）客人投诉心理分析（Psychological Analysis of Guest Complaints）

从消费者气质特征分析，可以把消费者的气质分为四大类：胆汁质型、多血质型、黏液质型和忧郁质型。经研究，大多数重复投诉的客人属于胆汁质型和多血质型客户，这两类气质客人的高级神经活动类型属于兴奋型和活泼型，他们的情绪兴奋性高，抑制能力差，特别容易冲动，因此，他们在投诉时的心理主要有三种：

From the perspective of temperament characteristics of guests, the temperament of consumers may be divided into four types: choleric type, sanguine type, phlegmatic type and melancholy type. As the study shows, repeated complaints are mostly made by choleric type and sanguine type of customers. The higher nervous activity of these two types of guests is excitatory and lively. They are easy to be excited and impulsive with poor self-control, so they may have the following three types of psychology when make complaints:

（1）求尊重的心理。客人在采取了投诉行动之后，都希望别人认为他们的投诉是对的、是有道理的，他们希望得到同情、尊重，希望有关人员、有关部门重视他们的意见，向他们道歉，并立即采取相应措施。

Seek for respect. After making a complaint, guests always want others to think that their complaints are right and reasonable. They aspire for sympathy and respect, and hope relevant persons and departments may attach importance to their opinions, apologize to them and take corresponding measures immediately.

（2）求发泄的心理。客人在碰到令他们烦恼的事情之后，或者被讽刺挖苦，或者被辱骂，心中充满了怨气、怒火，他们要利用投诉的机会发泄出来以维持心理平衡。

Seek for abreaction. When encounter with something bothersome, or be mocked or be abused, they will be filled with resentment and anger, and try to find mental balance by making complaints.

（3）求补偿的心理。客人投诉的目的在于补偿，包括财产上的补偿和精神上的补偿。当客人的权益受到损害时，他们希望不但在身心方面得到慰藉，而且在物质方面也有所获取。因此，客人投诉时，需要在这两方面都得到补偿。

Seek for compensation. The purpose of such kind of guest complaints is to seek for compensation, including both monetary compensation and mental compensation. When guests' rights and interests are damaged, they want not only physical and psychological relief, but also material one. Thus, guests should be compensated from the two aspects.

(二) 投诉产生的原因 (Reasons of Complaints)

(1) 主观原因：服务员本身素质原因引起，不尊重客人和工作不负责任或工作没按标准化、程序化和规范化进行操作而导致客人投诉。

Subjective reasons: personal qualities of the attendant. Do not respect guests, work irresponsibly or do not work according to standards, procedures or rules, leading to guest complaints.

对客人不尊重的主要表现有：

Main representations of do not respect guests are:

A. 待客人不热情、不主动。

Treat guests unenthusiastically or inactively.

B. 不注意语言的修养、冲撞客人。

Pay no attention to language usage or provoke guests.

C. 挖苦、辱骂客人。

Ridicule or insult guests.

D. 未经客人同意，闯入客人房间。

Break into the guest room without the consent of guests.

E. 丢物品给客人。

Throw items to guests.

F. 不尊重客人的风俗习惯。

Do not respect the customs of guests.

G. 无根据地怀疑客人。

Suspect guests without any ground.

H. 影响客人的休息。

Affect the rest of guests.

(2) 客观原因：指由于酒店环境设施出现问题而导致客人的投诉。

Objective reasons: refer to guest complaints arising from environmental facilities of the hotel.

A. 酒店的设备损坏后未能及时修理好（如空调坏了、太热、太冷或噪音太大，卫生间的抽水马桶坏了，餐厅的座椅不牢固摔倒客人，餐具破损了也不更换等）。

Untimely repair of damaged facilities (such as the air conditioner fails to run, is too hot or too cold, or produces much noise. The toilet is broken. The chair in the kitchen is infirm, making guests fall down. The tableware is broken and not replaced, etc.).

B. 基础设施不完善（电话不能打长途，客人使用的电器不便，门窗关不严，隐私得不到保护等）。

Inadequate infrastructure (long-distance call is not available, inconvenient electrical facilities, doors and windows are not tight, lack of privacy protection, etc.).

C. 服务收费不合理（如客人在就餐后或离店前结账时发现应付的款项和实际消费有出入或收费项目不明确，有欺骗客人的嫌疑等）。

Service fees are unreasonable (such as guests find there is unclear charges or discrepancy between the amount payable and the actual consumption amount at the time of dining or departure, the hotel is suspected to cheat guests).

由于客人气质性格的不同，处理问题的方式也不相同，当出现以上种种情况时，有的客人可能嘴里嘀咕几句就算了，有的客人虽有怨气也不一定发泄出来，只是心中想着以后再也不来这里就是了，但也有些性情急躁的客人，可能会大动肝火，找经理投诉。

Since different guests have different temperaments and qualities, ways of handling problems is also different. When the above circumstances occur, some guests may grumble or complain about the matter, but others will not vent out, just telling themselves not to come here in the future. However, some short-tempered guests may fly into a rage and make acomplaint to the manager.

二、客人投诉的处理（Handling of Guest Complaints）

在处理各种客人投诉时，保持冷静、耐心、微笑，采取果断、灵活而又令客人乐意接受的方式，妥善、及时地处理客人投诉，在不损害酒店利益的前提下，既能让客人感受到酒店的诚意，也能让客人觉得在酒店内受到重视，变不满意为满意，从而争取更多的回头客，带来更多的社会效益和经济效益。

When dealing with a variety of guest complaints, we should keep calm, be patient and take a smile to handle guest complaints properly and timely with a decisive, flexible and acceptable way. On the premise of not damaging the rights and interests of the hotel, we should make guests feel the sincerity of the hotel and value their opinions to turn their attitude from dissatisfied to satisfied, so as to attract more repeated guests and bring more social and economic benefits.

（一）客人投诉各类内容类型（Types of Guest Complaints）

1. 对设施设备的投诉（Complaints about Facilities and Equipment）

客人对酒店设备的投诉主要包括空调、照明、水电、家具等。即使企业建立了各种设备的检查、维修、保养制度，也只能减少此类问题的发生，而不能保证消除所有设备潜在的问题。服务员在受理客人有关设备的投诉时，最好的办法是立即去实地观察，然后根据情况，采取措施。事后，再次与客人电话联系，以确认客人的要求已得到了满足。

Complaints about facilities and equipment are mainly targeted to air conditioner, lighting, water and electricity, furniture and so on. Even if various inspection, repair and maintenance systems have been established, they can only reduce such problems, but cannot guarantee the elimination of all potential problems. When handle complaints about facilities and equipment, the attendant should better carry out on-the-spot observation immediately and then take corresponding measures depending on the circumstances. After that, contact with the guest to make sure his requirements have been met.

2. 对服务态度的投诉（Complaints about Service Attitude）

客人对服务员服务态度的投诉主要包括：粗鲁的语言，不负责任的答复或行为，冷冰冰的态度，若无其事、爱理不理的接待方式，过分的热情，待客不主动，不热情，不注意语言修养，冲撞客人，挖苦、辱骂客人；拿物品给客人不是“递”，而是“扔”或“丢”给客人；无根据地乱怀疑客人取走酒店物品，或者误以为他们没有结账就离开。

Complaints about service attitude are mainly directed against rude language, irresponsible response or behavior, emotionless attitude, indifferent and unconcerned reception, excessive enthusiasm, inactive and unenthusiastic hospitality, paying no attention to language usage, provoking guests, ridiculing or insulting guests; “throwing” or “tossing” items to guests rather than “handing over”; suspecting guests for taking away items without any ground, or mistakenly thinking they leave the hotel without checkout.

3. 对服务质量的投诉（Complaints about Service Quality）

客人对服务质量的投诉主要包括：服务员没有照客人要求提供服务，电话无人接听，取送物品不及时甚至送错，未经客人同意私闯客人房间，不尊重客人的风俗习惯，忘记或搞错了客人交代办理的事情，损坏、遗失客人的物品，房间床铺不干净、不换床单，房间浴缸内有头发丝或污垢等。

Complaints about service quality typically include the attendant fails to provide services as guests' requirement, no one answers the phone, untimely or wrongly delivery of items, break into the guest room without the consent of guests, do not respect the customs of guests, forget or make a mistake about things required by guests, damage or misplace guest items, the bed is not clean, do not change the sheets, there is hair or dirt in the bathtub, etc.

4. 对异常事件的投诉（Complaints about Abnormal Events）

对异常事件的投诉主要包括：停电、停水、偷窃、伤病、醉酒、电梯卡人、房内反锁等情况引起的投诉，要求服务员尽量在力所能及的范围内帮助解决，做好解释工作、协调工作、善后处理工作。

Complaints about abnormal events include complaints resulting from power or water cut, theft, injury, drunkenness, elevator get stuck, inverse locked door, etc. The attendant should try his utmost to handle such problems and do well the explanation, coordination and afterward disposal work.

（二）客人投诉类型分析（Analysis of Types of Guest Complaints）

1. 处理客人口头投诉（Handling of Oral Complaints）

（1）对待任何一位客人的投诉都要认真、耐心听取，表现出高度的负责态度，代表酒店向客人表示歉意与感谢。

Listen to guest complaints carefully and patiently, showing a highly responsible attitude and express apology and gratitude to the guests on behalf of the hotel.

（2）注意倾听客人具体的投诉（发生的时间、地点、经过、涉及人员等），并及时填写客人投诉记录表。如客人情绪激动，要有技巧性地将客人请到合适的地方进行交谈。

Pay attention to the detailed content of complaints (time, place, process, personnel concerned, etc.), and timely complete guest complaints record form. If guests are agitated, invite them to have a talk at the right place skillfully.

（3）在听取客人的意见时，避免怀有敌视情绪或与客人争论，对客人的遭遇应适时地表示理解并不失时机地表示歉意，让客人感到酒店是重视、理解其意见并且尽力帮助他们解决问题的。

When listen to the views of guests, avoid hostile emotion or controversy with guests. Express understanding with guests' experience and apologize timely to make guests feel the hotel values and understands their views and will try to help them solve the problem.

（4）在听取客人投诉时，要保持头脑冷静，在没有查明事件原因及经过的情况下，不可随便代表酒店承担责任，待弄清事情原委后，再做出判断。

When listen to guest complaints, we should stay calm. Do not take responsibilities on behalf of the hotel without identifying causes and circumstances. Make judgments only after finding out what is going on.

（5）与有关部门联系，对客人所投诉的事件进行调查处理，或随客人到出事地点处理问题，把将要采取的措施及所需要的时间告知客人并征求客人的同意。

Contact with the relevant departments and investigate the event complained by guests or deal with the problem on the site together with guests. Inform guests of the measures to be taken and the time required and seek for guests' consent.

（6）恰到好处地回答客人的疑问，如有可能，给客人提供几种选择的机会。

Answer guests' questions properly, if possible, give guests several options.

（7）对超过权限或解决不了的问题，要及时与上级联系以得到指令，不能无把握、无根据地向客人提出任何保证，以免妨碍事务的进一步处理。

Contact with the upper class timely and receive instructions to solve difficult problems or those exceed the limit of authority. Do not make any uncertain or unwarranted guarantee to guests so as not to impede the further disposal of problems.

（8）将客人的投诉意见及时通知有关部门，使问题得到及时妥善的解决。

Inform the relevant authorities of guest complaint to solve the problem promptly and properly.

（9）代表酒店管理部门采取补救措施，如赠送水果、礼品、致歉信等给投诉者作为礼貌性的致歉，使客人感到酒店的诚意，变不满意为满意。

Take remedial measures on behalf of the hotel management authorities, such as giving fruit, gifts, letter of apology to the complainant as a polite apology, to make guests feel the sincerity of the hotel so as to turn their dissatisfactory attitude to satisfactory attitude.

（10）对一些无理取闹的客人，在处理过程中要做到不卑不亢，坚持原则，但应注意态度、语言、举止要有礼貌，并根据情况采取有效措施。

For some troublesome guests, neither be haughty nor be humble and adhere to the principle during the process. Pay attention to language, attitude and behavior politely and take effective measures according to circumstances.

（11）将客人的投诉及处理经过详细记录在案，加强培训，避免类似的情况重复出现。

Record guest complaints and handling process in detail and strengthen training to avoid the recurrence of similar situations.

2. 处理客人书面投诉（Handling of Written Complaints）

（1）认真阅读客人投诉信件，了解客人不满之处。

Carefully read the letter of guest complaint to understand guest dissatisfaction.

（2）查阅客史档案，掌握有关情况。

Refer to guest history file to catch on relevant situation.

（3）约见被投诉服务点负责人，了解事情具体情况。

Have a meet with the responsible person for relevant service and understand the specific circumstances.

（4）如客人尚未离店，应尽快与客人联系，当面与客人沟通。

If the guest has not left the hotel yet, contact with the guest immediately to have a face-to-face communication with him.

（5）若客人已离店，则应代表酒店给客人写一份致歉信，在得到总经理的许可后再通过传真、邮寄或 E-mail 及时发送给客人。

If the guest has left the hotel, write a letter of apology on behalf of the hotel and send it to the guest by fax, mail or E-mail upon obtain the approval of the general manager.

（6）填写客人投诉记录表并发送到相关部门。

Fill the guest complaint record form and send it to relevant departments.

三、顾客投诉处理的原则（Principles of Guest Complaints Disposal）

（一）投诉语言要礼貌（Complaint Language Should be Polite）

客人向服务员投诉时，服务员绝不能说：不、不懂、不行、不对、不会、不知道、不是我管的。服务人员应该充分理解顾客的心情，同情客人的处境，满怀诚意地帮助客人解决问题。只有这样，才能赢得客人的信任和好感，才能有助于问题的解决。酒店要制定合理、行之有效的有关投诉处理的规定，以便服务人员在处理投诉时有所依据。自己不能处理的事情，要及时转交上级，要有一个引导交接的过程，不能使投诉中出现“空白”和“断层”。有些简单的投诉，凡本人能处理好的，更不能推诿和转移。否则，将会引起客人更大的不满。如果缺乏诚意，即便在技术上做了处理，也不能赢得客人的好感。

When guests make a complaint to the attendant, the attendant should never say: no, do not understand, no way, unlikely, do not know, not up to me. The attendant should fully understand the feelings of guests, show sympathy to them and help them solve the problem in all sincerity. This is the only way to win the trust and goodwill of guests so as to help them solve the problem. The hotel should develop reasonable and effective rules on the handling of complaints to provide basis for the attendant in handling complaints. As for those things that cannot be handled, the attendant should hand it over to the higher level. There must be a guiding process for handover, so as to avoid "blank" and "break" during the process. For some simple complaints that can be handled properly, the attendant should not shift responsibility onto others. Otherwise, it will lead to even greater dissatisfaction from guests. If we lack of sincerity, we cannot win the favorable impression of guests even if we have handled it technically.

接到客人投诉时，服务人员首先要能够站在客人的立场考虑问题：一定是我们的工作没做到位，给客人造成了麻烦，同时我们还要相信，没有一个客人会无事找事，他们投诉总会有他们的理由，因为客人永远都是正确的。这是一个非常重要的观念，有了这种观念，服务人员才会有必要的心理准备，即使客人使用过激的言语及行为，也会以平和的心态来处理客人的投诉，并且会对客人的投诉行为给予肯定、鼓励和感谢。

When receive guest complaints, the attendant should first be able to stand on the position of guests to consider the issue: there must be something wrong with our work. We cause trouble to guests. Meanwhile, we should also believe that no guest will find troubles intentionally. Guests must have their own reasons for complaints, because they are always right. This is a very important conception. With this kind of conception, the attendant will have necessary mental preparation. Even if encounter with aggressive language and behavior, they will remain calm in dealing with complaints from guests, and will show approval, encouragement and thanks for guest complaints.

（二）承认客人投诉的事实，认真听取意见（Recognize the Fact of Guest Complaints and Listen Carefully to Their Views）

当客人怒气冲冲前来投诉时，首先应适当地选择处理投诉的地点，避免在公共场合接受投诉；其次应该让客人把话讲完，然后对客人的遭遇表示歉意，还应感谢客人对酒店的关心。当客人情绪激动时，服务人员更应注意礼貌，绝不能与客人争辩。也不要试图说服客人，因为任何解释都隐含着“客人错了”的意思。态度鲜明地承认客人的投诉是正确的，能使客人的心理得到满足，尽快地把客人的情绪稳定下来，显示了酒店对客人的尊重和对投诉的重视，有助于问题的解决。

When guests make a complaint in a rage, firstly, choosing an appropriate place to handle the complaint and avoid receiving the complaint in public place; secondly, letting guests finish their words, and then show regrets to guests' experience and express thanks to their concern for the hotel. When guestsare agitated, the attendant should be polite and should neither argue with guests nor try to persuade them, since explanation implies "guests are wrong". Acknowledge that guests are right to satisfy their psychological feelings, and try to calm them down as soon as possible. This shows our respect for guests and concern about the complaint and will help solve the problem.

为了很好地了解客人所提出的问题，必须认真地听取客人的叙述，使客人感到酒店管理者十分重视他的问题。倾听者要注视着客人，不时地点头示意，让客人明白我们在认真听取他的意见，而且听取客人意见的代表要不时地说：我理解，我明白，我们一定认真处理这件事情！为了使客人能逐渐消气息怒，酒店部门主管或值班经理可以用自己的语言重复客人的投诉或抱怨内容，若遇上的是认真的投诉客人，在听取客人意见时，还应做一些听取意见的记录，以示对客人的尊重及对反映问题的重视。

For a good understanding of the issue raised by guests, listen carefully to guests' statement, making them feel the hotel manager attaches great importance to this issue. While listening, watch guests and nod from time to time to make guests understand that we are listening to their views carefully. The representative who listens to guests' views should say from time to time: I understand, I see, we will deal with this thing! In order to appease guests, the departmental director or manager on duty may repeat guest complaint in their own language. If encounter with a serious guest, do some recording while listening to views to show our respect and concern about the issue.

（三）充分理解客人（Fully Understand Guests）

处理投诉时应设身处地，站在客人立场，充分理解客人的心境及客人要求，积极为客人排忧解难，而不应推卸责任或转移目标。要让客人理解，我们非常关心对方的休闲环境以及所受服务是否令人满意。如果客人在谈问题时表示得十分认真，作为代表酒店，处理投诉事件的当事人，要不时地表示对客人的同情。

When handling complaints, the attendant should stand in the guests' position to fully understand their mood and requirements and take the initiative to solve their problems rather than shirk or shift responsibilities. Make guests understand that we are concerned about their leisure environment and services provided to them. If guests are serious when talking about the problem, as a representative of the hotel in handling complaints, we should express sympathy for guests from time to time.

如果客人投诉的事情属实，酒店要对此负责并要给予一定的补偿，这时要向客人表示歉意并说：我们非常抱歉，先生（女士），我们将对此事负责，感谢您对我们酒店提出的宝贵意见！

If the complaint turns out to be true, the hotel should take responsibility and give some compensation, and apologize to guests: We are very sorry, Mr. (Ms.), we will be responsible for this. Thank you for your valuable suggestions about our hotel!

（四）不损害酒店的利益和形象（Without Prejudice to the Interests and Image of the Hotel）

处理投诉既要真诚地为客人解决问题，保护客人的利益，也要注意保护酒店的正当利益，维护酒店的整体形象。服务人员和管理人员不能单单注重客人的陈述，讨好客人，轻易表态，给酒店造成一定的损失；更不能在安抚客人情绪时，顺着或诱导客人抱怨酒店某一部门，贬低其他服务人员，推卸责任，使客人对酒店的整体形象产生怀疑。对涉及经济问题的投诉，要以事实为依据，具体问题具体研究，使客人不会蒙受不应蒙受的经济损失，酒店也不会无故承担赔偿责任。仅从经济上补偿客人的损失和伤害不是解决问题的唯一有效方法，而应在尽量不损害酒店利益的前提下，谋求酒店利润与客人满意度的最大化。

When handling complaints, we should not only solve the problem for guests and protect their interests, but also protect the legitimate interests of the hotel and safeguard its overall image. The attendant and manager cannot simply focus on guests' statements and please them by declaring their stands, which will cause some damage to the hotel; nor induce guests to complain about a particular department, belittle other attendant or shirk responsibility when appeasing guests, or else guests will doubt about the overall image of the hotel. As with complaints related to economic issues, we should investigate on specific issue based on facts to avoid causing unnecessary losses to guests. The hotel should not assume liability of consumption without reason. The financial compensation for guests' loss and damage is not the only effective method to solve the problem. We should seek to maximize hotel profits and guest satisfaction on the premise of not damaging the rights and interests of the hotel.

在处理投诉时，既要一视同仁，又要区别对待，既要看投诉问题的情节，又要看问题的影响力，以维护酒店的声誉和良好形象。

When dealing with complaints, we should adhere to both equal and differentiated treatment, paying attention to both the whole story of the complaint and the influence of the problem, so as to maintain the reputation and good image of the hotel.

（五）同意客人要求决定采取措施，给予足够的关心（Agree with Guests' Request, Decide to Take Measures and Give Adequate Care）

当客人的抱怨和投诉属实，我们要表示同情和理解，同时当我们决定采取行动纠正错误时，一定要让客人知道并同意我们采取的处理决定及具体措施内容。

When guest complaints turn out to be true, we should express sympathy and understanding. When we decide to take actions to correct mistakes, we should inform guests of our corrective measures and make them agree with our decisions and specific measures.

如果客人不知道或不同意我们的处理决定，就不要盲目采取行动，要十分有礼貌地通知客人我们将要采取的措施，并尽可能让客人同意我们的行动计划，这样我们才有机会使客人的抱怨变为满意，并使客人产生感激的心情。

If guests do not know or do not agree with our decisions, do not take actions blindly, but inform guests of our measures politely and try to make them agree with our action plan, so as to make guests satisfied and grateful for us.

（六）感谢客人的批评指教（Express Thanks for Guests' Comments or Suggestions）

任何一位明智的酒店各级领导甚至是服务员要经常感谢那些对酒店服务水平或服务设施水准提出批评指导意见的客人，因为这些批评指导意见或抱怨，甚至投诉会协助我们提高管理水平和服务质量。

A wise leader or even attendant should always show their thanks to those guests who make comments on the service level or standards of service facilities, because these criticisms or even complaints will help us to improve the management level and service quality.

假如客人遇到不满意的服务，他不告诉我们，也不做任何投诉；但是，作为光顾过酒店的客人，会讲给他的朋友和身边的人，这样就会极大地影响酒店的未来客源市场，影响酒店的声誉。为此，凡是对我们提出批评、抱怨甚至投诉的客人，我们不仅要欢迎，而且还要感谢。同时，要把注意力集中在客人提出的问题上，不随便引申，不嫁罪于人，不推卸责任，绝不能怪罪客人。

If guests are not satisfied with the service, they do not tell us nor make any complaints; however, since they have visited the hotel, they will tell their experience to their friends and people around them. This will greatly affect the future guest market and the reputation of the hotel. For this reason, we should welcome and show thanks to those who criticize and even complain about us. Meanwhile, we should focus on the issues raised by guests and should not transfer guilt nor shirk responsibility and blame guests.

（七）记录要点，快速采取行动，补偿客人投诉损失（Record Main Points，Take Swift Action and Compensate for the Loss of Guests）

把客人投诉的要点记录下来，这样不但可以使客人讲话的速度放慢，缓和客人的情绪，还可以使客人确信，酒店对他所反映的问题是重视的。此外，记录的资料可以作为解决问题的根据。

Write down the main points of guest complaints. It will not only make guests slow down their speech, ease their mood, but also convince them that the hotel take their problems seriously. Furthermore, the recorded information can be viewed as the basis of solutions.

当客人完全同意我们所采取的改进措施时，我们就要立即行动，一定不要拖延时间，确保改进措施的进展情况。耽误时间只能进一步引起客人不满，此时，时间和效率就是对客人的最大尊重，也是客人此时的最大需求，要使服务水准及服务设施均处在最佳状态，否则就是对客人的漠视。最后，处理完客人反映的事情后，打电话或当面拜访客人问明客人的满意程度。

When guests completely agree with our corrective actions, we should take immediate action to ensure the progress. Do not delay and make sure the process of improved measures. Any delay will lead to the further dissatisfaction of guests. At this time, time and efficiency are the greatest respect for guests and also the biggest requirement of guests. Maintain the service standards and service facilities in the best condition, or else it will show our indifference to guests. Finally, after handling the issued reflected by guests, call them or pay visits to them to certify their degree of satisfaction.

四、处理客人投诉的程序（Handling Process of Guest Complaints）

酒店行业中有句行话“客人的满意就是我们的承诺”，客人的满意是酒店服务工作中所追寻的目标。但事实上无论是多么豪华、多么高档次的酒店，无论酒店管理者在服务质量方面下了多大的功夫，总会有某些客人，在某个时间对某件事、某物或某人表示不满。因此，投诉是不可避免的。作为酒店本身应对客人的投诉持欢迎的态度，并把处理客人投诉的过程视为改进管理与服务的机会。当客人投诉后，酒店要尽可能针对投诉，给予客人满意的答复。

As the jargon in the hotel industry goes “guests’ satisfaction is our commitment”, guests’ satisfaction is the goal of hotel’s service work. However, no matter how luxurious and superior the hotel is and no matter how much effort the hotel manager has spared in service quality, some guests will express their dissatisfaction on a certain matter, thing or person at a certain time. Accordingly, complaint is inevitable. The hotel should welcome guest complaints and view the handling process of guest complaint as an opportunity to improve its management and services. When guests raise complaints, the hotel should give them satisfactory replies as much as possible.

（一）认真听取客人意见（Listen Carefully to Guests’ Views）

在听完客人的投诉后，要对客人的遭遇表示抱歉（即使客人反映的不完全是事实，或酒店并没有过错，但至少客人感觉不舒服、不愉快），同时，对客人的遭遇表示同情和理解。这样，会使客人感觉自己受到尊重，自己来投诉并非无理取闹，同时也会使客人感到我们和他站在一起，而不是站在对立面与他讲话，从而减少对抗情绪。

After listening to the complaints of guests, the hotel should say sorry to guests (even if what guests said is not true, or the hotel is not to be blamed, the truth is that guests feel uncomfortable and unpleasant). Meanwhile, show sympathy and understanding about the experience of guests. In this way, guests will feel being respected. They are not trying to find troubles. This will make guests think that we are standing in their position rather than in opposition to them, thereby reducing the antagonism.

（二）保持头脑冷静（Keep Calm）

在投诉时，客人总是有理的。不要反驳客人的意见，不要与客人争辩。为了不影响其他客人，可将客人请到办公室，最好个别地听取客人的投诉，私下交谈容易使客人平静。投诉的最终解决只有在“心平气和”的状态下才能进行，因此，接待投诉客人时，首先要保持冷静、理智，同时，要设法消除客人的怒气。比如，可请客人坐下慢慢谈，同时，为客人送上一杯茶水。此时，尽量消除客人的怒气，不能出现使客人“气”上加“气”，火上浇油的效果。

Guests are always right when making a complaint. Do not refute their views. Do not argue with them. In order not to affect other guests, we may invite guests to the office to listen to their complaints privately. It is easy to make guests calm down during private conversation. Complaints can only be settled in a “calm” state. Therefore, when receiving guests who make complaints, we should remain calm and rational first and then try to relieve guests’ anger. For example, ask guests to sit down and talk slowly. Meanwhile, bring a cup of tea for them. After that, relieve guests’ anger and do not add “fuel” to the “fire” to make them become angrier.

（三）深表同情（Show Sympathy）

应设身处地考虑、分析问题，对客人的感受要表示理解，用适当的语言给客人以安慰，如“谢谢您告诉我们这件事”，“对于发生这类事件，我们感到很遗憾”，“我们完全理解您的心情”，等等。因为此时尚未核对客人的投诉，所以只能对客人表示理解与同情，不能肯定是酒店的过错。同时，不应该对客人的投诉采取“大事化小，小事化了”的态度。应该用“这件事情发生在您身上，我感到十分抱歉”诸如此类的语言来表示对投诉客人的关心。在与客人交谈的过程中，注意用姓名来称呼客人。并且，把注意力集中在客人提出的问题上，不随便引申，不嫁罪于人，不推卸责任，绝不能怪罪客人。

Considering and analyze problems by putting ourselves in guests’ position, express our understanding for their feelings and use appropriate language to comfort them, such as “Thank you for telling us about it”, “I’m sorry for this incident”, “I totally understand your feelings” and so on. Since we have not check out the complaint, so we can only express our understanding and sympathy. We cannot make sure that it is the hotel’s fault. At the same time, we should not take the attitude of “reducing major issues to minor ones and minor ones to nothing” toward guest complaints. Show our concern about guests by saying “I am very sorry for what happened on you”. In the process of talking with guests, address them by their names. Moreover, pay our attention to issues raised by guests. Do not extend the main points, transfer guilt, shirk responsibility or blame guests.

（四）记录要点（Record Main Points）

把客人投诉的要点记录下来，包括客人投诉的内容、客人的姓名、房号及投诉时间等，这样不但可以使客人讲话的速度放慢，缓和客人的情绪，还可以使客人确信，酒店对他反映的问题是重视的。此外，记录的资料可以作为解决问题的根据。并且，把将要采取的措施告诉客人并征得客人的同意，如有可能，要请客人选择解决问题的方案或补救措施。绝对不能对客人表示，由于权力有限，无能为力，但千万不要向客人作不切实际的许诺。

Record the main points of guest complaints, including the contents of guest complaints, guest name, room number and complaint time. It will not only make guests slow down their speech, but also convince them that the hotel take their problems seriously. Furthermore, the recorded information can be viewed as the basis of solutions. Moreover, inform guests of the measures to be taken and seek for their consent. If possible, ask guests to choose solutions to problems or remedies. Do not show guests that our power is limited and we could do nothing or make unrealistic promises to them.

（五）解决投诉问题（Settle Complaints）

要充分估计解决问题所需要的时间。最好能告诉客人具体的时间，不含糊其辞，切忌低估解决问题的时间。接待投诉客人的人，并不一定是实际解决问题的人，因此客人的投诉是否最终得到了解决，仍然是个问号。事实上，很多客人投诉并未得到解决，如果一时解决不了，应留下客人的姓名、联系电话，待事情解决后给客人一个回复，如果根本解决不了，也给客人一个答复，说明原因，询问客人是否需要其他帮助。因此，必须对投诉的处理过程进行跟踪，对处理结果予以关注。与客人进行再次沟通，询问客人对投诉的处理结果是否满意，同时感谢客人。

To fully estimate the time required to solve the problem. It is best to tell guests of the specific time. Do not be unambiguous and underestimate the time required to solve the problem. The person who receives guests is not necessarily the problem solver. So it is still uncertain as whether the complaint has finally been resolved. In fact, many guest complaints cannot be resolved promptly. In this case, record the name and contact number of guests and give them a reply after the problem is resolved. If the problem cannot be resolved, also give them a reply, indicating the reasons and asking if they have other needs. Therefore, we should track the whole process of handling complaints and pay attention to the final results. Communicate with guests again, asking whether they are satisfied with the results and express thanks for them.

（六）投诉的统计分析（Statistical Analysis of Complaints）

投诉处理完以后，有关人员，尤其是管理人员，不应对该投诉的产生及其处理过程进行反思吗？分析一下该投诉的产生是偶然的？还是必然的？应该采取哪些措施，制定哪些制度，才能防止它再次出现？另外，对这次投诉的处理是否得当？有没有其他更好的处理方法？只有这样，才能不断改进服务质量，提高管理水平，并真正掌握处理客人投诉的方法和艺术。

After the complaint is settled, is it necessary for the persons concerned, especially managers, to reflect on the complaint and the handling process? Is the complaint accidental or inevitable? What measures and systems should be developed to prevent the recurrence of such event? In addition, is the handling approach proper? Is there any other better approaches? Only in this way can we continuously improve our service quality and management level, and truly master the handling approach and technique of guest complaints.

客人投诉有助于酒店发现其服务和管理中存在的问题，是酒店提高服务质量和管理水平的杠杆，因此，酒店应十分重视客人投诉，加强对客人投诉工作的管理，做好客人投诉的记录等基础工作，建立宾客投诉档案，并定期由专人管理，及时进行信息整理、反馈及做好总结、反思工作，防止此类投诉再次发生。

Guest complaints are conductive to the hotel to find its service and management problems. It is the leverage for hotel to improve its service quality and management level. Therefore, the hotel should attach great importance to guest complaints, strengthen the management of guest complaints work, make a record of guest complaints, establish guest complaint file, appoint specific person to manage the file and carry out regular information collation, feedback, summary and reflection to prevent the recurrence of similar complaints.

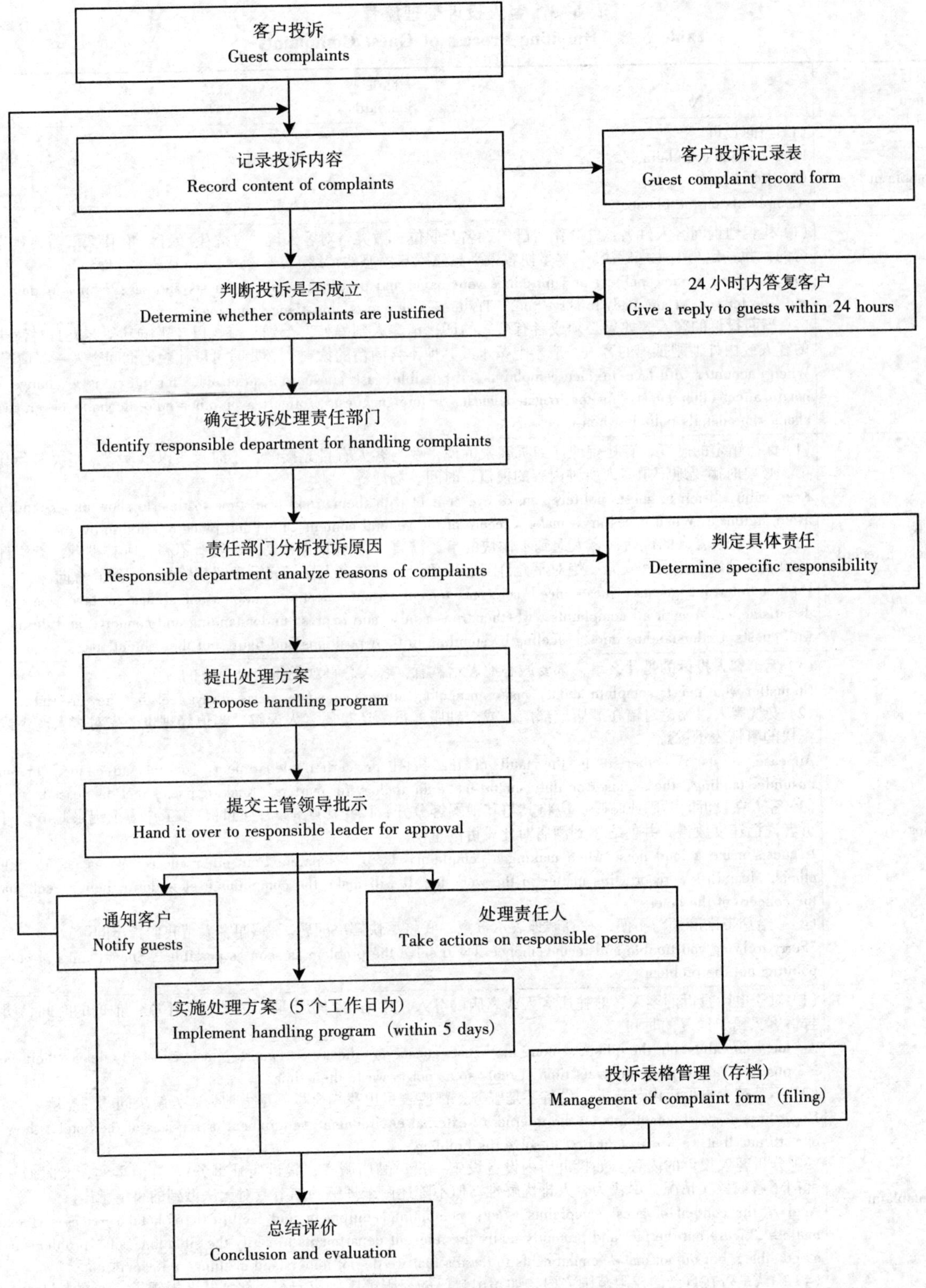

图 6-1　处理客人投诉流程

Figure 6-1　Flow Chart of Handling Process of Guest Complaints

表 6-3　客人投诉处理流程
Table 6-3　Handling Process of Guest Complaints

项目 Item	标准 Standards
1. 接到投诉 Receive a complaint	（1）当面投诉。 Face-to-face complaints. （2）电话投诉。 Complaints on the phone.
2. 保持冷静 Keep calm	（1）礼貌地询问客人姓名，并介绍自己的姓名及职位，微笑着对客人说："先生/女士，有什么事需要我为您效劳的，我一定马上为您解决。"尽量使客人平息急躁与愤怒的情绪。 Ask the guest's name politely and introduce your name and position, smile to guests and say: "Sir / Madam, what can I do for you, I am ready to serve you." Try to relieve guests' impatience and anger. （2）当面投诉的客人，如果必须或者有可能的话，请客人到静处，个别交流，以免影响其他客人，对情绪激动的客人或由外地刚抵埠的客人，应奉上茶水或其他不含酒精的饮料，必要时可以礼貌地询问客人一些情况。 When encounter with face-to-face complaints, if possible, ask guests to a quiet place for individual exchange, so as not to affect other guests. As for irrigated guests or foreign guests, offer tea or other non-alcoholic beverages. Ask about some details politely when necessary.
3. 倾听并记录 Listen and make a record	（1）保持镇定的态度，有礼貌地仔细听客人诉说，要与客人有目光接触，不时点头以示理解，坚决避免与其争辩。必要时摘要地记录客人所讲内容的梗概、时间、场地等。 Keep calm, listen to guests politely, make eye contact with them, nod from time to time to show understanding and avoid argument. When necessary, make a record of the general content, time and place referred to by guests. （2）不要打断客人的说话，客人遇到不愉快的事，需要一个倾诉的对象，以发泄不满。所有投诉，无论真假都必须表示理解、接受和安慰，绝对不允许与客人争论，站在客人立场表示理解其感受，了解其意向。 Do not interrupt guests. Guests need someone to talk when encounter unpleasant things to give vent to their dissatisfaction. Accept all complaints, whether true or false and express understanding and comfort, and do not argue with guests. Understanding guests' feeling by standing in their positions and figure out their intentions.
4. 致歉 Make an apology	（1）无论客人投诉的是什么事，都要诚心地表示歉意，客人总喜欢觉得自己是对的。 No matter what guests complain about, make an apology sincerely, since guests always feel that they are right. （2）安抚客人，无论对错在酒店或部门，或个别服务员，还是属客人误解，当值经理也要先对客人产生或引起不快的事情表示歉意。 Appease guests. Whether it is the fault of the hotel or certain department, or the attendant, or guests' misunderstanding, the manager on duty should make an apology for matters' making guests feel displeased. （3）客人在投诉时吵闹或喧哗，应将其与其他顾客分开，以免影响他人，同时，在工作簿上记录此事，可使投诉者说话速度放慢，并使之感到酒店对此投诉的重视。 If guests make a loud noise when making a complaint, keep it separate from other guests, so as not to influence others. Meanwhile, record this matter in the work log. It will make the complainant slow down their speech and feel the concern of the hotel. （4）"给您带来麻烦与不便，我真诚地表示歉意，我将尽快解决问题。"感谢客人帮我们指出问题。 "Sorry to bring you trouble and inconvenience. I will solve the problem as soon as possible." Show thanks to guests for pointing out the problem.
5. 分析投诉 Analyze the complaint	（1）对于电话投诉的客人，非住店客人或离店的客人，可请他们留下联系方式，为不耽误他们的时间，明确地告诉客人给予回复的时间。 As for complaints on the phone, non-in-house guests or check-out guests, ask guests to leave their contact information. Tell them of the exact time of reply so as not to waste their time. （2）不管客人投诉店内与店外，设备还是服务，都应表示出我们会尽心尽力地为客人解决问题的态度。 Regardless of guest complaints on the internal or external environment, equipment or services of the hotel, show them our attitude that we will try our best to solve the problem. （3）分析客人投诉的内容（如投诉店内设备设施；投诉酒店服务；投诉店外事务）。弄清事实，及时通知相关部门了解或核实情况，尽快为客人排忧解难，但不陈述尚未理解的细节或对无法做到的事情承诺。 Analyze the content of guest complaints (eg: complaints equipment and facilities; of hotel services; of external matters). Figure out the fact and promptly notify the relevant departments to verify the situation. Solve problems as soon as possible, but do not make commitments to details that we do not understand or things we cannot do. （4）确认是否在自己的权限范围之内，如超出自己的权限范围，应向客人解释并上报领导；如在自己的权限范围之内，应立即向客人提出解决方法。切勿轻易做出权利范围外的许诺。 Confirm whether the problem is within the scope of our power. Explain to guests and hand it over to the higher level if it is beyond our scope of power; if it is within our scope of power, propose solutions to guests immediately. Do not make commitments beyond our scope of power.

续表

项目 Item	标准 Standards
6. 协商并解决 Negotiate and resolve	(1) 如在自己的权限范围之内，值班经理可给客人优惠，或送客人礼品、鲜花、水果等表示歉意，告诉客人处理问题的办法，如有可能提供几种方法让客人选择，牢牢抓住抱怨问题的症结。 If it is within our scope of power, the manager on duty may make some discount or send guests gifts, flowers, fruits, etc. as an apology and tell guests the handling approach. If possible, provide several options for guests to choose. Firmly grasp the main point of complaints. (2) 如超出自己的权限范围，应向客人解释并上报领导请示处理方式，做出处理意见。 If it is beyond our scope of power, explain to guests and hand it over to the higher level for handling approach and advices. (3) 把调查情况与客人进行沟通，向客人作必要解释，争取客人同意处理意见。"先生/女士，您看这样解决好不好？" Communicate with guests about the investigation results, make necessary explanations and try to make guests agree with the results. "Sir / Madam, do you think the solution is proper?"
7. 修正问题 Modify the problem	(1) 如客人投诉店内设施设备，要把问题上报给部门领导和相关部门领导并在投诉报告上写明投诉的位置。通知相关部门马上补救；如需时间，一定要在投诉报告上注明。 If guests make a complaint about facilities and equipment, hand over the problem to departmental leader and leaders of relevant departments and state the specific location in the complaint report. Notify the relevant departments to make corrections promptly; if it requires much time, note it in the complaint report. (2) 如客人投诉服务，立即打电话至相关部门领导，将客人投诉内容告知，如客人提出相关部门人员道歉请求，马上要求相关部门领导协助解决。 If guests make a complaint about services, make a call to leaders of relevant departments immediately and inform them of the content of the complaint. If guests ask for an apology from person in relevant departments, coordinate with leaders of relevant departments to solve the problem immediately. (3) 如客人投诉店外事务，应帮助客人与店外投诉单位联系，并按投诉程序，帮助客人投诉。 If guests make a complaint about external matters, we should help guests to contact with the complaints unit and help them make complaints according to complaints procedure.
8. 记录 Record	在工作日志上详细记录投诉内容、处理方法、时间等并要填写投诉报告。复印给酒店相关部门并存档。如需继续跟进，由下一班值班继续关注。 Record the content, handling approach, time of complaint in the work log in detail and file out the complaint report. Send the copy to the relevant departments for filing. If follow up investigation is necessary, the next one on duty should continue with the and pay attention to the matter.
9. 反馈 Feedback	(1) 告诉客人对其投诉事件，酒店有关部门已经采取相应措施，并加以弥补和纠正，希望得到客人的谅解。 Tell guests that the relevant departments have taken appropriate measures and are correcting and compensating for the matter, hoping to obtain the guests' understanding. (2) 可以再次倾听客人的意见，以示酒店的重视程度。 Listen to the views of guests once again to show the hotel's concern for this matter. (3) 再次向客人致谢，欢迎客人给酒店提出宝贵意见。 Show thanks to guests once again and welcome them to propose valuable advices.
10. 输入电脑 Enter into the computer	(1) 如果住店客人投诉了，要将客人投诉相关内容输入客史档案，以备下次客人入住时酒店加倍重视所投诉的问题。 If the in-house guests make a complaint, enter the relevant content into the guest history file so as to pay particular attention to the issue when guests come the next time. (2) 当值经理要将整个事件过程简要向员工传达，让员工掌握此类案件应该如何处理及再次接待此类客人时应注意的事项。 The manager on duty should briefly communicate the entire process to the staff to make them comprehend the handling approach of such cases and things to be paid attention to when receive such guests the next time.

五、处理投诉注意事项（Notes to Handling of Complaints）

（1）快速反应。应在第一时间到达现场，并尽可能快地解决问题，给客人答复，不能拖延。这里提出 1∶10∶100 黄金管理定理。意思是：若客人提出问题当天就加以解决所需成本为 1 元，拖到第二天解决则需要 10 元，再拖几天就可能需要 100 元。

Swift response. Arrive at the scene at the first time and solve the problem as quickly as possible. Give guests a reply without delay. Here presented the Gold Management Theorem 1 : 10 : 100, that is if the problem is resolved on the day when it is raised, the cost will be 1 yuan. If it is delayed to the next day, the cost will be 10 yuan. And a few days later, it would be 100 yuan.

（2）在处理投诉时，注意倾听。倾听时注意“视觉接触”，同时注意自己的脸部表情。因为脸部表情反映着我们的感受。客人能从我们的脸部表情中感受到我们对此事的反应。如果处理投诉的管理人员满脸不耐烦，或者满脸不赞同，客人肯定不满意，对我们也会有敌意。管理人员要在客人的倾诉中去听、去看、去揣摩对方的态度是什么，他注重的是什么，他对我们有什么要求。

When dealing with complaints, pay attention to listening. Pay heed to "visual contact" while listening, as well as facial expressions. Since facial expressions reflect our feelings, guests may feel our response from our facial expressions. If the manager shows impatience and disagreement in his face while handling complaints, guests will certainly not be satisfied and will have a feeling of hostility towards us. The manager should learn to hear and observe while listening so as to figure out the attitude, main points and requirement of guests.

（3）处理投诉的程序因投诉客人类型的不同而有所不同。针对理智型客人的投诉，要认真聆听并记录，表示同情及理解，然后听取客人建议，采取行动，解决问题，解决落实后要将相关信息通知客人，并将投诉记录存档。针对冲动型客人的投诉，因为客人情绪比较激动，而投诉地点大多数在公众场合，所以要将客人请至专门的会客室，以免因处理不当而陷入被动境地，在客人未恢复理智前，进来安抚客人，平息客人情绪是首要的。尽量平息客人怒火，通过转移话题平息客人怒火，千万不要与客人争辩。对明显属于酒店的过错，不推脱，不狡辩。如有可能最好能和客人单独谈话。必要时可请更高级管理人员出面道歉。

Handling procedures vary depending on the types of guests. With respect to intellectual type of guests, listen carefully and make a record, express sympathy and understanding, and then listen to guests' suggestions and take actions to solve the problem. Inform guests of relevant information once the problem is solved and keep the complaint records in file. As for impulsive guests, since guests are irrigated and the complaint usually happens in public places, so invite guests to the reception room, so as to avoid being caught in a passive position due to improper handling. The most important thing is to comfort guests and appease their mood before they come to their senses. Try to relieve guests' anger by changing topics and do not argue with them. Do not shirk responsibility for problems caused by the hotel. If possible, it is best to talk with the guests alone. Ask a senior manager to make an apology when necessary.

（4）增强酒店员工与客人的沟通意识，提高沟通技巧，通过表单与工作程序的约束建立完善的制度，多渠道、多方位地加强与客人的沟通，通过与客人的及时沟通，最大限度地及时掌握客人的满意程度，缩小客人投诉态势的发展，并且增强、改进工作的主动性。

Enhance the communication awareness between hotel staff and guests, improve communication skills, establish sound system with the restriction of forms and procedures, strengthen communication with guests through various channels and in various aspects, maximize guest satisfaction through timely communication with guests, limiting the development trend of guest complaints and enhance the initiative of improvement work.

（5）真诚感谢投诉客人。处理客人投诉时一定要跟进，直到客人离开，直到客人满意。

Express sincere thanks to complainants. When dealing with guest complaints, follow up the progress until the guests leave or feel satisfied.

(6) 在与投诉客人谈判僵持不下时，可请第三方（客人的朋友）出面协调处理。

When come to a deadlock during the negotiation process，ask a third party (guests' friend) to coordinate.

(7) 当客人提出的要求超过自己的权限，无法处理时，应及时汇报上级解决。

When requests made is beyond the scope of power，report to the higher level promptly.

【实训与评价】【Training and Assessment】

[实训目的] [Training Goals]

1. 能够接受客人的合理建议。

Be able to accept reasonable suggestions from guests.

2.能够处理客人的投诉。

Be able to handle guest complaints.

3. 能够分析酒店前厅综合案例，找出合适的解决方案。

Be able to analyze integrated cases of Front Office and find the proper solution.

4. 培养学生积极思考、主动参与、共同探讨的协作意识。

Cultivate the collaboration awareness of positive thinking，active participation and mutual discussion among students.

5. 培养学生良好的服务意识，为客人提供优质服务。

Cultivatea good sense of service among students to offer quality services for guests.

[实训准备] [Training Preparation]

1. 前厅服务模拟场景、电脑、打印机、值班记录簿、入住登记单、账单等。

Service simulation scenarios at Front Office，computers，printers，duty log，check -in registration form，bill，etc..

2. 学生 6 人分为一组，教师讲解示范后，学生根据教师布置的任务进行实际操作。

Students are divided into a group of six. After demonstration，students implement practical operation according to tasks assigned by the teacher.

[实训方法] [Training Methods]

先观看教师播放的教学课件，然后由教师引导学生分析案例，学生 6 人一组，按照任务驱动的要求进行实际操作，教师巡回指导，实训结束前抽小组进行前厅服务模拟表演。

Watch the teaching courseware played by the teacher，and students analyze the case at the guidance of the teacher. Students are divided into a group of six to implement practical operation. The teacher should give guidance. After the completion of practical training，select a group of students to simulate service at Front Office.

[实训步骤] [Training Procedure]

第一步：教师演示课件，给出案例，提出问题，让学生思考。

The teacher display the courseware，show cases and put forward questions for students to think about.

第二步：学生分组讨论，由学生分析，指出正误。

Students are divided into groups to discuss，point out the right and wrong points and make analysis.

第三步：小组成员进行前厅服务模拟表演，通过角色扮演，深刻体会客人心理活动，设计出该案例的处理工作程序。

Group members simulate service at Front Office. Get a profound understanding of the mental activity of guests through role play and design the handling procedures for simulated cases.

第四步：各小组派代表宣读小组的设计结果，选出最佳设计小组展示处理客人投诉的过程。

The representatives of each group read the design results. Select the best design and show the handling procedures of guest complaints.

第五步：学生自评、小组评价、教师点评。

Student self-assessment, group evaluation, teacher evaluation.

［实训内容］［Training Content］

都是咖啡惹的祸？

Blame it on the coffee?

某日下午，李教授和他的一位朋友来到三亚湾红树林度假世界酒店大堂吧，坐定之后等服务员前来点要饮料。两人对坐闲聊了一会儿，服务员端来一壶现磨咖啡，外加两盅牛奶和数块方糖，朝着李教授说："我送来了您喜欢喝的咖啡。"（李教授是这里的常客，服务员都很熟悉他的爱好）谁知那天是李教授的朋友做东，他从来不喜欢喝现磨咖啡，而习惯雀巢速溶咖啡。李教授的朋友面露愠色地对服务员说："今天是我请李教授来此叙谈休息一下，你怎么如此不懂得待客的道理，竟自作主张！"服务员不肯认错，对李教授的朋友说："我了解李教授平时喜欢喝现磨咖啡，我料想您不会是忌喝咖啡的客人。"

One afternoon, Professor Li and his friend came to the lobby bar of Mangrove Tree Resort World Sanya Bay. They sat down and waited for the attendant to serve them beverage. They chatted for a while, then the attendant brought a pot of freshly ground coffee, plus two pots of milk and several cube sugar, and said to Professor Li: "I bring your favorite coffee."（Professor Li is a frequent visitor here, almost all the attendants know about his hobbies）. However, it was his friend that played the host that day and he was in favor of Nescafe instant coffee rather than freshly ground coffee. Professor Li's friend said with a displeased look: "Today I invite Professor Li to have a break here, how could you make decisions on what we want to drink?! You simply do not know how to entertain guests." The attendant refused to make an apology and said to him: "I know Professor Li like to drink freshly ground coffee, so I suppose you will not dislike it."

李教授听服务员这样讲，觉得对他的朋友有失尊重，于是批评这位服务员："你不应当在没有弄清主客之前就主观地下结论，即使今天我是主人，你也应当请问客人需要什么饮料嘛！"李教授的朋友接着讲："我恰好是向来不喝现磨咖啡，而是喝惯了雀巢速溶咖啡的人。"服务员讨好不成，反而遭到没趣，准备继续争论下去。这时大堂经理闻声前来……

Hearing this, Professor Li felt this was disrespect for his friend and criticized the attendant: "You shouldn't make subjective conclusion before figuring out who is the host. Even if I am the host today, you should ask what the guest like!" His friend added: "I happen to be the one never drink freshly ground coffee, but used to drink Nescafe instant coffee." The attendant tried to please Professor Li but was criticized by the two of them. At the time when he was about to argue about it, the assistant manager came...

［任务驱动］［Task-Driven Questions］

1. 假如你是酒店的大堂经理，你该如何解决上述问题？小组成员进行前厅服务模拟表演，通过角色扮演，深刻体会客人心理活动，合情合理处理客人投诉，让客人继续成为酒店的忠实客人。

If you are the hotel's assistant manager, how do you solve the problem? Group members simulate services at the Front Office through role play to get a profound understanding of the mental activity of guests and handle guest complaints reasonably, so as to make guests continue to become loyal guests of the hotel.

2. 通过本案例的场景回放和后续设计，你认为哪组处理问题最到位？请试着分析该案例，服务员在提供服务时应该注意哪些事项?

According to the scenario playback and subsequent design, which group do you think does the best? Please try to analyze this case and figure out what the attendant should pay attention to when providing services?

模块小结
Module Summary

1. 酒店建立客户档案的意义有哪些?

What is the meaning of establishing the guest history file?

2. 酒店如何建立完整的客户档案?

How to establish a complete guest history file?

3. 酒店的客户档案如何进行管理?

How to manage the guest history file?

4. 酒店客人投诉的原因有哪些，有哪些类型?针对不同类型的投诉，酒店该如何处理?

What are the reasons of guest complaints? Types of guest complaints? How should the hotel deal with different types of complaints?

5. 酒店处理客人投诉时的注意事项有哪些?

What should the hotel note when handling guests complaints?

模块七 前厅销售
Module VII Front Office Sales

【情境导入】【Scenario Introduction】

推销豪华套房
Promoting luxury suite

一天，三亚唐拉雅秀酒店前厅部预订员小夏接到一位美国客人霍曼从上海打来的长途电话，想预订每天收费180美元左右的标准双人客房两间，住店时间6天，3天以后来酒店。

One day, the reservation agent Xiaoxia from the Front Office of Sanya Tangla Hotel received a long-distante phone call made by an American guest Homan from Shanghai. He said that he wanted to book two standard double rooms charging about 180 USD per day for six days, and would be here in three days.

小夏马上翻阅预订记录，回答客人说3天以后酒店要接待一个大型会议的几百名代表，标准间已全部预订完，小夏讲到这里用商量的口吻继续说道："霍曼先生，您是否可以推迟3天来店？"霍曼先生回答说："我们日程已安排好，三亚是我们在中国的最后一个日程安排，还是请你给想想办法。"

Xiaoxia checked the reservation records immediately and answered that the hotel would receive hundreds of representatives of a large conference in three days, and all standard rooms were booked. And then, Xiaoxia asked in a consulting tone: "Mr. Homan, could you delay for three days?" "We have already made arrangements, and Sanya is the last stop in China, could you work this out?" answered by Homan.

小夏想了想说："霍曼先生，感谢您对我的信任，我很乐意为您效劳，我想，您可否先住3天我们酒店的豪华套房，套房是海景房，在房间可眺望三亚湾的优美海景，三亚湾是海南美景集中之地，室内有我们中国传统雕刻的红木家具和古玩瓷器摆饰；套房每天收费也不过280美元，我想您和您的朋友住了一定会满意。"

Xiaoxia thought for a while: "Mr. Homan, thank you for your trust. I am glad to help, could you live in our luxury suite for three days? It is a sea-view suite, from which you may overlook the beautiful scenery in Sanya Bay, the most beautiful place in Hainan. The room is equipped with the redwood furniture of traditional Chinese carvings and chinaware. Besides, it only charges 280 USD per day. I bet both you and your friend would be pleased."

小夏讲到这里，等待霍曼先生回答，对方似乎犹豫不决，小夏又说："霍曼先生，我想您不会单纯计较房价的高低，而是在考虑豪华套房是否物有所值吧。请告诉我您和您的朋友乘哪次航班来三亚，我们将派车去机场接你们，到店后，我们一定先陪你们参观套房，到时您再作决定好吗？我们还可以免费为您提供美式早餐，我们的服务也是上乘的。"霍曼先生听小夏这样讲，觉得还不错，想了想欣然同意先预订3天豪华套房。

Xiaoxia was waiting for the answer, but Mr. Homan seemed to be hesitating. Xiaoxia continued: "Mr.

Homan, I think you are considering about if the luxury suite is worth or not, rather than bothering about the price. Please tell me the flight number, we would pick you up at the airport, and then we would accompany you to visit the suite. You may make decisions at that moment. Is it ok for you? We can also provide American breakfast for you for free, and by the way, we offer superior service." Mr. Homan thought it was good, and he was glad to book the luxury suite for three days.

【情境分析】【Scenario Analysis】

在本案中，小夏在接待客人来电预订房间的整个销售过程中，做的很到位，体现了一名前厅服务员应有的良好的综合素质，这体现在以下几个方面：

In this case, Xiaoxia behaves quite professional in the entire room reservation process, fully reflecting the perfect comprehensive quality of a servant at the Front Office. It is mainly reflected in the following aspects:

1. 接待热情、礼貌、反应灵活、语言得体规范，做到了无"NO"服务，在接收霍曼先生电话预订的过程中，为客人着想，使客人感到自己受到重视，因而增加了对酒店的信任和好感。

Enthusiastic, polite, quick in mind, appropriate in language, and offering no-No service. When receiving the reservation call from Mr. Homan, she always considered for the guest, and as a result, the guest felt the attention from the servant, which enhanced the trust and favorable impression on the hotel.

2. 小夏在推销豪华套房的过程中，采用的是利益引诱法，即严格遵循了酒店推销的是客房而不是价格这个原则，因而在报价中报价委婉，采用了"三明治式"报价方式，避免了高价格对客人心理产生的冲击力，如：

During the process of promoting luxury suite, Xiaoxia employed the inducement method, namely, the hotel promotes guest rooms, instead of the price. Moreover, the price is given in euphemistic way, with the "sandwich way", which could avoid the impact force of high price on the mentality of guests, for instance:

（1）先介绍客房情况：A：先住两天我们酒店的豪华套房，套房是外景房，可以眺望三亚湾的优美景色；B：有中国传统雕刻的红木家具、古玩瓷器摆饰。

Introduce the condition of guest room first: A: you can live in the luxury suite of our hotel for three days at first, and it is a sea-view suite, from which you can overlook the beautiful scenery of Sanya Bay; B: It is equipped with the redwood furniture of traditional Chinese carvings and chinaware.

（2）报价委婉：豪华套房每天每套收费不过 280 美元。

Euphemistic offer: the luxury suite only charges 280 USD per day.

（3）在报价后，介绍选择后的好处，所提供的服务：A：我们到时派车去机场接你们；B：我们的服务是上乘的；C：免费提供美式早餐。

After making offers, advantages and services are introduced: A: We would send a car to pick you up; B: We offer superior service; C: We offer free American breakfast.

这里所讲的利益引诱法，并非是让客人上当受骗，而是一种促销技巧。在客人权衡以后，感到物有所值，因而接受其价格。小夏在巧妙销售豪华套房的过程中，并没有强求客人预订，而是巧妙而如实地介绍豪华套房情况及客人选择后可享受到的服务，这样客人才会欣然接受。最后小夏使客人还有一次选择决定的机会，如：到店后我们一定先陪你们参观，到时您再做决定好吗？这就更增加了霍曼先生对小夏及酒店的信任感。

The interest inducement method mentioned is a promotion skill, rather than cheating guests. The guest may accept it after considering about the price to value. Xiaoxia promoted the luxury suite perfectly instead of forcing the guests, while the guest accepted it happily after the introduction about the condition of luxury suite and services offered. Eventually, Xiaoxia also offered a chance for the guest to make decisions, for instance, we would accompany you to visit the suite, and you may make decisions at that moment, which enhanced the guest's trust on Xiaoxia and the hotel.

【案例分析】【Case Analyze】

小夏积极主动、成功地销售客房遵循了酒店销售的是客房而不是价格，在销售过程中，语言亲切，自然诚恳，善解人意，反应灵活，运用了心理学知识，提供了针对性服务，同时办事效率高，体现了小夏良好的思想素质和优秀的业务素养。

Xiaoxia saled the suite proactively and successfully, followed the principle in which the hotel sells guest rooms instead of the price. In the sales process, she was nice, sincere, considerate and flexible. Besides, she also offered targeted service with psychology knowledge. Moreover, she worked efficiently, showing excellent quality and perfect business accomplishment.

本案例的教学，使学生很容易理解了前厅服务工作的几个重、难点问题，懂得了作为一名前厅服务员应具备什么样的素质，也达到了很好的教学效果。

The teaching of this case allows students to understand the key and difficult problems in the services at the Front Office easily and to know what kind of quality a servant at the Front Office shall have. Besides, it receives perfect teaching effect.

【学习目标】【Learning Goals】

［知识目标］［Knowledge Objectives］

1. 掌握酒店房态类型、房态的检查及控制酒店房态的目的。

Grasp the status types, inspection and control over the status of hotel.

2. 掌握酒店房价构成与收费方式、影响房价的因素及定价方法。

Grasp the price and charging method of the guest room, factors impacting the price, and pricing method.

［能力目标］［Capacity Objective］

1. 熟练掌握推销客房的技能要求。

Grasp the promotion skills of guest room proficiently.

2. 具有处理突发事件的能力，如防止客人逃账的技能。

Grasp the ability of handling emergencies, for instance, the skills of preventing bill escaping.

【重点和难点】【Key Points and Difficulties】

1. 掌握酒店客房基本情况，了解酒店价格组成。

Grasp the basic conditions of the guest room, and learn about the prices of guest rooms.

2. 熟悉并掌握推销客房的技巧和艺术。

Familiar with and grasp the skills and art of guest room promotion.

任务一 客房状态控制
Task I Status Control of Guest Room

【情境导入】【Scenario Introduction】

租重房
Repeated check-in

一天，一位已经有预订的客人来到了三亚美高梅度假酒店前台，客人要求将原来的标准间改为套房，以方便会客，值台员小蔡查看了房态，正好有客人需要的套房，于是安排客人入住了916号套房，随后在客人的入住登记表上将标准间改为了916号套房，并且将原来客人预订的标准间在电脑上也做了空房修改，但是却忘记了在电脑上将刚才出租套房的房态改为已住房。到了晚上，小蔡下班时没有告诉接班的服务员小李换房的事，当有客人要求入住套房时，值台员小李将电脑上显示是空房而实际上已有住客的916号套房安排给了客人。

One day, a guest who had already booked a room at MGM Grand Sanya came to the reception desk, and demanded to change the original standard room to a suite, for the convenience of meeting visitors. The receptionist Xiaocai checked the status of guest rooms, and there was a room meeting the demands of the guest. Therefore, the guest was arranged in No. 916 suite, and afterwards, the check-in register form was altered to No. 916 suite, while the status of original standard room was changed to vacant. However, the receptionist forgot to change the status of the suite. At night, during the work shift, Xiaocai forgot to tell the other receptionist Xiaoli of the next shift about the room change. When another guest asked for a suite, Xiaoli arranged No. 916 suite to the guest, but the suite had already been arranged.

客人办完手续后上了楼层，随后就打电话下来质问是怎么回事，房间已经有人住了。听到此情况，小李一面向客人道歉，一面赶紧查看记录，然后将客人换到了该楼层的另一间套房，并且及时更改了房态。第二天，酒店向客人赠送水果以表歉意，并给了客人一个合理的解释。

The guest went upstairs after going through the check-in procedures, but they called to inquire why the room was occupied already. After hearing it, Xiaoli apologized to the guest and checked the records, and then changed another suite on the same floor for the guest and changed the room status. On the second day, the hotel sent free fruits to the guests to show apology, and gave a reasonable explanation.

【情境分析】【Scenario Analysis】

此案例的产生是由于前台员工小蔡没有按规定的程序处理工作信息而导致的工作失误，造成了电脑房态的显示错误，并致使接班服务员小李按照电脑资料安排另一位客人入住了已有客人入住的房间，以致不仅影响了酒店的形象，而且也给酒店带来了经济损失。

This case was a mistake made by the receptionist Xiaocai, for she failed to follow the regulated procedure and correct the room status on the computer, which resulted that Xiaoli arranged the occupied room to a new guest. Consequently, it not only impacted the image of hotel, but also resulted in economic loss for the hotel.

此案例中，问题发生后，小李及时为客人换到同一楼层另外一间套房，并且第二天酒店向客人赠送水果以表歉意，并给了客人一个合理的解释（例如电脑出现故障），相信能够取得客人的谅解。

In this case, when the problem occurred, Xiaoli changed another suite on the same floor for the guest, sent free fruits to show apology on the second day, and gave a reasonable explanation (for instance the computer breakdown), believing that the guest may forgive it.

此案例给酒店的启示是：

Revelations of the case to the hotel:

（1）酒店要在以后的工作中避免租重房间的情况发生。对容易出现租重房的几个前台操作环节要严格把关，逐级检查，特别要核对各种资料与实际房态的显示是否一致，注意随时变更的房态，做好记录。

It shall avoid the repeated rent of room in the future, grasp several links in which there may be repeated rent of room at the reception desk strictly, and inspect it step by step. It shall check if the data is in line with the real room status, pay attention to the change of room status and take records.

（2）作为前台服务员，知道酒店的客房状况随时都有变化，这就要求酒店服务员在交接班时，加强相互的信息沟通与协调，并能够根据客人的要求统筹安排，尤其是接班人员应对上一班的交接再次核实、确认，确保无差错。

The receptionist shall know that the room status may change at any time, which requires that the hotel servant shall communicate and coordinate with each other, and make arrangements according to the requirements of guests. Especially, the information shall be verified, confirmed and guaranteed during the change of work shifts.

一、客房状态的类型（Types of Guest Room Status）

客房房态是酒店专业用语，它是依据酒店的管理方式、工作程序、计算机管理软件的配置、员工的素质、服务质量的要求及客源市场等多方面因素来确定本酒店房态类型及房态控制方法的。它能够对酒店客房的占用、代售、清洁、维修等状态进行统计和动态显示。在世界各国酒店，客房房态类型及显示方法大致相同。在客人到店前，我们必须掌握房态报告，了解现时可出租的客房、稍候可能供出租的客房（如未清扫的空房），不可出租的客房（如维修房、走客房等）情况，并根据此报告排房，可避免给客人造成不便。

Guest room status is a technical word. The types and control method of hotel room status are confirmed from various aspects of factors, such as the management of hotel, working routine, configuration of computer management software, quality of employees, requirement of service quality, customer market, etc. It can conduct the statistics and dynamic display of the occupation, sale, cleaning, maintenance, etc. of hotel rooms. In hotels throughout the world, the types of guest room status and display methods are basically the same. Before the guest reaches the hotel, we shall grasp the room status report, learn about the available guest room, about-to-be available guest room (such as empty rooms that have not been cleaned yet), and unavailable room (such as rooms in maintenance, vacant dirty, etc.), and arrange rooms according to the report, so as to avoid the inconveniences to the guests.

酒店计算机联网系统，是用计算机设备系统综合显示客房状态最先进的一种方法，目前广泛适用于客房数量多、种类复杂、客流量大的大、中型酒店。在前台接待处、前台收银处以及客房值班中心配有联网的计算机终端机，各部位可通过操作终端机来了解、掌握、传递有关客房状态的信息。这不仅加快了相互沟通、联络的速度，更能提高工作效率，避免工作差错。同时，它还具有各种功能，如帮助酒店进行客史档案建立、客账管理、各种报表的形成、营业收入汇总等，这些可用于前台及整个酒店的管理工作。

Hotel computer networking system is the most advanced method that can display the room status with computer equipment system. At present, it is widely applied in large and middle-sized hotels with numerous diversified guest rooms. At the reception desk, cash desk and on-duty center, it is equipped with the networked computer terminals, so that each department can learn about, grasp and transfer the information related to the guest room status through the operation terminals. It not only accelerates the speed of mutual communication and connect, also improves work efficiency and avoids work mistakes. Besides, it also has other functions, for instance, helping hotel setting up guest archives, account management, formation of various statements, income summary, etc. All the functions can be applied in the management of the Front Desk and even the entire hotel.

目前酒店的客房状态显示系统一般有两种，即客房现状显示系统和客房预订状态显示系统。客房现状显示系统，又称客房短期状况显示系统，可显示每一间客房的即时状态。前台接待处的排房和房价等工作完全依赖此系统提供的状况。客房预订状态显示系统，又称长期状态显示系统。在未使用计算机联网系统的酒店，这一系统是通过“客房预订汇总表”及预订情况显示未来某一时间内，相对某种类型客房的可销售量。

At present, the guest room status display system consists of two categories, including the guest room status display system and guest room reservation status display system. The guest room status display system, also called the short-term status display system, can show the instant status of each guest room. The room arrangement and price at the reception desk rely on the information provided by the system completely. The guest room reservation status display system, also called long-term status display system. In hotels without the computer networking system, this system can display the sales volume of a certain type of guest room in a certain period in the future through the "guest room reservation status summary" and reservation condition.

不同酒店管理软件定义的客房房态可能略微有差异，不过，万变不离其宗，客房房态无外乎以下几种：

Different hotel management software may define the guest room status differently, but it is basically the same, and there are the following types of room status:

（1）住客房。指已经出租，正由住店客人使用的客房。

Occupied (OCC), referring to rooms that have already been rent and used by guests.

（2）空房。已清扫整理、经检查可供出租的房间，也叫可售房。

Vacant clean (VC), referring to rooms that have already been clean and available or rent, also called available room.

（3）走客房。亦可称为 Check -out 或 On change，客人已结账离店，客房正处于清扫整理阶段。

Vacant dirty (VD), also called Check-out or On change, meaning that the guest has already left and the room is being cleaned.

（4）待修房。硬件出现故障、正在进行维修而暂停出租的客房。

Out-of-order, referring to rooms with mal-function in hardware and in maintenance that suspended renting.

（5）保留房。指某个房间已在某时期为某位客人保留，以防将其出租给其他客人。这是一种内部掌握的房态，对于一些大型团队或会议客人，酒店需要提前为他们预留所需的客房；还有些客人（尤其是常客）在订房时，常常会指明要某个房间，或处于某个位置、具有某种景观的客房。前台人员应在计算机上做好标志，防止将其出租给其他客人而引起麻烦。

Blocked, referring to rooms that have been reserved for a certain guest in a certain period, for preventing from being rent to others. It is a room status that shall be grasped, and it shall be reserved for some large teams or conference guests. Hotels shall reserve guest rooms for them. Some guests (especially the frequent caller) would appoint a certain room, or the rooms with certain location or landscape. The servants at the reception desk shall mark it on the computer, for preventing the troubles caused by the rent to someone else.

（6）散客房。去异地独立旅游者，两人以下包括两人入住一间客房的客人。

Room for individual guest, tourist traveling at a strange place, less than two or two guests living in one room.

（7）同住房。多人一同开房不属于旅行团，但是要求一个账户结账。

Living together room, several people rent rooms together, but they do not belong to a tour group, and they require the settlement in one account.

（8）团队房。旅行团带领游客以旅行团的名义开多间客房。

Room for teams, tour group usually rent several rooms in the name of tour group.

（9）自用房。酒店内为内部需要自己占用客房，这种房不计入出租率，不计入房租。

Self-use room, the hotel may occupy rooms for its own demands, and it will not be included in the occupancy rate or rent.

（10）免费房。酒店因为某种原因不收取该客房的房费，但是计入出租率。

Free room, hotels will not charge the rent for some reason, but it shall be included in the occupancy rate.

下列几种房态是楼层在进行客房状况检查时，要注意掌握并通知前台的：

The following kinds of room status shall be grasped during the room status inspection, and shall be informed to the reception desk:

（11）外宿未归房。如果住客在外过夜，前台接待员应在计算机上对该房做外宿未归标记，同时，将此信息通知大堂副理及客房部。大堂副理应锁住该房间，并作记录，以保证该房安全。

Sleep Out, if the guest sleeps in other place, the receptionist shall mark it on the computer. Meanwhile, it shall be informed to the assistant manager and housekeeping department. The assistant manager shall lock the room and take records for guaranteeing the safety of the room.

（12）携少量行李的住客房。为了防止发生逃账等意外情况，客房部应将此种客房状态通知前台。

Occupied with light luggage. In order to prevent the bill escaping, the housekeeping department shall inform the status of such guest room to the reception desk.

（13）请勿打扰房。客人为了不受干扰，在门把手挂有或灯光显示“请勿打扰”字样时，服务员就不能进房为客人提供服务。请勿打扰房通常应该是住客房，但也有可能是走客房或空房。所以有必要对此种房态加以关注。到了酒店规定的时间，前台或客房部应打电话与住客联系，以弄清情况。

Do Not Disturb (shorted as DND). The guest may hang the plate or lighting “do not disturb” on the handle for preventing disturbance. At this moment, the servant shall not enter the guest room to provide service. DND are usually the occupied guest rooms, but it may be VD or VC. Therefore, it is necessary to focus on such room status. Till the stipulated time, the reception desk or housekeeping department shall make phone calls to contact the guests to figure out.

（14）双锁房。住客为了不受干扰，在房内将门双锁，服务人员用普通钥匙无法开启。对双锁房要加强观察与检查，因为客人有可能生病，甚至死亡。有时，当酒店发现房内设备严重受损，客房内有暴露的贵重物品或发生刑事案件时，酒店管理部门也会做出双锁客房的决定。

Double Locked. The guest may double lock the room to prevent disturbance, and the servant cannot open the door with ordinary key. For double locked rooms, it shall strengthen the observation and inspection, for the guest may get sick, or even die. Sometimes, if the devices in the room are severely damaged, or there are valuables in the room, or there are criminal cases, the hotel management department will also double lock the door.

二、控制房态的目的（Purpose of Guest Room Status Control）

（一）提高排房效率及预订决策力（Improving Room Arrangement Efficiency and Reservation Decision）

前台、预订部、总台等部门清楚地了解房态，就知道哪些房间是可以租售的，哪些房间目前不能租售出去，并且能更好地与客人进行沟通，促进租售。

The reception desk, reservation department and information desk shall be clear about the room status, know which rooms can be rent, which rooms cannot be rent for now, so as to communicate with guests better and promote the sales.

（二）方便为客人调换房间（Convenient for Room Changes for Guests）

当客人对当前房间不满投诉时，可以更快地安排让客人满意的房间（客人投诉说房间小了、空调坏了、有味道、有工程问题、朝向不好、跟一起来的朋友房间相隔太远等，当大堂副理协调好，决定给客人换房时，服务员要做好前台和客人的向导，提供最好的换房建议）。

When guests are complaint about the current rooms, please arrange other rooms to satisfy guests as soon as possible (for instance, the guests complain that the room is too small, the air-conditioner is broken, smelly, there are problems in projects, the orientation is bad, far away from friends, etc. When the assistant manager coordinates with the guests and decides to change rooms for guests, the servant shall guide the guests and offer best suggestions for room change).

（三）有利于安排每天的工作任务（Favorable for Arranging the Daily Task）

领班或主管每天要给服务员安排工作任务，通过了解不同的房态，该维修的安排维修，该打扫的安排打扫，洗过地毯的房间该恢复房态的恢复房态。

The foreman or supervisor shall arrange tasks for servants every day, such as maintenance, cleaning, or recovery of status for rooms with clean carpet, etc. through learning about the room status.

（四）有利于安排打扫房间的顺序（Favorable for Arranging the Sequence of Rooms for Cleaning）

服务员拿到分房表后，根据房态的不同，打扫房间的顺序是不一样的。一般的打扫顺序是：

When the servant receives the room assignment table, the sequence of room cleaning is different. Generally, it is:

（1）客人口头或电话提出要打扫的房间。

The guest asks for the room cleaning orally or through telephone.

（2）挂了请即打扫牌的房间。

The guest hangs the plate of “room cleaning”.

（3）前台或总台通知要打扫的房间。

The reception desk or the information desk requires the cleaning.

（4）贵宾住客房。

Rooms of distinguished guests.

（5）走客房。

VD.

（6）普通住客房。

Ordinary guest room.

（7）空房。

Vacant room.

（8）长包房、自用房或被用作办公室的房间约定时间打扫。

Long-term compartment, self-use room or office rooms shall be cleaned at the appointed time.

（五）方便领班查房，放房（Convenient for Being Inspected or Released by the Foreman）

领班根据初始房态来检查房间，查看有无差异、漏项，衡量清洁程度，跟进工程，决定是否放房给前台销售。

The foreman shall check the room according to the initial room status, check if there are any differences or missing terms, measure the cleanness degree, keep up with the project, and decide if the room shall be released for rent.

（六）方便统计住客率和调整销售策略（Convenient for Accounting the Occupancy Rate and Adjusting the Sales Strategy）

房态体现了住店客人的多少，酒店通常会根据淡季、旺季或者住客率的高低调整相关的价格或销售方式。

The room status of the hotel reflects the number of guests, and the hotel will usually adjust the related price or sales mode according to the slack season, busy season or occupancy rate.

三、客房状态的核对与检查（Check and Inspection of the Guest Room Status）

由于前台的工作量大，且客房时常处于变化之中，虽然很多酒店通过计算机查询，可知目前的房态情况，但为了避免由于工作上可能出现的差错，而造成前台接待处的房态与楼层实际房间状态的不符，出现“重房”或“漏房”现象，造成前台客房销售及客房服务的混乱，及时对房态的核对、检查是十分必要的。对于房态的检查，是计算机查询与参考相关客房状况报表并用的。对于以手工方法显示房态的酒店，则比较复杂，且容易出错。除掌握客房状况显示架运行方法外，还应借助于控制房态的表格以及加强房态信息的有效沟通。有效的房态控制，有利于客房的销售和最佳利用。

Due to the huge workload of the reception desk, and the guest room status may change at any time. Although it can be checked through computer in many hotels for learning about the room status, in order to prevent the errors in work, the room status at the reception desk may not be in line with the practical room. As a result, the rooms may be rent repeatedly or missed, resulting in the chaos in guest room sales and guest room service. Consequently, it is extremely important to check and inspect the room status. As for the inspection of room status, it can be inquired through the computer or related guest room status statement. For hotels displaying the room status manually, it is relatively complicated, and it may go wrong easily. Besides grasping the guest room status display frame, it shall also refer to the room status table and strengthen the effective communication of room status. Effective room status control may be favorable for the sales of guest room and optimal utilization.

检查核对客房预订情况：①预订的复核确认情况；②预订住客的航班情况，掌握到达时间；③预订变更及取消情况；④预订不到情况的预计。

Check the reservation of guest rooms: ① Re-check for confirming the reservation; ② Flights of the reserving guests, grasp the arrival time; ③ Changes of reservation and cancellation; ④ Prediction of no shows for the reservation.

检查核对预期离店客房情况：①无变动的预期离店情况；②延期离店情况；③提前离店情况。

Check the condition of rooms with expected check-out: ①expected check-out with no changes; ②delayed check-out; ③check-out in advance.

检查核对可出租房：①可出租房的整房情况；②复核可出租房房态。

Check the available guest room: ①Condition of the available room; ②Re-check the room status for rent.

检查核对次日必须首先保证的客房情况：①贵宾房；②团队房；③酒店方违约的客人次日入住房间；④保证预订住客的预订房间。

Check the guest room that must be guaranteed on the second day: ① Distinguished room; ② Team room; ③Guest room for guests with which the hotel break the contract; ④Guarantee the room reserved for the guest.

无论计算机还是手工制作的客房状态报表大致包括：

The room status statement made by the computer or manually shall include the following parts:

（1）客房状态报告。客房状态报告是接待处根据计算机所显示的客房状态以及订房资料，每天定时制作的。制作此表的目的，是通过定时统计来确定客房的现状以及预订状况。

Guest room status report. The guest room status report is made at a given time every day according to the guest room status and reservation data displayed by the computer. It is mainly made to confirm the status of the guest room and reservation condition.

（2）客房状态调整表。客房状态调整表是将未经预订，直接抵店、延期离店和换房等情况汇集起来，形成客房状态调整表。它的作用主要体现在两点：一是用于预订处与接待处之间的信息沟通，使预订处依据调整表中的内容，更改并建立新的客房预订汇总表。二是调整表上的统计数字，可以使接待处掌握有多少临时取消住店、已预订但未到店、提前离店和逾期离店的客人，以及他们所占客源的百分比。这些数字对客房的销售起了很大作用。

Guest room status adjustment table. The guest room status adjustment table is mainly formed by integrating the unreserved room, delayed check-out rooms and change of rooms, etc. It is reflected by two aspects. Firstly, It is mainly applied for the information communication between the reservation and reception, so as to adjust the contents for the reservation place, change and create new guest room reservation table. Secondly, it is applied for adjust the statistic in the table, so that the reception desk may grasp the guests who cancel the reservation temporarily, who make the reservation but fail to show up, who leave in advance and who delay the check-out, as well as the percentage. These figures play a vital role for the sales of guest room.

（3）接待情况汇总表。接待情况汇总表是指接待处将计算机中所显示出的客房状态记录下来而形成的接待情况报告。它主要是为制作客房营业报表以及前厅的统计分析报表提供资料。

Reception summary table. The reception summary table refers to the report of reception formed according to the records of room status displayed by the computer, and it mainly provides data for the guest room operation statement and Front Office statistical analysis statement.

表 7-1 客房状况调整表
Table 7-1 Guest room status adjustment table

星期 Day（ ）日期 Date（ ）

序号 Room No.	类型 Type	姓名 Name	需作调整的日期 Adjusted date		备注 Remarks
			自 From	至 To	

备注 Ref：未经预订，直接抵店 N/R =Non Reservation（Walk-in）
延期离店 Ext =Extension（Overstay）
取消 Cnl =Cancellation
提前离店 Ux-dep =Unexpected Departure（Undetstay）
订了房，但未抵店 Nx =No shows

表 7-2 每日接待情况表
Table 7-2 Daily reception table

每日到达 Daily Arr	如期离开 Ori. Dept		提早离开 Adv. Dept		延期至 Ext. Till		取消预订 Canc	转房 Room _ Change				表格数 number of tables	备注 remark	当事人签字 Signed by principal
	房号 No.	日期 date	房号 Room No.	日期 date	房号 Room No.	日期 date		由 from	到 to	-	+			

VIP 或团队名单。VIP 或团队名单是接待员根据客房状态显示系统提供的资料制作而成的。它的作用是使酒店及时掌握在店的和即将抵店的贵宾、团队客人的信息，以便酒店做好各方面的准备工作。

VIP or team list. VIP or team list is made according to the data provided by the guest room status display system. It allows the hotel to learn about the information of about-to-arrive distinguished guests and team guests in time, so that the hotel can get prepared.

住店客人名单。住店客人名单，就是将所有住店客人的姓名记录下来。一般酒店编制住客名单主要采用两种方法：一是按照酒店客房房号的顺序排列；二是按住客姓名的首写字母的顺序排列。制作住店客人名单的作用，是为了便于前台各部门的对客服务。

List of guests. The List of guests mainly takes record of all names of guests. Generally, the compilation of the list of guests mainly adopts two methods: one is to follow the guest room number, and the other is to follow the first letter of the guest name. The list may make it convenient for the guest-oriented service offered by departments of the Front Desk.

预期离店客人名单。预期离店客人名单是根据客人在填写入住登记表时填写的离店日期汇总而成的。此表一般是按楼层、房号的顺序排列，其主要是为前台各部门和为客房部提前做好客人离店准备工作和客房的重新预订销售提供依据。

List of the expected check-out guest. The list of the expected check-out guest is formed according to the check-in date on the check-in register table. Generally, it is ranked by the room number and floor number, and it can provide basis for all departments of the reception desk and housekeeping department to het prepared for the check out and re-reservation of guest room.

四、影响房态的因素（Factors Impacting the Room Status）

（1）排房：包括保留房和锁房。

Arranging rooms: including the reserved room and locked room.

1）排房顺序为：团体客人，VIP客人和常客，已付定金的预订客人，要求延期离店的客人，普通预订客人并有准确航班号或抵达时间，无预订的散客。

The rooms shall be arranged in such a sequence: team guests, VIP guests and frequent guests, guests reserving with down payment, guests requiring the delay of check-out, ordinary reservation guest with accurate flight number or arrival time, unreserved individual guest.

2）排房方法：团体客人安排同一楼层，采用相对集中排房的原则；内外宾有不同语言和生活习惯的分别安排在不同楼层；行动不便（残疾人、老人、带小孩）的客人尽量安排在离电梯较近的房间；常客和有特殊要求的客人应予以照顾，满足其要求；敌对国家的客人尽量不要安排在同一楼层或相近的房间；应注意房间号码的忌讳。

Room arranging method: the team guest shall be arranged on the same floor, and it shall follow the relative concentration principle; foreign guests of different languages and living habits shall be arranged on different floors; guests inconvenient in action (the disabled, the old and the one with kid) shall be arranged in rooms near the elevator; frequent guests and guests with special demands shall be taken care of and satisfied; guests from countries hostile to others shall not be arranged on the same floor or near each other; please pay attention to the number of room.

（2）入住：可售房变住客房。

Check-in: available room shall be changed to occupied room.

（3）换房：住客房变走客房或可售房或待修房。

Changing rooms: occupied room shall be changed to VD or available room or room for maintenance.

（4）退房：住客房变走客房。

Check-out: occupied room shall be changed to VD.

（5）待修房。

Room for maintenance.

（6）关闭楼层。

Floor closed.

前厅销售人员应随时、准确地掌握这些变动的信息，及时传递、变更房态变化的信息。

The salesman at the Front Office shall grasp the varying information at any time accurately, and transfer and change the information of room status in time.

五、客房状况的转换（Transformation of Guest Room Status）

（1）客人入住与退房。由于客人的入住与退房，产生客房状况的转换。

Check-in and check-out, since the check-in and check-out may result in the transformation of guest room status.

（2）离店日期的变更及延迟退房处理。客人因事需提前或延迟退房，接待员应及时与预订处、收银处等取得联系，填写及传送有关通知单。

Changes of check-out date and delayed check-out. If the guest shall delay the check-out or leave in advance, the receptionist shall contact the reservation desk, cash desk, etc. in time, fill in and deliver related letter of notice.

（3）换房处理。应首先弄清（或向客人解释）换房原因；再向客人介绍准备调换的客房情况，并确定换房的具体时间；填写“客房、房租变更通知单”，并送往有关部门，经签字确认换房信息已经收到；更改客房状况，并将换房信息记录在客史档案上。

Room change. Please figure out the reason of room change (or explain to the guest), and then introduce the condition of the guest room that will be changed, and confirm the specific time of room changing. Fill in the *Guest Room and Rent Changing Notice*, and send it to related departments, and it will be confirmed as received after being signed; change the guest room status, and note the room change information on the guest history file.

【实训与评价】【Training and Assessment】

［实训目的］［Training Goals］

1. 熟悉酒店客房的各种状态。

Familiar with various status of the guest room.

2. 能够熟练掌握客房状态控制的有效方法及手段。

Grasp the effective means and methods of controlling the guest room status proficiently.

3. 规范自己的言行，正确使用礼貌用语和敬语；能有礼有节、不卑不亢地处理突发事件。

Standardize the statements and actions, use polite language and deferential language, and be able to deal with emergencies at ease.

［实训准备］［Training Preparation］

1. 前厅服务模拟场景、电脑、预订登记簿、值班记录簿、学生到各酒店调研时收集的相关资料等。

The Front Office service simulation site, computer, reservation register, on-duty recorder, related data collected during the investigation in hotels, etc.

2. 学生 6 人分为一组，教师讲解示范后，学生根据教师布置的任务进行实际操作。

Students are divided into groups of six, and after the illustration, students shall practice according to the tasks assigned by teachers.

［实训方法］［Training Method］

先观看教师播放的教学课件，然后由教师引导学生分析所收集到的相关资料，学生 6 人一组，按照任务驱动的要求进行实际操作，教师巡回指导，实训结束前抽小组进行点验结果的汇报。

Watch the teaching courseware displayed by the teachers, and then analyze the related data collected under the guidance of teachers. Groups of six shall conduct the practical operation according to the task-driven requirement, and teachers shall guide students and extract groups to report the examination result before the end of training.

［实训步骤］［Training Procedure］

第一步：教师向学生展示前厅客房状况显示系统和客房状况显示表，让学生有一定的感性认识。

Teachers shall display the guest room status display system and guest room status display table, so that students can gain sensible understanding.

第二步：学生分成 4 人一组讨论如何有效地控制客房状态，由学生分析，指出正误。

Students are divided into groups of four to discuss the effective control of guest room status, analyze it and point out the mistakes.

第三步：由学生继续讨论，列出几个实行方案。

Students shall continue to discuss, and list several practical plans.

第四步：各组学生代表发言，其他各组学生评价。

Representative of each group shall make statements, and other students shall evaluate.

第五步：教师评价与回答问题。

Teachers shall evaluate and answer the questions.

[实训内容][Training Content]

1. 如何有效、准确地控制客房状态？

How to control the guest room status effectively and accurately?

2. 到某星级酒店了解客房状态控制工作过程及具体内容（这环节课前进行），并写出一份调研报告（以小组的形式在班里进行汇报）。

Learn about the guest room status control process and specific contents at a star hotel (it shall be conducted before the class), and write an investigation report (report in groups in the class).

[实训评价][Training Evaluation]

客房状态控制调研任务评分标准如表 7-3 所示。

Grading standard for the guest room status control investigation task is shown in Tadle 7-3.

表 7-3　客户状态控制任务评分标准

Table 7-3　Grading standard for the guest room status control investigation task

姓名：
Name: 　　班级：
Class: 　　时间：
Time:

分数 Score / 要求 Requirements	应得分 Reserved score	小组自评 Self-evaluation	其他组评分 Grading by other groups
调研对象符合要求 The investigation target meets the requirements	10		
调研内容明确 The investigation is explicit in content	20		
调研报告文字达标 The investigation report is standard in writing	25		
汇报时表达流畅 The report representation is smooth	25		
小组合作融洽，分工明确 The group cooperation is harmonious and the division of labor is clear	20		
教师评语： Comments from teachers:			

任务二 酒店房价
Task II Hotel Rates

【情境导入】【Scenario Introduction】

再给 8.8 折的优惠
Twelve percent off

某日，一位新加坡的常客来到三亚喜来登度假酒店前台要求住房。接待员小王见是常客，便给他 9 折优惠。客人还是不满意，他要求酒店再多给些折扣。这时正是旅游旺季，酒店的客房出租率甚高，小王不愿意在黄金季节轻易给客人让更多的利，新加坡客人便提出要见经理。

One day, a frequent guest from Singapore came to Sheraton in Sanya and demanded for a room. The receptionist Xiaowang found that he was a frequent guest, and offered 10% discount. But the guest was not satisfied, and asked for more discounts. Since it was the busy season with high occupancy rate, Xiaowang did not want to give more discounts in the golden season, and the guest from Singapore asked to meet the manager.

其实，酒店授权给前台接待员的房价折扣不止 9 折，小王原可以把房价再下浮一点，但他没有马上答应客人。一则他不希望客人产生如下想法：酒店客房出租情况不妙，客人可以随便还价；二则他不希望给客人留下这样的印象：接待员原来可以再多打一些折扣，但他不愿给，只是客人一再坚持后他才无可奈何地退让，这会使客人认为大酒店员工处理问题不老实。于是小王希望通过酒店再次让利让客人感到前厅经理对他的尊重。小王脑中闪过这些想法后，同意到后台找经理请示。他请新加坡客人先在沙发上休息片刻。

Actually, the hotel authorized that the receptionist with more than 10% of discount, and Xiaowang could have gave more discounts, but he did not promise the guest immediately. On one hand, he did not expect such opinion from guest: the guest room did not sell well, and the guest can bargain easily. On the other hand, he did not want to leave such an impression on the guest: the receptionist could give more discounts, but he was not willing to give it, and he had to make a concession in front of the insistence, which may result that the guest though the receptionist was not honest, then Xiaowang wished that the hotel could give more discounts to show the respect from the manager to him. With these ideas, he agreed to ask for the manager, and he invited the gust from Singapore to rest on the Sofa for a while.

数分钟后，小王满面春风地回到总台，对客人说："我向经理汇报了您的要求。他听说您是我店常客，尽管我们这几天出租率很高，但还是同意再给您 8.8 折的优惠，并要我致意，感谢您多次光临我店。"小王稍作停顿后又说："这是我们经理给常客的特殊价格，不知您觉得如何？"

Several minutes later, Xiaowang came back with smiles, and said to the guest: "I have reported your requests to the manager, and he heard that you are the frequent guest of our hotel. Although we enjoy high occupancy rate in recent days, we still agree to give you 12% more discount. Besides, he also asks me to show our gratitude to you." He continued: "this is a special price given to the frequent guest from our manager. How do you think?"

新加坡客人计算一下，9 折的基础上再打 8.8 折，这样他实际得到了优惠折扣便是 7.9 折，这对于位于三亚亚龙湾地区，又处旅游旺季的五星级酒店来说，已经是给面子的了。客人连连点头，很快便递上身份证办理入住手续了。

The guest calculated, with 10% discount and 12% more, he actually enjoyed 21% discount, which was quite face-saving in the five-star hotels in Sanya Yalong Bay. He nodded repeatedly, and handed over the identity card to go through the check-in procedures.

【请你分析】【Please Analyze】

1. 案例中，小王在推销过程中，哪些策略是值得我们学习的？

In this case, what strategies are worth learning in the promotion process?

2. 客房销售过程中存在哪些销售技巧？案例中的小王，运用了哪些技巧？

What kind of sales skills are there in the promotion process? How many skills does Xiaowang apply in this case?

【情景分析】【Scenario Analysis】

全员促销是酒店成功销售产品的重要手段。酒店所有员工都有推销产品的可能和职责，但机会大小不一。一般来说，总台接待员、餐厅点菜员和歌舞厅、商场、酒吧、咖啡厅等一线部门的服务员有更多的机会。各酒店应像这个酒店的总经理那样经常向员工灌输促销意识，因此酒店还应在部门内加强促销技巧的培训。

The total sales promotion is a significant approach of successful product sales. All employees of the hotel shall take the product promotion as the responsibilities, but there are various distinct opportunities. Generally speaking, the receptionist, waitresses, and servants in the dancing hall, supermarkets, bars and coffee house, etc. have more chances. All hotels shall infuse the promotion consciousness to employees frequently like the general manager of the hotel. Moreover, the hotel shall also enhance the training of promotion skills.

本例中的接待员小王在转入后台之前的一段思索是正确的。他有权给客人超过 9 折的优惠，但他没一下子把这个权用尽，只要有可能，他总是想法为酒店多创一分利。后来客人提出再给优惠的要求，他又借口去请示经理，显得极为成熟老练。这样处理还有两点更深的含义：一是表明小王为此已经尽了很大的努力，使客人深感酒店是把他作为重要客人来对待的；二是再给 8.8 折优惠是前厅部经理的决定，如欲进一步提高折扣，其可能性将是微乎其微，这将有助于刹住客人继续要求降价的欲望。

In this case, the consideration of the receptionist before shifting to the backstage was correct. He had the right to offer more than 10% discount, but he did not use it, for as long as it is possible, he always wanted to create more profits for the hotel. Later, the guest asked for more discount, he used the excuse to apply for it from the manager, which was quite mature and experienced. The treatment also showed that: firstly, Xiaowang had made great efforts, which made the guest think that they were important. Secondly, 12% more discounts were given by the manager, and it was impossible to give more discounts, which would help stop the guest's desire for more reduction in price.

如果客人对此仍不满意，而接待员的折扣权限已经到顶，接待员还是应该向经理请示。每个上门的客人都要尽最大努力留住，尤其是常客，不能因为是旅游旺季而拒绝他们并不过分的要求。常客为酒店带来巨大财富，万万不可轻率地把他们推到自己的竞争对手那儿去。

If the guest was still unsatisfied and the receptionist had already given all discounts, he shall still ask for instructions from the manager. Each guest shall be reserved, especially the frequent guest, and please do not refuse the unexcessive demand due to the busy season, for the frequent guest may bring substantial fortune for the hotel. Please do not hesitate to push them to our competitors.

一、酒店房价构成与收费方式（The Room Rate Composition and Charging Method of Hotel）

酒店客房价格是由客房商品的成本和利润构成的。其中客房商品的成本包括建筑投资及由此产生的利息和客房设备折旧费、修缮费、物资用品消耗费、土地资源使用费以及经营管理费、客房服务人员工资福利、保险费、营业税等。利润则包括所得税和客房利润。

The room rate consists of the cost and profit, in which, the cost includes the construction investment and interest incurred, depreciation of equipment, repairing charge, material consumption cost, land resource application cost, as well as the operating management cost, housekeeping servant salary and welfare, insurance expenses, business tax, etc., while the profit includes the income tax and guest room profit.

（一）欧洲式（European Plan，EP）

包含房价，不包括餐费的收费方式，为国际上大多数酒店所采用。

Including the room rate, excluding the charging of meal fee, and it is mainly adopted by most hotels throughout the world.

（二）美国式（American Plan，AP）

不仅包含房费，还包括一日三餐费用，被称为“全费用计价方式”，多为远离城市的度假性酒店或团队客人所采用。除了包含与欧陆式早餐所有的项目比如咖啡或茶、黄油、果酱、面包和果汁外，还包括英式早餐中的煮黄豆、德式早餐中的香肠，还有麦片、谷物粥类、鸡蛋类、肉食类等食品。

It includes the room rate, as well as the meal fee, and it is called “total cost pricing manner”. It is adopted by vacation hotels or team guests far away from the city. Besides all items in the continental breakfast, such as coffee or tea, butter, jam, bread and juice, it also includes the boiled soybean in British breakfast, sausage in German breakfast, cereal, grains, eggs, meat, etc..

（三）修正美式（Modified American Plan，MAP）

包含房费和早餐费用，此外，还包括一顿午餐或晚餐（两者任选其一）的费用，多为普通旅游客人所采用。

Including the room rate and breakfast, in addition, it also includes a lunch or dinner (any one), and it is mainly adopted by ordinary tourists.

（四）欧洲大陆式（Continental Plan，CP）

包括房费及欧陆式早餐。星级酒店中的“欧陆式早餐”也叫“简单早餐”，而美式早餐相对项目繁多，因此也被称为“复杂式早餐”和“全早餐”。欧陆式早餐包含的项目一般只有咖啡或茶、黄油、果酱、面包、麦片、果汁、水果和沙拉。

Including the room rate and Continual breakfast. In tart hotels, CP is also called “simple breakfast”, but the American breakfast is diversified in varieties. Therefore, it is also called “complicated breakfast” and “full breakfast”. CP includes coffee or tea, butter, jam, bread, cereal, juice, fruit and salad.

（五）百慕大式（Bermuda Plan，BP）

包含房费及美式早餐。美式早餐除包括欧陆早餐的内容外，通常还包括鸡蛋、火腿、香肠、咸肉等肉类食品。

Including the room rate and American breakfast, which not only covers the CP, but also includes eggs, ham, sausage, bacon, etc.

二、房价类型（Room Rate Types）

房价种类一般有门市价、商务合同价、团队价、小包价、折扣价、家庭租用价、免费、淡季价、旺季价、白天租用价、加床价等。酒店房价由酒店决策者合理制定，其市场交易价格一般可分为以下几种类型：

Generally, the room rate includes Rack rate, Commercial rate, Group rate, Package rate, Discount rate, Family plan rate, complimentary rate, slack season rate, Busy season rate, Day use rate, Extra bed rate, etc. The hotel rate is made by the decision makers properly, and the market transaction rate generally consists of the following types:

1. 门市价（牌价、标准价、公布价）［Rack Rate（List Rate, Standard Rate, Release Rate)］

在价目表上明码公布各类现行价格，按照国际通行的计价方式（欧洲式、美国式、修正美式、欧洲大陆式、百慕大式），一般以欧洲式计价为多，21世纪以来，在欧洲式基础上加自助早餐的较多。

Publish the current rate on the rate card, according to the international rating method（European plan, American plan, modified American plan, Continental plan, Bermuda plan）, generally, EP dominates; since this century, most hotels adopt the EP and buffet breakfast.

2. 商务合同价（Commercial Rate）

酒店与有关机构签订售房合同，优惠幅度视情而定。

The hotel sign sales contract with related authority and the preferential margin depends.

3. 团队价（Group Rate）

酒店给旅行社等提供的一种折扣房价，优惠幅度也视情而定，有的高出门市价的40%以上。

Hotel may provide a discount to the travel agency, and the preferential margin also depends. Some is even about 40% higher than the rack rate.

4. 小包价（Package Rate）

即一揽子报价，一般包括房费、餐费、交通费、游览费等项目以方便客人。

Namely the package rate, including the room rate, meal fee, and traffic and traveling cost, etc. in order to make it convenient for guests.

5. 折扣价（Discount Rate）

酒店向常客、长住客或其他特殊客人提供的优惠价。

The hotel may offer discount rate to frequent guests, long stay guests, and other special guests.

6.家庭租用价（Family Plan Rate）

酒店对携带小孩的父母提供的折扣价格，如提供免费小床等，以刺激其他消费。

The hotel offers discount rate to parents with children, for instance, free small bed, to stimulate other consumption.

7. 免费（Complimentary Rate）

一般用以接待友好往来单位，免费范围视情而定。

It is usually applied for receiving the friendly exchanging unit, and it depends.

8. 淡季价（Slack Season Rate）

一般优惠的幅度大。在营业淡季，酒店为经营需要而采用刺激需求、吸引客人的价格，一般在标准价的基础上下浮一定的百分比。

It is quite favorable. In slack season, hotels shall adopt the price that may stimulate the demand and attract the attention from guests, and it usually decreases by certain percentage based on the standard price.

9. 旺季价（Busy Season Rate）

一般优惠幅度小甚至加价。

The preferential margin is small, and it even increases.

10. 白天租用价（Day Use Rate）

（1）凌晨抵店。

Arrives early in the morning.

（2）超过离店时间。

Exceeding the check-out time.

（3）钟点房。

Hour room.

11. 加床价（Extra Bed Rate）

酒店一般会视情而定。

It depends on actual situation of hotels.

三、影响房价的因素（Factors Impacting the Room Rate）

制定房价是酒店自主的经营活动，可以自由地选择定价目标。但由于内外环境和条件的制约，使酒店定价自由度受到一定的限制。因此，酒店定价必须充分考虑内在和外在因素。酒店定价时除考虑酒店硬件设施设备以外，还应考虑其服务质量的高低。

The room rate is the independent right of hotel, and the hotel can choose the rate freely. However, due to the restrictions of internal and external environment and condition, the rate freedom degree may be restrained to a certain level. Therefore, the hotel rate shall fully consider the internal and external elements. During the room rate, besides the hardware equipment, the hotel shall also consider about the service quality.

（一）定价目标（Room Rate Objectives）

客房定价的目标有追求利润最大化、提高市场占有率、应付和防止竞争以及实现预期的投资收益等。定价目标是指导酒店进行客房定价的首要因素。这是酒店确定经营方针的重要依据。

The room rate objectives include the pursuit for profit maximization, increase of market share, dealing with and preventing competition, and realizing the expected income from investment. The rate objective is the primary factor guiding the room rate, and it is also the significant basis for the hotel to confirm the guideline for management.

1. 追求利润最大化（Pursue for the Maximization of Profit）

追求利润最大化应该是客房商品最基本的定价目标。但利润最大化分为短期利润最大化和长期利润最大化，追求短期利润最大化和长期利润最大化会使酒店管理者在不同的时期，确定不同的价格水平。酒店管理者应以长期利润最大化为追求目标，而不应鼠目寸光，采用杀鸡取卵的定价方法。

The pursuit for profit maximization shall be the basic rate objective. But it consists of short-term profit maximization and long-term profit maximization. The pursuit of the two objectives may make hotel managers to confirm different rate levels in different stages. Hotel managers shall pursue for the long-term profit maximization, instead of being shortsighted.

2. 提高市场占有率 (Increase the Market Share)

提高市场占有率意味着客房销售量的增加，酒店客房及其他设施设备的利用率的提高，经营成本的降低，以及酒店市场竞争力的提高，因此，是很多企业追求的目标。采用低价策略，酒店决策者应考虑到以下事实。

The increase of market share means the increase of guest room sales, increase of utilization of guest rooms and other facilities, decrease of operation cost, as well as the increase of market competitiveness. Therefore, it is the objective pursued by many enterprises. Hotel decision makers shall consider about the following facts before adopting the low rate strategy.

(1) 有时，降低价格并不一定能增加客源，提高市场占有率。

Sometimes, the decrease of price may not increase the guests, and increase the market share.

(2) 低价可能有损酒店形象，影响服务质量。

Low rate may do harm to the image of hotel and influence the service quality

(3) 低价促销可能引来同行竞争的报复，导致价格战，结果两败俱伤，也使提高市场占有率的计划落空。

Low rate promotion may draw the revenge of peers, resulting in price war and loss at both sides, and meanwhile, the plan of increasing market share may fail.

3. 应付或防止竞争 (Deal with or Prevent the Competition)

(1) 与竞争者客房同价。

The same room rate as the competitors.

(2) 高于竞争者的客房价格。

Higher than the guest room rate of the competitors.

(3) 低于竞争者的客房价格。

Lower than the room rate of competitors.

4. 实现预期投资收益率 (Realize the Expected Income from Investment)

(二) 成本水平 (Cost Level)

价格应确定在成本之上，成本往往是价格的下限。这是影响客房价格水平的基本因素。如建筑成本回收期的长短，以及目标利润率的高低，都会对房价的制定产生影响。在进行客房定价时，必须考虑成本水平。包括：

The room rate shall be above the cost, which is usually the lower limit of rate, as well as the basic elements impacting the guest room rate. For instance, the period of construction cost recovery, the target rate of return, etc. may impact the room rate. When determining the room rate, the cost level must be considered, including:

(1) 折旧、水电、空调、低值易耗品等 (物化劳动的转移价值)。

Depreciation, water and electricity, air conditioner, low cost and short lived articles (transfer value of the materialized labor).

(2) 员工工资、福利 (活劳动支出中的必要劳动价值)。

Salary and welfare of employees (necessary labor value in the direct labor expenditure).

(3) 非营业部门费用分摊 (物化劳动的转移价值)。

Non-operating department cost allocation (transfer value of materialized labor).

（三）市场供应关系（Market Supply Relation）

市场供求关系是不断变化的，处于动态状况。供大于求，降低价格，供不应求，提高价格。当供过于求时，酒店业不得不考虑降低价格；当供不应求时，酒店业要考虑适当提高价格。客房商品的价格随供求关系的变化而调整。

The market supply relation is ever-changing in dynamic condition. When the supply exceeds the demand, the price can be reduced, or it can be increased. When the supply exceeds the demand, the hotel has to consider about the reduction in price, or it can consider about the increase of price. The room rate can be adjusted with the supply-demand relationship.

（四）酒店地理位置（Geographic Position of the Hotel）

酒店所处地理位置是影响房价的又一因素。地理位置对于酒店经营的确非常重要。位于市中心区，繁华商业区，距离机场、火车站比较近等交通便利的酒店，其房价的制定或调整的条件就会有利一些。而位于市郊、远离繁华商业区、交通条件等地理位置较差的酒店，虽然地价便宜，经营成本低，但由于其对客人的吸引力差，因此房价会相应低一些，以提高酒店的竞争能力。

The geographic position of hotel is another factor impacting the room rate, and it is extremely important for the hotel management. Hotels with convenient traffic, such as in the downtown, busy commercial district, close to the airport or train station, etc. may be much more favorable in the room rate and adjustment. However, for hotels with poor geographic positions, such as in the suburb, far away from busy commercial district, poor traffic condition, it is less attracting despite of its low price and operation cost. Therefore, the price may be relatively lower, for improving the competitive capacity of the hotel.

（五）竞争对手价格（Room Rate of the Competitor）

制定房价，应首先了解本地区同等级的其他酒店的房价。竞争对手的价格是酒店制定房价时的重要参考依据。

As for the room rate, it shall lean about the room rate of other hotels in the same region in the first place, and the room rate of competitors shall be the significant reference basis for the room rate.

因为在定价过程中，定价人首先要调查本地区同等级、同档次、具有同等竞争力的酒店的房价，做到“知己知彼”。

For in the process of room rate, the rater shall investigate the room rate of hotels with same level, same grade and equal competitive force, trying to “know both ourselves and our adversaries”.

（六）客人的消费心理作用（Consumer Psychology）

客人的消费心理也是进行客房价格定价时应予以重点考虑的因素，尤其是客人对某一种商品价格能够接受的上限和下限。

The consumer psychology is also the element that shall be considered during the room rate, especially the upper limit and lower limit that can be accepted.

（七）有关部门和组织的价格政策（Rate Policy of Related Department and Organization）

旅游经济具有脆弱性，其产品具有不稳定性、波动性。一个稳定、繁荣的社会政治及经济环境对以旅游经济为其重要收入来源的酒店来讲是至关重要的。

Tourist economy is fragile, and its product is unstable with fluctuations. A stable and flourishing social politics and economic environment may be critical for hotels that take tourist economy as an important source of income.

客房房价还受本地区政府主管部门以及行业协会等组织和机构对酒店价格政策的约束。例如某地区对所在地区酒店客房价格的最高上限要求。

The room rate shall also be restrained by room rate policies of the competent department of district government and industry association, for instance, the upper limit requirement of the room rate in the district of hotel.

四、客房定价方法（Guest Room Rate Method）

客房定价的基本原理：客房价格一般以供给价格为下限，以需求价格为上限，实际市场成交价格受市场竞争的影响在上/下限间波动。特殊时期市场成交价格可能会低于客房产品成本价格。其中，客房产品的价值决定供给价格，客人支付能力决定需求价格，市场竞争决定市场成交价格。

The basic principle of room rate: the guest room price usually takes the ordinary supply price as the lower limit, and demand price as the upper limit. The actual market transaction price may fluctuate between the upper and lower limit due to the influence of market competition. In special period, the market transaction price may be lower than the cost price of the guest room. The value of guest room decides the supply price, the payment capacity of guests determines the demand price and the market competition determines the market transaction price.

（一）千分之一法/建筑成本定价（Thousandth Method / Construction Cost Pricing）

根据客房造价来确定房间出租价的一种方法，即将每间客房的出租价格确定为客房平均造价的千分之一。特别是用来指导酒店（尤其是新建酒店）的客房的定价，判断酒店现行客房价格的合理程度。该方法是人们在长期的酒店建设和经营管理实践中总结出来的一般经验，可以用来指导新建酒店客房的定价，判断酒店现行客房价格的合理程度。每日客房价格=酒店建造总成本/酒店客房总数/1000。

It is a method that can determine the room rate according to the construction cost, namely the room rate of each guest room is determined as thousandth of the average construction cost. Especially, it can be applied for guiding the room rate of hotels (especially newly-built hotels), and judge the reasonable degree of the current room rate. The method is the ordinary experience summarized from the long-term hotel construction and operation management practice, and it can be applied to guide the rate of newly-built hotels, and judging the reasonability of current room rate. The daily room rate = total construction cost of the hotel / total rooms / 1000.

例如，某酒店有客房400间，总造价4000万美元，若每间客房布局统一，则平均每间客房的造价为10万美元，按千分之一规律，房价应为：

For instance, a hotel has 400 guest rooms, and the total construction cost is 40 million USD. If the rooms are arranged uniformly, the construction cost of each guest room shall be 100000 USD, if following the thousandth rule, the price shall be:

客房价格=40000000/（400×1000）=100000/1000=100美元

Room rate = 40000000 /（400×1000）= 100000 / 1000 = 100 USD

千分之一定价法的运用，其科学性和合理性受以下两个条件制约：

As for the application of thousandth rate method, the scientificity and reasonability is restrained by the following two conditions:

一是酒店客房类型、面积、设计设备的豪华程度等基本相同（平均房价）。

Firstly, the types of guest rooms, area, luxury degree of equipment are basically the same (average room rate).

二是酒店客房、餐饮及娱乐等规模和投资比例适当。

Secondly, Hotel guest rooms, catering and entertainment, etc. scale and investment shall be proper.

注意：使用千分之一法定价，需要满足以下三个前提条件：

Notice: if thousandth method is applied, it shall follow the three premises:

（1）客房的年平均出租率要达到70%。

The average annual occupancy rate reaches 70%.

（2）其他部门（如餐饮、商品部等）能够提供一定的利润。

Other departments (for instance catering, commodity department, etc.) can provide certain profits.

（3）酒店的营业毛利率要达到55%。

The gross profit of hotel shall reach 55%.

如果上述这些都能做到，在扣除其他费用以后，房租的收入可以使酒店每年还本6%。使用千分之一法，酒店管理人员可以迅速做出决策，也可以作为衡量一家酒店收费是否合理的重要参考依据。但是千分之一法把房价和过去的建筑费用联系在一起而不考虑当前酒店的各项费用，如上缴税金、获取酒店的合理利润等。因此它的可行信大打折扣，一般酒店基本不采用。该方法具有明显的局限性，只考虑了酒店客房的成本因素，没有考虑供求关系及市场竞争状况，因此只能仅供参考。

If he above mentioned can be attained, the rent income can also repay 6% of the principal after the deduction of other cost. With the thousandth method, hotel managers can also make decisions soon, and it can be the significant basis measuring if the hotel's charging is reasonable or not. However, thousandth method connects the room rate to the past construction cost, without considering the current costs of the hotel, such as the payment of taxes, acquisition of reasonable profit, etc. Therefore, its feasibility is discounted, and it is seldom adopted by the ordinary hotels. It has obvious limitation, for it only consider about the cost factor of hotel, instead of the supple-demand relationship and market competition. Therefore, it can only be used as references.

（二）赫伯特定价法/成本核算定价法（Hubbart Formula / Cost Accounting Pricing Method）

赫伯特定价法是20世纪50年代，美国酒店和汽车旅馆协会主席赫伯特主持发明的。它是以目标收益率为定价的出发点，在已确定计划期各项成本费用及酒店利润指标的前提下，通过计算客房部应承担的营业收入指标，进而确定房价的一种客房定价法。

Hubbart formula was invented by the chairman of American Hotel and Motel Association Hubbart in the 1950s. It is a guest room rate method that can determine the room rate through calculating the operation revenue index undertake by the housekeeping department, by starting from the target yield on the premise of confirming all costs and hotel profit index.

与千分之一法相比，赫伯特定价法要合理得多。它是根据计划的营业量、固定费用及酒店所需达到的投资收益率来确定每天客房的平均房价。

Compared to the thousandth method, Hubbart formula is much more reasonable. It is the average room rate confirmed according to the planned business volume, fixed cost and return on investment.

一般而言，新建酒店往往采用此种方法定价。

Generally speaking, newly-built hotels usually adopt this method for room rate.

$$\text{平均每间客房租价} = \frac{\text{预期投资收益} + \text{固定费用（税、折旧、利息等）} + \text{未分配费用} - \text{其他营业部门利润} + \text{客房部营业费用}}{\text{计划的营业量（预计客房出租间数）}}$$

Average guest room rate = Expected income from investment + fixed charge (tax, depreciation, interest, etc.) + undistributed cost - profits of other departments + operation cost of housekeeping department / planned business volume（predicted rent rooms）

该公式的缺陷在于客房部必须承担实现计划投资收益率的责任。由分子看出，其他部门盈利高，房价可低些，一旦其他营业部门亏损，房价则上升。因此，其他部门经济效益低，不应由高昂的、缺乏竞争力的房价来弥补。同时，其他部门的高额利润也不应成为制定过低房价的理由。

The flaw of this equation lies in that the housekeeping department must undertake the responsibility of realizing the planned return on investment. It can be seen from the numerator that if the profit of other department is higher，the room rate can be lower，once other operating departments suffer from loss，the room rate will increase. Therefore，the low economic benefit of other departments shall not be compensated by the high and less competitive room rate. And meanwhile，the high profits of other departments shall not become the excuse of low room rate.

早期的酒店客房定价一般以成本为导向，酒店管理者在进行价格决策时，主要关注的是投资回报。千分之一法和赫伯特定价法属于成本导向定价法。

The early hotel room pricing is generally guided by the cost. When hotel managers make price decisions，they mainly focus on the return of investment. Thousandth method and Hubbart formula belong to the cost-oriented pricing method.

以上两种成本导向定价法的最大缺陷是忽略了市场因素，没有考虑供求关系、顾客需求及市场竞争状况。

The greatest disadvantages of the above two cost-oriented method are that the market factors are neglected，and it fails to consider the supply-demand relationship，customer demand and market competition.

（三）客房面积定价法（Room Area Pricing Method）

通过确定客房预算总收入来计算单位面积的客房应取得的收入，进而确定每间客房应取得的收入来进行定价。假设计划期内，客房预算总收入为 y，计划期天数为 n，客房总面积为 M，某间客房的面积为 m，预计计划期客房出租率为 r，那么，客房价格=y/（M×n×r）×m。

例如，某酒店 2014 年 6 月的客房预算总收入为 160000 美元，总客房面积为 2000 平方米，预计客房出租率为 70%，那么面积为 20 平方米的客房价格应为：

For instance，the total budget of guest room in June 2014 of a hotel is about 160000 USD，and the total area is 2000 square meters. The predicted occupancy rate is 70%，and then the room rate of 20-square-meter guest room shall be：

客房价格 = y /（M×n×r）× m =（160000/2000×30×70%）× 20 = 76 美元

Guest room rate = y/（M×n×r）× m =（160000 / 2000×30×70%）× 20 = 76 USD

这种定价方法主要受客房预算收入的影响，取决于经营者预算收入的准确度是否符合实际。如果预算收入高，则客房价格也高；但如果市场不接受，或预算收入低，则会给酒店经营和预期利润率带来负面影响。该方法对市场竞争情况及供求关系考虑不足，科学性值得怀疑，使用较少。

Such pricing method is mainly impacted by the budget income of guest rooms，relying on if the accuracy of budget revenue meets the reality or not. If the budget is too high，the guest room rate will also be high. But if it is not accepted by the market，or the budget income is low，it may bring negative influence on the hotel management and expected profitability. This method is insufficient in the consideration of market competition and supply-demand relationship. The scientificity is doubtful，with little application.

（四）收益管理定价法（Yield Management Pricing Method）

收益管理（Yield management）或收入管理（Revenue management），是指运用信息系统和定价策略，在合适的时间、合适的地点，以合适的价格将产品销售给合适的顾客。

Yield management or Revenue management refers to the application of information system and pricing strategy at appropriate time and place, and it can be sold to proper guest in appropriate price.

它将客房出租率和平均房价两个指标结合起来，追求整体的收益最大化。收益管理定价法（市场导向定价法）的目标在于通过价格变化平衡供求关系，寻求市场供需水平的匹配，从而保证任何一个时点上生产资源和能力都能得到最优配置和利用。

It combines two indexes, including the occupancy rate and average room rate, and pursues for the profit maximization. The Yield management pricing method (Market-oriented pricing method) mainly targets at balancing the supply-demand relationship through price variation, and seeking the market supply and demand level, so as to guarantee that the production resources and abilities can be allocated and utilized properly.

（五）随行就市法（Market-based Method）

以酒店业的平均价格或现行价格水平作为酒店的定价标准。将同等档次竞争对手的客房价格作为定价的依据，从而制定出本酒店客房价格的一种定价方法。适用于自身产品无特殊性，竞争者众多的酒店。使用目的：用集体智慧，减少风险。

It takes the average rate or current rate level of the hotel industry as the rate standard of the hotel, and room rate of competitors of the same grade as the basis of room rate, so as to make a pricing method of room rate for the hotel. It is applicable for the hotel without any particularity, and there are numerous competitors. Application objective: use collective intelligence to reduce risks.

比如目前经济型连锁酒店的客房价格：如家快捷、莫泰 168、锦江之星、7 天。

For instance, the room rate of current economical chain hotels, such as Home Inn, Motel 168, Jinjiang Inn, 7 Day Inn, etc.

五、客房经营统计分析（Guest Room Operating Statistics Analysis）

（一）客房出租率（Guest Room Occupancy Rate）

客房出租率是酒店实际出租的客房数在酒店可供出租的客房总数中所占的比例。

$$\text{即，本期客房出租率} = \frac{\text{本期实际出租客房数（间·天）}}{\text{可出租客房总数} \times \text{本期天数}} \times 100\%$$

Guest room occupancy rate is the proportion of actually rent guest rooms among the total available guest rooms.

Namely, the occupancy rate of guest room = actually rent guest room (rooms·days) / Total available guest rooms × days of this period × 100%

例如丽园酒店是拥有 300 间客房的中档酒店，2013 年该酒店出租的客房数为 76650 间·天，那么丽园酒店 2013 年客房出租率是：

For instance, Theme Park Hotel is a middle-end hotel with 300 guest rooms. In 2013, the actually rent guest room was 76650 (rooms·days), then, the occupancy rate of Theme Park Hotel in 2013 was:

$$\text{客房出租率} = \frac{76650\text{ 间·天}}{300\text{ 间} \times 365\text{ 天}} \times 100\% = 70\%$$

Occupancy rate = 76650 (rooms·days) /300 rooms × 365days × 100% = 70%

一般来讲，酒店经营者总是设法提高客房出租率，以期提高酒店的经济效益。但客房出租率并非越高越好，理想的年平均客房出租率应在85%左右，最多不超过90%，否则，就属于“破坏性接待”，这是因为：

Generally speaking, hotel managers usually manage to increase the occupancy rate of guest room for improving the economic benefit of the hotel. However, high occupancy rate may not be good, and the idea average occupancy rate shall be about 85%, and 90% at most, or it belongs to “destructive reception”, for:

（1）酒店及客房设施设备需要保养维修，过度使用会使其功能失灵，建筑物寿命缩短。这样不仅影响酒店的经济效益，而且将直接影响对客人的服务质量，进而影响酒店的长远利益。

Hotel and guest room facilities shall be maintained and excessive application may result in the failure of functions, and shorten the life span. Consequently, it will directly impact the economic benefit of the hotel, as well as the service quality, and long-term interest of the hotel.

（2）长年过高的出租率会使包括客房服务员在内的酒店员工被牢牢地固定于工作岗位，无暇参加旨在提高员工素质的各种培训，以致使服务质量下降，对管理工作也会造成很大的压力。

Long-term excessive occupant rate may get employees of the hotel, including guest room attendants, fixed to the posts, and they may be too busy to join various trainings targeting at improving their quality, which may lead to the declining service quality, and pose a great pressure on the management.

全年平均客房出租率最高不能超过85%，除了上述原因外还有以下几个方面的因素：

The average annual occupancy rate shall not be higher than 85%. Besides the above mentioned reasons, there are also the following aspects of elements:

（1）酒店是一种服务行业，因此与酒店本身有业务往来关系的人士来往很频繁，这样就需要留少量的免费客房，用来接待相关客人，这既是一种不可缺少的社会交际，也是酒店的一种业务广告。

Hotel is a kind of service industry, so it is closely related to businessmen that the hotel has connection with. In this way, some complimentary rate rooms shall be reserved for receiving related guests. It is not only the indispensable social interaction, but also a kind of advertising.

（2）酒店的经营要求，对客人只能回答“Yes”，而不能回答“No”。所以必须留一定的客房来保证计划以外客人的需求。

Hotels can only say “Yes”, rather than “No” to guess. Therefore, certain number of rooms must be reserved for guarantee the demands that are beyond the plan.

（3）要有一定的客房用来做紧急情况下的调用。如接待重要会议、一些重要客人来酒店下榻等。

Certain number of guest rooms must be reserved for emergencies, such as receiving significant meetings, significant guests, etc.

比较理想的客房出租率应该在75%~80%，最高不能超过85%（全年平均客房出租率），但是要灵活机动，全年每个月的出租率根据实际情况，可高可低，例如旅游旺季客房出租率可达90%以上，甚至100%。而淡季则要相对少一些。使全年的平均出租率保持在75%~80%这个水平上是最理想的。

The ideal occupancy rate should range between 75% and 80%, and 85% at most (average annual room occupancy rate), but it shall be flexible, and the monthly occupancy rate can fluctuate according to the practical conditions, for instance, in busy season, the occupancy rate may be above 90% or even 100%, while in slack season, it can be relatively smaller. Above all, 75% to 80% of the annual average occupancy rate is the most ideal.

（二）双开率（Occupancy Rate of Rooms Lived by Two People）

双开率是指在已出租客房中，双人使用的房间数所占的比例。

Occupancy rate refers to the proportion of rooms lived by two people in the total rooms rent to guests.

双人使用的房间数 = 客人总数 - 已出租房间数

Number of rooms lived by two people = total guests - number of rooms rent

双开率 = 双人使用房间数/已出租房间总数 × 100% = （客人总数 - 已出租房间数）/已出租房间数 × 100%

Occupancy rate of rooms lived by two people = number of rooms lived by two people / total number of rooms rent × 100% = (total guests - number of rooms rent) / number of rooms rent × 100%

例如，某酒店共接待住宿客人 390 人，当时出租客房 280 间，其双开率为：

[(390 - 280)/280] × 100% = 39.3%

For instance, a hotel receives 390 lodgers, and about 280 rooms are rent, and then the occupancy rate of rooms lived by two people shall be:

[(390-280)/280] × 100% = 39.3%

双开率指标可以反映酒店客房的利用状况，是酒店增加收入的经营手段。其前提是一个房间（单人间除外）划出两种价格，比如一个标准间住一位客人房价 90 美元，住两位客人每位只收 60 美元，这样客人节省，酒店也增收，西方酒店往往这样操作。

Occupancy rate of rooms lived by two people may reflect the utilization of hotel guest room, and it is an operating approach of increasing the income. The premise is that there are two kinds of rates for a room (excluding the single room), for instance if one person livesin a standard room, the room rate would be 90 USD, but if two people live in one room, each would be charge by 60 USD. In this way, it may save money for guests and increase income for hotels. Western hotels usually practice it in this way.

（三）实际平均房价（Actual Average Room Rate）

这是在酒店经营统计分析中仅次于客房出租率的指标。

It is the index only second to the room occupancy rate in the operating statistical analysis.

实际平均房价 = 客房总收入/出租房间数，即已出租房间的平均房价，也称为日平均房价；也可指一定时间内，酒店每个可售房间的平均收益，即可售房的平均房价。

Actual average room rate = total income of guest room/number of rooms rent, namely the average rate of rooms rent (ADR), also called daily average room rate. It can also refer to the average yield of each available room (Rev, PAR), namely the average room rate of rooms available for sale.

影响酒店实际平均房价的主要因素：

Main factors impacting the actual average room rate:

(1) 实际出租房价：一般低于门市价。

Actual room rate: generally lower than the rack rate.

(2) 客房出租率：客房出租率与实际平均房价一般会成反比例。

Guest room occupancy rate: the guest room occupancy rate is usually in inverse proportion to the actual average room rate.

(3) 销售客房类型结构：一般以标准间为主，约占 80%，接近平均房价。否则就会波动较大。

Structure of guest rooms sales: it is mainly dominated by standard room, about 80%, close to average room rate. Or the fluctuation may be huge.

（四）理想平均房价（Ideal Average Room Rate）

理想平均房价是指酒店各类客房以现行牌价按不同的客人结构出租时可达到的平均房价。计算理想平均房价时，要结合计划期内的客房出租率，双开率及客房牌价进行（尽量避免“破坏式经营”）。其计算方式为：针对一定时间内，从计算最低价到最高价出租客房和从最高价到最低价出租客房而得出的客房价格平均值。

The ideal average room rate refers to the average room rate reached in the rent for different guest structure according to the current list price. When calculating the ideal average room rate, it shall combine the guest room occupancy rate in the planning period, occupancy rate of rooms lived by two people and list price (please avoid the "destructive operation"). The calculation mode is: targeting at a certain period of time, it is the average room rate obtained by calculating the rooms from the minimum rate to the maximum rate, and from the maximum rate to the minimum rate.

在实际运作中，若酒店实际平均房价高于理想平均房价，说明酒店经济效益好，酒店可获得较为理想的盈利。这种比较也能在一定程度上反映酒店牌价是否适应市场的实际状况。若两者相差甚远，则说明牌价过高或过低，酒店应作适当调整。

In practical operation, if the actual average room rate is higher than the ideal average room rate, it means that the economic return is good, and the hotel can achieve ideal profit. Such comparison can also reflect if the rack rate adapts to the practical situation of the market at a certain degree. If there is a huge difference, it means that the rack rate is too high or too low, and the hotel shall make adjustments.

（五）收益管理（Yield Management）

收益管理核心是通过制定一套灵活的且符合市场竞争规律的价格体系，再结合现代化的微观市场预测及价格优化手段对酒店资源进行动态调控，以期获取最大收益。收益管理的主要功能有：

The core of yield management is to make a set of flexible rate system that is in line with the market competition rules. Meanwhile, hotel resources are controlled dynamically by combining the modern micro-market prediction and rate optimization, for gaining maximum profit. The main functions of the field management are:

（1）顾客分类及需求预测。

Classification of customers and demand prediction.

（2）优化控制。

Optimization of control.

（3）节假日价格需求控制。

Price demand control at holidays or festivals.

（4）动态价格设定。

Dynamic rating.

（5）超额预订控制。

Excessive reservation control.

（6）团体和销售代理管理。

Team and sales agent management.

（7）酒店附设资源管理。

Attached resource management.

（8）经营状况比较。

Comparison of operation conditions.

任务三 销售程序与技巧
Task III Sales Procedure and Skills

【情境导入】【Scenario Introduction】

总经理的朋友要打折
Discount shall be offered to friends of the general manager

一天，某酒店总台来了一位自称是总经理朋友的客人，要求总台接待员小陈给他一间特价房，可是按照酒店的规定，没有批示，服务员就没有给特价房的权利。由于小陈没有接到通知，所以没有立即接受客人的要求，同时因为未确认该客人的身份，也没有贸然拒绝。可是客人已经不高兴了，说连总经理的朋友也不买账，一定要到总经理那里投诉小陈。

One day, a guest claimed that he was a friend of the general manager came to the information desk, and demanded the receptionist Xiaochen to offer a room of bargain price. However, according to the stipulations of the hotel, if there was no instruction, the servant had no right to offer bargain price. Since Xiaochen had not received any notice, she did not accept the demands immediately, and meanwhile, she did not refuse hastily before confirming the identification of the guest. However, the guest was unhappy, claiming that he would complain Xiaochen at the general manager.

于是，小陈首先向客人表示歉意，可能是同事忘记通知她了，并请客人先到大厅休息一下，她这就与总经理联系，并给客人递上了一杯茶和一份当日的报纸。然后，小陈马上与前厅经理取得了联系，询问此事的处理办法，前厅经理在与总经理联系后，总经理告知只是一个有一面之交的朋友，给一个优惠价就可以了。

Therefore, Xiaochen made an apology to the guests at first that maybe her colleague forget to notice her, and asked the guest to rest in the hall for a while, saying that she would contact the general manager. Meanwhile, she handed in a cup of tea and a newspaper. Later, Xiaochen contacted the Front Office manager to ask for advice. When the Front Office manager contacted the general manager, the general manager said it was only an acquaintance, and a preferential price might be good.

小陈得到指示后，请客人来到总台，首先对让客人久等了表示歉意，然后告诉客人，由于没有接到通知，同时与总经理又联系不上，自己没有给客人特价房的权利，但是考虑到客人是总经理的朋友，可以特别给予一个优惠价，客人听后欣然同意。

After receiving instructions, Xiaochen invited the guest to the information desk, and showed her apology for making the guest waiting for a long time. Later, she told the guest that since she had not received any notice, and meanwhile, she failed to contact the general manager, and she had no right to offer bargain price. However, considering that the guest was a friend of the general manager, a preferential price might be given. The guest was quite satisfied.

【情境分析】【Scenario Analysis】

对酒店总台接待员来说，经常会遇到客人要求打折优惠的情况。此例中小陈的做法较为可取。在没有接到总经理批示，不能确认客人真实身份的情况下，没有轻易地接受或拒绝客人的要求。为了避免给客人和总经理之间制造麻烦，小陈还很聪明地请客人到大厅等候，然后再打电话进行请示。因为此客人可能是总经理的重要朋友，也可能是一般朋友，甚至可能根本就不是朋友，面对不同的情况，总经理肯定会不同地对待。小陈的做法，避免了由于总经理直接面对客人而可能发生的两难境地，使得总经理可以很轻松地做出决定，而又不得罪朋友。同时也给客人留了面子，不是总经理不给特价房，而是联系不上，并且饭店还给了特别的优惠价。

As for the receptionist of hotel, there are always conditions in which guests require a discount. In this case, the practices of Xiaochen are acceptable. Without the instructions from the general manager and the identity of guest cannot be confirmed, she did not accept or refuse the demand easily. In order to avoid the troubles between the guest and the general manager, Xiaochen was smart to invite the guest to wait in the hall, and then make phone calls for instructions. Since the guest may be a significant or ordinary friend, or he may not be friend, the general manager may treat it differently in different situations. The practices of Xiaochen avoid the dilemma of direct contact between the general manager and the guest, which may make it easy for the general manager to make decisions, without offending the friend. Meanwhile, it also saved faces for the guests. It was not because the general manager didn' t offer room of bargain price, just because they couldnot be in touch with the general manager. The hotel also gave special preferential price to the guest.

但是对酒店来说，应该有一个健全的价格管理体制，否则会给管理带来混乱，影响经济效益，严重的还会导致经营的失败。因此，酒店应该有明文规定，上到总经理，下到服务员，都应该按酒店规定行事，作为总经理更要带头做好此项工作。当然，有的时候，需要灵活性，特殊情况也可以特殊处理。

However, as for the hotel, there should be a perfect rate management system, or it may bring chaos to the management and influence the economic benefit, and it may even result in the failure of operation. Therefore, there should be explicit stipulations that both the general manager and servant shall follow the rules, and the general manager shall also take the lead. Of course, it shall be flexible sometimes, and special conditions can be handled in a special way.

一、前厅销售的内容（Contents of Front Office Sales）

（一）酒店的地理位置（Geographic Condition of the Hotel）

酒店所处位置是影响客人选择所住酒店的重要因素之一，前厅部服务人员应充分利用现有的地理位置进行积极推销。

The geographic condition of hotel is one of the significant factors impacting the selection of guest. Therefore, the Front Office servants shall make full use of the current geographic condition to promote actively.

（二）酒店的设施设备（Facilities of Hotel）

酒店齐全有效的设施设备、过硬的有形产品是开展销售的重要条件。为此，前厅部服务人员应娴熟地掌握酒店所拥有的设施设备及其有别于其他酒店的特点。

The effective facilities and tangible products are the important conditions of the launch of sales. Therefore, the Front Office servants shall grasp the features of facilities that are different from other hotels proficiently.

（三）酒店的服务（Services of Hotel）

服务是酒店所销售产品中最为重要的部分。

Service is the most significant part of the promoting products.

（四）酒店的形象（Image of Hotel）

酒店的形象是最有影响的活广告。前厅部服务人员应灵活运用，自觉维护。它主要包括酒店的历史、知名度、信誉、口碑、独特的经营作风、优质的服务等。

Image of hotel is the most influential advertisement. The Front Office servant shall apply it flexible and maintain it consciously. It mainly includes the history, reputation, credit, public praise, unique practices, and excellent service, etc.

（五）酒店的气氛（Atmosphere of Hotel）

酒店的气氛是客人对酒店的一种感受。前厅部处于酒店最显眼的地段，又是留给客人第一印象和最后印象的所在地，故其所创造的气氛十分重要。

The atmosphere of hotel is the feeling of guest to the hotel. The Front Office is in the most remarkable part of the hotel, which may leave the first and last impression on the guests. Therefore, it is quite important to create atmosphere.

二、客房销售报价艺术（Offer Art of Guest Room Promotion）

"报价"是一种艺术，巧妙的报价方式，可提高酒店产品的推销与营业收入。报房价，不仅要报全价，还要主动向客人介绍产品的特点，要对房价差异产生的因素有所了解，使决定权潜意识地转向我方，运用口头描述技巧，引起客人的购买欲望，借以扩大销售的一种推销方法，其中包含着推销技巧、语言艺术、职业品德等内容，在实际推销工作中，非常讲究报价的针对性，只有适时采取不同的报价方法，才能达到销售的最佳效果。掌握报价方法，是搞好推销工作的一项基本功，以下是酒店常见的几种报价方法：

"Offer" is a kind of art, and the ingenious offer may improve the product promotion and operation revenue of hotel. Besides the offer, the receptionist shall also introduce the features of product, know the factors causing the differences of room rate, turn the decision-making power to the hotel unconsciously, apply the word picture, and give rise to the purchase desire of guest, so as to enlarge the sales. It covers the promotion skills, language art, occupational morality, etc. In practical promotion, receptionist shall be particular about the pertinence of offer. Only by adopting different offer methods, can it reach the optimal effect of sales. It is fundamental to grasp the offer for promotion. The following are several common offer methods:

（1）"冲击式"报价。即先报价格，再提出房间所提供的服务设施与项目等，这种报价方式比较适合价格较低的房间，主要针对消费水平较低的顾客。

"Impacting" offer. Namely make offers first, and then the service facilities and terms provided by the room. Such offer method is applicable for low room rate, targeting at customers of low consumption level.

（2）"鱼尾式"报价。先介绍所提供的服务设施与项目，以及房间的构造特点，最后报出价格，这种报价方式适合价格较高的房间，突出物美，加深客人对物美的第一印象，减弱高价对客人的影响。它较适合消费水平高、有一定地位和声望的顾客。

"Fishtail" offer. It will introduce the service facilities and projects offered, as well as the features of room, and finally the price. It is applicable for high room rates, targeting at highlighting the materials, and deepening the first impression, and weakening the impact of high price on the guest. It is applicable for the guests with high consumption level, certain status and reputation.

(3)"夹心式"报价。将房价放在提供服务的项目中间进行报价。这种方式适合中档房，先介绍房间类型再报价，如果客人觉得比较贵再补充介绍特点，加强美的印象，从两面冲弱价格的强度。

"Sandwich" offer. Make offers between the services provided. It is applicable for the middle-class hotels. The room category can be introduced at first and then the offer. If the guest thinks it expensive, extra features will be introduced to strengthen the materials feature impression, so as to weakening the intensity of room rate.

(4)高低趋向报价。这是针对讲究身份、地位的客人设计的，这种报价法首先向客人报明酒店的最高房价，让客人了解酒店所提供高标准房间及与其相配的环境和设施，在客人对此不感兴趣时再转向销售较低价格的客房，接待员要善于运用语言技巧说动客人，高价伴随的高级享受，诱使客人做出购买决策，当然，所报价格应相对合理，不宜过高。

High-low trend offer. It is designed for guests who are particular about the identity and status. The receptionist would give the highest room rate of the hotel to the guest, so as to let them know the high standard rooms and the corresponding environment and facility. If the guest is not interested, lower rate can be introduced. The receptionist shall be good at persuading guests with language skills. High rate with advanced enjoyment may induce the guests to make decisions. Of course, the offer shall be reasonable, instead of being too high.

(5)低高趋向报价。这种报价可以吸引那些对房间价格做过比较的客人，为酒店带来广阔的客源市场，这种报价法有利于酒店的竞争优势。

Low-high trend offer. It may attract guests who have compared the room rates, and it may bring broad guest source market. It will be favorable for the competitive advantage of hotels.

(6)排列报价法。这种报价法是将酒店所有现行价格按一定排列顺序提供给客人，即先报最低价格，再报最高价格，最后报中间价格，让客人有选择适中价格的机会。这样做，酒店既坚持了明码标价，又维护了商业道德，既方便客人在整个房价体系中自由选择，又增加了酒店高价客房的出租，获得更多收益的机会。

Arrangement offer. The offer mainly gives all current room rates to the guest according to certain sequence: namely the lowest rate, and then the highest, and finally the middle rate, which may allow the guest to choose. In this way, the hotel not only insists on the expressly marked price, but also maintains the business morality. It will not only be convenient for the guests to select in the entire room rate system, but also increase the rent of high rate rooms, and gain more profits.

(7)选则性报价。采用此类报价法要求前台操作人员善于辨别抵店客人的支付能力，能客观地按照客人的兴趣和需要，选择提供适当的房价范围，一般报价不能超过两种以上，以体现估量报价的准确性，避免选择报价时犹豫不决。

Optional offer. It requires that the receptionist shall be good at telling the payment ability of gusts, and provide appropriate room rate range according to the interest and demands of guests. Generally, there should not be more than two offers, so as to reflect the accuracy of offer and to avoid the hesitation of offer.

(8)利益引诱报价。这是一种对已预订到一般房间的客人，采取给予一定附加利益的方法，使他们放弃原预订客房，转向购买高一档次价格的客房。

Interest induction offer. It is a method taken for guests making reservations. Since it provides certain additional benefit, the guests may give up the original reservation and turn to higher rate of guest rooms.

(9)弱化价格重要性报价。此类报价是将价格置于所提供的服务项目中，以减弱直观价格的分量，增加客人购买的可能性，此类报价一般由前台接待人员用口头语言进行描述性报价，强调提供的服务项目是符合客人利益的，但不能太多，要恰如其分。

Price significance weakening offer. The offer is placed in the service projects provided, for weakening the weight of perceptual intuition and increase the possibilities of purchase. Such offer is usually described by receptionist orally, emphasizing that the service is applicable for the benefit of guests. It shall not be too much, but it shall be appropriate.

(10) 灵活报价。灵活报价是根据酒店的现行价格和规定的价格浮动幅度，将价格灵活地报给客人的一种方法。此报价一般是由酒店的收益管理中心决定，根据酒店的具体实际情况，在一定价格范围内适当浮动，灵活报价，调节客人的需求，使客房出租率和经济效益达到理想水平。当然，价格什么时候报，报几种，要针对不同客人的特点与消费心理，切不可夸大其辞，否则会适得其反。

Flexible offer. Flexible offer is a kind of method that may make offers flexibly according to the current rate and stipulated rate fluctuation range. It is usually decided by the yield management center of the hotel according to the practical situations of the hotel, and it can fluctuate within certain price range, and it shall offer flexiblely to adjust the demands and get the occupancy rate and economic benefit to an ideal level. Of course, when shall the offer be made, how many offers can be made, etc. shall be based on the features and consumption psychology of different guests and exaggerations shall be avoided, or it may make the situation worse.

三、客房销售程序（Guest Room Promotion Procedure）

(一) 前台销售的一般工作要求（General Job Requirements of the Front Desk Sales）

1. 销售准备（Sales Preparation）

(1) 仪表仪态要端正，要表现高雅的风度和姿态。

Right appearance, elegant demeanor and posture.

(2) 前台工作环境要有条理，使服务台区域干净整齐，不零乱。

The work environment of Front Office shall be in order, and get the service counter clean and tidy.

(3) 熟悉酒店各种类型的客房及其服务质量，以便向潜在客人介绍。

Familiar with all kinds of guest room types and service quality, for the convenience of introduction to potencial guests.

(4) 了解酒店所有餐厅、酒吧、娱乐场所等各营业场所及公共区域的营业时间与地点。

Know the business hours and sites of all places of business and public regions, including the restaurants, bars, entertainment sites, etc.

2. 服务态度（Service Attitude）

(1) 要善于用眼神和客人交流，要表现出热情和真挚。

Be good at make eye contacts to communication with guests, show enthusiasm and sincerity.

(2) 要面部常带微笑，对客人表示：“欢迎，见到您很高兴。”

With smiles, to show “welcome, nice to meet you” to the guests.

(3) 要礼貌用语问候每位客人。

Greet each guest politely.

(4) 举止行为要恰当、自然、诚恳。

The behaviors shall be appropriate, natural and sincere.

(5) 回答问题要简单、明了、恰当，不要夸张宣传住宿条件。

Answer questions simply and appropriately, without exaggerating the lodging conditions.

(6) 不要贬低客人，要耐心向客人解释问题。

Do not belittle the guest and explain problems to the guests patiently.

一个有礼貌、训练有素的前台人员是酒店经营最宝贵的财富之一，他所造成的客人对酒店的第一印象，将决定客人是否再次光顾，甚至会自动为酒店宣传，扩大酒店的影响。

A polite and well-trained receptionist is one of the most valuable fortunes of the hotel management, and the first impression on guest left by him may decide if the guest will come to the hotel again, and it will even advertise for the hotel automatically, and enlarge the influence of hotel.

3. 销售工作 (Sales)

(1) 要善于用描述性语言向客人提供几种客房的优势，说明能给客人带来好处以供客人选择，但不要对几种客房作令人不快的比较。

Be good at describing the advantages of several types of guest rooms, show the benefits brought to the guest, and please do not compare several types of guest rooms unhappily.

(2) 不要直接询问客人要求哪种价格的房间，应在描述客房情况的过程中，试探客人要哪种。

Please do not inquire the guests of the room they wanted directly, and instead, please explore what kind of rooms they want during the process of describing the conditions of guest rooms.

(3) 要善于观察和尽力弄清客人的要求和愿望，有目的地销售适合客人的客房。

Be good at observing and trying to figure out the demands and wishes of guests, and promote the guests rooms required by the guests with purpose.

(4) 不要放弃对潜在客人推销客房。必要时可派人陪同他们参观几种不同类型的客房，增进与客人之间的关系，这将有助于对犹豫不决的客人促成销售。

Please do not give up the promotion to potential guests. Accompany them to visit several types of guest rooms if necessary to enhance the relationship with guests, which may help promoting the sales to hesitating guests.

4. 服务工作 (Services)

(1) 要保证客人到店后所有的信函和留言得到发送。

Guarantee that all correspondence and message shall be delivered when guests arrive at the hotel.

(2) 提供叫醒服务要有记录，确保准时，避免疏漏。

Provide morning calls with records, and it shall be accurate in time and avoid careless omission.

(3) 避免前台工作出现“停顿”。如果确定下了某位客人的预订，在有现房的情况下，可先安排客人住宿，然后再处理预订单，不要让客人久等。

Prevent the “stop” of work in the information desk. If the reservation of a certain guest is confirmed, accommodation can be arranged in advance when there are rooms available, and then the reservation order can be processed. Please do not make the guests wait for so long.

(二) 销售程序 (Sales Procedure)

(1) 把握特点。前厅服务人员应充分了解酒店目标市场的客人类型及其需求，并有效利用已建立的客史档案资料，把握客人的需求特点，采取针对性、个性化的销售方法。

Grasp features. The receptionists of Front Office shall fully know the guest types and demands of the target market, and make full use of the established guest history file, grasp the features of guest demand,

and take targeted and individual sales methods.

（2）介绍客房。前厅服务人员应根据客人的不同特点介绍酒店客房，应注意察言观色，生动描述房间的特点、给予客人的便利条件以及各种附加的心理方面的满足，以减弱客房价格的分量。

Introduce the guest room. The receptionist of Front Office shall introduce the hotel guest room according to different features of guests, pay attention to the practices and words, describe the features of room vividly, give conveniences to the guests and satisfy their additional psychology, so as to weaken the weight of room rate.

（3）洽谈价格。在对客房特点给予恰当的形容和强调后，前厅服务人员应让客人认同酒店所销售客房的价值，并解答客人最希望了解的关键问题，有技巧地与客人洽谈价格。

Negotiate the price. After describing and strengthening the guest room features, the receptionist of Front Office shall let the guests realize the value of guest room, answer key problems of guests, and negotiate with guests skillfully.

（4）展示客房。若客人仍有疑虑，前厅服务人员应将事先准备好的客房宣传册、图片等直观资料展现给客人。

Display the guest room. If the guests still have doubts, the receptionist of Front Office shall display the prepared brochures and pictures of guest rooms to the guests.

（5）促成购买。在观察到客人对所推荐的客房发生兴趣时，前厅服务人员应倍加努力，采取有策略的语言和行为，促成客人做出最终选择。

Urge the purchase. After observing the interest of guest in the room promoted, the receptionist of Front Office shall double the effort and adopt strategic language and action to urge the final selection of guests.

四、客房销售技巧（Guest Room Pomotion Skills）

所有的销售技巧，包括宾馆客房的销售技巧，可以简单地浓缩成一句话：促使顾客达成交易的关键是满足顾客的欲望，产品是什么并不重要，重要的是通过产品这个媒介，顾客可以得到某种欲望的满足。

All promotion skills, including the promotion skills of guest room can be shortened into a sentence: the key to urge the transaction is to satisfy the guest's desire. The product may not be important, but it is important that with the product, the guests can satisfy their desire.

（一）把握客人的特点（Grasp the Features of Guests）

不同的客人有不同的特点，对酒店也有不同的要求。前台人员要注意从客人的衣着打扮、言谈举止以及随行人数等方面把握客人的特点（年龄、性别、职业、国籍、旅游动机等），进而根据其需求特点和心理，做好有针对性的销售。

Different guests have different features and distinct requirements on the hotel. Receptionists shall pay attention to the dressing style, behaviors and number of accompanying people to grasp the features of guests (age, gender, occupation, nationality, motivation of traveling, etc.), so as to make targeted promotion according to the features and psychology.

（1）商务客人通常是因公出差，对房价不太计较，但要求客房安静，光线明亮（有可调亮度的台灯和床头灯），办公桌宽大，服务周到、效率高，酒店及房内办公设备齐全（如安装有宽带网和直拨电话以及电脑、打印机、传真机等），有娱乐项目。

Businessmen usually go on business trips, without caring about the room rate. But they demand for quiet and bright rooms（with adjustable table lamp and bedside lamp），wide office table，considerate service with high efficiency，and well-equipped rooms（for instance，internet，telephone，computer，printing machine，fax machine，etc.），as well as entertainment items.

（2）旅游客人要求房间外景色优美，房间内干净卫生，但经济承受能力有限，比较在乎房间价格。

Travelers require beautiful sceneries outside the window. The room shall be clean，but due to the limited economic foundation，they may care about the price of room.

（3）度蜜月的客人喜欢安静，不受干扰且配有一张大床的双人房。

Guests on honeymoon prefer quiet and undisturbed double room with a big bed.

（4）知名人士、高薪阶层及带小孩的父母喜欢住套房。

Celebrities and high-salaried stratum，as well as parents with children prefer the suite.

（5）年老的和有残疾的客人喜欢住在靠近电梯和餐厅的房间。

The aged and the disabled like to live in rooms near the elevator and restaurant.

（二）熟悉客房（Familiar with the Guest Rooms）

前台员工在销售客房时应明确自己是在销售客房，而非销售价格。因此前台员工应熟悉客房，在销售时，应多做客房的具体描述，而尽量少提及价格。同时，要强调客人受益。由于客人对产品价值和品质的认识程度不一样，相同的价格，有些客人认为合理，而有些客人则感到难以承受，在这种情况下，前台人员将价格转化为能给客人带来的益处。如套房，就强调方便，便于会客；外景房，就强调风景宜人；内景房，就强调幽静等。强调客人受益，增强客人对产品价值的理解程度，从而提高其愿意支付的价格限度。具体如下：

When promoting the guest rooms，the receptionist shall know that he is promoting the guest room，rather than the price. Therefore，receptionists shall be familiar with the guest rooms，and describe the guest room specifically during the promotion，instead of mentioning the rate frequently. Meanwhile，they shall emphasize on the benefit of guests. Since guests have different understandings about the product value and quality. As for the same price，some guest may think it reasonable，while some think it unbearable. Under such circumstances，the receptionist can turn the price to be the benefits that can be brought to the guests，for instance，the suite，emphasizing that it is convenient to meet friends，scenery-view room，emphasizing on the beautiful sceneries；indoor setting room，emphasizing on the peacefulness，etc. Stressing on the benefits of guest，and enhancing the guests' comprehension of product value，it may increase the payment limit of guests. Specifically，it is shown as follows：

（1）前台人员在销售客房时，为了增加客房产品的魅力，多使用描绘性语言，像类似“24 小时热水、中央空调、IDD 电话”等销售用语，肯定是不能吸引客人的；同时，选择使用不同的报价方式：夹心式、鱼尾式和冲击式，以减弱客房价格的分量，突出客房能够满足客人需要的特点。

When receptionists promote the guest rooms，they may use describing language to enhance the enchantment of guest room，just like the common promotion expressions，“24-hour hot water，central air-conditioner，IDD telephone” etc. which is certainly unappealing. Meanwhile，different offer methods can be selected，such as the sandwich style，fishtail style，impact style，for weakening the weight of room rate and highlight that the guest room may satisfy the demands of guests.

（2）前厅销售过程中，常出现的一个误区是只谈房价而不介绍客房的特点。比如，不能只说：“一间 198 元的客房，您要不要？”而应说“一间刚装修过的、宽敞的房间”、“一间舒适、安静、能看到美丽湖景的客房”、“一间具有民族特色的、装修豪华的客房”，等等。这类形容词是无穷无尽的，只有这样才容易为客人所接受。

During the sales, a common mistake shall be the discussion of room rate, instead of the discussion of guest room features. For instance, the receptionist shall not say "do you want a room about 198 Yuan", and instead, he can describe it in this way, "a newly-decorated and spacious room", "a comfortable, quiet and beautiful lake-view guest room", "a characteristic and luxury guest room", etc. There are numerous adjectives, and it may be accepted by the guest easily.

（3）要准确地描述客房，必须首先了解客房的特点。这是对前台员工的最基本要求之一，比如带他们参观客房，并由专人讲解客房的特点，以加深印象。

In order to describe the guest rooms precisely, please learn about the features of the room in the first place, and it is one of the basic requirements on the Front Office receptionist, for instance, showing them the guest rooms, and illustrating the features of guest rooms, for deepening the impression.

（三）从高到低报价（Make Offers from High to Low Rate）

在前台销售服务过程中，不可避免要谈到房价，向客人报房价也需要一定的技巧，即要从高到低报价。从高到低报价可最大限度地提高平均房价，但并非接待每一位客人都要从"总统套间"报价。而是应在客人所能接受的价格范围内，从高到低报价，尽可能将客人所能接受的最高房价的客房销售给客人。

In the promotion process, the negotiation of room rate is unavoidable. And the making of offers shall also be skillful, namely form high rate to low rate. It may increase the average room rate to a maximum limit, but there is no need to make offers from the "presidential suite" to every guest. And instead, it shall be within the acceptable range, and try to promote the rooms with acceptable high rates.

（1）前台人员可根据客人的特点，向其推荐两种乃至三种不同价格的、可供比较的客房，让客人自己选择。如果客人没有具体说明需要哪种类型的客房，那么客人可能是第一次来到本酒店，也可能希望选择一种过去没有住过的客房。前台人员可根据客人的特点，推荐两三种不同房型、价格的客房，供客人比较、选择，激发客人的潜在需求，增加酒店的收益。如一个看上去很有身份的商人，要订一个普通标准间，接待人员除报价外，还应试探性地向其推荐商务客房或套房，并用描述性的语言说明商务客房的便利，可能会收到比较好的效果。

Receptionist can recommend two to three guest rooms of different rates to the guests for comparison, and ask them to select by themselves. If the guest does not illustrate the type of guest room he wants specifically, it might be his first time to arrive this hotel, or he might want to select a guest room he has not lived so far. The receptionist can recommend two to three different types and price guest rooms according to the features of the guests for comparison and selection, so as to inspire the potential needs and increase the profits of hotels. If a businessman who seems to be with high status wants to order an ordinary standard room, the receptionist can also recommend other business guest rooms or suite to him besides the making of offer, and describe the conveniences of business rooms, which may receive better effect.

（2）如果是推荐一种客房，就会使客人失去比较的机会，推出价格范围，应考虑到客人的特点。

If only one kind of guest room is recommended, the guest may not have the chance to compare; when making offers, please consider about the features of guests.

（3）高码讨价法。是指在客房销售中向客人推荐适合其地位的最高价格的客房。根据消费心理学，客人常常接受接待员首先推荐的房间。如果客人不接受，再推荐价格低一档次的客房，并介绍其优点。这样由高到低，逐层介绍，直到客人做出满意选择。这种方法适合向未经预订、直接抵店的客人推销。一般来说，报房价由高价格到较低价格比较适宜。例如，可以说"靠近湖边新装修的客房是328 元"、"别墅式的客房是 198 元"、"环境安静、景色优美、在四楼的客房是 168 元"，然后问客人，

·“您喜欢哪一种?”

High-code bargain method. It mainly refers to recommend the highest rate guest room applicable for the guest. According to the consumer psychology, guests usually prefer the first room recommended by the receptionist. If the guest does not accept it, lower rate rooms can be recommended, and then the advantages can be introduced. In this way, it can be introduced from layer to layer till the guest makes satisfied decisions. This method can be applied to walk-in guests without reservations. Generally speaking, it is relatively appropriate to recommend rooms from high rate to low rate, for instance, “the newly-decorated lake-view guest room costs 328 Yuan”, “the villa-style guest room costs 198 Yuan”, “the quiet and beautiful guest room on the fourth floor is 168 Yuan”. And then ask the guest, “which one do you like?”

(4) 由高价向低价报，而不是由低价向高价报，能使多数客人选择前几种较高价格的客房。至少，客人在有可能选择最低价格的情况下，会选择中间价格，因为人们往往避免走极端。由高价向低价报，还可以使服务人员在觉察到客人认为价格太贵的情况下，有推出低价格的余地。

From high rate to low rate, instead of from low rate to high rate, it may enable most guests to select the front several high rate guest rooms. At least, the guest who will possiblely choose the lowest rate may select the middle rate rooms, for people always avoid the extremes. It may also allow the receptionist to promote lower rate rooms when he realises the guest thinks it too expensive.

(5) 价格分解法。有时客人一听到前台接待员的报价，就可能被吓退，而拒绝入住，此时就要将价格进行分解以隐藏其“昂贵性”。例如，某类型客房的价格是580元，报价时可将80元免费双早和100元免费餐费从房价中分解出来，告诉客人实际房价是400元；假如房费包含免费洗衣或免费健身等其他项目，同样应进行价格分解。这样，客人心目中高价的概念就会被大大弱化，更易打动客人，促成交易。

Rate decomposition method, Sometimes, the guest may be frightened by the offer made by receptionist and refuse to check in. At this moment, the rate shall be decomposed to hide “valuableness”, for instance, if the room rate is 580 Yuan, the 80 Yuan of free breakfast for two people and 100 yuan of free meals can be decomposed from the room rate, so the receptionist can tell guest that the actual room rate is only 400 Yuan. If the room rate also includes the free laundry or fitting fee, it shall also be decomposed. In this way, the concept of high room rate would be weakened greatly, and it may move the guests and promote the transaction.

(6) 在口头推销中，向客人推荐的价格一两种为宜，最多不能超过三种，因为价格种类太多，客人记不住。在接待过程中，经常会遇到客人抱怨房价太贵了，询问“能不能打折”，对确实无法承受门市价格的客人，适当给予优惠也是适应市场、适应竞争的重要手段。但要注意接待员要在授权范围内给客人一定优惠幅度，但尽量不以折扣作为达成交易的最终手段，多销售全价房。

In the verbal promotion, recommending one or two kinds of room rates is proper please do not recommend more than three kinds of room rates, for the guest may not be able to remember them all. During the reception process, receptionist may hear the complaints of guests about the expensive room rates often, and the guest may ask “if there is any discount?” For guests who cannot really bear the rack rate, the offer of preferential price may be a significant approach for adapting to the market and competition. However, please pay attention that the receptionist shall give preferential price within the authorized range, and try not to regard the discount as the final approach of concluding the transaction and try to sell full rate rooms.

（7）在洽谈房价的过程中，前台服务人员的责任是引导客人、帮助客人进行选择，而应避免将自己的观点强加于客人，过分的“热情”往往会适得其反，要尊重客人的选择。客人可能会因为不喜欢某类客房而找托辞，前台人员不要坚持为自己的观点辩护，更不能贬低客人的意见，对客人的选择要表示赞同与支持。要使客人感到自己的选择是正确的，即使客人最终选择了一间便宜的或档次相对较低的客房。

During the rate bargaining process, receptionist shall be responsible to guide the guests and help them to make choice, and avoid exerting opinions on the guests. Excessive “enthusiasm” may receive counter effect, and instead, please respect the selection of guests. The guests may find excuse if they do not like the guest room, so the receptionist shall not defend for himself, or belittle the opinions of guests, and instead, he shall agree or support the choice of guests. To make guests feel that their selections are correct, even if they select cheaper or lower grade of guest rooms.

（四）注意使用适当的推销语言（Pay Attention to Use Appropriate Promotion Language）

前台员工在推销客房时，应注意掌握听的艺术，只有通过听，才能得知客人的要求，全面把握客人的意图和心理需求；接待客人时，最好采用正面说法，善于将客房或客房所处环境的不利因素转化为给予宾客的便利因素，说话不仅要有礼貌，而且要讲究艺术性，称赞对方的选择，应避免使用“不走运”、“只剩下”等类词语。比如，应该说：“您运气真好，我们恰好还有一间漂亮的单人房！”而不能说：“单人房就剩这一间了，您要不要？”在与客人谈话过程中，不要出现打断其思路或显出烦躁不安的表现，更不应随意评论、反驳或争辩。

When promoting guest rooms, the receptionist shall pay attention to the art of listening. Only through listening, can the receptionist learn the requirements of guests, and fully grasp the intention and psychological demand of guests. When receiving the guests, positive statement would be better, it may transfer the unfavorable factors of guest rooms and their position to those that can bring convenience to guests. Please be polite and particular about the speaking art, praise the choice, and avoid the negative words, such as “unlucky”, “only left”, etc. Instead, we may say “it's lucky that we have a beautiful single room”, rather than “we only have one single room, would you like it or not?” During the conversation, please do not interrupt the guest or be unrest, or even comment, refute or argue freely.

（五）多提建议（Make More Suggestions）

客人犹豫不决时，是客房销售能否成功的关键时刻，此时，前台接待员要正确分析客人的心理活动，耐心地、千方百计地去消除他们的疑虑，多提建议，不要轻易放过任何一位可能住店的客人。这种时候，任何忽视、冷淡与不耐烦的表现，都会导致销售的失败。前台人员在必要时还可以建议客人进房参观。

When the guest is hesitating, it is a critical moment of the success or failure of guest room sales. At this moment, the receptionist shall analyze the mental activities of guests correctly, eliminate their doubts patiently by all means, make more suggestions, and please do not let off any possible guest easily. At this moment, any ignorance, unconcern or impatient expression may result in the failure of sales. The receptionist can also suggest guests to visit if necessary.

对犹豫不决的客人可以多提建议。许多客人并不清楚自己需要什么样的房间，在这种情况下，接待员要认真观察客人的表情，设法理解客人的真实意图，了解客人的特点和喜好，然后按照客人的兴趣和爱好，有针对性地向客人介绍各类客房的特点，消除其疑虑。假若客人仍未明确表态，接待员可以用语言和行为来促使客人下决心住下来。例如，递上入住登记表说：“这样吧，您先登记一下……”或“要不您先住下，如果您感到不满意，明天我们再给您换房”。也可以在征得客人同意的情况下，陪同客人实地参观几种不同类型的客房，让客人对酒店客房产品有个感性认识。当他们亲自看了客房设施后，可能会迅速做出住宿的决定，即使客人不在这里住宿，也会记住酒店的热情服务，可能下次来投宿或推荐给其他亲友。

Make more suggestions to hesitating guests. Many guests do not know what kind of rooms they want. In such circumstance, receptionists shall observe the expression of guests carefully, and manage to learn about the real intentions of guests, as well as the features and hobbies of guests. And then, they can introduce the feature of guest rooms to eliminate the doubts according to the interests and hobbies of guests. If the guest still fails to make decisions, the receptionist can urge the guest to made decisions with language and behavior, for instance, hand in the check-in registry form and say: "you may register first", or "you may check in, and if you are not satisfied, we can change it for you tomorrow". Also, the receptionist can also accompany the guest to visit several types of different guest rooms on the premise of permission, so that the guest may gain a perceptual knowledge about the guest room. When they see the facilities, they may make quick decisions. Even if they do not live here, they may remember the enthusiastic service and come in the next time or recommend it to friends.

（六）展示客房（Display the Guest Room）

前台在销售客房时，应适时展示客房，在展示客房过程中，要自始至终表现得有信心、有效率、懂礼貌，并注意对客人的称呼，及时解决客人存在的疑虑。如客人不打算租用酒店的客房，前台人员也应对客人的光临表示感谢，并告诉客人，欢迎他以后有机会再来。

When promoting the guest rooms, the receptionist can display the guest room at appropriate time, and during this process, the receptionist shall be confident, efficient and polite, pay attention to address the guests and solve the doubts of guests in time. If the guests do not plan to rent the room, the receptionist shall also thank for the presence of guests, and tell him that he will be welcomed at any moment.

（七）达成交易（Reach the Transaction）

前台人员与客人达成交易是销售客房的最后一项工作，也是销售客房的关键。当前台人员意识到客人对所推荐的客房感兴趣时，应强调现在就订的好处，用提问的方式，促使客人做出选择。例如，可以用这样的方式结束推销："××先生，您试试这间客房可以吗？""您会认为花这个价钱是值得的。""您愿意试住一个晚上吗？××先生，如果不满意的话，我明天再为您换一间。""您现在要办理入住登记手续吗？"

The conclusion of transaction between the receptionist and guest shall be the final work of guest room promotion, and it is also critical in the promotion of guest rooms. When the receptionist realizes that the guest is interested in the room recommended, we shall emphasize on the advantages of reservation, and urge guests to make decision in questions. For instance, "Sir ××, will you try this guest room?" "You may think it is worth of spending the money", "Would you like to try one night? Sir ××, if you are not satisfied, we can change another room for you." "Would you go through the check-in procedures at this moment?"

达成交易后，前台人员还应诚挚地向客人表示谢意，应尽量缩短客人等候时间，给客人办理入住登记手续。在入住登记时，前厅接待人员可抓住二次销售的机会，采用利益引诱法，亦称由低及高法。是对已预订到店的客人采取的给予一定附加利益使他们放弃原预订客房，转向高一档次价格客房的方法。建议客人只要在原价格基础上稍微提高，即可得到更多的好处或优惠。例如，"您只需要再多付50元，就可以享受包价优惠，除房费外，还包括免费早餐和午餐。"如果客人接受了前台人员的建议，其结果是酒店增加了营业收人，客人同时也享受到了更多的实惠。

After concluding the transaction, the receptionist can also show gratitude to the guests, but try to shorten the waiting time and go through the check -in procedures. During the check -in process, the receptionist can take the chance of secondary sales, with interest induction method, namely low -high method. Additional benefit can be given for urging guests making reservations to give up the original reservation and adopt the higher grade of guest room. The receptionist can suggest to the guest that a little increase on the basis of the original price may help gain more advantages or benefits. For instance "Pay 50 Yuan more, you may enjoy the contract price privilege, excluding the room rate, it also includes the free breakfast and launch". If the guest accepts the suggestions, it actually increases the operating income of hotel, and meanwhile, the guest indeed enjoys more benefits.

（八）推销酒店的其他设施和服务（Promote Other Facilities and Services of the Hotel）

在宣传推销客房产品的同时，不应忽视推销酒店的其他服务设施和服务项目，如餐饮、娱乐、商务等设施和服务，以使客人感到酒店产品的综合性及完整性。因为客人住店，不仅仅是为了满足其休息的生理需要，往往还有其他方面的需求，如果接待人员不向客人介绍推荐，就有可能使某些设施设备长期无人使用或很少使用，不但使酒店的营业收入受到损失，而且造成设备资源的闲置浪费。所以在预期客人需要的前提下，向客人提供有关信息，不仅是一种积极的销售技巧，还可增加酒店的营业收入，改善与宾客的关系。不过，在推销酒店的其他服务设施和服务项目时，应注意时间和场合。如客人深夜抵店，可以向客人介绍 24 小时咖啡厅服务或房内用膳服务；如客人经过长途旅行后抵达酒店，很可能需要洗衣和熨烫外套，这时应向客人介绍酒店的洗衣服务等。

During the process of promoting guest rooms, please do not neglect the promotion of other service facilities and service projects, such as catering, entertainment, commercial facilities and services, so that guests may feel the integrity and completeness of hotel products, for guests may not just satisfy the psychological demand for rest, they may also have other demands. If the receptionist fails to introduce them to the guests, some facilities may not be applied for a long time. As a result, the hotel may suffer the loss, and it is also a waste of resources. Therefore, please offer related information to guests on the premise of expected demands, which will not only be a positive promotion skill, but also increase the income of hotels, and improve the relationship with guests. However, when promoting the other service facilities and services, please pay attention to the time and occasion, if the guest arrives late in the night, 24-hour café house service or dining service can be introduced to the guest; if the guest arrives the hotel after long-distance trip, they might need to do some laundry or iron their clothes, so laundry service can be recommended to him.

表 7-4 防止客人逃账流程

Table 7-4 Procedures of Preventing Bill Escaping

项目 Project	标准 Standard	流程内容 Flows
1	灵活应对 及时上报 Deal with it flexibly and report in time	前台收银处发现客人不愿交定金，一方面要礼貌地请客人交预付款，并做好解释，另一方面要将情况报告值班经理 The cash desk finds that the guest is not willing to pay down payments. On one hand ask the guest politely and make explanation, on the other hand, report it to the duty manager in time

续表

项目 Project	标准 Standard	流程内容 Flows
2	及时上报 密切关注 Report in time and pay close attention	收银处输单时若发现客人一次性高额签单，应报告财务主管，并查清客人的情况，密切注意客人的以后消费，若有可疑情况及时报告值班经理 During the cashing, it is found out that the guest signs a contract with high amount of bills, please report it to the financial manager, and figure out the condition of guests. It shall pay close attention to the suspicious condition and report it to the duty manager if possible
3	确认无误 及时上报 Affirm and report in time	对于证实确实已离开营业场所的逃账客人，由财务部将逃账客人的详细资料（客人情况、消费情况）提供给安全保卫部。如需立案侦查的，由总经理批准后，安全保卫部开展侦查工作 For the proved bill-escaping guests, the financial department will provide the details of guests (such as the guest condition, consumption condition) for safety department, if it needs to be investigated, it shall be launched by the security department after the approval of general manager

[实训内容] [Training Contents]

1. 向客人推销中档价格的客房。

Recommend middle-price guest rooms to guests.

2. 向客人推销价格较低的客房。

Recommend low-price rooms to guests.

[实训准备] [Training Preparations]

前厅部前台或模拟场地；酒店简介、价目表等有关的宣传资料；模拟客人。

Reception desk of the Front Office or simulation sit; introduction of the hotel, price list, etc.; simulation of guests.

实训具体标准和测试表分别如表 7-5 和表 7-6 所示。

The specific standard of training and test chart are shown in Table 7-5 and Table 7-6 respectively.

表 7-5　实训具体标准

Table 7-5　Specific standard of training

实训内容 Content of Training	操作要领 Operation points	评分标准 Standard for evaluation
仪表仪容 Appearance	服务牌佩戴在外衣左上方、服装整洁、鞋袜洁净，头发、指甲、饰物等均符合职业要求 The service plate shall be worn on the top left of the coat, the clothing shall be clean, the shoes and sock shall be clean, the hair, nail, accessory shall meet the occupational requirements	有一项不符合要求，扣 2 分，扣完为止 If one item is not satisfied, 2 points will be deduced, till it is deduced completely
仪态 Bearing	行走、站姿正确，行为规范有礼 Walk and stand in correct posture, and behavior politely	有一项不符合要求，扣 2 分，扣完为止 If one item is not satisfied, 2 points will be deduced, till it is deduced completely
主动迎宾 Initiative meeting	对客人微笑、行注目礼、用敬语问候客人 Smile to the guest, make eye contact and greeting guests with deferential language	每遗漏一项扣 6 分；有一项没到位扣 2~4 分，扣完为止；累计两项没做到位，扣 6 分 6 points will be deduced for each missed item, and 2-4 points shall be deduced if one is not performed well, till it is completely deduced. If two items are not performed well, 6 points will be deduced

续表

实训内容 Content of Training	操作要领 Operation points	评分标准 Standard for evaluation
推销客房 Promoting guest room	根据客人的愿望和要求，正确使用报价方法；主动将有关的宣传资料展示给客人，并准确介绍客房设施、设备、朝向等情况；采用正面的说法称赞客人的选择，并能适时抓住成交机会 Use correct offering method according to the wishes and requirements of guests. Display the advertising data to guests initiatively, and introduce the equipment, facility, orientation, etc. of the guest room accurately, praise the choice of guests and grasp the transaction opportunity at proper time	有一项不符合要求，扣 10 分，扣完为止 If one item is not satisfied, 10 points will be deduced, till it is deduced completely

表 7-6　测试表
Table 7-6　Test Chart

姓名：　　内容：　　组别：　　时间：
Name:　　Contents:　　Group:　　Time:

序号 No.	项目 Project	分值 Score	自评分 Self-scoring	小组评分 Group-scoring	建议 Suggestions
1	仪表仪容 Appearance	20			
2	仪态 Bearing	10			
3	主动迎宾 Initiative meeting	10			
4	推销客房 Promoting guest room	60			
总成绩（星级） Total points (level)		100			
备注 Remark	星级评定： Star-level rating: 一般（50~60）★较好（61~74）★★良好（75~85）★★★ Ordinary (50~60) ★Good (61~74) ★★Well (75~85) ★★★ 优秀（86 以上）★★★★ Excellent (above 86) ★★★★				

模块小结
Module summary

1. 酒店客房房态主要包括哪些种类，影响房态的因素都包括哪些？

What kinds of hotel guest room status are there? How many factors impacting the room status?

2. 酒店控制房态的目的是什么？

What's the purpose of controlling hotel room status?

3. 酒店工作人员在核查房态时应注意什么？

What shall the hotel employees notice during the inspection of guest room status?

4. 酒店房价类型与收费方式主要包括哪些？

What kinds of hotel room rate and charging method?

5. 影响酒店房价的主要因素包括哪些？

What are the main factors impacting the hotel room rate?

6. 酒店客房定价方法主要包括哪些？

What kinds of hotel room rate methods are there?

7. 酒店工作人员销售客房时的流程包括什么？销售技巧有哪些？

What are the procedures of hotel guest room sales? What are the sales skills?

模块八　安全保障
Module VIII　Safety Guarantee

【情境导入】【Scenario Introduction】

假冒的美籍华人的朋友
A Counterfeited Friend of the Chinese American

一天傍晚，海口星海湾豪生大酒店总机的电话铃响了，服务员小姚马上接听，对方自称是住店的一位美籍华人的朋友，要求查询这位美籍华人。

One evening, the telephone of Howard Johnson New Port Resort Haikou rang. XiaoYao, receptionist of the hotel, picked up the phone immediately. The caller claimed that he was a friend of an American Chinese guest of the hotel and required XiaoYao to have a check.

小姚迅速查阅了住房登记中的有关资料，向他报了几个姓名，对方确认其中一位就是他要找的人，小姚不假思索，就把这位美籍华人的所住房间号码818告诉了他。

XiaoYao quickly checked the check -in record of the hotel and offered some names. The caller determined that one of the guests was actually the guest he wanted. Without hesitation, XiaoYao told the caller that the American Chinese lived in Room 818.

过了一会儿，酒店总机又接到一个电话，打电话者自称是818房的“美籍华人”，说他有一位谢姓侄子要来看他，此时他正在谈一笔生意，不能马上回来，请服务员把他房间的钥匙交给其侄子，让他在房间等候。接电话的小姚满口答应。

Later on, the hotel received another call. The caller claimed that he was the “American Chinese” in Room 818. He said that his nephew with the family name of Xie would come to visit him but he couldn't get back as he was in a business negotiation. So he asked the receptionist to give the key of his room to his nephew and ask him to wait in the room. XiaoYao consented readily.

又过了一会儿，一位西装笔挺的男青年来到服务台前，自称小谢，要取钥匙。小姚见了，以为果然不错，就毫无顾虑地把818房钥匙交给了那位男青年。

A moment later, a young man in business suit came to the Reception Desk. He introduced that he was XiaoXie and asked for the key. Without any suspicion, XiaoYao immediately give the key of Room 818 to that young man.

晚上，当那位真正的美籍华人回房时，发现一只高级密码箱不见了，其中包括一份护照、几千美元和若干首饰。

At night, when the real Chinese American went back, he found that a high grade code case was missing, including a passport, several thousand of dollars and several jewelries.

以上即是由一个犯罪青年分别扮演“美籍华人的朋友”“美籍华人”和“美籍华人的侄子”而演

出的一出诈骗酒店的丑剧。

In this case, the young criminal respectively acted as "the friend of the American Chinese", "the American Chinese" and "the Nephew of the American Chinese" by himself and successfully committed a fraud.

几天后，当这位神秘的男青年又出现在另一家酒店用同样的手法搞诈骗活动时，被具有高度警惕性，严格按酒店规章制度、服务规程办事的总台服务员和总台保安员识破，当场被抓获。

Several days later, when the mysterious young man tried to commit fraud with the same trick to another hotel, he was perceived by the Attendant and Safety Guard at the Reception Desk who had high sense of alertness and worked strictly according to the rules, regulations and service procedures of the hotel and finally he was caught on site.

【情境分析】【Scenario Analysis】

冒名顶替是不法分子在酒店犯罪作案的惯用伎俩。相比之下，本案中的这位犯罪青年的诈骗手法实在很不高明。总台服务员只要提高警惕，严格按规章制度办事，罪犯的骗局完全是可以防范的。

Masquerading is a common trick to commit crimes in hotels by bad guys. In comparison, the trick played by the young criminal in this case is not wise in nature. And such fraud may be completely prevented as long as the Attendant at the Reception Desk is on the alert and works strictly according to the rules and regulations.

首先，按酒店通常规定，为了保障入住客人的安全，其住处对外严格保密，即使是了解其姓名等情况的朋友、熟人，要打听其入住房号，总台服务员也应谢绝。变通的办法可为来访或来电者拨通客人房间的电话，由客人与来访或来电者直接通话；如客人不在，可让来访者留条或来电留言，由总台负责转送或转达给客人。这样既遵守了酒店的规章制度，保护了客人的安全，又沟通了客人与其朋友、熟人的联系。本案例中打电话者连朋友的姓名都叫不出，令人生疑，总台服务员更应谢绝要求。其次，“美籍华人”电话要总台让其“侄子”领了钥匙进房等候，这个要求也是完全不能接受的。因为按酒店规定，任何人只有凭住宿证方能领取钥匙入房。凭一个来路不明的电话“委托”，如何证明来访者的合法性？总台服务员仅根据一个电话便轻易答应别人的“委托”，明显地违反了服务规程，是很不应该的。总台若能把好这第二关，犯罪的诈骗阴谋仍然来得及制止。

First, as a general rule of hotel, to guarantee the safety of the residing guest, the hotel should regard the residing place of the guest as high confidentiality. In case that someone asks about the room number of the guest, the attendant at the Reception Desk should decline politely, even to the friends or acquaintances knowing the name of the guest. A flexible method is to ask the visiting or calling guest to dial the room telephone of the guest and have the guest to talk directly with the visitor or the caller. In case that the guest is not in, ask the visitor or the caller to leave a message and the Reception Desk should be responsible to relay the message to the guest. This not only follows the rules of the hotel, protect the safety of the guest, but also maintain the connection between the guest and his/her friends or acquaintances. In this case, the caller failed to tell the name of his "friend" . This is doubtful and the attendant at the Reception Desk should also decline his request. Secondly, the "American Chinese" called the Reception Desk to give the key to his "nephew" and ask him to wait in the room. This request is fully unacceptable. According to the rules of the hotel, room keys can only be given to those who present the certificate of residence. So, how can the attendant prove the legitimacy of the visitor just based on the entrustment of an unauthentic call? The attendant of the Reception Desk accepted the "entrustment" of others easily just according to a call.

Obviously, this is against the service procedures and is quite ridiculous. If the Reception Desk can make proper control, the trick still could be stopped.

【学习目标】【Learning Goals】

［知识目标］［Knowledge Objectives］

1. 掌握酒店安全管理的重要性。

Master the importance of hotel safety management.

2. 掌握酒店各岗位安全控制事项。

Master the matters related to safety control on each post of the hotel.

3. 掌握酒店消防安全的主要隐患地方。

Get to know the main hidden dangers of the fire safety of the hotel.

［能力目标］［Capacity Objectives］

1. 熟练掌握排查酒店安全隐患的能力。

Fluently master the ability to check the hidden safety dangers of the hotel.

2. 具有处理突发事件的能力，如失窃、火灾等。

Be capable to dispose sudden events such as burglary and fire.

【重点和难点】【Key Points and Difficulties】

1. 掌握酒店各岗位安全控制注意事项，能够消除各项安全隐患。

Master he precautions on safety control of each post, be capable to eliminate various types of hidden safety dangers.

2. 具备处理酒店突发事件（如失窃、火灾等）的能力。

Be capable to dispose sudden events such as burglary and fire.

任务一　服务安全
Task Ⅰ　Service Safety

【情境导入】【Scenario Introduction】

能否随便给访客开门
Does it make sense to open the door for the visitor without authorization

某日，一位客人带着一个小孩在酒店的楼道里走来走去，看见正在打扫卫生的服务员就走过来，让其打开3408房。该员工依照酒店开门程序对这位客人进行询问：“先生，您是住客还是要找人？”“我找人!”“对不起，先生! 在没有得到房间主人的许可下，我们是不能为您将门打开的，请谅解!”但客人坚持说只是把一个包放在房间里就走，不会逗留。该员工一想也不会使住店客人有什么损失，况且自己跟着进房间，便询问来访者要找的客人姓什么？客人毫不犹豫地说自己姓孔。经过客房中心核实身份，此房间客人确实姓孔。于是员工敲门，听房间内无人回应，便直接打开房门并让来访者进去，自己也跟了进去。但是没有想到客人正在房间内休息，场面非常尴尬。客人相当生气且来到大堂大声投诉说，为什么没有经过他同意就给来访的人开门！经大堂经理和值班经理出面，向房间客人进行了道歉，客人情绪才稍缓和。

One day, a guest walked around in the corridor of a hotel with a child. On seeing the cleaner, the guest came up and asked the cleaner to open Room 3408 for him. The cleaner enquired the guest according to the door opening procedure for the hotel: "Sir, are you a guest or a visitor?" "Visitor." "Sorry, sir. we cannot open the door for you without the permission of the guest of the room. Please understand." However, the guest insisted that he just wanted to leave a bag inside and would not stay. The cleaner thought that this would not cause trouble to the guest, besides that he would be accompanied by the cleaner. So the cleaner asked the visitor about the family name of the guest. The visitor replied that the family name of the guest is Kong without hesitation. The cleaner verified the identity of the Room Center and confirmed that the family name of the guest was Kong. So the cleaner knocked the door and there was no reply from within. So the cleaner opened the door and followed the visitor in. However, beyond the expectation of the cleaner, the guest was resting in the room. The scene was quite embarrassing. The guest was quite angry and complained loudly in the lobby that the door was opened for visitors without his authorization. The Assistant Manager and the Duty Manager apologized to the guest. The guest was slightly calmed.

【情境分析】【Scenario Analysis】

此案例中，服务人员视酒店规章制度不顾，擅自答应访客打开宾客房门，是一种安全意识淡薄和纪律观念差的表现；服务人员必须本着对酒店、对客人高度负责的态度，强化规范化操作，强化安全意识，制度严明，不可有麻痹大意、自作主张的思想，否则会使服务工作陷入被动。

In this case, the staff ignored the rules and regulations of the hotel and opened the guest room without authorization. This is the representation of poor safety consciousness and concept of discipline. The service staff must bear high sense of responsibility for the hotel and the guests, enhance normalized operations and sense of safety, and strictly obey the rules and may not be lack of vigilance or self-assertive. Or, the service would be in passivity.

一、酒店安全管理的重要性（Important of Hotel Safety Management）

常常有人认为酒店的安全工作是依附于服务而产生的，它不直接产生利润，属于非生产部门，因而将之作为“二线”服务而轻视之。这种看法无疑是片面的，酒店安全工作的好坏，不仅直接关系到酒店的正常运转，也在很大程度上影响酒店的效益。

Often some people regard safety of the hotel as "second-line" service and ignore it as it is attached to the hotel services and it does not create profits directly and belongs to non-production department. The perspective is definitely one-sided. The safety performance of the hotel not only bears direct relationship with the normal operation of the hotel, but affects the benefits of the hotel greatly.

（一）安全管理是提高客人满意度的重要保证（Safety Management is the Important Guarantee to Enhance Guest Satisfaction）

安全是人类的一个最基本的需求。酒店住客如同其他任何人类一样，具有免遭人身伤害和财产损失，要求自身权利和正当需求受到保护和尊重的安全需求，而且，住客身处异地他乡，他们对自己的生命安全、财产安全和心理安全的关注与敏感，其期望程度比平时更甚。因此，从经营的角度而言，为住客提供安全的环境以满足客人对安全的期望，是酒店正常经营管理工作和提高服务质量的一个基础。

Safety is the basic demand of the humans. Just as other people, hotel guests also have the safety demands to prevent personal harms and property losses and require the protection and respect of their own rights and rightful demands. In addition, as the guests are remote to their hometowns, their concerns and sensitivity on the life safety, property safety and sense of safety as well as their expectation on safety is even greater than usual. Therefore, from the aspect of operation, to provide safe environments to meet the demands of guests on safety is the basis for the hotels to make normal operation management and enhance service quality.

（二）安全管理直接影响酒店的社会效益和经济效益（Safety Management Bears Direct Influence on the Social Benefits and Economic Benefits of the Hotel）

住客来酒店消费，酒店经营者有义务制定出能保证消费者安全的服务标准，具备能够保证消费者安全的服务设施。否则，酒店经营者将面临安全问题而引起的投诉、索赔直至承担法律责任，从而影响酒店的社会效益和经济效益。因此，从法律的角度而言，酒店在经营管理工作中，必须牢固树立安全意识，确保酒店所有人员及所有财产的安全。这里的“所有人员”，既包括住客，也包括从业人员及所有合法在酒店的其他人员；“所有财产”包括住客财产、酒店财产，也包括从业人员的财产。

For the guest residing and consuming in the hotel, the operator of the hotel should have the liability to formulate service standards sufficiently guarantee the safety of the consumers and provide service facilities to safeguard the safety of the consumers. Or, the hotel operator would have to face complains, claims or even assume legal liabilities arising from safety issues, which would further adversely influence the social benefits and economic benefits of the hotel. Therefore, from the legal aspect, during the operation management, the hotel must establish firm sense of safety and guarantee the safety of all personnel and property of the hotel. “All personnel” herein involve not only the guests but also the staff as well as other personnel legally staying in the hotel; “all properties” involve not only the properties of the guests and hotel but also the practitioners.

（三）安全管理有助于提高员工积极性（Safety Management Contributes to Enhancement of Staff Enthusiasm）

安全管理不仅是对客人安全、酒店财产安全的管理，同时也包括对员工安全的管理，如果酒店在生产过程中缺乏各种防范和保护措施，将不可避免地产生工伤事故，使员工的健康状况受到影响，很难使员工积极而有效地工作。

Safety management involves not only management on guest safety and hotel property safety, but also the management on staff safety. If the hotel lacks of various types of preventive and protective measures in the process of production, occupational injury accidents would be unavoidable. This would affect the health status of the staff and make it hard for the staff to work positively and effectively.

二、酒店各岗位安全控制事项（Matters Related to Safety Control on Each Post of the Hotel）

（一）入住登记安全控制事项（Safety Control Precautions of Check-in Registration）

（1）前台接待员负责接待住客住宿登记工作，每天 24 小时当班服务。

The Receptionist at the Reception Desk is responsible for the check-in registration of the guests residing in the hotel and be on duty in shifts around the clock.

（2）所有中、外住客必须凭有效身份证件如实填写《客人住宿登记单》，登记合格率 100%。同时，住客应与所登记的姓名、人数、性别相符，如有增减换人情况，应提醒客人与前台接待联系。

All the domestic and foreign guests must fill in the *Guest Check-in Registration Form* with valid identity documents according to the fact. The conformity rate of registration should be 100%. Meanwhile, the guests residing in the hotel should be consistent with the names, number of people and sex recorded in the registration form. In case that the guests living in are increased/decreased or changed, remind the guest to contact the Reception Desk.

（3）对零散住客实施登记时必须做到“三清，三核对”。“三清”即字迹清、登记项目清、证件检验清。“三核对”即核对住客本人和证件照片是否相符、核对登记年龄和证件的年龄是否相符、核对证件印章和使用年限是否有效。

When making check-in registration for individual guests, “Three Clearness and Three Checks” must be made. “Three Clearness” refers to: Clear handwriting, clear registration items and clear credential inspection “Three Checks” refer to: Check whether the appearance of the guest is consistent with the photo on the credentials; whether the registered age is consistent with the age on the credential; check whether the seal and the validation period of the credential has expired.

（4）旅行团体客人的住宿登记可由旅行社陪同或销售代表代办填报。

Check-in registration of tourist group guests may be made with the company of the travel agency or filled by the sales representative.

（5）VIP 客人可先领进房，在房内办理登记手续或由省、市接待部门代为登记。

VIP guests may be guided into the room first and proceed check-in formalities in the guest room or their check-in registration may be made by the provincial or municipal level reception unit.

（6）严格按照前台钥匙管理制度的规定为客人准备钥匙。

Prepare the keys for the guests strictly according to the key management rules of the Reception Desk.

（7）在输入客人资料时，建立新的客人档案，核查此客人是否是公安局协查的查控人员，如客人信息与电脑记录中查控人员的信息相符，发现可疑人员采取内紧外松，先安排入住，前台接待员应立即通知本部门或当值经理，双方确认无误后立即通知酒店保安部对此客人进行监控，并迅速与公安机关联系，避免打草惊蛇。

When inputting the guest information, create new file for the guest, check whether the guest is being investigated or wanted by the public security bureau. If the guest is listed into the investigated or wanted personnel in the computer system, treatment may be intense inside and relaxed outside to the suspicious personnel. The Receptionist of the Reception Desk may first arrange the guest to check in and then immediately notify the Department Manager or Duty Manger. Upon confirmation, notify the Security Department to monitor the guest, and immediately contact the public security bureall. Do not act rashly and alert the guest.

（8）按时向公安机关申报，每日输入电脑的情况要准确无误；不能漏输或不输，保证及时发送，谁输入谁负责。同时，住客资料和公安机关下发的有关通缉协查对象应及时输入电脑准确无误，以便核查。

Report the information to the public security bureall on time. Ensure there're no errors and omission in daily computer input. Ensure the timely transmission. The personnel making the input should take the responsibility. Meanwhile, the guest information and the list of investigated and wanted personnel issued by the public security bureau should be timely and accurately input into the computer for examination and verification.

（9）接待员在办理住宿登记的同时，应提醒旅客贵重钱财、证件可免费保管。

When handling check-in registration formalities, the receptionist should remind the guests that cash, valuables and credentials may be deposited for free at the hotel.

（10）按照公安部门规定：访客须登记，访客时间不超过23时。

As stipulated by the public security bureau, visitors must register at the hotel and the visits should not be later than 23：00.

（11）如有店外客人查询客人信息，前台接待员有对住宿客人信息保密的义务，不经客人本人同意不可将客人房号及有关信息告知他人。

If the guest information is requested by other personnel out of the hotel, the receptionist of the Reception Desk must keep the guest information confidential. Without the consent of the guest in person, no disclosure should be made on the room number and other related information to others.

（12）如客人到前台办理延住手续，首先核对客人是否为住店客人，前台接待员可以请客人出示证件，请其说出本人身份证件上所属的地址、出生日期及证件号码并与电脑核对；如客人证件在房间，请当值经理陪同客人上楼确认其身份，确认无误后，方可将重新做的钥匙交给客人。

If a guest comes to the Reception Desk to extend his/her stay, first check whether the guest is a residing guest of the hotel. The receptionist of the Reception Desk may ask the guest to present his/her credentials, enquire the guest to tell the address, date of birth and number of the identity document and check with the computer record. If the credential of the guest is in the guest room, the Duty Manager should go upstairs with the guest to check his/her identity. In case that nothing suspicious is detected, give the new key to the guest.

（13）前台接待员应提醒客人将自己的房卡钥匙保存好，以防丢失。离开房间时，将房门锁好。

The receptionist of the Reception Desk should remind the guest to keep the room card and key properly to avoid losing. Lock the room properly when leaving the room.

（14）客人如随身携带贵重物品应存放在酒店提供的保险箱中。

Valuables with the guest should be deposited in the hotel safe.

（15）以上内容均须严格遵守。谁主管，谁负责。谁当班，谁负责。每日早、中班检查当日登记单及当天PSB的输入情况。夜班负责最后把关，将资料发送到公安机关。

Strictly abide by the above mentioned provisions. The staff in charge should take responsibility. And the staff on duty should take responsibility. The morning shift and middle shift every day should inspect the daily registration record and the PSB input for that day. The night shift should make the final check and send the data to the public security bureau.

（二）访客接待安全注意事项（Precautions for Visitor Reception Safety）

（1）如有访客，前台接待员应首先根据访问者提供的情况进行核实，核实无误后，打电话征求客人意见，在得到住店客人同意后方可告知来访者住店客人的房号。

In case of visitors, the receptionist of the Reception Desk should first make verification according to the information provided by the visitor. If the information is correct, call the guest to ask for his/her opinion. Inform the visitor the room number of the guest only upon the consent of the guest.

（2）如发现电脑中客人有保密要求，应根据客人要求对来访者做相关解释。

If the guest requires confidentiality according to the computer record，make explanations to the visitor according to the requirements of the guest.

（3）如遇特殊情况请与当值经理联系解决。

Contact the Duty Manager in case of special circumstances.

（三）钥匙安全管理注意事项（Precautions for Key Safety Management）

设计周密的钥匙系统是酒店最基本的安全硬件。为了有效地运用钥匙，钥匙要定期更换、改变。如传统的锁应定期更换锁芯。当然，使用电子计算机控制的电子门锁更换的频率更高。钥匙安全管理注意事项如下：

Elaborate key system is the most fundamental safety hardware of the hotel. For effective utilization of keys，the keys should be replaced or altered in a scheduled manner. Periodically replace the lock cylinders of traditional locks. Of course，the replacement frequency of computer-controlled electronic locks is higher. Precautions on key safety management are as follows：

（1）前台接待员为住店客人提供房间钥匙，每间房最多提供两把钥匙（有加床提供三把），不得多做。

The receptionist of the Reception Desk provides room keys to the guest. Maximally two keys should be provided for each room（three in case of extra bed）.

（2）如遇客人找不到房间钥匙或将房间钥匙丢失时，前台接待员首先确认此客人是否为住店客人，请客人出示有效证件并认真与电脑核对是否一致；如客人未带证件，请其说出本人的身份证所属的地址、出生日期及证件号码与电脑核对是否一致；询问客人的钥匙是否丢失，还是忘在房间。接待员在核实确认后为客人重新做钥匙。同时应提醒客人使用新钥匙，旧钥匙已作废。

In case that the guest cannot find or loses the room key，the receptionist of the Reception Desk should first check whether the guest is a residing guest of the hotel，then ask the guest to present the valid credential，and check for consistency with the computer. If the guest doesn't bring the credential，ask the guest to provide the address，date of birth and number of the credential，and check on the computer for consistency. Ask the guest whether the key is lost or forgotten in the room. After verification and confirmation，the receptionist should remake a key to the guest. Meanwhile，the receptionist should remind the guest that the new key should be used and the old key would be disabled.

（3）如客人离店时，想保留钥匙做纪念，前台接待员应收回旧钥匙，给客人一把新的空钥匙。

If the guest wants to keep the key as a souvenir when the guest checks out，the receptionist of the Reception Desk should collect the old key and give a new and invalid key to the guest.

（4）前台接待员不得私自配钥匙、上楼层打开房门或把钥匙交与非住店人员。

The receptionist of the Reception Desk is prohibited to make a key，open the door or give the key to the non-residing personnel without authorization.

（5）员工对自己的钥匙机密码保密，不得泄露。

The staff should keep the password of the key machine confidential and shall not disclose the password.

（6）磁卡钥匙应专项专用，不得挪做他用。

The magnetic card key should be designated for specific use and cannot be used elsewhere.

（四）行李服务安全注意事项（Precautions for Luggage Service Safety）

1. 行李房安全管理注意事项（Precautions for Safety Management of Luggage Room）

（1）礼宾员在取送宾客行李进入客房时，要有该客房服务员或客人在场，礼宾员不得单独进入客房取行李。同时，坚持行李寄存卡片同行李牌相结合，禁止随意翻动客人寄存的物品。

When the Concierge Attendant delivers or collects the luggage in the guest room, the Room Attendant or the guest should be present. The Concierge Attendant cannot enter the guest room to collect the luggage alone. Meanwhile, the luggage deposit card and the luggage tag should be consistent. Do not rummage the articles deposited by the guest.

（2）对客人寄存的行李、物品要认真履行登记手续，过夜行李要放在行李房内，暂存在大厅的行李要用绳索串联拴好并用网罩覆盖，并派专人看守，防止丢失。对行李房内客人长期存放的行李，一定要登记准确，库房钥匙由专人管理。坚持一丝不苟地办理寄存及领取手续，切实做到四对（对房号、对牌号、对件数、对签名）。

Work on registration formalities carefully on the luggage and articles deposited by the guest. Overnight luggage should be stored in the Luggage Room. Luggage deposited temporarily in the lobby should be tied up on rope and covered with net. Specific personnel should be assigned to guard the luggage to avoid missing. For luggage stored for a long term in the Luggage Room, accurate registration should be made. The key of the storeroom should be managed by specially assigned personnel. Deposit and retrieval formalities should be handled meticulously and "Four Checks" should be made (Check on room number, tag number, number of luggage and signature).

（3）礼宾部在接收客人行李时，注意发现有无枪支弹药或易燃易爆等危险物品，一经发现立即报告保安部，并做好当时的保护工作。同时，警惕住客将危险物品夹在行李中寄存，坚持现金与贵重物品需放进保险箱。

When receiving the guest luggage, the Concierge Department should attach importance to hazardous goods such as firearms, ammunition, inflammable or explosive articles. Once such materials are detected, the Concierge Department should immediately report to the Security Department and take proper protective measures. Meanwhile, be alerted that some guest might deposit hazardous articles by mingling them into luggage. Insist that the cash and valuables should be deposited into the safe.

（4）对贵重物品、烟酒食品、动物牲畜一律不予寄存。

Valuables, liquor, tobacco and animals should not be deposited.

（5）禁止任何人在行李房内外生明火、吃东西、休息、吸烟。

No one shall light open fire, eat, rest or smoke in and out of the Luggage Room.

（6）行李房内严禁吸烟和无关人员进入，行李房随时保持干净整齐，要定期对行李房进行清理，寄存的行李要摆放整齐。

Smoking is strictly prohibited. And unrelated personnel should be kept away from the Luggage Room. The Luggage Room should be kept clean at any time. Tide the Luggage Room periodically. The deposited luggage should be placed in order.

（7）礼宾师和副礼宾师对客人行李物品的登记要核收核发，对前往客房取送行李的礼宾员要记载并存档备查。

Chief Concierge and Assistant Chief Concierge should check the acceptance and retrieval registration of the luggage; the Concierge Attendant should record and archive the luggage delivered to or collected from the guest room for further reference.

（8）对于宾客信件包裹要有登记、收发、签字手续，任何人不得私拆、扣压、毁弃。送信员工要将送信时间、房号、姓名进行认真登记并存档备查。

Registration, reception and dispatching and signature formalities should be ready for letters and packages of the guests. No one should open, withhold or destroy without authorization. The staff delivering letters should make careful registration on the delivery time, room number and name, and archive such information for further reference.

(9) 对于件数较多的行李存入行李房时，须加盖网罩，以便区别。

If the luggage to be deposited is relatively great in number, the luggage must be covered with net to make distinction.

(10) 行李房要定期检查安全隐患，并及时排除。同时，行李房不允许存放员工的私人物品。

The hidden safety dangers should be checked periodically and removed timely in the Luggage Room. Meanwhile, personal belongings are not allowed to be deposited in the Luggage Room.

(11) 坚持交接班有记录。

Shift handover must be recorded.

2. 行李寄存处安全防火管理注意事项（Precautions for fire safety management in Luggage Office）

(1) 非当班人员严禁入内，当班人员由主管指派方可为客人存取行李。

Off-duty staff are strictly prohibited to enter the Luggage Room. The on-duty staff should deposit or retrieve the luggage for the guest only if he/she is assigned by the Supervisor.

(2) 不得存放易燃易爆物品，也不得给客人存放枪支、弹药、化学剧毒、放射性物质等物品，如当时未发现，事后发现要及时报告部门主管和保安部。

Inflammable or explosive articles should not be stored in the Luggage Room. Do not deposit firearms, ammunition, chemical poison, radioactive articles, etc. for the guests. If such articles are not detected at the time of deposit, the Department Supervisor and Security Department should be reported timely upon detection later on.

(3) 不准堆放废纸物，严禁在行李寄存处吸烟，带入明火。

Do not stack wasted paper in the Luggage Room. Smoking and open fire is strictly prohibited.

(4) 要制定存放行李的规定，用中英文在明显处写出指标牌（存放行李须知）。

Formulate provisions for luggage deposit; put on notice board at visible position in both Chinese and English (Luggage Deposit Instructions).

(5) 工作人员要熟记就近灭火器材的存放位置，掌握灭火器材的性能、作用及使用方法，保持灭火器的清洁。灭火器材存放的位置不能随意移动。

The work staff should be familiar with the storage positions of the nearby firefighting equipments; master the properties, functions and usage of the firefighting equipments and maintain the cleanness of the firefighting equipments. The storage positions of the firefighting equipments cannot be moved randomly.

(6) 发现火情及时报警和扑救。

Make alarms and take control measures timely in case of fire.

(7) 不得在行李房内逗留，关门前一定要先关灯。

Do not stay for a long period in the Luggage Room; turn off the lights before closing the door.

(五) 收银服务安全 (Cashier Service Safety)

1. 酒店收银工作方式、程序、规格（Work Styles, Procedures and Specifications of Cashier Work of Hotel）

(1) 上班必须做好备用金、发票、凭据、客用保险箱、各类钥匙、文具用品，重要事宜的交接签收工作。

Prepare revolving fund, invoice, credentials, guest safes, various types of keys and stationary before starting work; sign for handover of important matters.

（2）前台收银：

Reception Desk Cashier:

A. 检查前厅接待处交来的入住登记单及有关资料是否正确齐全，并利用电脑进行查询核对无误后在入住登记单上签名，将入住登记单放入相应的入住登记单袋中，符合要求的入住登记单要退回前厅接待处。

Check whether the check-in registration form and related data passed by the Reception Desk at the lobby is correct and complete. Check on the computer to confirm that there's no error. Sign on the Check-in Registration Form. Put the Check-in Registration Form into corresponding Check-in Registration Form Bag. Check-in Registration Form with reference information meeting related requirements should be returned to the Reception Desk.

B. 订金。根据入住登记单上批示，按酒店规定向客人收取订金，同时开出暂收款凭证，将凭证号码填写在入住登记单卡上并签名，将第一联交给客人，第二联入机后放入客人资料袋中，并打印账单，第三联做下班对账用。

Advance Payment. Collect advance payment from the guest according to the provisions of the hotel as instructed on the Check-in Registration Form. Issue Temporary Receipt Voucher. Fill in the voucher number onto the Check-in Registration Form Card and sign on the card. Put the first copy to the guest; input the second copy into the computer, and put it into the information bag for the guest and print the bill; keep the third copy for account checking at shift handover.

C. 信用卡。若客人用信用卡结账，应事先在接待处压卡，并将身份证号码抄写在签购单上，收银员必须查黑名单，再审查信用卡资料，取得适当的信用额，正确无误后要在入住登记单交接簿上签名，然后放入客人资料袋中。

Credit Card. If the guest selects to pay the bill with the credit card, he/she should have the credit card detained at the Reception Desk. Copy the identity card number onto the slip. The cashier must review the blacklist first and double check the credit card information to obtain appropriate credit amount. If no errors are detected, sign on the handover book of the Check-in Registration Form and then put it into the information bag of the guest.

D. 应收账。核对有关的应收资料是否正确齐全。

Accounts receivable. Check whether the related data receivable is correct and complete.

E. 支票。核对该客户是否同酒店签有“可接受支票协议书”，获取客人的有效资料，并知会上级。

Cheque. Check whether the guest has signed “Agreement on Acceptable Cheque” with the hotel; obtain the valid data of the guest and inform the superior.

F. 房租。低于正常房价的租金是否有酒店授权人批准签名。

Room Rate. Check whether room fees lower than normal room rates have been approved and signed by the authorizer of the hotel.

G. 免费房。核对是否有申请免费房的通知及批准人的签名。

Free Room. Check whether there's notice on free room application as well as the signature of the authorizer.

H. 团体。核对清房数、人数、房租、付款方式、结账人、用餐情况、来离日期等内容，将团体安排表及团体名单等资料放入团体资料袋中，并知会收银主管。

Group. Check contents such as the number of rooms, number of people, room rates, payment method, payer and dining conditions as well as the arriving and departure date. Place data such as the group schedule and group list into the group information bag and inform the Cashier Supervisor.

I. 职员房。核对是否有酒店授权人批准。

Staff Room. Check whether the room has been approved by the hotel authorizer.

2. 入住人数（Entry）

（1）每收到各营业点送来或报来的单据应首先同客人入住登记单等资料及电脑记录查对清楚，及时准确输入电脑，金额过大的要知会主管，经同意后方可入数。

When receiving the vouchers submitted or reported by each business unit, first check the computer record on data such as the Check-in Registration Form. Timely input the information into the computer; inform the Supervisor on large sums; make entry upon consent.

（2）将单据第一联放入客人资料袋中，第二联作交班核查用。

Put the first copy of the voucher into the guest information bag; keep the second copy for check at shift handover.

（3）各个营业部门送来或报来的单据要做好登记记录下来，互报姓名、工号或单号并打钟卡，以明确责任。

Record the vouchers submitted or reported by each business department; report the name, job number or voucher number and punch the card to clarify the responsibilities.

3. 退房（Check Out）

（1）接过客人钥匙，从资料袋中拿出客人资料，同时打电话通知楼层查房，并将回复电脑的分机号码知会楼层服务员及说出双方工号，以便跟进工作。

Receive the key from the guest; pick out the guest data from the information bag; call corresponding floor to check the room; inform the extension number of the guest room to the floor attendant and exchange the job numbers to facilitate follow-up.

（2）问清客人的结算方式，利用电脑熟练操作，打出账单交客人审阅并签名（连同所有小单一起交客人），检查客人的签名是否同 RC 的签名一致。

Ask the settlement method of the guest; operate on the computer skillfully, print the bills, have the guest check the bills and sign on the bills (give the bills to the guest together with the slips); inspect whether the signature of the guest is consistent with RC signature.

（3）根据实情收支款，注意找换的准确及检验货币的真伪，填写退款凭证，须客人签名。

Receive and disburse the funds according to the facts; give the change correctly and inspect the authenticity of the cash; fill in the refund vouchers and ask the guest to sign the vouchers.

（4）用信用卡结账的要注意严格按接受信用卡的程序进行操作，超过限额的要先取得授权，正确填写金额及货币符号，并将信用卡资料压印在账单上，核对卡的签名是否一致。

In case of credit card settlement, operation should be made strictly according to the credit card procedures. If the amount exceeds the limit, authorization should be obtained first. Fill in the amount and currency symbols correctly; press the credit card information onto the bills; verify whether the signature of the card is consistent.

（5）以挂账方式结算的要审核所有应收资料是否正确齐备，用酒店金卡的要在账单上压上金卡的资料，并核对签名，所有的小单一定要跟齐。

In case of account settlement on credit, examine and review whether the data to be collected is correct and complete. In case of gold card of the hotel, information about the gold card should be pressed onto the bills and the signature should be checked. All the slips must be complete.

（6）团体退房要知会主管，收齐钥匙，人完散数，根据团体安排表上的结算指示准确结算。

Group check-out should be informed to the Supervisor. Collect all the keys and then make inventory. Make accurate settlement according to the settlement instructions according to the group schedule.

（7）所有退房的账单必须有入住登记单资料跟在其后，以便夜、日审核查。

All check-out bills must be attached with information about Check-in Registration Form to facilitate night and day examination.

（8）所有退房的账单必须有客人的签名，签名必须与入住登记单的签名一致，发现签名不一致，或客人遗失订金收据立即知会上司或上报大堂经理协同处理。

All check-out bills must be signed by the guest. The signature must be consistent with the signature on the Check-in Registration Form. In case that the receipt is not consistent the guest loses the receipt on advance payment, immediately inform the superior or report to the Assistant Manager for coordinative treatment.

任务二　消防安全
Task II　Fire Safety

【情境导入】【Scenario Introduction】

火灾案例集
Fire Case Set

酒店是火灾青睐的重点之一。全球酒店业每天都有火灾发生，酒店火灾关系到人们生命财产的安全，关系到社会的稳定，关系到酒店的生死存亡。所以，从事酒店事业的全体员工，必须认真探讨火灾的规律；切实做好深入细致的消防工作，把火灾这只“猛虎”消灭在“下山”之前。通过对 15 年来全球酒店火灾的案例研究，我们认为，三个 70%是其中重要的规律。

Hotels are likely to be attacked by fire. Fire breaks out every day in the hospitality industry globally. Fire in hotels has the direct bearing on the life and property safety, social stability and is of vital importance for the survival of the hotel. Therefore, all staff working on hospitality must carefully discuss the rules of fires, practically make in-depth and detailed fire prevention and to nip the “Fire Tiger” in the bud. Based on case studies on fires in hotels globally for the past 15 years, we deem that the “Three 70%s” is an important rule within.

【情境分析】【Scenario Analysis】

一、70%的火灾是由电器引发（70% of the Fires are Triggered by Electronic Causes）

由于现代化酒店的主要能源是电，电线如网，用电设备多，整个酒店是一个大的带电体，用电设施的缺陷、线路的老化、人员造作的失误都易造成短路起火，电器的管理、使用不当是酒店火灾的头号杀手，占酒店火灾的70%以上。

The major energy supply of modernized hotels is electricity. electricity lines are just like nets. The electricity equipments are intensive in hotels. And the entire hotel is a big "electrified body". Defects in electricity consummation facilities, aging of electricity lines and errors of personnel operations would easily cause short circuit and fire. Improper electronic management is the first killer of hotel fires and accounts over 70% of the hotel fires.

例如，2005年6月10日，汕头市华南酒店，由于电器线路短路故障引燃可燃物，造成特大火灾事故，造成31人死亡，28人受伤，过火面积2800平方米，直接经济损失81万余元。

For example, On June 10, 2005, in Shantou Huanan Hotel, an extraordinarily serious fire accident was caused as inflammable goods were ignited by electric circuit shortcut, resulting in 31 deaths and 28 injuries. The burned area was 2800 m^2 and the direct economic loss was over 810000 yuan.

又如，2010年7月16日凌晨，伊拉克北部苏莱曼尼亚中心一家酒店，由于电器短路造成特大火灾，造成43人死亡，23受伤。

Another example, Early on the morning of July 16, 2010, in a hotel of the Sulaymaniyah Center in the north of Iraq, an extraordinarily serious fire accident was caused by electrical short circuit, resulting in 43 deaths and 23 injuries.

所以，用电设施的规划布局，设备的完好，合格的人员的电器操作和管理是减少和杜绝酒店火灾的关键之一。

Therefore, the proper planning and layout of the power consuming facilities, consummation of equipments and proper electric operation and management are key to reduce and eliminate hotel fires.

二、70%的火灾是用火不慎（70% of the Fires are Triggered by Careless Fire Use）

火不只给人们带来光明，同时也会给人们带来灾难，这里的关键是谨慎正确的用火，所有用火人员都必须严格操作规程，百分之百的慎之又慎，用火设施任何时候都必须处于良好状态，否则就容易酿成大祸。

Fire not only brings brightness to people but also causes disasters. The key is cautious and correct fire use. Therefore, all personnel dealing with fires must strictly follow the operation procedures and pay 100% alertness. Fire using facilities must be in good conditions all the time, or serious accidents would be easily caused.

例如，2004年2月1日，洛阳经济开发区深森酒店，由于值班人员用煤炉取暖，煤炉引燃值班人员的大衣而造成特大火灾，烧死10人，其中女服务员7人，烧伤摔伤16人。

For example, On February 1, 2004, in Shensen Hotel of Luoyan Economic Development Zone, staff on duty used coal stoves to keep warm and ignited the coat of the staff. An extraordinarily serious fire accident was caused, resulting in 10 deaths, including 7 female attendants, as well as 16 burned and fallen injuries.

2007年7月26日晚，辽宁省朝阳市百姓楼酒店，酒店人员擅自使用一个没启用的柴油灶，操作严重违规，导致重大火灾，造成11人死亡，16人受伤。

On the evening of July 26, 2007, in Baixinglou Hotel, Chaoyang, Liaoning Province, the hotel staff used a diesel stove not used before without authorization and seriously breached the operation rules. An extraordinarily serious fire accident was caused, resulting in 11 deaths and 16 injuries.

所以，涉火人员的安全防范意识要十分高，九分不行，九点九分也不行，非十分不可。再加上不断检查维修用火设施，严格执行操作规程，是防止酒店火灾的重要环节。

Therefore, sense of fire prevention of fire related personnel must be 100%. 90% or even 99% will not do. Such efforts, plus continuous inspection and maintenance on fire use facilities, strictly implementation of operation procedures, form important links to prevent hotel fires.

三、70%的火灾发生在早、晚和零散人员身上（70% of the Fires Break in Mornings, At Nights and On Scattered Personnel）

早晚、节假日易造成管理松懈，是管理漏洞的多发时节，也是火灾隐患经常出没之时。零散人员是管理的死角，是领导管理的“灯下黑”，因此许多酒店的火灾容易发生在管理松懈的早晚和节假日，以及疏于管理的零散人员身上。

Mornings, nights and holidays are periods that would easily cause loose management, frequent management leakage as well as hidden fire dangers. Scattered personnel are dead corners in management, which are also the “blind areas” for leadership management. Therefore, many hotel fires would easily occur in mornings, at nights and on holidays when the management is loose as well as on scattered personnel where the management is less intensive.

例如，1997 年 1 月 29 日，燕山酒家保安员使用酒精炉煮东西吃，违反操作规程发生火灾，造成 40 人死亡，重伤 27 人，轻伤 62 人，烧毁建筑面积 1/10——997 平方米。直接经济损失 92 万元。

For example, On January 29, 1997, the security guard in Yanshan Hotel cooked with a spirit stove. The guard breached the operation rules and caused a fire accident, resulting in 40 deaths, 27 serious injuries and 62 light injuries. The burned area was 997 m^2, one tenth of the building area. The direct economic loss was 920000 yuan.

2003 年 2 月 2 日 17 时 59 分，黑龙江哈尔滨市天潭大酒店，一名酒店服务员用汽油代替煤油燃料添加取暖炉引发特大火灾，造成 33 人死亡，10 人受伤，其中服务员有 7 人死亡，2 人重伤，他们都是来自农村的青年人，进酒店之后未曾接受过防火知识的教育培训。

At 17: 59 on February 2, 2003, in Tiantan Hotel of Harbin, Heilongjiang Province. An attendant added the heater with petroleum instead of kerosene. An extraordinarily serious fire accident was caused, resulting in 33 deaths and 10 injuries, including 7 deaths and 2 injuries among the attendants. All of them were youth from rural areas, and they'd never received training on fire protection.

所以，全时控、全员懂、全过程的严格管理，是防止酒店火灾的必需，是消除火灾隐患的根本大计。火灾虽然是无情的，但也是有规律可循的，只要我们加强防范，严格管理也是可以避免灾难发生的。

Therefore, it is a must for the hotel to conduct all time, entire staff and overall process strict fire control, which is the root to eliminate hidden fire dangers. Fire is ruthless, but it also has some rules to follow. As long as we enhance prevention and make strict management, disasters may be avoided.

一、酒店消防安全的主要隐患（Main Hidden Dangers of the fire Safety of the Hotel）

（一）违规装修施工（Decoration Construction Against Rules）

一些酒店进行装修改造施工，由于用火、用电、用气设备点多量大，加上个别施工材料不符合消防安全的规定，一旦工人操作失误或处理不当，容易引发消防安全事故。

In the fitment and reconstruction of some hotels, as the numbers of equipments and locations of fire use, electricity use and gas use are great, plus that some construction materials do not conform to fire safety provisions, in case of mistaken or improper operations by the workers, fire safety accidents would likely occur.

（二）电器设备老化（Aging of Electric Apparatuses）

一些酒店电器线路老化或配备不合理，容易引发火灾。如大量使用单层绝缘绞线接线板，这种电线没有护套，易因挤压或被动物咬噬而发生短路；客房内的电熨斗、电暖气、热得快等电热器具，客人使用不当、违章接线或忘记断电而使电器设备过热引燃周围可燃物造成火灾。

Electric lines in some hotels are aged or irrationally arranged, fire would be easily caused. For example, if single layer insulation stranded wire terminal boards are intensively used and the wires are provided with no sheaths, shortcut would easily occur caused by extrusion or biting of animals. For electric appliances such as irons, electric heaters and electric boilers used in the guest rooms, fires would also be caused in case that improper use, line connection against rooms or forgetting to cut off the power makes the electric appliance overheating and ignites the inflammables nearby.

（三）厨房违规操作（Operation Against Rules in Kitchen）

如在炉灶上煨、炖、煮各种食品时，浮在上面的油质溢出锅外，遇火燃烧；在炉灶旁烘烤衣物或用易燃液体点火发生燃烧或爆炸。此类火灾蔓延速度快，扑救困难，特别是油类火灾，无法用水进行扑救。

In case of stewing, boiling or baking various types of foods on stoves, the oil floating on the food spills out of the cooker and burns with fire. Fire or explosions would be caused by baking the clothes besides the stove or igniting fire with inflammable liquid. Such fires spread fast and are hard to be put out. Especially for oil fires, they cannot be put out with water.

（四）住客客人安全意识不强（The Sense of Safety of the Guests is not Strong）

客人在酒店卧床吸烟是诱发火灾的重要因素；少年儿童如无同行成年人的监督，容易因玩火而引发火灾，且事后易惊慌失措，到处躲藏，隐瞒火情，错过遏制火情的有效时机。

Smoking in bed of the guest is an important factor to trigger fires. For young people and children, if they're out of the supervision of the adults, fire would easily be caused as they play with fire. In addition, they would be frightened. They would even hide everywhere and conceal the fire. This would restraint the effective opportunities to control fire.

（五）施救设备不全或失效（Incomplete or Invalid Rescue Equipments）

目前，一些酒店存在安全出口锁闭或数量不足，疏散通道被堵塞、占用，消火栓被圈占、遮挡，自动报警、喷淋设施损坏或未按要求安装，疏散指示标志不足，应急照明损坏，灭火器过期等现象，一旦发生火灾，得不到及时扑救，最终酿成事故。

Presently, there're some problems existing in hotels, such as locked or insufficient exits, blocked or occupied evacuation exits, enclosed or sheltered fire hydrants, damaged or improper installed automatic alarming and sprinkling facilities, insufficient evacuation indicatory signs, damaged emergency lighting and expired fire extinguishers. In case of fire, accidents would be caused if the fires cannot be put out in time.

此外，消防安全制度不健全，责任制落实不到位等，也是引发酒店火灾发生的原因之一。

In addition, factors such as unsound fire safety systems and insufficient implementation of responsibility systems are also causes for hotel fires.

二、酒店火灾的危害性（Hazard of Hotel Fires）

（一）火灾荷载大（Great Fire Loads）

酒店内部存在大量的可燃、易燃装饰材料及生活用品，一旦发生火灾，大量可燃材料将导致火灾迅速蔓延；大多数可燃材料在燃烧时还会产生有毒烟气，给住店客人逃生造成极大不便。

There're a great number of combustible and inflammable decoration materials as well as living goods. In case of fire, massive combustible materials would make the fire spreading rapidly. Most combustible materials would generate poisonous fume in burning, causing great inconvenience for the escape of the guests.

（二）火势蔓延迅速（Rapid Spreading of Fire）

影响酒店的火灾蔓延速度的因素很多，一是没有良好的防火分隔和隔阻烟火措施。二是客房的封闭性很强，起火后不易及时发现。三是内部楼梯间、电梯井、电缆井、垃圾道等竖井林立，一旦发生火灾，极易产生“烟囱效应”。

There're a great number of factors that affect the spreading of fire. One is there're no favorable fire separation and smoke separation measures. Secondly, the guest rooms are relatively tightly enclosed. Fire would not be easily detected in case of fire. Thirdly, there're dense vertical shafts within the hotel, such as the stair wells, elevator shafts, cable shafts and refuse channels. In case of fire, chimney effect would easily occur.

（三）火灾扑救难度大（Great Fire Suppression Difficulty）

酒店多为高层建筑，发生火灾后火势蔓延迅速、供水困难、疏散救人和控制火势难等诸多因素，扑救难度大。

Most of the hotels are high-rise buildings. In case of fire, due to various factors such as rapid spreading of fire, difficult water supply, people evacuation and rescue, and hard fire control, the difficulty to control the fire is great.

（四）疏散和施救困难（Difficult Evacuation and Rescue）

酒店人员多且较为集中，进出频繁，且大多数是暂住的客人，对建筑物内的环境、出口和消防设施等情况不熟悉，同时，发生火灾时，被困人员心情紧张，极易迷失方向，拥塞在通道上，造成秩序混乱，给疏散和施救工作带来困难，往往造成重大伤亡。

The personnel in the hotel are relatively concentrated and the turnover is frequent. Most of them are guest temporarily residing in the hotels and they are not familiar with environments within the buildings, exits and fire facilities, etc. of the hotel. Meanwhile, in case of fire, the trapped personnel are quite nervous. They would easily lose their directions and be jammed on the exit channels, causing disorder and difficulty in excavation and rescue. Generally, heavy casualties would be caused.

三、酒店的防火制度和报警处理程序（Fire Systems and Alarm Processing Procedures of Hotels）

（一）酒店防火制度（Fire System of Hotel）

（1）严禁携带易燃、易爆物品进入酒店客房或公共区域。酒店营业需要的易燃易爆品，要由专人保管，严格执行采购、运输、保管易燃易爆物品的审批、监控制度。

Inflammable and explosive articles are strictly prohibited to be carried into the hotel guest rooms or public areas. Inflammable and explosive articles required for business operation should be kept by specially assigned personnel. The examination, approval and monitoring systems for purchase, transportation and keeping of inflammable and explosive articles should be strictly carried out.

(2) 除厨房和餐厅外，任何部门与个人不得在酒店内动用明火，如有特殊情况，须报经消防中心批准，并在有消防人员监控的情况下按程序进行。

Any departments or individuals other than the kitchens and restaurants should not use open fires in the restaurant. In case of special circumstances, reporting should be made to the Fire Center for approval. And situations must be handled according to the procedures under the monitoring of the firc control operators.

(3) 不准随地丢烟头、火柴棒。

Do not litter cigarette butts and matchsticks randomly.

(4) 安全走火通道不准堆放物品或作其他用途。

Fire exits may not be stacked with articles or used for other purposes.

(5) 禁止在酒店内燃放烟花爆竹。

Setting off fireworks and crackers in the hotel are strictly prohibited.

(6) 不准在仓库、机房、客房、洗衣房等地吸烟、用火或乱拉电源。

Smoking, fire or dragging power lines randomly in the warehouse, machine room, guest room, laundry, etc. is strictly prohibited.

(7) 非电工，不准擅自接电或拆电线、电源。

Personnel other than electricians are prohibited to connect power or remove the power lines and power sources without authorization.

(8) 行政人员下班时，要认真检查办公室内的安全情况，关闭门窗，切断电源方可离开。

When the administrative personnel is about to leave work, the personnel should inspect the safety conditions of the office, close the doors and windows, cut off the power supply before leaving the office.

(9) 在重点部位值班的员工，要坚守岗位，不得擅离职守，防止火灾的发生。

Staff on duty at key positions should stick to their posts and should not be absent without leave to avoid fires.

(10) 在厨房和餐厅工作的员工，要严格按照安全操作规程使用明火，并且每周要对气体管道、阀门、开关、电源检查一次，发现故障及时汇报。

Staff working in kitchens and restaurants should use open fires strictly according to the safety operation precautions; inspect the gas pipelines, valves, switches and power supplies on weekly basis; and report failures in time.

(11) 酒店工程施工需要使用明火时，必须经过严格的申报审批程序，经批准后，要在消防人员的监控下使用。

Where open fire is required in construction of hotel engineering, strict reporting, examination and approval procedures must be followed. Upon approval, open fire should be used under the monitoring of the fire control operators.

（二）酒店报警处理程序（Hotel Alarming Disposal Procedures）

表 8-1 消防酒店紧急报警处理程序

Table 8-1 Emergency Alarm Disposal Procedures for Hotel Fire Control

程序 Procedures	标准 Standards
1. 接到报警 Receiving alarm	(1) 认真仔细听清报警地点、报警人姓名。 Carefully listen to the alarming point and name of the personnel reporting the alarm. (2) 重复报警地点及报警人姓名。 Repeat the place and the name of the caller. (3) 把报警迅速准确记录下来。 Quickly and accurately record the alarm.
2. 通知部门 Informing departments	(1) 如消防酒店在出事地点报二级火警，应通知当日值班经理、保安部经理、客房部经理、工程部经理、医务室、车队。 If the hotel reports secondary alarm of fire safety on the spot, the hotel should inform the Duty Manger for that day, Manager of Security Department, Manager of Room Department, Manager of Engineering Department, Clinic and Fleet. (2) 如消防酒店在出事地点报一级火警，除应通知上述 6 个部门有关人员外，还需通知酒店总经理。 If the hotel reports primary alarm of fire safety on the spot, more than related personnel in the above mentioned departments, the General Manager of the hotel should be notified. (3) 如有客人询问火灾情况，应告知"有关人员正在现场处理"，不必做过多解释。 In case that the guests enquire the progress of the first, inform them that "relative personnel are making treatment on the spot" without giving excessive explanations.
3. 填写记录 Filling in records	(1) 报警时间、地点及报警人姓名。 Alarming place and the name of the caller. (2) 记下通知上述 6 个部门接到报警电话人的姓名。 Note down the names of the personnel receiving the alarming calls in the abovementioned six departments. (3) 接线员姓名。 Name of the telephone operator. (4) 等待并记录消防酒店通知的报警原因。 Wait and record the cause of the fire alarm caused by the hotel. (5) 火灾灭后，方可交接班。 Shift handover should be made only after the fire is put out.

表 8-2 处理报警器报警程序

Table 8-2 Disposal Procedures on Alarming by Alarms

程序 Procedures	标 准 Standards
1. 接到报警 Receiving alarm	报警器蜂鸣，立即察看事故的地点、回路名称，记录报警时间、地点。 The alarm buzzes; immediately view the place of the accident, name of the circuit; record the alarming time and place.
2. 通知部门 Informing departments	(1) 报保安部实地查询，记录受话人姓名、时间。 Report to the Security Department to make site inspection; record the name and time of the personnel receiving the call. (2) 报告当值大堂经理。 Report to the on-duty Lobby Manager.

续表

程序 Procedures	标 准 Standards
3. 等待处理结束 Waiting for the completion of disposal	(1) 在保安部未确认事故原因前不能消音。 Do not erasure until the Security confirms the cause of the accident. (2) 待故障处理后方可消音。 Erasure only after the failure is removed. (3) 如果是火警，按火警程序处理。 Dispose according to fire alarm procedures in case of fire alarms. (4) 将处理结果及时间登记在工作日志上。 Timely record the disposal results and time onto the work log.

四、火警的处理程序（Disposal Procedures of Fire Alarm）

1. 火警报告（Fire Alarm Report）

（1）立即使用最近电话拨“消防值班电话”，或用对讲机告知火警情况。

Dial the “Fire Watch Number” with the nearest telephone, or inform the fire alarm information with walkie talkie.

（2）通知总机房，通知时须清楚说明：火警发生详细地点及何种物品引发火灾；火势情况；自己的姓名及部门、职位；叮嘱总机员工报“119”并询问对方的姓名。

Inform the Telephone Exchange Room and clearly indicate the following information: The detailed place of the fire alarm, the material triggering the fire; the fire behavior; the name, department and post of the caller; urge the staff of the exchange room to dial “119” and ask the name of the personnel answering the call.

（3）通知时，须保持冷静，避免引起客人恐慌。

Keep clam when giving notice to avoid panic of the guests.

2. 组织扑救（Organize Fire Fighting）

（1）通知完毕后，迅速返回火警发生处并在附近寻求其他同事协力灭火。

After the notice is finished, quickly return to the fire site and try to find other colleagues nearby to put out the fire.

（2）使用最近而适合的灭火器具尝试将火势扑灭，或尽量控制火种蔓延。

Use the nearest and appropriate fire fighting appliances to put out the fire or control the spreading of the fire as possible.

（3）不论火势能否扑灭，报告者须驻守于火势不至于蔓延的最近而安全的范围，待有关部门主管，值班大堂经理或高级行政人员到场后，决定下一步行动。

Whether or not the fire can be put out, the reporting personnel must stay at the fire site to prevent the fire from spreading to the nearby safety ranges; further actions may be determined after the supervisors of related departments, on-duty Assistant Manager or senior executives arrive at the site.

（4）待火势扑灭后，报告者将发生火警详细情况以书面形式向保安部报告。

The reporter should report the detailed information of the fire on paper to the Security Department after the fire is put out.

（5）火警情况代号为“1001 情况”。

The fire alarm information code is "1001 Case".

3. 采取措施（Take Measures）

（1）大堂经理值班台须有一人驻守，以便回答客人、酒店各部门的各种咨询，如遇有客人询问时，一律按标准答复："情况正在进行调查中，调查后将会进一步通知阁下。"

There must be one staff available at the Assistant Manager On-duty Desk to answer various consultations of the guests and different hotel departments. Apply standardized reply in case of guests inquiry: "The case is under investigation. We'll keep you posted."

（2）当接到总指挥疏散酒店内人员的命令后，大堂经理立即将大堂所有玻璃门打开。

Upon receiving the command of evacuation of personnel in the hotel by the Commander-in-chief, the Assistant Manager should immediately open all the glass doors of the hotel.

（3）请接待部立即提供残疾人员房号、客人姓名，通知有关人员进行特别关注和帮助。

The Reception Department should immediately offer the room numbers and names of persons with disability to related personnel for special care and assistance.

（4）连同保安部值班经理携带万能钥匙及紧急钥匙从客房逐栋逐间房巡查，确保房内无人。

Work with the On-duty Manager of the Security Department, carry master keys and emergency keys to check the guest rooms building by building and room by room, ensure that there're no guests in all rooms.

（5）确定房间无客人滞留后，再知会工作人员撤离。

Inform the work staff to evacuate after it is determined that no guests are in the rooms.

4. 密切联络（Keep Close Contact）

（1）与保安部、工程部密切联系，随时了解事态的进展。

Contact with the Security Department and Engineering Department to know the progress of the case from time to time.

（2）在紧急情况未处理完前，不准离岗，暂停交接班，要坚守大堂经理岗位。

Do not leave the post before the emergency is fully removed; suspend shift handover and stick to the post of Assistant Manager.

5. 客人返回（Organize the Guest to Return）

（1）当接到总指挥返回酒店的命令时，大堂经理负责知会客人并安排他们返回房间，进房时，将由房务部核对证件进入房间。

Upon receiving the command of returning to the hotel by the Command-in-chief, the Assistant Manager should be responsible to inform the guest and arrange them to return to the guest rooms. The Room Department should check the credentials when the guests enter the room.

（2）不断提醒客人在返回房间的过程中请勿拥挤，礼让为先。

Keep reminding the guests not to crowd and give precedence to others when returning to guest rooms.

（3）返回大堂值班台后，立即知会总机，并负责处理客人提出的各种问题。

Immediately inform the Exchange Room when returning the On-duty Desk of the Lobby; be responsible to response various types of questions proposed by the guests.

（4）告知客人酒店大堂备有免费饮料供应。

Inform the guests that there's free drink available at the Lobby.

（5）有关当天房租问题将根据实际情况请示酒店领导，做出灵活处理。

For rate refunding problems for that day, ask the hotel leadership for instructions as the case may be and dispose in a flexible manner.

（6）连同保安部值班经理/主任返回火警现场拍摄现场情况。

Return to the fire site to take photos together with the Duty Manager/Director of the Security Department.

五、加强酒店消防安全的措施（Measures to Enhance Fire Safety of the Hotel）

（一）按有关规定建设完善消防设施（Construct and Consummate Fire-fighting Equipments According to Related Provisions）

酒店客房内所有装饰、装修材料均应符合消防的相关规定。要设置火灾自动报警系统、消火栓系统、自动喷水灭火系统、防烟排烟系统等各类消防设施，并设专人操作维护，定期进行维修保养。要按照规范要求设置防火、防烟分区，疏散通道及安全出口。安全出口的数量，疏散通道的长度、宽度及疏散楼梯等设施的设置，必须符合规定，严禁占用、阻塞疏散通道和疏散楼梯间，严禁在疏散楼梯间及其通道上设置其他用房和堆放物资。

All decorations and finishing materials in the guest rooms in the hotel must conform to related fire fighting provisions. Establish various types of fire fighting facilities such as automatic fire alarm system, hydrant system, automatic sprinkler system and smoke control system; specially assign personnel for operation and maintenance; make periodical maintenance. Design fire and smoke bays, evacuation exits and emergency exits according to standard requirements. The amount of emergency exits, the length and width of the evacuation exit and arrangement of facilities such as emergency staircases must conform to related provisions; do not occupy and block evacuation exits and excavation staircases; do not design other rooms or stack materials in the emergency staircases and the passageways.

（二）建立健全消防安全制度（Establish and Consummate Fire Safety System）

酒店要落实消防安全责任制，明确各岗位、部门的工作职责，建立健全消防安全工作预警机制和消防安全应急预案，完善值班巡视制度，成立消防义务组织，组织消防安全演习，加大消防安全工作的管理力度。

The hotel should put into practice the fire safety responsibility system; clarify the work responsibilities of each post and department; establish and consummate fire safety pre-warning mechanism and fire safety emergency plans; consummate on-duty inspection system; establish voluntary fire safety team; organize fire drills and enhance the management on fire safety.

（三）强化对重点区域的检查和监控（Enhance Inspection and Monitoring on Key Areas）

酒店消防安全责任人和楼层服务员要加强日常巡视，发现火灾隐患及时采取措施。餐厅应建立健全用火、用电、用气管理制度和操作规范，厨房内燃气燃油管道、仪表、阀门必须定期检查，抽烟罩应及时擦洗，烟道应每半年清洗一次。厨房内除配备常用的灭火器外，还应配置灭火毯，以便扑灭油锅起火的火灾。

The responsible personnel for fire safety and floor attendants of the hotel should enhance daily inspection and take timely measures in case of hidden fire dangers. The dining room should establish and consummate managerial systems and operation norms for fire use, power use and gas use. Periodical inspection must be made on the gas and oil pipelines, meters and valves; the smoke hood should be cleaned timely; the flue should be cleaned every half a year. More than common fire extinguishers, the kitchen should also be equipped with fire blanket to put out the fire caused by the burning pan.

（四）加强对员工的消防安全教育（Enhance Fire Safety Education to the Staff）

酒店要加强对员工的消防知识培训，提高员工的防火知识，使员工能够熟悉火灾报警方法、熟悉岗位职责、熟悉疏散逃生路线。要定期组织应急疏散演习，加强消防实战演练，完善应急处置预案，确保突发情况下能够及时有效地进行处置。

The hotel should enhance training on fire safety knowledge to the staff; enhance fire safety knowledge of the staff; enable the staff to be acquainted with fire alarming methods, post responsibilities and excavation and escape routes. Periodically organize emergency excavation drills; enhance practical drills on fire safety; consummate emergency disposal plans; ensure timely and effective disposal in case of emergencies.

（五）加大消防监管力度（Intensify Fire Control Supervision）

消防部门要按照《消防法》的规定和国家有关消防技术标准要求，加强对酒店的监管和检查；旅游行政主管部门要通过行业标准等手段，实施对酒店的消防安全监管。

The fire department should enhance supervision and inspection on the hotels according to the provisions of the *Fire Protection Law* as well as related national fire technical standards; the administrative tourism department should make supervision on fire safety of hotels by measures such as industrial standards.

（六）强化对客人消防安全的提示（Enhance Prompts on Fire Safety to Guests）

要加强对住店客人消防安全提示，要设置禁止卧床吸烟和禁止扔烟头、火源入废纸篓的标志；要告知客人消防紧急出口和疏散通道的位置，要提醒住店客人加强对同行的未成年人和无行为能力人的监护，防止其不甚引发安全事故。

Enhance fire safety reminders to the residing guests; set up signs of “No smoking on Bed”, “Do not Litter Butts and Fire into Waste Bin”; inform the guest the locations of fire exits and excavation exits; remind the guest to enhance the monitoring of minors and persons incapable of disposing to prevent inadvertent safety accidents.

六、消防安全基本常识（Common Sense on Fire Safety）

（一）消防及火灾的定义（Definition of Fire Control and Fire Disaster）

（1）消防：消灭火灾和预先防范，防止火灾发生的社会行为。

Fire Control: The social behavior to put out fire, make proactive prevention and avoid the occurrence of fire disaster.

（2）火灾：指在时间上或空间上失去控制的燃烧所造成的灾害。

Fire Disaster: Disaster caused by uncontrolled fire in terms of time or space.

（二）燃烧和灭火的原理（Principles of Combustion and Extinguishment）

燃烧是有发光发热的化学反应，多数燃烧都会产生烟雾，它必须具备（即燃烧三要素）：可燃物、助燃物（氧气）、着火源（火种）构成所谓的燃烧三角形。灭火原理即破坏燃烧的三角形，切断三者之间的联系。

Combustion is the chemical reaction emitting light and heat and in most cases it generates smokes. Combustion must be provided with the following three elements: Combustible material, comburent (oxygen) and ignition source (kindling material). The three elements compose the so-called “Combustion Triangle”. The extinguishment principle is to destroy such “Combustion Triangle” and cut off the links thereof.

（1）容易引起火灾的火源有烟头、电源开关、打火机等。

What is the combustion sources resulting fire: Butt, power switch, lighter, etc.

（2）酒店容易着火的部位：客房、厨房、发电机房、变压器房、锅炉房、机房、仓库各种电器及插座。

Easily ignitable parts of the hotel: Various types of electronic appliances and sockets in guest room, kitchen, generator room, transformer room, boiler room, machine room and warehouse.

酒店易燃品包括：家具、布草、纸张、塑料用品、酒精、煤气、油漆及各种油（可燃物）。

Combustible materials in hotel involve: Furniture, linen, paper, plastic, alcohol, coal gas, paint and various oil (consumables).

（3）消防的“三知”和“三会”：“三知”包括知消防法规、酒店消防安全制度，知防火常识，知灭火常识；“三会”包括会报警、会扑救初起火灾、会自救逃生和疏散人员。

“Three Knows and Three Ables” in fire control: “Three Knows” involve knowing fire laws and regulations and the safety systems of hotel fire control; knowing common senses in fire protection; knowing the common sense of fire extinguishment; “Three Ables” involve being able to give alarms; being able to put out initial fires and being able to make self-excuse and excavation.

其中，会报警，（拨打消防支队电话）首先拨打119，然后讲清街道门牌号码，起火楼层部位及有无危险物品和人员围困，最后报上自己的姓名和报警使用的电话，派人到十字路口接消防车。其次，会使用灭火器材，首先提起灭火器上下摇动，拨掉保险销，右手握住皮管顶端，左手握住压把，离火苗2~3米距离，对准火苗根部喷射。最后，会自救逃生和疏散人员，包括平时注意大厦安全通道环境；发生火灾时不能乘坐电梯；尽可能用湿布条保护鼻子，沿安全通道往下跑；在无照明中，弯腰沿墙壁前行；无法逃生，回房间用布条封堵门缝，再用水浇湿，然后开窗向外呼救；无条件逃生，可跑向房顶。

“Being able to giving alarms” means the ability to dial the number of the firehouse branch. First, dial 119 and clearly tell the street name and door plate number, the fire location, hazardous articles and trapped personnel (if any); and finally tell the name of the caller and the telephone number used to give the alarm. Assign the personnel to receive the fire truck at the crossing. Secondly, be able to use the fire equipments. First lift the fire extinguisher and shake upwards and downwards; remove the safety pin; hold the top of the tube with the right hand and grasp the handle with the left hand; spray the bottom of the flame at a distance of 2-3 m to the flame. Finally, be able to make self-rescue and evacuate the personnel, for example: pay attention to the exit passageway environments at ordinary times; do not take elevation in case of fire; cover the nose with wet strips of cloth as possible; run down along the exit passageway; if there's no illumination, bend down and walk along the walls; if no escape is available, go back to the rooms and block the door slots of the room with strips of cloth, wet the cloth with water, then open the window and ask for help; if there's no escaping conditions, run to the top of the building.

（4）灭火的最佳时机：发现起火的最初5~7分钟内为最佳灭火时刻，烟雾少，能见度好，及时扑救和报警就能避免火灾。火灾最怕的是惊慌失措和烟雾，据统计，火灾伤亡80%以上是二者造成的。

Best opportunity of extinguishment: The first 5-7 minutes upon detection of the fire is the optimal period to extinguish a fire. During this period, the smoke is few and the visibility is good, timely fighting and alarming will avoid the fire disaster. The most dreadful things in fire are panic and smoke. According to statistics, over 80% of the fire casualties are caused by both factors.

（三）酒店发生火灾如何处理（Disposal of Hotel in Case of Fire）

酒店的任何员工在酒店范围内任何地方如发生灾情时应根据火势的大小而定，如果是力所能及的小火就应立即解决而后向上司书面报告。如火势较大应就近找到电话拨打总机（0）或酒店消防监控中心（任何员工没有总经理的授权都不允许私自拨打 119），报警时语言要清晰，讲清楚火灾位置、火情类别、自己所属的部门及姓名。如找不到电话时应就近找到消防栓，打碎消防栓的报警按扭玻璃进行报警，并关闭电闸。

If any staff detects fire disaster at any place within the range of the hotel, as the case may be, small fire within the power should be immediately put out; and written report should be made to the superior later on. If the fire is relatively great, dial the exchange (0) or the Fire Monitoring Center of the hotel (No staff should dial 119 without the authorization of the General Manager). When reporting the fire, explicate the location and nature of the fire as well as the department and name of the caller. If no telephone is available, find the nearest fire hydrant; break the glass of the alarm button of the fire hydrant to sound the alarm; turn off the power switch.

（四）发生火灾如何自救（How to Make Self-rescue in Case of Fire）

发生火灾时不要急于打开现场门，先用手摸一下门的温度，如果门的温度过高，就千万不能打开门，报警并寻找其他自救法。如果被困在房间里要用湿抹布堵住门缝和空调孔，防止浓烟进入房间，然后通过电话和其他方式呼救。离开房间时要关门，火灾时千万不要使用电梯，如果浓烟较大，要爬行，因为这时近地面才有新鲜空气，还可用湿毛巾捂住口鼻。

If the fire is detected, do not hurry to open the doors at site. Touch the temperature of the door. Do not open the door if the door temperature is excessively high. Make the alarm and find other self-rescue methods. If being trapped into the room, block the door slots and AC hole with wet rags to prevent dense smoke into the room. Then call for help by telephone and other methods. Close the door when leaving the room; do not use the elevator in case of fire; crawl in case of dense smoke as fresh air is only available near the floor. Also may cover the mouth and nose with wet towel.

（五）灭火的方法（Fire Extinguishment Methods）

冷却法：主要是降低火灾现场的温度来灭火的一种方法，可用水冷却和净化碳灭火器进行灭火。

Cooling Method: It is a method to lower the temperature of the fire site, fire extinguishment may be achieved by water cooling and purifying carbon fire extinguisher.

窒息法：主要是让火灾处于无空气的状态下来灭火的一种方法，可用泡沫干粉灭火器。

Choking Method: It is a method to put out the fire by isolating the fire with air, foam dry powder fire extinguishers may be used.

隔离法：主要是将火源与着火物隔开，防止火势的加强导致更大的损失和伤害。

Isolation Method: It is a method between the source of ignition and the burning material to avoid more damages and harms caused by enhanced fire behaviors.

采用以上三种方法将火势控制，不让火势延伸至酒店的消防设施。

Take the above mentioned three measures to control the fire behaviors, do not have the fire extend to the fire-fighting equipments of the hotel.

（六）酒店的消防设备（Fire-fighting Equipments of the Hotel）

酒店应设有灭火器、消防栓、手动报警系、烟雾感应器、温度感应器、喷淋系统、隔离卷闸门、走火通道、防毒面具、灭火器、送风排烟系统、消防电话报警系统、电梯监控系统、消防火警检测屏。

The hotel should be provided with fire extinguisher, fire hydrant, manual alarming system, smoke sensor, temperature sensor, sprinkler system, isolation rolling gate, fire exit door, respirator, fire extinguishers, smoke evacuation system, fire call alarm system, elevator monitoring system and fire alarm detection screen.

其中，灭火器的类型包括干粉灭火器（油类、油漆）、干粉灭火器（固体、柴油、煤油、气体燃烧、油漆等任何火灾）、1211（气体灭火器，不会留下痕迹，但不环保，精密仪器、文物档案适用）、二氧化碳（干冰灭火法，不能扑灭电器火灾，-80摄氏度，会报毁，不带电物质的火灾）、泡沫灭火器（扑灭油类火灾，大型工厂、油库适用）。

The types of the fire extinguishers involve dry powder extinguisher (for oil and paint), dry powder extinguisher (for solid, diesel fuel, kerosene, gas combustion, paint and any other fire disasters), 1211 (gas fire extinguisher, without traces, but not environmental friendly, suitable for precise instruments, cultural relics and files), carbon dioxide (dry ice fire fighting method, cannot put the fires on electric appliances, -80℃, suitable for uncharged materials fires), foam extinguisher (for oil fires, suitable for large-sized factories, oil depots).

灭火器的使用方法：首先把灭火器的保险插销拉出，然后把灭火器喷管对准火源的根部，压下开关即可进行灭火。

Usage of fire extinguishers: First pull out the safety pin of the fire extinguisher, align the nozzle of the fire extinguisher to the root of the flame, press the button to extinguish fire.

消防栓的使用方法：把消防栓门打开，拿出水带和枪头；将水带往火场方向铺开；把水带一头接到消防栓接头处，再把总开关阀打开，并在奔跑时接上枪头，对准火场即可进行灭火。

Usage of fire hydrant: Open the door of the fire hydrant; pull out the water tape and the spray nozzle; extend the water tape towards the fire site; connect one end to the connection of the hydrant, turn on the main switching valve, connect the nozzle while running; aim at the fire site to extinguish the fire.

防毒面具的使用方法：取出面具；一手抓住面具的口鼻部位，另一手抓住面具的后部，由头顶上方向后下拉；迅速调整口罩眼窗位置；搭上尼龙搭扣即可使用。

Usage of respirator: Pull out the respirator, grasp the mouth and nose position of the mask with one hand and grasp the rear part of the mask. Pull downwards from the top; quickly adjust the eyes position of the mask; buckle the nylon fastener tape to use.

自动喷淋的作用：在楼内99%的地方，红色管路连接装置，又称花洒系统。自动喷淋系统是一种固定式的消防保护装置，它具有火灾探测、报警、喷水启动等多功能的灭火系统，当喷淋头探测到周围温度达到68摄氏度时整个系统即可自动喷水灭火，具有报警和灭火的双重作用。

Functions of automatic spraying: The automatic spraying system is also called sprinkler system, which connects the devices with red pipelines and covers 99% of the building. The automatic spraying system is a fixed fire protection device. It is a fire fighting system with multiple functions such as fire detection, alarming and spraying starting. When the spraying head detects that the surrounding temperature reaches 68℃, the system would spray water to extinguish the fire automatically. The system is provided with dual function of alarming and extinguishing.

烟雾感应器的作用：烟雾感应器主要是对火灾有预防和报警的作用，当周围烟雾达到一定的浓度时，即会向消防监控报警箱发出报警指令，使火灾得到及时有效的扑救。

Functions of smoke sensor: The smoke sensor is provided with prevention and alarming functions. When the smoke in surrounding areas reaches a certain concentration, it would issue alarming instruction to the fire alarming box to enable timely and effectively extinguishment of the fire.

应急灯的作用：当发生火灾停电时，应急灯起到紧急照明的作用。

Functions of emergency lamps: In case of power failure caused by fire, the emergency lamps should provide emergent illumination.

出口指示牌的作用：起到在火场内疏散被困人员的作用。

Functions of exit indicators: Evacuate the trapped personnel in the fire.

（七）烟雾感应器和温度感应器（Smoke Sensor and Temperature Sensor）

在楼内90%的地方，安装在天花板下的白色圆形为烟雾感应器报警探头，当周围的烟雾或烟尘达到一定浓度时，圆形物上的红色指示灯亮起来并把信号在火警监探中显示出来。在厨房、车库和一些地方的天花板下白色圆形物为温度感应器报警探头，温度变化超过15摄氏度时，红灯亮起来，与烟雾感应器报警过程相同。

The white round devices installed under the ceiling of 90% of the building are smoke sensor alarming probes. When the smoke or dust reaches a certain concentration, the red indication lamp on the round device lights up and transmit the fire alarm to the fire alarm monitor. Some white round devices under the ceilings of the kitchen, garages and some other places are temperature sensor alarming probes. When the temperature variation exceeds 15℃, the right lamp will light on, the process is the same as smoke sense alarming.

（八）送风，排烟（Ventilation and Smoke Removal）

楼层走廊天花板上的条形排气孔（不同于空调的方形孔或长形孔）是楼层排烟孔，其自动开关在火警中心，其作用是在火灾时排除楼层内的烟雾。

The bar exhaust vent (different from the square and rectangle holes of AC system) under the ceiling of the floor corridor are smoke removal holes for the floor. The automatic switch is in the Fire Alarm Center. The function is to remove the smoke of the floor in the fire site.

（九）火场自救（Self-rescue of Fire Site）

（1）当身上着火时的处理办法：尽快把着火衣服或帽子脱下，如来不及脱，可就地打滚或叫在场人员用棉被或大衣包住使空气与火隔绝而熄灭，或用水淋熄。

Disposal methods in case of body fire: remove the burning clothes or hat as soon as possible; if it's unavailable to do so, roll on the ground or ask other personnel onsite to wrap the body with cotton quilt or coat to extinguish the fire by insulation of air and fire, or put out the fire with water.

（2）当处在浓烟中时的处理办法：首先要想办法逃走，烟雾不浓时可俯身行走，烟雾很浓时必须卧地爬行。其次要设法用水淋湿头发和衣服，避免冲过火焰时衣服和头发着火。

Disposal in case of dense smoke: Firstly, try to escape; bend to move forwards if the smoke is not dense; crawl on the floor if the smoke is dense. Secondly, Manage to wet the hair and clothes with water to avoid that the clothes and hair catches fire when rushing through the flames.

（十）火场的疏散（Excavation of Fire Site）

（1）人员的疏散：各楼层服务台值班员，在火灾紧急情况下，必须负责引导住客迅速安全转移；听到疏散警铃或紧急广播后，当班服务员要立即分头去检查卫生间和套间的所有房间，确认房间无人时，要把房间的所有门都关上，并加以标记；疏散时，要通知客人走最近的安全通道，千万不能使用电梯。

Personnel evacuation: In case of fire emergency, the on-duty attendants of each floor should be responsible to guide the residing guests to make removal quickly and safely. Upon hearing the excavation bells or emergency broadcasting, the on-duty attendants should respectively check the toilets and all rooms in the suites. If it is confirmed that there're no people inside, close all the doors of the room and make marks. In case of evacuation, inform that guest to take the nearest exit passageway and not to use the elevator.

（2）火场需要疏散的物品有：首先要疏散有爆炸危险的物品；要优先疏散性质重要、价格昂贵的物资；要及时疏散影响灭火战斗的物资（例如纸箱等）。

Articles to be excavated from the fire site: First, excavate articles with explosion hazard; give priority to materials with important nature and high value; timely excavate materials affecting the fire fighting battles (e.g. cartons).

模块小结
Module Summary

1. 酒店安全管理的重要性包括哪些内容？

What is the importance of hotel safety management?

2. 酒店各岗位安全控制事项包括哪些？请分别说明。

What are the precautions of post safety control of the hotel? Please list them in details.

3. 酒店消防安全的主要隐患包括哪些内容？一旦发生火灾，有哪些危害？

What are the main hidden dangers of hotel fire safety management? What are the hazards in case of fire?

4. 如何加强酒店消防安全的措施？

What are the measures to enhance fire safety of the hotel?

5. 酒店消防安全基本常识包括哪些内容？

What are the basic common senses of hotel fire safety?